MW01620532

RUSSIAN ART
IN THE NEW MILLENNIUM

RUSSIAN ART
IN THE NEW MILLENNIUM

EDWARD LUCIE-SMITH
& SERGEI REVIAKIN

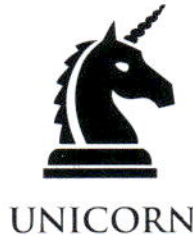

UNICORN

CONTENTS

ACKNOWLEDGEMENTS

Dmitry Azarov
Leonid Bazhanov
Alexander Borovsky
Andrey Cheglakov
Mikhail Dedinkin
Konstantin Dudakov-Kashuro
Viktor Fedotov
Peter Lukacs
Igor Sukhanov
Rustam Suleymanov
Olga Sviblova
Terebenin family
Irina Tsvetkova
Maria Vishnyak
Irina Yazykova
Jupiter Foundation
R – Pharm

Authors would like to thank the State Russian Museum, the State Pushkin Fine Arts Museum, the Moscow Museum of Modern Art, the Multimedia Art Museum, the Gazprombank Corporate Collection, the Moscow Manege, Artwin Gallery, Anna Nova Gallery, Babylon Gallery, DiDi Gallery, Ovcharenko Gallery, Pop/oof/art Gallery, Triumph-Gallery, Victoria Gallery, 11.12 Gallery, Kompass Projects, Siberian Printing House and Kinovar Icon Workshop

Special thanks to Natalia Kambarova-Odoevskaya

FOREWORD

BY EDWARD LUCIE-SMITH

It has now been thirty years since the fall of the Soviet Union. During that period, Russian visual culture has developed considerably, and has become in many respects unlike that of the previous era – less controlled by the state and much more diverse geographically. During this period, developments in Russian art have been widely misunderstood in the West, although Russian art has also been influenced by now more readily available Western sources, in particular the younger Russian artists featured in this book. At the same time, however, Western attention has become increasingly focused on so-called 'dissidents' – that is to say, artists who seemed to court trouble with the post-Soviet regime.

Western attention was also directed towards artists who, during the last years of the Gorbachev period, left Russia to establish studios elsewhere, though without completely disassociating themselves from their homeland, where they often continued to exhibit. In doing so, they followed a tradition that had begun in the mid-nineteenth century, long before the rise of Communism, when both artists and major literary figures – Ivan Turgenev (1818-1883), for example – moved out of Russia for a freer life. This pattern continued after the Revolution. One such example is the career of Natalia Goncharova (1881-1962). As a young woman she acquired great fame in the very last years of Imperial Russia as a painter. During the First World War she moved to Switzerland, and then on to Paris, where she forged a new career for herself, not so much as an independent painter but more as a leading designer for Sergei Diaghilev's (1872-1929) exiled, and by now fully international Ballets Russes.

Another expatriate of this era was Zinaida Serebriakova (1984-1967), a member of the Benois family, who did not leave Russia until 1924. She too settled in Paris, but also travelled widely, taking French citizenship in 1947. She was unable to resume contact with her family in Russia until the 1960s. At the very end of her life, in 1966, she staged an immensely successful touring exhibition in Russia, seen in

Moscow, Leningrad and Kiev. She was never truly a committed Modernist, like Goncharova.

It is perhaps notable that both of these artists were female. Today, female artists continue to be strongly represented in Russia, as can be seen from the work illustrated in this book.

This new generation of Russian artists is also noteworthy in that their work is extremely varied, covering a wide variety of different Modernist styles. None of them can be described as being in any way academic or conformist. Nearly all of the artists illustrated here live and work in Russia but cannot be considered to be cravenly obedient to the current regime. They freely express personal feelings and ideas. Sometimes they absorb ideas from the West – an example is the painting here by Ludmila Konstantinova (born 1980), *Portrait of a Weeping Girl*, from her *Degenerreotype* series. This obviously owes something to the American Pop artist Roy Lichtenstein (1923-1997). Many other recent international stylistic categories, in addition to Pop, are represented in contemporary Russian art: Abstraction, Surrealism, Conceptual Art, Installation. Satires and examples of street art – i.e. graffiti – have become increasingly important in recent years; in contrast to Western hit-and-run equivalents, they are quite often officially 'blessed'. In 2013, when Moscow held a festival called 'Best City on Earth', numerous artists, including a group of non-Russians, were invited to produce large-scale open-air paintings.

A strong feeling continues to exist in Russia that artworks should be publicly accessible statements, rather than being locked away in the salons of the rich. While art collecting continues to exist, with a market for contemporary Russian works provided by a few auction rooms and galleries now based within Russia itself, prices in the salerooms do not each the giddy heights that are regularly achieved in New York and London. Expressed in terms of US dollars or sterling, top lots occasionally reach six figures, but never seven or eight.

Russia now has an increasing number of large official and semi-official art galleries, scattered over an enormous area – not just the so-called 'big four': the Hermitage and State Russian in St Petersburg and the Tretyakov and the Pushkin in Moscow. During the past twenty years, art centres throughout the country have multiplied and diversified, a fact reflected in this book.

One artist, among quite a number now working in Russia who embrace these attitudes is Arseny Zhilyaev who was born in Voronezh in 1984 but is now listed as living and working in Moscow. As he says on his personal website: 'I guess I first realised that an exhibition (and more generally, a museum) is an ideal media for artistic self-expression back in 2007 when I visited the former Museum of the Russian Revolution in Moscow.'[1] He is a member of the Russian Socialist Movement, as is indicated by the titles of some of his earlier series – *Market Labour, Radio October* – but his art doesn't look like a product of the Communist past. In 2010 he was a winner of the Innovation Prize – one of the major Russian awards for contemporary artists – in the 'New Generation' category. He has exhibited quite frequently abroad: for example, in the Biennial of Lyon (2015), in the Kwanju Biennial, South Korea (2016) and the Liverpool Biennial (also 2016).

There are also, in addition to artists who are recognisably contemporary but still with some links to the Soviet past, others who belong to categories that in a much broader sense seem peculiarly Russian, for instance, contemporary icon painters. Icons never completely disappeared under the officially atheist Soviet regime. They continued to be made in provincial centres, if not in Moscow or what was then Leningrad (now St Petersburg). Icon painting, of all forms of visual art, has the longest continuous tradition in Russia. Leading contemporary icon painters, living and working in the country, are currently widely recognised outside Russia itself.

Certain other factors also seem especially Russian. One is the lingering memory of the Second World War, which devasted Russia more than anywhere else in the world, and cost millions of lives. This conflict, and its aftermath – the threat of the atomic bomb – continue to resonate in Russian art but are now largely absent from Western equivalents.

Another theme is an abiding love for the Russian landscape, and for Russian nature, sometimes directly expressed in works such as Anton Zabrodin's (born 1980) *Pine Trees on the Baltic Shore*, which owes much to Russian nineteenth-century landscape painting by artists such as Isaac Levitan (1860-1900); it is sometimes also expressed with ironic intent, such as Oleg Borodin's (born 1988) representation of a landscape, painted as an exterior mural on the walls of a dull skyscraper.

If women are very much present in Russian contemporary art, the racial themes that are now so prevalent in Western art, particularly in Britain and also in the United States, are largely absent in Russia. Many nationalities and ethnic minorities are incorporated within Russia, but there is nothing like the sharp racial divisions that exist in Western societies. Racial issues, therefore, tend to play only a minor role in the art now being made in Russia.

Official recognition and promotion of black artists, in compensation for past wrongs, is less relevant in Russia as there is no comparable history of African slave-trading. Africans were occasionally present at Tsarist courts however: the nineteenth century poet Alexander Pushkin (1799-1837) had an African great-grandfather. Much has been made of this in recent American studies of Pushkin, but they have found little resonance in Russia itself.[2] Pushkin's name is of course attached to one of the four major official museums in Russia that exhibit modern art: the Pushkin State Museum of Fine Arts in Moscow.

The relationship of Russian contemporary art to the big international auction rooms and to major museums, both inside and outside Russia, is also different from Western artists. When Russian contemporary, or near-contemporary paintings are offered at auction, these sales now almost invariably take place domestically. The very highest international price tier is rarely offered, occupied instead by works from the United States and Western Europe, with occasionally works by Japanese, or more even more rarely, Chinese artists. Work by Russian artists, when included in these international sales, belongs to the earlier years of the Modern Movement and is usually the work of expatriate artists, such as Wassily Kandinsky (1866-1944) and Mark Chagall (1887-1985). The most contemporary Russian work has almost no presence at all.

Major auctions, now often conducted online, take place at various locations in the United States, Europe and increasingly often in China. Russian collectors – usually expatriates and not resident in Russia itself – are occasionally present at these sales, but not necessarily as buyers of recent Russian art.

Where the Russian state museums are concerned – the big four in particular – the pattern of financing differs from that in the West, where institutions pay at least some of the cost themselves. In Russia, museum exhibitions of contemporary art at the big four invariably have to be subsidised from outside. It is sometimes easier to obtain these subsidies from promoters of non-Russian artists, looking to obtain a prestigious venue, than to acquire local financial backing.

Russian contemporary art, like Latin American contemporary material, and also to some extent contemporary art from the Middle East, currently exists as a separate category. It communicates with other art worlds but maintains its independence from those other artistic spheres.

During the Gorbachev period, just before the fall of the Soviet Union, a sudden enthusiasm arose in the West for the art then being produced in Russia. During the past thirty years that enthusiasm has tended to die away. The artists now working in Russia, especially the younger ones, who have had little or no direct experience of the Soviet system, are correspondingly little known outside their own country. In many ways this book contradicts the ossified view of Russian art still prevailing in the West, which is based on what happened in the Gorbachev period and immediately after. What we hope to do here is to correct that view and offer a study of what is happening in Russian art at the present time. Russia is a very large country: an artistic universe in itself.

FOREWORD

BY SERGEI REVIAKIN

The extraordinary changes to what was once one of the two world superpowers led to the creation of the modern Russia in 1991. Devoid of the ideology and private travel bans of the predecessor state, its people embraced this new reality, which affected all aspects of their daily life, including culture and art, with the 'dashing' nineties leading to the formation of a class of the newly rich and the appearance of new personalities in politics.

The Russian art world underwent a dramatic change too. The artists who were considered 'non-conformist' in the Soviet Union finally received high recognition not only from outside their home country, where they had been known and collected from the 1960s, but also in Russia itself. Most of them were already well established through their connections with international art galleries. It is not surprising that the majority of the newly emerged Russian collectors almost without exception turned to buying Russian pre-Revolutionary, Soviet and non-conformist art.

Other Russian artists were left to their own devices. The Artists' Union of the USSR, which had been effectively providing work to most of the country's artists, was dissolved in January 1992, when financial support to their members ended. Harsh economic realities and a rapid decrease in living standards forced many prospective graduates and young artists to pursue different careers or to take up a non-art-related job for a living. The commercial market barely existed, with only a few galleries like Marina Gisich in St Petersburg or Regina (now Ovcharenko) and XL galleries in Moscow specialising in contemporary art and artists often selling directly to collectors sometimes at highly discounted prices.

As it happened, support came from the state in the form of the provision of exhibition spaces and the opening of new venues. In St Petersburg, this role was taken by the Contemporary Art Department of the State Russian Museum. The Department, run by Alexander Borovsky and housed in the Marble

Palace on the bank of the Neva River, is the oldest in Russia and has been providing continuous support to young artists by organising regular contemporary art exhibitions since the end of 1980s. Erarta, a private museum dedicated to contemporary art, opened its doors in St Petersburg in 2010.

In Moscow, the National Centre for Contemporary Art, the Moscow House of Photography (later to become the Multimedia Art Museum, Moscow) and the Moscow Museum of Modern Art were founded in 1992, 1996 and 1999 respectively, and the Ekaterina Cultural Foundation, the Art4 and the Garage Museums of Contemporary Art opened their spaces in 2007 and 2008. Upon its foundation, the Multimedia Art Museum launched the Moscow Photobiennale and later opened the Rodchenko School of Photography and Multimedia in 2006. The National Centre of Contemporary Art went on to open regional contemporary art centres in eight cities across the country, including Kaliningrad, Nizhny Novgorod and Samara. It also established (together with the Moscow Museum of Modern Art) the Festival of Young Art (now called the Moscow International Biennale for Young Art) and, in 2005, launched an all-Russian visual art innovation competition. Although the Centre has become a part of the larger museum, the Biennale is flourishing and the competition was officially endorsed as the Innovation State Prize in Contemporary Art. It has nine nominated categories and is now one of the most sought-after contemporary art awards in Russia.

The other two prestigious contemporary art awards are the privately funded Kandinsky Prize, launched in Moscow in 2007 and the Kuryokhin Prize, founded with the support of the city government in St Petersburg in 2009. The Kandinsky Prize, named after the world-famous Russian abstract artist, has three nominations where 'any Russian artist without exception may be the candidate for the Kandinsky Prize: the receipt of applications from the participants based on the principle of self-nomination.'[1] The Sergey Kuryokhin Prize, named after Sergey Kuryokhin (1954–1996), a short-lived but influential composer and experimental artist who made his career in St Petersburg, is held during the annual 'Art-Mekhanika' festival and is one of the major cultural events of Russia's 'second capital'.

It is notable that all three prizes have independent juries made up of international and Russian art critics, curators and academics whose decisions are based on novelty and artistic merit rather than political agenda or social needs. Most contemporary artists in Russia reflect the world around them and challenge the problems of daily life in their work, using the visual and artistic means they can best master. In doing so, they follow a long-lasting tradition set up by the country's leading intellectuals in the nineteenth century and continued throughout the twentieth. Hence, the avant-garde art displayed in this book is rich in irony and double meaning when dealing with nostalgia about the past, climate change, political and social ills and even nature. In order to understand it, and modern Russia, it requires an open mind, rather than bias and prejudice, but the effort is worth it.

Interest in contemporary art was growing not only in the capital, where the Garage Museum of Contemporary Art launched its own Triennial of Russian Contemporary Art in 2017, but throughout the whole country. Among the new institutions are the Museum of Contemporary Art in Perm, near the Ural Mountains; the Typography Contemporary Art Centre in Krasnodar, in southern Russia; Ploschad Mira (Square of Peace) Museum Centre in Krasnoyarsk, in eastern Siberia, and the Zarya Centre for Contemporary Art in Vladivostok, the largest Russian city in the Far East. The city of

Yekaterinburg hosts the Ural Industrial Biennial of Contemporary Art which has become the most important contemporary art event outside Moscow and St Petersburg. With its sixth edition in 2021, entitled 'Time to hug and shy away from hugs', it rephrases the Book of Ecclesiastes and references the Covid pandemic.

The fact that most contemporary artists in Russia are motivated by professional recognition, unlike many of their counterparts in the US, China or elsewhere, who are influenced by the pressure of pure commercial interests, explains a lot. In this sense, it makes the Russian contemporary art world more democratic, with low entry barriers for young artists and, to a great extent, excludes money-propped bad art from entering and dominating its playground.

This is not to say that there is no art market. It has been growing with the increased interest in national contemporary art. The Winzavod Contemporary Art Centre was opened in Moscow to house contemporary art galleries and the Cosmoscow contemporary art fair was launched in 2010. It aimed to bring international art to the country and, even more so, to show Russian art to the outside world. Auction house Vladey, specialising in Russian contemporary art, began selling in 2013. Many new galleries, like Artwin, chose to have a distinctive online presence and to exhibit their artists in prestigious, though temporary, spaces. Helped by the continuing process of digitalisation, most artists created comprehensive internet sites of their own or began to sell directly via social media sites like Facebook and Instagram. It also allowed local galleries across Russia to sell regional art to clients throughout the country.

Another important and increasingly decisive factor contributing to the promotion and the support of contemporary artists financially are private institutions and foundations. To name but the few, Breus Foundation created and runs the aforementioned Kandinsky Prize with substantial monetary awards, the Garage Museum provides grants for the artists, V-A-C Foundation, set up in 2009, not only extends financial support to individual artists but has its own exhibition space at the Palazzo delle Zattere in Venice and converted the former GES-2 power plant into a vast exhibition space at the heart of Moscow.

It is worth mentioning that *The Art Newspaper*, a major source of international art news, has been owned since 2014 by the Russian collector Inna Bazhenova. It has a Russian-language edition extensively covering the national contemporary art scene. In November 2018 *The Art Newspaper*, jointly with AFF (The Aksenov Family Foundation, an art and cultural foundation, established in 2012) launched *Art Focus*, a monthly online newsletter in English, with the aim to support and promote Russian art worldwide.

In the last twenty years, contemporary art in Russia has clearly created a unique and fascinating world, perhaps one of the most distinctive on the international stage, as the authors of this book have discovered. It has quietly grown out of the non-conformist art scene of the Soviet days, when unofficial art was exhibited in small flats with artists, journalists, prospective buyers and art lovers in attendance. These venues, with their spirit of camaraderie and belonging, have now been replaced by spacious exhibition venues housing spectacular art events where collectors, artists and art professionals mix together, exchanging views and ideas; this is where the new art world is born.

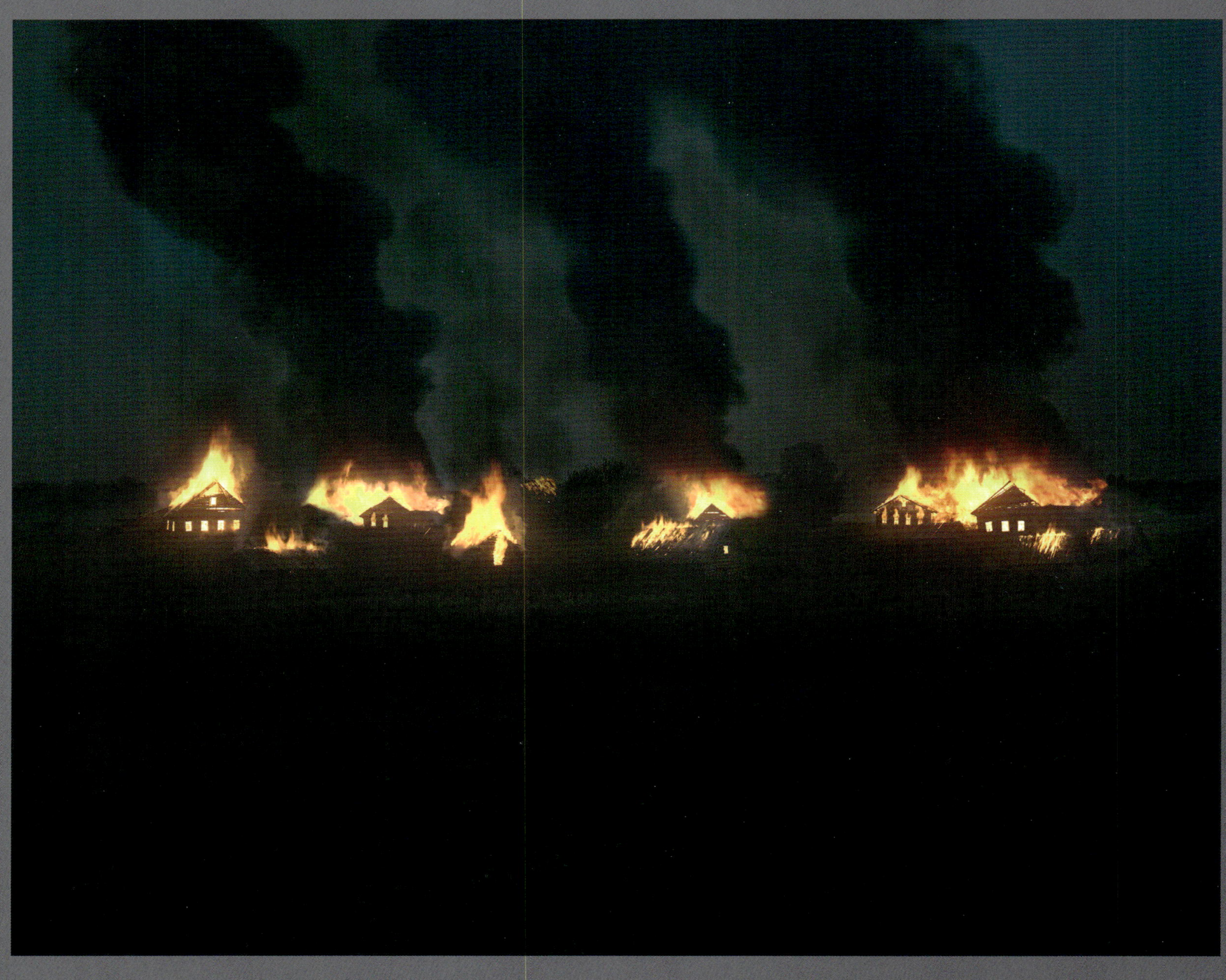

1 FROM PAST TO PRESENT

For Russian society, even today, the Second World War is very much seen as recent history. It hasn't faded from popular memory to nearly the same extent as it has in Western European or American society. There is also nostalgia for some of the scientific and technological achievements of the post-war Soviet Union. Unsurprisingly, contemporary Russian art, from recent decades, continues to refer to both of these.

Take, for example Alexander Gronsky's (born 1980) twinned photographs, one dated 2006 and the other 2016. They memorialise contemporary Russia's gradual passage out of Soviet drabness. The large building on the right of the scene has been repainted pink, the street kiosk beside it is now paired with a structure sheltering a bench and used to display posters, and the sapling beside the building has flourished and become a tall tree.

Dimitri Venkov (born 1980), in a video called *Hymn of Moscovy* shows a grand official building upside down. This is somehow reminiscent of the series of self-portraits by the German artist Georg Baselitz (born 1938), in which he shows his own image inverted. Venkov inverts not himself, but the pomposity of official architecture.

Danila Tkachenko (born 1989) is less forgiving. In a work called *Motherland*, which he describes as 'a nostalgia and a commemorative project – a parting with dead and no longer functional structures,'[1] he depicts a whole village of old wooden huts: the right way up, but in flames.

The artworks included in this section are rich in ironic commentary. For example, Roman Mokrov's (born 1986) *Another Day In Paradise*, offers a laptop almost buried in the midst of a table loaded with plastic bottles in an old Soviet-style room. Some may be mineral water or soft drinks, but most seem to be beer or wine bottles. The walls of the surrounding space carry a graffito of waves, implying that what is shown is a substitute for a day at the beach. Mokrov comments: 'You no longer remember

←
Tkachenko, Danila
Motherland, Nr.1
2016, print

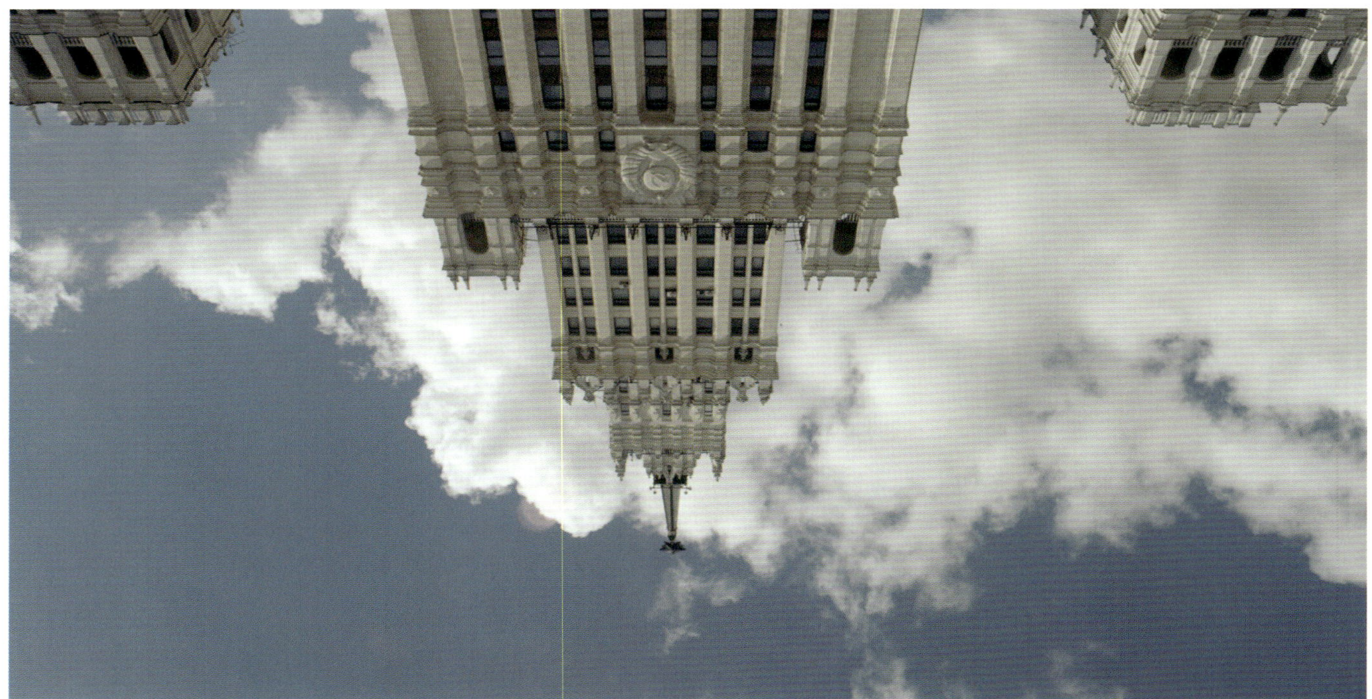

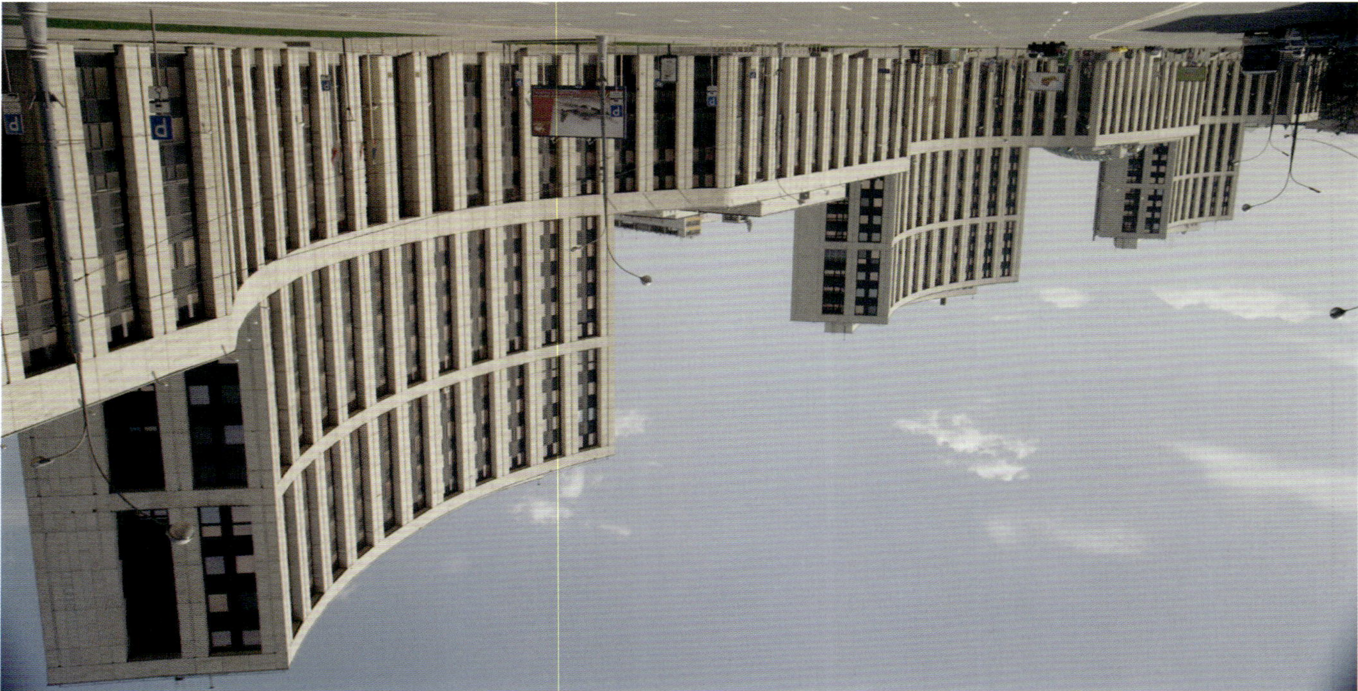

↑↑
Venkov, Dimitri
The Hymns of Moscovy
2018, video still

↑
Venkov, Dimitri
The Hymns of Moscovy
2018, video still

→
Gronsky, Alexander
Untitled, Scheme Series
2006-2015, pigment print on paper

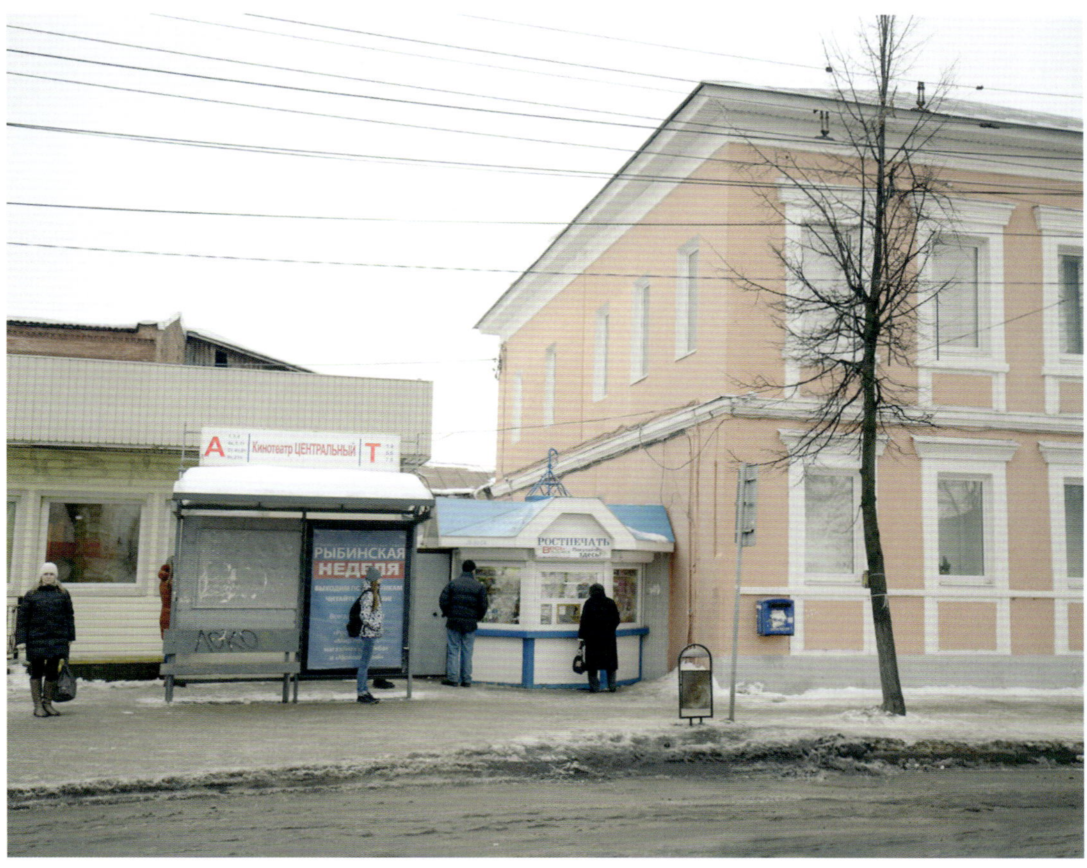

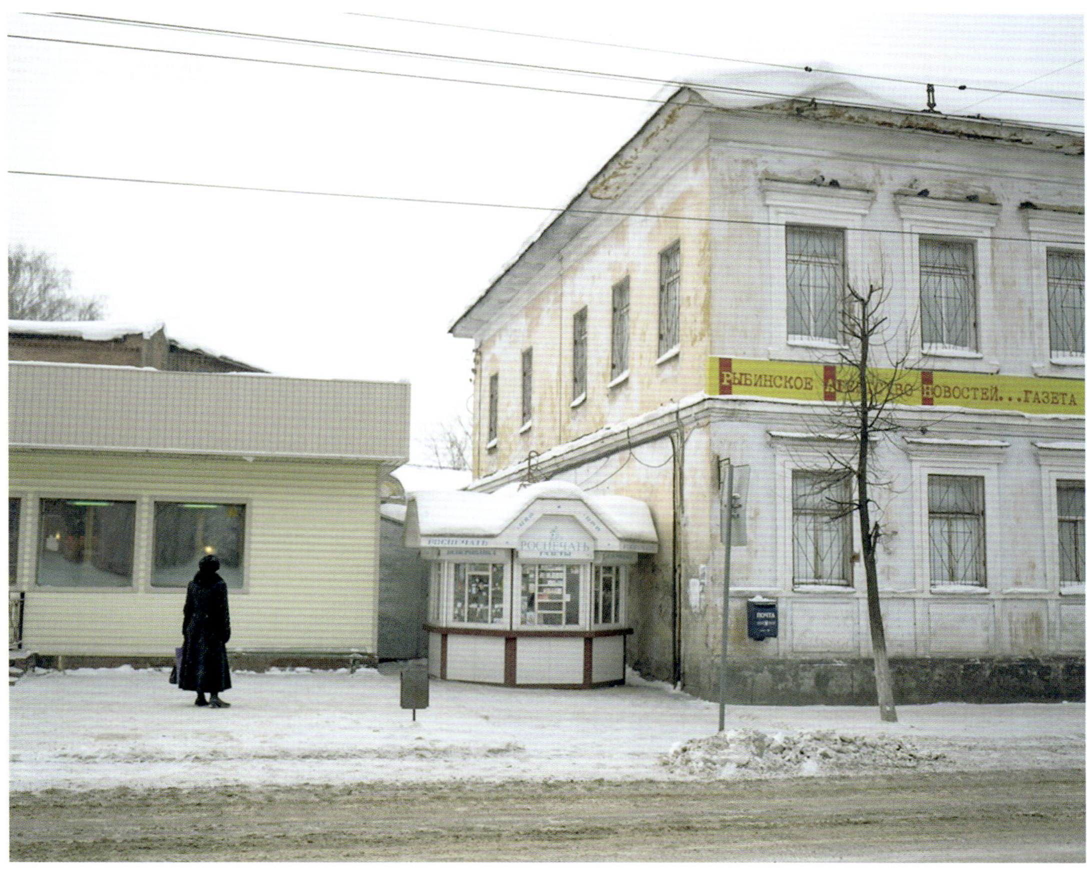

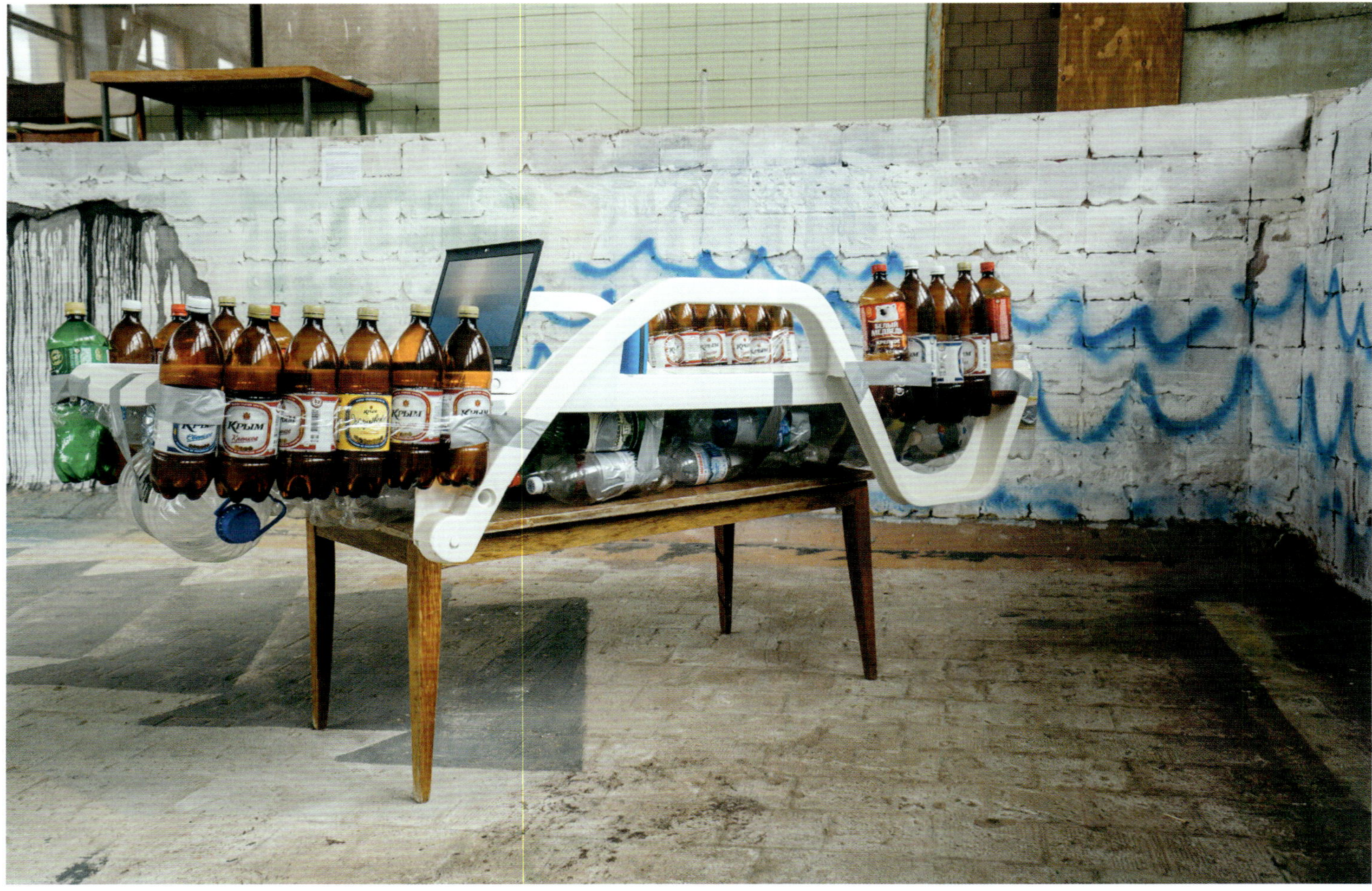

who you are, whether you are old or young, how long you've been here, and where your home is. Don't worry, you are already home, welcome to eternity!'[2]

Irony is also very much present in Pavel Otdelnov's (born 1979) 2014 painting *Stonehenge*. It depicts a residential tower block rising from a thick field of smog.

Alexandra Paperno's (born 1978) *Colourization, In Memory of Sergei Eisenstein's Film Battleship Potemkin* is a homage, also with a tinge of irony, to one of the masterpieces of Soviet cinema. An old black-and-white photograph of a crowd waiting outside a large building, presumably where the film is due to be shown, is adorned with red flags, commemorating the dead-and-gone Communist regime.

More concise is Konstantin Reshetnikov's (born 1985) sculpture *Turnip 200* (from the series *Substitution of Import*, 2020), which shows the dome of an Orthodox church being used as a rocket warhead.

Sergey Poteryaev's (born 1988) *Staraya Utka (Old Duck) Village* (2017) also offers the image of an Orthodox church, seen through a lace-curtained window. Its crowning dome is askew and trails of smoke are rising around it, perhaps referring to Soviet times when churches were destroyed or converted into factories.

Equally to the point is Taisia Korotkova's (born 1980) *Transport of Radioactive Waste* (2014), a tempera painting on a gesso ground: one of the most traditional ways of creating a painted image and much favoured by icon painters. This elegant still life 'celebrates' these lethal substances which place the whole planet in danger.

←
Mokrov, Roman
Another Day in Paradise
2017, installation

↓
Otdelnov, Pavel
Stonehenge
2013, oil on canvas

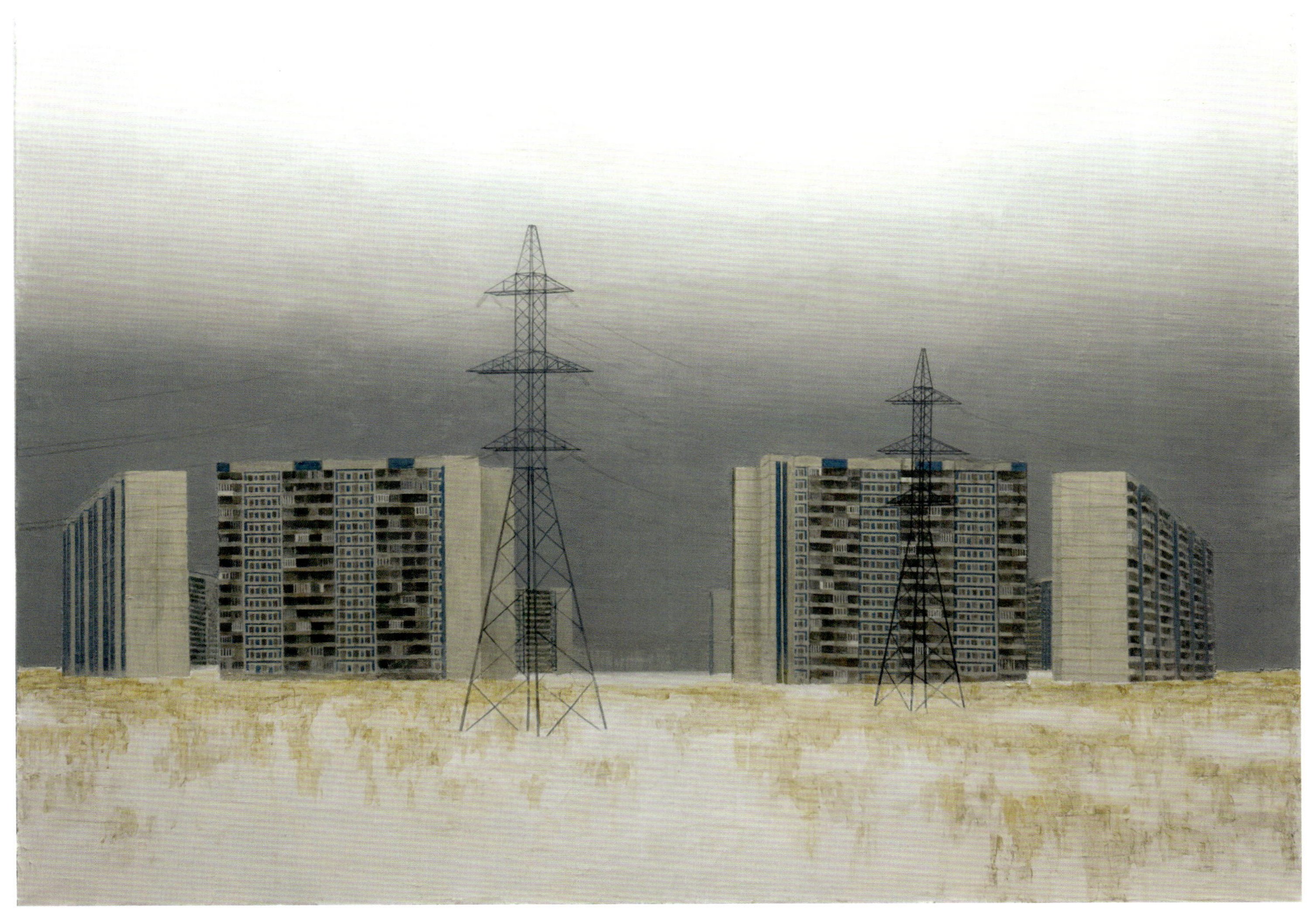

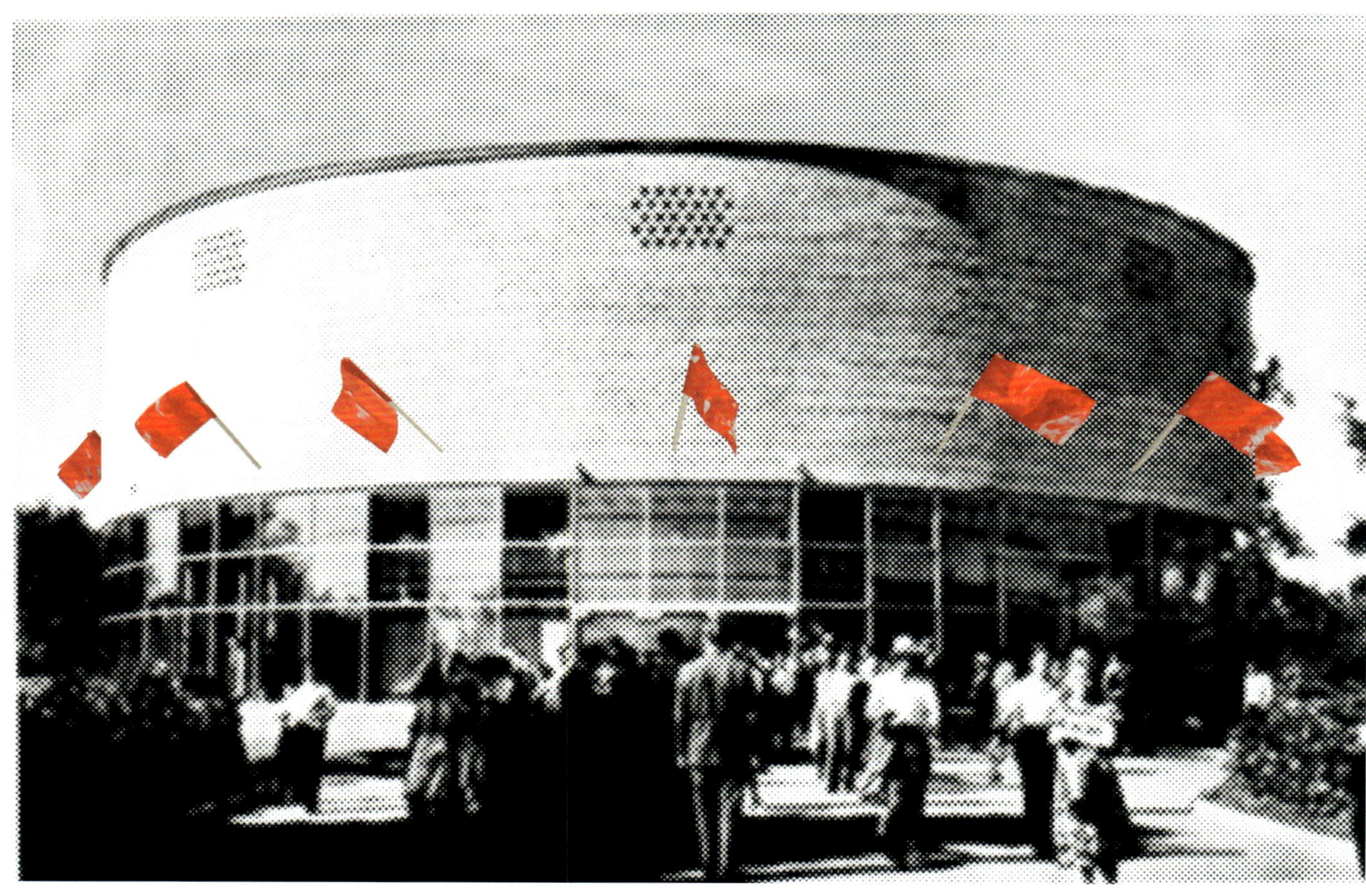

↑
Paperno, Alexandra
Colourization, Cinema of the Repeat Film Project
2015, installation

The sequence of images in this opening section acts as a reminder that Russian art being produced today remains deeply embedded in both recent and – as with the references to the Orthodox Church – apparently more remote Russian history.

Western commentators frequently fail to understand that Russian history and Russia's traditional culture remain part of the national identity: ever present and ever resonant. All too often the cry is 'Why can't they be just like us? With the same preoccupations and obsessions and maybe some of the same prejudices?'

Russian art has now become much more varied than even a short time ago. It also seems to be created in a much greater number of different locations, situated throughout the vastness of Russia. Not surprisingly, these locations often have their own preoccupations and characteristics, but nevertheless they remain quintessentially Russian. The levelling down of Russian society brought about by the now-vanished Soviet regime has been followed by the creation of a very small and very wealthy oligarch class, some of whom of which live abroad in tax havens such as Monaco, but the majority in Russia itself, close to the seat of power.

There is, nevertheless, a kind of populism in much of the art now being produced in Russia, but it is not rigidly enforced. There are aspects of Russian art today that could be credibly described as 'elitist'. But the elite which this describes is not one of wealth. It is, rather, a kind of art that seems to address itself to fellow intellectuals. It does so through an ever-increasing number of public spaces, which now exist in various forms throughout Russia, not just in Moscow and St Petersburg.

→
Reshetnikov, Konstantin
Turnip 200, Import Substitution Series
2020, steel, welding, turning and milling, paint, varnish

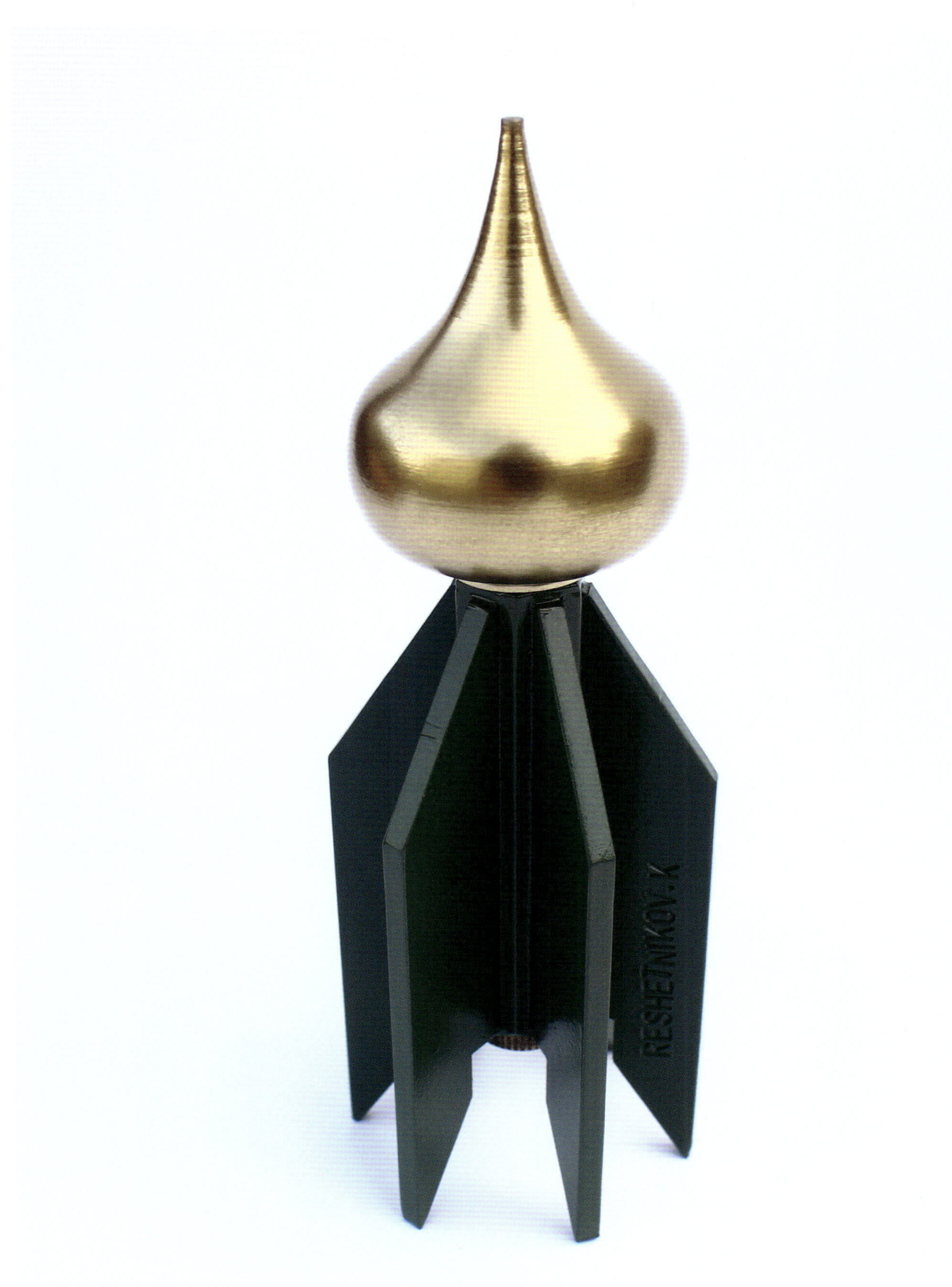
RESHETNIKOV.K

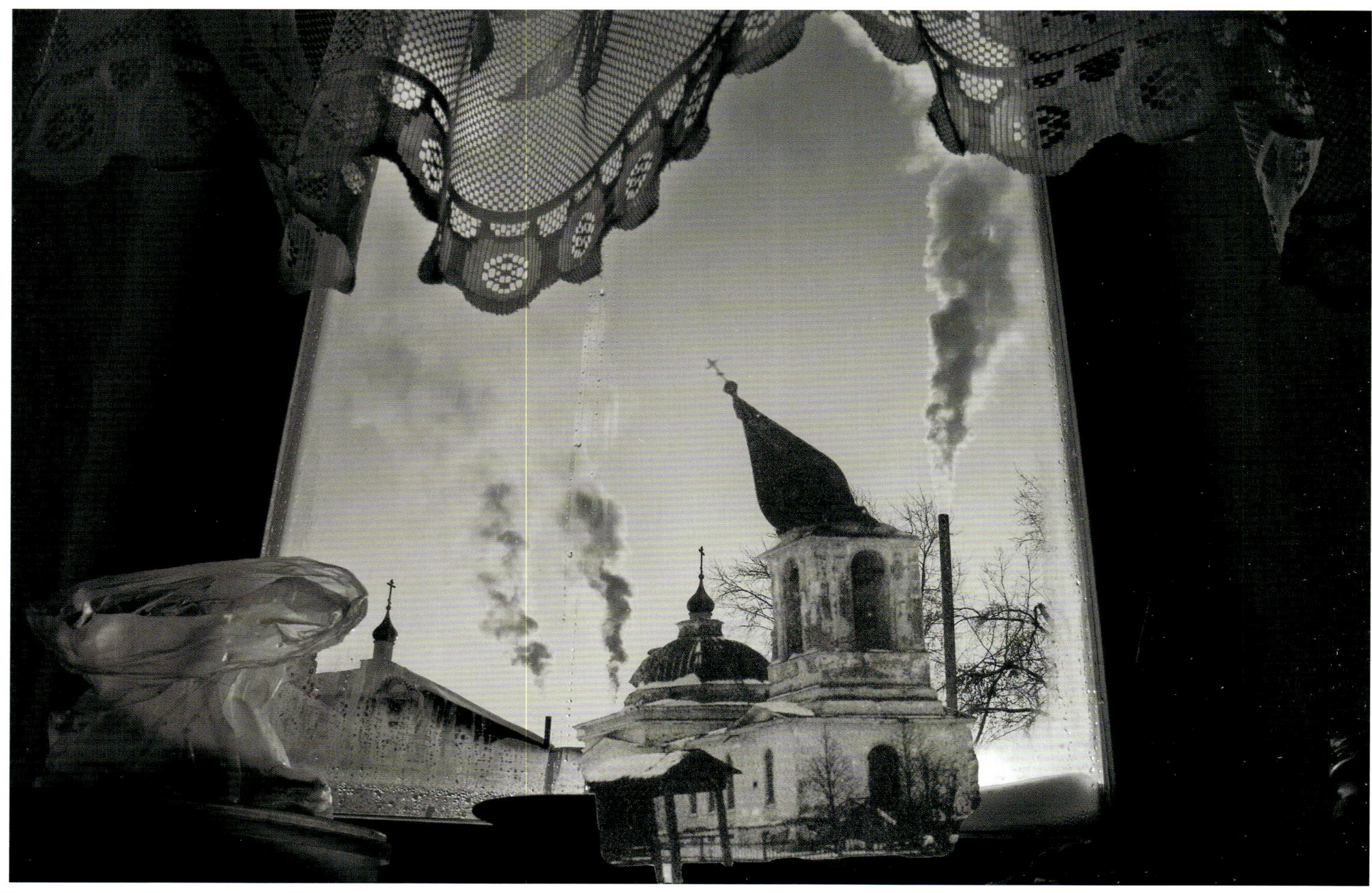

No rigid stylistic diktat has existed in art created in Russia since the Millennium, and more especially during the last ten to fifteen years. It is not a prisoner of realism. It is fully aware of the range of Modernist experiments and styles, back to their very beginnings in the first years of the twentieth century, and sometimes seems to use these as a dictionary for its own experiments. It is also fully aware of recent technological progress in making images. It is by no means the poor relation of technologically experimental art in the West.

In many ways it seems more varied than the art now being produced in the West. In addition, for Western viewers, it may seem surprisingly prompt in its embrace of seemingly 'dissident' opinions. Very often, when there are hints of political trouble, the artist or artists concerned come bouncing back. Russia now has an increasingly elaborate system of official prizes and awards for contemporary artists. An artist can be in trouble with the official system at one moment, and winner of a major award the next.

↑
Poteryaev, Sergey
Untitled, Staraya Utka Series
2013, photoprint

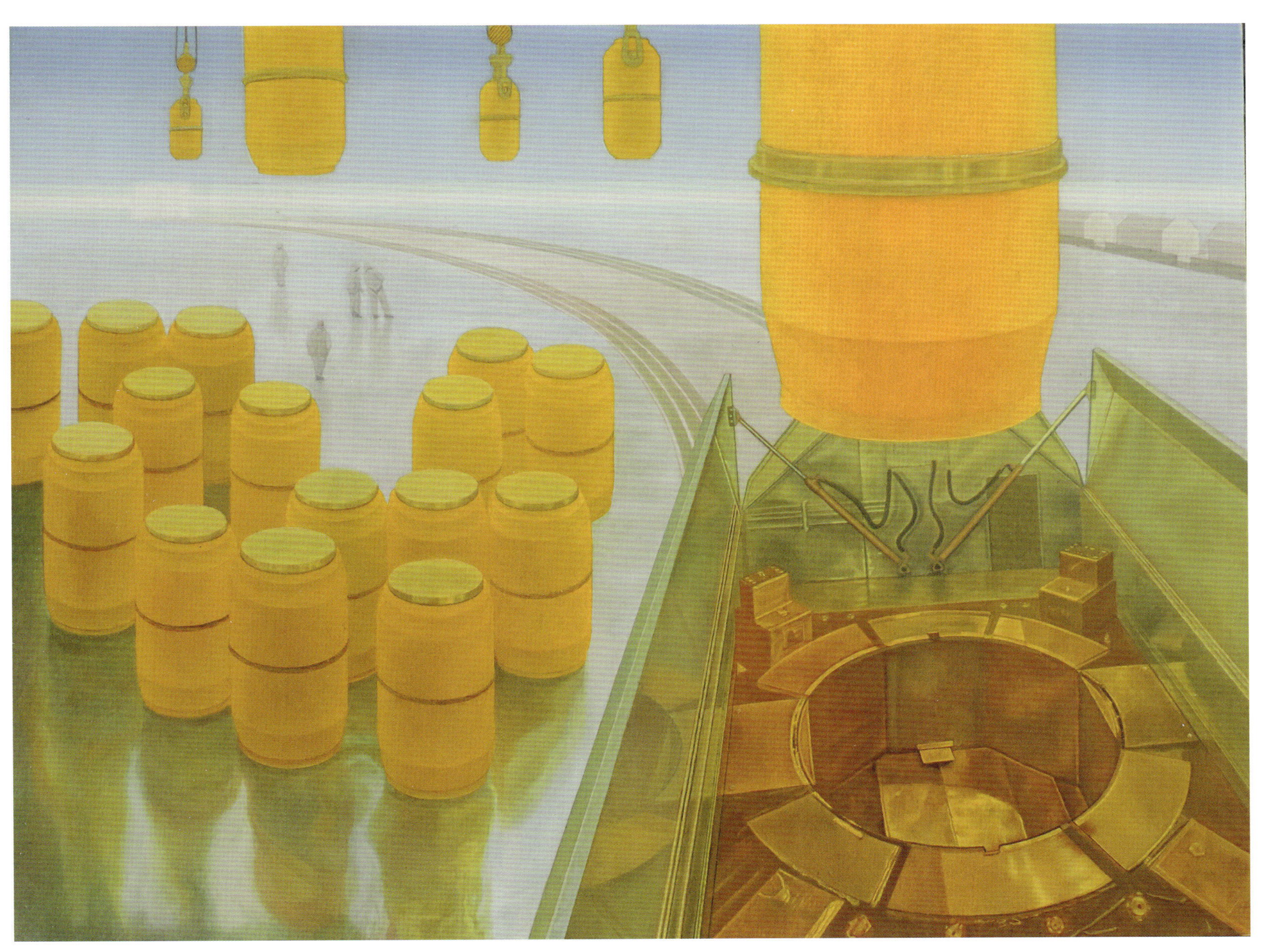

↑
Korotkova, Taisia
Transport of Radioactive Waste
2014, wood, tempera, gesso ground

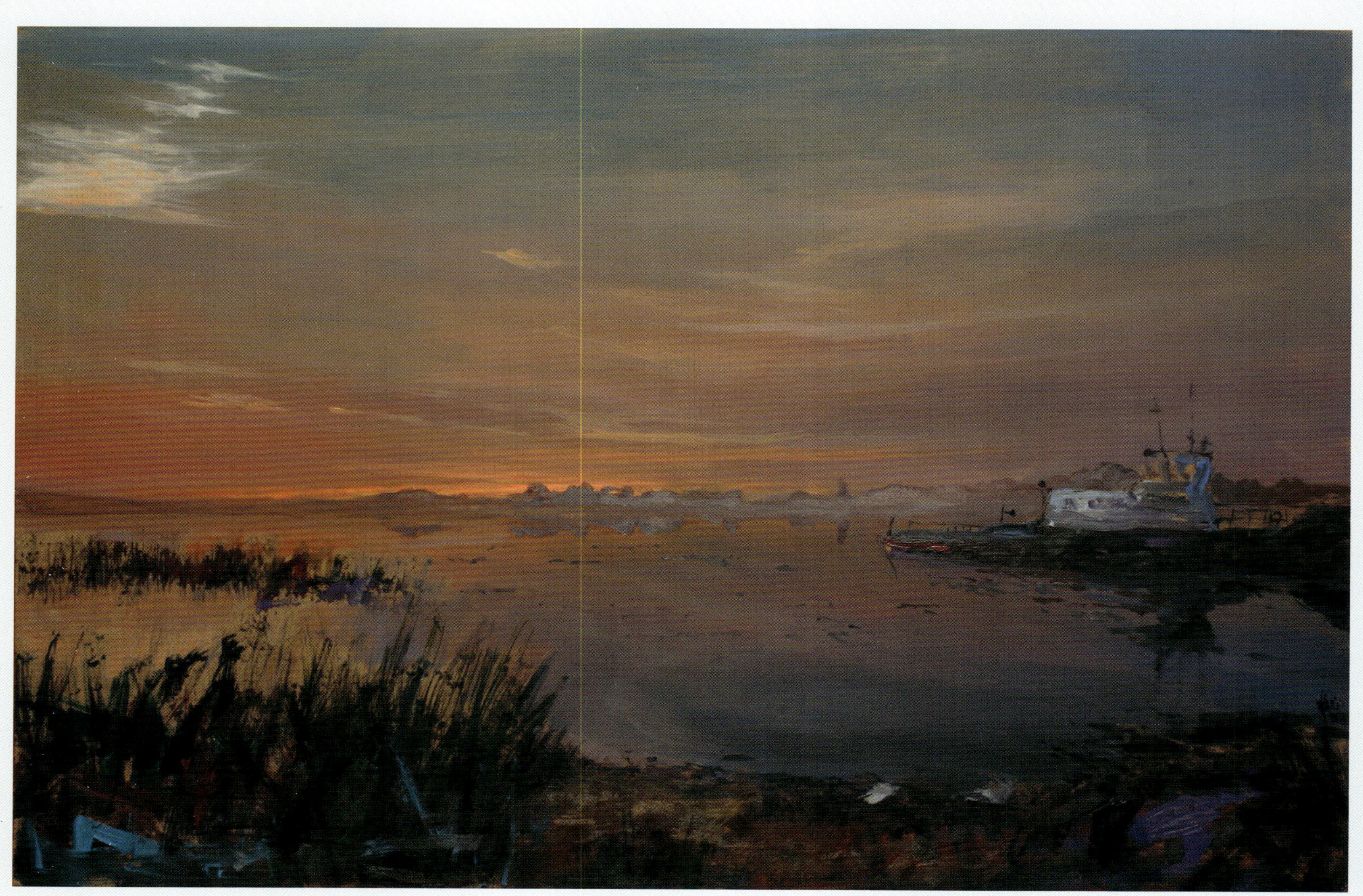

2 NATURE & LANDSCAPE

Landscape painting no longer plays a prominent role in the Western art world – at least not among artists who enjoy major contemporary reputations. There are of course a few celebrated artists who continue to produce work of this kind. Chief among them is the veteran British artist David Hockney (b.1937). Now living in France, he currently produces pictures that are perhaps best described as being 'Monet without the chimney-stacks'.

In Russia, landscape established itself as a major subject for art in the mid-nineteenth century and has never really been absent since. The pioneers were a group of artists who called themselves the Wanderers or Itinerants, who set up a series of popular touring exhibitions in the Russian provinces, as a challenge to art in tsarist St Petersburg. Their paintings were not simply images of landscapes, but pleas for social justice and a celebration of peasant life. As such, they made a fairly easy transition to the new society established by the Soviet government, though the man who was perhaps the most prominent member of the Wanderers disassociated himself from Russia after the Bolsheviks came to power. This was Ilya Repin (1844–1930) who was internationally famous by the time the Revolution broke out in 1917. He owned an estate on the other side of the border that now divided Russia from Finland and decided to retain his residence there. However, Repin remained on cordial terms with the new government, and in 1925 a major exhibition of his work was held at the State Russian Museum in what was then Leningrad. His work continued to be held up as an example to Soviet painters after his death. Its influence is still felt today.

The artists included in this section are quite widely separated in age. The oldest, Ilgiz Gimranov, was born in 1960. The youngest, Stanislav Miroshnikov, was born in 1985. They all nevertheless have great similarity of style. Most of the group belong to a generation too young to have known much at first hand, or indeed anything at all, about the then dissolving Soviet art world. What they

←
Gimranov, Ilgiz
Life Like a Dream
2018, acrylic on hardboard

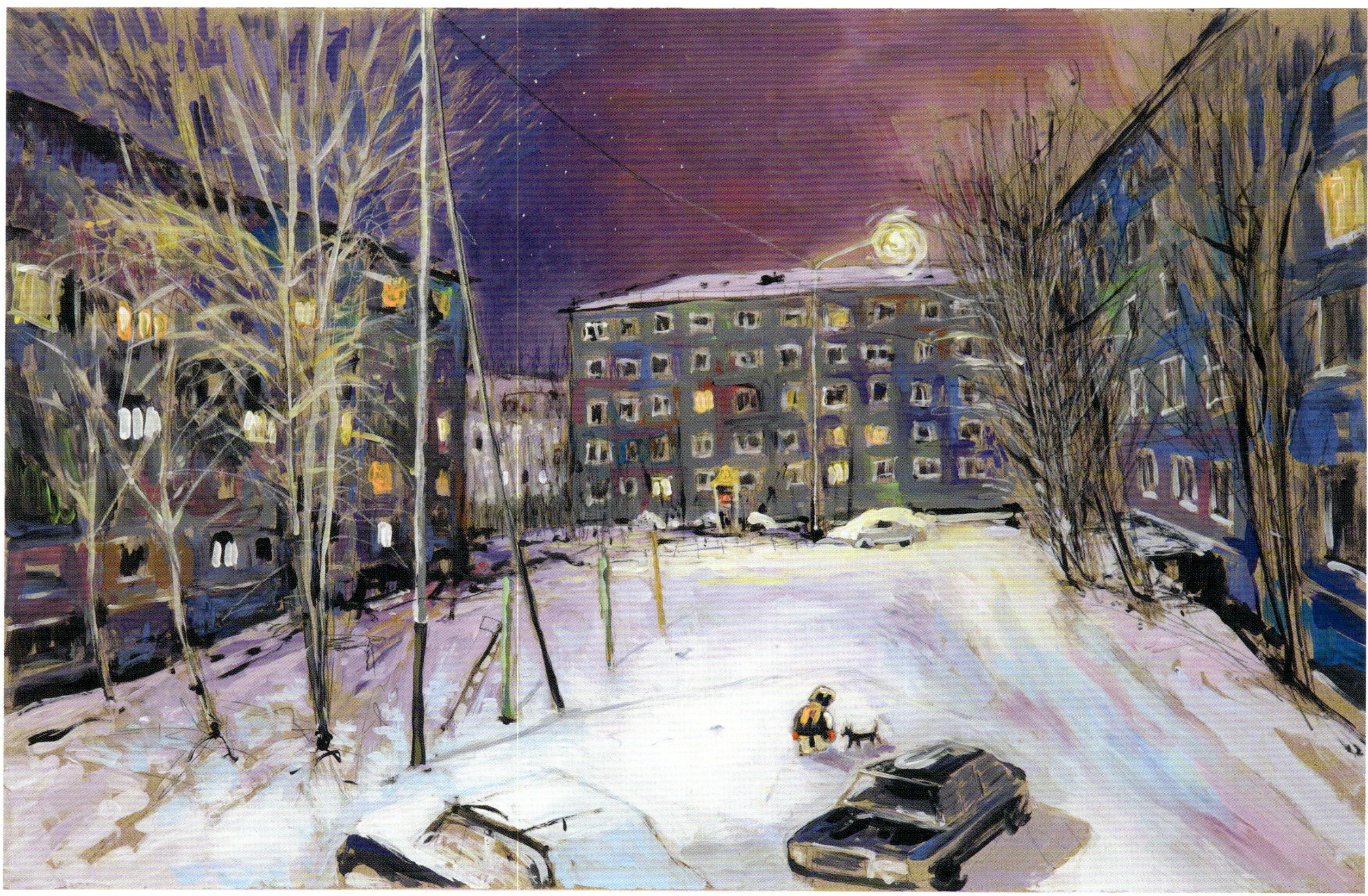

do perhaps show is the professionalism of the training system that the Soviets inherited from the academies of the nineteenth century, and which the Russia of the new century was in no hurry to discard. Gimranov's *Life Like a Dream* (2018) takes the viewer to the banks of the Volga, the largest river in European Russia. His *Aren't Your Paws Frozen*, dated 2017, picks up on themes already familiar from Soviet landscape art – winter, the urban environment, large blocks of flats where collective lives are lived.

Almost as neutral in attitude is Dmitry Shorin's (b. 1971), *Simeiz* (2020), a reference to the famous Black Sea resort, and *Pushkin,* (2018), a winter landscape of the park in Pushkin, a town near St Petersburg. It was named Tsarskoye Selo or Tsar's Village and was an imperial residence during the time of Elizabeth, the Empress of Russia in 1741-1762. The most famous Russian poet Alexander Pushkin studied at Tsarskoye Selo Lyceum, an elite school for Russian nobles, housed in a wing of her magnificent palace, at the start of the 19th century.

It is, of course not surprising that contemporary Russian landscape painting is rich in scenes featuring snow.

Some of the landscapes are less studiedly neutral, but are instead confident continuations of the nineteenth century Romantic tradition. This is the case, for instance, with Vitaly Pushnitsky's (b. 1967) *The Death of Orpheus* (2018) – an overgrown thicket with an abandoned chair.

↑
Gimranov, Ilgiz
Aren't Your Paws Frozen?
2017, acrylic on hardboard

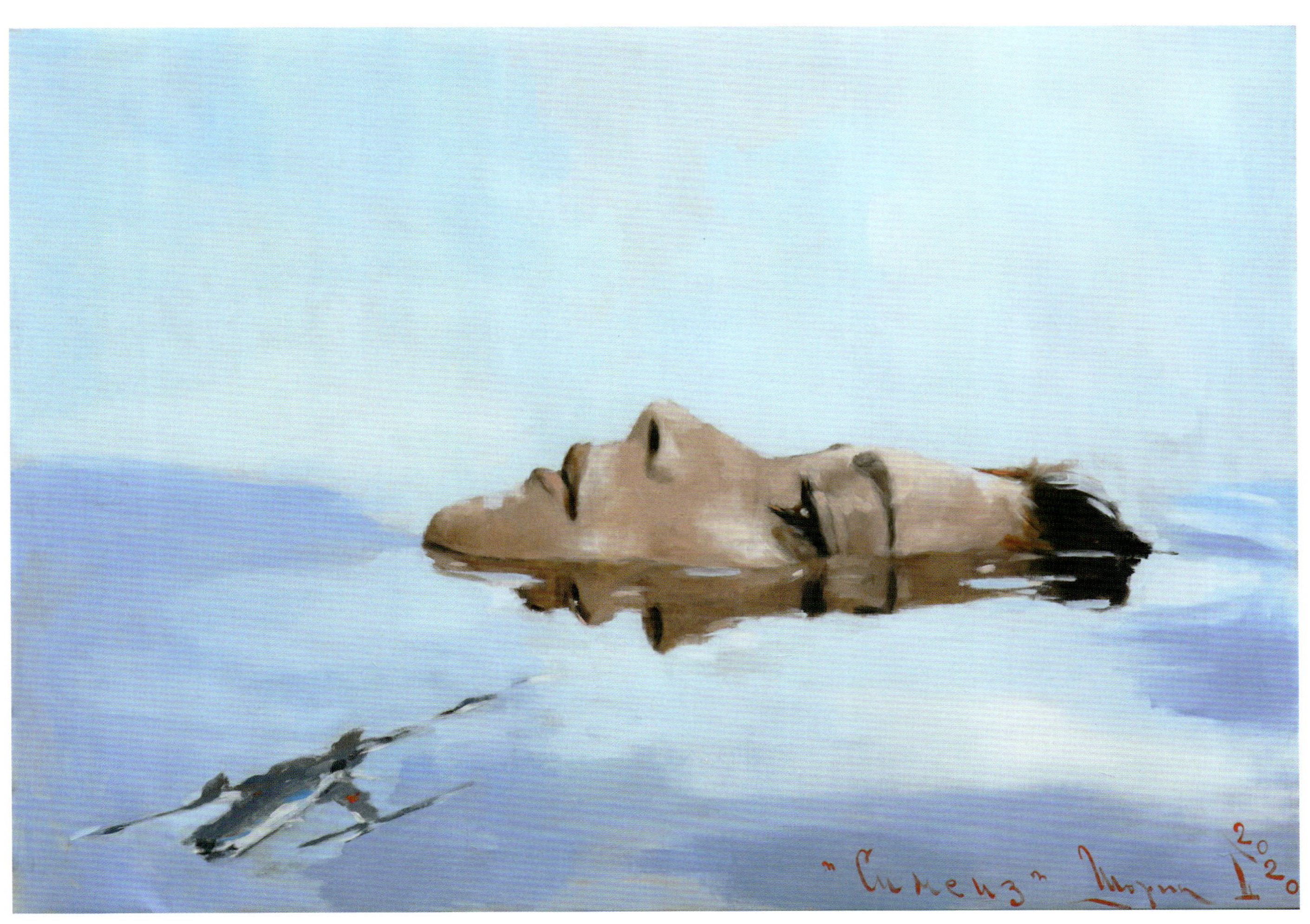

↑
Shorin, Dmitry
Simeiz
2020, oil on canvas

↓
Shorin, Dmitry
Pushkin
2018, oil on canvas

→
Pushnitsky, Vitaly
The Death of Orpheus Nr. 1
2018, oil on canvas

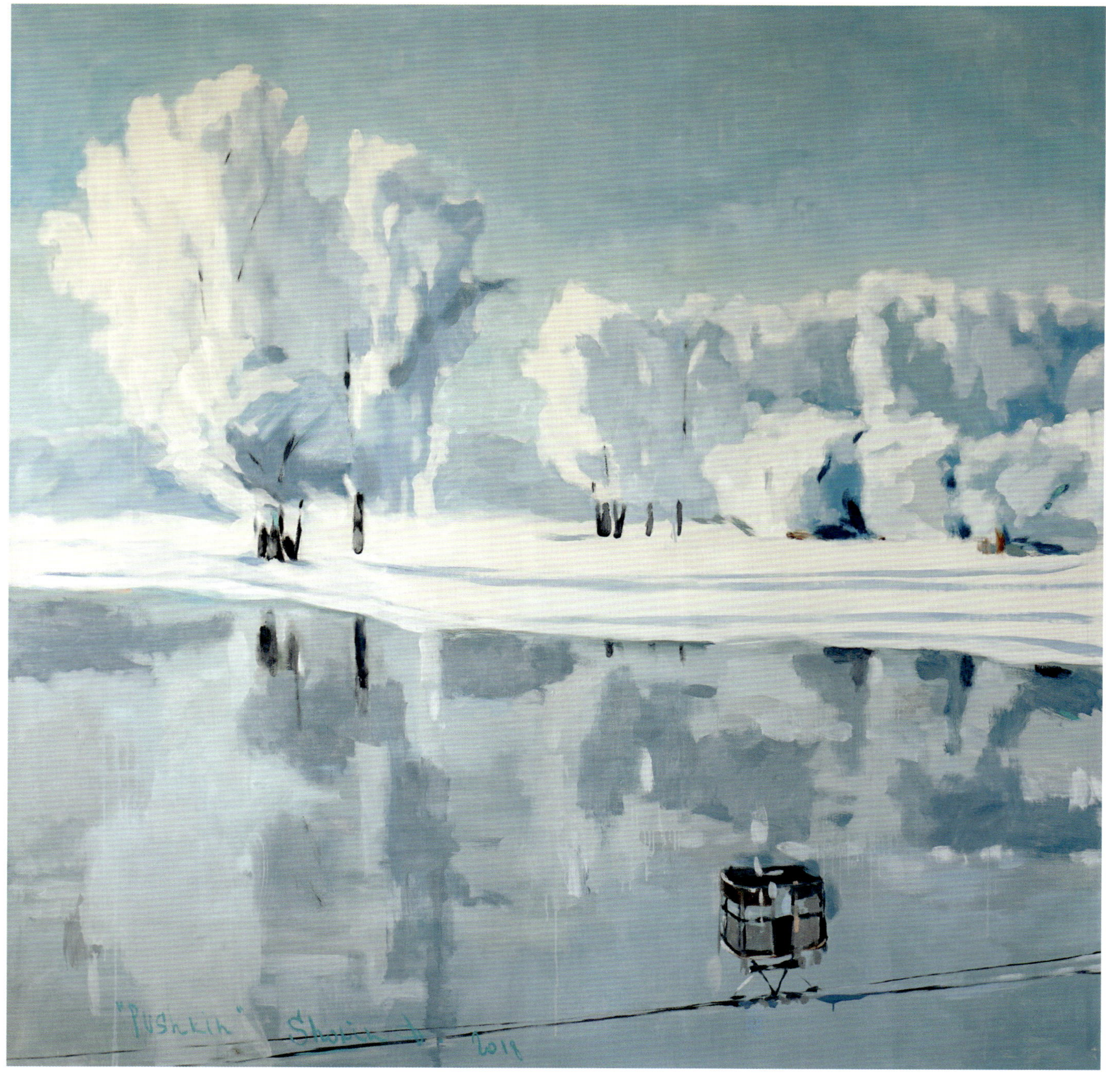

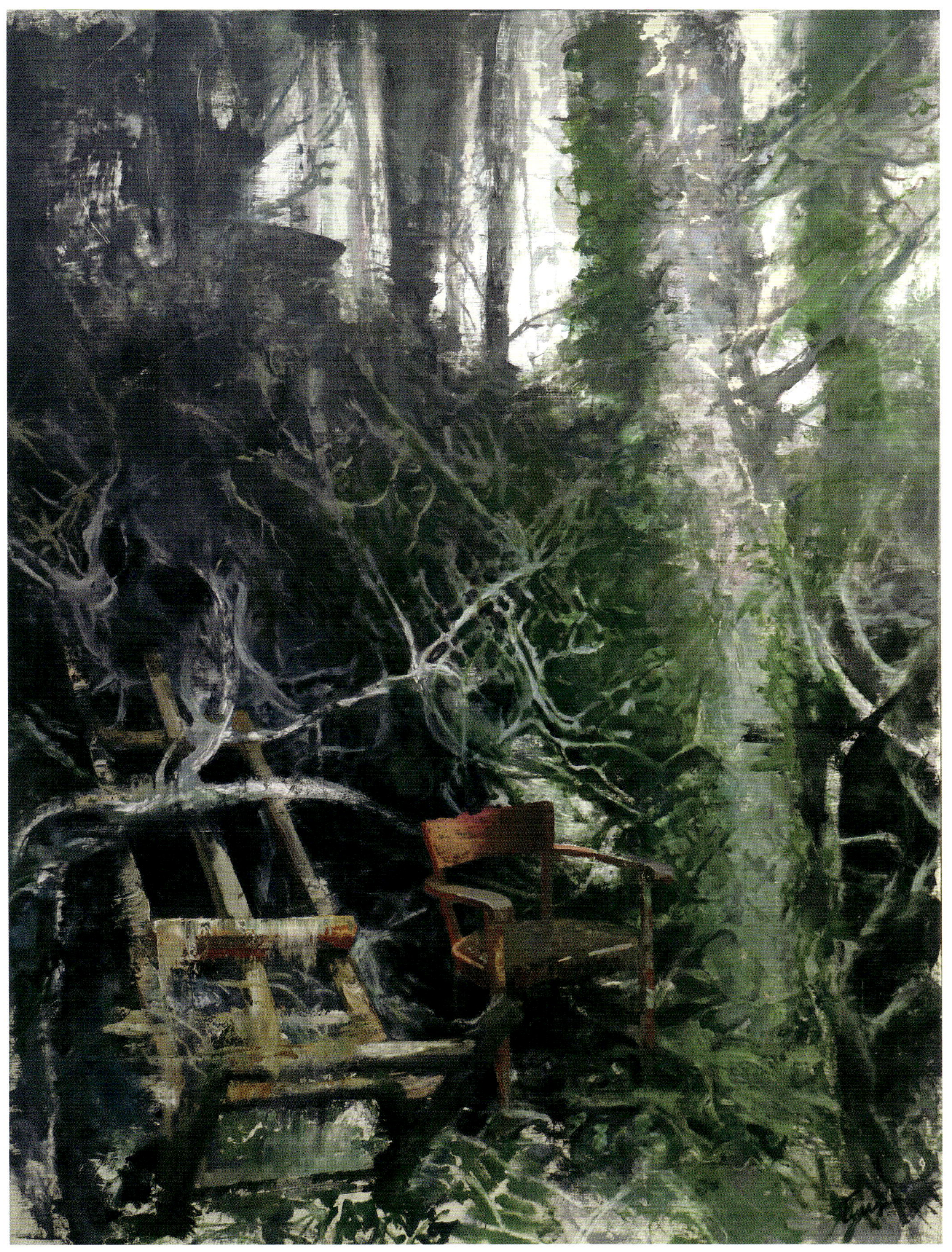

Vasily Kuraksa (b. 1981) offers a studiously national image of the Russian North. His *Solovetsky Island* (2018) is dominated, at the background of the composition, by a towering Solovetsky Monastery, a northmost Orthodox Christian stronghold, founded in the first half on the 15th century. During its long history the monastery was used as a fortress, a prison and housed a biological science station. The winter cityscape is of Yuryev-Polsky, an old Russian town which still has St. George's Cathedral (1230-1234), the last white-stone church built in Russia before the Mongol invasion[1]. Kuraksa is well-established. He is a member of the Union of Artists of Russia, the Moscow Union of Artists, the Association of Painters, a corresponding member of the International Academy of Culture and Arts and of the Russian Academy of Arts.

In contrast to this, Oleg Borodin, in the context of the exhibition *Irony as a Landscape* (mentioned earlier), offers a landscape painted on the side of a towering apartment building, with other, similar buildings clustered in the background and a row of automobiles parked on the snowy road in front of it. Borodin describes himself as a collagist who was previously a photographer.

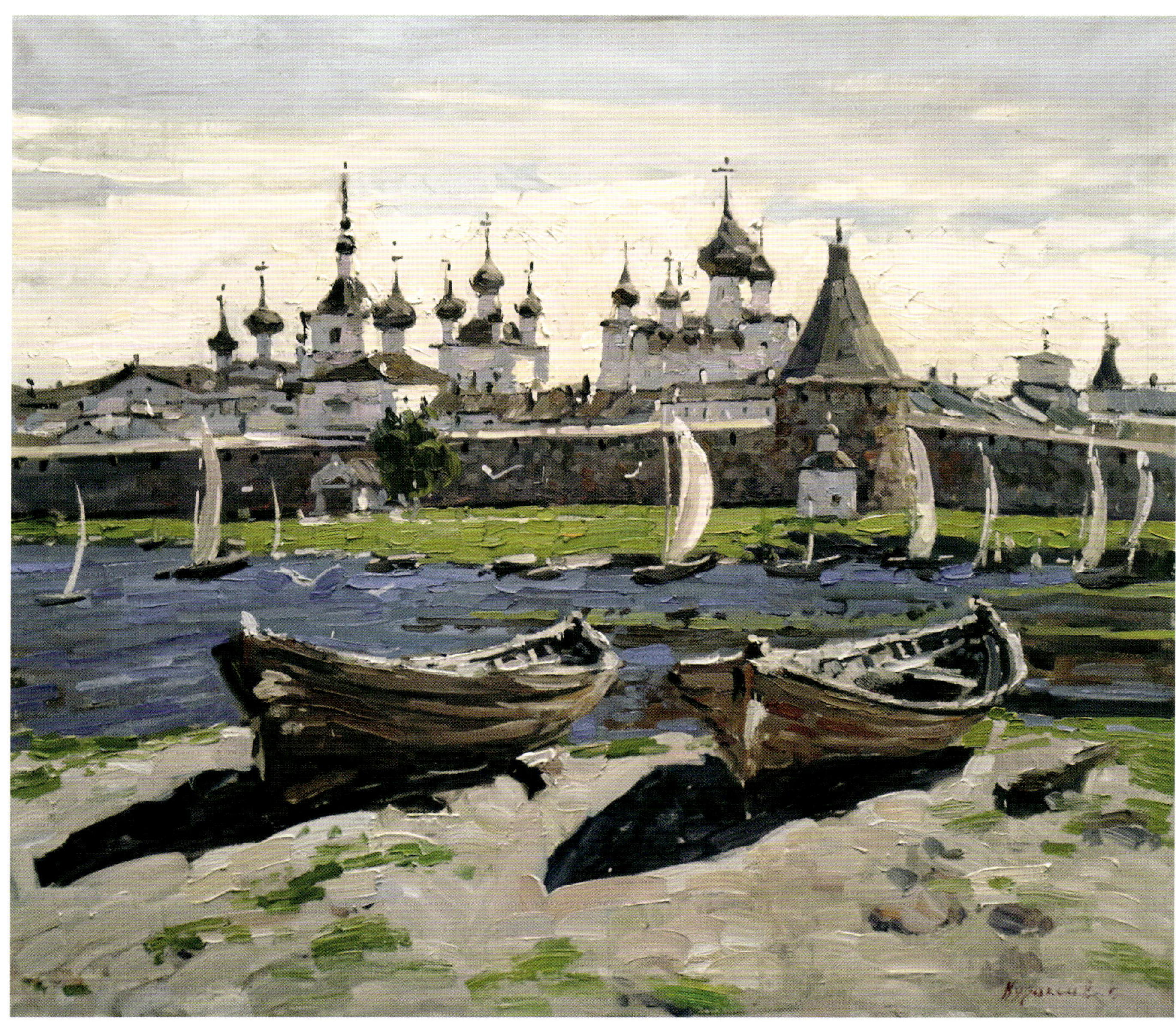

←
Kuraksa, Vasily
Solovetsky Island
2018, oil on canvas

↓
Kuraksa, Vasily
Yuryev-Polsky
2018, oil on canvas

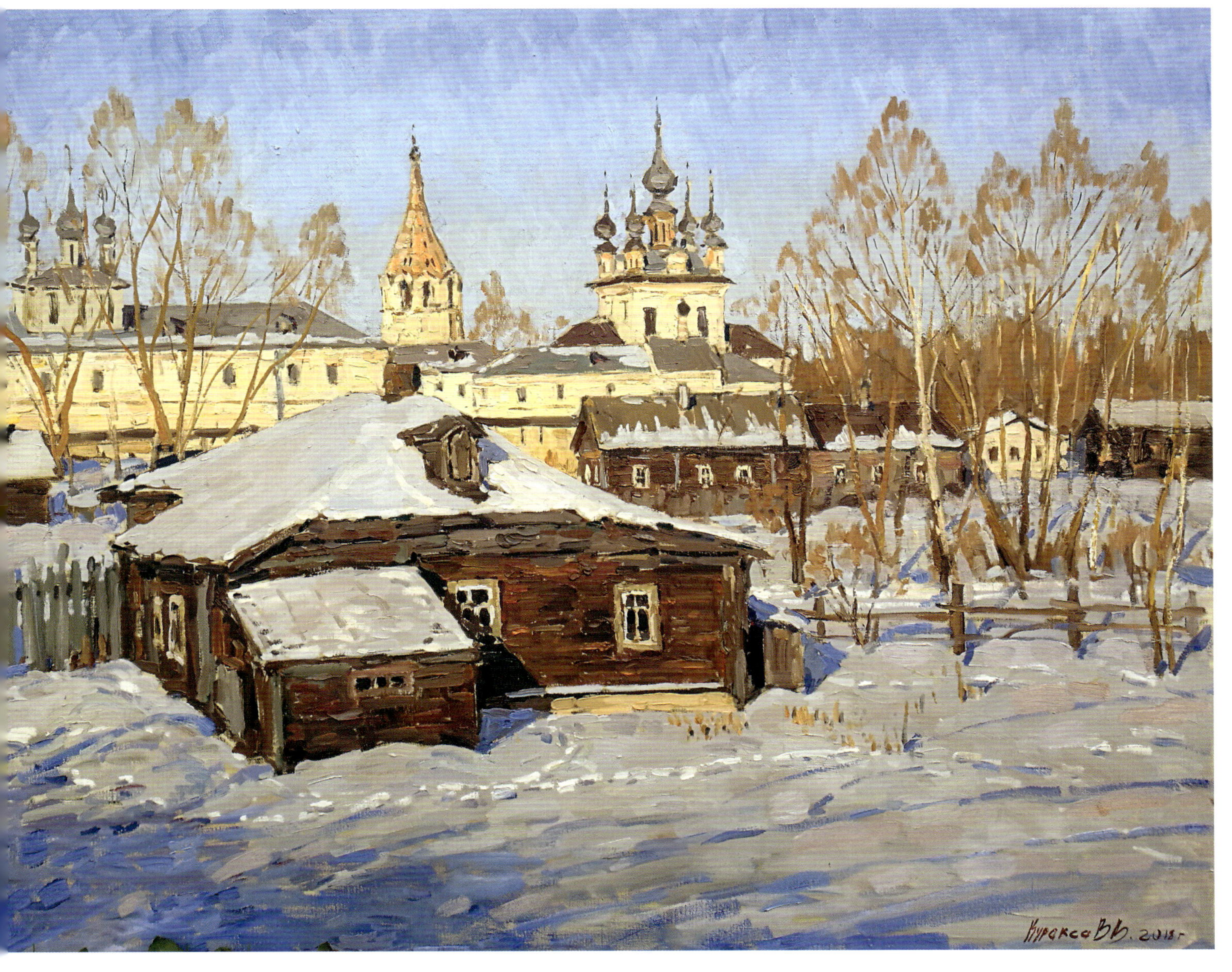

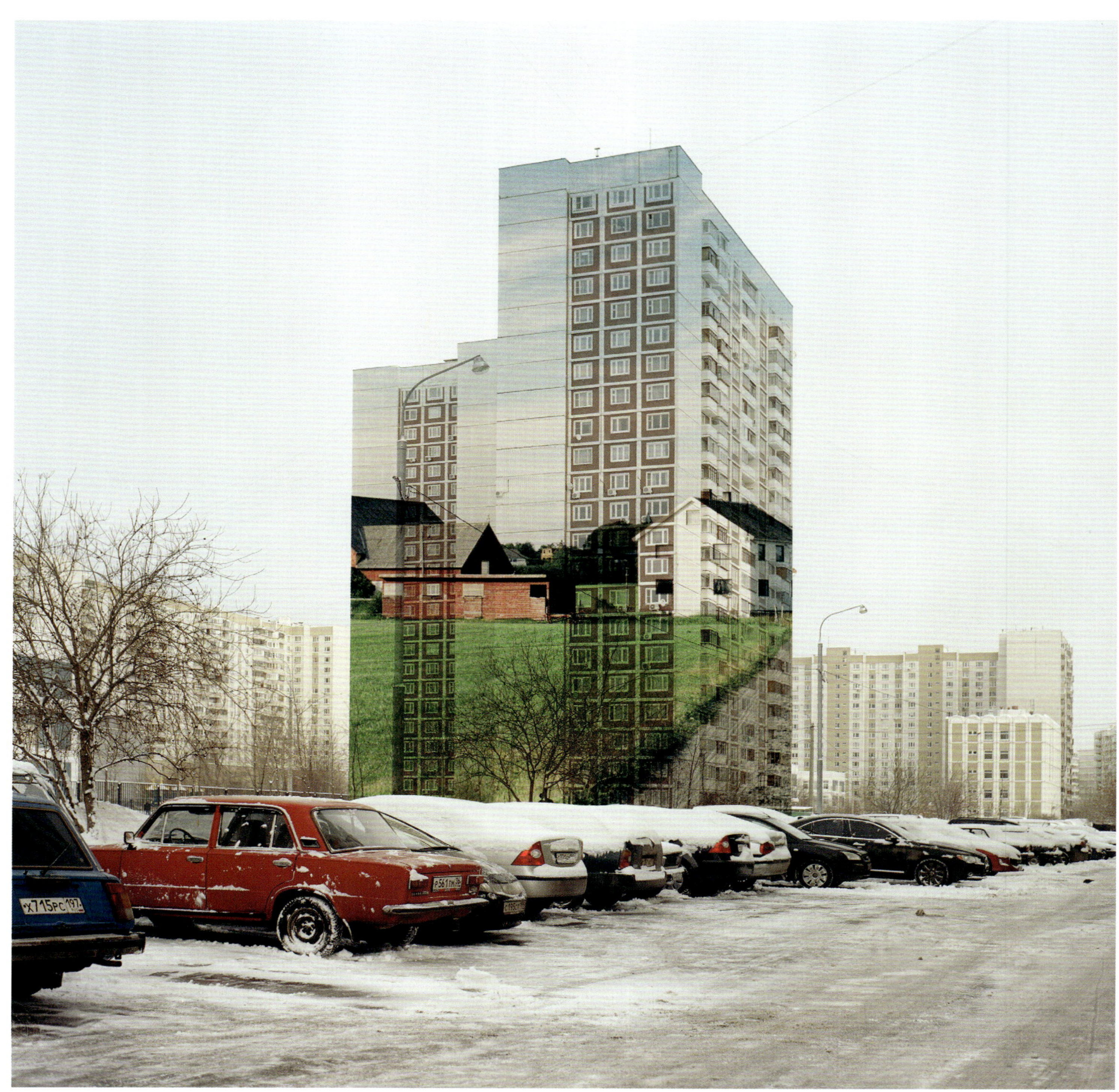

↑
Borodin, Oleg
Untitled, Irony as a Landscape Series
2016, colour printing on paper

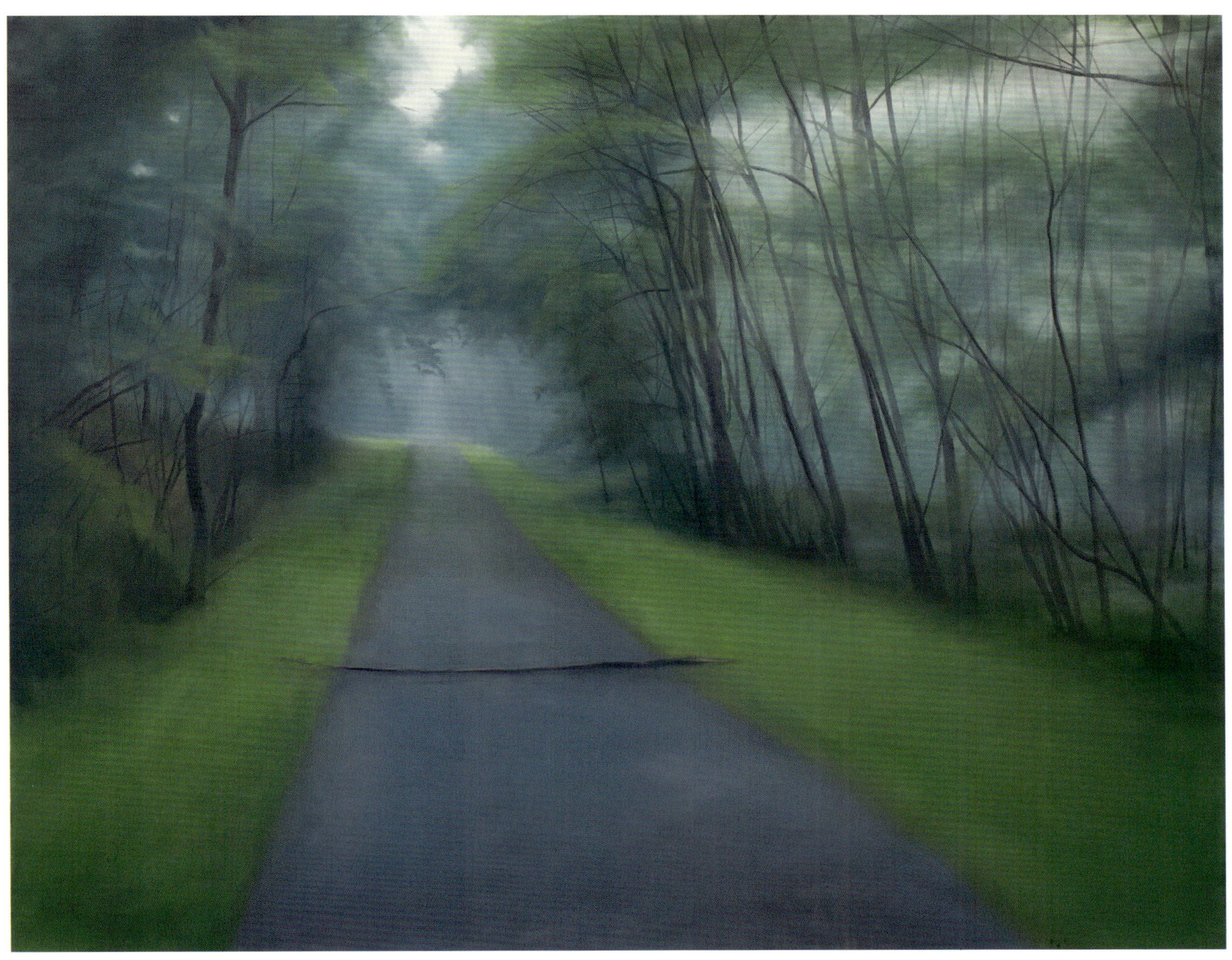

↑
Buravleva, Evgeniya
Rain
2017, oil on canvas

He says, in an interview: 'The exhibition [was] a rather important project for me, which took place just at the transitional stage between photography and collage… On the whole, the exhibition became a kind of landmark event – the end of my photography practice, after which I went even more into collage and never really returned to photography in its pure form.'[2]

The image offers a skilful blend between two different kinds of reality, one urban and the other pastoral and rural. It suggests the conflict that exists in contemporary Russian society between these two realities.

Some images here, like Evgeniya Buravleva's (b. 1980) *Rain* (2017) seem to pick up a vibe from the Symbolist Movement at the end of the nineteenth century. This influence is even more obvious in Stanislav Miroshnikov's (b. 1985) canvas *Dream* (2018), with its beautiful female dreamer asleep high up on a green hill overlooking a river at sunset. This might even, at first glance, be a painting by a late nineteenth century British Pre-Raphaelite.

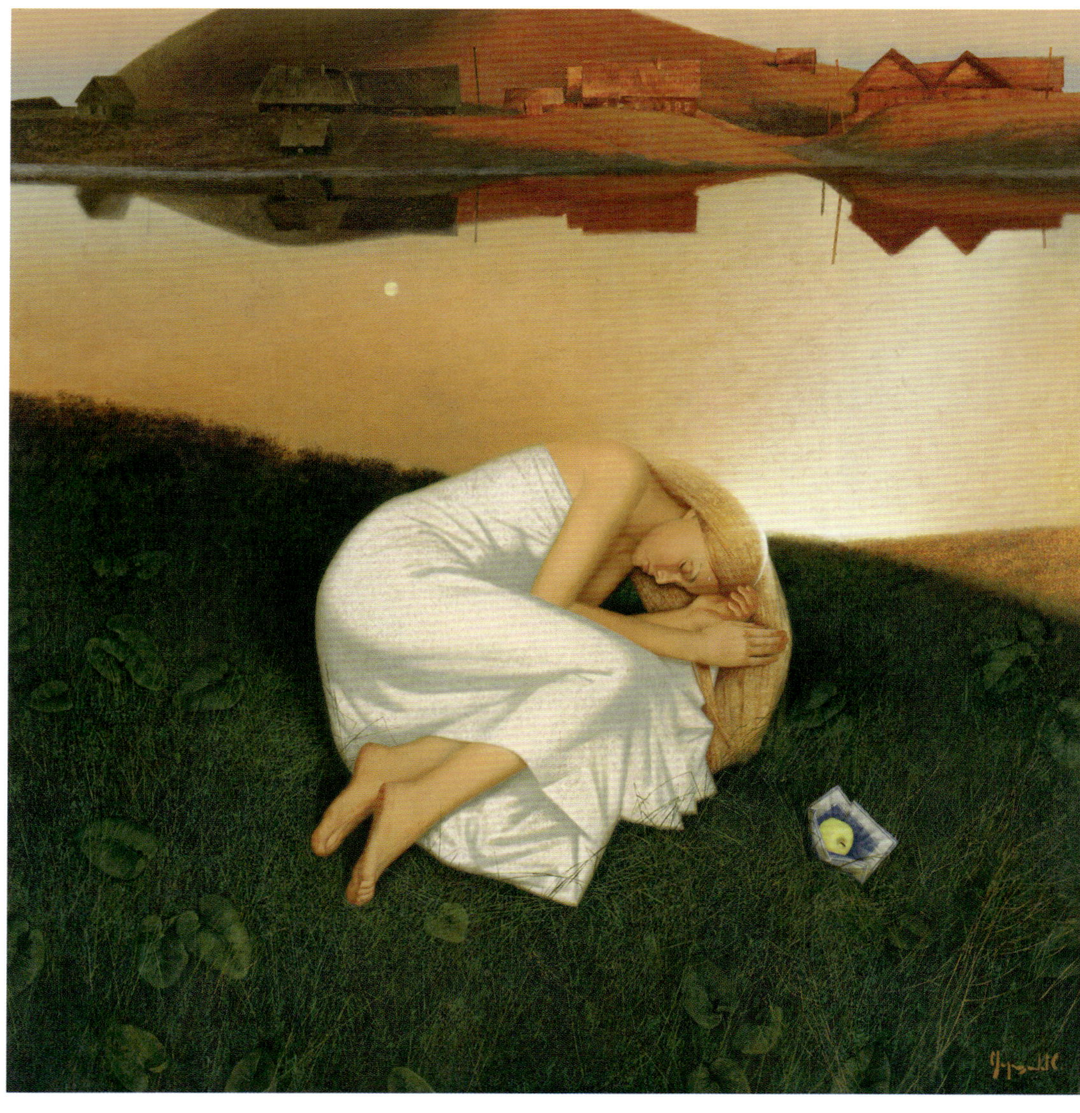

←
Miroshnikov, Stanislav
Dream
2018, oil on canvas

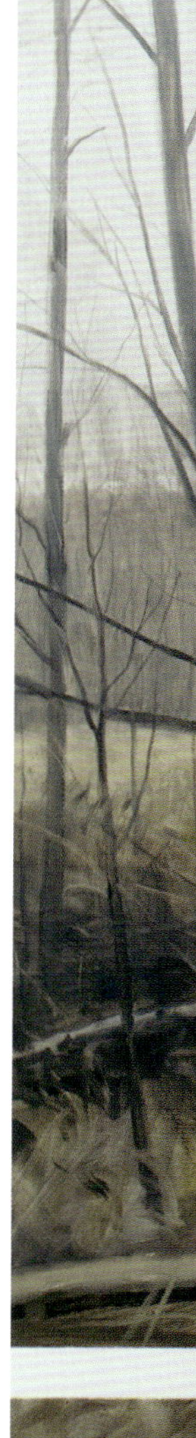

The Russian contemporary painters featured have a secure grasp of the basic technical skills that are needed in order to produce the images they have in mind: more so, perhaps, than most young painters now working in the West. In the training they have received in Russian, and in some cases also in European art schools, there also seems to have been no element of the 'Oh, we must leave them to find themselves' approach now so universally prevalent in British and American institutions of the same type.

Even when the mood is quite bleak the works are projections of "a dream-like reality from which neither the protagonist nor the viewer can escape" as, for example, in Egor Plotnikov's (b. 1980) *Second Half of the Day* (2020), a view through a window of saplings stripped of all their foliage, but not yet blanketed in snow[3]. Egor graduated from the Moscow Surikov State Academy Art Institute (studio of Pavel Nikonov (b.1930), one of the founders of so-called "Severe Style"[4]). in 2006 and makes figurative painting and sculptures often presented as combined installations.[5]

↓
Plotnikov, Egor
Second Half of The Day
2020, oil on canvas

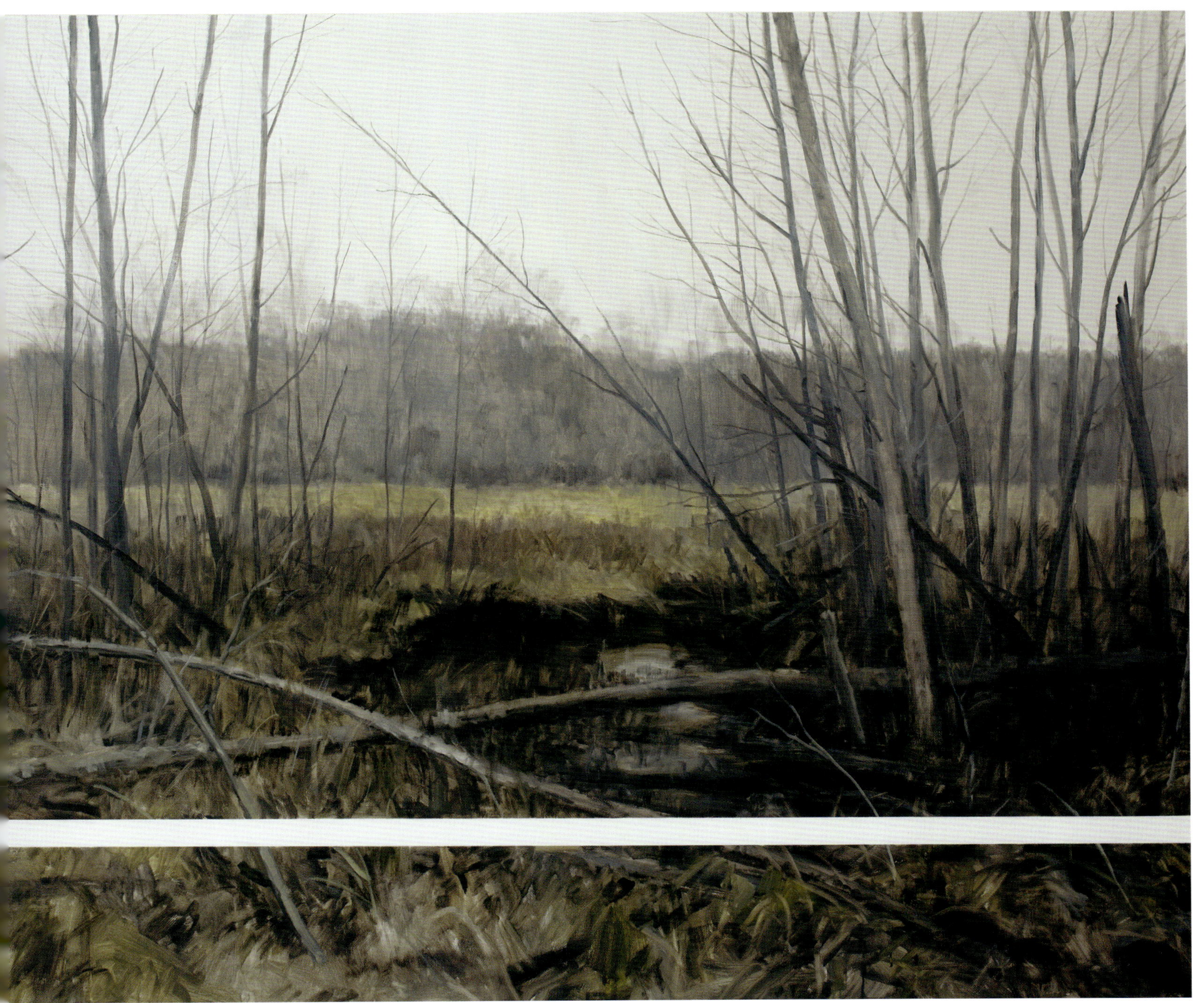

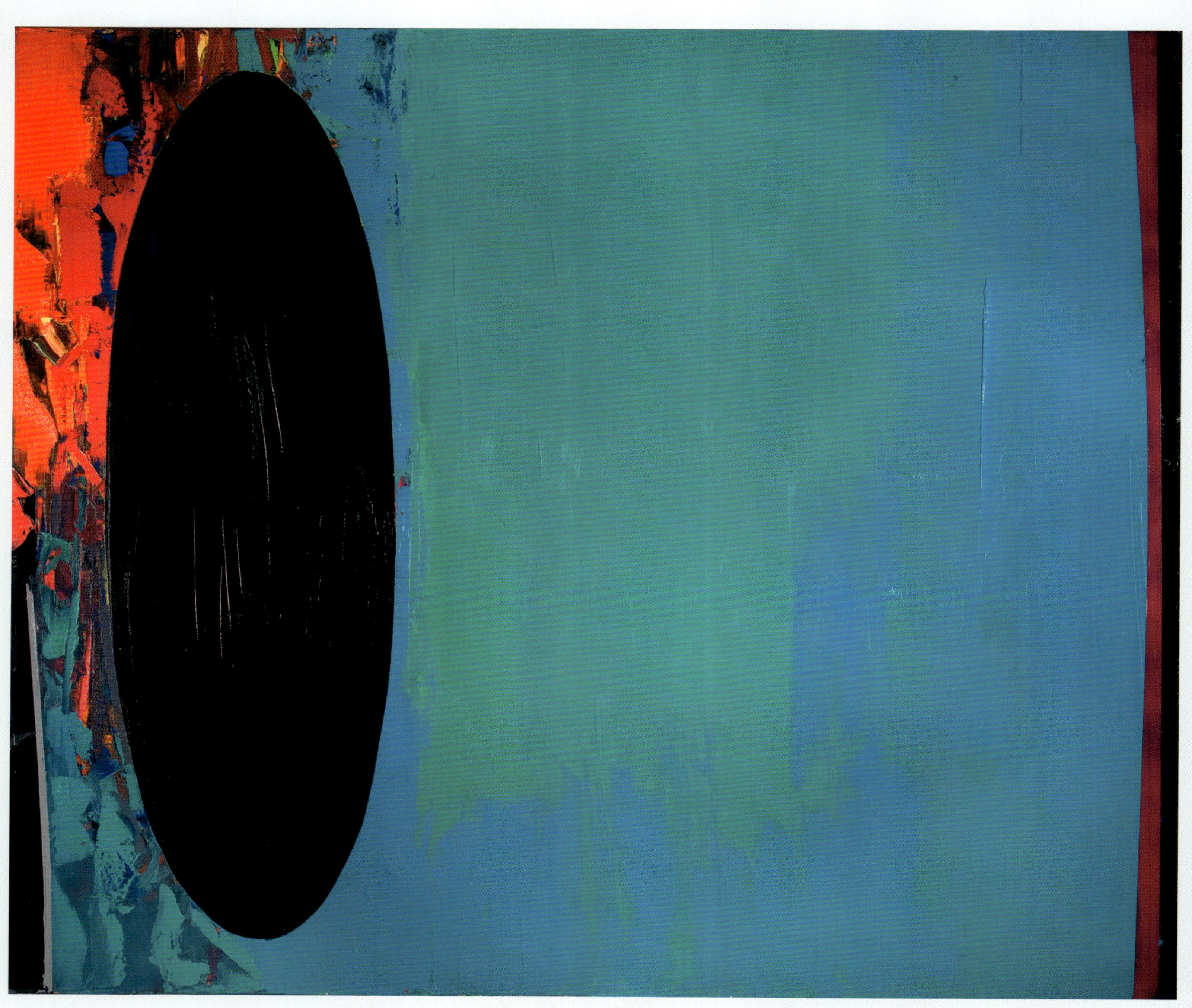

3 ABSTRACT & SURREALIST ART

In a recent essay, Alexander Borovsky, head of the Contemporary Art Department of the State Russian Museum in St Petersburg, pointed out that abstract art, supposedly banned in Russia during most of the Soviet period, had never really disappeared. Instead it had simply gone into hiding. In the case of works by leading abstractionists of the Early Modern epoch, such as Kazimir Malevich (1879-1935), this hiding place was very often the storerooms of great official museums. This was also true of the works of the abstract and figurative artists who were exhibiting their art in the Soviet Union unofficially in the 1960s and became widely known as Nonconformists.

As Soviet control over the visual arts began to crumble in the Gorbachev era, increasing numbers of Russian artists began to look with interest at the heritage of European Modernism. This interest became more fully liberated when the Soviet regime fell apart in the 1991 and is increasingly visible in Russian art today. Ironically, this is happening just at the time when young artists in the West seem to be losing faith in classic Modernist doctrines, and to be turning instead to various forms of populism.

In this section of the book, we want to illustrate the work of contemporary Russian artists who can either be classified as abstract, or else who seem to be allied, in one way or the other, to the heritage of Surrealism.

It is noticeable that two of these artists, Andrey Volkov (b. 1968) and Rinat Voligamsi (also b. 1968) are considerably older than most of those featured in this book – that is to say, closer to the Soviet past, though their artistic careers did not fully begin until after the Soviet Union collapsed. Volkov first exhibited as an artist in 1985 but did not graduate from the Stroganoff Academy of Art and Industry in Moscow until 1993. He became a member of the Moscow Union of Artists in 1995 and was a participant in the Fifty-First Venice Biennale in 2005. His work can now be found in the collection of the State Russian Museum in St Petersburg.

←
Volkov, Andrey
Family Secrets
2007, oil on canvas

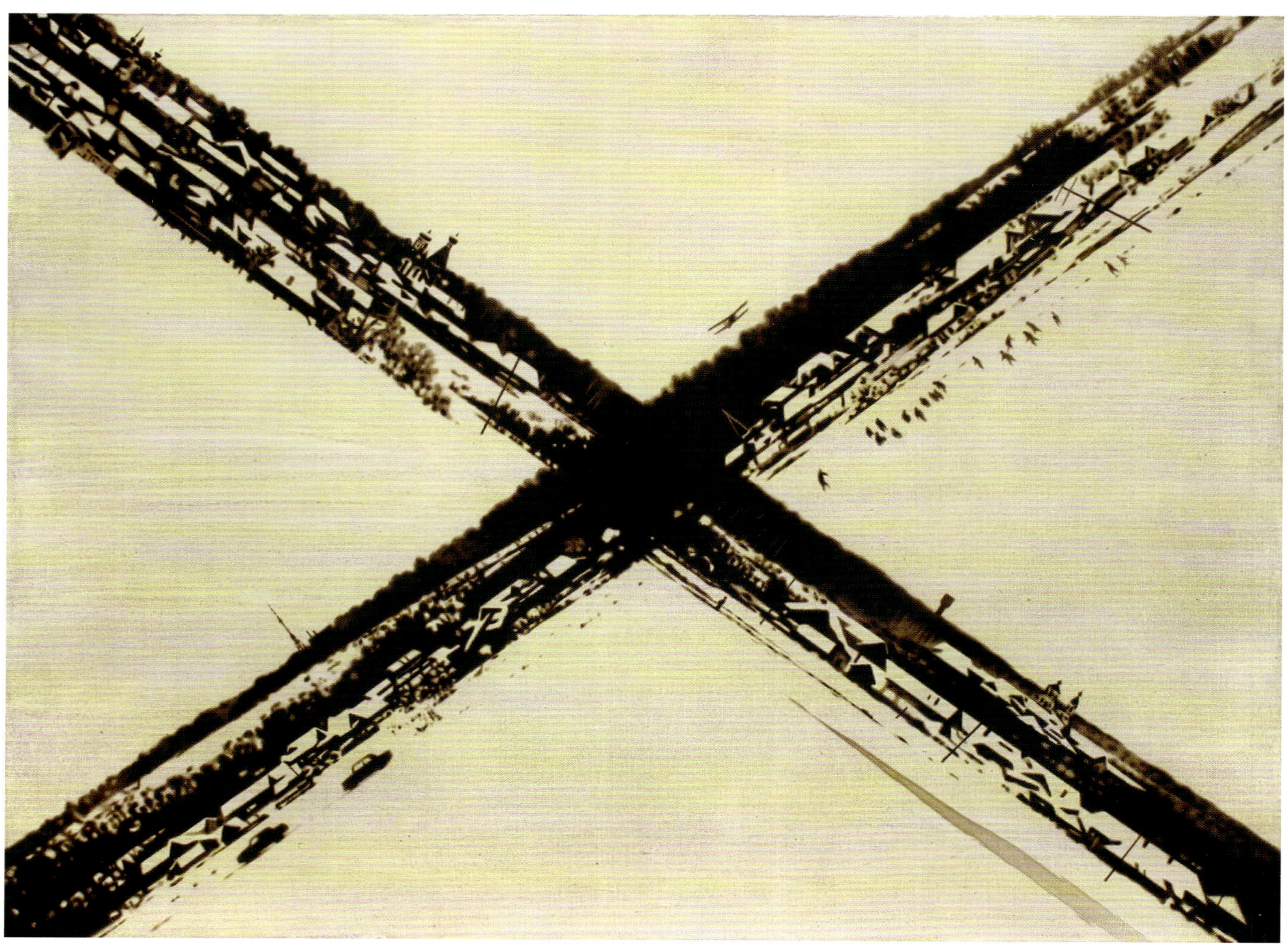

In an interview with art critic Anastasia Martynova about his work, Volkov had this to say:

> I would like to 'slow down' the viewer. 'Slow art', as it were. In the endless stream of changing visual images, photographs, primarily, the value of the image is devalued. I would like the material density of the painting to create a kind of gravitational effect, a slowdown, so that the viewer senses time itself. I've had interesting coincidences happen where someone has come up to me, complete strangers, looked at my work, and told me what I myself had been feeling. My Facebook friend came to my exhibition in Italy in the summer of 2016, and we had never met in real life before. And he suddenly began talking about the works in the same exact words I would have used myself, although there were no specific commentaries on the works at the exhibition.[1]

Rinat Voligamsi is partly self-taught. He entered the Ufa State Technological University in the Architecture Department in 1984, but did not graduate until 1989, due to an interval as a conscript in military service. He was awarded the State Prize of Russia in 2005, and gained international attention the following year with a project called *Unofficial Album*: a fictitious biography of Lenin and his supposed twin brother Sergei. Lenin did in fact have an older brother, not a twin, who was called Alexander ('Sasha') Ulyanov. He joined a terrorist group that plotted to assassinate Tsar Alexander III. They were rounded up and hanged before they could make the attempt.

↑
Voligamsi, Rinat
Cross-landscape
2013, oil on canvas

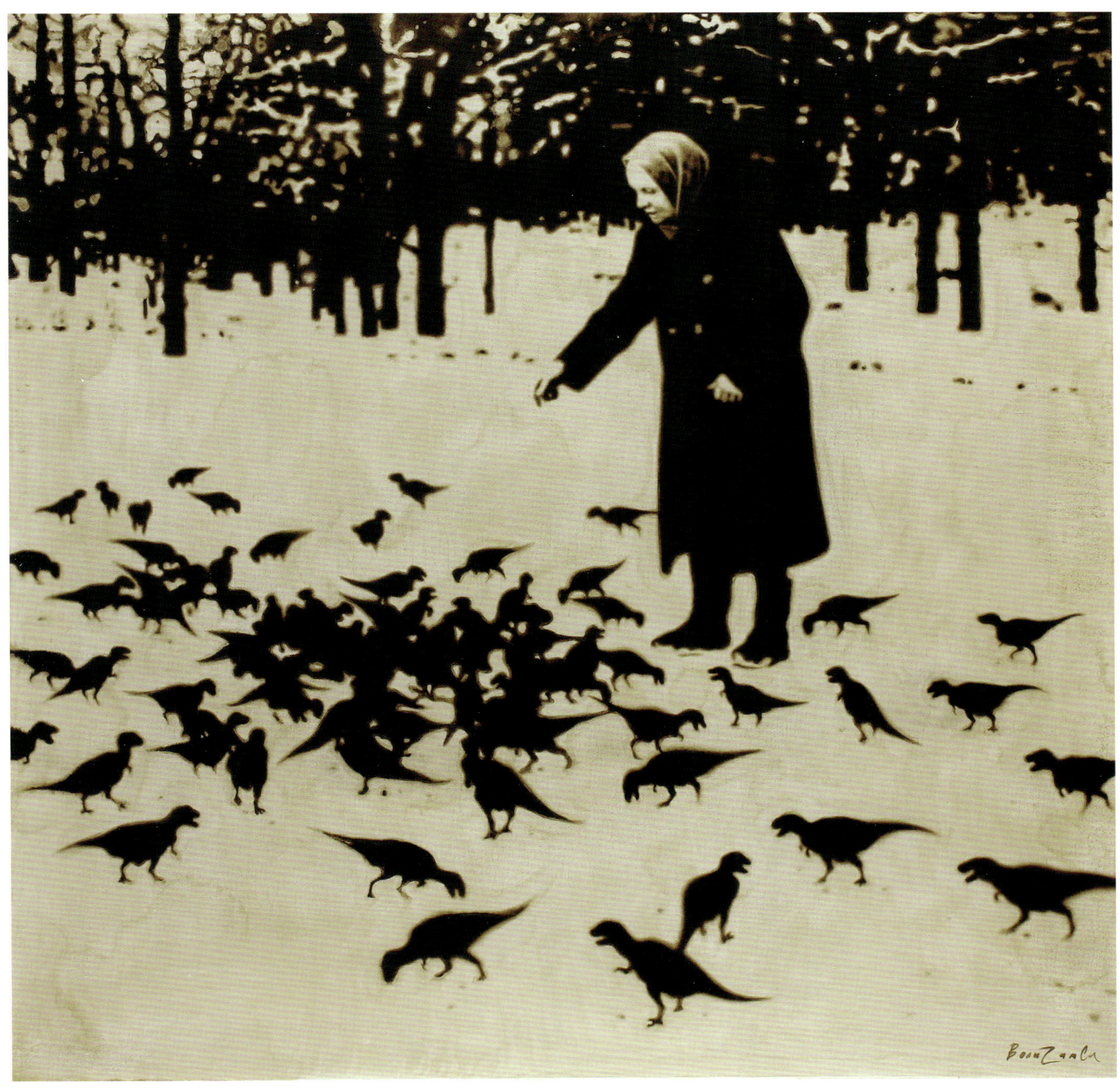

↑
Voligamsi, Rinat
Winter Day
2015, oil on canvas

In Voligamsi's work, as the internet commentary relates, 'The kingdom of dreams takes over reality. The author's quasi-documentary method closely examines the universe though a surrealistic lens. There can be no doubt in the veracity of the grotesque... no protective mechanism works, and a viewer is compelled to surmise: what if this "alternative fantasy" is real?'[2]

His *Cross-landscape* (2013) appears to intertwine the past and the present. The other painting, *Winter Day* (2015), shows a warmly clad woman feeding little dinosaurs as if they are little chicks.

Voligamsi's work can now be found in a number of important Russian collections, among them those of the State Russian Museum in St Petersburg, the Moscow Museum of Modern Art and the privately owned Erarta Gallery in St Petersburg.

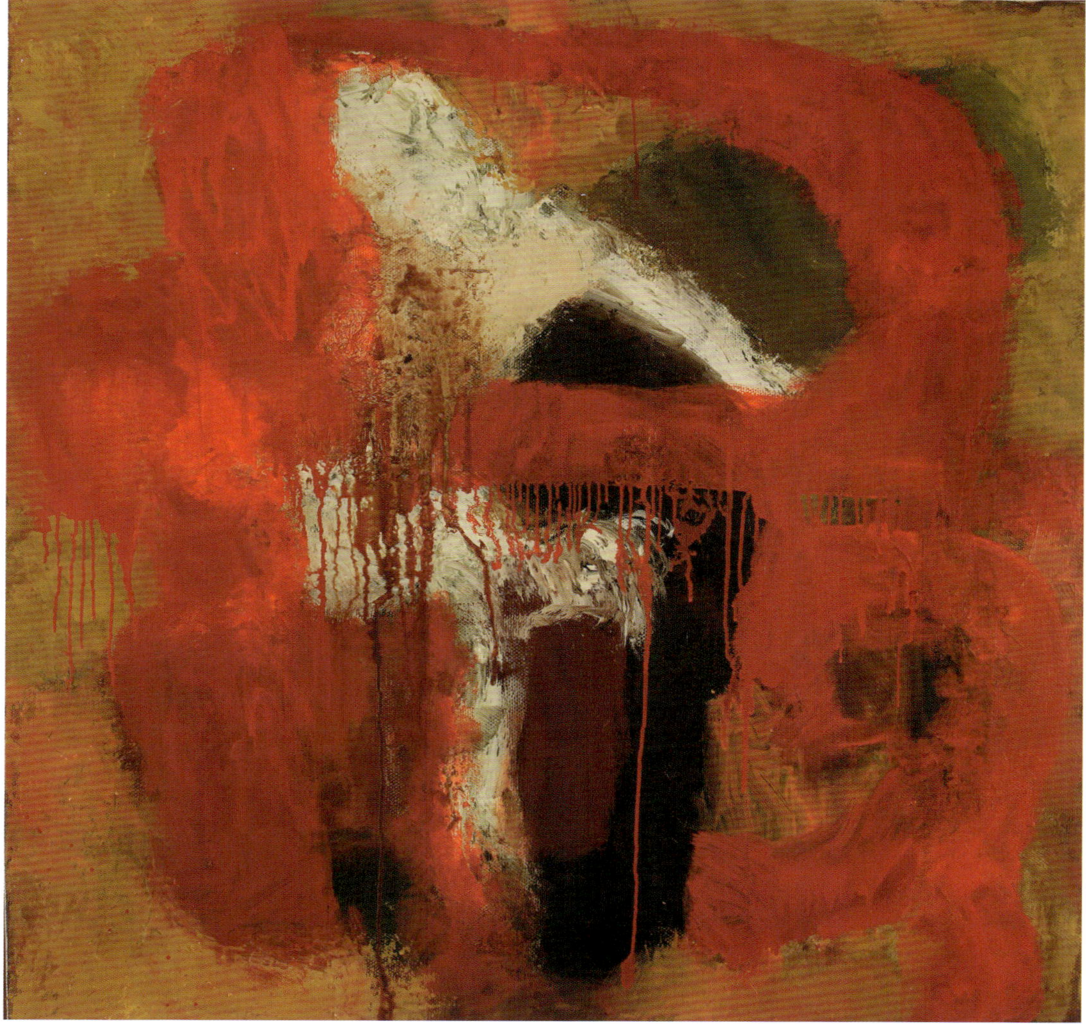

←
Sitnikova, Natalia
Solar Wind-4
2009, oil on canvas

Natalia Sitnikova, born in 1978, is a decade younger than the two artists just discussed. From 2005 onwards she held a large number of exhibitions in Russia, some solo and others shared. Perhaps the most significant of these was in 2011 at the Pushkin Fine Art Museum in Moscow, shared with the sculptor Georgy Frangulyan (b.1945), who is more than three decades older than Sitnikova.

As a recent review in the *Wall Street International* magazine states, Frangulyan is famous for 'his constant search for new figurative solutions reflecting and organizing the surrounding space'.[3] The Pushkin show was called *Abstraction: from flatness to volume*. It is obvious, when one studies Sitnikova's flattened, abstract forms, what her role in this dialogue is likely to have been. She is one of the examples, in terms of Russian art as it currently exists, of a total commitment to abstract forms. Her substantial list of exhibitions nevertheless indicates that she has a firmly established place in the contemporary Russian art world.

Another abstract or quasi-abstract Russian artist of this generation is Victor Alimpiev (b. 1973), also known as a video artist. His abstract forms have more easily recognisable figurative overtones than in Sitnikova's work. Alimpiev describes his paintings as a 'single event in a carefully prepared space'. He also talks of the star-shaped elements that appear in some of his paintings as 'an act of vandalism desecrating the beautiful space. It is like a kiss which is irreversible. They (the elements) have something... scandalous about them.[4]

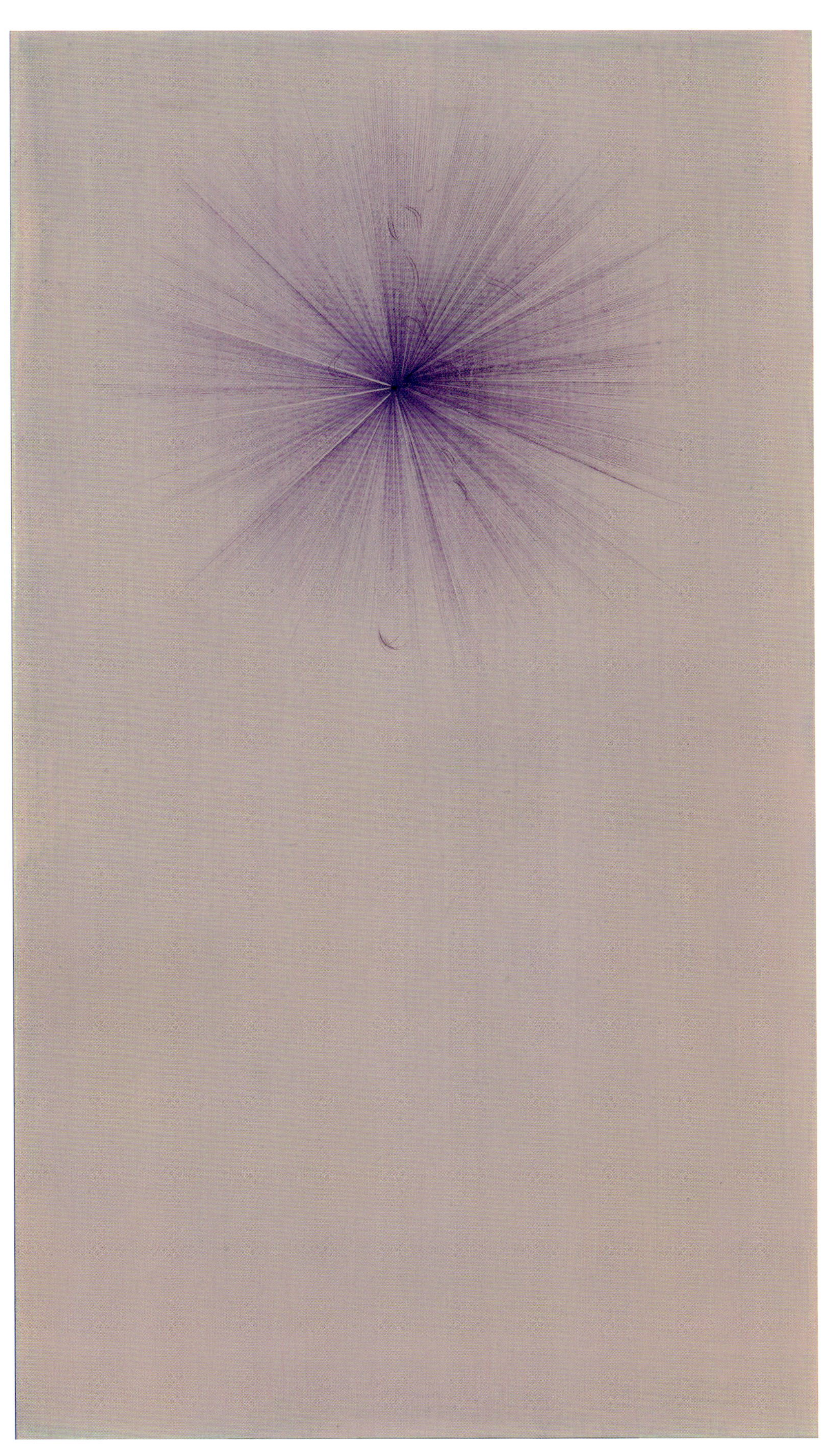

→
Alimpiev, Victor
Kathleen Ferrier
2015, acrylic on canvas

Alimpiev, who lives and works in Moscow, has a substantial list of exhibitions outside of Russia: for example in the Badischer Kunstverein, Frankfurt; Modern Art Oxford; the Studio la Città, Verona; the Ikon Gallery, Birmingham; the Passerelle Centre d'art contemporain, Brest, and the High Line in New York. In 2017 he featured in the Triennial of Contemporary Russian Art held at the Garage Museum of Contemporary Art in Moscow,

Ivan Novikov (b. 1990) belongs to a much younger generation than the four artists thus far discussed but shares their experimental spirit. Despite his youth, he also has a long list of exhibitions to his credit, stretching back to 2011, and an equally impressive list of grants and awards. He was a nominee for the Kandinsky Award in 2015 and received grants from the Garage Museum in Moscow both in that year and in 2016. In 2018 he won an Innovation Award in the 'Regional Project' category. His background is international. Novikiov graduated from the Moscow Surikov State Academic Art Institute, has an MA in History from the University of Manchester in the UK and lives in Russia and Vietnam.

His work tends to be radically abstract, as in the example illustrated here. The exhibition booklet for his exhibition at the Moscow Museum of Modern Art in 2020 relates that the show took its title, *Against the Grain*, from a 2017 book by the American political scientist and anthropologist James Scott called *Against the Grain: A Deep History of the Earliest States*. This was a study of 'the grassroots resistance towards oppression' of the inhabitants of the mountainous regions of South East Asia. The booklet goes on to say that:

Novikov, Ivan
I Want to Be Afraid of the Forest
2014, dry plants, tempera on canvas

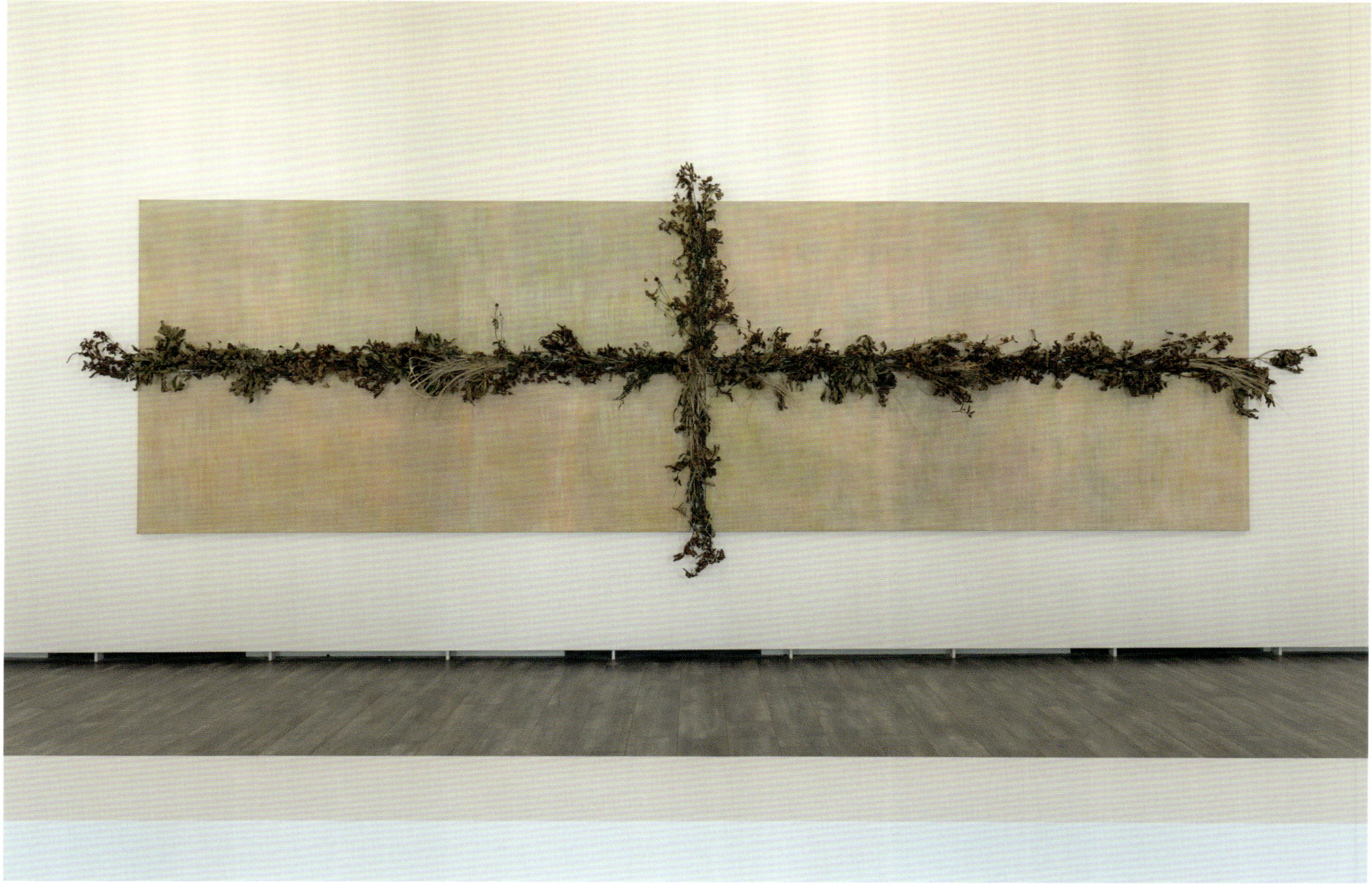

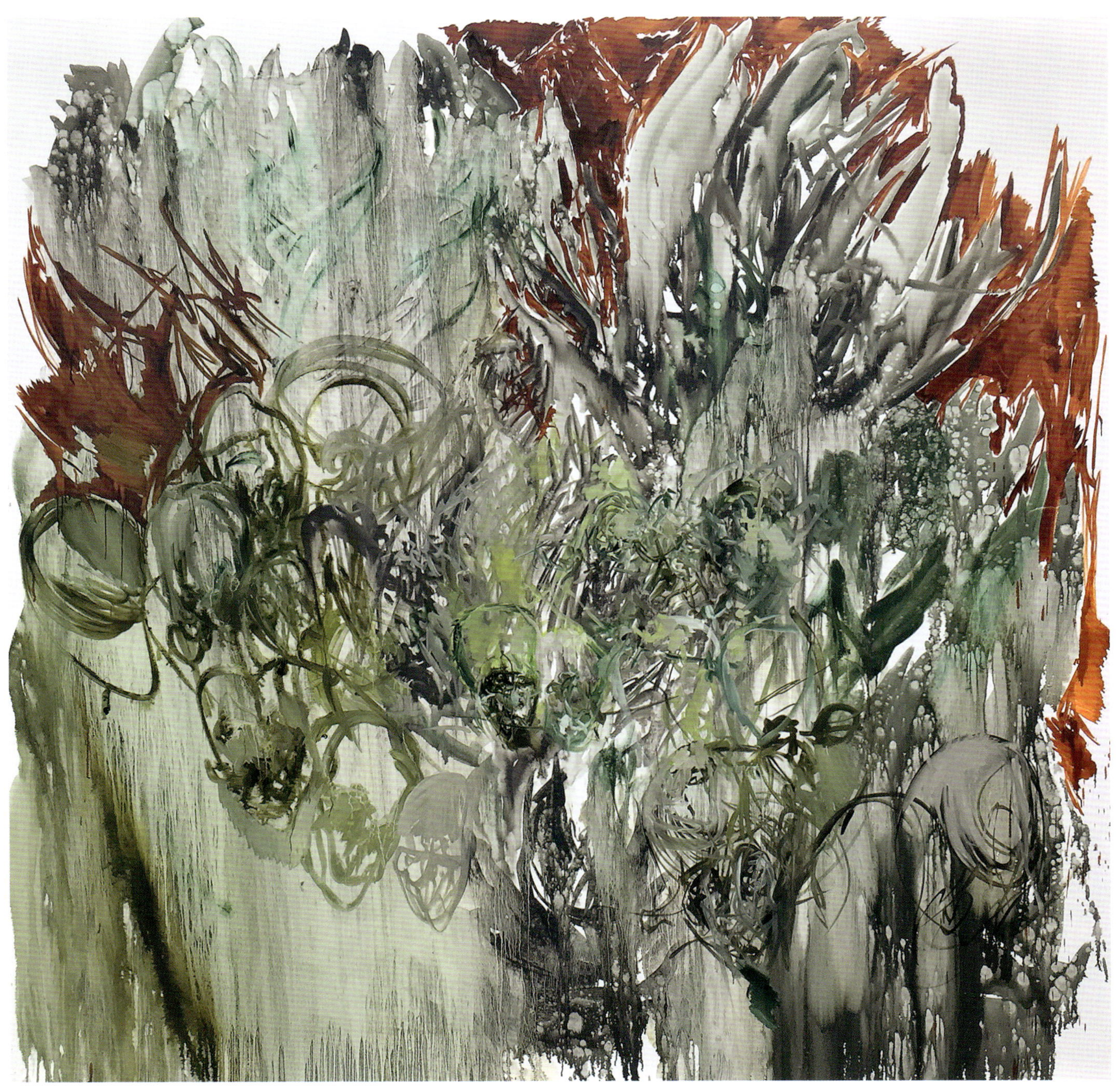

> The artist reflects on these tragic subjects in the light of modern-day post-colonial and ecological research and correlates them, paradoxically, with the affective scope and theoretical challenges of abstract painting... Precisely, painting becomes for him the medium that, in its very structure and physical composition — canvas, ground, binding agents, textures and colours — equally reveals the natural and the anthropogenic.[5]

↑
Kulkov, Vlad
Untitled
2019, oil on canvas

Novikov therefore combines some of the political and social preoccupations typical of many phases of twentieth and twenty-first-century Russian art with their apparent polar opposite: an interest in pure abstraction.

A somewhat similar but less drastically abstract artist of the same generation living and working in Russia is the Latvian-born Vlad Kulkov (b. 1986), now resident in St Petersburg. He is a graduate

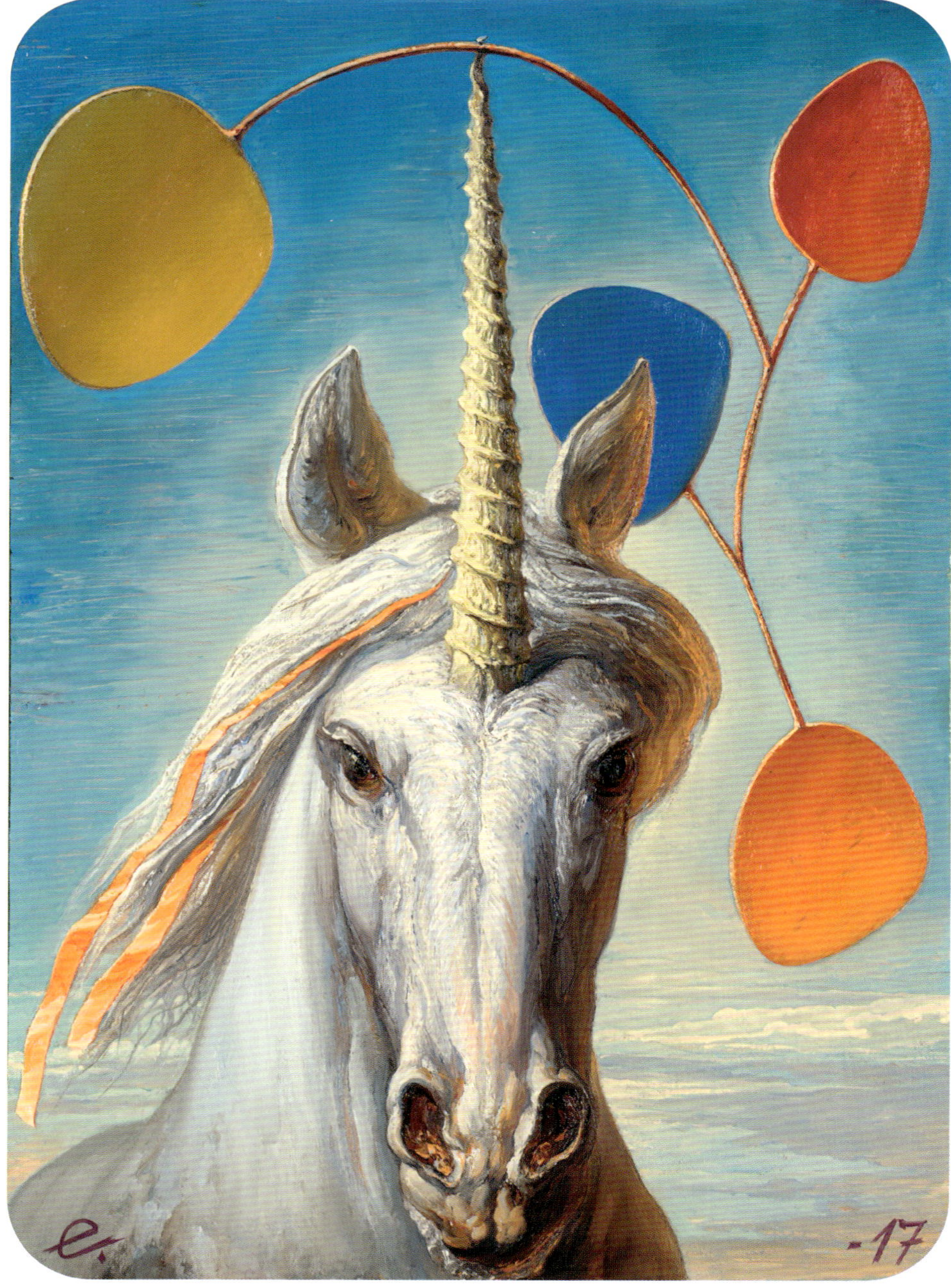

←
Koshelev, Egor
Snowball
2017, oil on canvas

of the Stieglitz Academy of Art and Design. While he is based in Russia, he has also taken the opportunity to travel widely during the past fifteen years. Most of his travels have been in Latin America – Mexico, Argentina and Peru – but he has also been to Death Valley in the USA, which straddles the California-Nevada border, and to Los Angeles. He has also visited Nepal. In this sense he is representative of the increasing cosmopolitanism of the Russian art world that he now inhabits. The references in his paintings are to nature and objects discovered in nature but without specific descriptions of natural scenes.

Egor Koshelev (b. 1980), living and working in Moscow, takes a somewhat different route. His art is figurative but offers playful references to the past of the International Modern Movement. The painting illustrated, for example, shows a unicorn with what appears to be a Calder mobile swinging on the tip of its horn. A website comments with some justification that his world resembles a dream, in which mythology collides with images of mass culture and new technologies.[6]

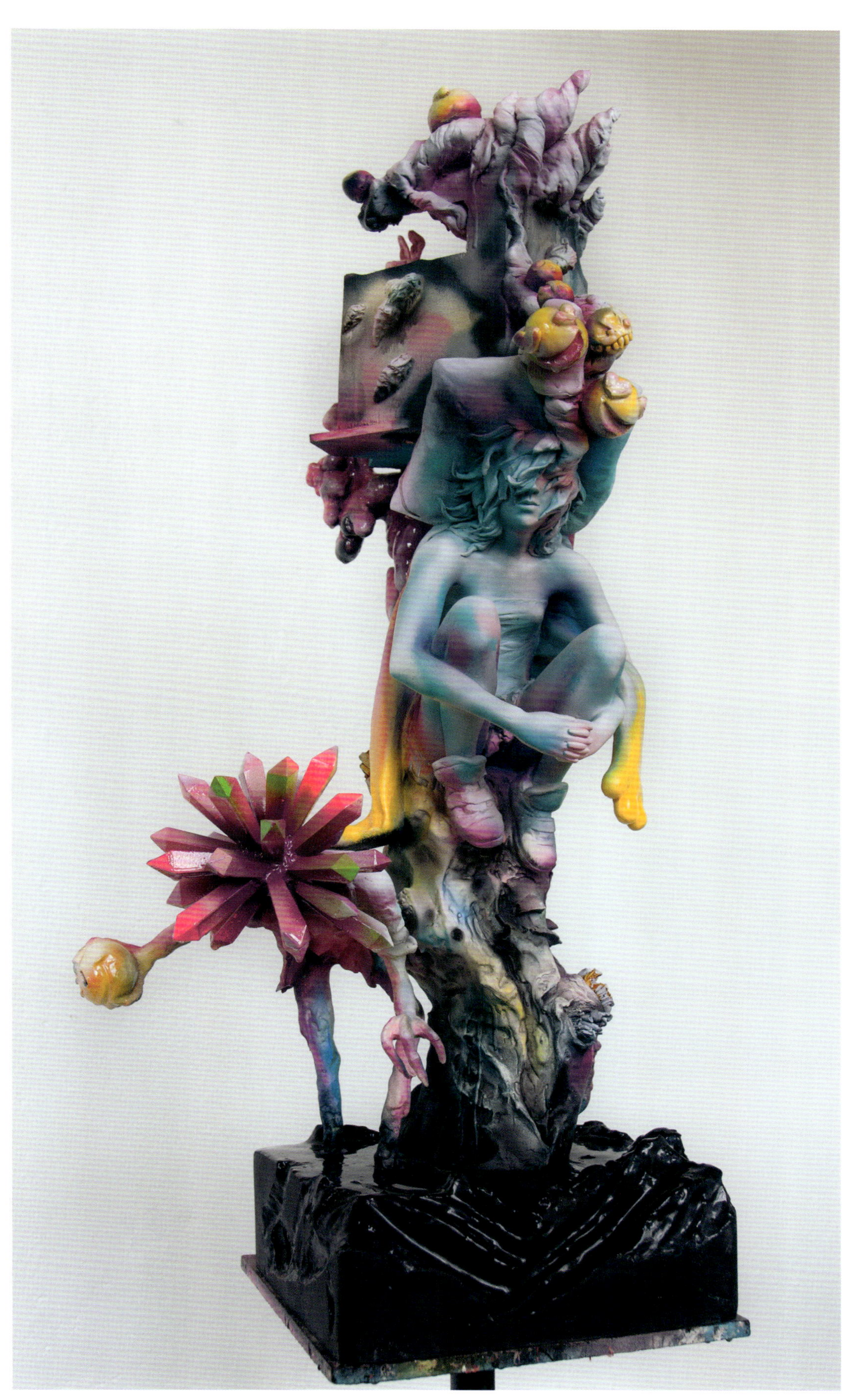

→
Crocodile Power
My Mind Says No
2018, plastic, resin

This nails down a basic difference between what one might call the Modernism of tradition and the kind that exists today. Modernism is now just one alternative amongst a very large spectrum of styles. It exists, not in its own right but as a type of commentary.

A Moscow-based group called Crocodile Power is fully aware of this new situation. Founded in 2011, it consists of just two artists: Peter Goloshchapov (b. 1982) and Oksana Simatova (b. 1979). Both are graduates of the Stroganov State University in Moscow, and both later studied at St Martin's in London.

In an artists' statement they say:

> We perceive contemporary reality as a moveable, flexible space in which the past, present and future simultaneously exist and mix. We are interested in the process, which excites us with its unpredictability, in which a person simultaneously takes on the role of the creator and the laboratory mouse. Creativity becomes a game in which each new step brings us closer to the limits of conventional everyday life.

They are therefore attempting to achieve what they call 'augmented reality', where what is fictional 'is so organically built into a reality we know, that its existence seems possible (either in the past, present and future).'[7]

In 2015 an exhibition of the Crocodile Power works was held at the Moscow Museum of Modern Art.

Another artist who works in a quasi-surrealist vein is Anna Andrzhievskaya (b. 1989), who lives and works in St Petersburg, a member of the North-7 group. Her work covers a wide range of activities – painting, sculpture, graphics and performance – and she is interested in the ways in which contemporary art is now perceived by its audience; this has led her to experiment with ideas such as making edible sculptures. In creating more permanent works she often chooses to use materials and techniques that are perceived as being populist, such as coloured gel pens and gold markers.

In an artist's statement written for a show at the Sample Gallery she defined her intentions thus:

> I would like to paint as simply as the drops flow down the misted glass. I want the lines to be as clear and confident as broken glass or the first ice on the pond.

At the same time, I want to forget myself and find myself in a different place with verified drama and a twisted plot. There, each character would not be like anyone else, but at the same time would resemble a forgotten friend. There would be undiscovered fantastic plants and objects, whose function could be understood only intuitively. I would like the viewer to perceive my work as a film with a non-linear narrative, as a fragment of the most vivid dream.[8]

On the accumulated evidence now available, there can be no doubt that Russian art has renewed its ties with the Modernist Movement, to which it was such a major contributor in the early years of the twentieth century.

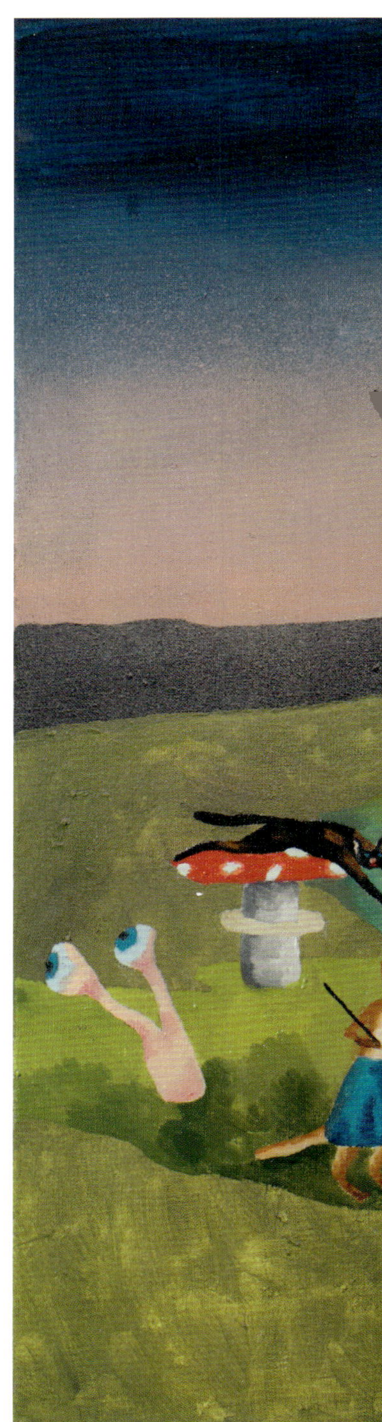

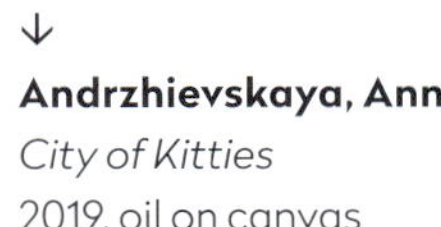

Andrzhievskaya, Anna
City of Kitties
2019, oil on canvas

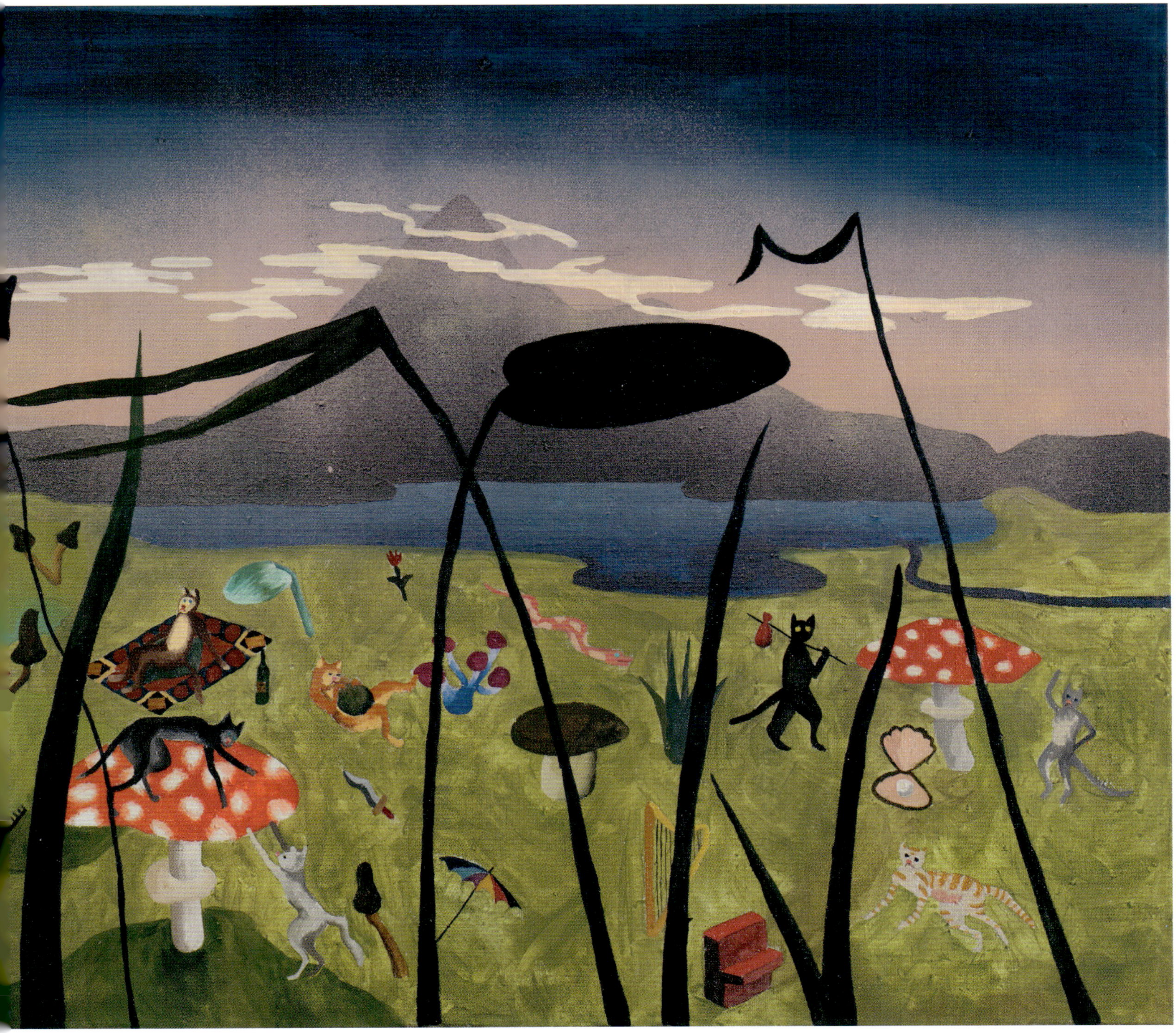

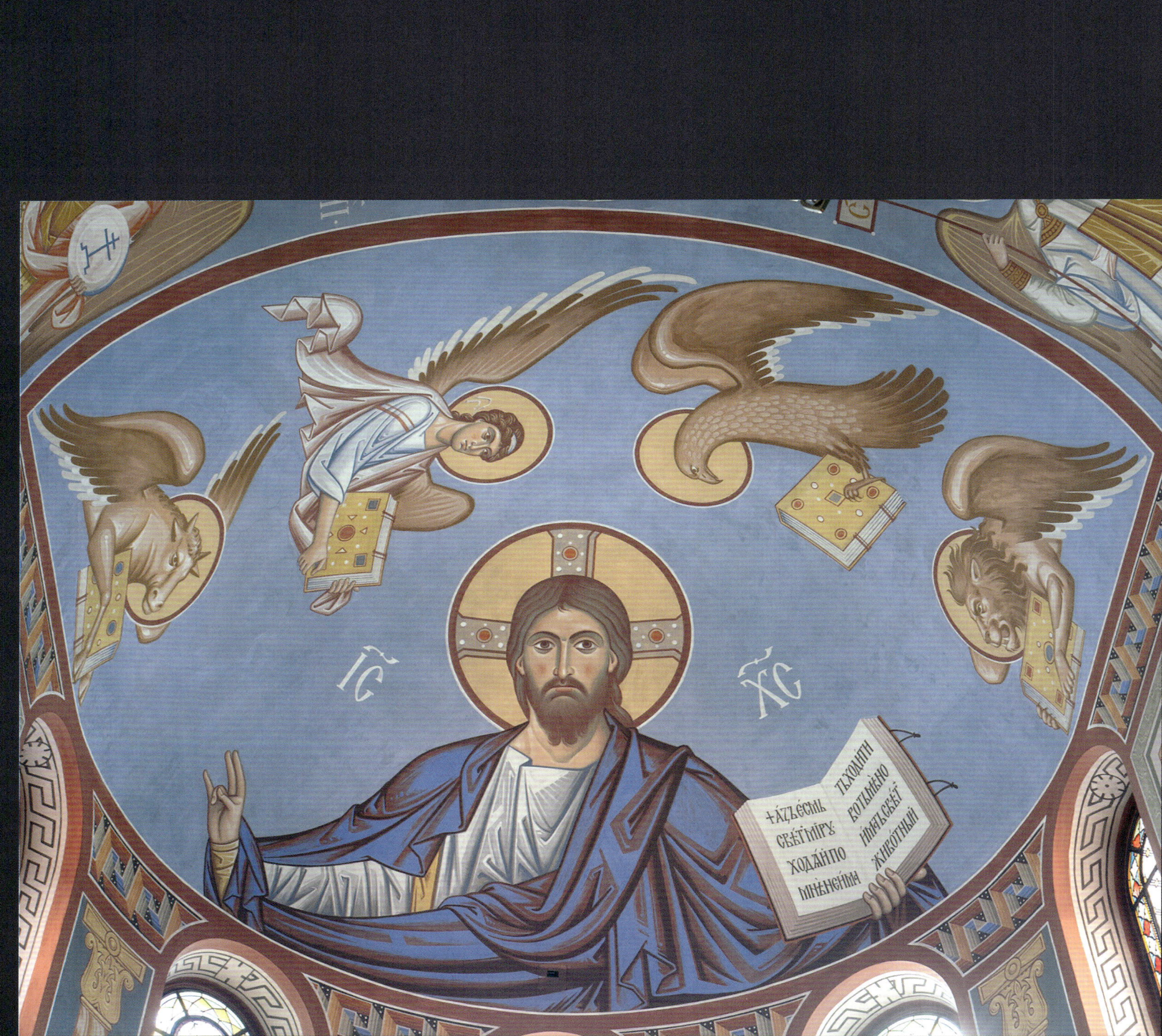
IC
XC
+АЗЪ ЕСМЬ
СВѢТ МІРУ
ХОДАЙ ПО
МНѢ НЕ ИМА
ТЪ ХОДИТИ
ВО ТЬМѢ НО
ИМАТЬ СВѢТ
ЖИВОТНЫЙ

4 ICON PAINTERS

Icons occupy a special place in the history of Russian art. Originally imported from Byzantium, when the regions that we now identify as 'Russia' converted to Christianity, icons have the longest continuous history of any form of painting made there. This history was never completely interrupted under the officially atheist Soviets. The icon painting re-emerged into view in the 1970s and were almost fully acknowledged officially during the final years of Soviet rule in the 1980s.

A distinction needs to be made between icons made as folk products, a category which includes battered older paintings rescued from the junk heap and spruced up to look new, and the images made by contemporary Russian artists, moved by religious faith and striving to carry forward the tradition they have inherited. A key figure in this category is Archimandrite Zinon (Theodor) (b. 1953). Father Zinon was already extremely active in the 1980s, producing art for major Russian churches and not simply small panels for private devotional use.

Since the Orthodox faith is not confined to Russia, his work can also be found outside national boundaries, for example in Finland, Belgium, Austria and even on Mount Athos in Greece, where at one time he took up residency at the Simonopetra Monastery.

←
Archimandrite Zinon (Theodor)
View of the frescoes inside the Cathedral of St Nicholas the Miracle-Worker in Vienna, Austria
2006 – 2008

Like a number of the other artists featured here, father Zinon is influenced not by the strictest Russian tradition, but follows – as his residence in Athos suggests – ideas from other eras and locations of Orthodox art. In the mid-1990s he allowed the Catholic priest Romano Scalfi, Italian president of the Christian Russian Centre, to celebrate Latin mass in an unconsecrated chapel at the Orthodox monastery of Mirozh, where father Zinon was head of the painting school. He also on this occasion received communion himself, thus breaking Orthodox rules. For this he was banned by the archbishop in charge of his diocese.

The ban was lifted in 2001 but continued de facto. In 2005, father Zinon left for Austria, moving on

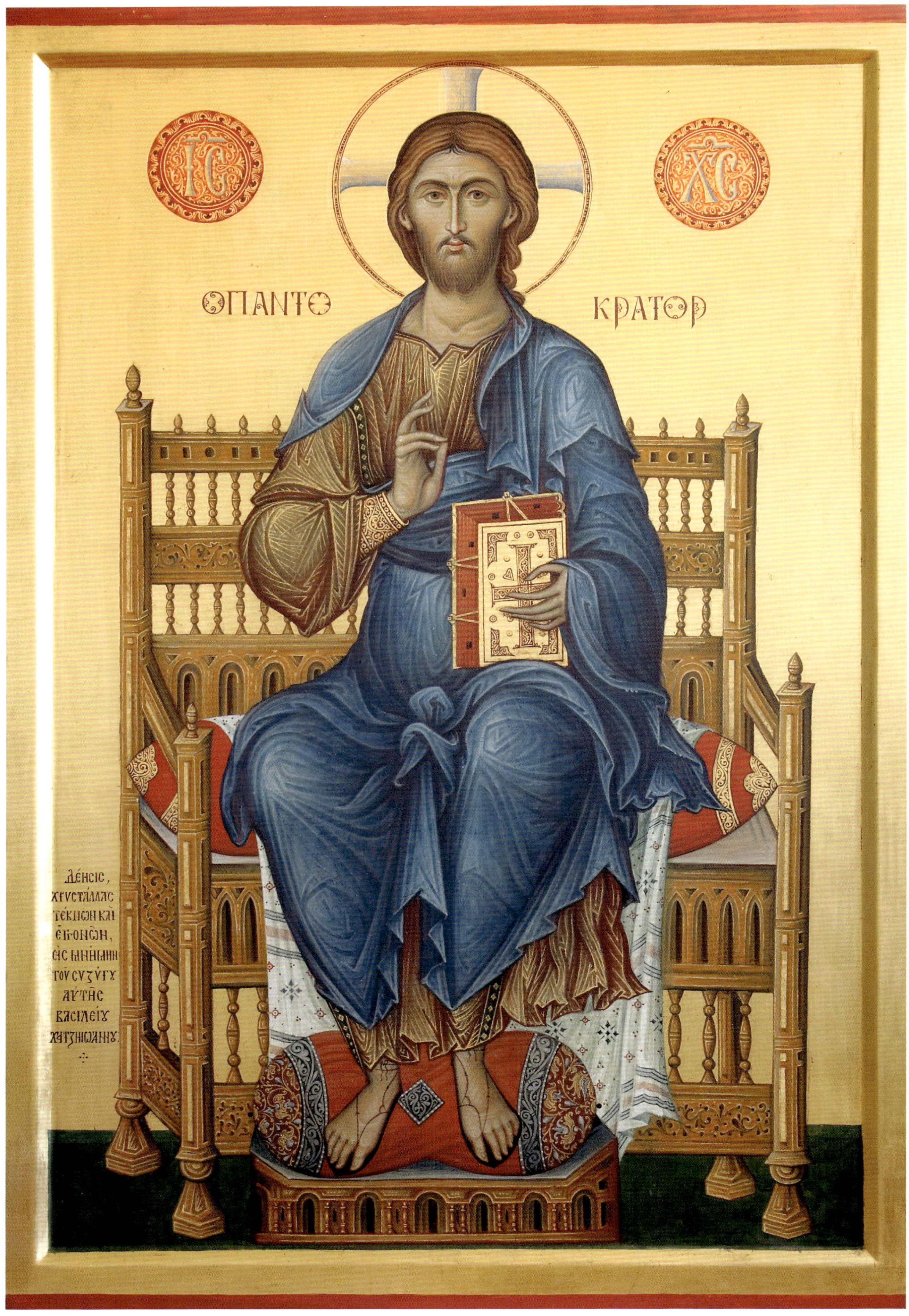
IC XC
Ο ΠΑΝΤΟ ΚΡΑΤΩΡ
Δέησις,
Χρυστάλλας
τέκνων καὶ
ἐγγόνων,
εἰς μνήμην
τοῦ συζύγου
αὐτῆς
Βασιλείου
Χατζηιωάννου

→
Sokolov, Alexander
Icon of the Mother of God the Inexhaustible Chalice
1993, silver riza, egg tempera, gesso on wood

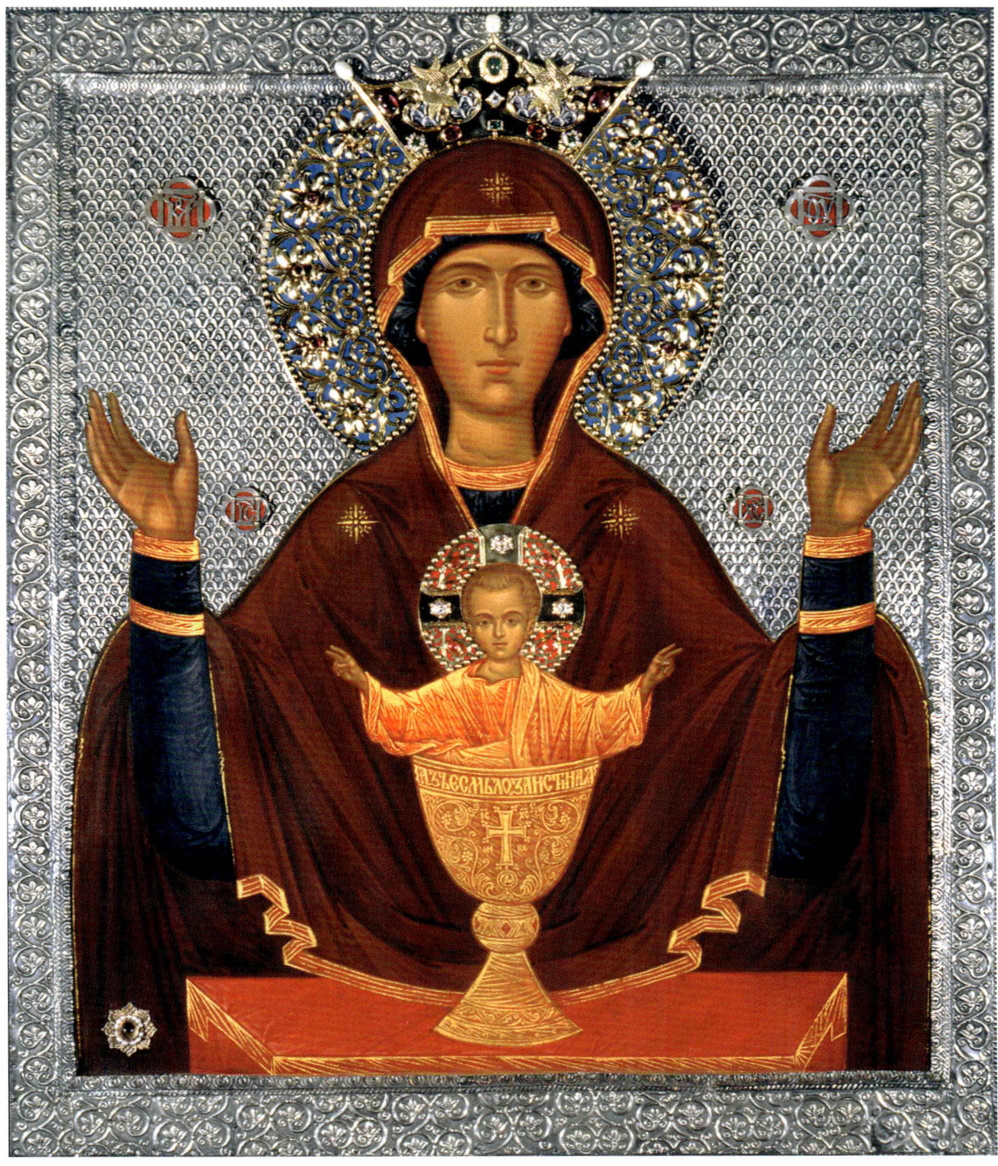

subsequently to Mount Athos. This somewhat turbulent events in his career happened after he was awarded the State Prize of Russia for his contribution to church art in 1994. Father Zinon was the first church figure to receive it.

Another very senior figure is Alexander Lavdansky (b. 1952), founder of the Cinnabar workshop, who in 1970s was ranked as a leading avant-gardist. This changed, when, towards the end of the decade, he received a commission to produce church murals from the then bishop of Sukhumi, the chief city of Abkhazia, which is part of Georgia. In Soviet times Sukhumi was famous as a subtropical beach resort, with palm trees and citrus plantations. Since then Lavdansky has become a major practitioner of icon painting. His work has been seen both in Moscow and in prominent Christian sites outside Russia, for example in the USA, Greece and Cyprus. A website devoted to his work notes that it is devoted to a search for proportion and harmony, rooted in Byzantine as well as in purely Russian forms.

It also notes that, 'Lavdansky's formation as a master was also influenced by the fact that from the beginning of his icon-painting career he worked not only individually, but in a team with other icon painters.'[1]

←
Lavdansky, Alexander
Icon of Christ Pantocrator
2014, egg tempera, gilding on gesso and wood

A third member of this senior generation was Alexander Sokolov (1959–2015). He is now chiefly remembered for his miracle-working icon of the *Mother of God the Inexhaustible Chalice* at the Vysotsky Monastery in Serpukhov, near Moscow. This revered image replaced a medieval icon with the same subject that was destroyed in Soviet times. The new work proved to have the same power. Questioned about this in an interview, Sokolov replied: 'What is a miraculous icon? It is a mysterious and inexplicable presence of Divine power, that manifests itself in response to people's hopes, aspirations and requests. He continued:

For a person who participates in the ordinances of the Church, miracles are common. If we believe in the miracle through which bread and wine are transformed into the Flesh and Blood of God, we also believe that through Communion we ourselves partake of eternal life... The process of icon-painting is regulated. Through each action, through the repetition of some formulae, some symbols, a person becomes involved in what he is doing. Ideally the work of an icon painter should be a meaningful ministry, with meaning filling every step, starting with the choice of material.[2]

Sokolov had a widespread international career. He painted for churches both in Russia and elsewhere: in Poland, Japan, USA, Greece, Azerbaijan, Cyprus and Sicily. He also held personal exhibitions outside Russia: in Japan (1997), India (1998), Luxembourg (1998), the USA (1998), and Finland (2006).

A contemporary painter of church art who rivals Zinon in influence, but who has a less controversial reputation, is Alexander Soldatov (b. 1965). He started his career as a decorative painter and did not begin to train as an icon painter until 1991 when he enrolled in the icon-painting school at the Moscow Theological Academy, graduating in 1994. He is now the head of the school, with a large number of major church commissions to his credit. He is also head of the Andrei Rublev Centre for Temple Art and has recently worked on frescoes and the iconostasis of the Church of the New Martyrs and Confessors of the Russian state in the city of Beslan, Republic of North Ossetia-Alania.

A considerable number of other artists currently produce modern icons in Russia. There are at least fourteen officially recognised icon-painting workshops. The majority are situated in Moscow and St Petersburg with others in Yekaterinburg, Arkhangelsk and Dubna, which is approximately 125km north of Moscow. This city is also home to the Joint Institute for Nuclear Research, one of the largest scientific foundations in Russia.

Icons are produced by both male and female artists. Among the leading female painters of icons are Irina Zaron, Svetlana Rzhanitsyna and Darya Kiryanova. Irina Zaron is married to the sculptor Sergey Antonov, who produces icon-like reliefs. She has been a member of the Union of Artists since 1982. She and her husband first met as art students. Neither of them, at that time, were much interested in sacred art. She remembers, however, accompanying Antonov to the Rublev Museum, and also visiting the Trinity Lavra of St Sergius. This, 70km north-east of Moscow, is the spiritual centre of the Russian Orthodox church. In the church itself they 'were allowed to climb the scaffolding and I was then already seven months pregnant. Therefore, our son went there in the womb.'[3]

By the end of the 1980s the couple were already successful in material terms but searching for something else. They met the Archpriest Alexander Men' and attended a series of his lectures on baptism. Shortly before his death Father Alexander baptised the whole family. Immediately after her baptism Irina began painting icons. 'Why? I wanted to do something that would be needed. There was tremendous joy when I began to paint the first icon... there [was] some meaning in this.[4]

Darya Kiryanova (b. 1969) was not interested in art at school, but became fascinated with early Russian painting while at Moscow University. After studies at various icon-painting schools during the 1990s, she has worked from 2004 as a restorer in the art restoration workshops of the Danilov Monastery, the official residence of the Patriarch of Moscow, while at the same time pursuing an independent career of her own. She has produced paintings for numerous churches in the Moscow region as well as for churches in Italy, France and California, and has executed many private commissions. She says her chief influences are the paintings made in Moscow from the fourteenth

→
Sokolov, Alexander
Icon of the Holy Trinity
2014, egg tempera, gold leaf, gesso on wood

Overleaf, left
Soldatov, Alexander
Icon of the Mother of God
2018, fresco

Overleaf, right
Soldatov, Alexander
Icon of Christ the Savior
2018, fresco

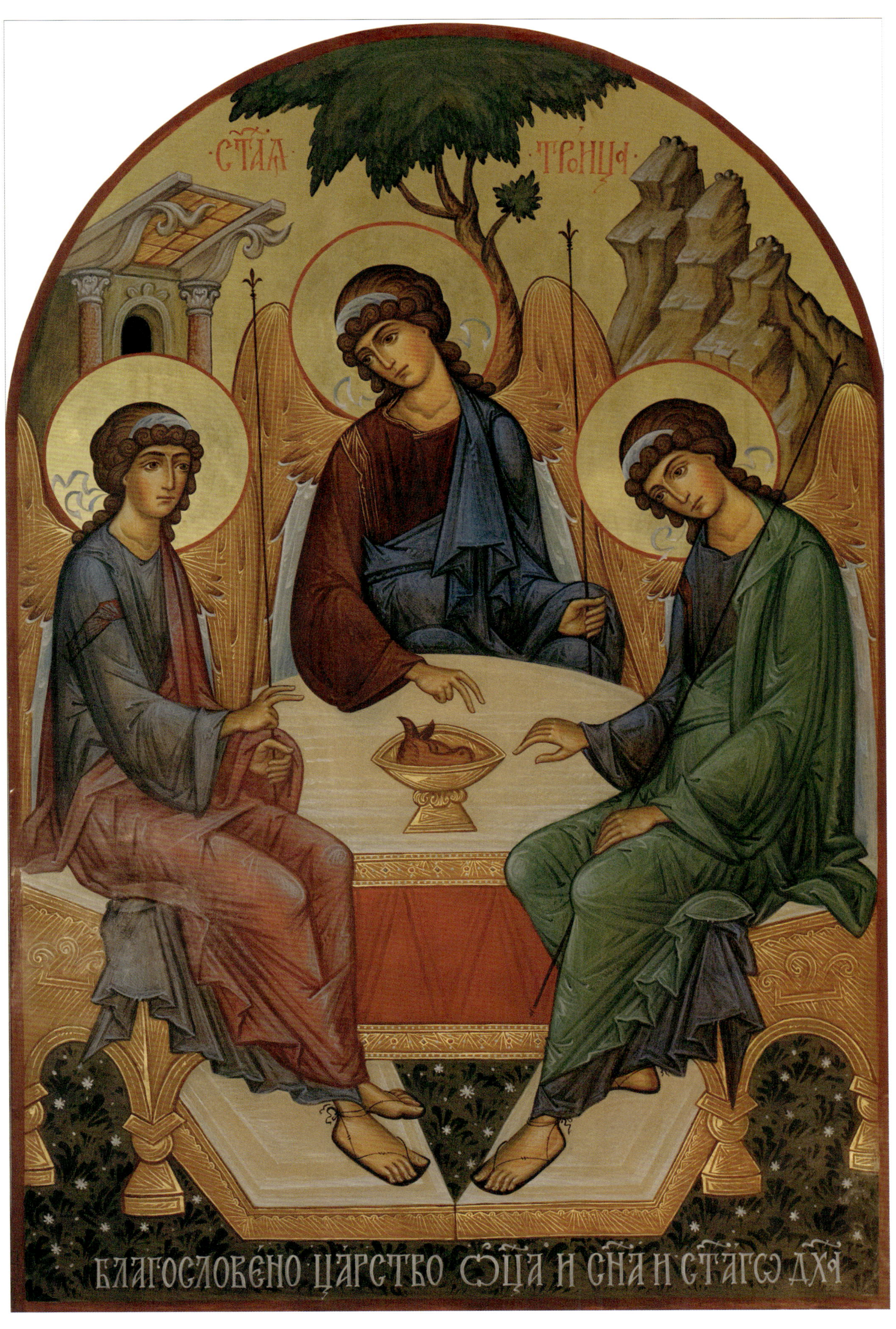
·СТАѦ· ·ТРОИЦА·
БЛАГОСЛОВЕНО·ЦАРСТВО ѾЦА И СНА И СТАГѠ ДХА

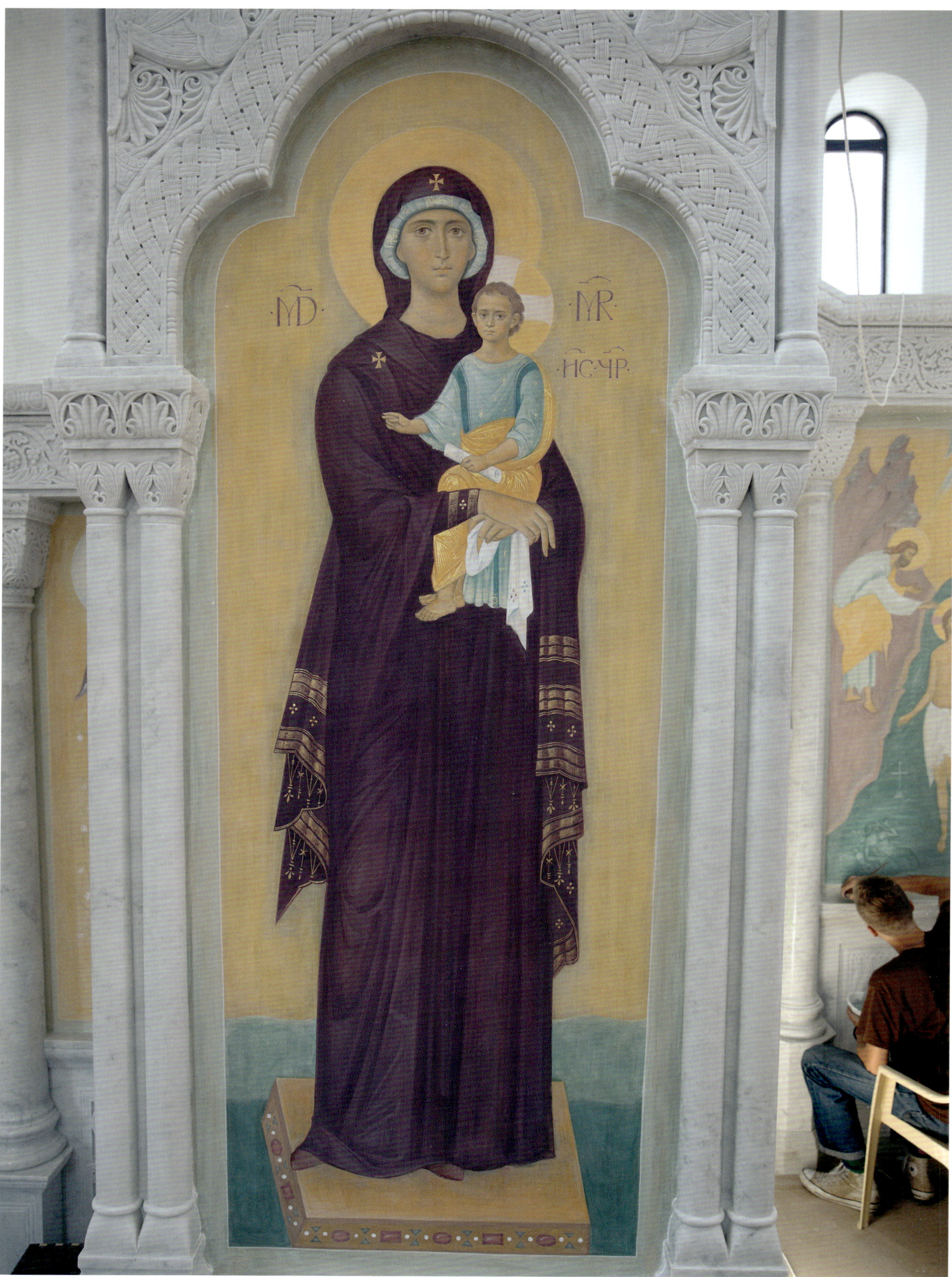

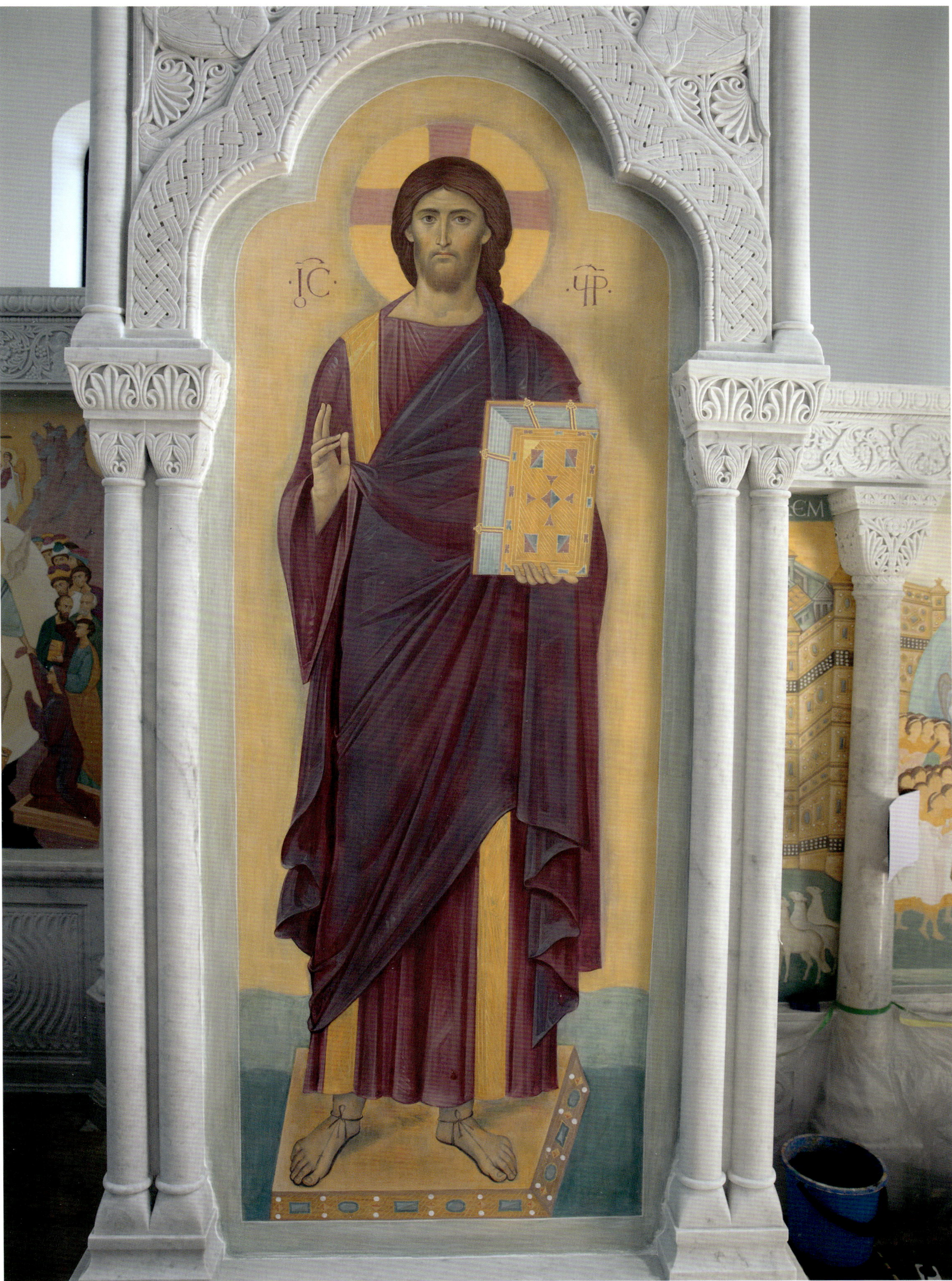
IC

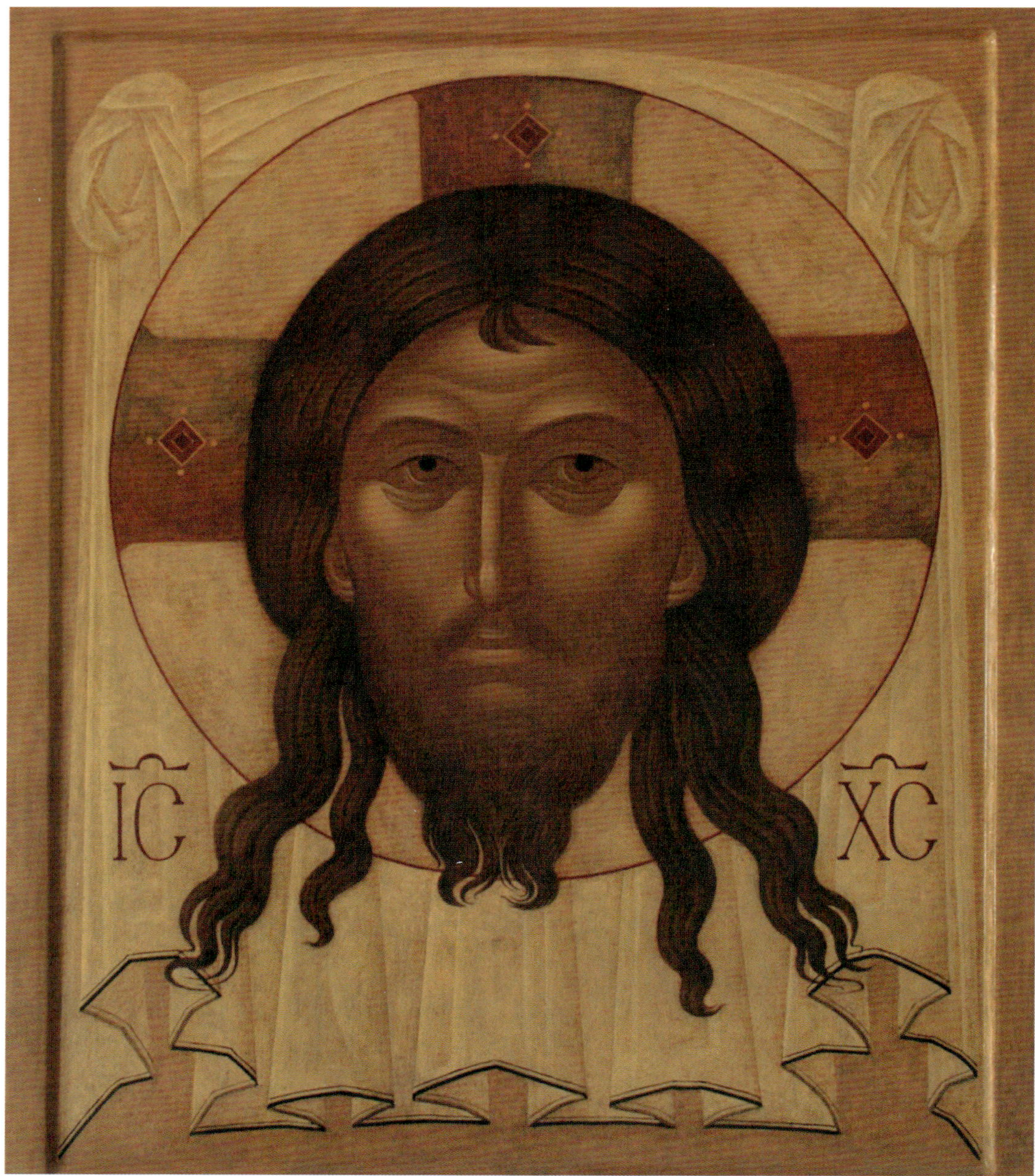

←
Zaron, Irina
Icon of the Image of Edessa (the Mandylion)
2015, egg tempera, gesso on wood

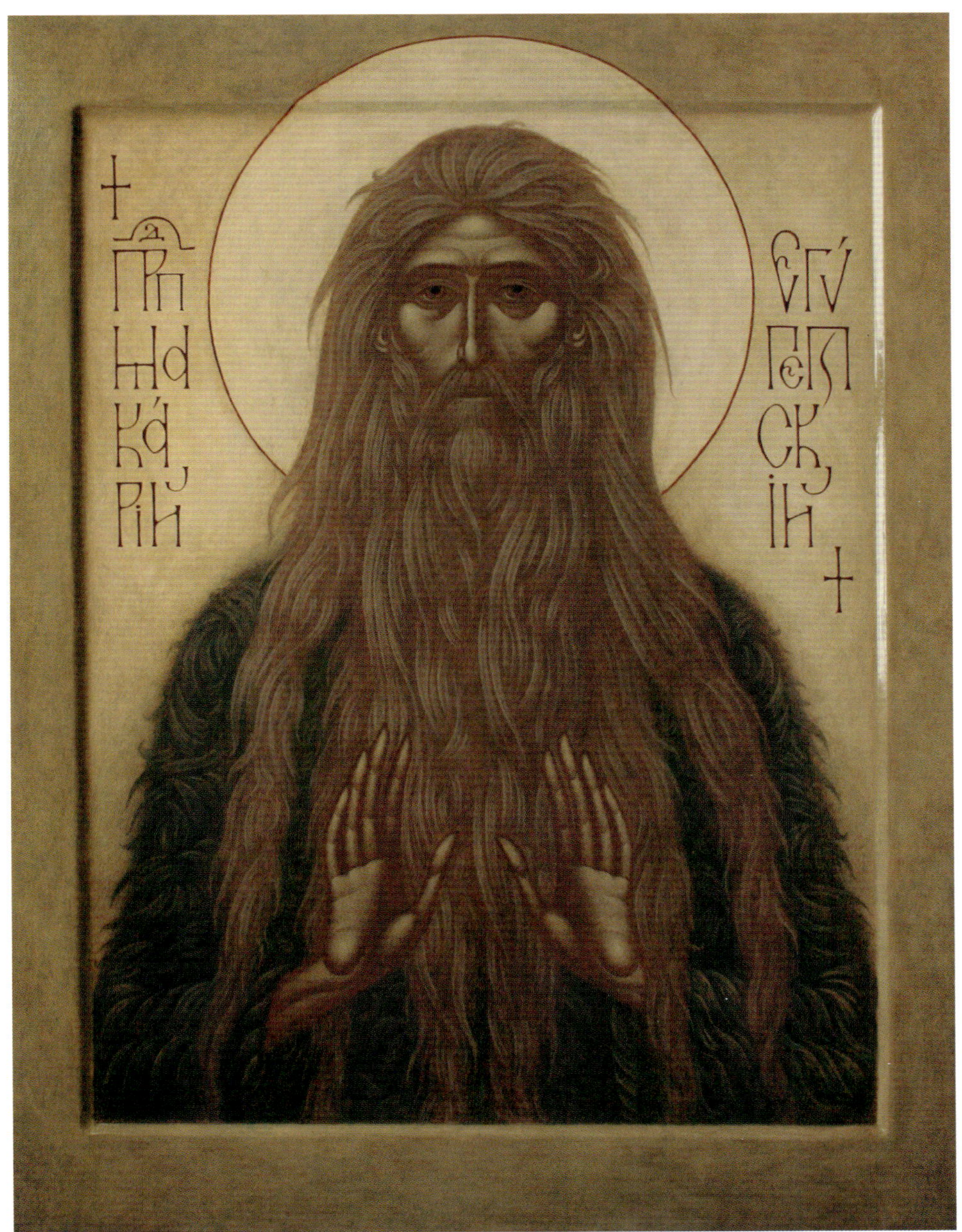

→
Zaron, Irina
Icon of St. Macarius of Egypt
2015, egg tempera, gesso on wood

to the sixteenth centuries, but that she also takes inspiration from early Byzantine art, as well as from images made in Novgorod and Pskov, close to the border with Estonia.

Svetlana Rzhanitsyna (b. 1967) says that she always liked to draw when she was a child, and also made a vow when she was twelve to paint 'the best sacred image of Our Lord': a promise she rapidly forgot. She studied at the Surikov Art Institute in Moscow, benefitting from remarkable teachers. She only remembered her promise made to God after she left. 'I was not a believer at that time,' she says. 'I wanted to believe, but it was difficult for me. I was very happy when I understood: that God exists as a reality.' She also says that it was initially hard to find a way into icon painting, but also asserts, 'Now I am very happy – I am trying to carry out my promise, given to God.'[5]

Andrej and Phillip Davydov and Olga Shalamova form a family group of contemporary Russian icon painters. Andrej Davydov (b. 1957) is a painter-priest, who is currently head of the icon-painting workshop at the Nikolskaya church at Suzdal, one of the oldest Russian towns, around 140 miles east of Moscow. He first started painting icons in 1978 and was ordained as a priest ten years later. He has worked at Suzdal since 2007. Before he was ordained, he trained as a stage designer at the Moscow Art Theatre School. In addition to creating icons, and also icon-like reliefs in bronze, he paints frescoes, and is a writer, producing texts on theology as well as on the art of icon painting. He travels outside of Russia and regularly teaches both practical and theoretical masterclasses in Italy, the Netherlands, Germany and the USA. His icons have also been widely exported. They are made using the ancient encaustic (hot wax) technique. His aim is to celebrate the long continuity of this tradition of religious image-making.

It is also continued in the work of his son Philip Davydov (b. 1975) and his daughter-in-law Olga Shalamova (b.1977) who now have a joint workshop in St Petersburg called the Sacred Murals Studio. While sticking to the strict rules that continue to govern Christian religious art in Russia, they have evolved their own personal style. In an interview with the two younger artists published in 2014 in the *Orthodox Arts Journal*, Philip Davydov was careful to separate his own approach from that of his father, while still expressing gratitude for the background his father provided. He describes the gap between 'what you want to do and what you really can do'. He continues thus:

Rzhanitsyna, Svetlana
Icon of Christ the Savior on the Throne
2021, egg tempera, gold, gesso on wood

Rzhanitsyna, Svetlana
Icon of the Mother of God with the Child on the Throne
2021, egg tempera, gold, gesso on wood

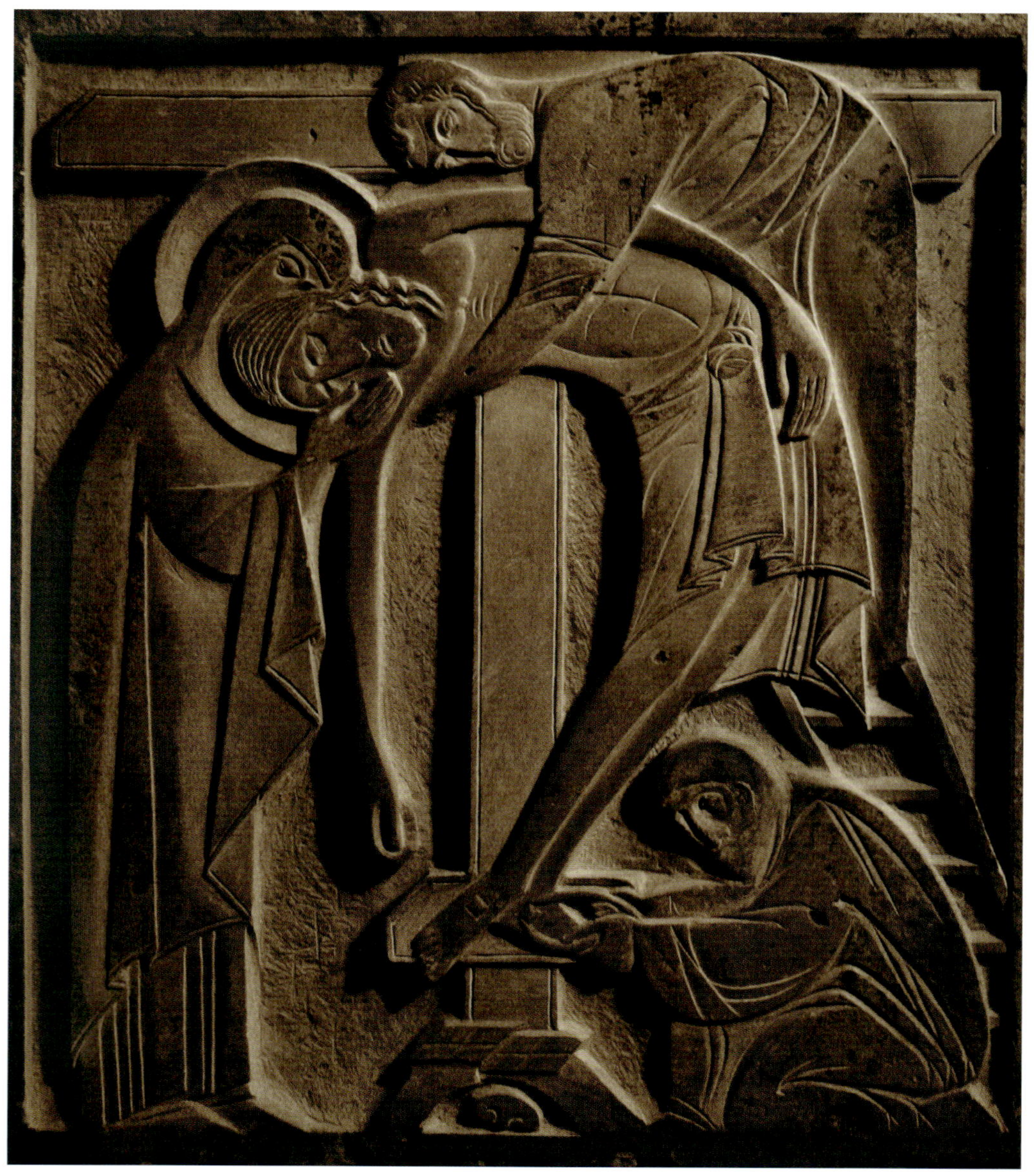

←

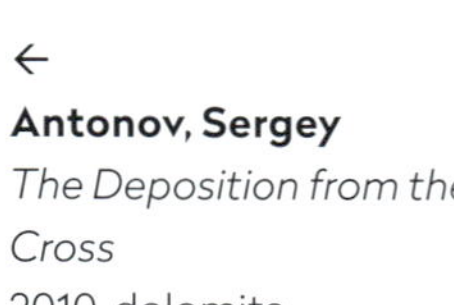

Antonov, Sergey
The Deposition from the Cross
2010, dolomite

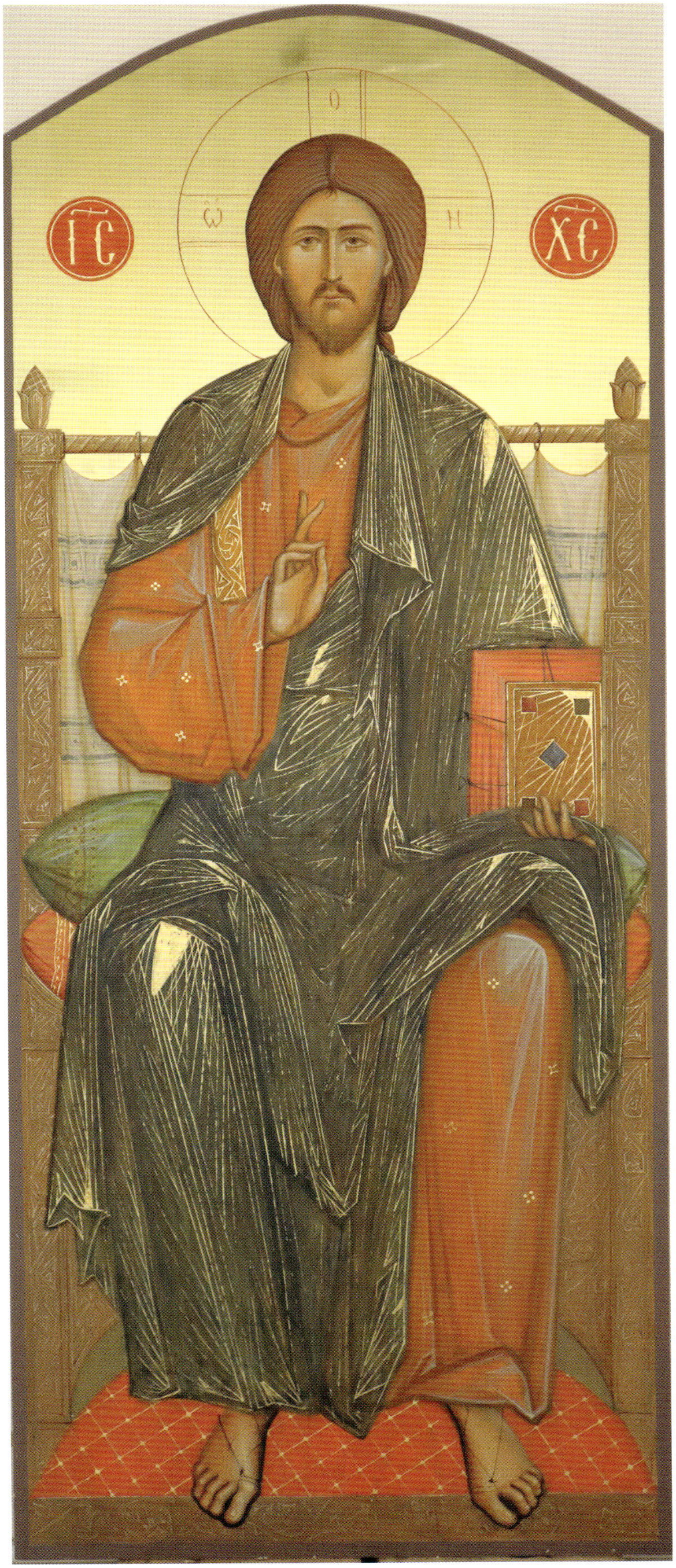

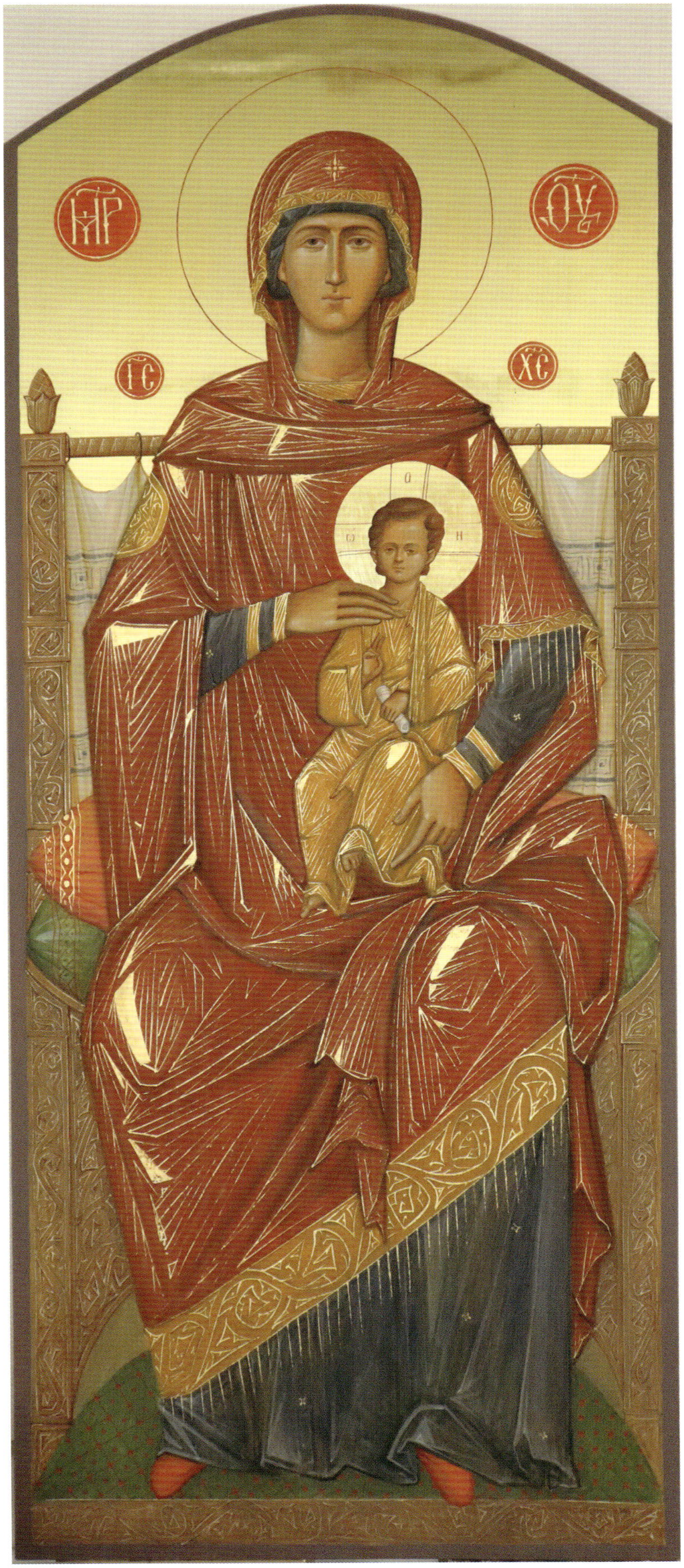

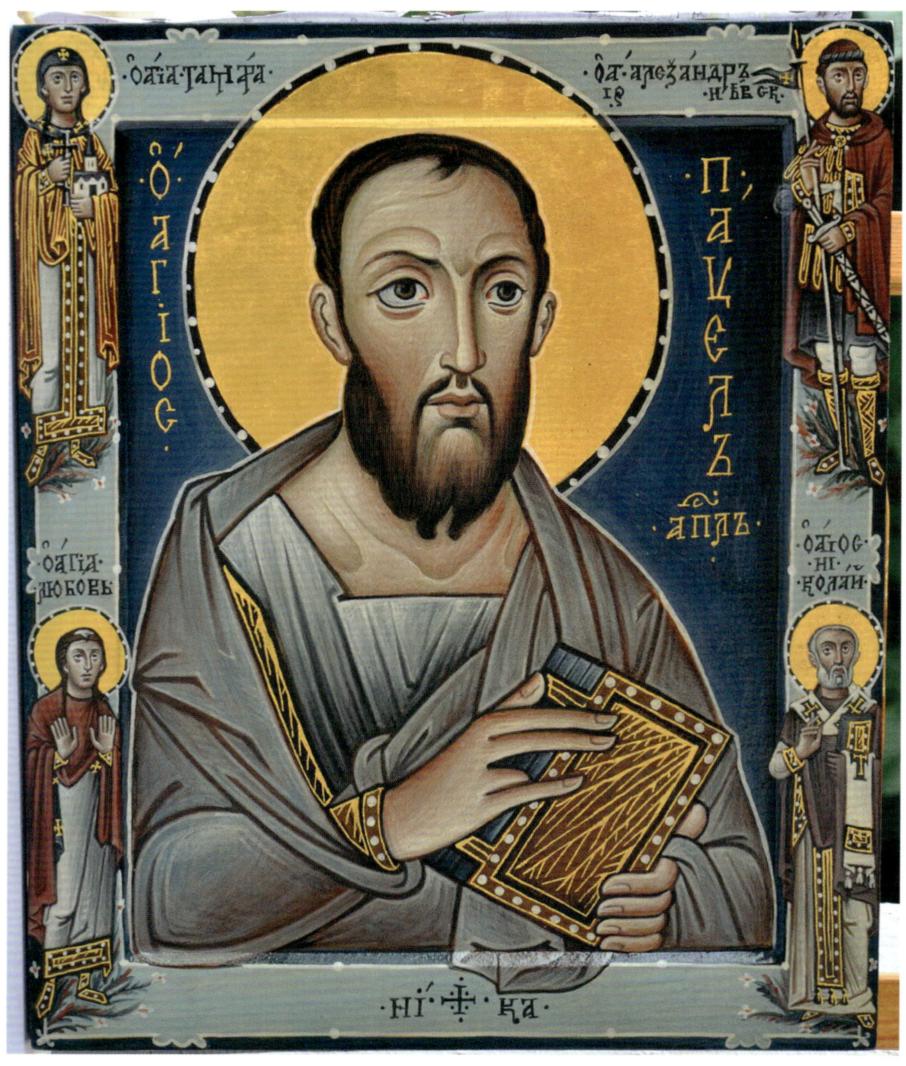

←
Davydov, Andrej
Icon of St Paul with Saints
2018, encaustic painting on wood

In our days this is even more notable. Everyone is striving to do his or her best; this 'best' can be very different. We may master our skills and technique, or we may try to communicate something very important, and these are two different approaches. Comparing twelfth-century Constantinople icons with nineteenth-century Russian provincial icons would demonstrate an unbelievable diversity, but they also share the same goal – to create an icon as an image of God and a window to heaven, but not as a decorative object.[6]

This sums up the dilemma facing many of the leading Russian icon painters of this younger generation. It is certainly one that has also confronted Philip Davydov's wife, Olga Shalamova. In the same text she says, 'I started as an artist, but at a certain point I understood that to continue this path was going to be a very hard task. So, I enrolled at the Fine Art Academy, faculty of Theory and History of Art.'

Eventually, however, she repented of this decision: 'I am not,' she says, 'the kind of person who can make copies. I am just unable to do it.' She adds: 'I just work and to a greater or lesser extent out comes what I conceived.' However, she still has generous thoughts about those who preceded her in the Soviet period, saying, 'I would like to preserve the memory of these people, who worked in iconography at such a difficult time. In ten to fifteen years it will be impossible to gather any material about them.'[7]

The continuity of Russian church and icon-painting, after the comparatively brief break under

→
Davydov, Andrej
Icon of the Nativity of Jesus
2019, encaustic painting on wood

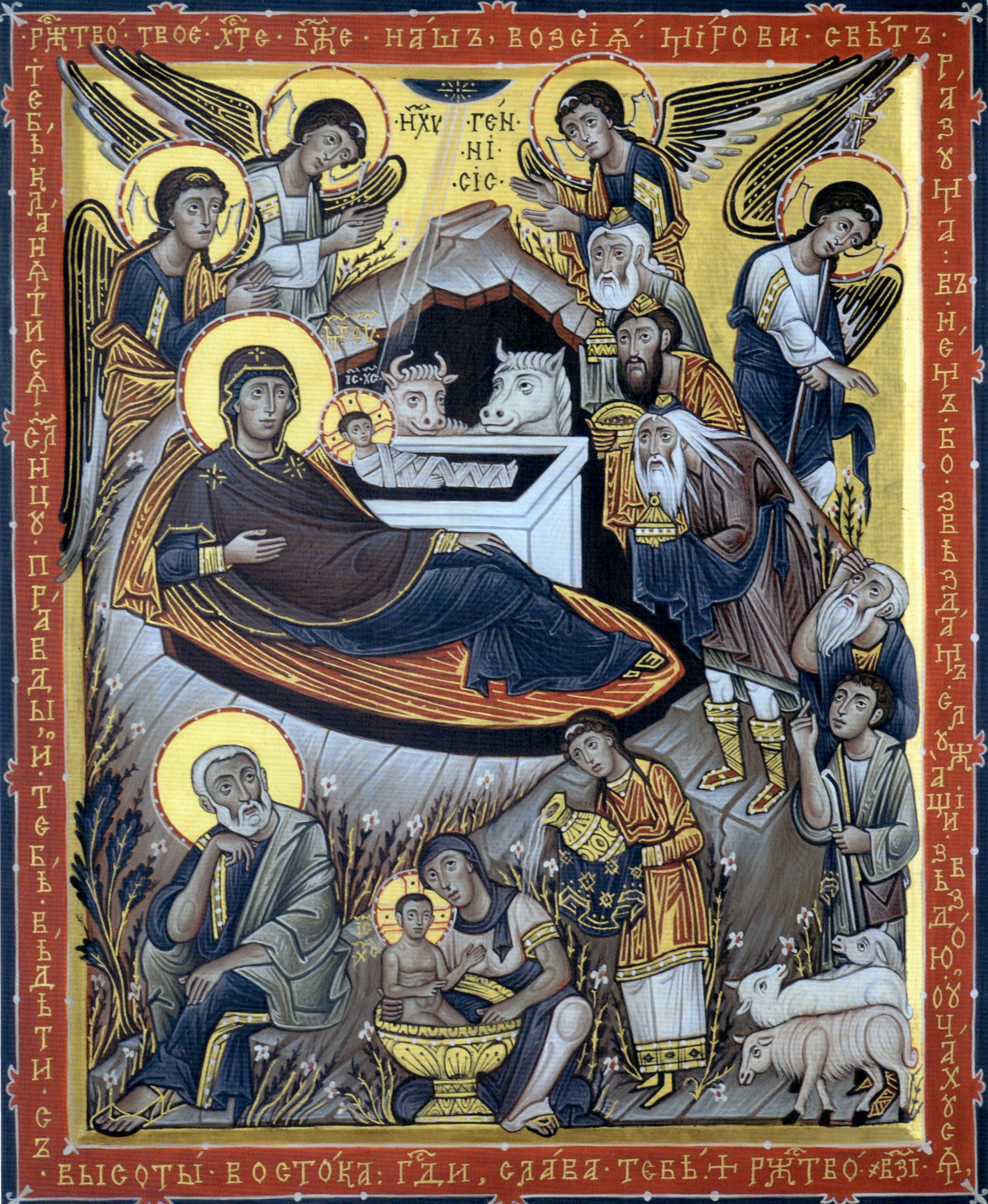
Р҃ЖТВО ТВОЕ ХР҃ТЕ Б҃ЖЕ НАШЪ, ВОЗСІА МІРОВИ СВѢТЪ
РАЗУМА: ВЪ НЕМЪ БО ЗВѢЗДАМЪ СЛУЖАЩІИ ЗВѢЗДОЮ УЧАХУСЯ
ТЕБѢ КЛАНЯТИСЯ СЛНЦУ ПРАВДЫ, И ТЕБЕ ВѢДѢТИ СЪ
ВЫСОТЫ ВОСТОКА: Г҃ДИ, СЛАВА ТЕБѢ. + Р҃ЖТВО ХВ҃

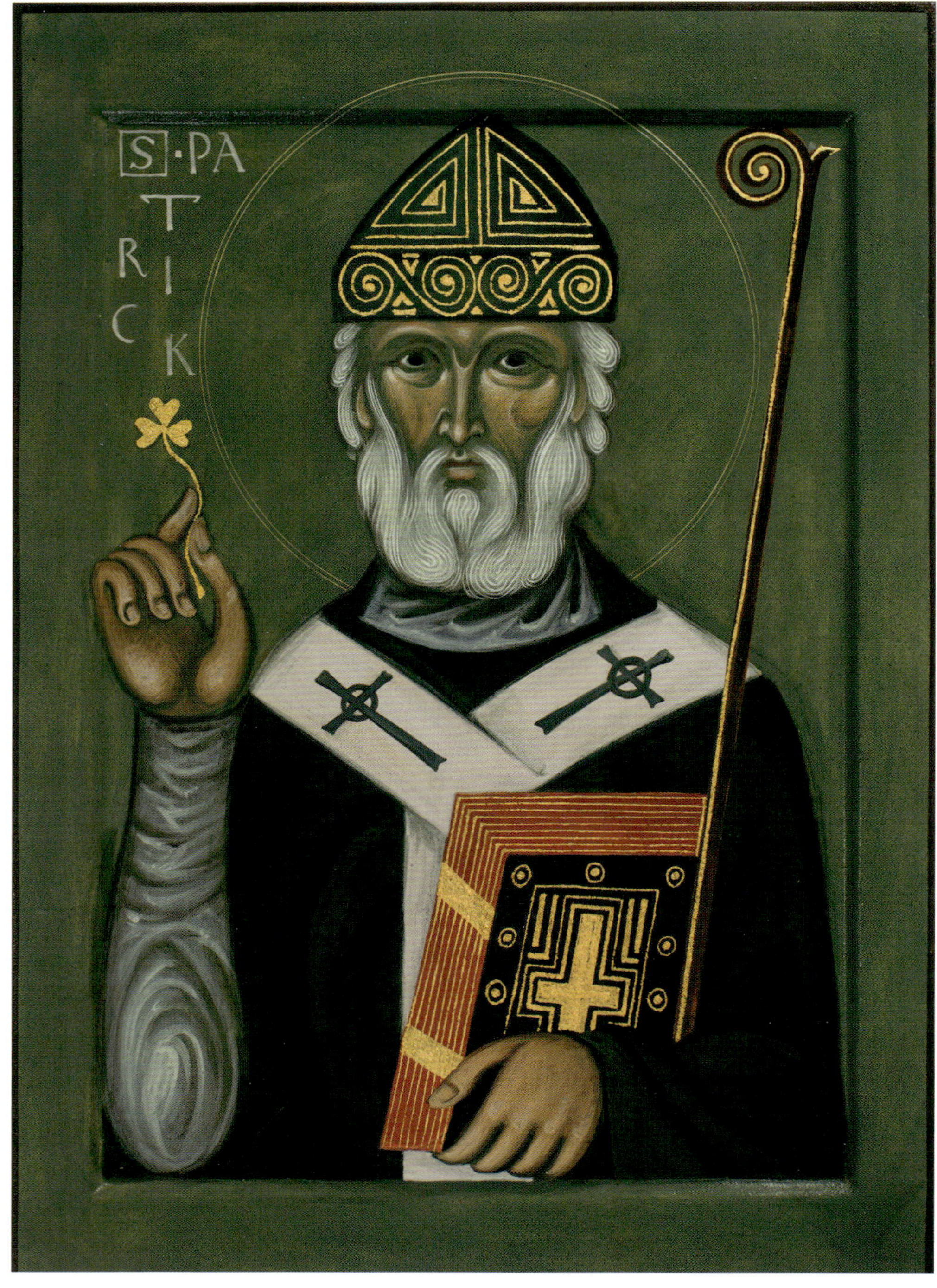

←
Davydov, Philipp
Icon of St Patrick
2017, egg tempera, gilding, gesso on wood

→
Shalamova, Olga
Icon of St Hilda
2016, egg tempera, gesso on wood

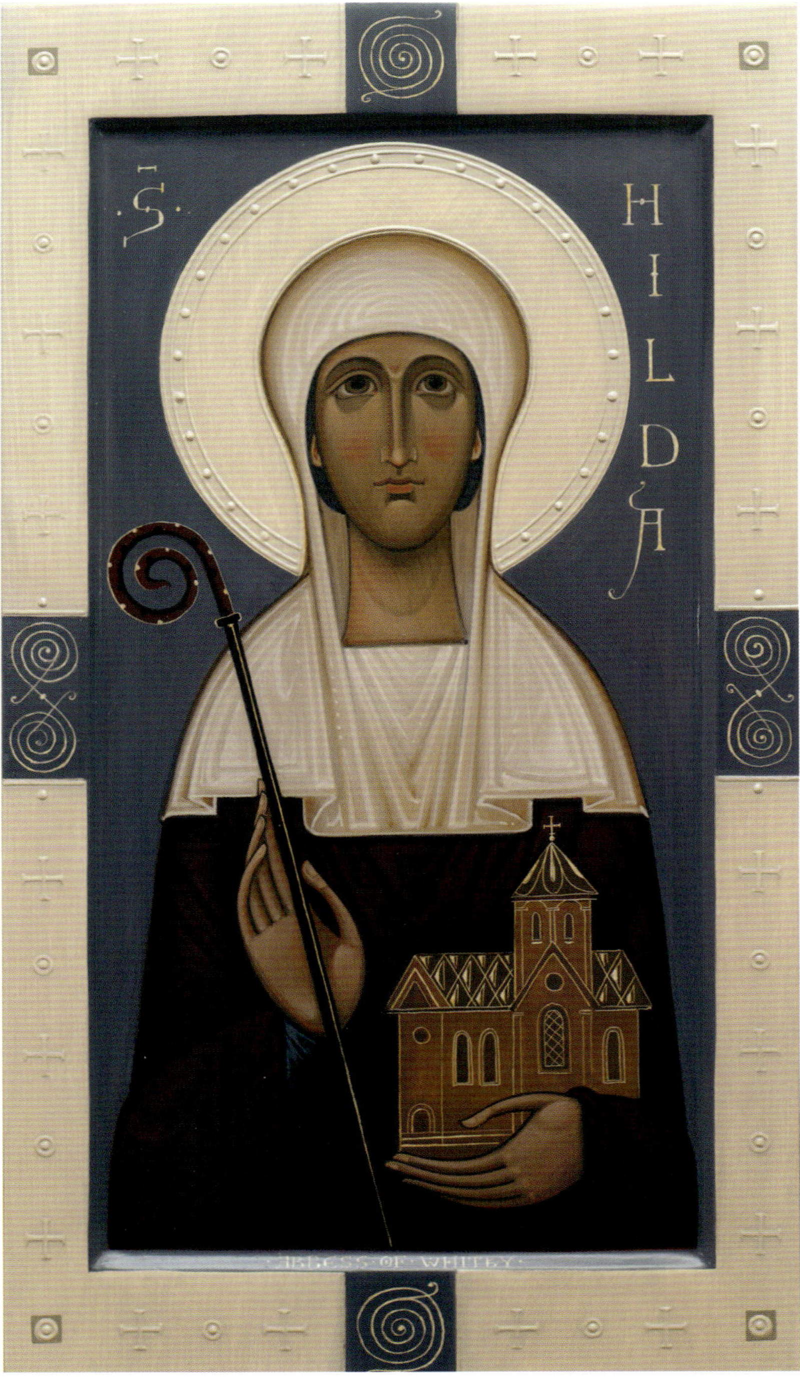

the Soviets, is impressive. So too has been the determination of leading practitioners to evolve stylistically, paying homage to the achievements of the past without being wholly constrained by them. Russian church art is a public statement. It asserts the continuing importance of the church in post-Communist society. In this sense it is a political, not a purely devotional product. Portable icons are, for their owners, individual declarations of faith.

It is also important to note that both icon painting and church art, while being generated in Russia, are an aspect of contemporary Russian culture that experiences no barriers when the artists concerned reach out internationally. They are welcomed wherever the Orthodox faith has a presence.

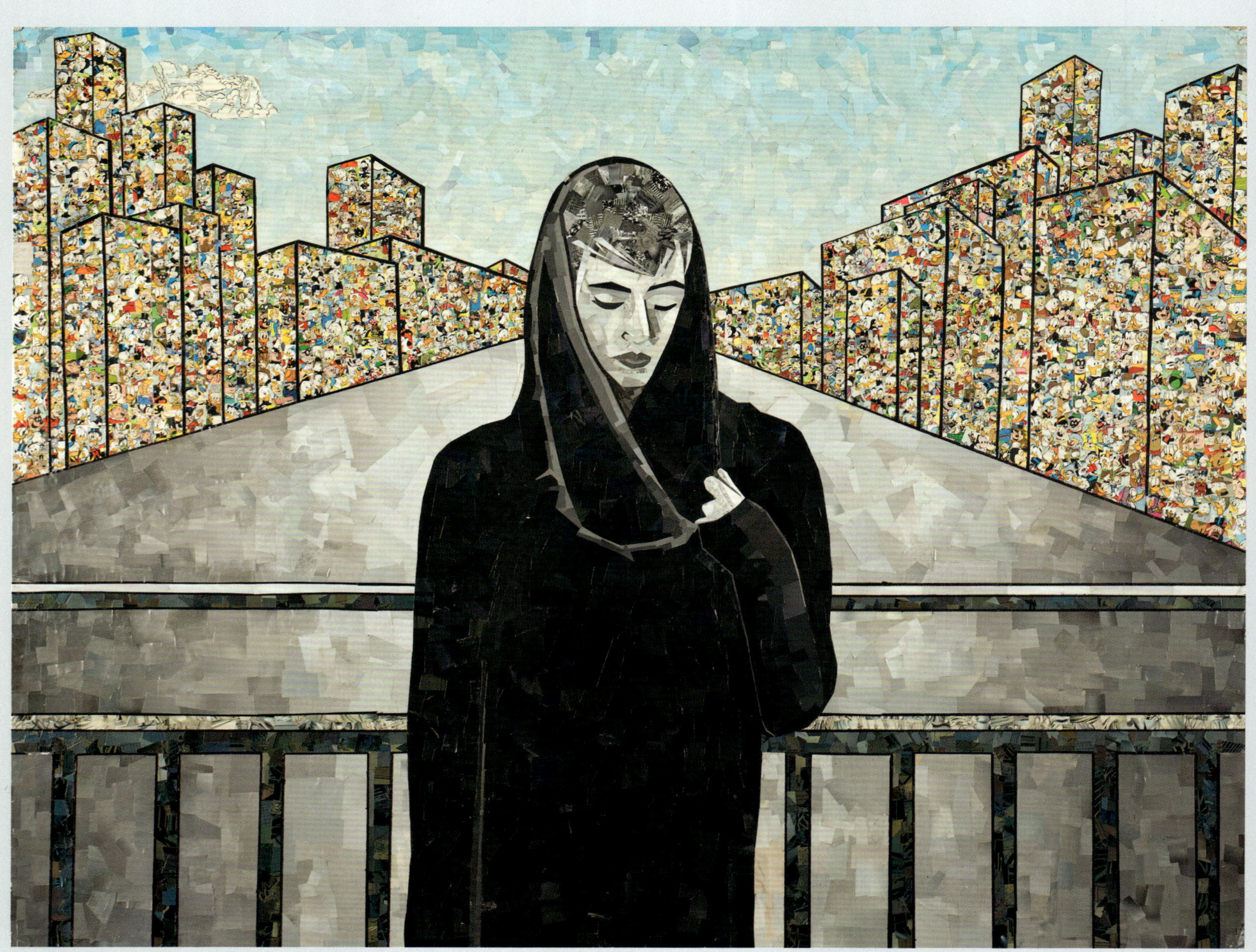

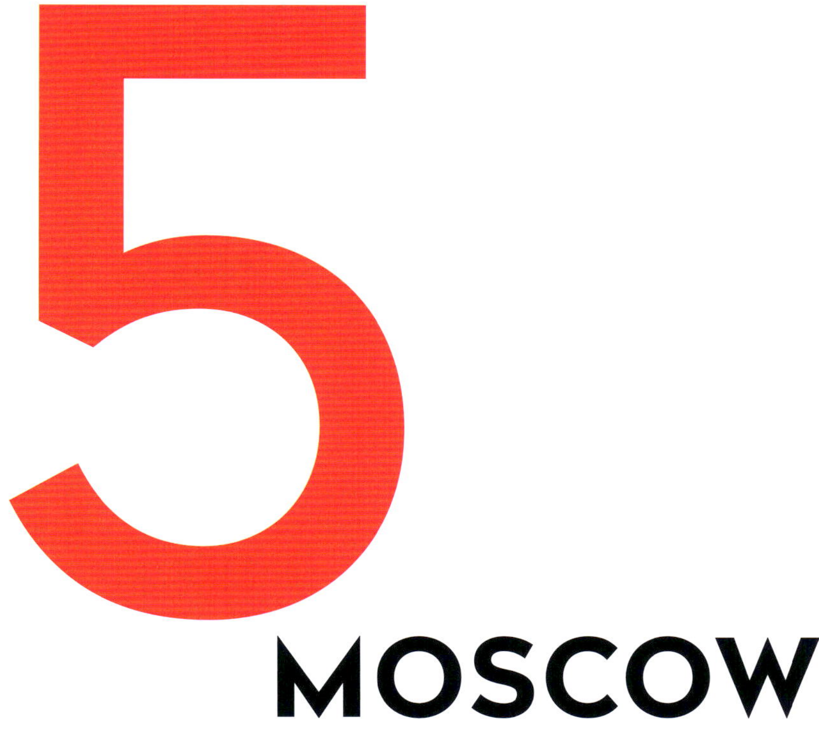

MOSCOW

The images made by Moscow-based artists are, as one might expect, urban and sophisticated. Some of the artists were born in Moscow, others have migrated there for the sake of their art. Interestingly, many of these Moscow-based artists are female. It is equally fascinating to note that a substantial proportion of the artists featured – maybe most of them – have exhibited their work outside Russia, as well as in many varied leading Russian institutions. The subject matter they use covers a wide range.

Olga Kroytor (b. 1986) has exhibited in France, Wittenberg (Germany) and in Baku (Azerbaijan). In 2015, she was the winner of the Kandinsky Prize in the 'Young Artist' category. In 2017 she was part of a special project organised by the Pushkin Museum in Moscow for the Venice Biennale. In the same year she was one of the participants in an International Performance Art Festival held in Vilnius, Lithuania. She works in a wide variety of different media. The image shown here, *Long Way*, is an evocation of urban loneliness.

Svetlana Shuvaeva (b. 1986) studied first at the Samara State University of Architecture and Construction. She moved to Moscow in 2010 and opened an 'apartment gallery' there in 2013. Later she linked up with the Garage Museum and was a participant in the Triennial of Russian Contemporary Art held there in 2017. Her painting, *Panic at the Pool*, from her series *Crowd Character*, shows a host of very active figures, gender unspecified, in a huge swimming pool. They are seen from behind, but we can feel the strength of their emotions by the movements of their arms and bodies. Their heads are brightly coloured blobs, perhaps suggesting the waterproof caps that swimmers wear. Individuality is lost. The painting reads at first glance like an abstraction. There is, however, also a distant echo of the realist pictures of sportsmen and sportswomen produced by official artists in the days of the Soviet Union.

←
Kroytor, Olga
Long Way
2011, collage on cardboard, magazines

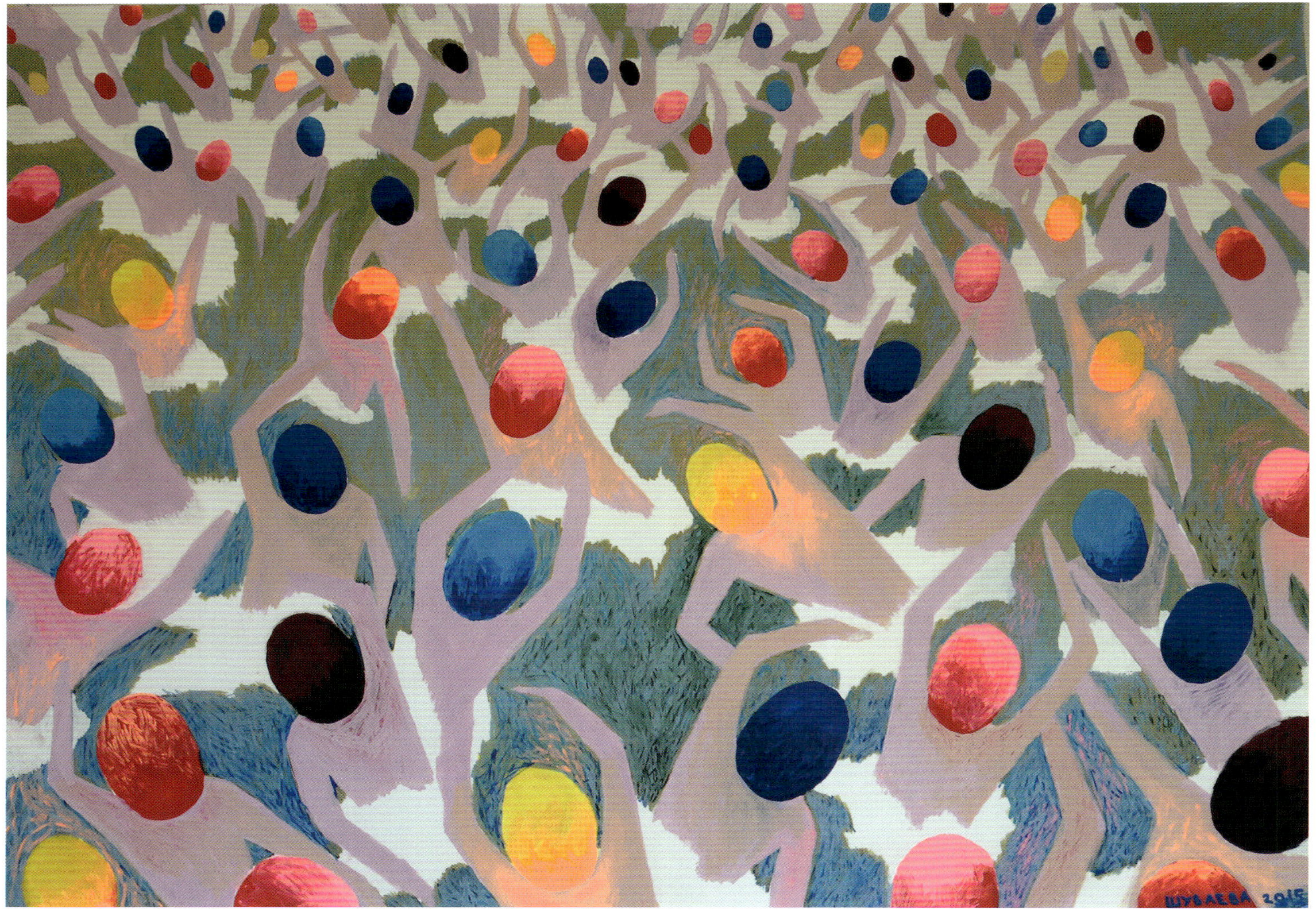

Stanislav Shuripa (b. 1971) studied at the University of History and Culture in Moscow from 1993 to 1997. Later he studied for an MA at the Valand Academy at Gothenburg in Sweden. In 2014 he was one of the co-founders of a group called the Agency of Singular Investigations. His work is displayed in major Russian collections of contemporary art: the Moscow Museum of Contemporary Art, the State Tretyakov Gallery, and also the Garage Museum in Moscow. With *Evening*, he offers another modernised Soviet echo: what appears to be a vast industrial building under an ominously red sky, with a searchlight beam cutting across it.

Irina Korina (b. 1977) graduated in 2000 from the Russian Academy of Theatrical Art. Later, like Stanislav Shuripa, she studied at the Valand Academy at Gothenburg in Sweden, as part of an exchange programme. Later still, she studied in the media class at the Academy of Fine Arts in Vienna, Austria. She has often worked in the theatre. In 2007 and 2014 Irina won the All Russia Innovation Prize awards, in 2011 and 2014 she was a finalist of Kandinsky Prize and in 2009 and 2017 participated in Venice Biennale. She has exhibited at the Brooklyn Academy of Music in the United States, in 2014 at Ostrava in the Czech Republic and other countries.[1]

↑
Shuvaeva, Svetlana
Panic at the Pool, Crowd Character Series
2015, acrylic markers on paper

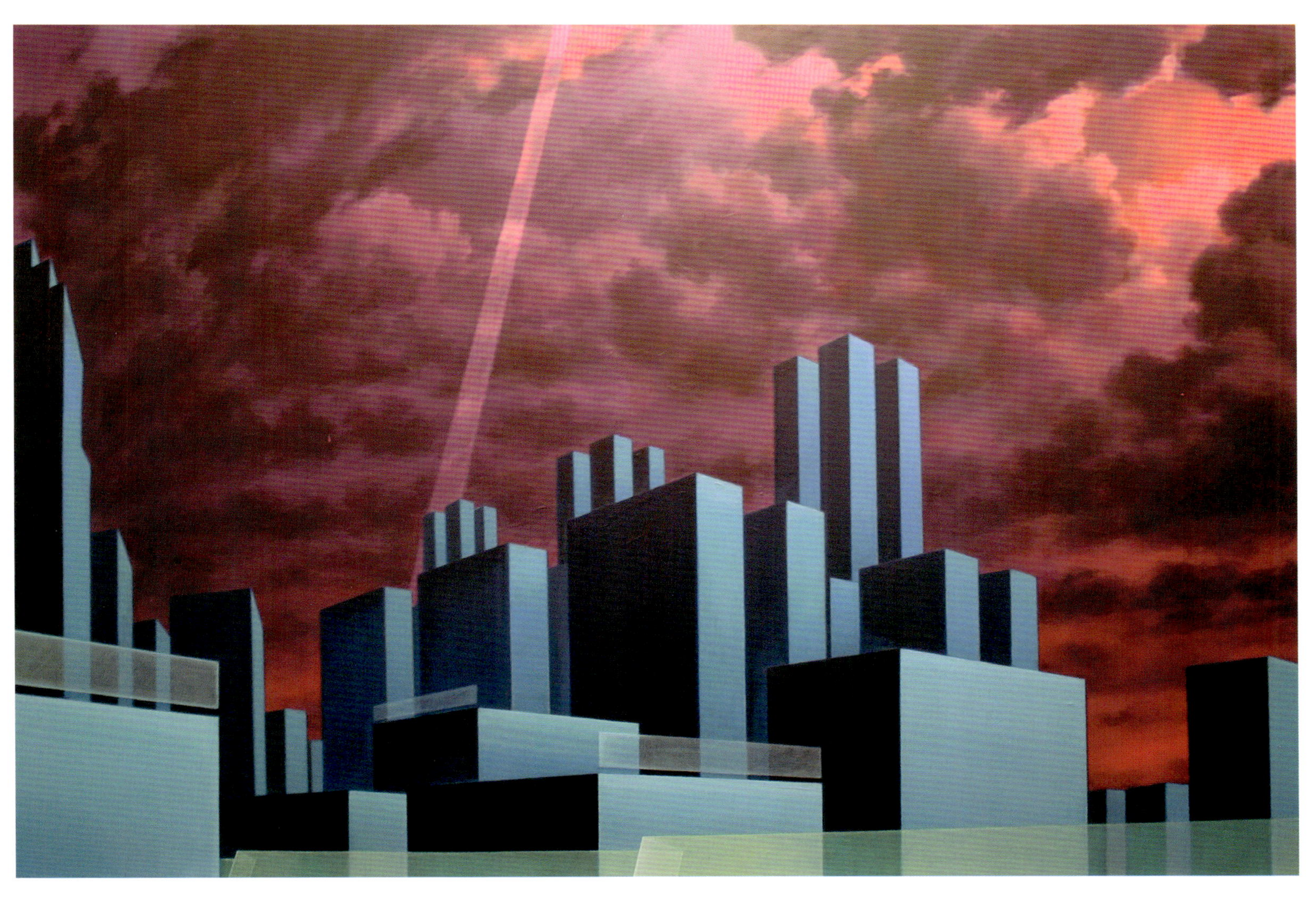

↑
Shuripa, Stanislav
Evening, Cityscapes series
2008, acrylic on canvas

In her sculptural installation *On Vacation*, she has moved fully into the present. This is a luxurious modern corporate headquarters, in which the dutifully abstract sculptures used for prestigious decoration are in the most literal sense taking over the space from humans. One sculpture is still on its pedestal. Another reclines in a fragile-looking armchair.

Diana Machulina (b. 1981) has been active not only as an artist, but as a curator and as an art critic. She graduated from the Moscow Academic Art Lyceum in 1998, then studied scenography at the Russian Academy of Theatrical Art. In 2002 she had an internship at the Stuttgart Academy of Fine Arts, before graduating in 2004 from the Surikov Institute in Moscow. In 2008 she won the 'Young Artist of the Year' Kandinsky Prize. She has participated in exhibitions both in Russia and abroad. These include shows at the Tretyakov Gallery in Moscow; in Sofia, Bulgaria; in Paris, including *Russian Counterpoint* at the Louvre; in Rennes; in Boden, Sweden; and at the American Academy in Rome. The work illustrated here is an installation entitled *Body of Labour*.

Anna Parkina (b. 1979) lives and works in Moscow but trained outside Russia, at the Art Centre College of Design in Pasadena, California, and at the École des Beaux-Arts in Paris, from which she graduated in 2006. During her time in Paris she ran one-day shows, performances and conferences in her apartment and published books by artists, under the imprint Tramway Editions. In 2005 she had a solo show of her work at Galerie Meerrettich in Berlin. In 2009 she held her first show in Moscow. In the same year her works were featured at the Venice Biennale.

→
Machulina, Diana
Body of Labour
2013, installation

Korina, Irina
On Vacation
2019, installation

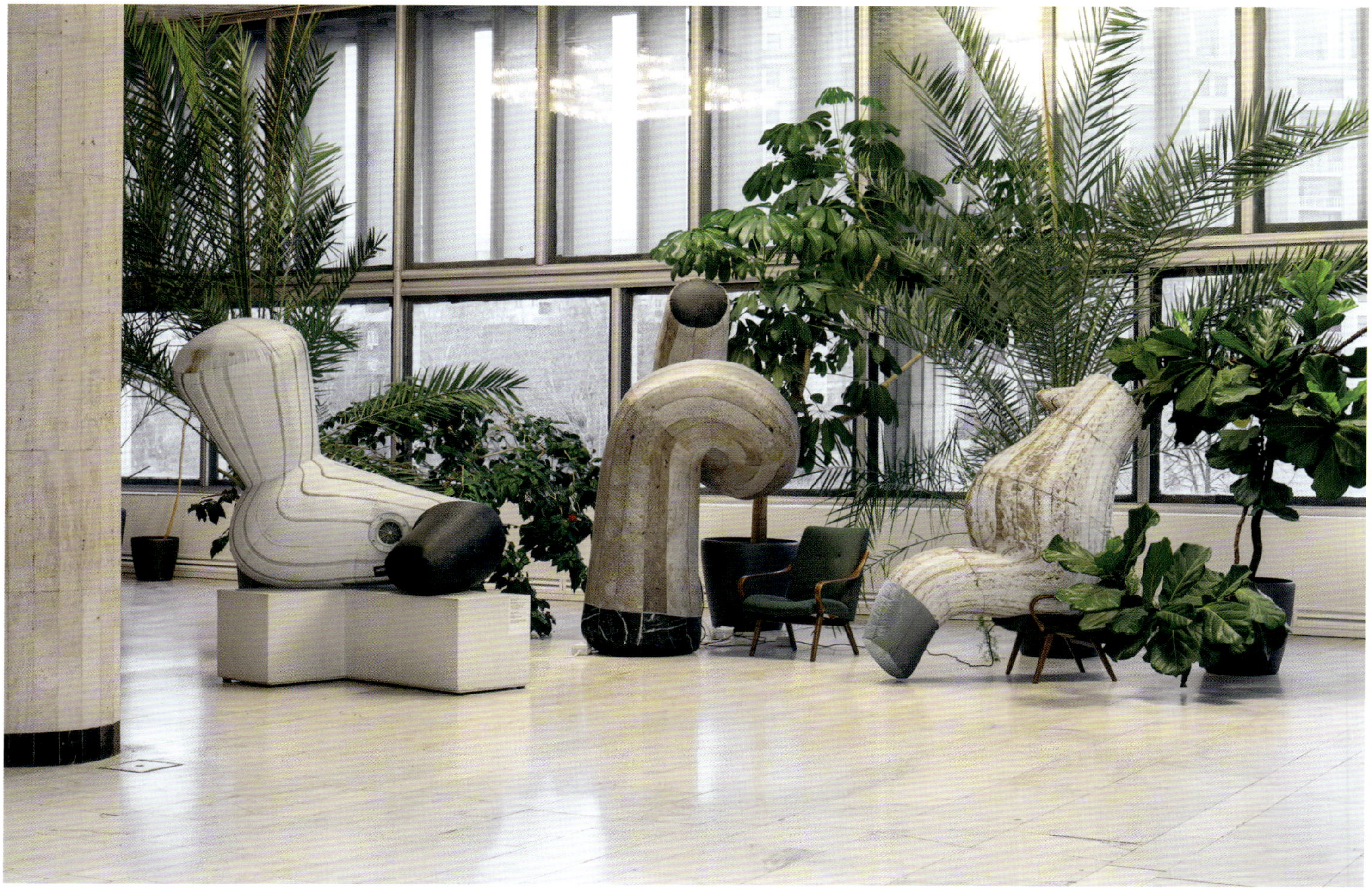

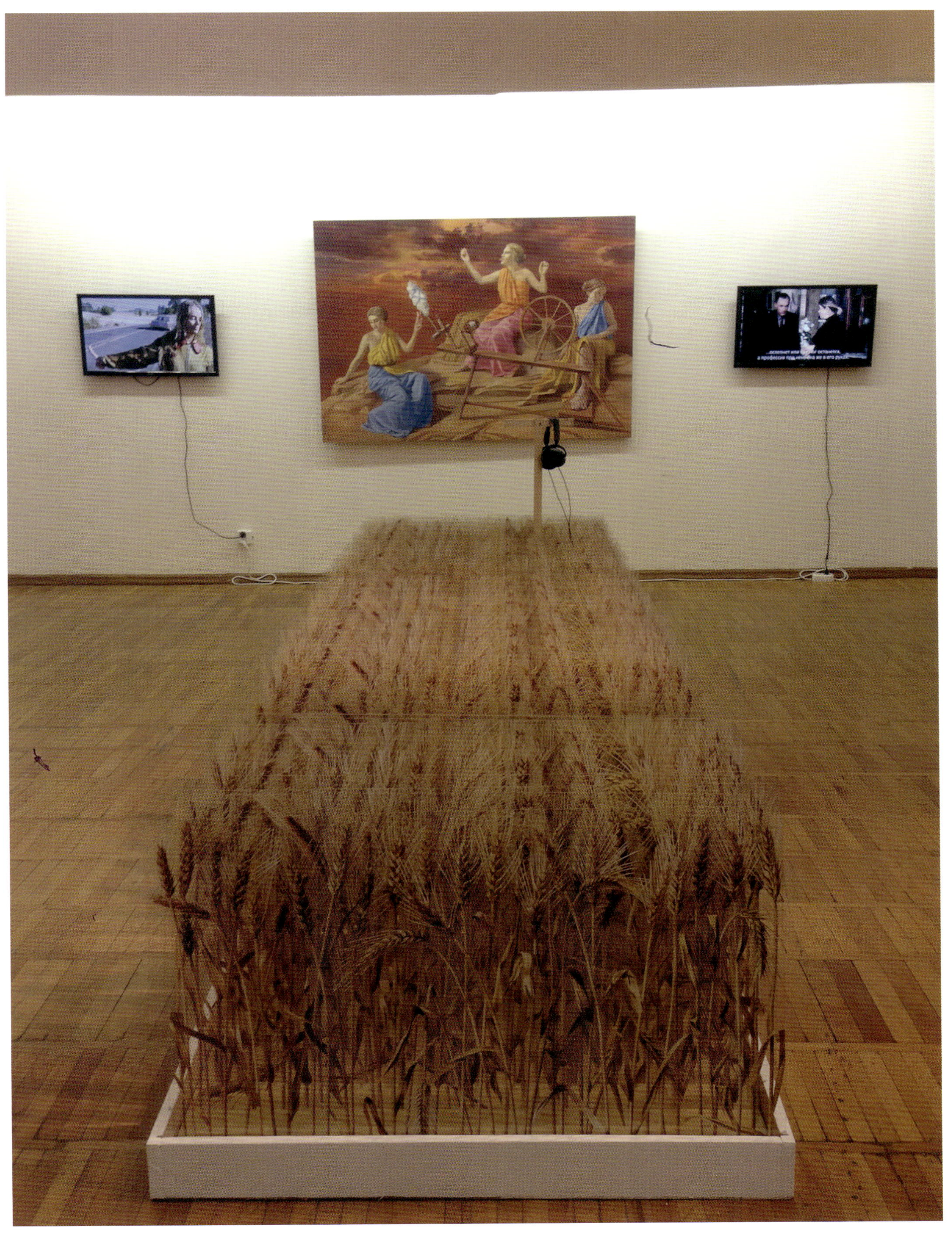

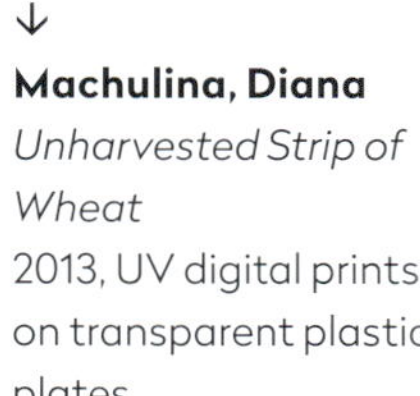

↓

Machulina, Diana
Unharvested Strip of Wheat
2013, UV digital prints on transparent plastic plates

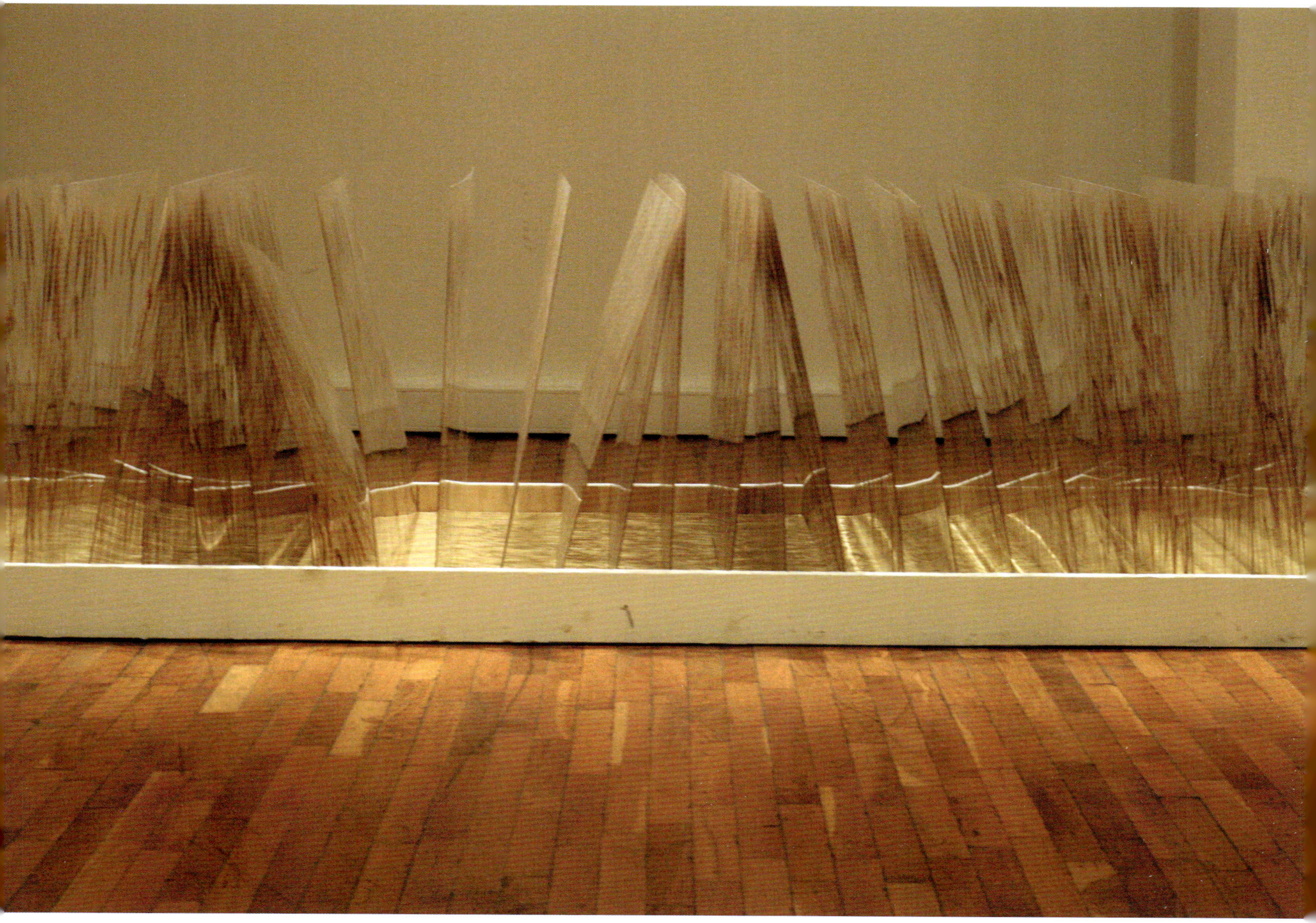

↓
Machulina, Diana
The Fates
2013, oil on canvas

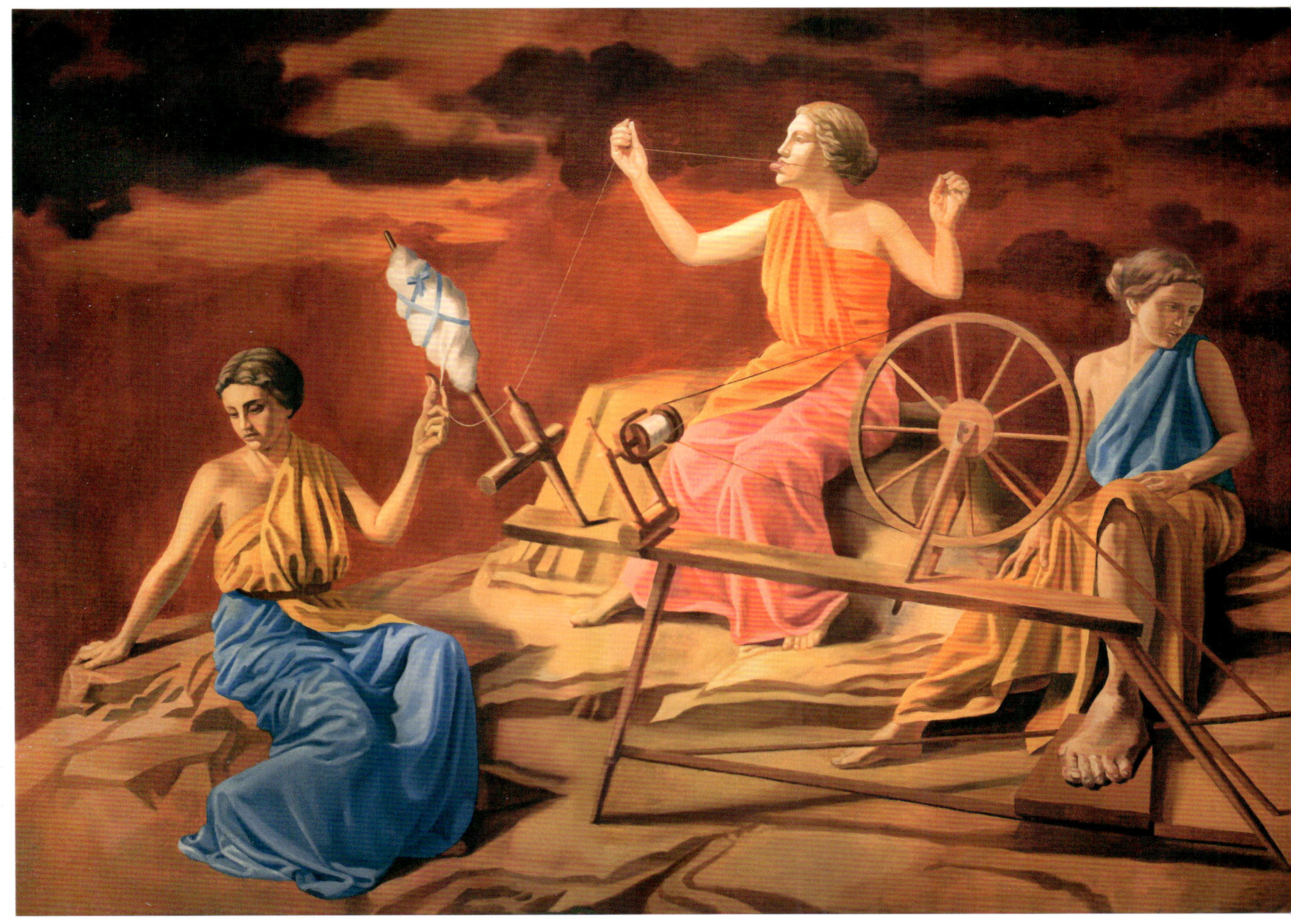

She has continued to show her work widely since then: in 2010, at the exhibition *Modernikon: Contemporary Art from Russia* in Turin; in 2011 with a solo show at the San Francisco Museum of Modern Art entitled *Fallow Land*; and in London, with exhibitions at the Wilkinson Gallery in Brewer Street. Anna has participated in a long list of group shows and performances. Her art is compared to the collages of the German artist Kurt Schwitters (1887-1948), the British artist Richard Hamilton (1922-2011) and even to Kazimir Malevich,[2] but they can also be seen as unique and original. The untitled illustration shown is an example of her work in collage, dating from 2011.

Dima Rebus (b. 1988) is another Moscow-based artist who has held solo exhibitions in London and Brussels, and has participated in group events in Patagonia, Argentina (2011), and at the UN Biennale in Berlin. The bulk of his work is in watercolour, and 'floats between reality and surrealism'.[3] The work shown here, *The Woman*, is from Rebus's SPAM | 2015 series described as *'Everybody keep their mouth shut, while my mom plays bingo'.*[4]

↓
Parkina, Anna
Untitled
2011, collage on paper

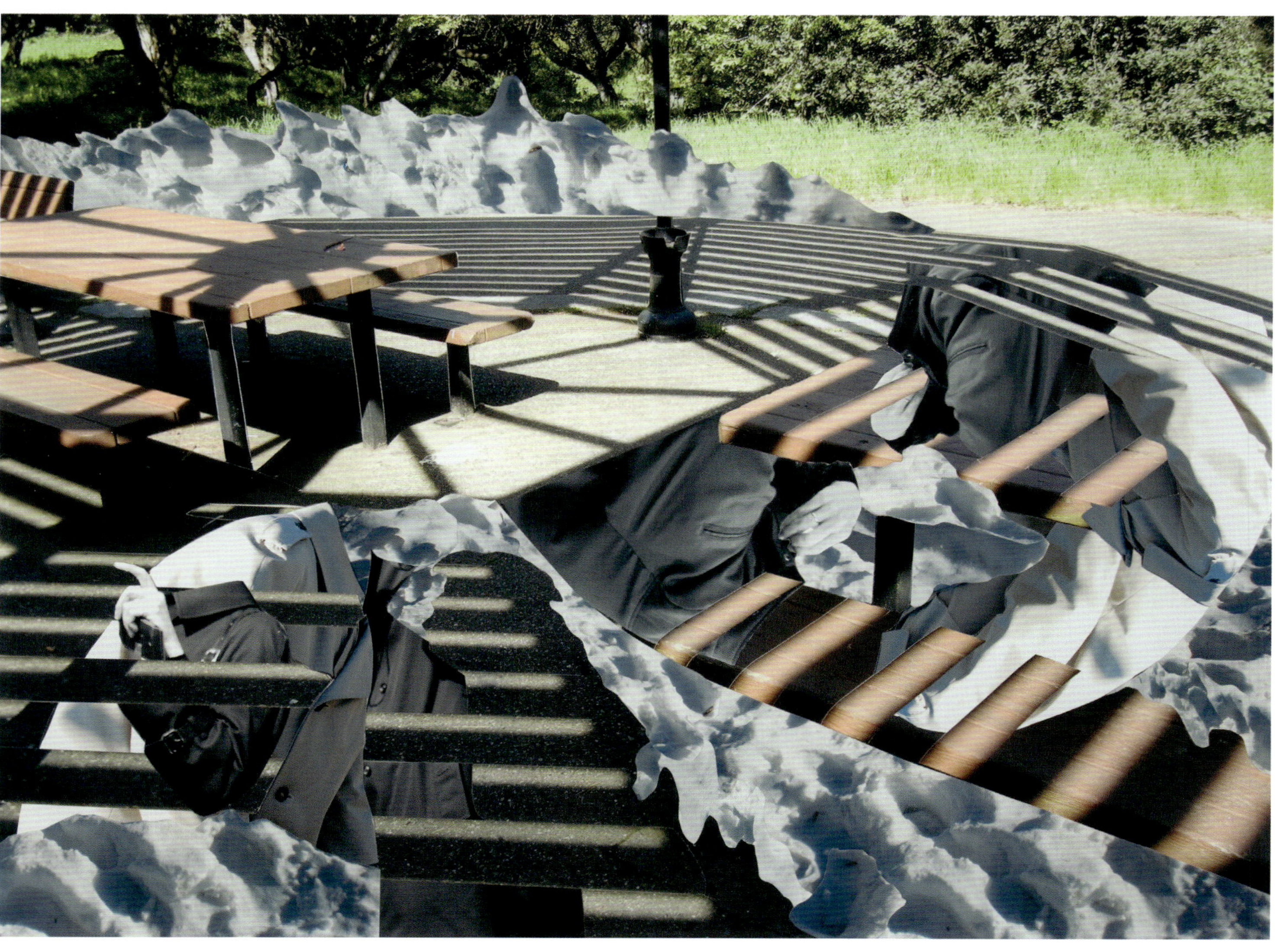

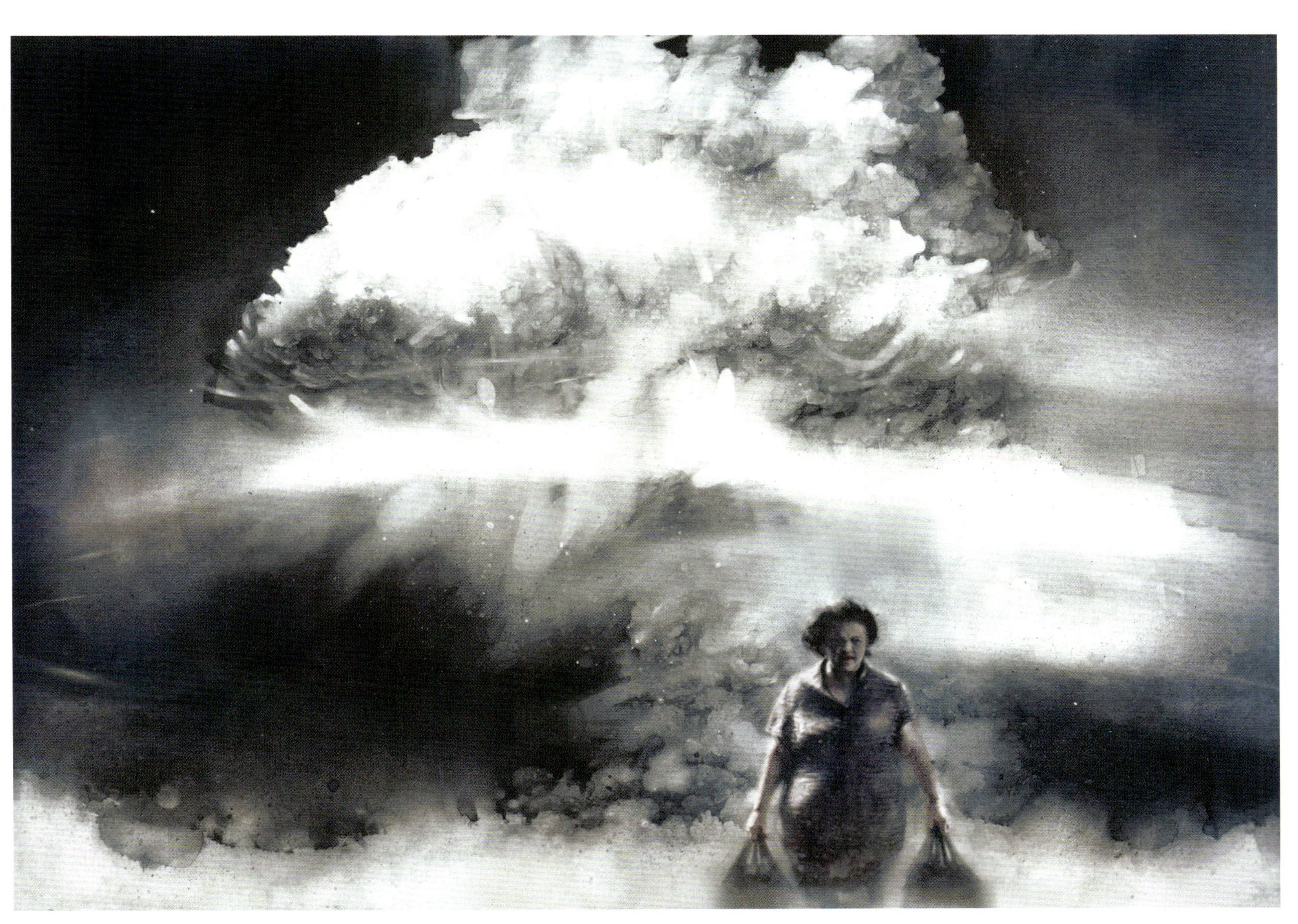

↑
Rebus, Dima
The Woman
2015, watercolour on paper

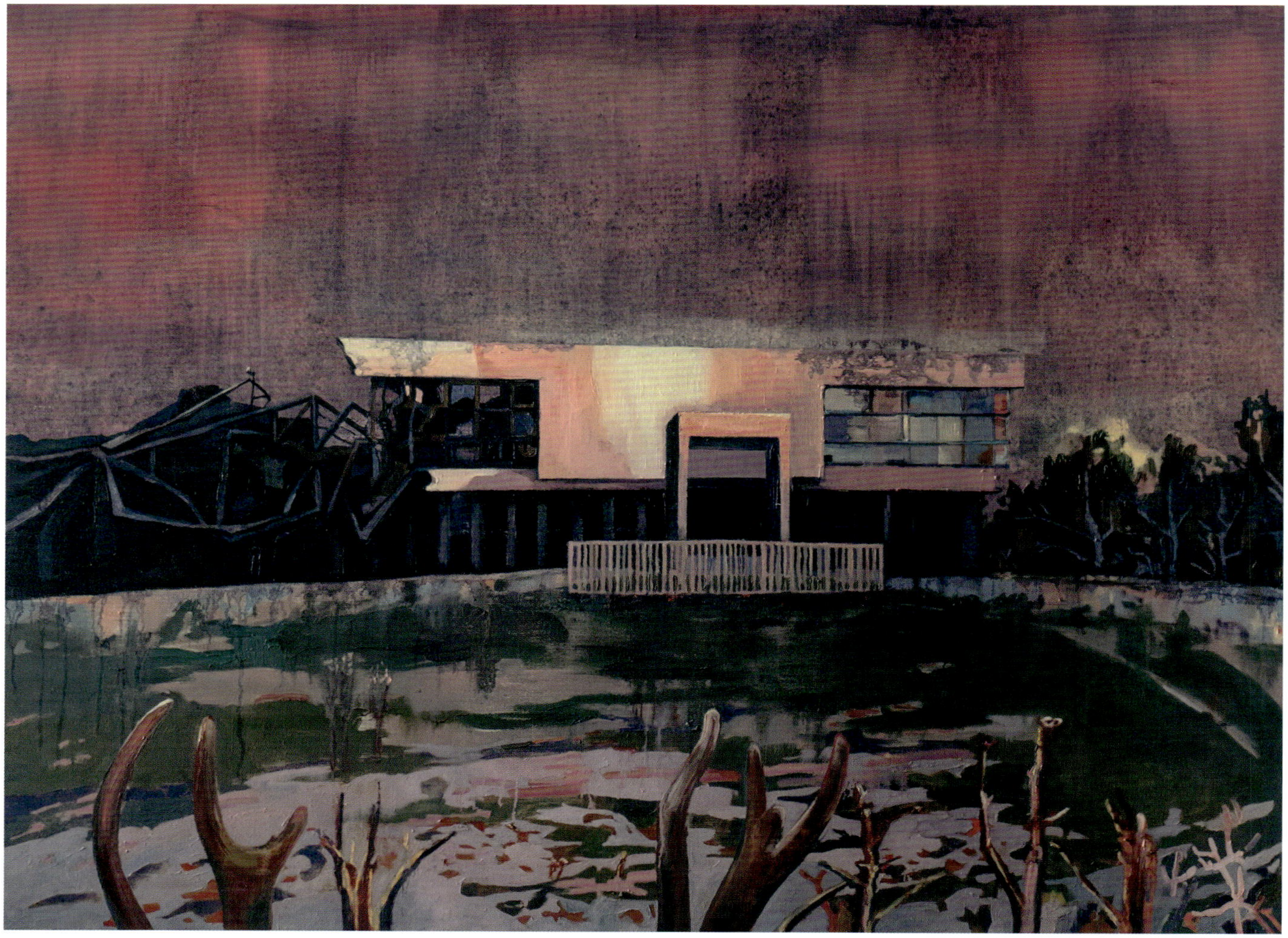

Mika Plutitskaya (b. 1983) describes herself as 'interested in tropes, stipulations and unspoken experiences within Soviet culture regarded from a contemporary perspective.'[5] She was born in the final decade of the USSR and studied psychology before completing a course at the Moscow State College of Theatre and Character Animation and receiving a BA (Hons) in Fine Arts degree from the University of Hertfordshire in 2019. The works shown here are from her *Like a Merry-Go-Round in Childhood* series, 'a painterly series about haunted memories of Soviet childhood on the borderline of reminiscence and imagination.'[6]

David Ter-Oganyan (b. 1981) was born in Rostov-on-Don. He moved to Moscow in the 1990s where his father, the provocative artist Avdey Ter-Oganyan (b.1961), became a gallery director and, eventually, from 1995–98, the director of the School of Contemporary Art, where David was a student. Avdey ran into trouble because of a performance piece called *Young Atheist* which involved him chopping up reproductions of Orthodox icons. He was charged with spreading religious hatred and he emigrated in 1998. He returned to Moscow in 2019 when his case was dismissed and he could not think of himself outside of Russia anymore.[7]

David's art is less provocative than that of his father, but is still, as these images of his works demonstrates, very much High Modernist in style. He participated in the 32nd Parisian Fair of Contemporary Art 'FIAC' in 2005 with his project *This is not bombs* and became the first Russian artist to receive the Henkel Art Award in 2011. David also took part in a number of international group shows: the *Manifesta 4* Biennial in Frankfurt; the Tenth Istanbul Biennial; *Ostalgia* in the New Museum in New

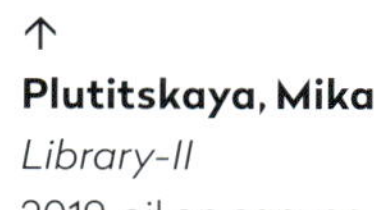

↑
Plutitskaya, Mika
Library-II
2019, oil on canvas

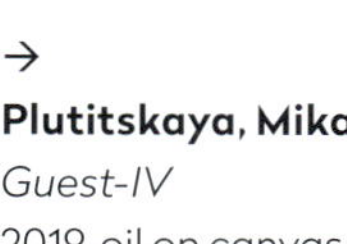

→
Plutitskaya, Mika
Guest-IV
2019, oil on canvas

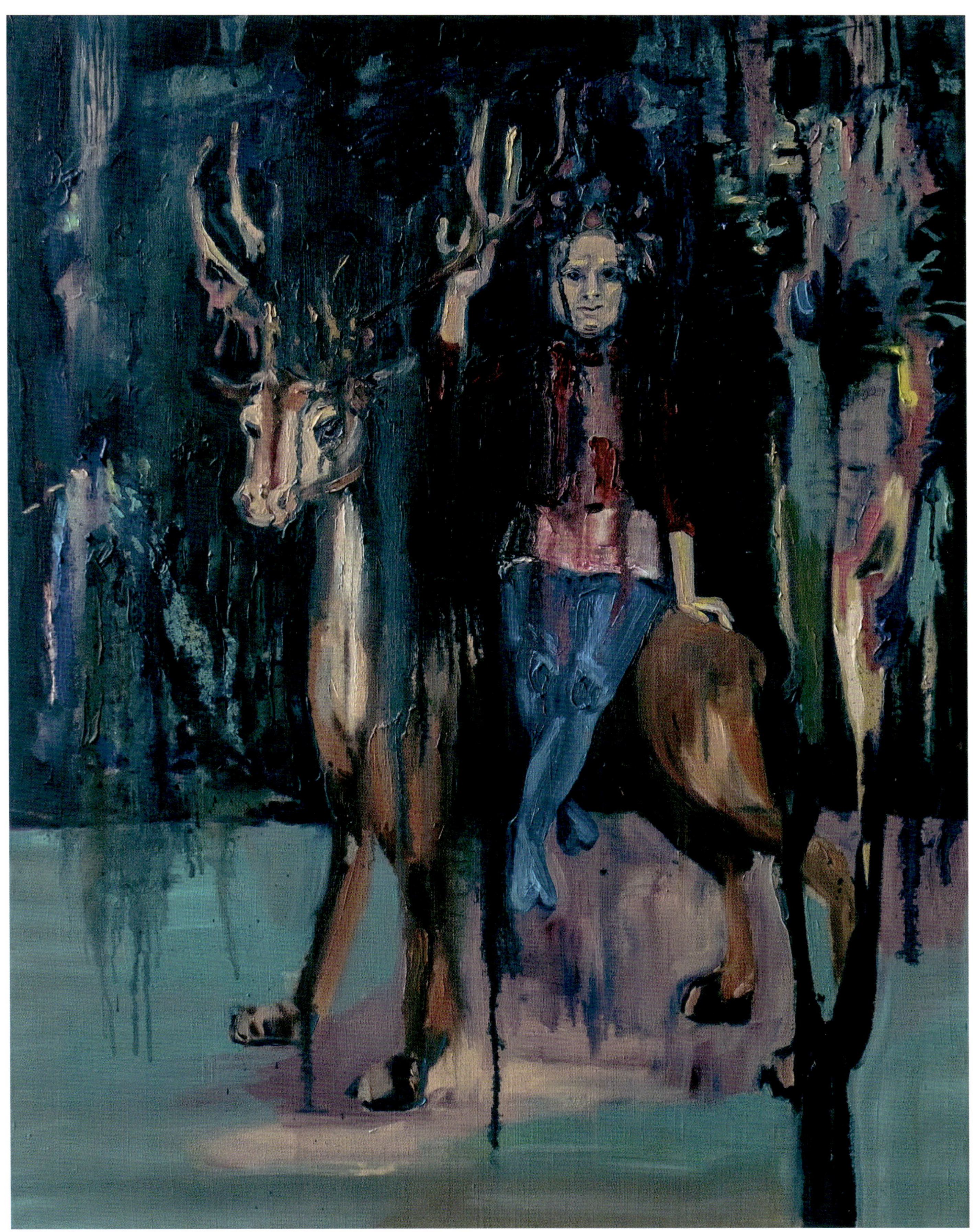

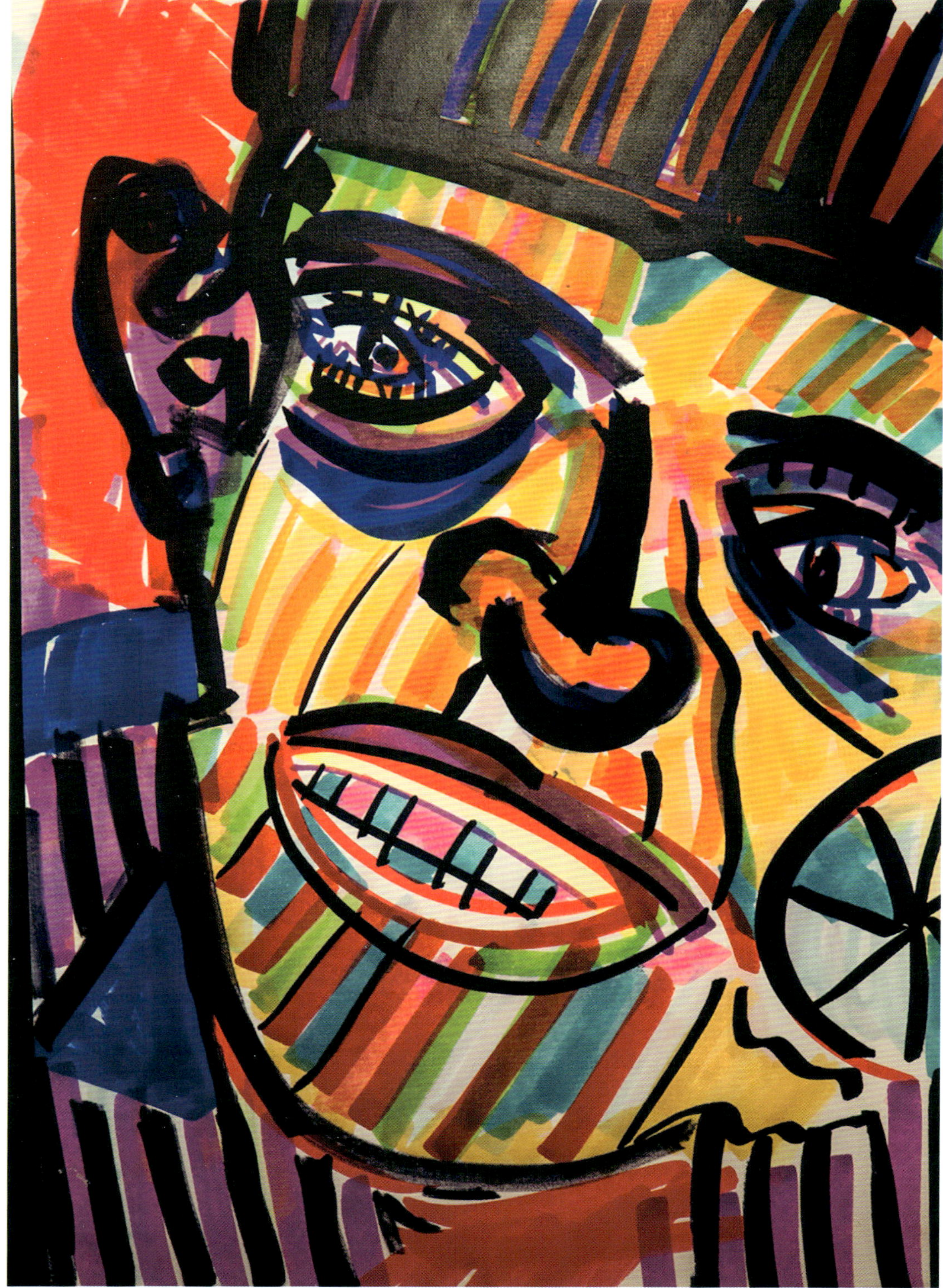

←
Ter-Oganyan, David
Face
2014, C-print on canvas

→
Ter-Oganyan, David
Beach
2014, C-print on canvas

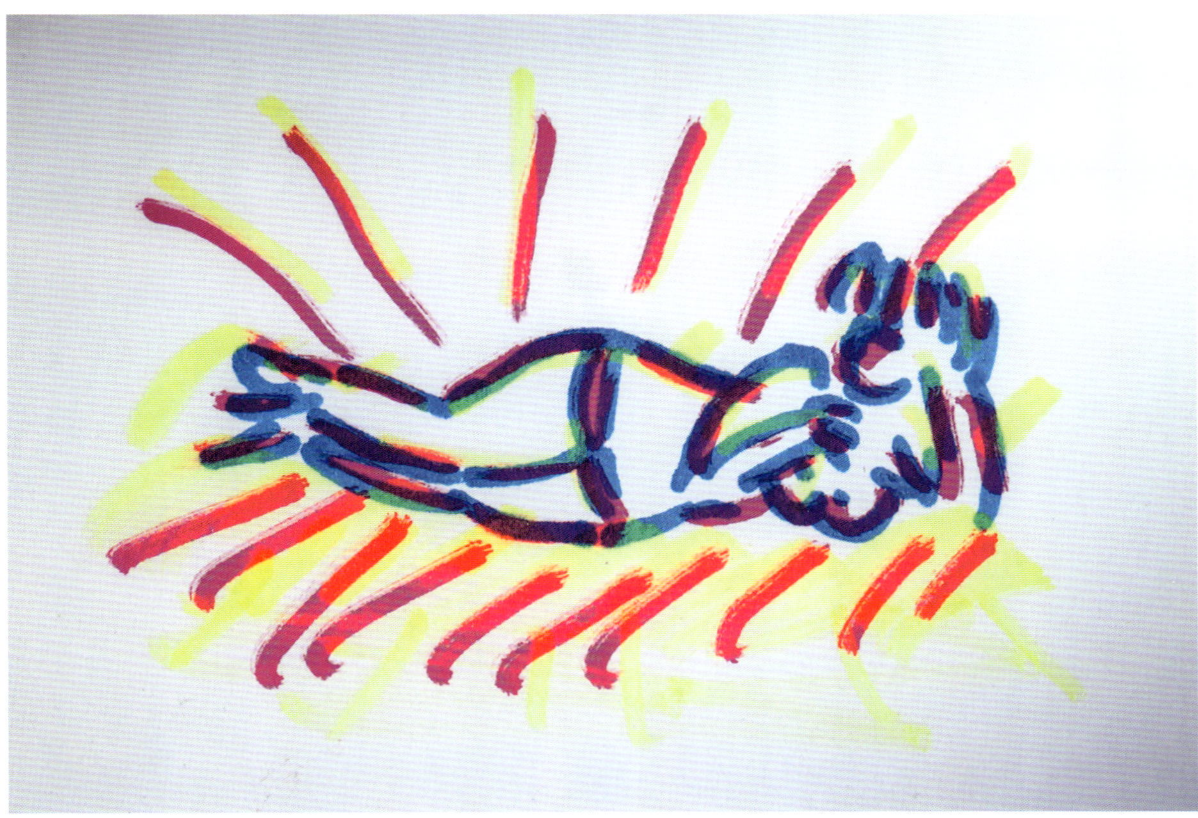

York; *Modernikon* in Turin and the *In the Heart of the Country* show at the Museum of Contemporary Art in Warsaw.

Roman Sakin (b. 1976) is another restlessly experimental Moscow modernist who graduated from the Moscow State Stroganov Academy of Design and Applied Arts. He gives a detailed account of the genesis painting illustrated, entitled *How to Become a Good and Even Holy Person*, or *Antennas and Semicircles*:

> Rambling as a child through the countryside, I used to come across a dilapidated church and would always climb into it. It was very interesting inside. I was always longing to find an old Bible and an iron cross there. However, there were of course only empty spaces. But these empty spaces were no less exciting than the undiscovered Bible or the cross. Semi-circular spaces especially: they seemed to perfect you by their design. You only had to step into this semi-circular coverage area. I also liked the dome and roof frames a lot. They appeared as antennas, enhancing the impact of the church semicircles. Rickety crosses looked very convincing as antennas, since our TV antenna was also tilted and its angle could not be altered even by a millimetre. Once as a guest I even saw a TV with a hanging meat grinder to stop the antenna moving. And this hyper-respectful attitude to the antenna's position made it dominant in space, more important than the TV itself. A switched-off TV with a convex kinescope and a cruciform antenna somehow reminded me of a church. Drawing a house or sculpting one from plasticine I would always place antennas on its roof, this was the most essential element… Remembering that time now, I realise that only two things have been sacred for me – antennas and church semicircles.[8]

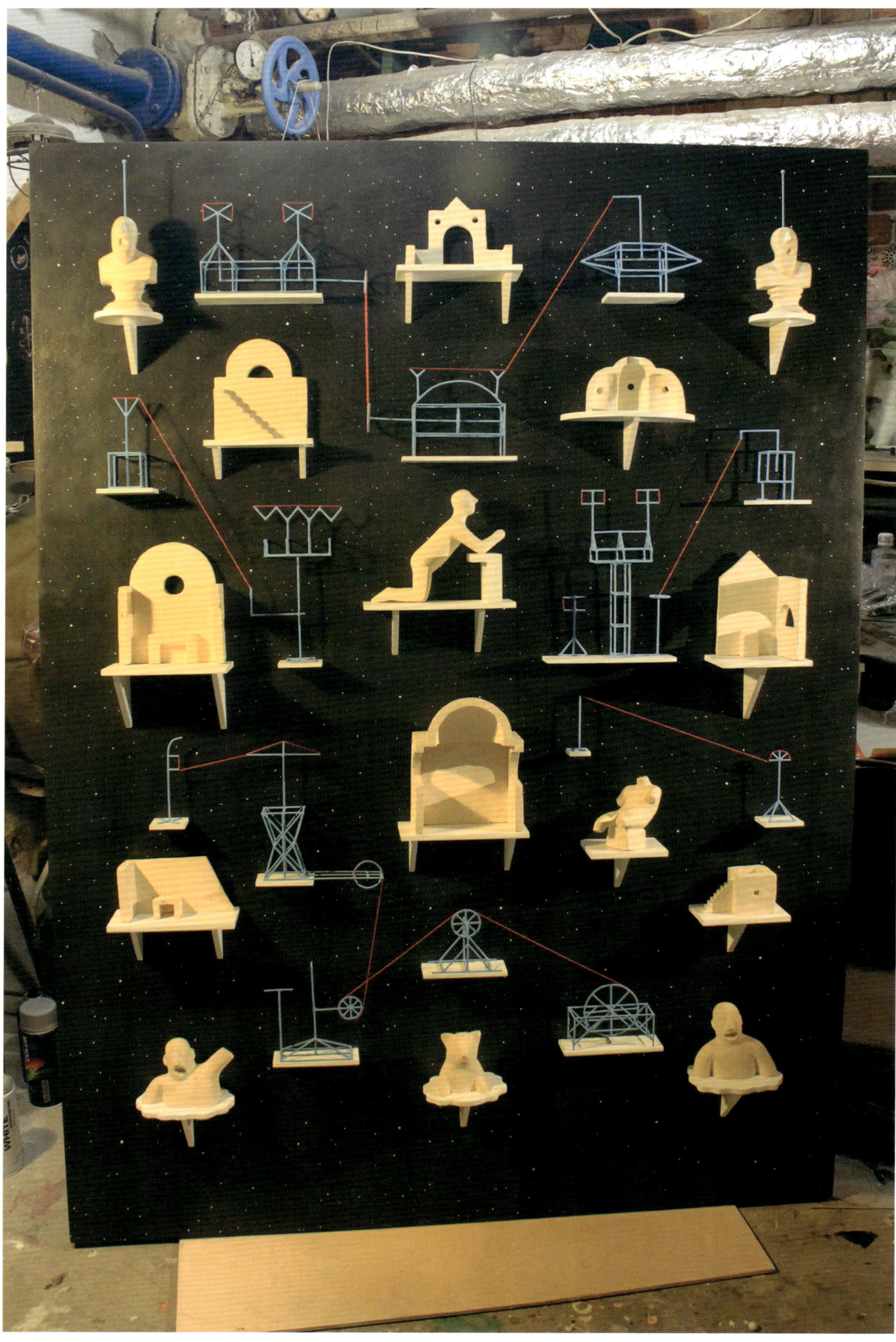

←
Sakin, Roman
How to Become a Good and Even Holy Person, or Antennas and Semicircles
2016-18, chamotte, paint and thread on wood

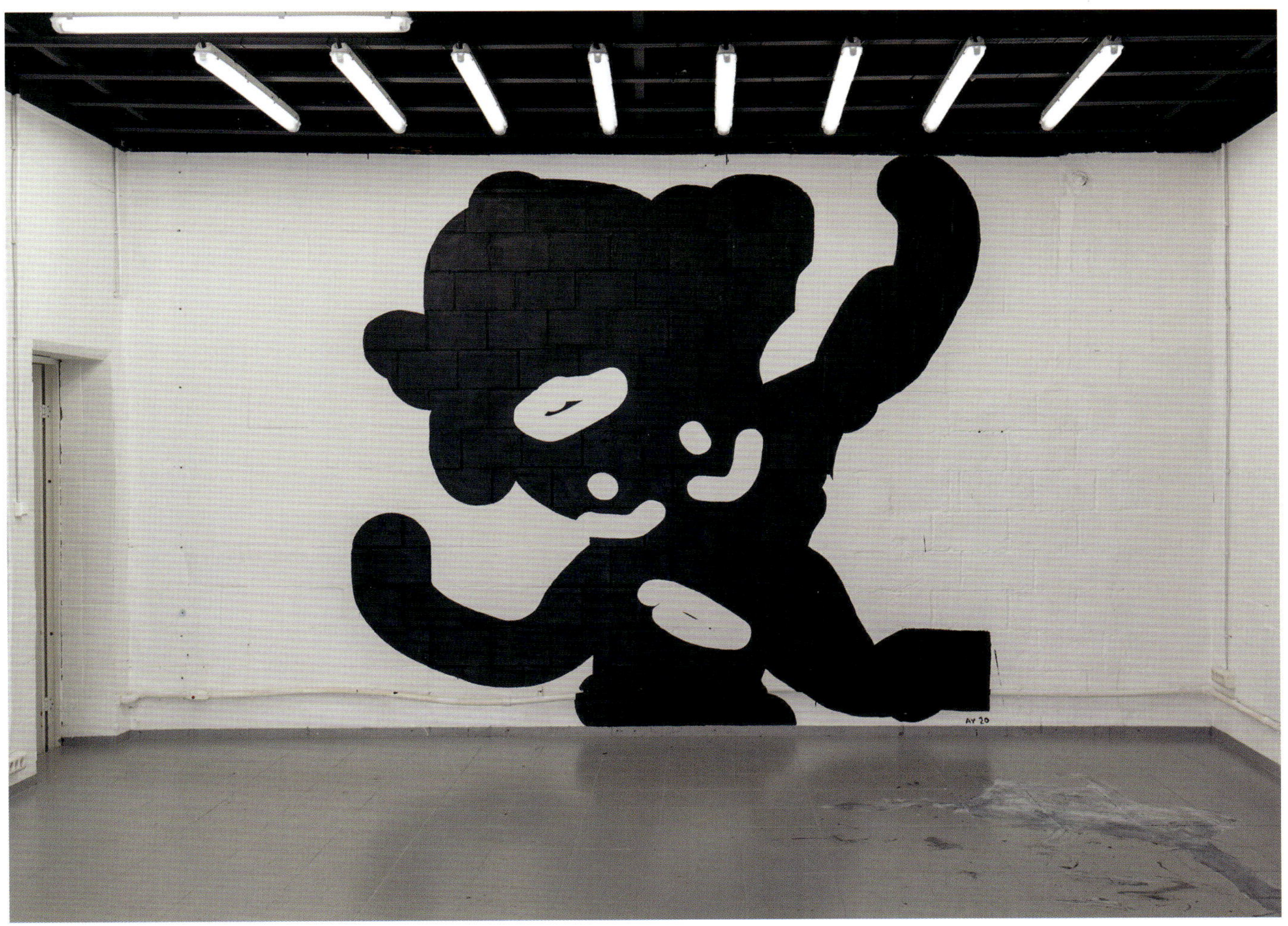

↑
Yoffe, Alisa
Mama
2021, acrylic on tiled wall

Finally, in this section, there is Alisa Yoffe, born in Tashkent, Uzbekistan in 1987. She creates her graffiti-like images on iPhone and transfers them onto walls, canvas or paper. Some of them remain in digital form on social media. Her future plans include also presenting her works as NFTs (Non Fungible Tokens). The images she makes are best described in a statement by *The School Without Centre*, an ad hoc operation situated on the borders of the Moscow city area. The official description reads thus:

> For *School Without Centre* Alisa Yoffe uses her expressive black and white wall paintings to make urgent past-and-present socio-political questions visible in the exhibition space. They deal with [the] (im)possibilities of individuals within the system, with freedom of information and censorship of creativity and thought. A special interest lies in the relationship between people and machines. In reference to forms of protest in the public urban space, to temporary communities and dissident communication, Yoffe creates a series of tools for resistance and care. These soft and nomadic images are to be worn on bodies or carried and stuck to walls as flags or used for covering tables, pillows or eyes.[9]

It is perhaps the final noun in the concluding sentence that has the strongest resonance in contemporary circumstances. The Moscow-based artists featured here are engaged in acts of 'seeing again'. The whole turbulent history of Modern art, from its beginnings more than a century ago, is open to them, ready for use. They combine what they find to suit themselves.

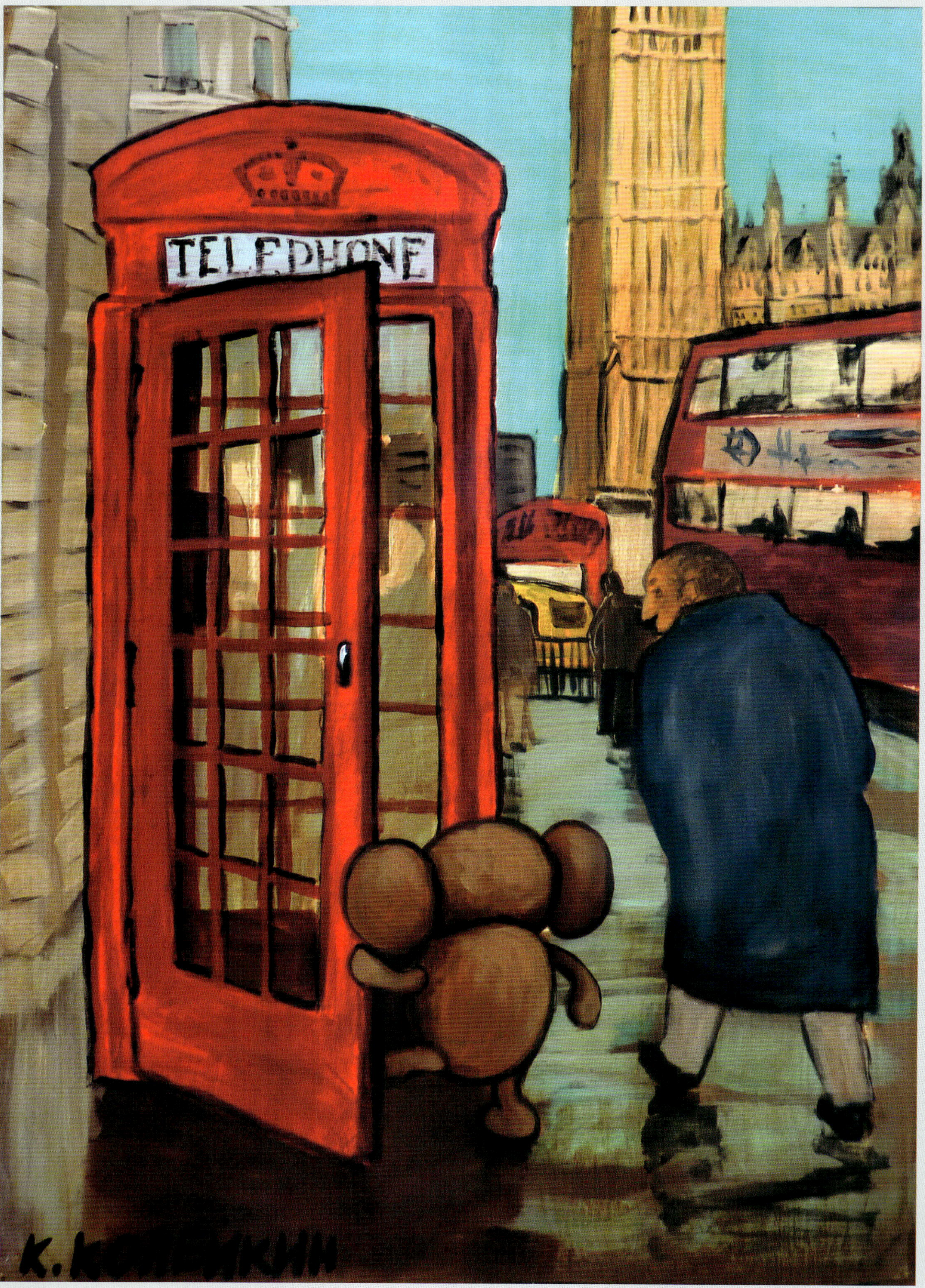
TELEPHONE

6 SAINT PETERSBURG

The works by St Petersburg artists are more varied and have perhaps a wider range of references than those from Moscow. *The War of the Worlds*, 2009, by Nikolay Kopeikin (b. 1966) shows a fight between children's and comic books heroes while his other work, *Mister Cheburashka*, 2012, features a beloved Russian cartoon character entering a London phone box, where he lives in the cartoon narratives. Kopeikin is also a filmmaker and has been a participant in both national and international film festivals. In addition, he has, since 1999, worked with NOM, a popular 'joke rock' act with cult underground status in Russia. His artistic influences range from French Fauvism to German Expressionism, and he mocks both international events and everyday Russian affairs.

Many of the works in this section seem more painterly than those from Moscow. Kirill Makarov's *Conversation*, for example, dated 2010, bears quite a close family resemblance to the work of Zinaida Serebriakova, produced during her long years of exile in France, and belatedly celebrated in Russia during her brief return there in the late 1960s. Makarov (b. 1988) is a generation younger than Kopeikin. He graduated from the Stieglitz Academy in St Petersburg in 2011, afterwards taking up an artist residency at the Abbaye de La Prée, in France.

Flowers, 2018, by Ivan Plusch (b. 1981), is more experimental with paint. It shows a vase of flowers, placed on a chest. A figure standing next to the vase is composed of airy blots of paint, creating the impression that it is ready to float in space. This can be read as a sophisticated reminiscence of some of the effects originally pioneered by the German Expressionists. His other work, *Glass Disease*, 2015, is equally challenging. Plusch studied at the St Petersburg Roerich Art School (1997–2001), and then at the Stieglitz State Academy of Art and Design in 2003–2009. He won the Innovation Prize in 2013 and the Sergey Kuryokhin Prize in the same year.

Wooden Danae, 2020, by Nestor Engelke (b. 1983), with a nude female figure gesturing at a bat,

←
Kopeikin, Nikolay
Mr Cheburashka
2012, acrylic on
cardboard

is, in contrast to the Plusch piece, a contemporary paraphrase of Rembrandt's work from Engelke's *Wooden Hermitage Walks* series. The innovative aspect is the unexpected material from which it has been made.

Engelke was one of the founder members of the North-7 Group. He comes from a family of the St Petersburg intelligentsia, and is the son and grandson of famous architects and art historians. From early childhood he was associated with the Academy of Arts.

As an architect, Engelke loves and values wood and prefers a 'tree with history' as a basis for his work. The tree, understood as a natural entity, has become the main theme of his art. He says of it: 'I am interested in the tree itself – it is alive, it is a piece of flesh. There is a frozen movement in its growth. There is just a branch, and I'm interested in finding a place for it in a person's life. When wood is only a material for chairs and cabinets, then it is not the most important ingredient. And if, for example, I swing an axe at it, then it will show itself, the essence will climb out of it, it will be released from the closet, from the nightstand, from the wall.'[1]

In contrast to this, Alexander Dashevsky's *Swimming Pool* (2013) offers a version of the architectural themes used by artists working in Moscow, but with a stronger air of desolation. The pool is empty. The raised portion nearest the spectator is strewn with debris. It hasn't been cleaned for a long time. Windows along one side of the building, and at the end of the pool, reveal a desolate urban landscape. This is a painting with a contemporary social message

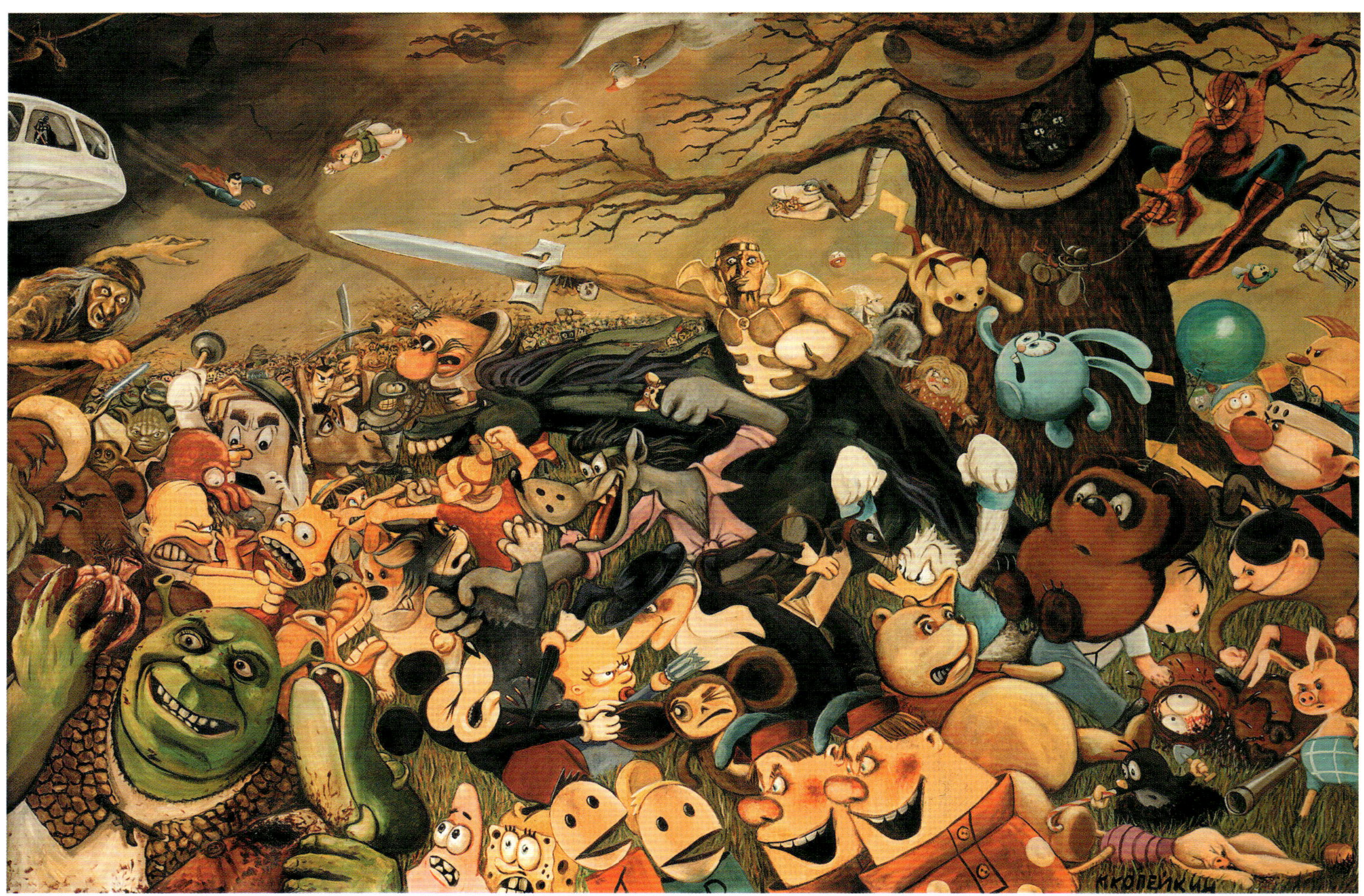

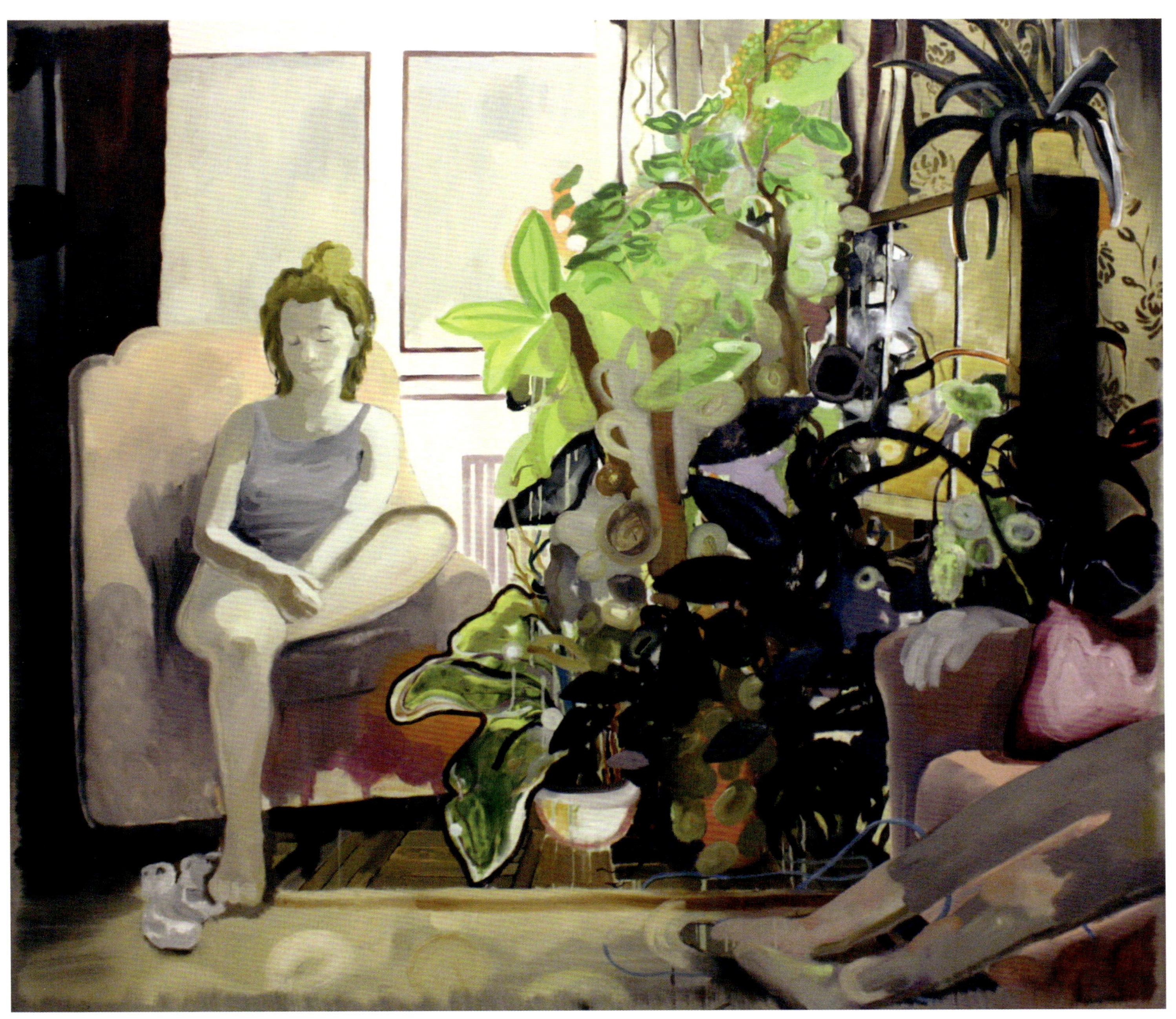

←
Kopeikin, Nikolay
The War of the Worlds
2009, acrylic on canvas

↑
Makarov, Kirill
Conversation
2010, oil on canvas

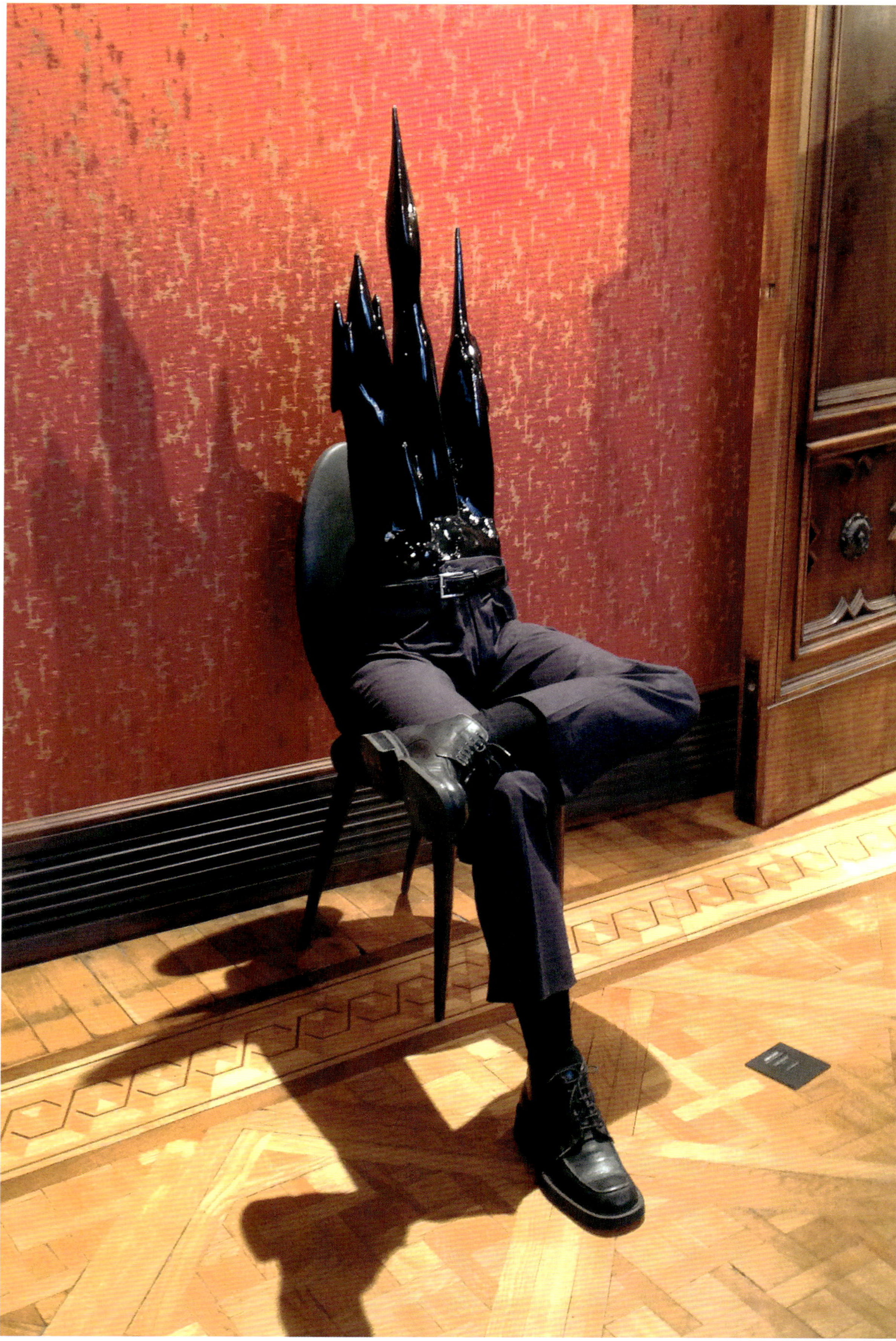

←
Plusch, Ivan
Glass Disease
2015, wood, glass, leather, textile

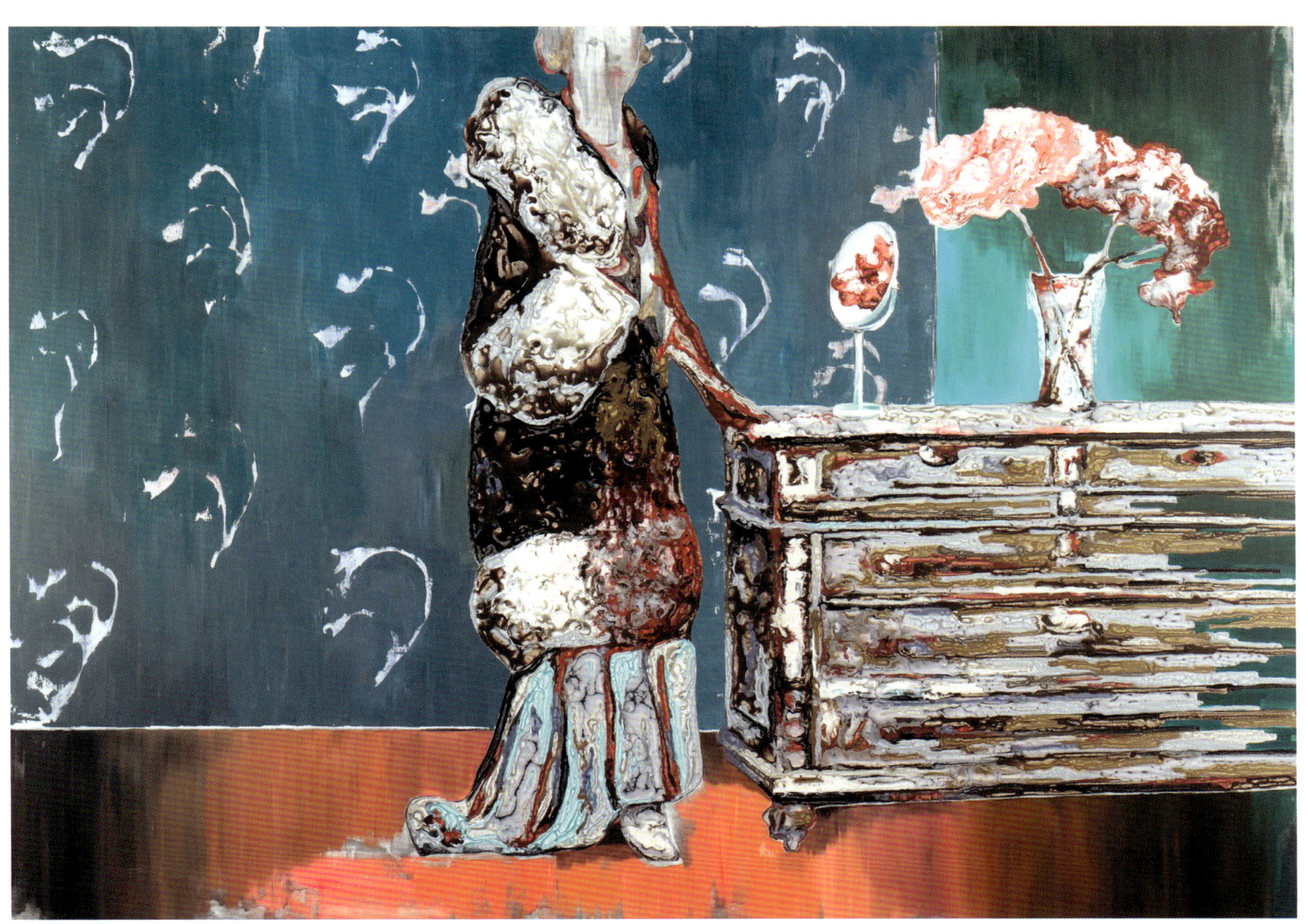

↑
Plusch, Ivan
Flowers
2019, oil and acrylic on canvas

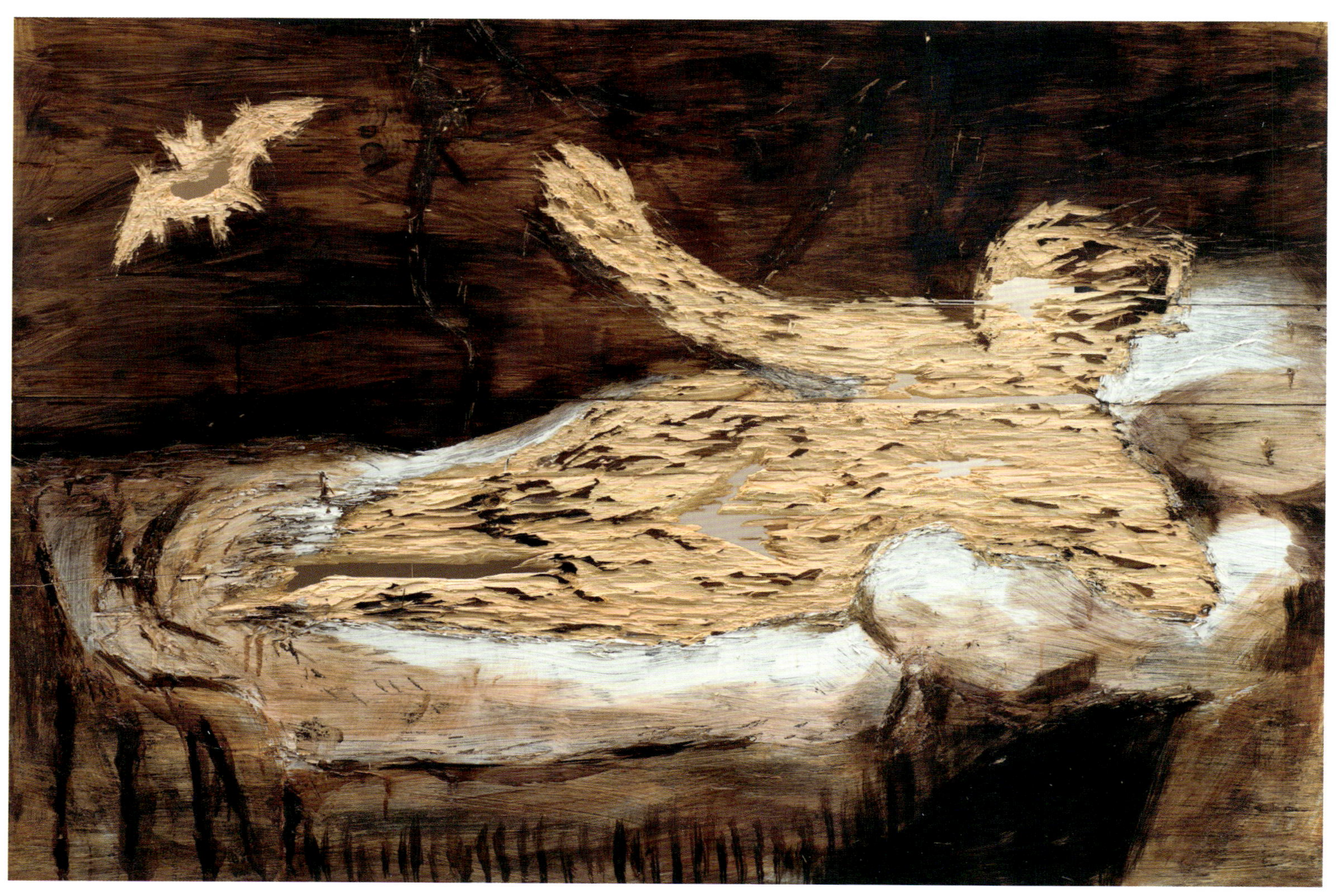

↑
Engelke, Nestor
Wooden Danae
2020, wood

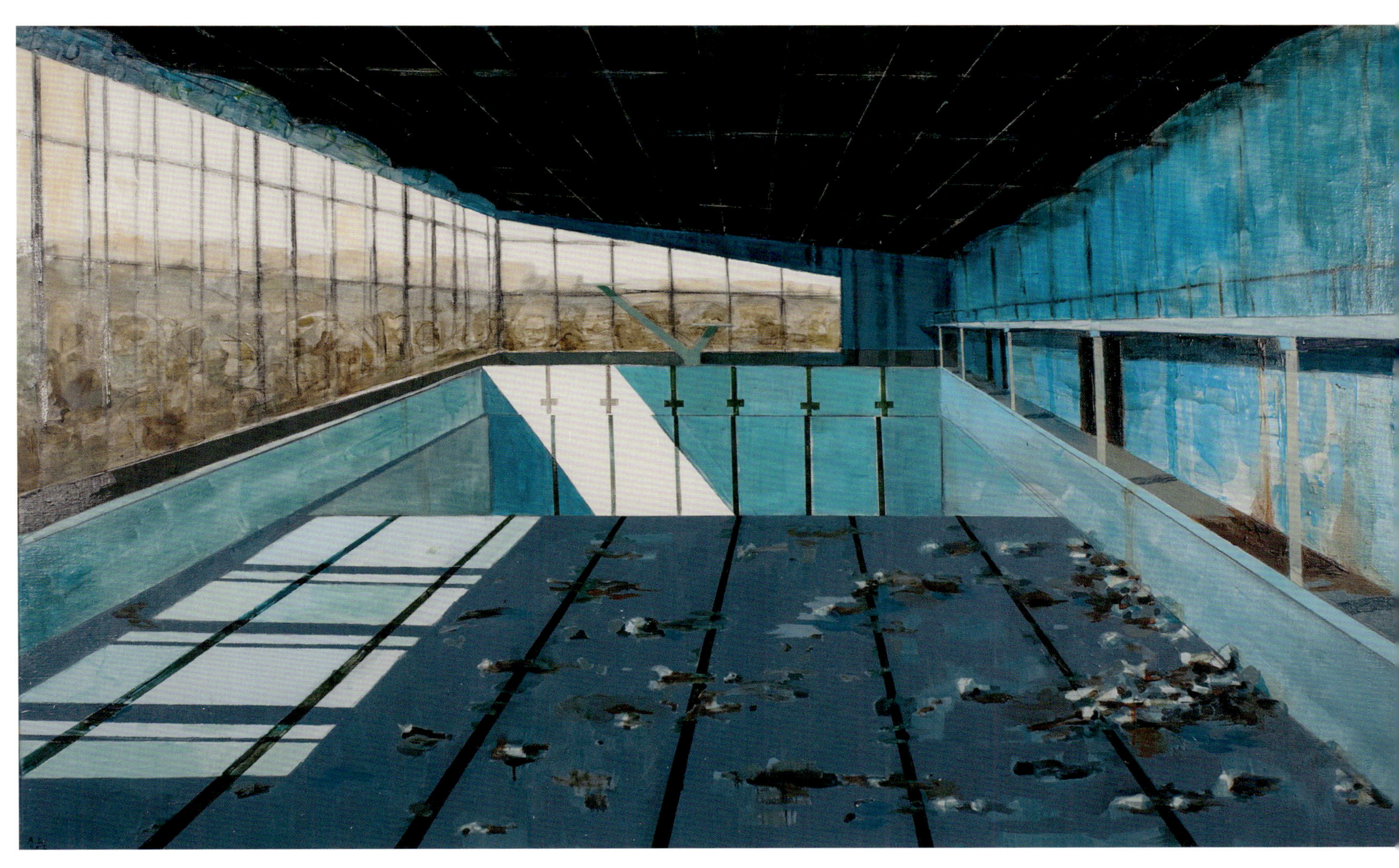

↑
Dashevsky, Alexander
Swimming Pool
2012, oil on canvas

Dashevsky (b. 1980) originally graduated from the Economics Department of the St Petersburg University of Film and Television. He then studied at the faculty of theory and history of arts at the State Academic Institute of Painting. He has work in the collections of the Moscow Museum of Modern Art and at the State Russian and Erarta Museums in St Petersburg.

Phillip Dontsov (b. 1972) is up-to-the-minute in a slightly different way. He uses the materials and technologies of product design and industrial model-making in his paintings, sculptures and installations exploring the interplay of form and light. His *Red Works* paintings in polymer on aluminium depict the human body in a fashion derived from photography, though at first glance they seem to be abstract. The glossy surface of the polymer emulsion seems to shift the images from positive to negative, the back again. A website suggests that the suspended animation of these

Dontsov, Philipp
Red Work RM-31
2002-2003, acrylic, resin, aluminium board

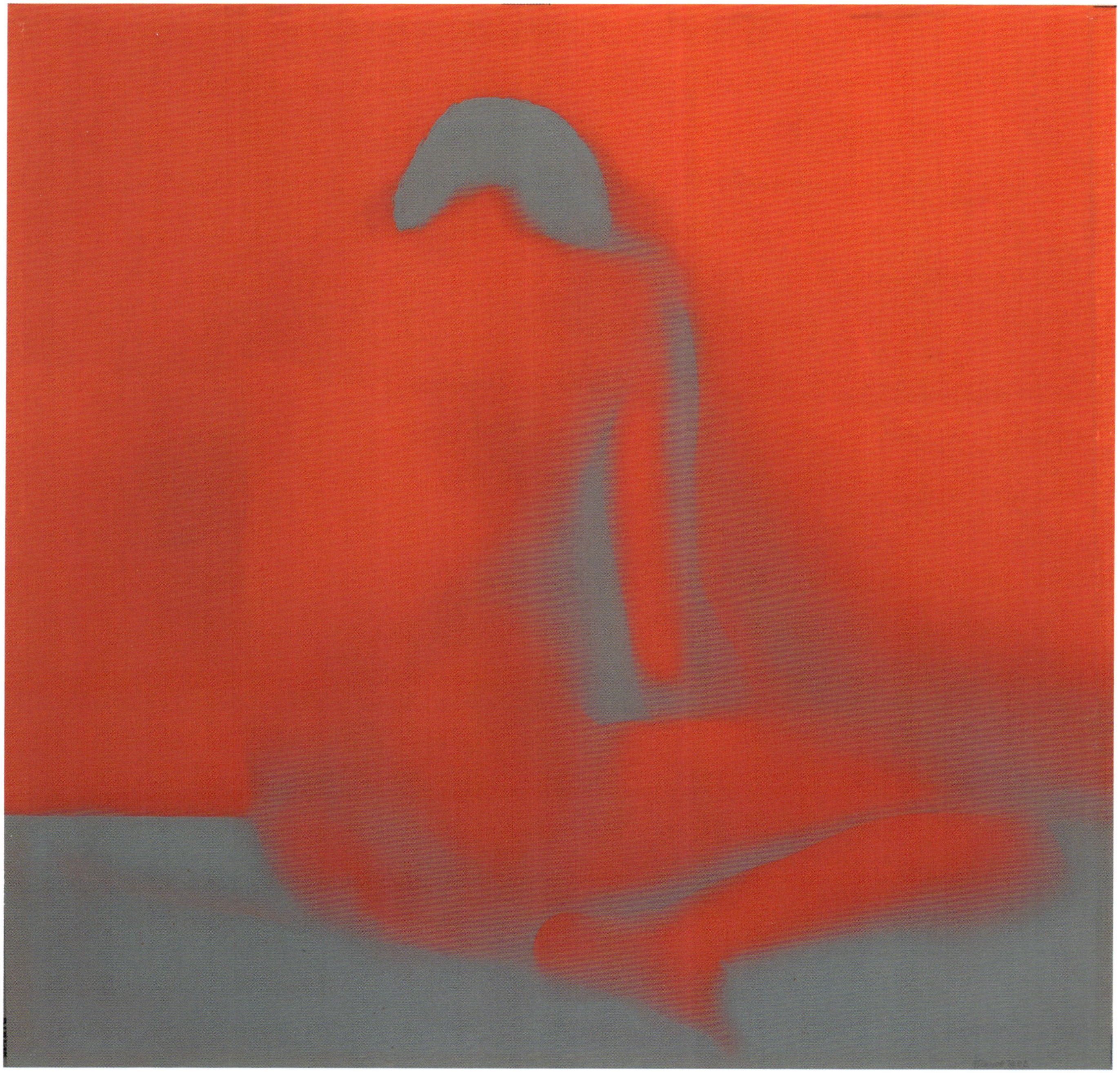

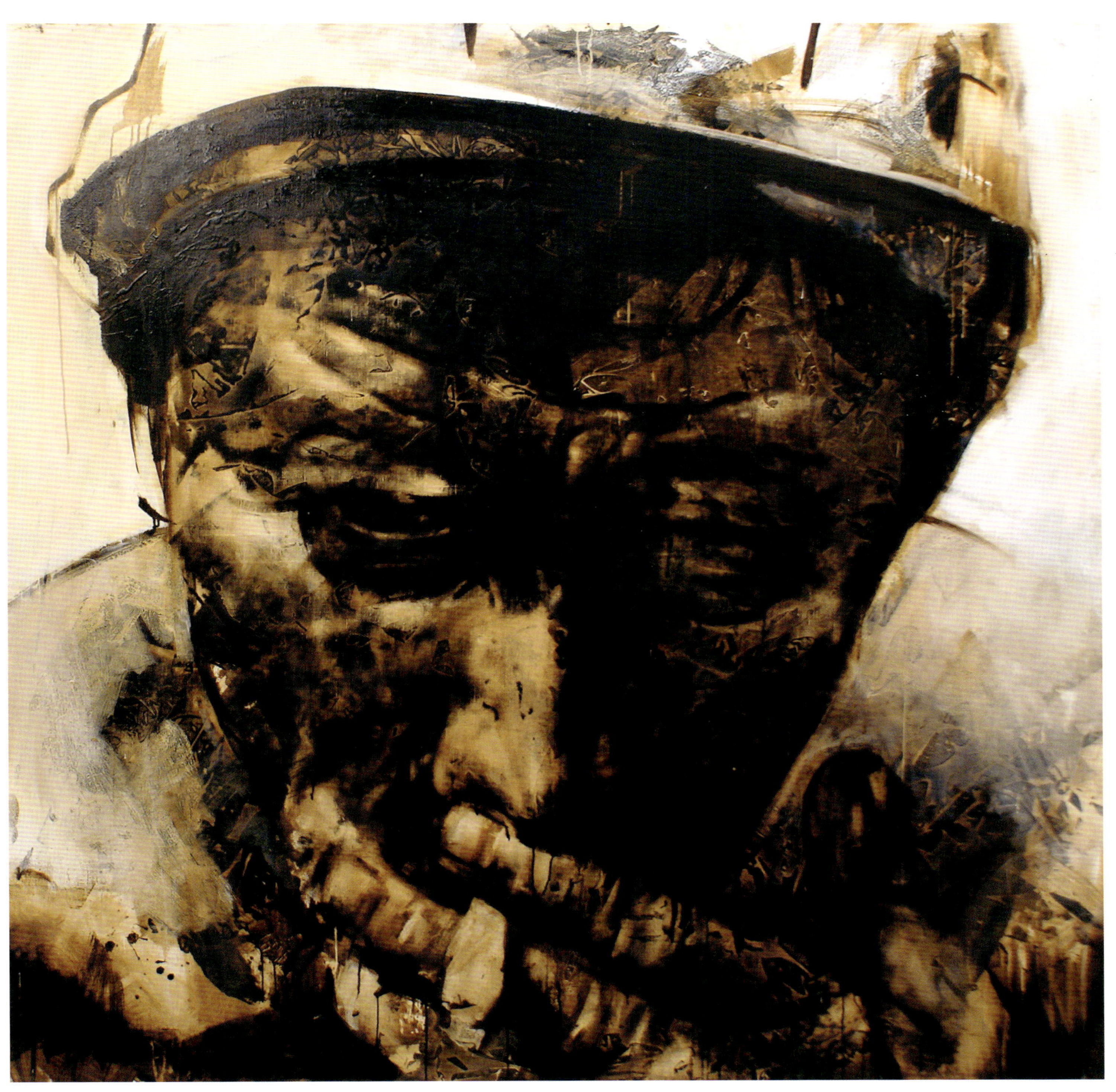

↑
Gaponov, Ilya
Kuzbas Parallel
2007, bitumen on canvas

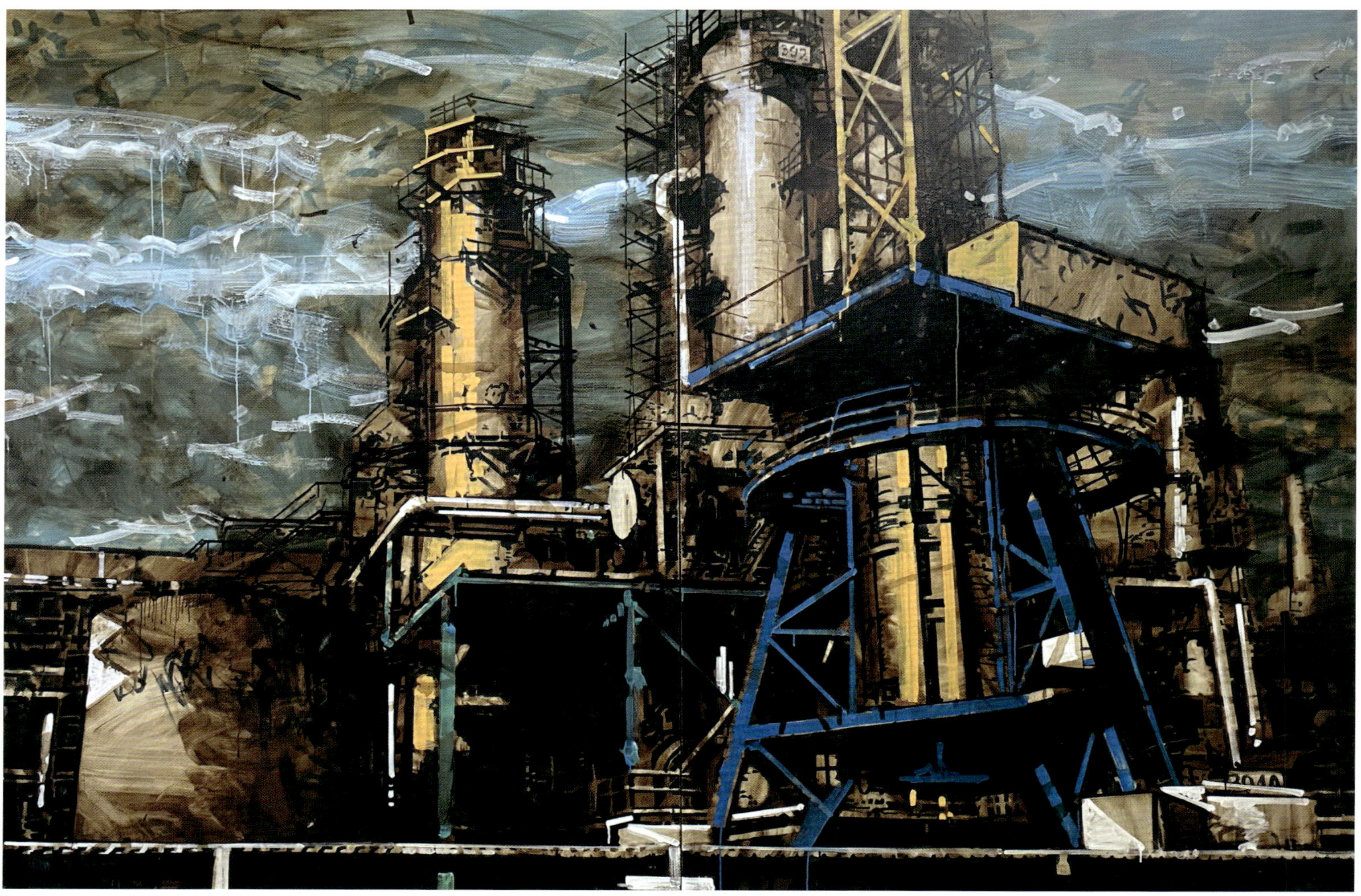

images 'recalls a near-death experience in the artist's youth when he "died" after a choking accident and was resuscitated after thirty minutes'.[2]

His work is represented in the collections of the Victoria & Albert Museum (London), the State Tretyakov Gallery (Moscow), the State Russian Museum (St Petersburg), the Moscow Museum of Modern Art and also at the Kirsten Kear museum in Denmark.

Ilya Gaponov's (b. 1981) approach to painting has its roots in the Russian realist tradition. He uses bitumen varnish as a medium because it was everywhere in his native town in the heartland of one of Russia's coal-mining regions. It was also used as *imprimatura* by some of the Wanderers, a nineteenth-century Russian realist artist group. In his *Miners* project, Gaponov, who worked on mosaics in churches in his native Kemerovo, compares the work routine of miners to religious Mass and the bell towers of mines to churches.[3] After graduating from the Kemerovo School of Fine Arts he studied at the École nationale supérieure des beaux-arts in Paris and the Stieglitz State Academy of Art and Design in St Petersburg, where he now lives. His works have been exhibited in London and at the State Tretyakov Gallery in Moscow.

Leonid Tskhe (b. 1983) adopts a more fluid strategy than most of the artists represented here. He

↑
Gaponov, Ilya
Ammonia
2021, bitumen and acrylic on canvas

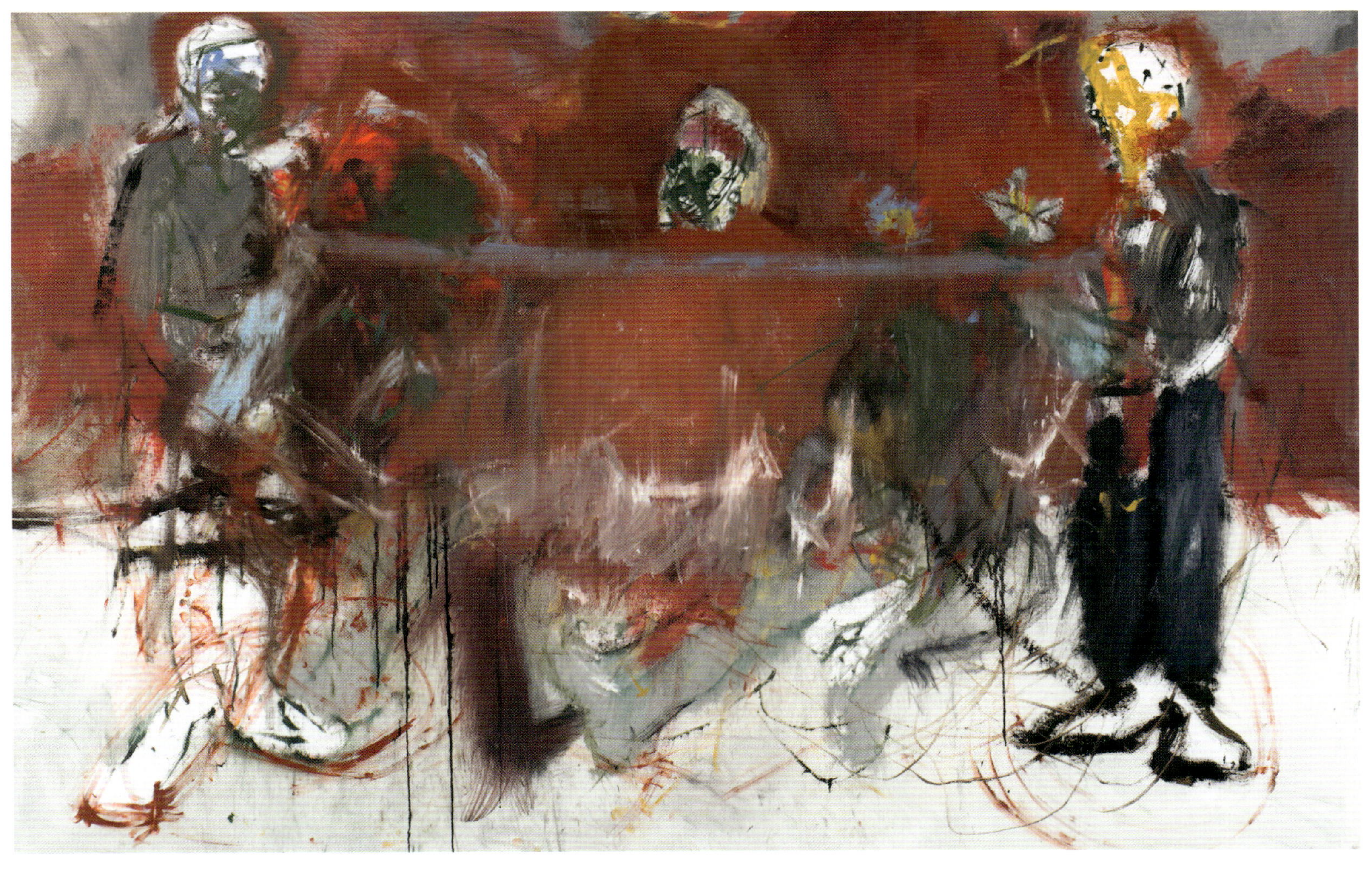

studied in the graphics department of the Repin State Academy of St Petersburg, and became a lecturer there in 2010, also that year becoming a member of the Union of Artists of Russia. Since 2007 he has also worked with DETGIZ, the State Publishing House for Children's Literature. The fluidity of his drawing produces artwork that seems to be in a constant state of becoming.

Also, in tune with the contemporary, but in a more hermetic fashion, is the art being produced by Andrey Gorbunov (b. 1979), who teaches at the St Petersburg Stieglitz State Academy of Art and Design in the department of monumental and decorative painting. The illustration here comes from his *Vertex* series, which shows complex geometric forms apparently floating in the blackness of space. The name *Vertex* should, as the artist points out, suggest to the spectator 'something steadfast, unshakeable, a starting point'.

Yet, as he also notes: 'This swarm of asteroids is made up of body parts, fragments of mechanisms and scraps of printed text. All of these pieces are drawn to one another, sticking to the surface of crystal-like formations.' He adds: 'These not-quite objects are cramped by the global library of human knowledge, squeezing between the pages of discourse into the thinnest of sheets.'[4]

This is certainly work, as the accompanying text suggests, of a far-reaching, ambitious kind. At the

↑
Tskhe, Leonid
Ruler
2019, oil on canvas

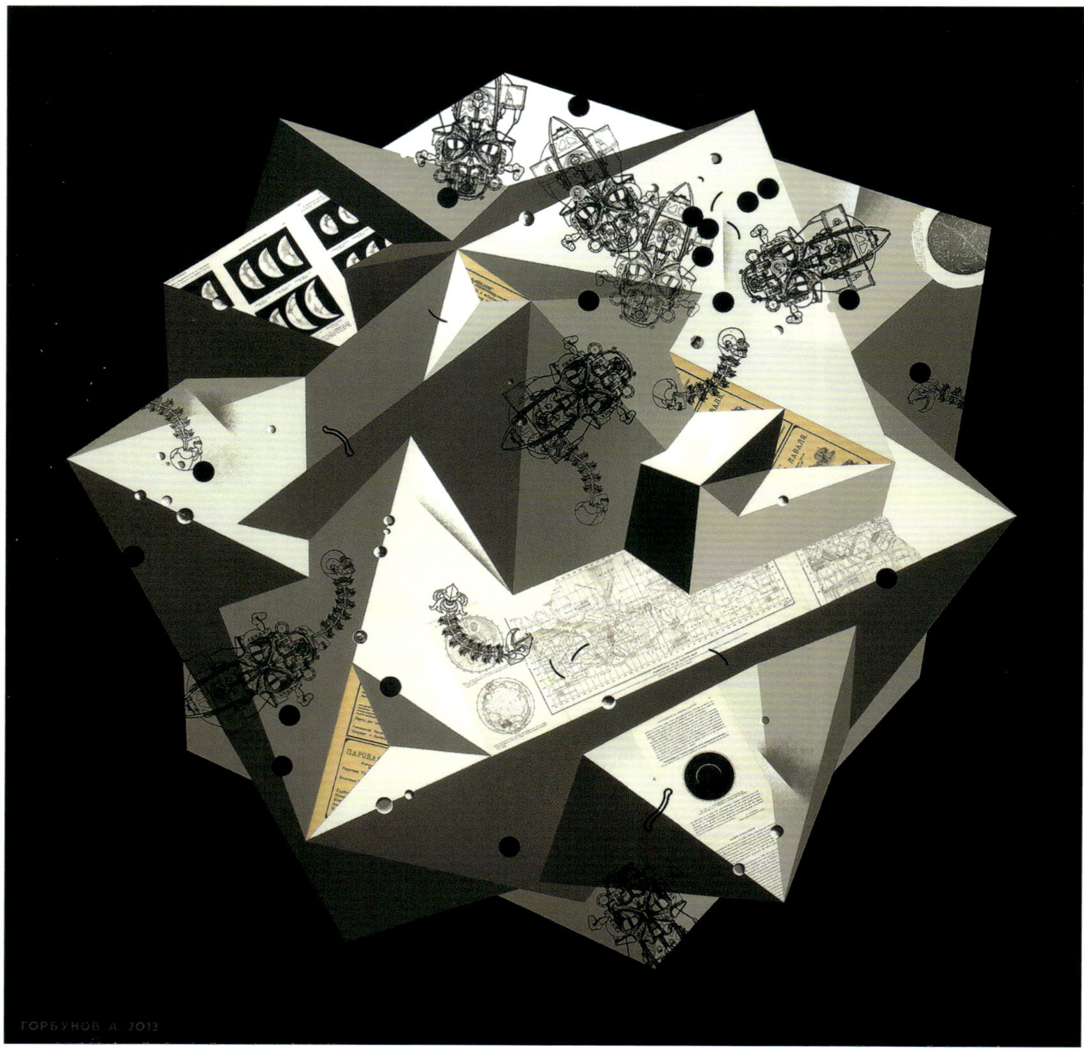

←
Gorbunov, Andrey
Transformation 3
2013-2014, acrylic, marker, vanish, paper on canvas

same time, it isn't in any way populist, however one chooses to use that elastic adjective.

Fedor Hiroshige – real name Irina Fedor (b. 1982) – is another member of the North-7 art group. She also belongs to the Parasit Art Group, a 'democratic community of living-thinking artists' that avoids establishment norms. She has participated in more than forty so-called 'corridor exhibitions' as well as many Parasite touring projects.[5] Among the materials and techniques she employs are not only traditional pencil and watercolour but pyrography, birch bark and sawdust.

Yet another openly non-conforming St Petersburg artist, but one of a very different sort, is Alexander Tsikarishvili (b. 1983). He is a co-founder and permanent member of North-7: a painter, sculptor and graphic artist. A recent show of his work, which opened at the Ovcharenko gallery In Moscow in December 2019, was entitled *Funny Soil Frutti Land*.

The accompanying website states that it involved '[Immersion] in a personal study of the phenomenon of «private eclecticism» – modern forms of spontaneous folk art and embellishment, which are characterised by an impulse to create collages of images, textures and scattered elements lacking their usual functionality.'

It goes on to say that Alexander Tsikarishvili 'became interested in their perception as "exotic", as well as how these forms are created due to cravings for something "exotic". So, by raising the question of the exotic as such, we can say that it is the inevitable flip side of any attempt to talk about the national.'[6]

→
Tsikarishvili, Alexander
Return of the Prodigal Son
2019, mixed media (acrylic, oil, pastel, soil, textile) on canvas

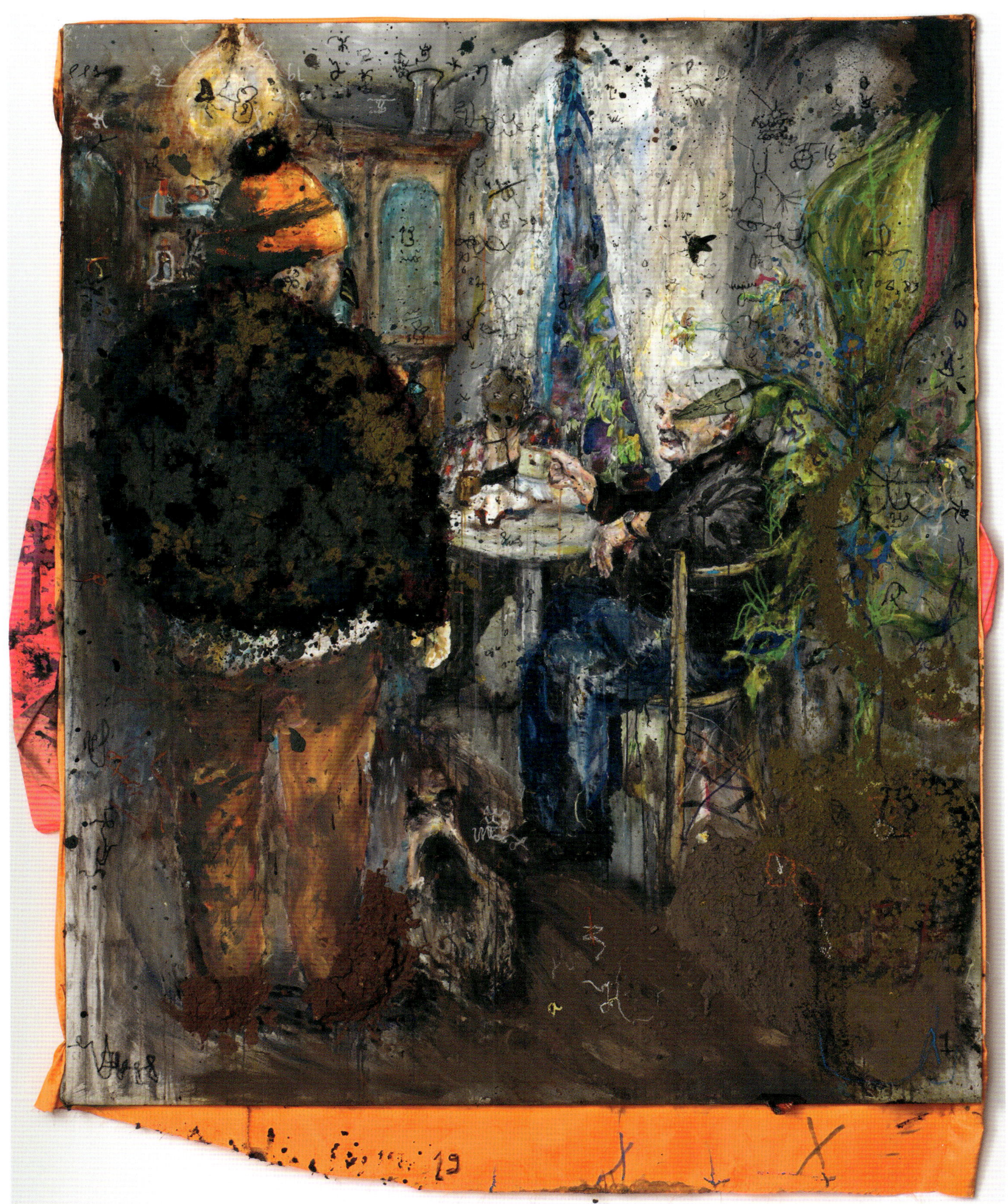

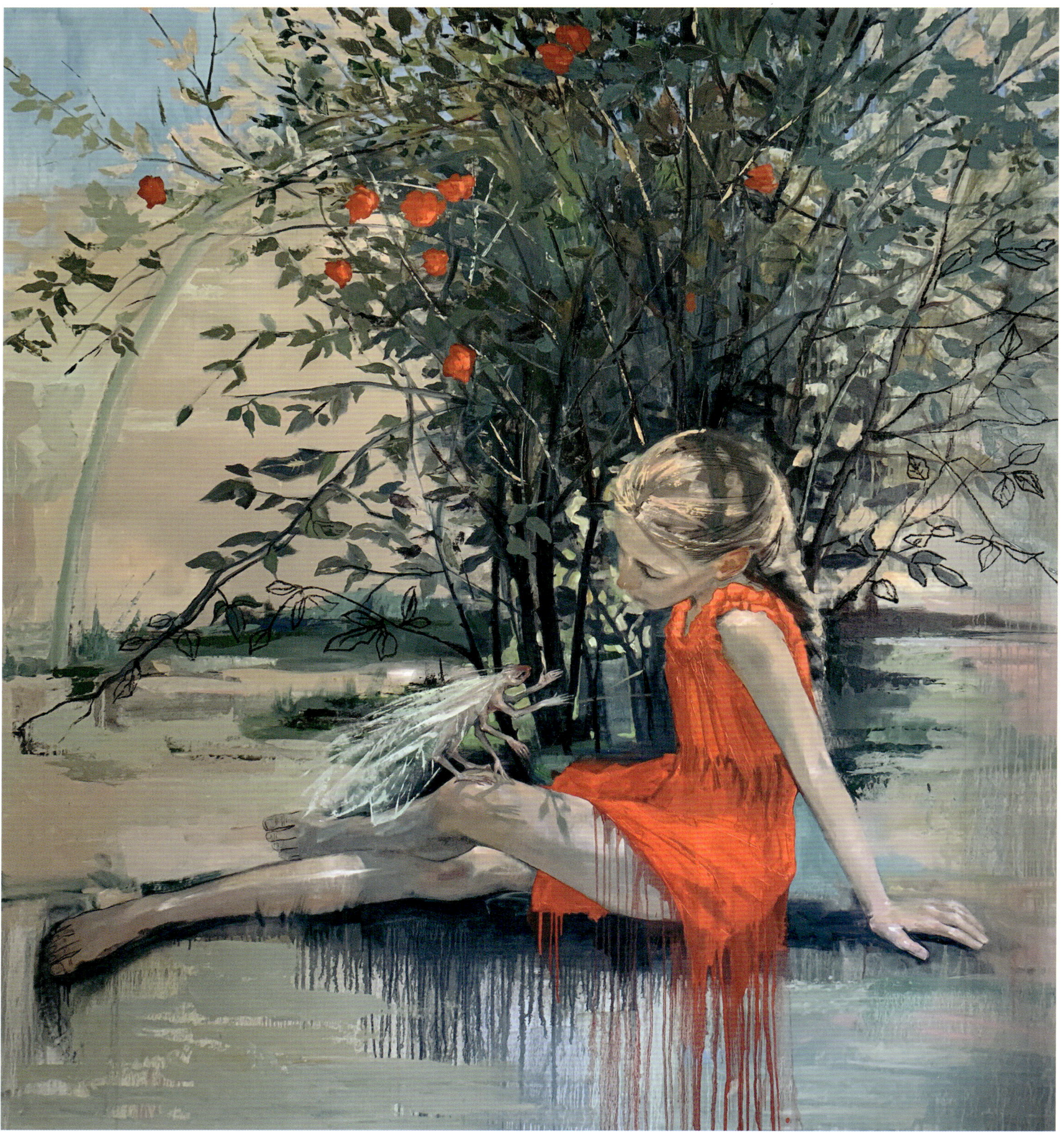

→
Drozd, Irina
Praying Squid
2020, synthetic ceramics

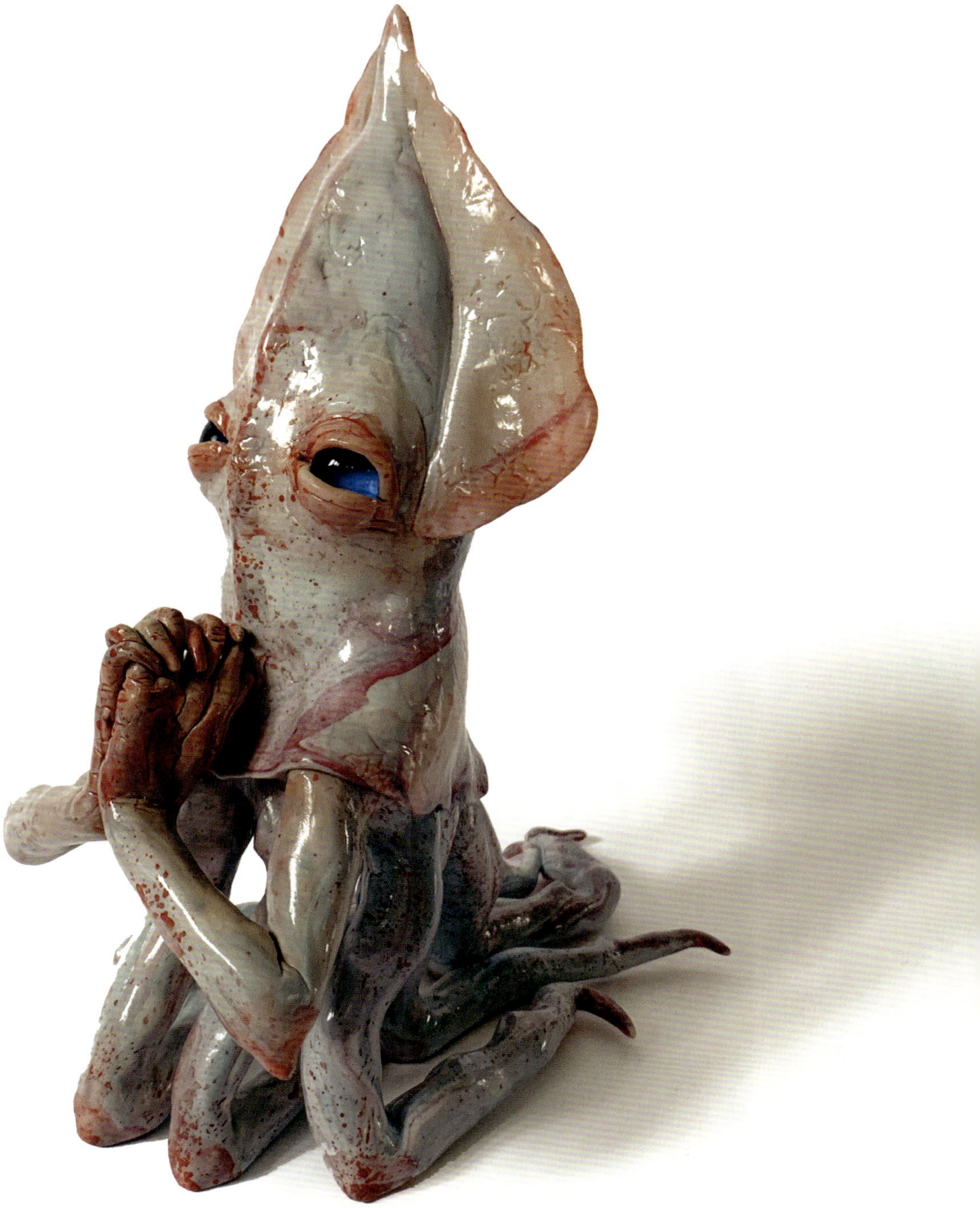

Even more light-hearted is the work of Irina Drozd (b. 1983), as is suggested by the illustration offered here. It refers to Buzzy Wuzzy Busy Fly, a verse fairy tale about the adventures of an amiable fly who is kidnapped by an evil spider at her birthday party but then rescued by a knightly mosquito whom the fly eventually marries. It was written by Korney Chukovsky in 1923 and has become an iconic text still read by all Russian children. Drozd lives and works in St Petersburg and has work exhibited in the collections of the Moscow Museum of Modern Art and the National Centre for Contemporary Art and is represented in a large number of public and private collections, not only in Russia, but in Germany, Italy and the USA. She has had residences in Paris, Berlin and Groningen in the Netherlands. Much of her work features images of young people, as the chosen picture suggests. Irina also is a sculptor. *Praying Squid* (2020) shown here is made of synthetic ceramics.

Not by any means all of the art now being produced in Russia takes itself seriously. Its willingness to deal with social issues is fully matched by a willingness to ignore them.

↖
Drozd, Irina
Buzzy-Wuzzy Busy Fly
2019, oil on canvas

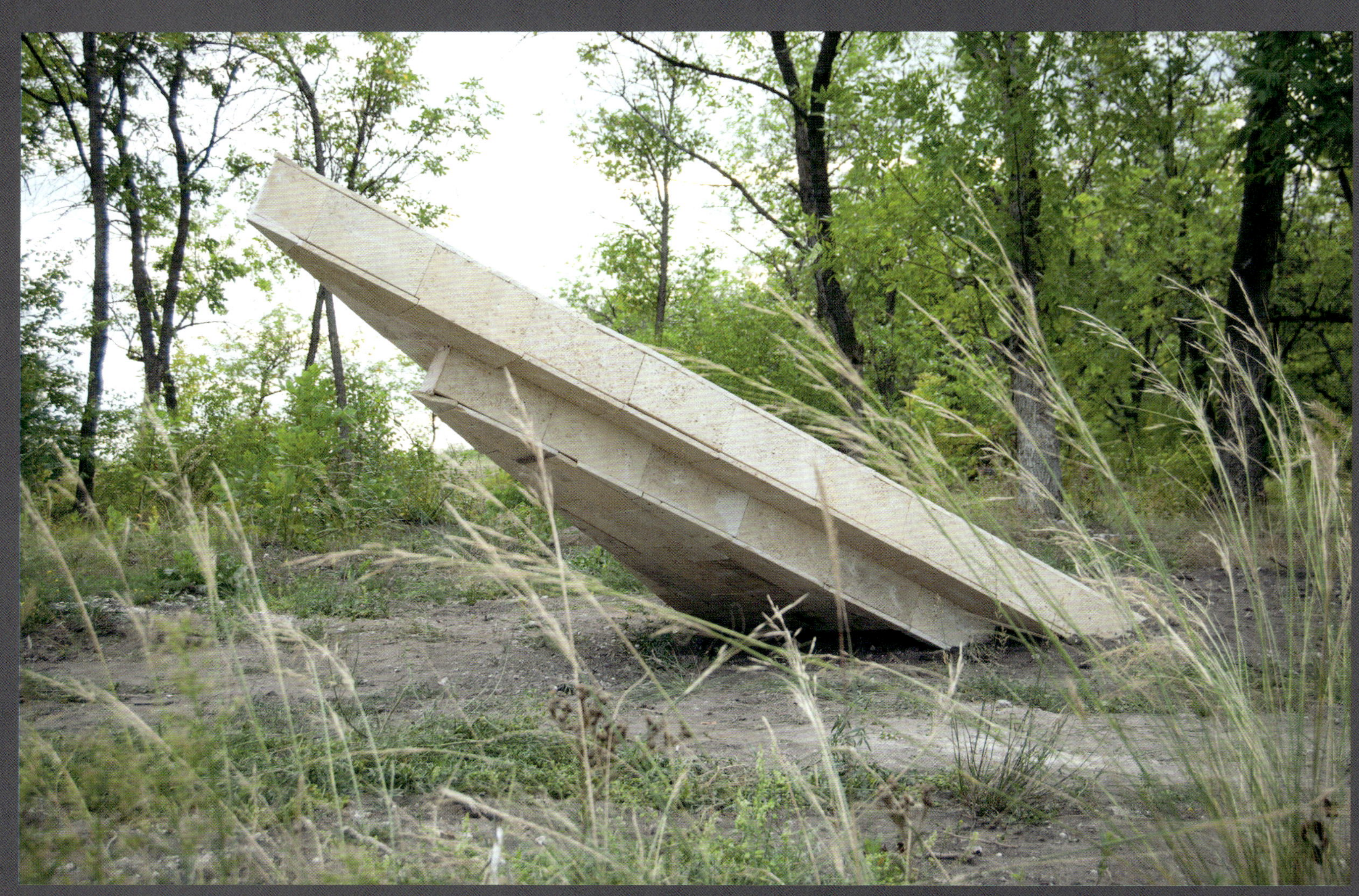

7 CENTRAL RUSSIA

Two institutions, both located in Russian provincial cities, have had a unique impact on the recent development of contemporary art in Russia, unlike anything in the West. It is worth elaborating on what occurred in some detail.

The history of the Voronezh Centre for Contemporary Art began in 2004 with the activities of a creative association called 'PPI' ('Popular Borderline Research' in Russian), which included the artists Ivan Gorshkov, Arseny Zhilyaev, Nikolai Alekseev, Maria Chekhonadsky, Alexander Sinozersky and Ilya Dolgov. Artists staged apartment exhibitions and performed network provocations. However, the association fell apart, since most of its members left for Moscow.

In 2008, a gallery named Kh.L.A.M (or 'junk' in Russian)[1] and the Voronezh Centre for Contemporary Arts[2] opened in Voronezh where former participants of 'PI', as well as representatives of naive art, were exhibited. The Centre's members at first created art events before it had even been established as a legal entity. They did not have permanent premises, a budget, infrastructure or any kind of official support.

As an institution with premises of its own, the Centre took shape in 2013, when it was provided with a free-of-charge location on Revolutsii Avenue. A new exhibition was held every month, mainly shows for non-resident artists. The geographical range was impressive: the Centre exhibited artists from Moscow, Perm, Petersburg, Volgograd and other Russian cities, as well as from Estonia, Great Britain, Germany, Austria and the Netherlands.

One of the three largest projects undertaken by the Centre was an exhibition held in 2018, entitled *History of the Present*. It featured more than thirty artists: from Russia, France, Sweden, Finland and Germany, among them well-known contemporary names.

The Voronezh Centre sought to create something that was significant not only for Voronezh, but

←
Alekseev, Nikolay
Shell
2014, steel, shell rock, wood

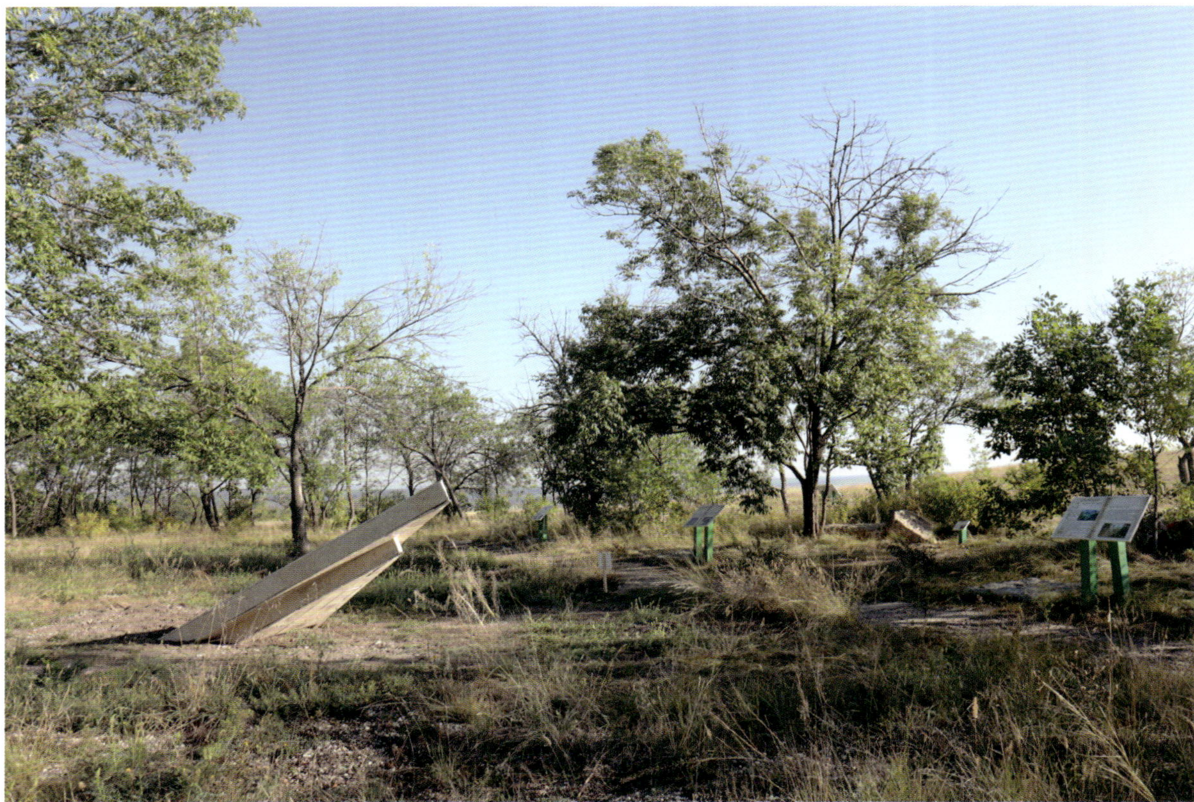

←
Alekseev, Nikolay
Shell
2014, steel, shell rock, wood. Overview

also for Russia as a whole. To some extent, they succeeded. During its existence, exhibition projects at the Centre were nominated three times in a row for the national Innovation prize in the field of contemporary art. Ivan Gorshkov and Nikolai Alekseev were made Fellows of the Garage Museum of Contemporary Art.

Ivan Gorshkov and Arseny Zhilyaev, founders of the Voronezh Centre, were also included in the *Forbes* magazine list of promising artists for the formation of a contemporary collection.

Among the artists who now live and work in Voronezh is Nikolay Alekseev (b. 1986), co-founder of the Voronezh Centre for Contemporary Artists. He is a graduate of the Voronezh Art College. He works with found objects and video, and creates fictional, fairy-tale narratives. He has been a nominee for the Kandinsky Prize in the Young Artist category and also for the Innovation Prize. His work is represented in the collection of the State Tretyakov Gallery.

His work *Shells*, shown here, is made for the exhibition «What if...» at the geological part of the Divnogorye open-air museum and nature reserve in Voronezh oblast, Russia.

As a Kandinsky Prize finalist in 2011 he exhibited a series of 'geometric bodies', which were in fact «plaster casts of the empty places found in packing foam, used to protect consumer electronics items».[3]

'Gathered together', as the official website for the Kandinsky Prize recorded, these 'reveal parallels with architecture, the avant-garde, nature and visual history. Researching, spelling out these parallels, we can discover a kingdom of mute forms that lives by its own laws'.[4]

A point of interest here is not simply the use of found objects – now a commonplace of contemporary avant-garde art – but the fact that these objects are the detritus of a sophisticated consumer society.

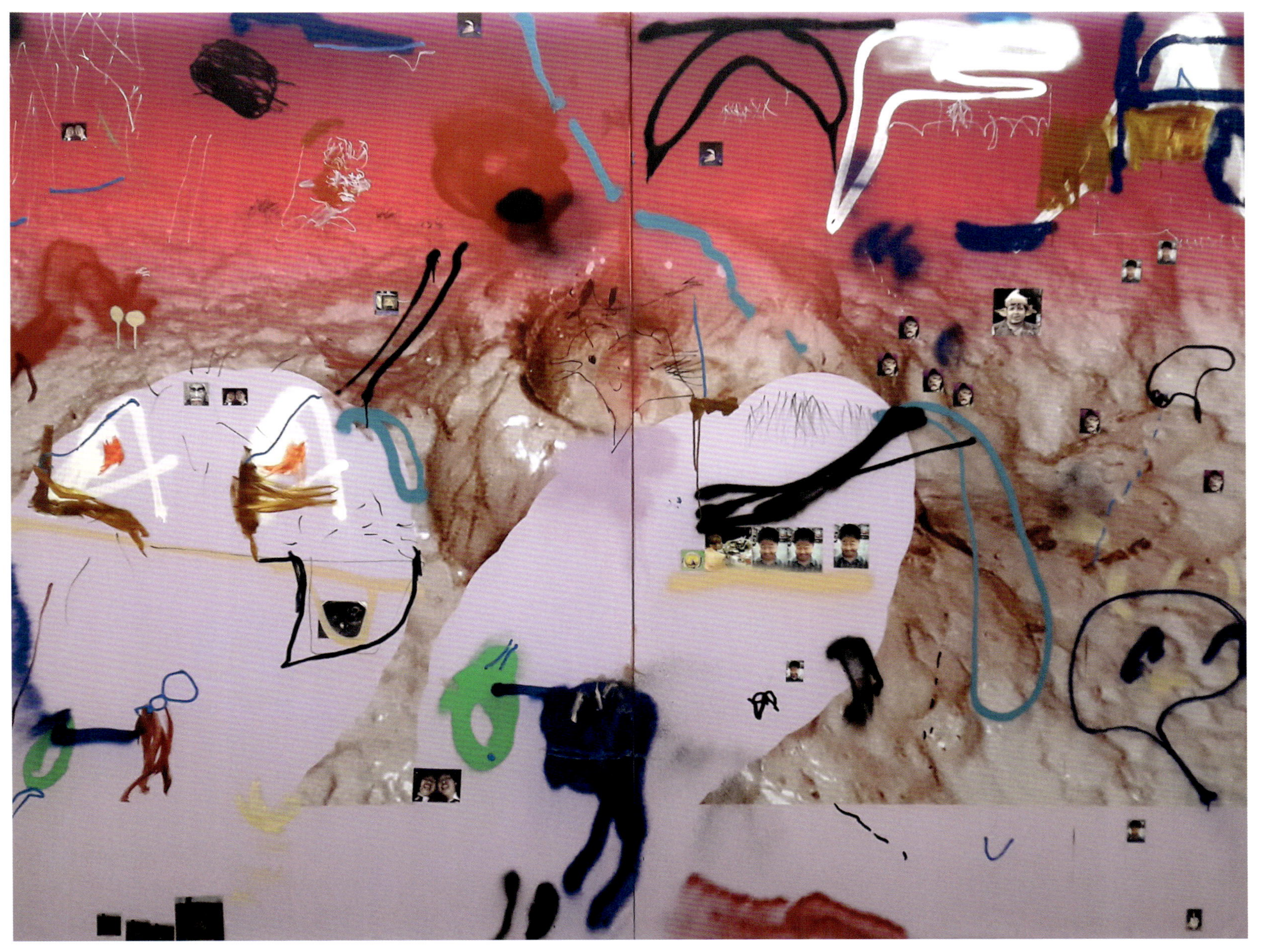

↑
Gorshkov, Ivan
Untitled, Hyper-Jump and the Anteater Series
2016, oil, spray, digital printing, stickers, felt on canvas diptych

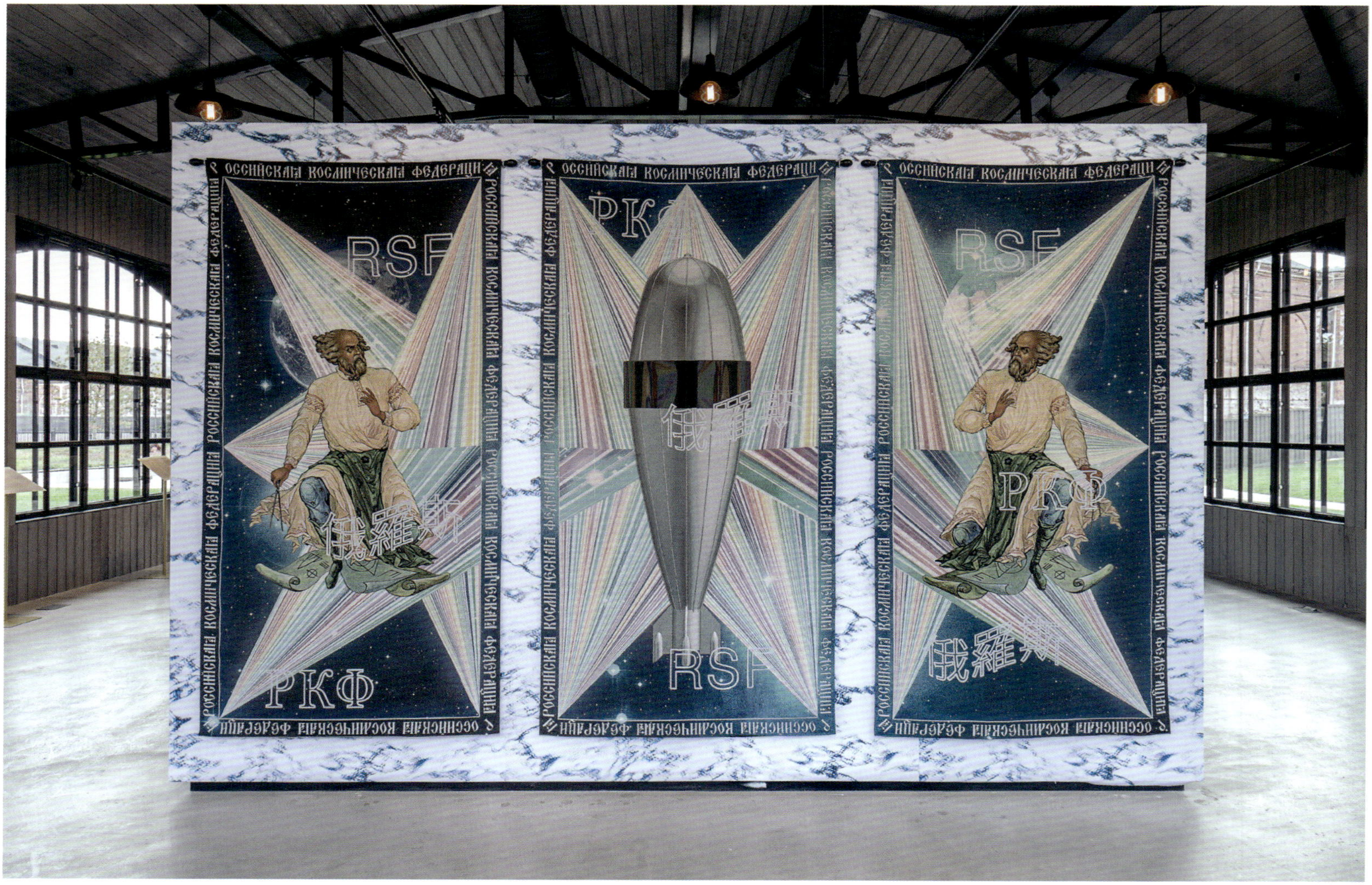

Ivan Gorshkov (also b. 1986), another co-founder, who also continues to live and work in Voronezh, has three times been a scholar of the Garage Museum support programme for young artists. In recent years he has begun to exhibit quite widely outside Russia, with shows in Berlin, Paris, Vienna and Budapest.

He took part in the *The Fountain of Everything* show, held at the Moscow Museum of Modern Art in 2019, where he was 'rethinking traditional artistic means – painting and sculpture – in a bold "hooligan" manner.' The exhibition website speaks of 'The effortless combination of materials, textures and visual languages in Gorshkov's works [which] creates dynamic, transformative images... Something turns into something, and, conversely, something suddenly turns into something else. Metal sculptures become inflatable, and picturesque canvases turn out to be LED displays... a place of objects with overhead synthetic curls and rags inhabited by plastic animals...'[5]

Arseny Zhilyaev (b. 1984) was also born in Voronezh, though he is now sometimes listed as a Moscow artist. He graduated from the faculty of Psychology and Philosophy at Voronezh in 2006, and later studied at the Moscow Institute of Contemporary Art and at the Valand Academy in Gothenburg in Sweden.

Another artist from Voronezh, Kirill Garshin (b. 1990), 'while aiming to continue the Russian painting tradition... also makes reference to current international trends.'[6] He graduated from the Voronezh Art College in 2010 and took part in the Leipzig International Art Program in 2013 and the Garage Triennial 2017. Responding to growing ecological problems, Garshin published a manifesto entitled 'Organic painting or creation of a new painting from plant juices and environmentally processed materials'.[7]

Zhilyaev, Arseny
Tsiolkovsky, Second Advents, part of the installation
2016, mixed media

Garshin, Kirill
A Bear, Tanais Series
2017, acrylic on canvas and board

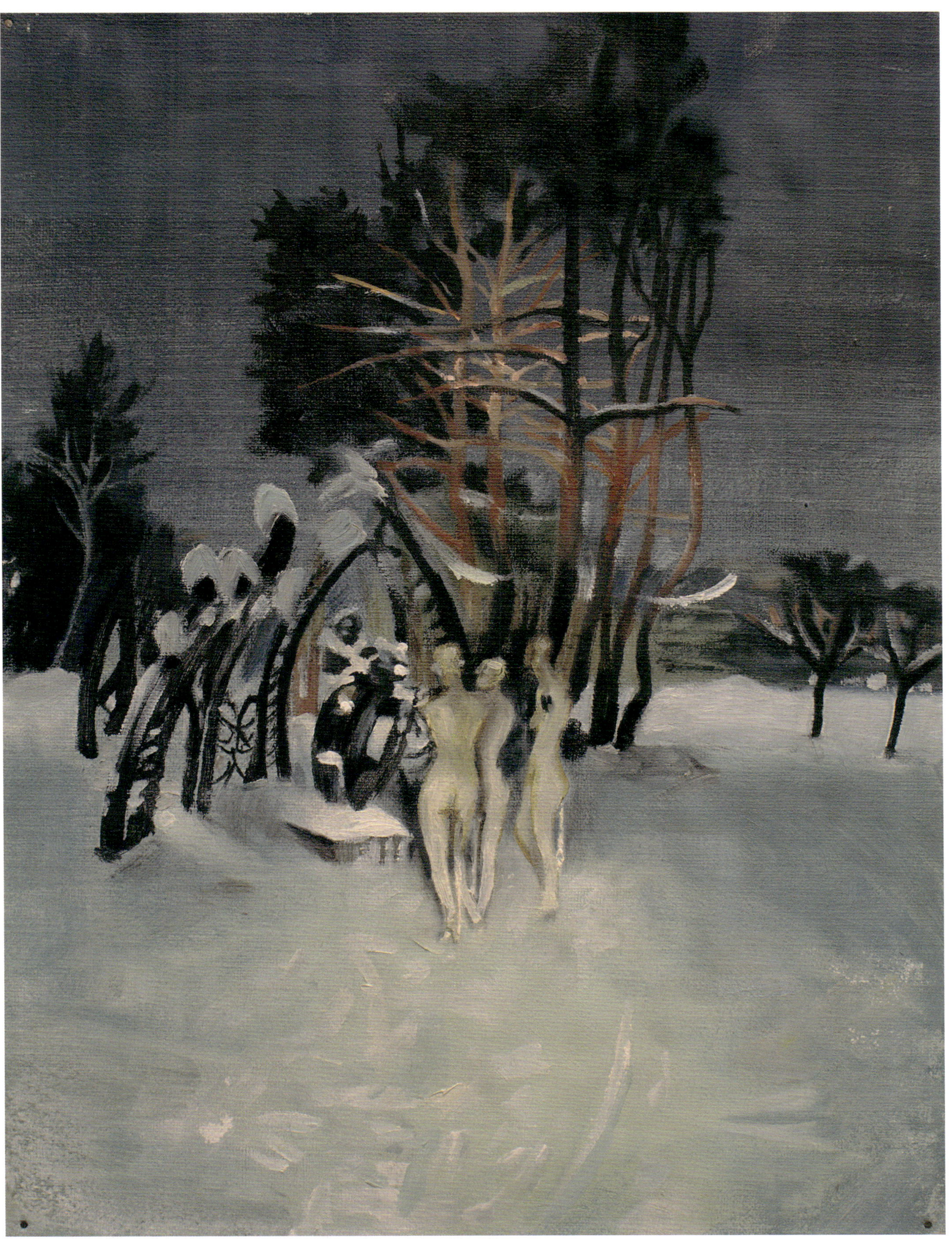

Toptunova, Elena (Lena Lisitsa)
Three Townswomen
2016, acrylic on board

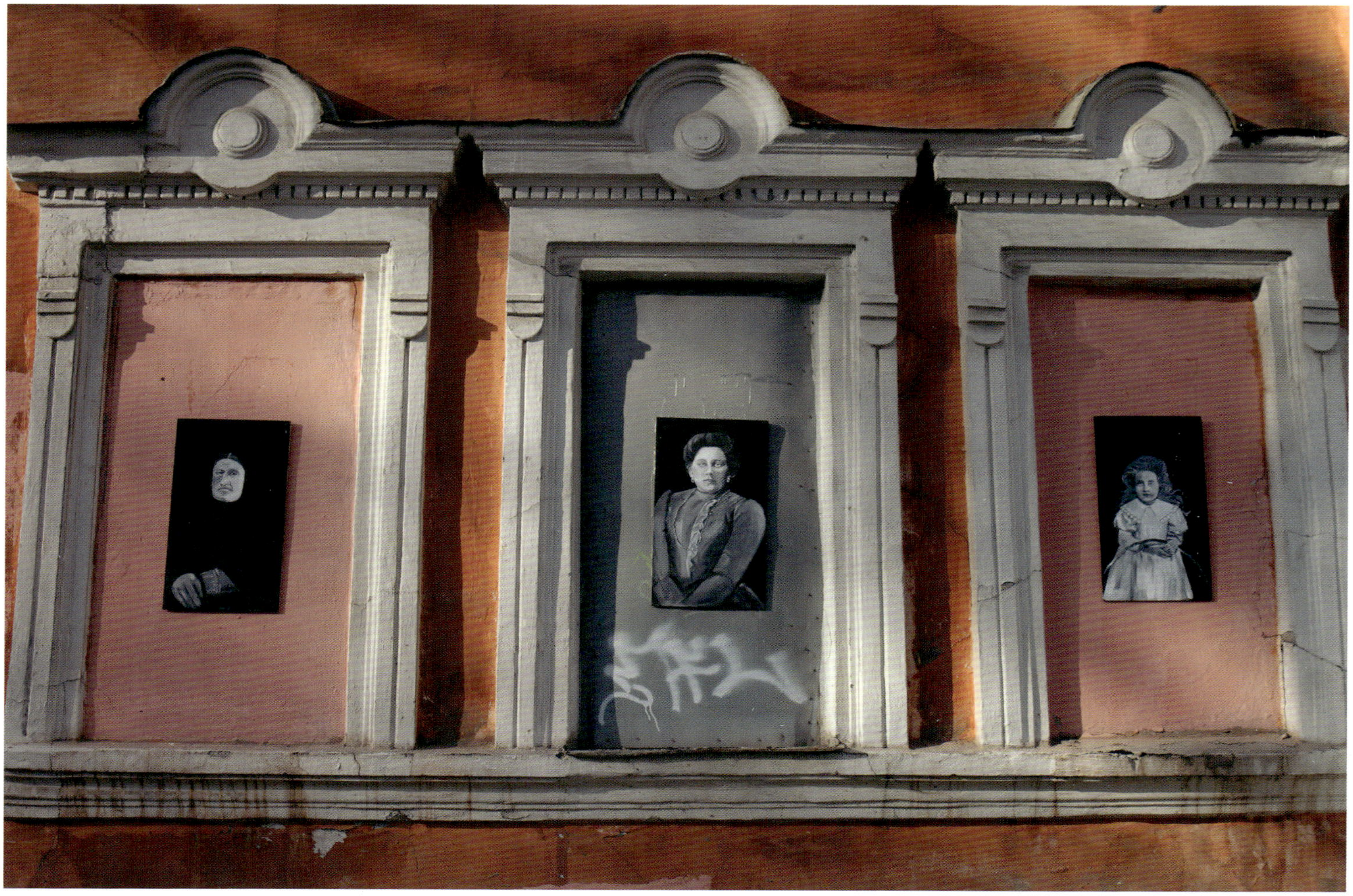

The other city that pioneered major changes in the world of contemporary Russian art, in a perhaps more informal way, is 800-year-old Nizhny Novgorod. This is due to a street-art festival called 'Mesto' ('Spot' in English). This, as its name suggests, was developed in order to create new street art on the spot in a contemporary urban environment. The festival, launched in 2017, has an educational element. It includes workshops, artist talks with iconic representatives of street art, screenings of documentary movies and street art excursions.

Since then, more than sixty new street artworks by leading practitioners have been created, and these function as attractions for visitors to the festival, with art tours that regularly attract hundreds of participants. No similar tours, fully sanctioned by the local authorities, seem to exist in comparable Western European or North American cities.

In 2020 plans for the Nizhny Novgorod street-art festival included the creation of at least twenty-five new street-art projects, plus a parallel programme of exhibitions, lectures, masterclasses,

Nomerz, Nikita
The Detail
2013, spray paint on wall

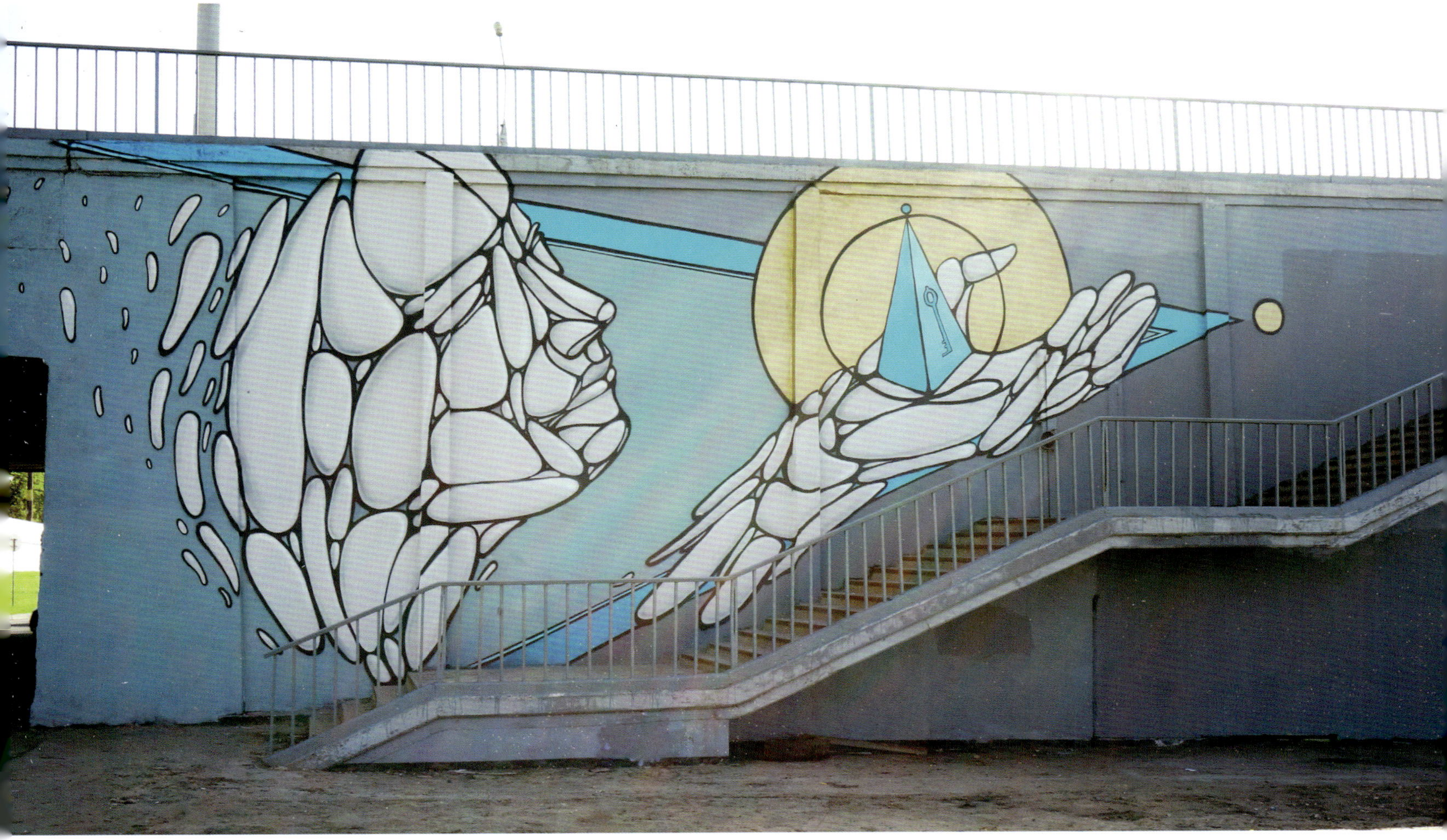

excursions, music parties and screenings of relevant documentaries – in fact, everything needed to inform, and, at the same time, entertain visitors.

Not unexpectedly, however, street art remains the dominant theme. It takes a wide variety of forms and appears on an equally wide variety of surfaces. For example, a mural called *Carpenters' Lunch* (2014) by a group called TOY Crew, formed in 2012, rather fittingly finds a place on a traditional wooden building. Sometimes, as in this series of three portraits by Elena Toptunova (b.1991), a series of images occupy separate niches in a nineteenth-century classical building.

Just occasionally, as in Nikita Nomerz's (b.1990) ambitious design showing a large female head with an equally huge hand holding a metronome in its palm, the designs for the wall paintings are ambitiously Modernist in style. Equally occasionally, as with Vasya Basyo's (b.1985) (in collaboration with Vladimir Abikh (b.1987) and Dmitry Drenin (b.1989) aka Zloyproduct) image of a book on a ruined fragment of wall, entitled *Easy Way to Stop Being A Street Artist*, they mock the whole idea of street

↓

Basay, Vasyo; Abikh, Vladimir and Dima Zloyproduct
Easy Way to Stop Being a Street Artist
2019, spray paint on wall

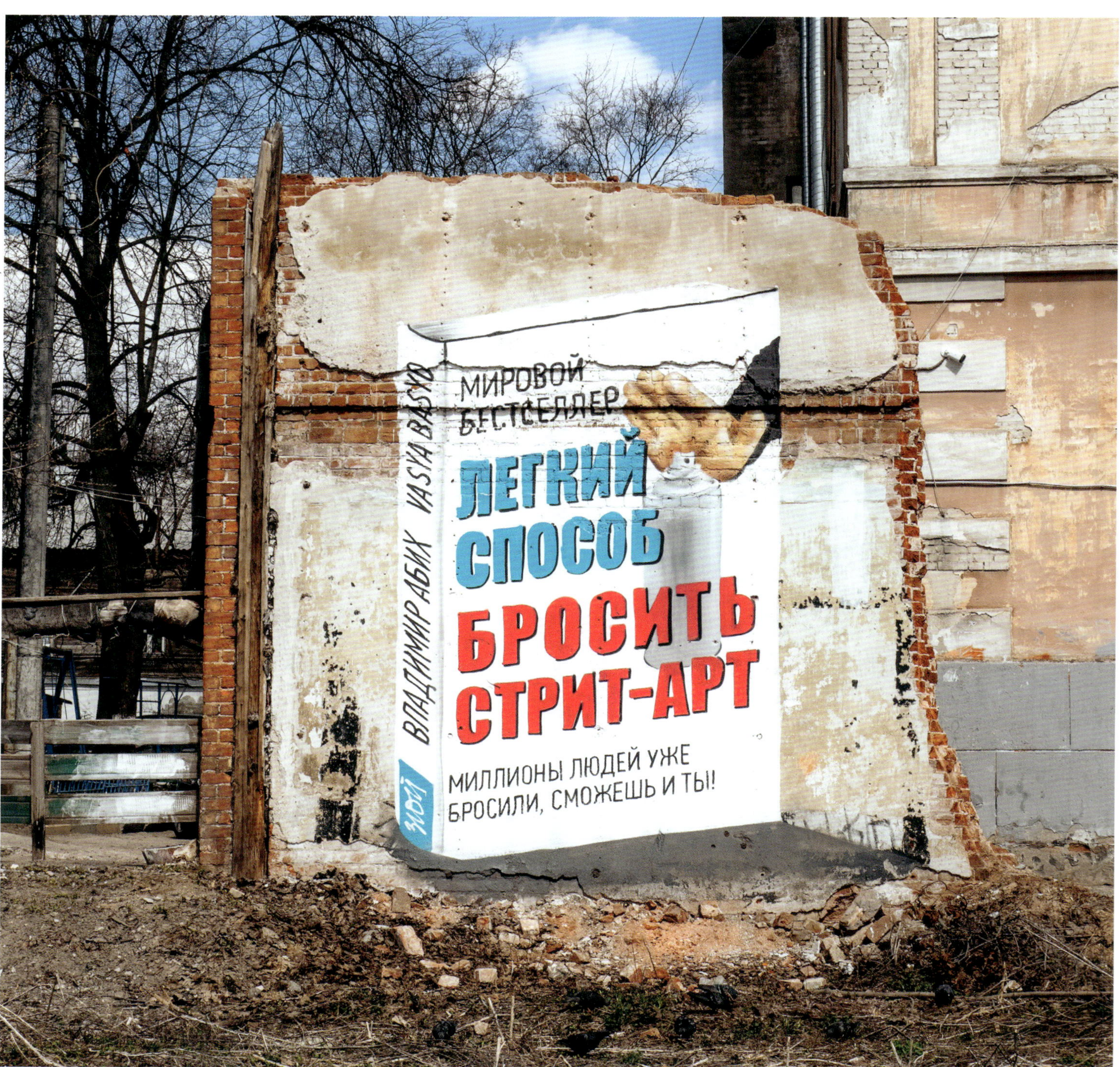

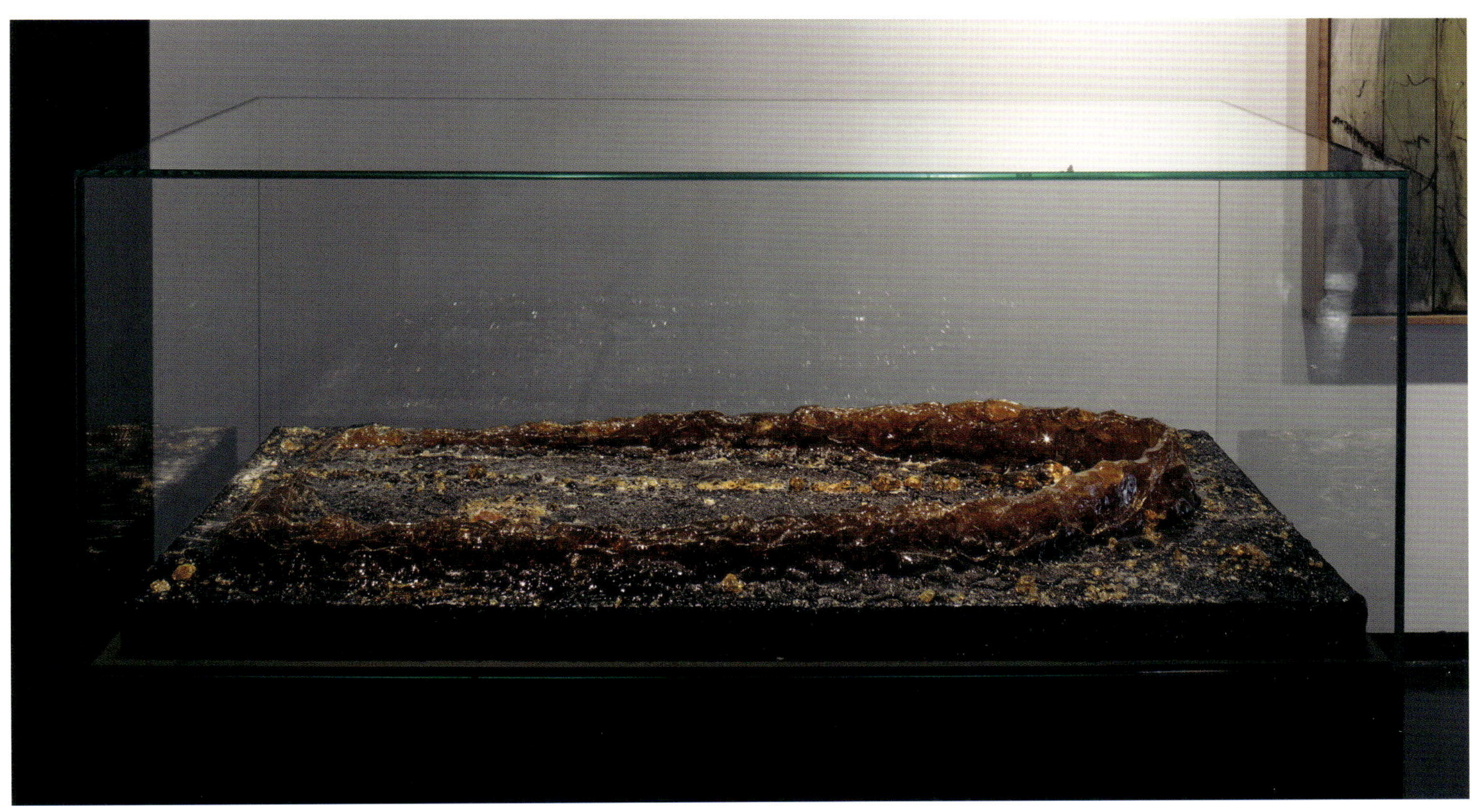

↑
Chernyshev, Vladimir
Boat
2017, resin, tar

art. There are three-dimensional works, such as Vladimir Chernyshev's (b.1992) *Boat* (2017) that somehow resist the idea of being thought of as sculpture.

Alexey Korsi (b. 1986), the winner of the Innovation award special prize in 2013[8], and Artem Filatov (b. 1991) created their *Name Garden* project, exploring the fear of death, in a local crematorium in 2019. Filatov was awarded two Innovation prizes for the 'Best regional project' in 2018 and in the 'New generation' category in 2020. He also, together with Alisa Savitskaya, co-authored a *Brief History of Nizhny Novgorod Street-Art*, published in 2019.[9]

There are several things that perhaps need to be remembered here. One is that populist street art is a relatively new phenomenon in Russia – one that has happened within the space of a very few years, but with great potential for growth. In the Soviet epoch, there were large public images of the likes of Lenin and Stalin, happy citizens, children, and sportsmen and women, all approved by the Communist Party, but not much else.

Nizhny Novgorod is not the only Russian city that has embraced the presence of populist murals. Sometimes, indeed, paintings on walls, out of doors, open to the popular gaze, have disturbed the political authorities with dissident messages. More often, it now seems that they are being accepted as a typical feature of everyday life in Russia. Much more art of this kind is illustrated elsewhere in this book. Street art in Nizhny is encouraged as a tourist attraction, something that brings money into the local community.

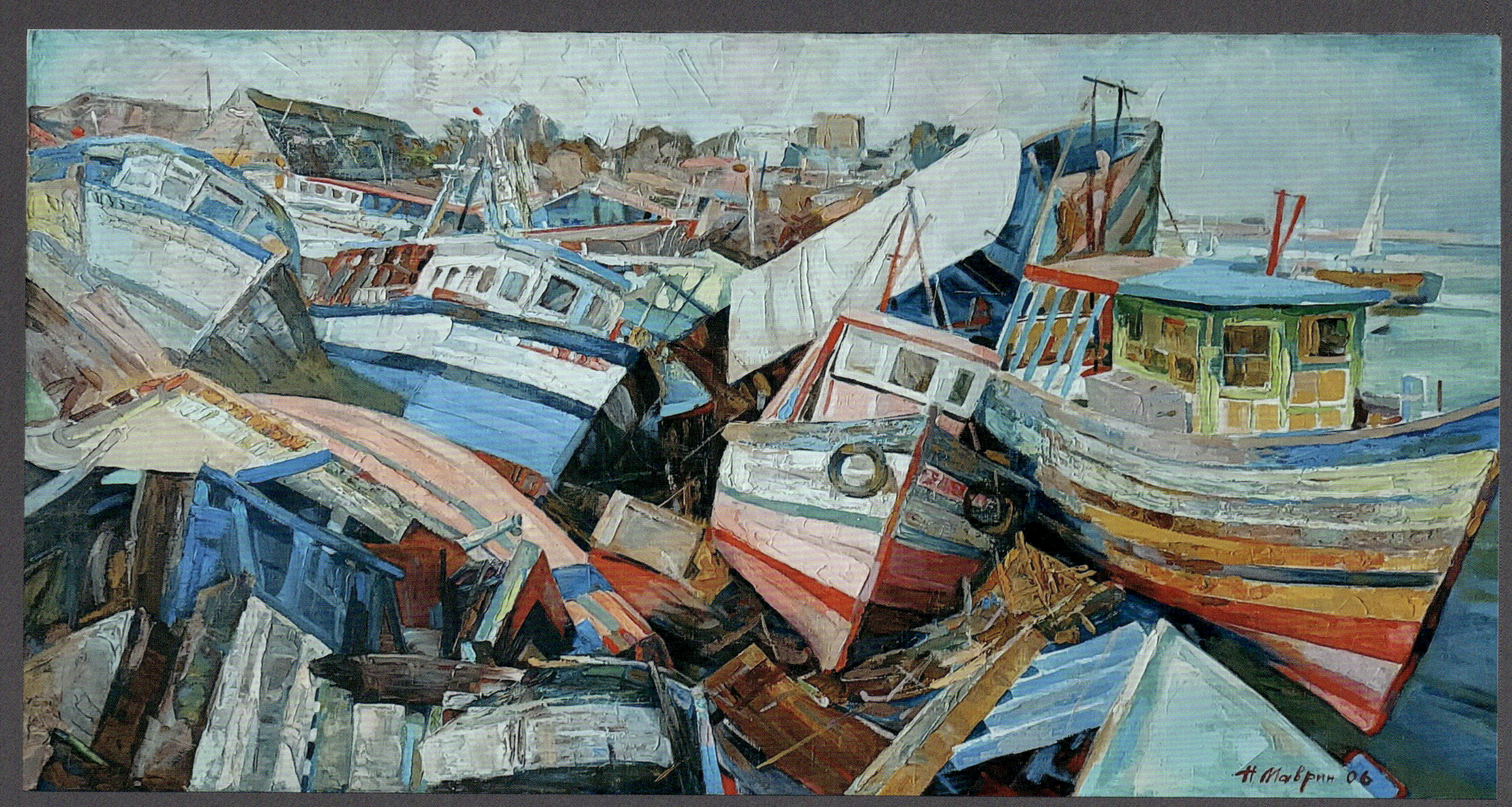
Н Маврин 06

8 ALONG THE VOLGA

The Volga is the longest river in Europe. Its course lies almost entirely within the borders of Russia. Among the major cities along its course are Kazan, Ulyanovsk, Samara and Saratov. Navigable canals link the cities on the Volga to Moscow, other regions of Russia, the Baltic and the Black Sea.

The art currently being produced in Kazan, the capital of the Republic of Tatarstan, sometimes called the 'third unofficial capital of Russia', is on the whole less experimental than that of Moscow and St Petersburg. An exception was the 'Like It. Art' street art festival in 2012, where forty-five artists from nine countries took part in a five-day event in Kazan, a 1000-year-old city. The event was initiated by the artist Dmitry Kudinov (b.1986), a native of Nizhnekamsk on the Kama river, an industrial town in Tatarstan, built in 1961 around the local petrochemical company, the largest in Europe.

In 2015 Kudinov organised and initiated a creative art project called *Supernova Art Embassy*. The artists involved found themselves in the thick of it when Kazan hosted some of the games of the FIFA Confederations Cup in 2017 and FIFA World Cup in 2018. Soccer stars such as Ronaldo, Messi and Neymar were depicted on the facades of buildings. The images appeared in the world media. As Kudinov noted, tourists rushed to take pictures, to confirm that they were indeed 'there'.[1] One of Kudinov's last works, *The Essence*, according to the artist, "had a fragment of the full of energy abstract work by the German artist Raphael Gerlach (aka SatOne) in the centre and Chernushka, the Soviet space dog and a symbol of human thought in the development of the unknown, as one of the important elements of the painting. The dog was launched into space and successfully landed in a field near the village of Old Tokmak in the Zainsk district of Tatarstan on March 9, 1961"[2]

A strong classical feeling is also to be found in the region. For example, Sergei Tsarev's (b.1985) accomplished Art Deco-like *Annunciation* or *They All Ate and Were Satisfied* have nothing about them to classify them as in any way provincial. The artist, who studied at the Ilya Repin St Petersburg

←
Mavrin, Nikolay
After Storm in the Harbour
2006, oil on canvas

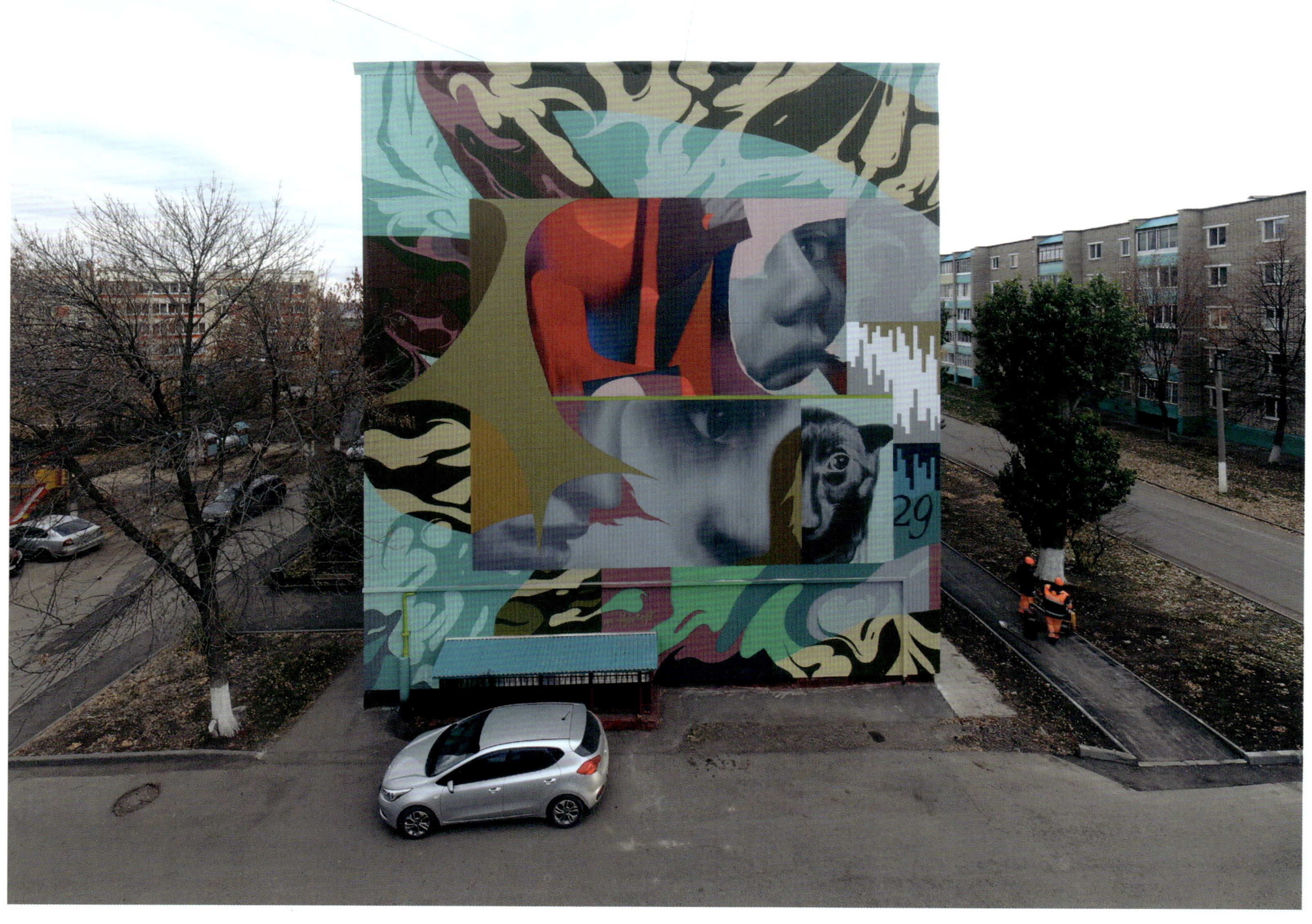

↑
Kudinov, Dmitry (aka LIL-DEE)
The Essence
2021, spray paint on wall

State Academy of Arts, was born and still lives in Zelenodolsk ('Green Valley' in Russian), 35km from Kazan. This town, situated on the Volga River, has boasted an important shipbuilding yard since the end of the nineteenth century. During the Cold War it was a secret development base for warships. Future development plans for the area suggest that Zelenodolsk will become part of Kazan.

Ulyanovsk, the birthplace of Vladimir Lenin, was formerly known as Simbirsk and is one of the few Russian cities that has not reverted to its original, pre-Revolutionary name. Parts of the old town, where Lenin lived as a child in the 1870s and '80s, have been carefully preserved; there is also a huge concrete Soviet-built Lenin memorial complex. It was once a place of pilgrimage for Soviet citizens but became a popular travel destination for Chinese tourists after the break-up of the USSR. Ulyanovsk has a small but elegant Fine Art Museum in the city centre and a house-museum dedicated to Arkady Plastov (1893-1972), one of the most renowned Russian Socialist Realist painters, in a small village 60 km to the west.

Nikolay Mavrin (b. 1960), a maverick artist, had his personal show and became a local celebrity

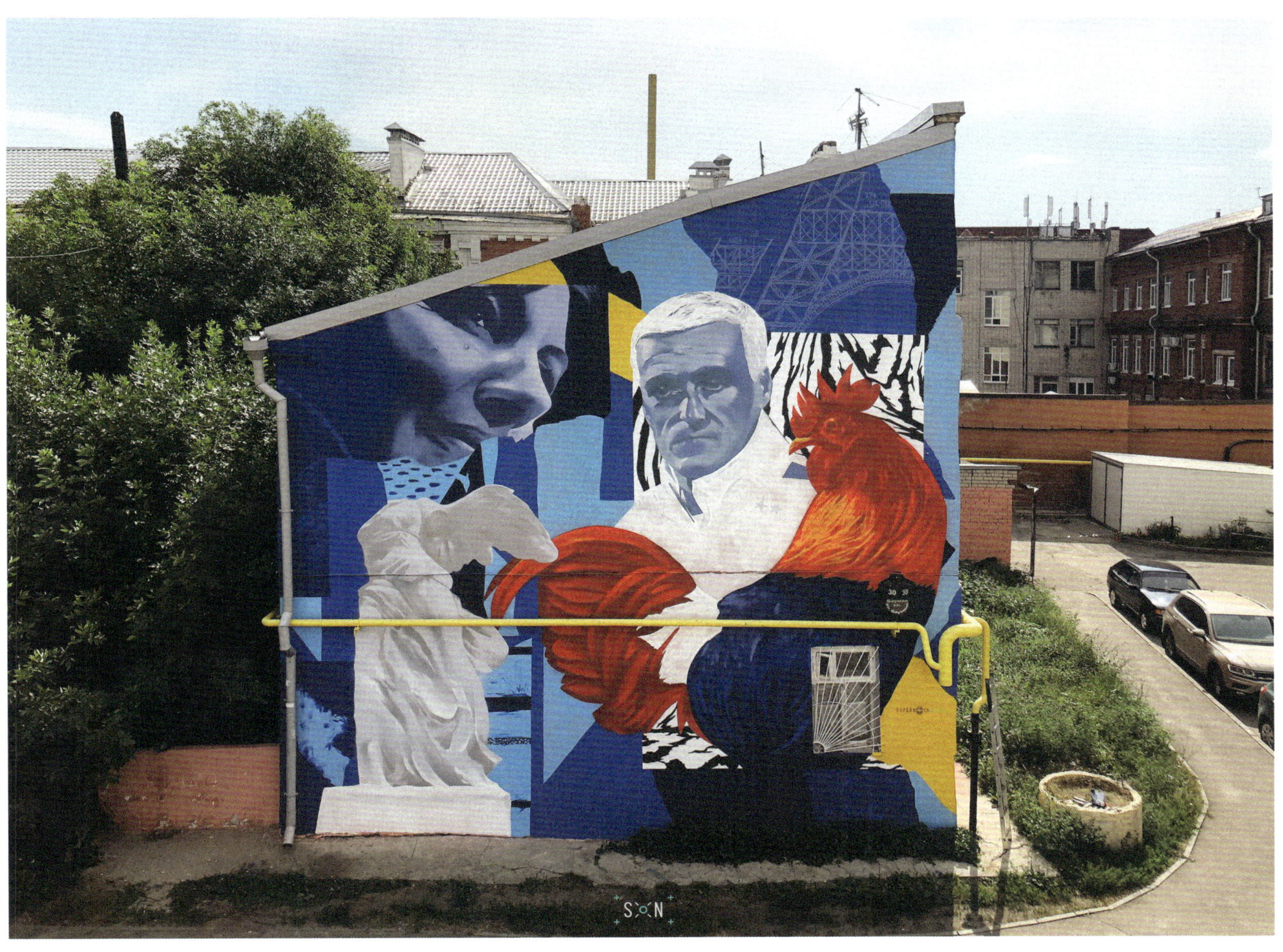

in 2021.[3] Retaining academic professionalism, he paints in a variety of styles and depicts local and familiar themes. In contrast, his sculptures and assemblages represent a new departure. They are made of found objects reminiscent of the Surrealists and Joseph Cornell (1902-1973), but taking an individual visual approach linked to Mavrin's strong national roots.

Samara, a city of over one million people, was a closed zone during the Soviet era and was chosen as its alternative capital during the Second World War and still has the Stalin's war shelter deep underground which can be visited by tourists. Samara has a surprisingly large number of churches and religious buildings serving different faiths and communities: Orthodox Christian (the majority), Armenian Apostolic Christians, Catholics, Protestants, Muslims and Jews. Samara has also many buildings devoted to cultural events: an opera and ballet theatre, several drama theatres, a concert hall, and a number of museums – the Fine Art Museum with an important collection of Russian avant-garde art from the beginning of the twentieth century, a museum devoted to the city's contribution to the aerospace industry, a large local history museum and a small museum of Art

↑
Kudinov, Dmitry and Sergey
Viva La France
2018, spray paint on wall

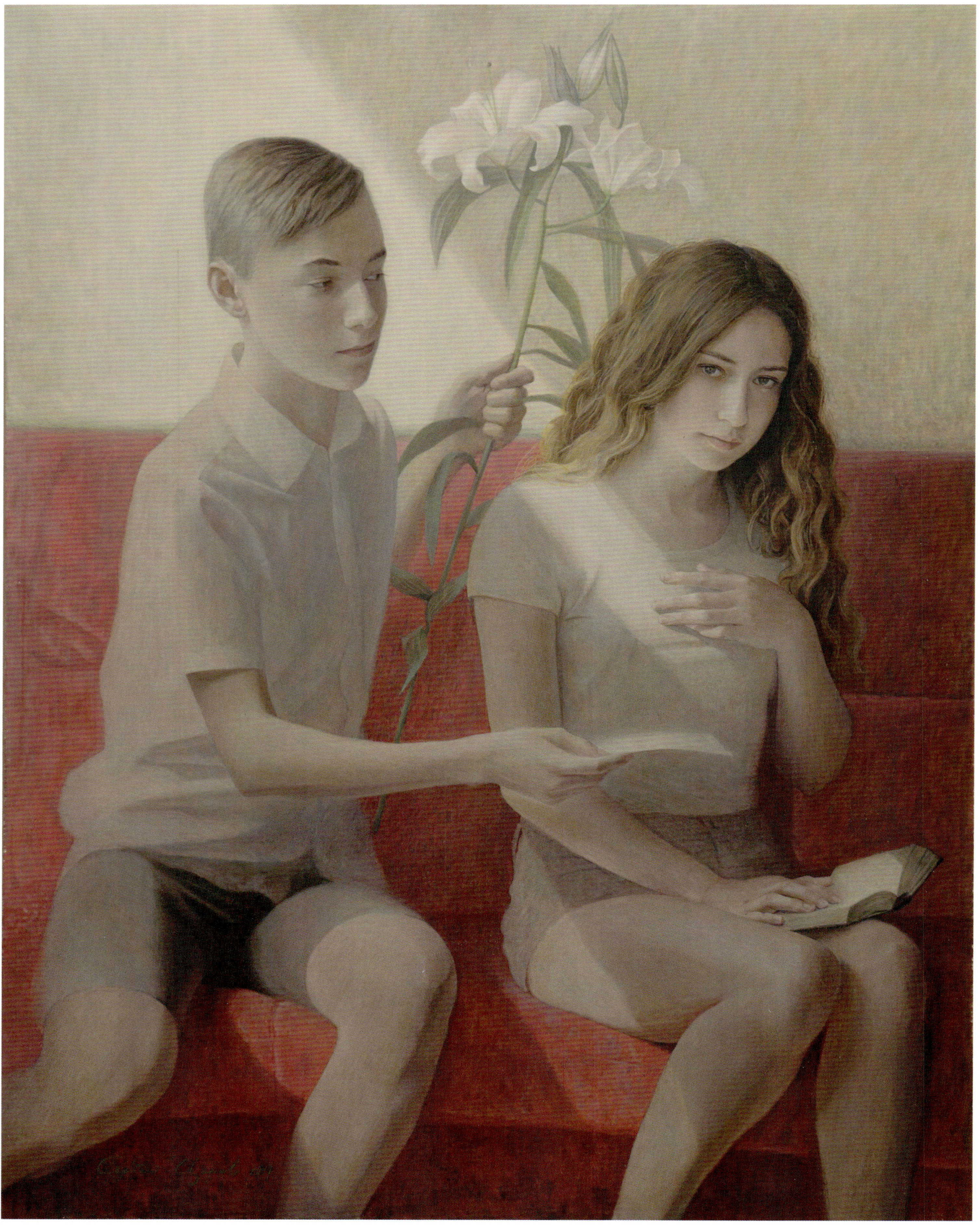

Tsarev, Sergei
They All Ate and Were Satisfied
2015, egg tempera and gesso on board

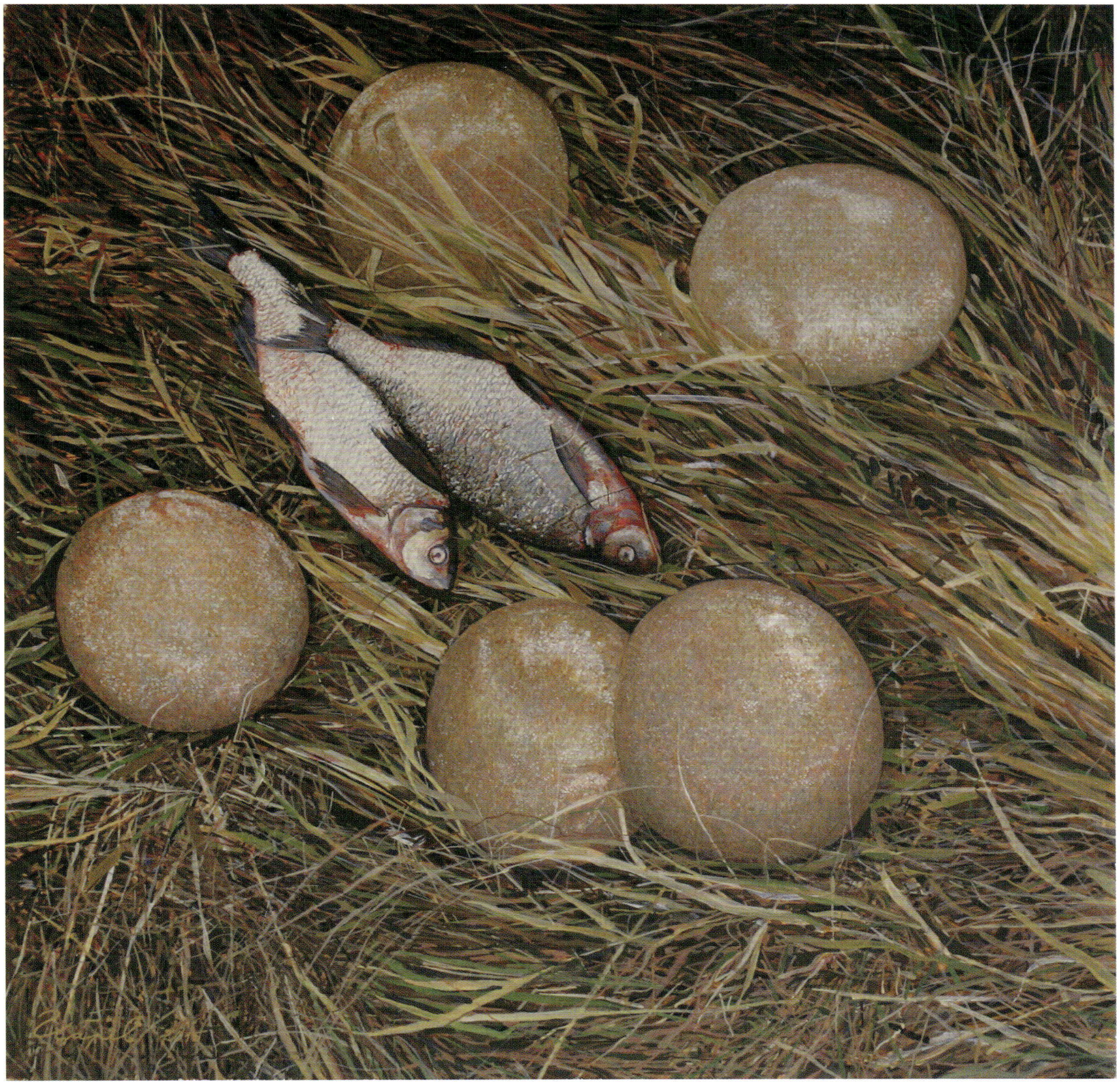

Nouveau, opened in 2012. The latest major tourist attraction became the Samara branch of the State Tretyakov Gallery. It is housed in the hammer and sickle shaped building of a former kitchen-factory constructed in 1932. The hammer and sickle was the main state emblem of the Soviet Union and is a symbol that represents the unity of workers and peasants. Its first cultural event, a series of theatrical performances "Utopia for Dinner", specially created for the opening, took place in September 2021.[4]

A group of young artists who became known as 'Samara Wave' has put the city decisively on the map of contemporary art centres in Russia. Most but not all of these artists are interested in abstract art: amongst them are Alexander Zaytsev, Vladimir Logutov, Andrey Syaylev, Svetlana Shuvaeva and others.

Tsarev, Sergei
Annunciation
2017, egg tempera, gesso on board

Alexander Zaytsev (b. 1986) explores the geometry of the urban environment and city landscapes. He says about himself, 'My work is an attempt to study the environment, plunge into a complex urban space, translate it into a field of abstract images, into a field of subtle connections and non-verbal references.'[5]

Vladimir Logutov (b. 1980) has twice been a nominee for the Kandinsky Prize and was declared Artist of the Year after winning the Innovation Prize in 2018. In one work he placed the silhouettes of two onlookers in front of an abstract painting. Was this philosophical or ironic? Clearly, he can be both.

Andrey Syaylev (b. 1982) studied at the Samara Art College where he met Vladimir Logutov. The pair organised the Art Chaos festival in 2004 and were the core members of the Laboratory art group in Samara in 2010–2014. By 2016 Syaylev had become the best-known contemporary artist from Samara. In 2019, his 'Pillars' were erected in different districts of the city of Krasnoyarsk as decorations beside large modern apartment buildings. What do the pillars commemorate? According to the artist, "the work thematizes the image of the soil in the model of the geological cut — core. Similar to the cultural strata going into the deep, the «pillar»-object captures a historically extended stream of time, from the new constructions at the top, through soviet modernism, to the Stalin's architecture and the first barrack buildings in the lower part".[6]

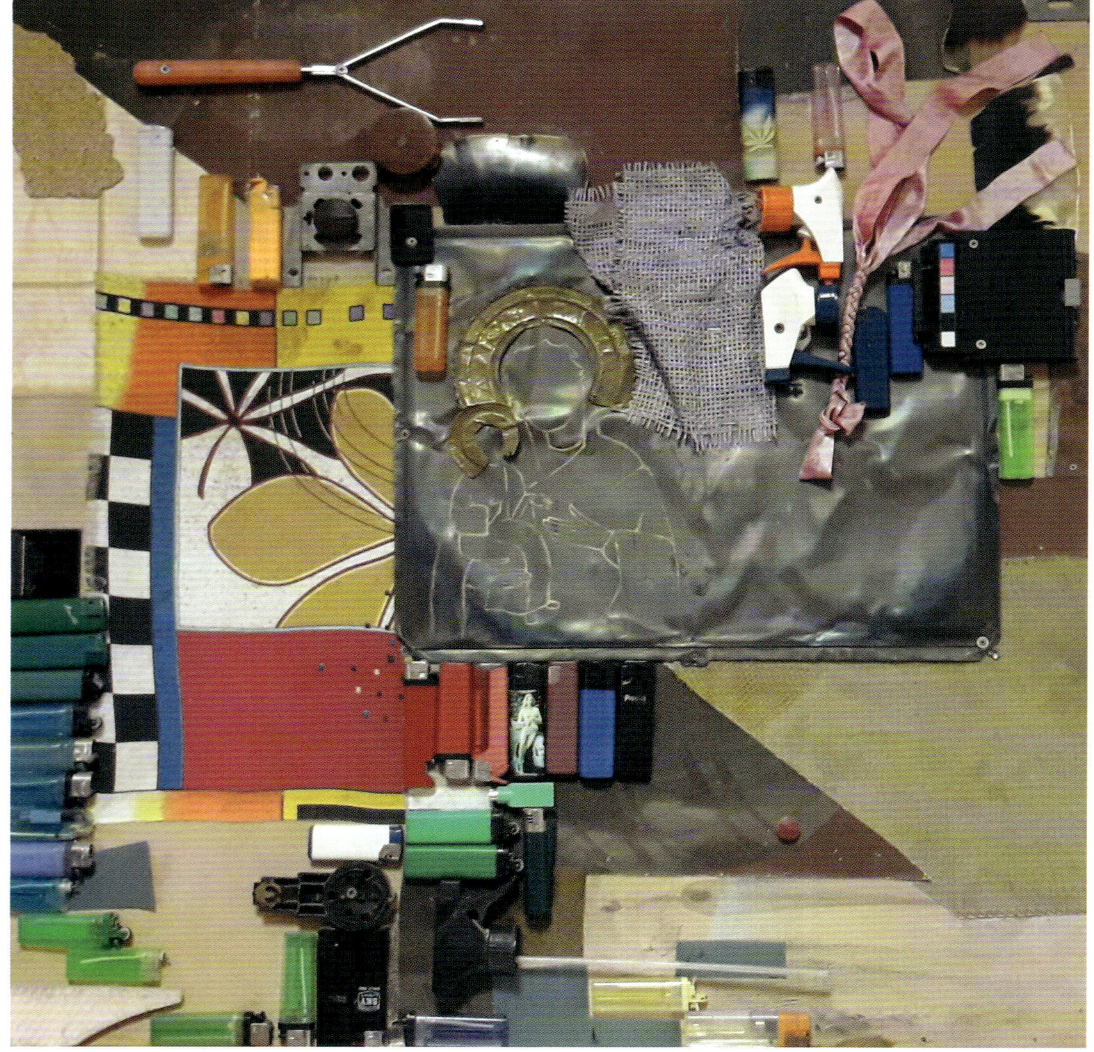

←
Mavrin, Nikolay
Mundane and Spiritual
2011, mixed media, found objects on board

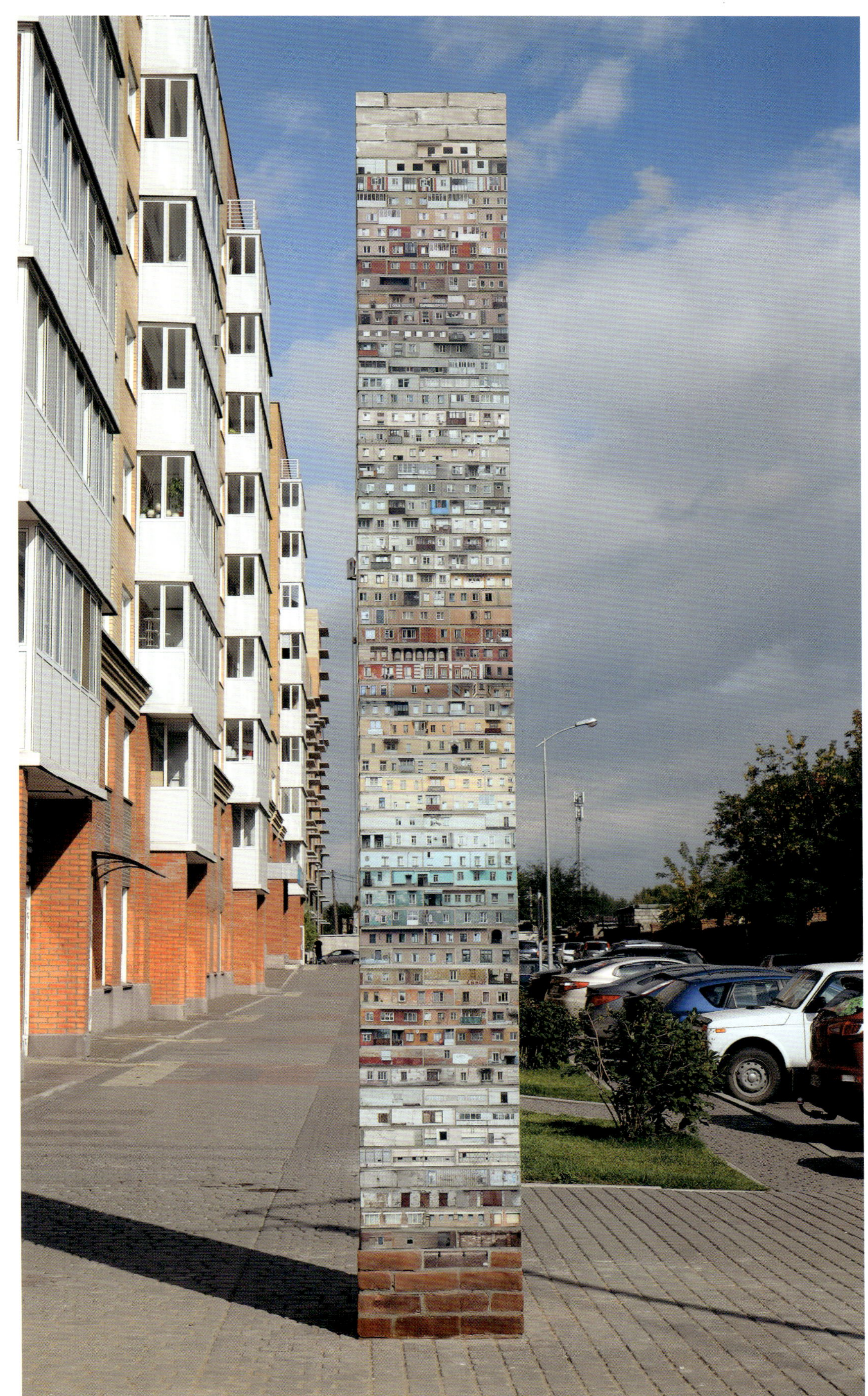

→
Syaylev, Andrey
Pillars of Krasnoyarsk
2019, UV printing, two-component acrylic polyurethane varnish, ceramic tiles, tile adhesive, bricks

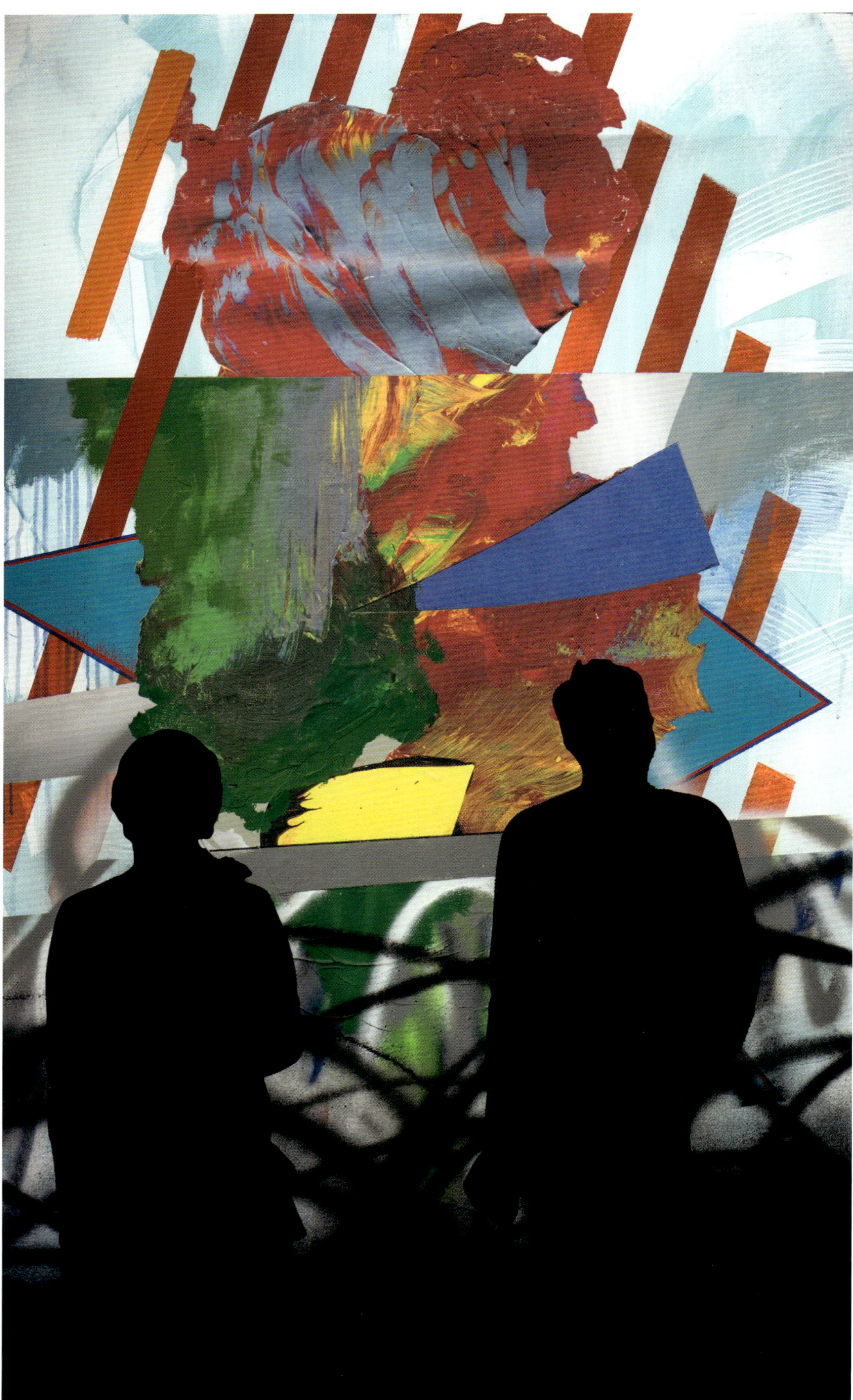

←
Logutov, Vladimir
Untitled, Encounters series
2017, acrylic, airbrush, inkjet printing, mixed media on canvas

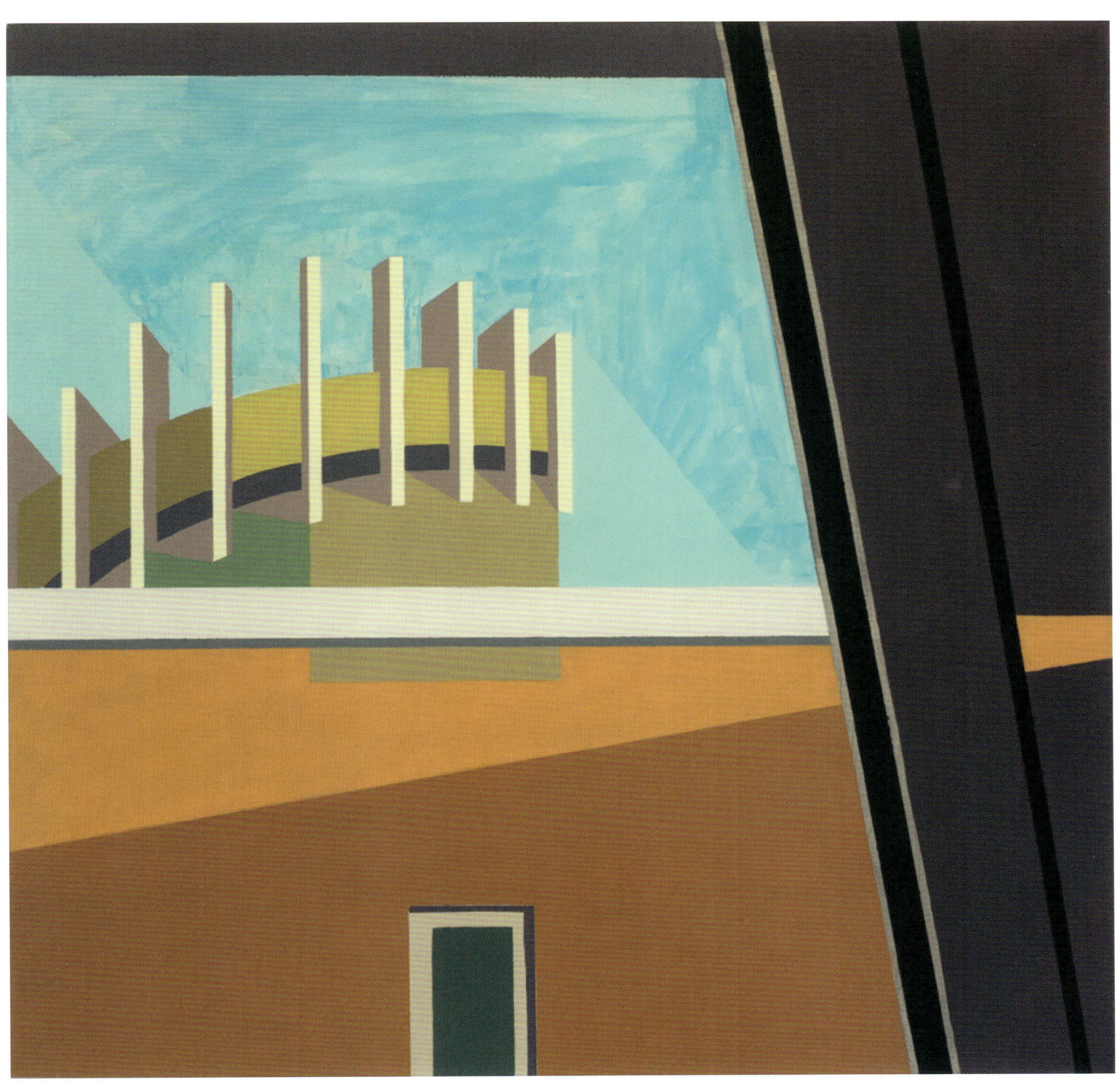

↑
Zaytsev, Alexander
Untitled
2016, acrylic on canvas

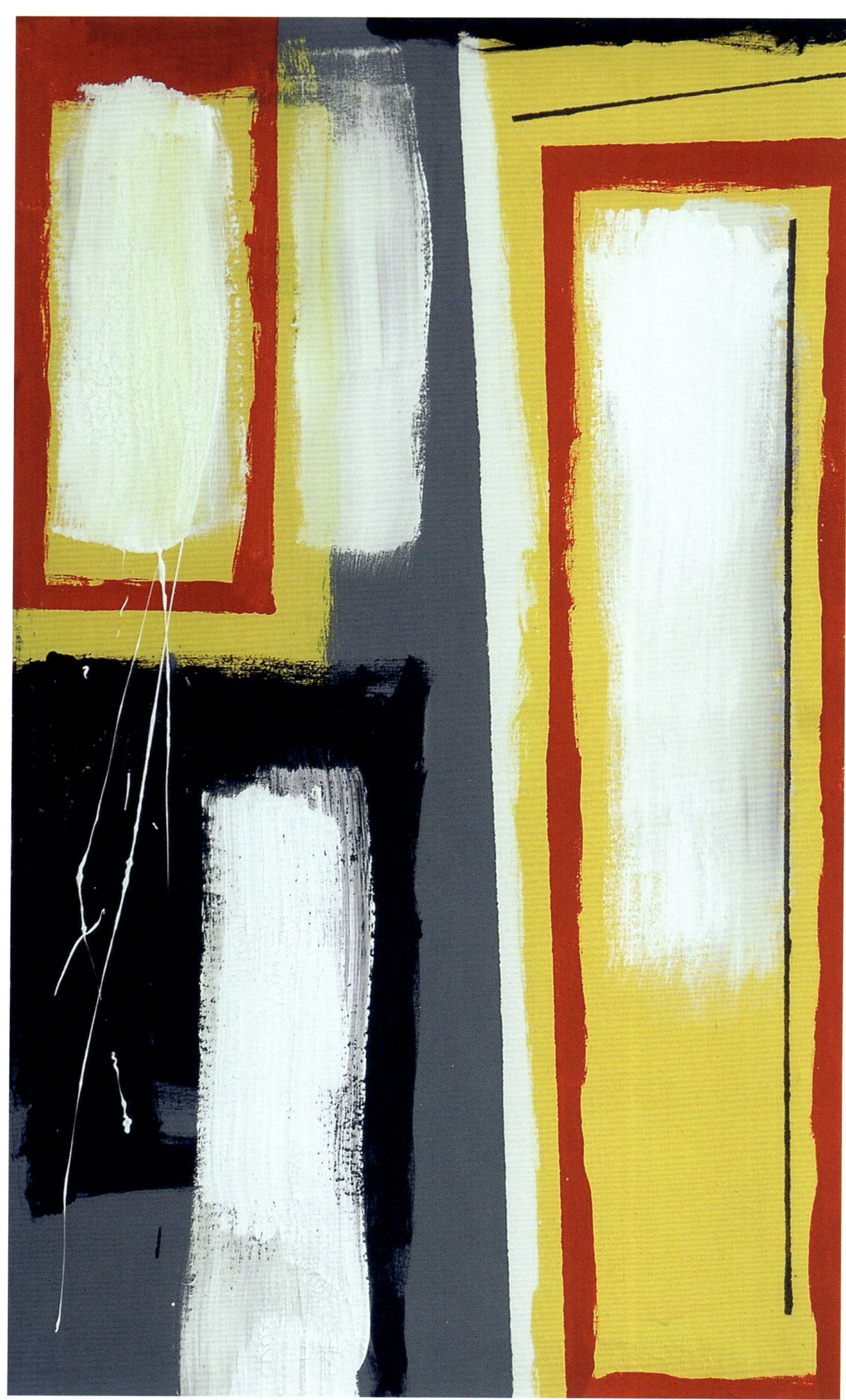

←
Lezin, Mikhail
Untitled
2014, acrylic on canvas

→
Lezin, Mikhail
Untitled
2016, acrylic on paper

Mikhail Lezin (b. 1974) from Tolyatti, the second largest town in the Samara region and the home of Russia's largest car manufacturer, AvtoVAZ (Lada), is, in his own words, 'interested in the interaction between pictorial componentry and technical drawing and the possibility of co-existence and discussion of incipient shapelessness and geometrical structures'.[7]

The younger generation of Samara artists have chosen their own ways to explore the non-objective. Anfisa Dobrokhodova (b. 1992) pushes her figurative image so far towards abstraction that the figurative intention is barely recognisable.

Art Abstractov (b.1988), also known as Anton Eager, who was born and lives in Samara and whose works can be seen in Moscow, St Petersburg, Barcelona, Rotterdam and Tel Aviv, started painting graffiti in 2007, but after a few years he realised that it did not bring him any aesthetic pleasure and

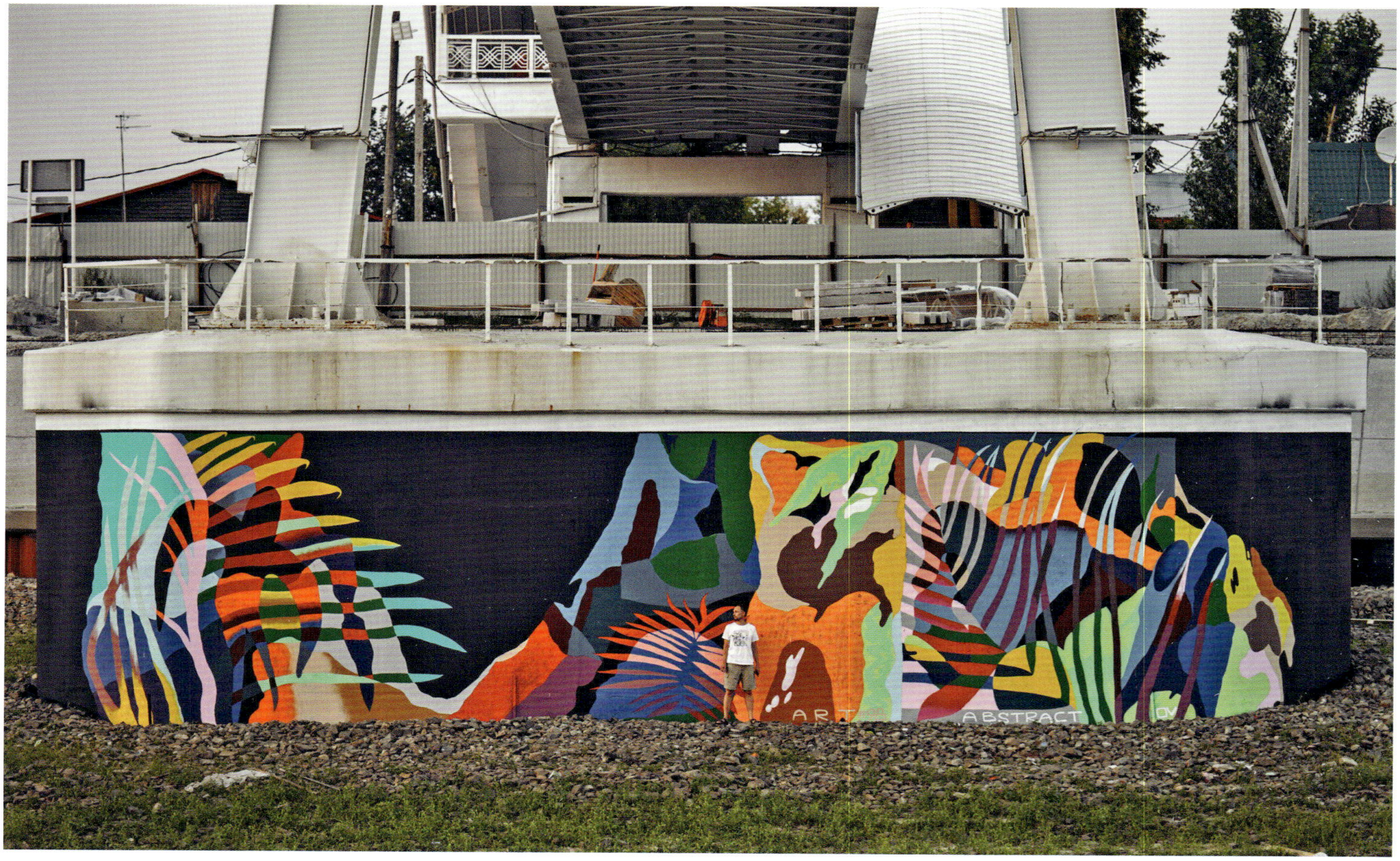

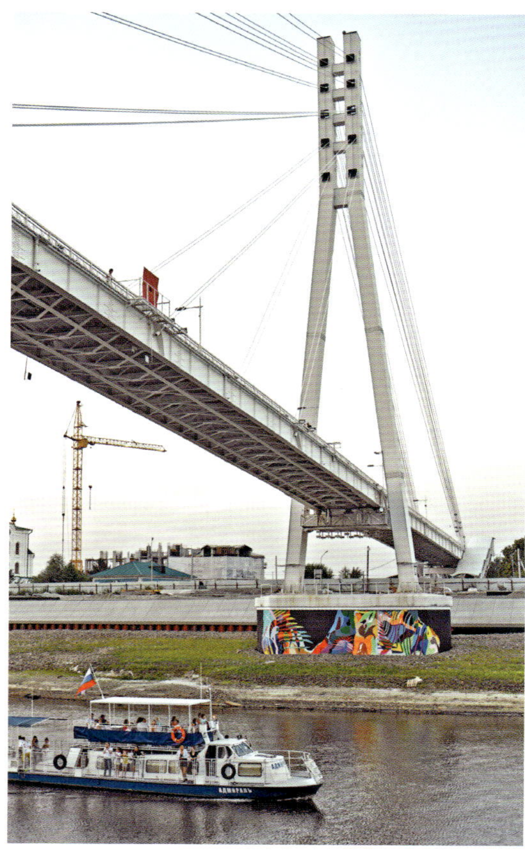

←
Art Abstractov
Avantgarde Series 98
2020, spray paint on wall, overview

↑
Art Abstractov
Avantgarde Series 98
2020, spray paint on wall

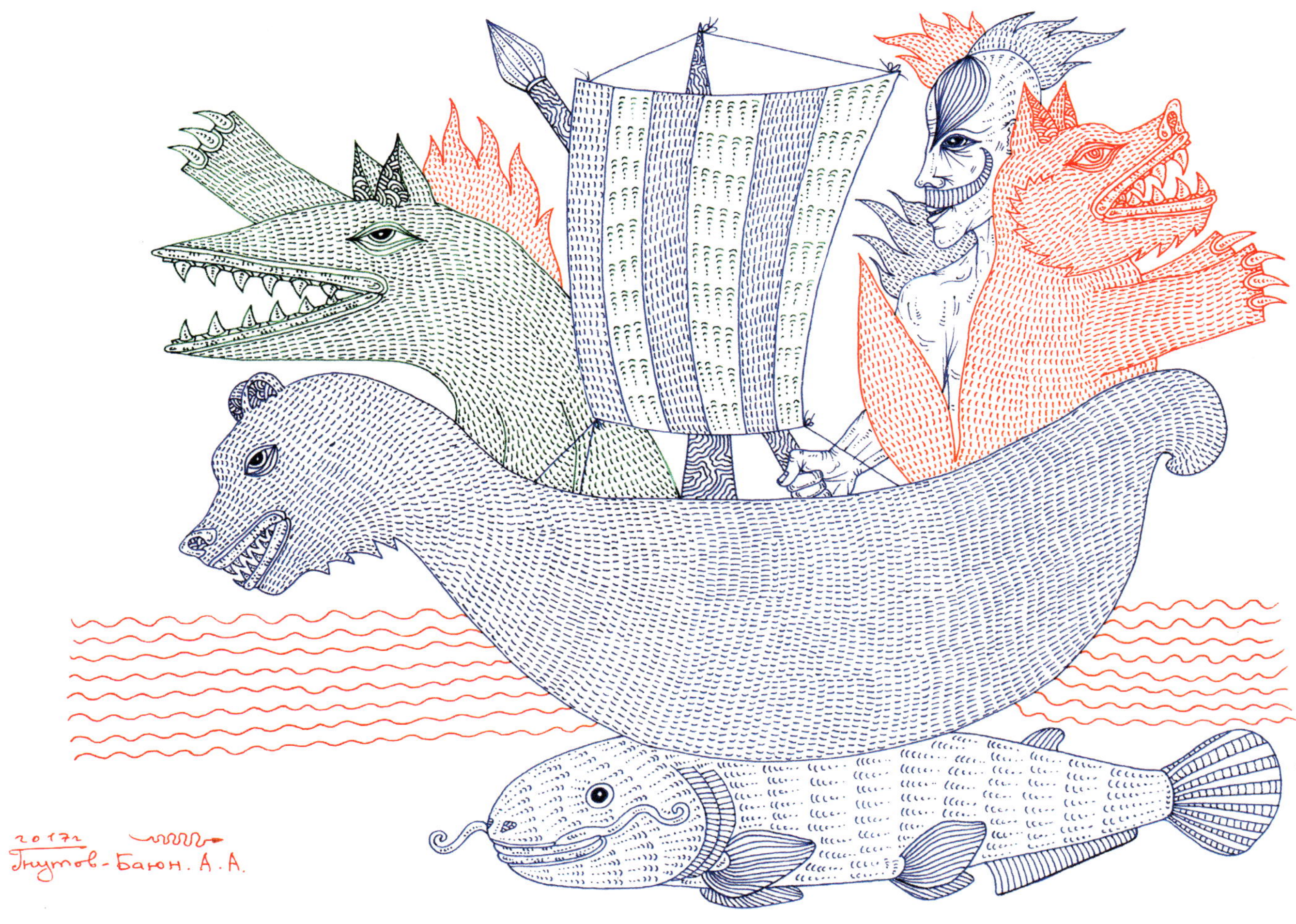

↑
Gnutov, Alexander
Ushkui (flat-bottomed boat)
2017, multicolour gel pens on paper

decided to create abstract motifs on the wall surfaces.[8]

The final two artists mentioned in this chapter are from Saratov, a town on the Volga nearly 450km south of Samara. This also was a closed city under the Soviets. It boasts the Radishchev Fine Art Museum, reputedly the first museum opened to the public in Russia – in 1885 – and is the birth place of Victor Borisov-Musatov (1870-1905), the creator of the Russian Symbolist style, along with Mikhail Vrubel (1856-1910). The art of Borisov-Musatov inspired Pavel Kuznetsov (1878-1968) and Alexander Matveev (1878-1960), both born in Saratov, to establish the Blue Rose, an influential Russian symbolist art group, in Moscow at the beginning of the twentieth century.

Alina Belousova (b. 1982), a graduate of the Saratov Art College named after A.P. Bogolyubov, set up her own project, *Digitalina*, to make decorative and art objects from disused computer parts.[9] A series of her works – entitled *Fabergé Neo-Incubators* – offers an ironic link between the Fabergé imperial-epoch Easter eggs with their tiny precious surprises inside and the eggs present in computer games as surprises – the player walks around various locations to find them.

To conclude, here is an elegant Surrealist drawing by Alexander Gnutov (b. 1976), also a graduate of the Saratov Art College. The artist is keenly interested in martial arts and concerned with the transformation of ancient Slavic bird and animal totems into body language and modern art forms.[10] His art recalls traditional Russian fairy tales, and at the same time the atmosphere of some of the ballets mounted by Diaghilev.

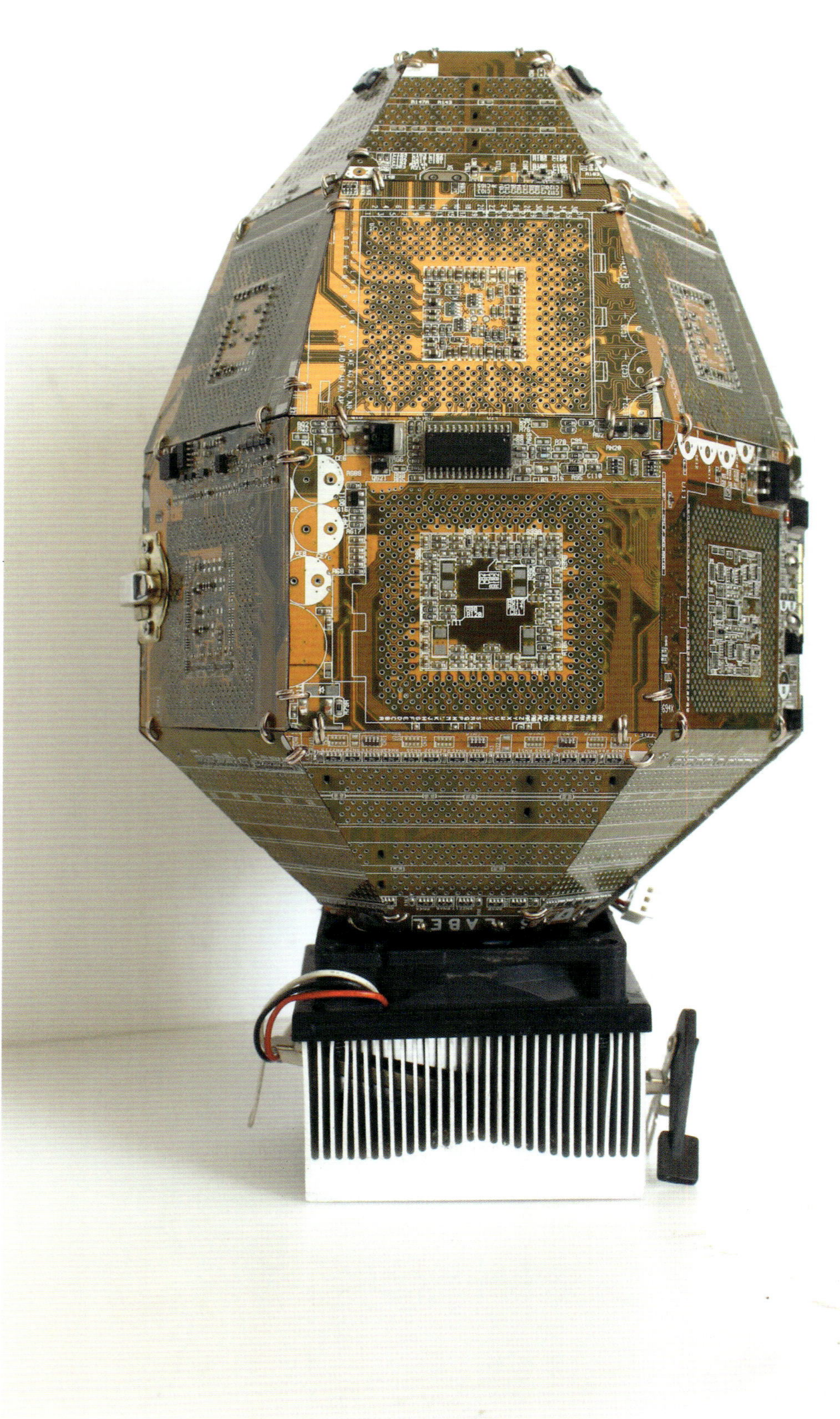

←→
Belousova, Alina
Neoincubator No. 13
2019, printed circuit boards, radiators

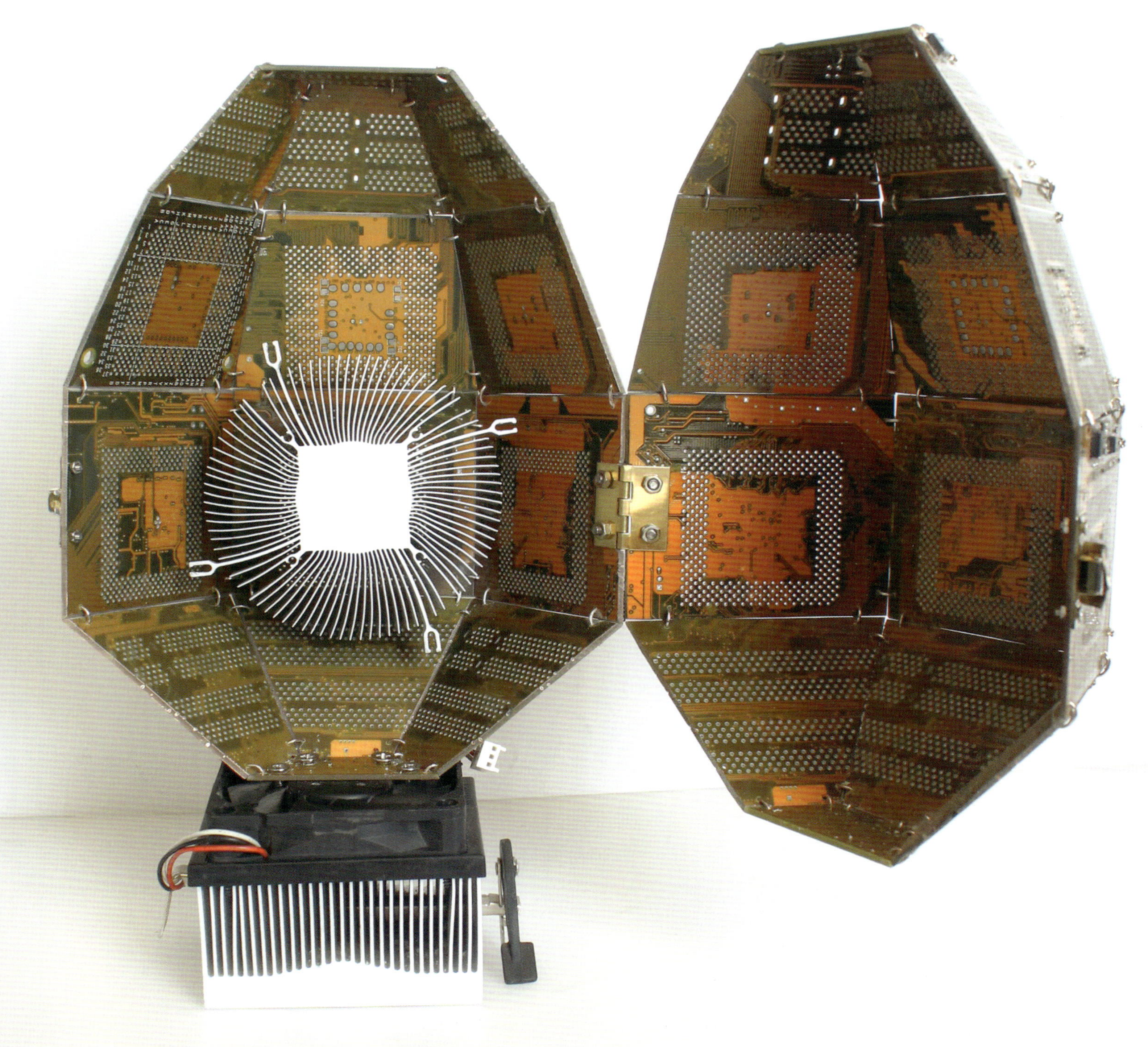

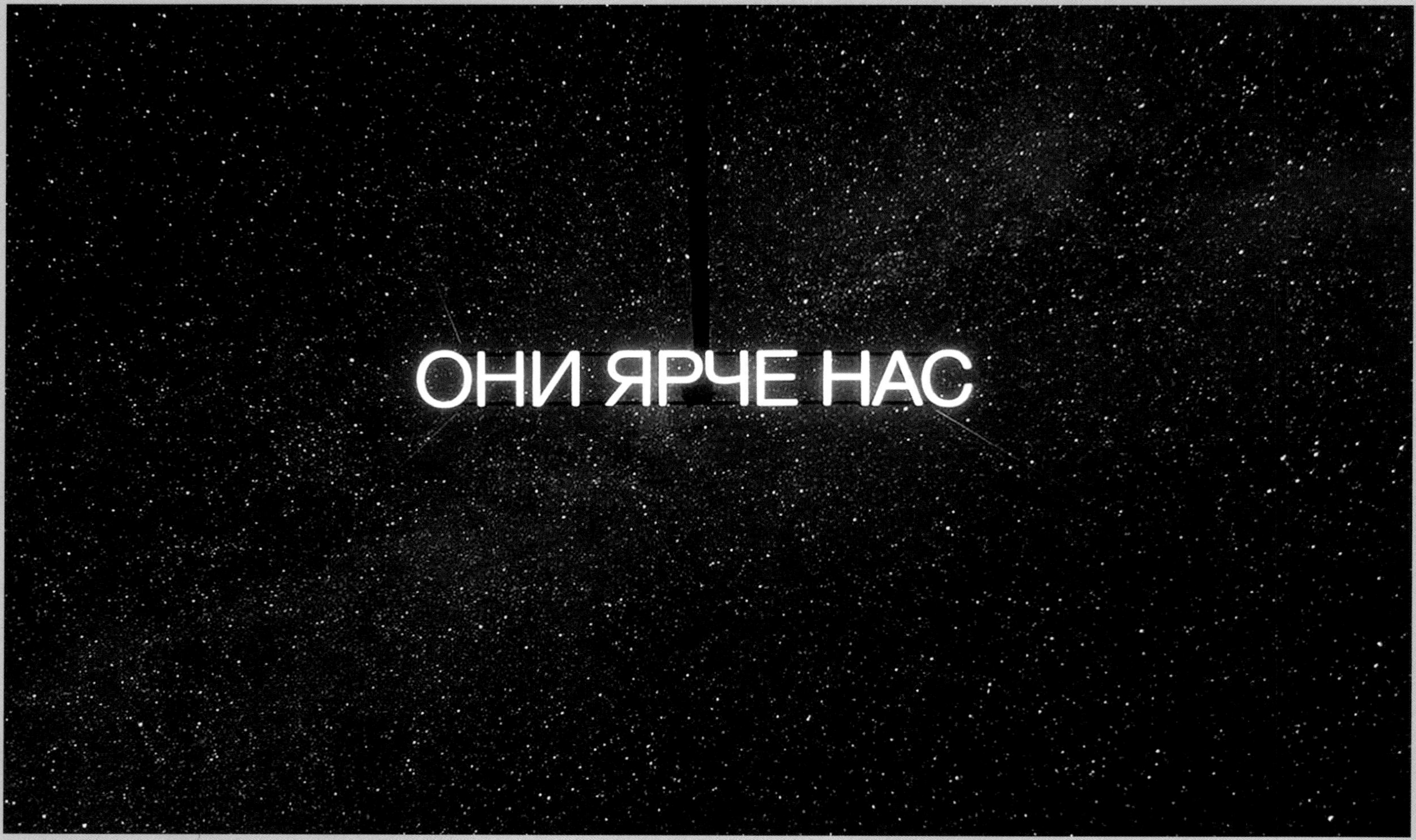

ОНИ ЯРЧЕ НАС

9 AROUND THE URALS

Yekaterinburg, named after the Empress Catherine I, wife of Peter the Great, is situated more than 1,000 miles (1,667km) east of Moscow. It enjoys a doleful celebrity, as the place where the last tsar, Nicholas II, and members of his family, were executed in 1918. It is situated on the eastern slope of the Ural Mountains, and is a major industrial centre. During Soviet times it was a centre for research into chemical and biological warfare. It is a major railway junction – the Trans-Siberian railway runs through it, and it houses a number of important centres both for higher education and also for scientific research, among them the Urals branch of the Russian Academy of Sciences. In addition, it is now an important cultural centre, with a large number of working artists.

It is not surprising to find that the art now being produced there often has links to science and technology. For example, Vladimir Seleznyov's (b. 1973) *Metropolis*, a night-time pseudo-aerial panorama of the city of Kazan (2010–2019) makes use of everyday objects, light-accumulating paint and digital technology. The artist was born in Nizhny Tagil, an industrial town in the Middle Urals, eighty miles north of Yekaterinburg. It is the centre of Russian tank production. Seleznyov worked as a welder at the Nizhny Tagil metallurgical plant before forming Zehr Gut, his own art group, and moving to Yekaterinburg, where he now lives.

Tima Radya's (b. 1988) view of a sky sparkling with a myriad of stars is entitled *Brighter Than Us*. It is made for his Observatory project in 2016 and consists on the neon lights mounted on the arrow of the crane next to the special astrophysics' laboratory of the Russian Academy of Science in the Northern Caucasus. You can only see the phrase when looking up the sky. In this work the artist who studied to be a philosopher, reinterprets the famous phrase by Chuck Palahniuk, a renowned American author: "Look up into the stars and you're gone"[1]

In the *Collector* project (2015), the Where Dogs Run artists' group, formed by 4 artists, Vlad Bulatov

←
Radya, Tima
Brighter Than Us
2016, installation

↓
Seleznyov, Vladimir
Metropolis, Kazan
2013, light-accumulating paint, bulb, light switch, household waste.
Daylight view.

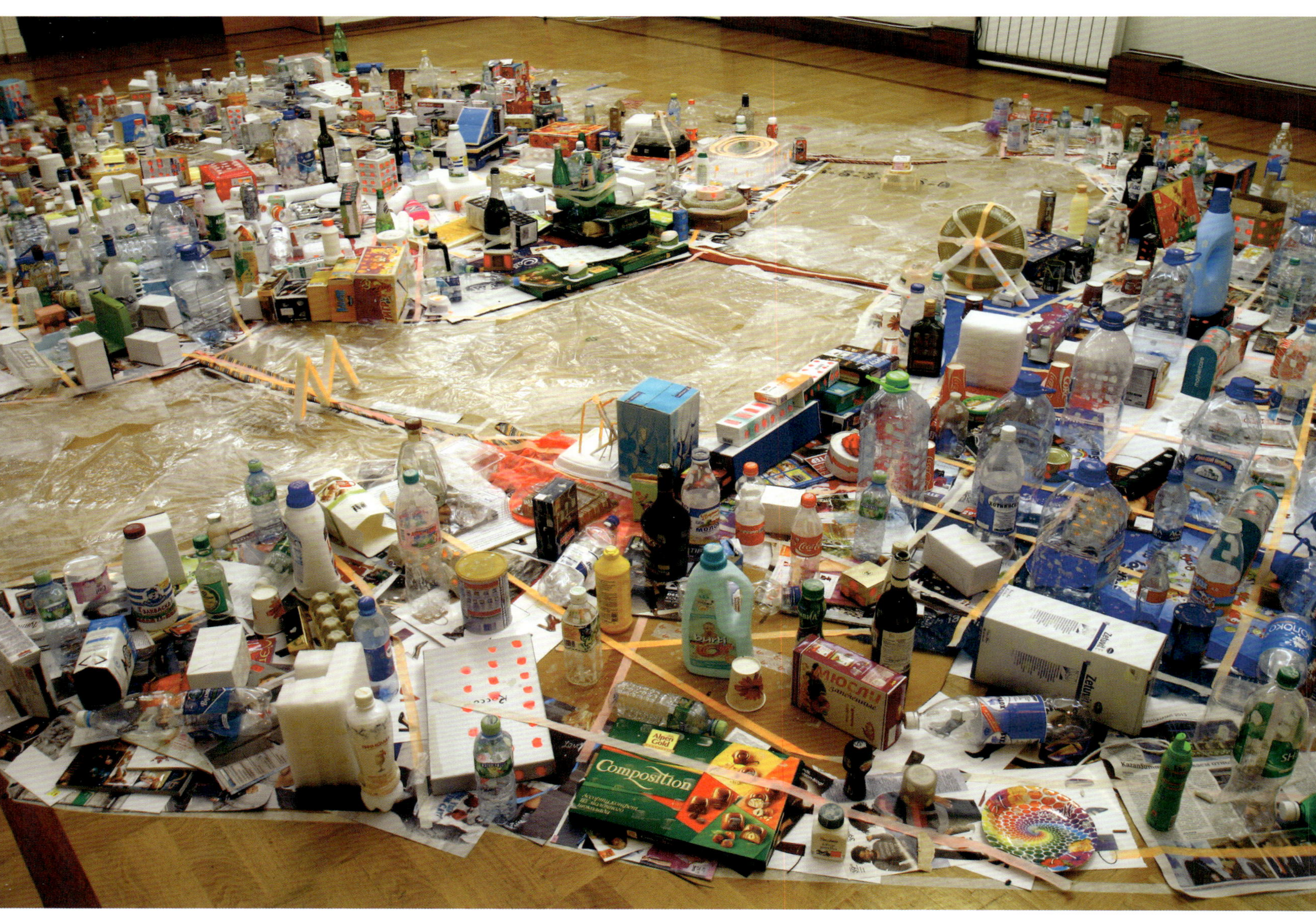

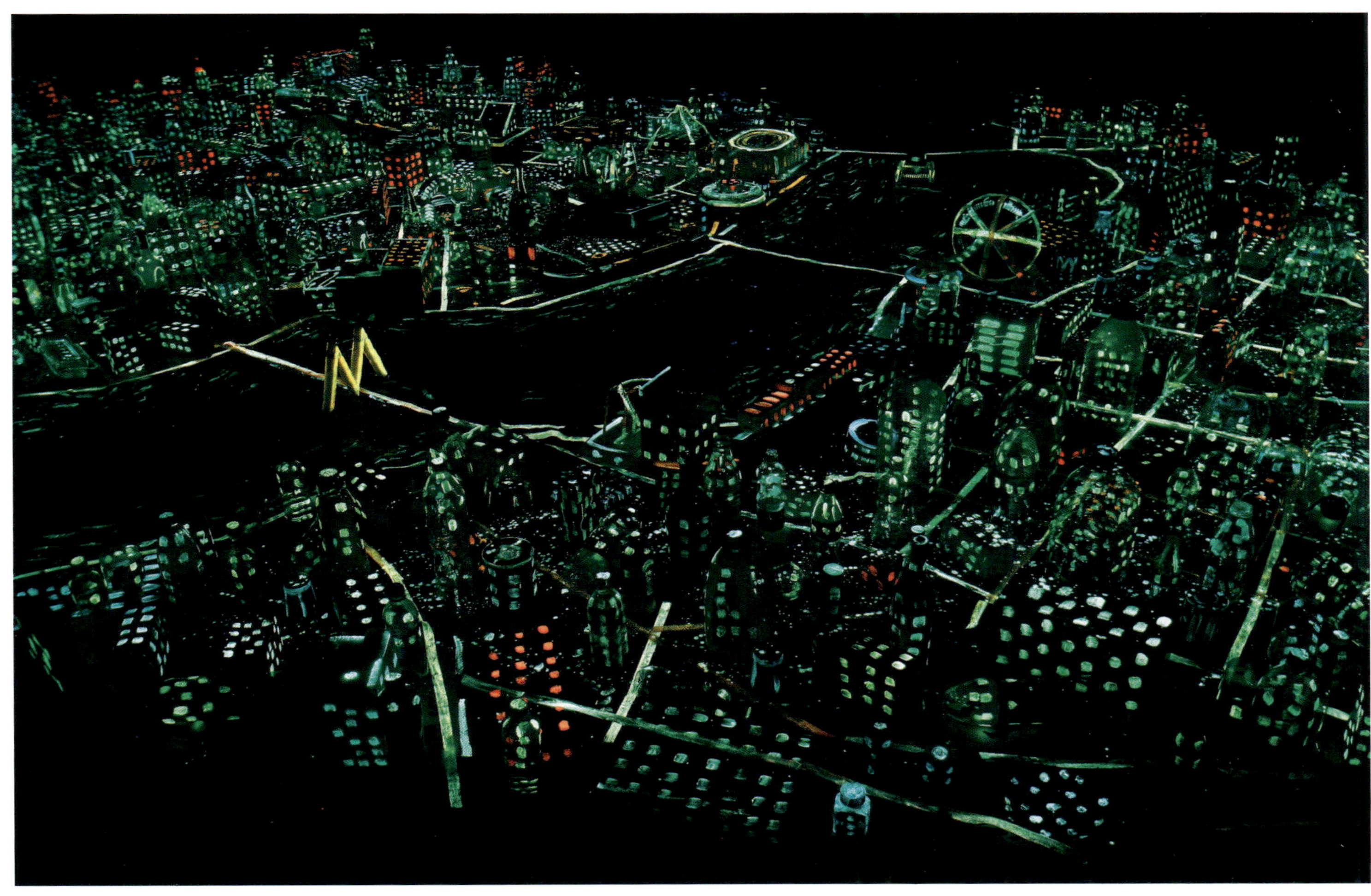

↑
Seleznyov, Vladimir
Metropolis, Kazan
2013, light-accumulating paint, bulbs, light switch, household waste

(b. 1975), Natalya Grekhova (b. 1976), Olga Inozemtseva (b. 1977) and Aleksei Korzukhin (b. 1973), in Ekaterinburg in 2000, transforms human interaction with nature by erasing the boundaries between art and science. The use of scientific instruments and computer technology allows a media artist to create music almost literally out of thin air.[2] The group often collaborates with scientists and has participated in major art shows in Russia and abroad, including the State Hermitage in St Petersburg, the State Tretyakov Gallery in Moscow and MHKA in Belgium.

Another rather ironic comment comes from Elena Slobtseva (b. 1981) in *The Cities* ('Gorodki'). In this she offers a drastically simplified city image based on a Russian folk game where, as Wikipedia relates, 'the aim... is to knock out groups of skittles arranged in various patterns by throwing a bat at them'.[3] In this case the skittles are simplified elements representing an urban panorama with toppling skyscrapers. The actual location portrayed may be Perm, where the artist resides. Perm is another industrial city in the Urals, identified by a map projected on the wall behind the installation.

Irony surfaces yet again in a sequence of four photographs by Fyodor Telkov (b. 1986) entitled *Ural Mary, Traditional Garments* (2010–2018). The two images in the top row show people in folk costumes. That on the left perhaps shows a newly married couple, enclosed for the photograph in a gilt frame.

Where Dogs Run
Collector
2015, photograph of the media artist during the project

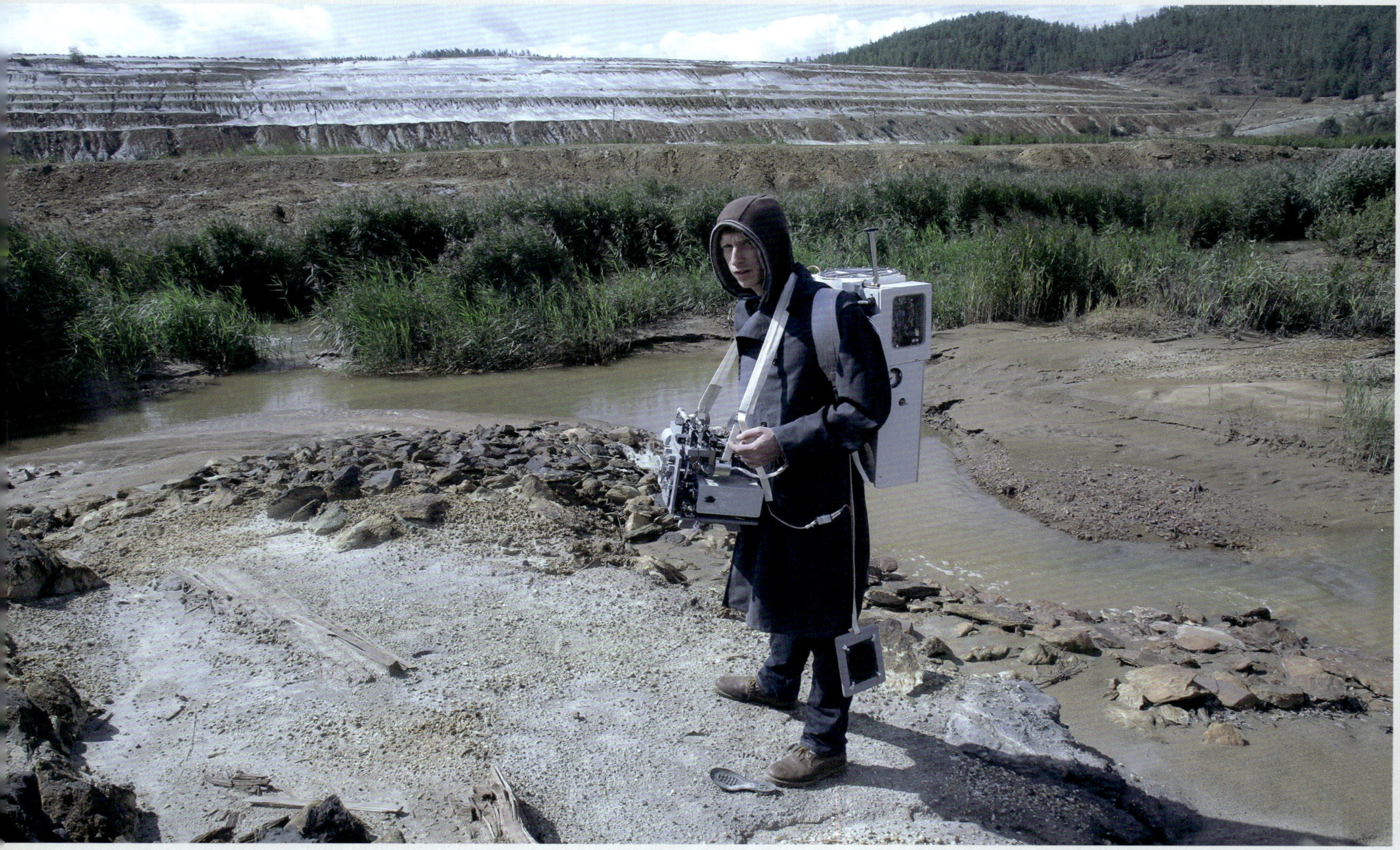

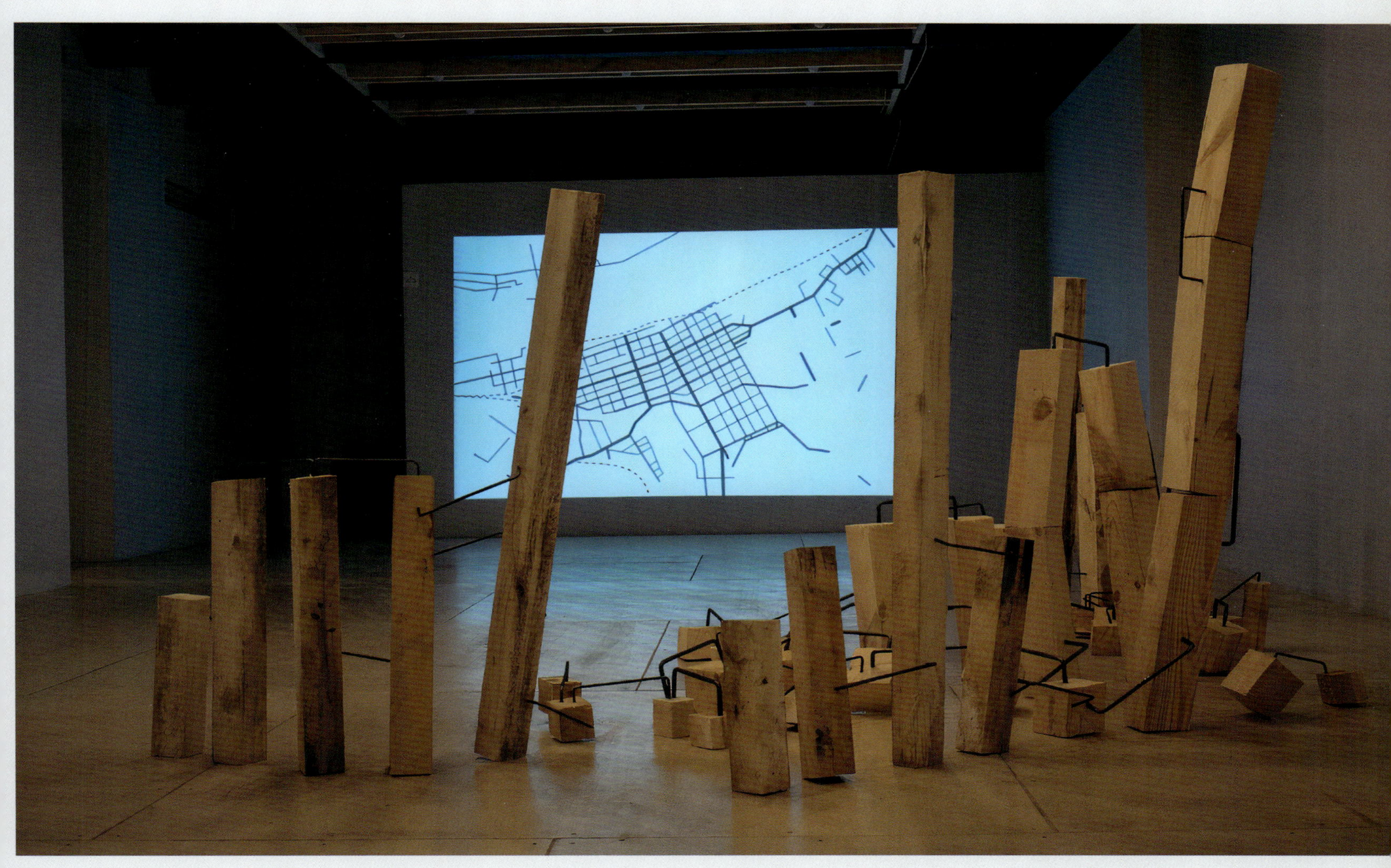

↑
Slobtseva, Elena
Gorodki (Skittles)
2017, wooden and steel wire sculpture

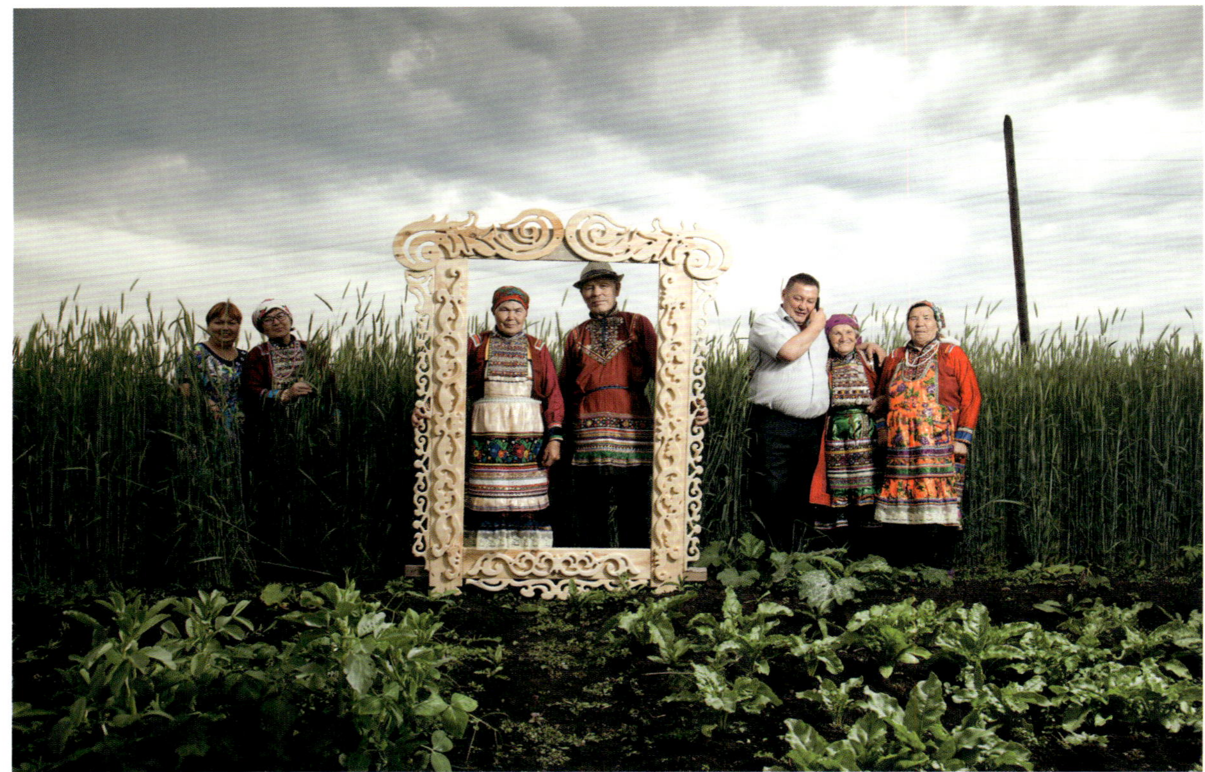

←
Telkov, Fyodor
Carpenter with his Wife, Relatives and Friends, Sarsy village
2017, digital image

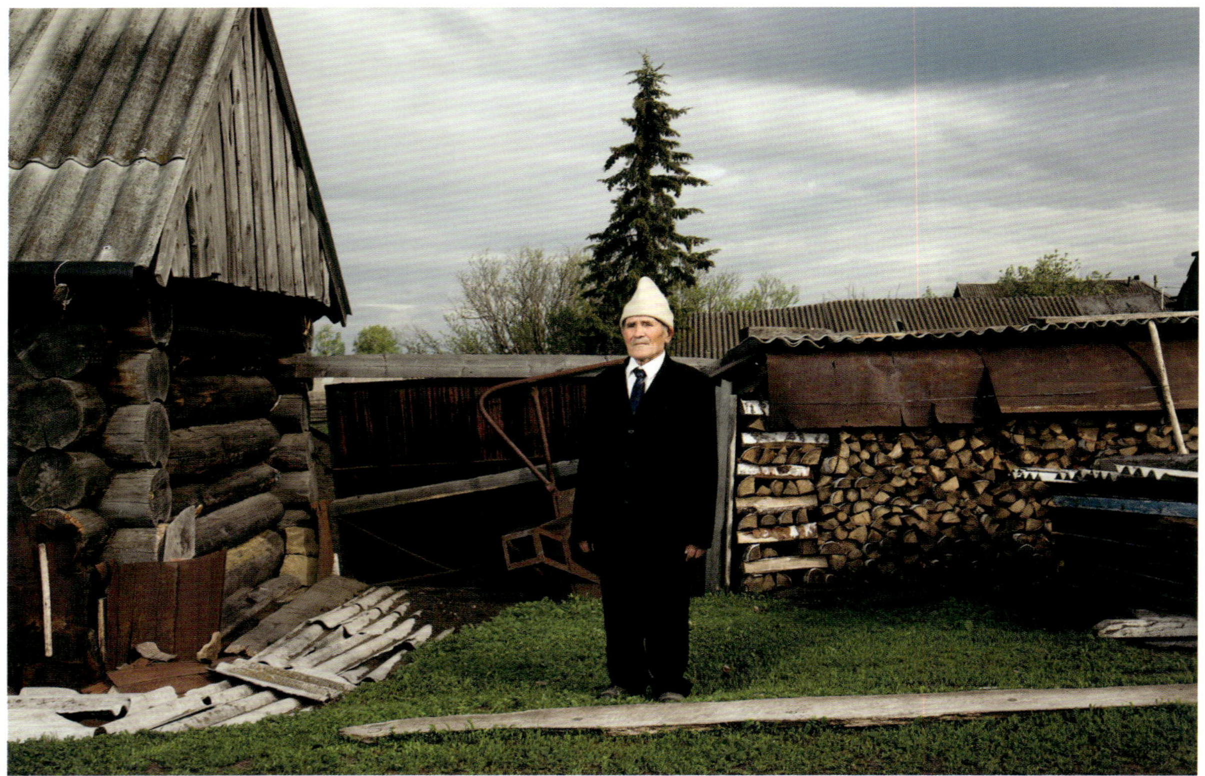

←
Telkov, Fyodor
Priest, Mary Karshi village
2017, digital image

→
Telkov, Fyodor
Women of Kurki village
2017, digital image

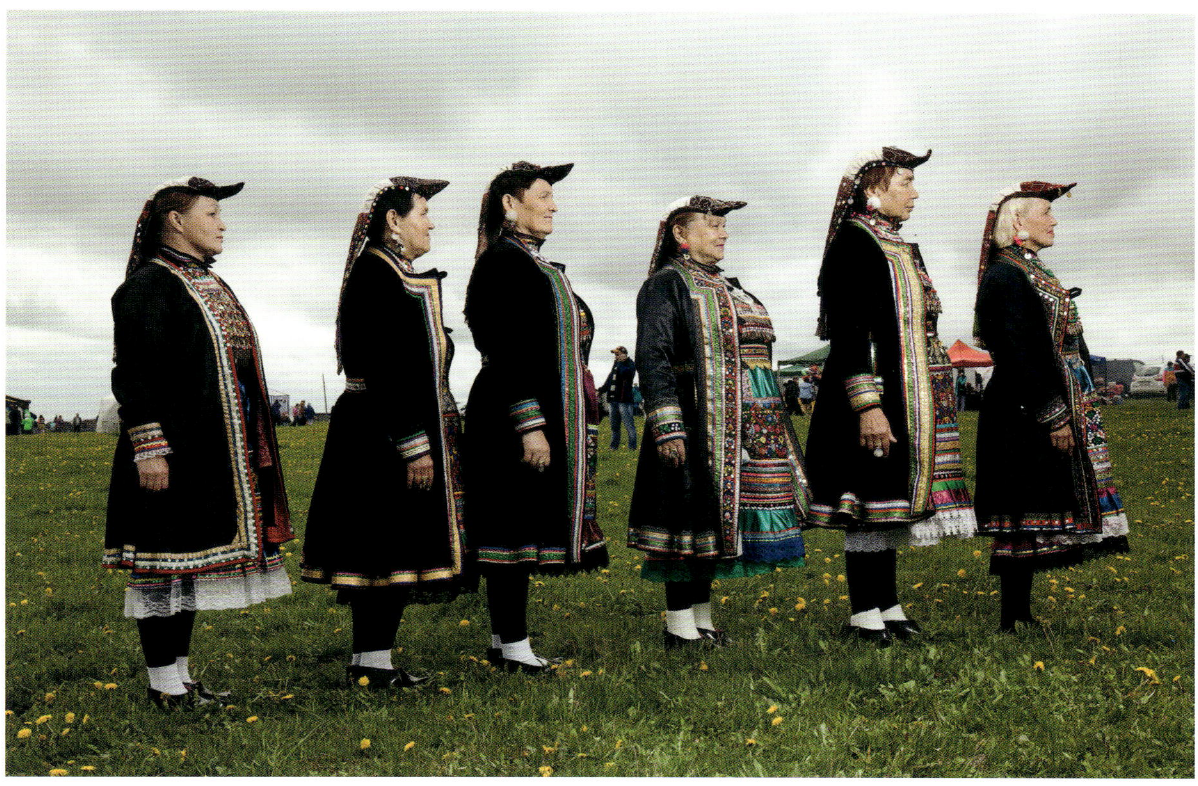

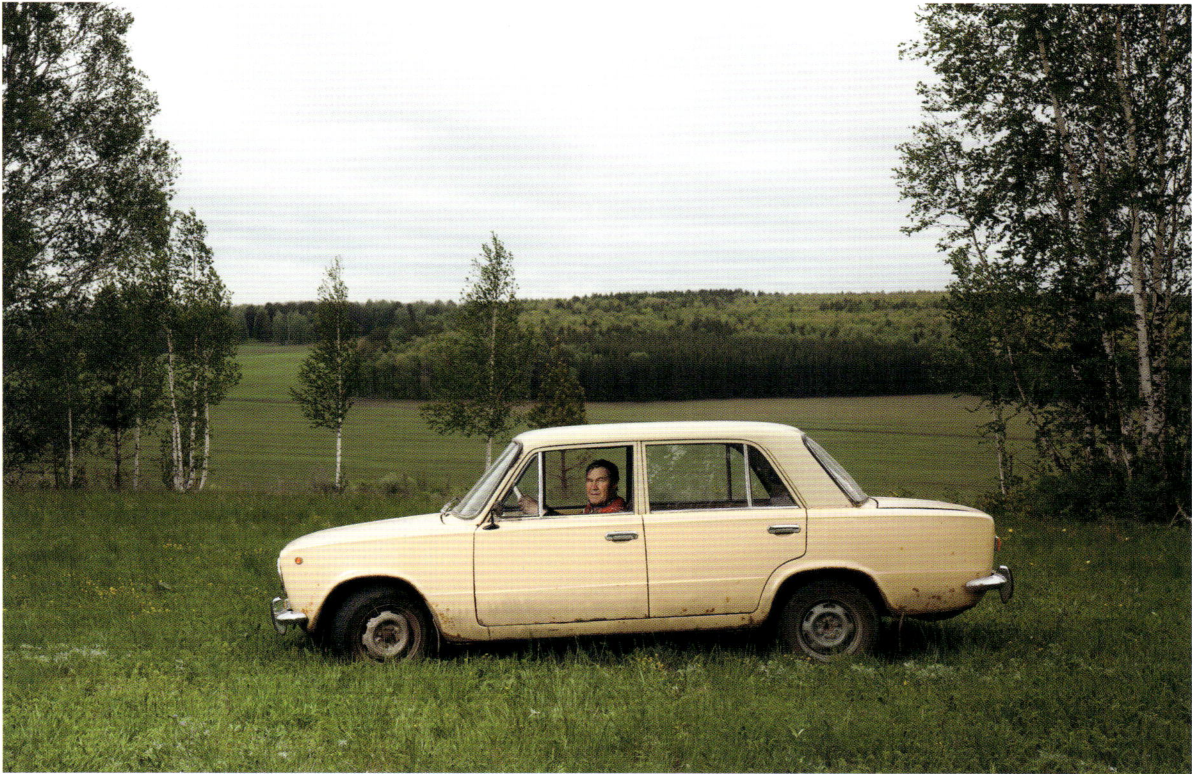

→
Telkov, Fyodor
Local Historian, Big Tavra village
2017, digital image

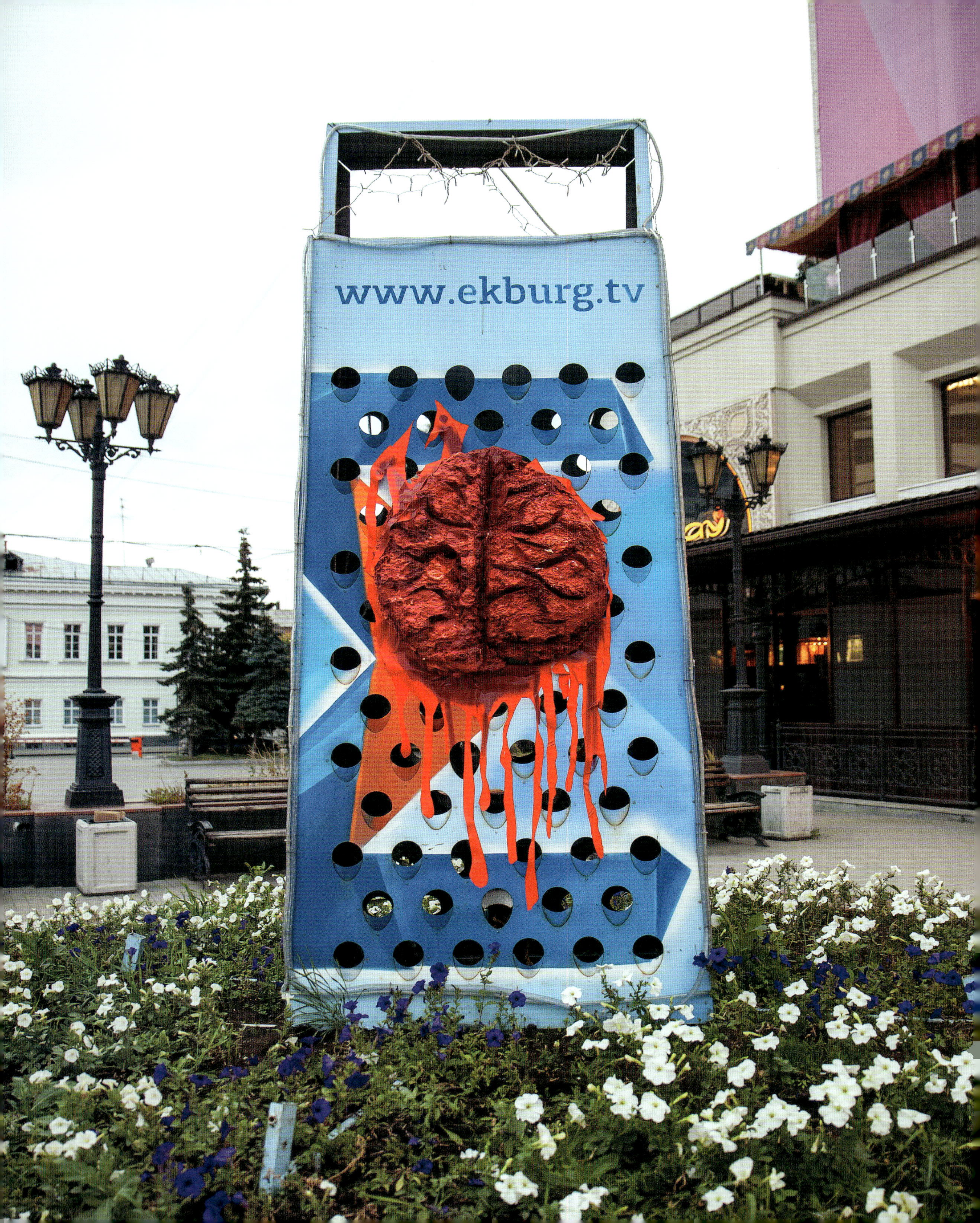
www.ekburg.tv

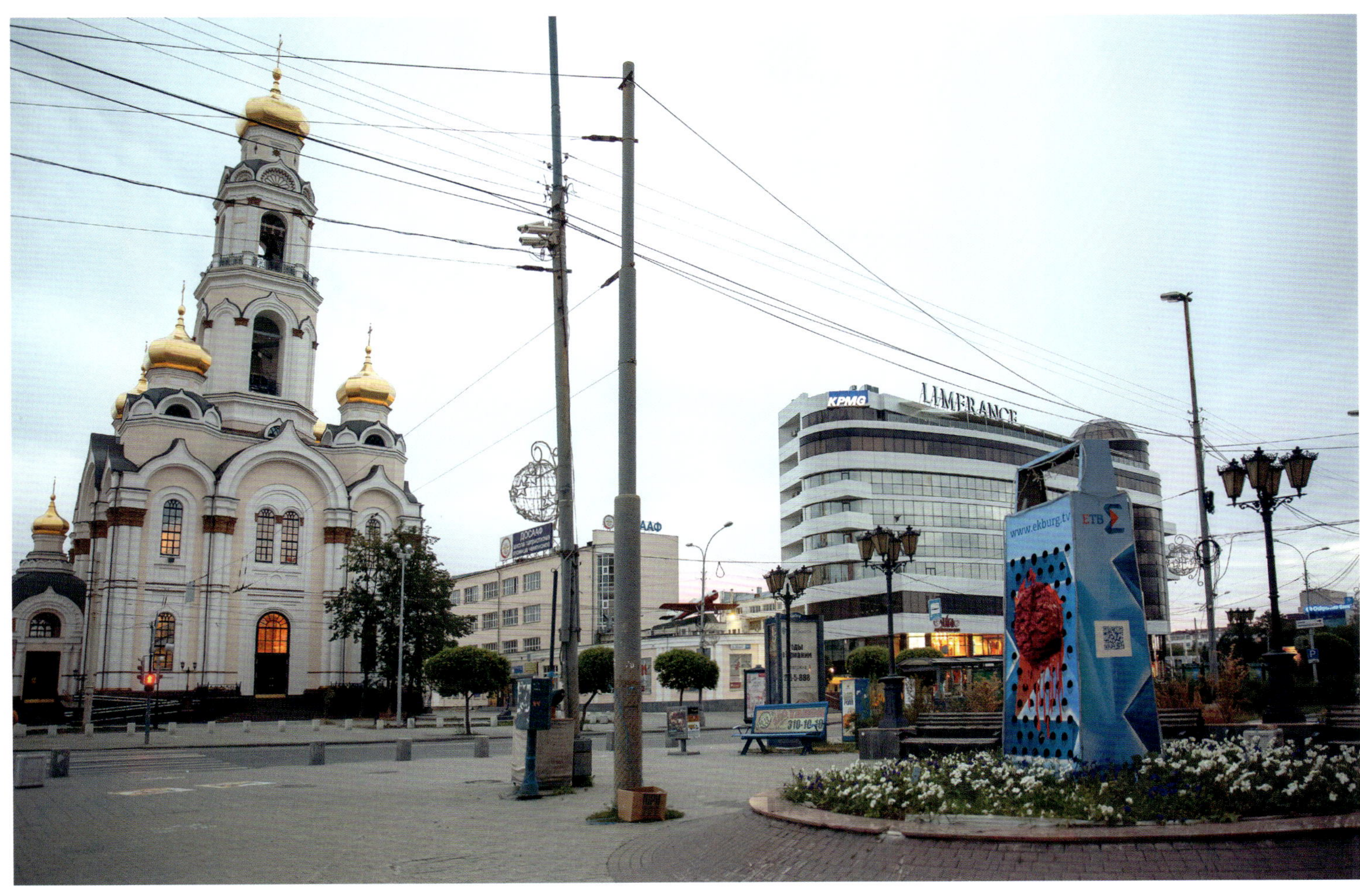

↑
Zlye (Evils), art group
Brainwash
2013, spray paint, mounting foam, self-adhesive film, tin. Overview.

←
Zlye (Evils), art group
Brainwash
2013, spray paint, mounting foam, self-adhesive film, tin

The two lower pictures show one man in a business suit, although still in a rural setting, and another, possibly the same individual, in an undistinguished-looking motor car, perhaps a Lada. This message is in support of the small number of Maris who live in the Urals, outside of their own Mari El Republic in the Upper Volga region of Russia.[4]

This ironic spirit is even more brutally expressed in *Brainwash* (2013), an outdoor sculpture by the Yekaterinburg art group Zlye ('Evils' in Russian), formed in 2004.[5] A giant grinder is exactly what it is, with a bleeding brain painted in the centre of the object. At the top of the grinder is an inscription in Latin, not Cyrillic, characters, reading 'www.ekburg.tv' – the website of the official local TV and news channel.

Anna (b. 1989) and Vitaly (b. 1990) Cherepanovy were also born in Nizhny Tagil. Apart from being an industrial centre, the town also hosts more than twenty ethnographic, historic and art museums including the Fine Art Museum. It houses *The Holy Family or Tagil Madonna*, once attributed to Rafael Santi (1483-1520) but now believed to be the work of his pupil.[6] The Cherepanov House is dedicated to the father and son team who built Russia's first steam train and railway in the nineteenth century.

↓
Cherepanov, Anna and Vitaly
Cherepanov Set
2021, mixed media
65X40X12 cm

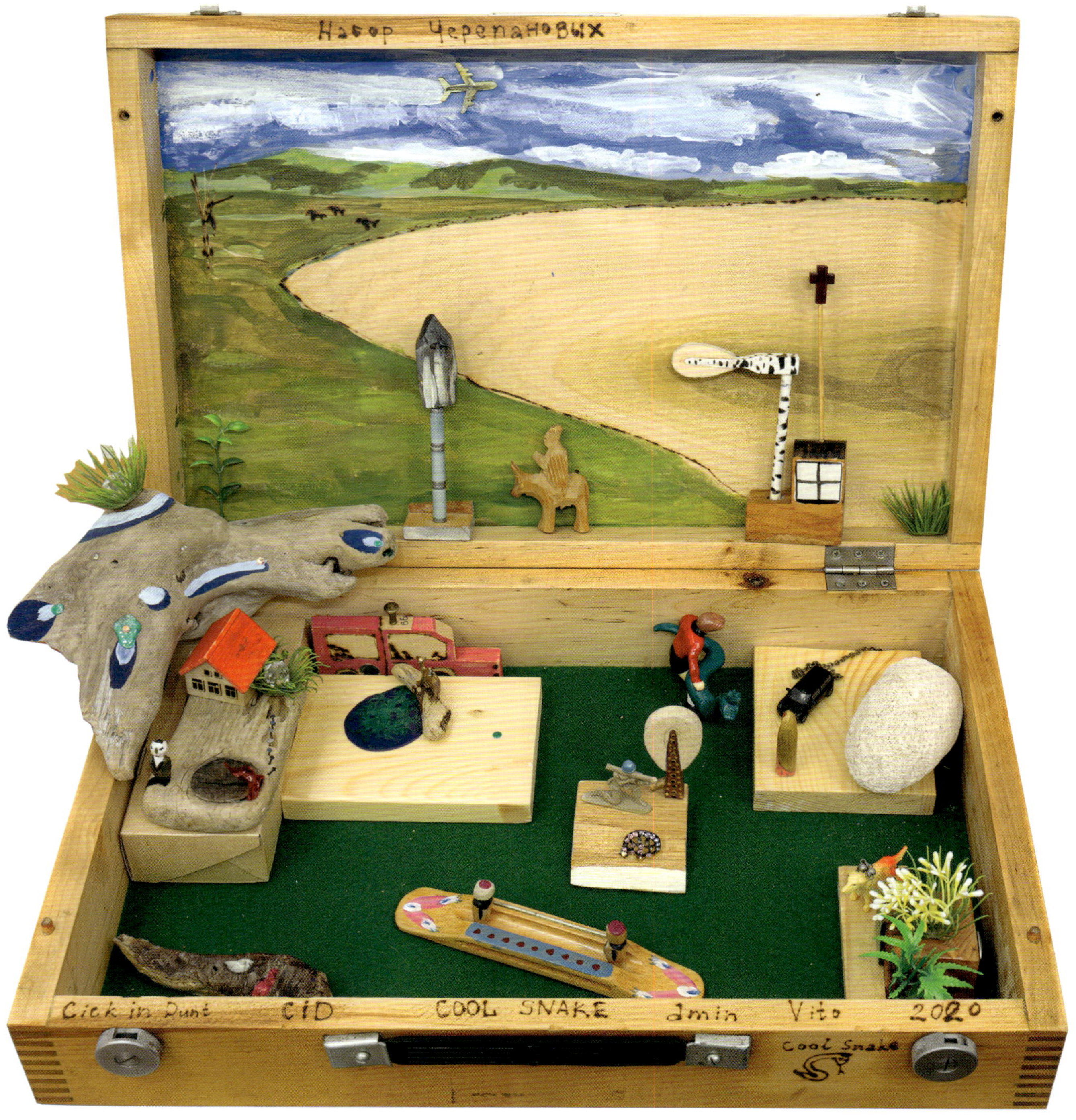

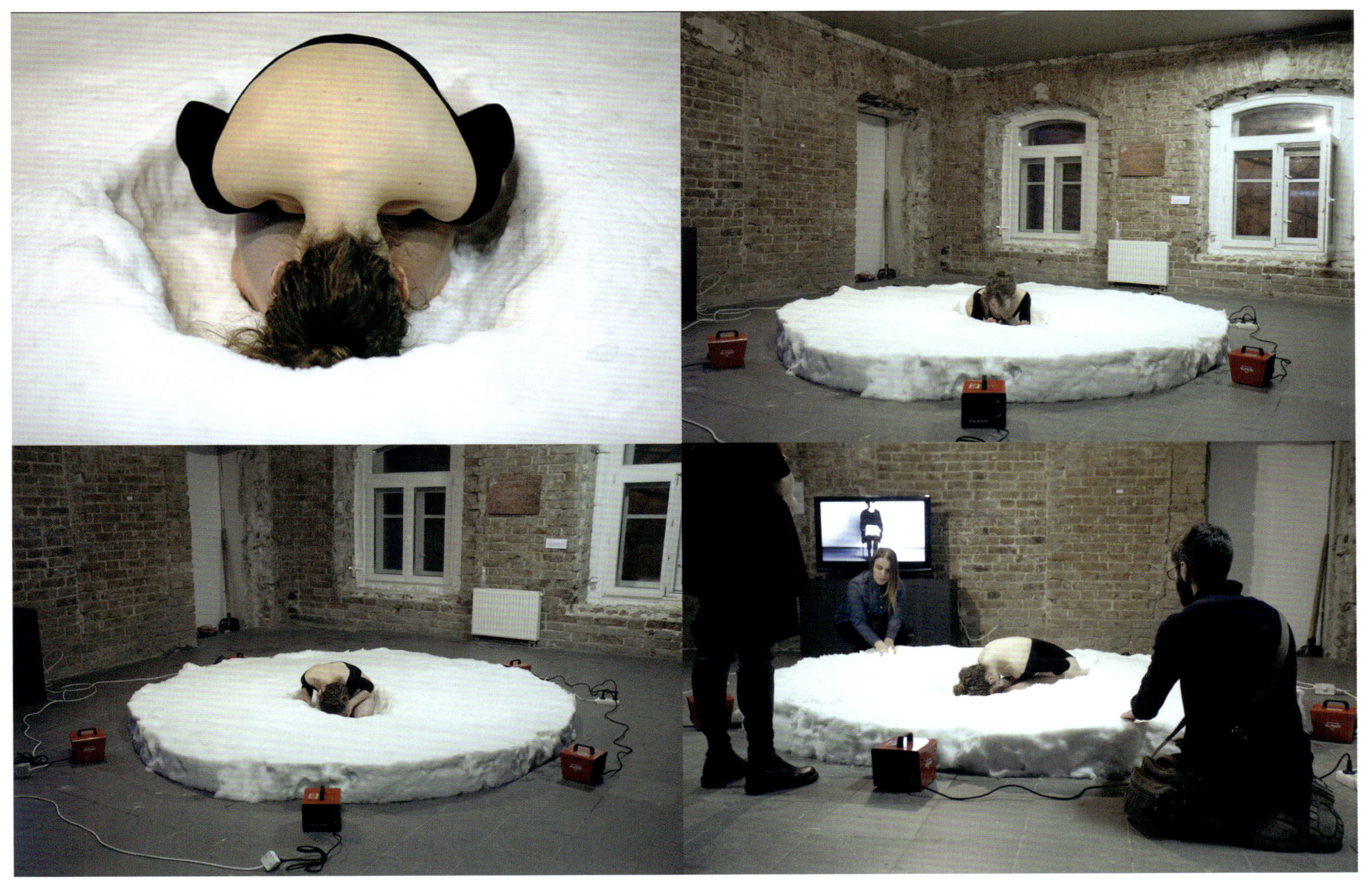

↑
Spirina, Svetlana
6 Hours of Melting Snow
2016, performance video still

Anna and Vitaly were the founders of the 'Life as Performance' (abbreviated ZhKP in Russian) art group and displayed their art at a disused former military base. They run *Action Dice*, an auction created by the artists and described as a work of art in itself.[7] The work shown here is one of the Cherepanovys' sets, a mini sculpture in the form of a toy created for private use.

To conclude is the video-performance piece, *Six Hours of Melting Snow* (2016), in which the artist, Svetlana Spirina (b. 1990), has immersed herself, partly naked, in a great disk of snow, which slowly melts around her crouching figure. " Each of the performances focuses on a separate topic: emptiness, memory, expectations, balance-and speaks about the interaction of the inner world of a person with the outside world, embodied in specific objects".[8] This kind of masochism is common in recent examples of European performance art. It recalls some of the work of Marina Abramovic.

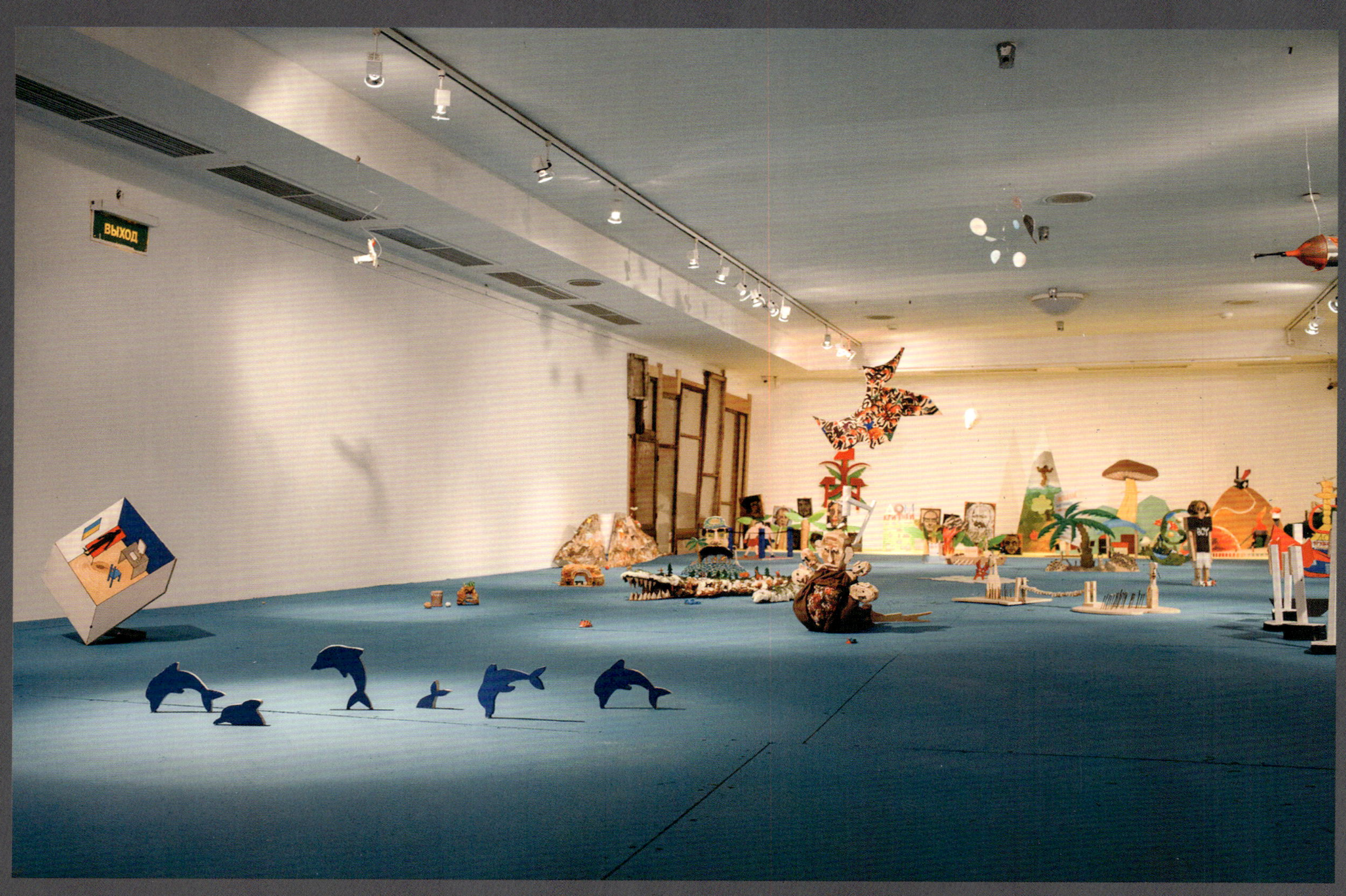
ВЫХОД

10 ACROSS THE COUNTRY

The artists featured here are from regions as diverse as southern Russia, the northern Caucasus, Siberia and the Far East. They illustrate the wide geographical range of contemporary Russian art, and also the tendency of younger artists to cluster together in groups, according to their geographical location.

Zip, a group of three street artists, Evgeny Rimkevich (b.1987), brothers Vasily Subbotin (b.1991) and Stepan Subbotin (b.1987), was formed in 2009 and is based in Krasnodar in southern Russia. They have been seen very widely in Russia, but also in Amsterdam, Buenos Aires, Kyiv, Tromso (Norway), and Almaty in Kazakhstan. They often choose to work informally, outdoors. A 2017 'intervention' (and a film) in Rijeka, Croatia, made in collaboration with local artists, saw them performing in a city square, on a makeshift wooden stage. A favourite protagonist is a performer dressed as a dolphin, and the text on the group website describes it as follows:

> This work is a translation from the theme of the city to identity as a social performance, which identifies a person (or Dolphin) as belonging to one collective or another: how you look, what clothes you wear, how you behave, how you cross the road, what gestures you use, what kind of talk you have, what kind of eye shape, skin colour – all of this constructs our image, which can be read as 'ours' or 'not ours'.[1]

←
Zip Art Group
Layout of Utopias
2017, part of installation, mixed media

Recycle Art Group was formed in Krasnodar in 2008. It consists of just two artists – Andrey Blokhin (b. 1985) and Georgy Kuznetsov (b. 1987). The group were the winners of the Kandinsky Prize in 2010 and participated four times at the Venice Biennale. A text published in connection with a show at the Pushkin Museum in Moscow in 2017 describes their artistic technique:

The Recycle Group artists play a unique game with visitors by placing their objects and sculptures in the space of a classical museum. They offer works of art that visually resemble pieces of ancient artefacts but in reality are made of polyurethane and plastic. They are actually post-industrial waste, and at the same time a subtle reflection about the 'personal dimension' in the virtual reality age.

Relics of 'classical art' (or, at least, something that a modern viewer could interpret as an element of 'high culture') become part of the 'archaeology of the future'.[2]

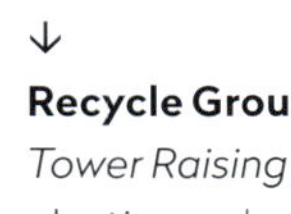

↓
Recycle Group
Tower Raising II
plastic mesh

The example of their work illustrated, *Tower Raising* (2014-2015), is impeccably classical in style but is made from plastic mesh.

33+1 is an art group that originated in Vladivostok in the Far East of the country in 2003, but whose influence has spread to other cities through exhibitions, performances and debates. It was created by Pavel Shugurov, born in 1978, comprising thirty-three fictional artists who supposedly lived or worked in Vladivostok. In reality, the group unites artists from all over the country. Pavel Shugurov was a Chief Artist of Vladivostok and said in a 2016 interview:

> The main thing is that our contemporary culture does exist!" The city is very creative – several exhibitions open weekly, musical groups present their material at various venues – a unique situation for cities with a million-plus population. There are many different artists here, including those working in their own style on the streets of the city. And the people themselves live here in a very interesting way. All this determines the urban culture, and if all this was properly administered, one could find some kind of exclusive 'Vladivostok cultural idea' ...to increase the synergistic nature of Vladivostok as a tourist attraction'.[3]

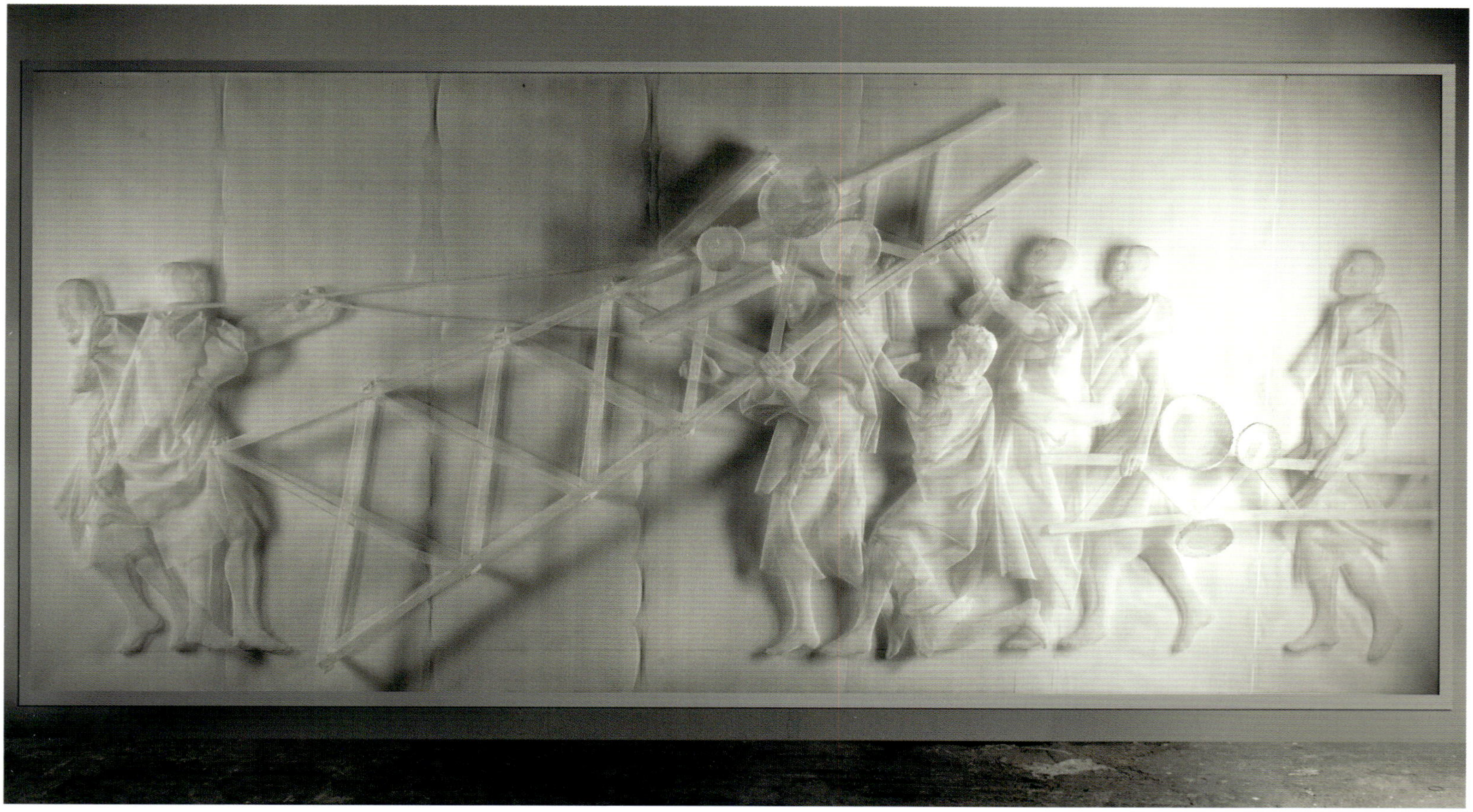

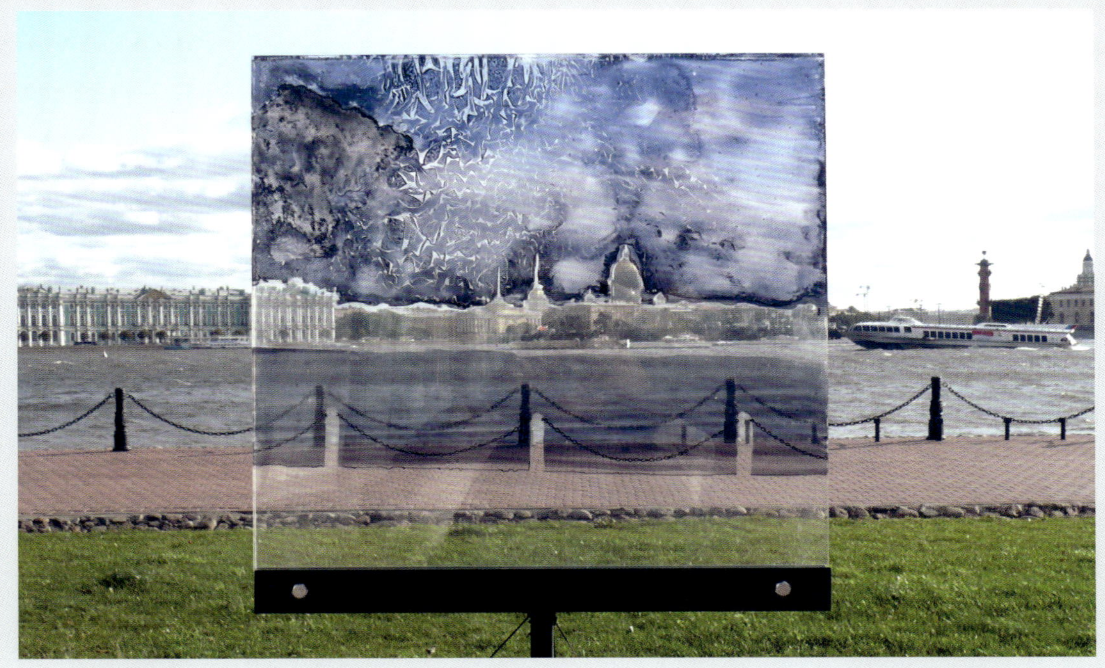

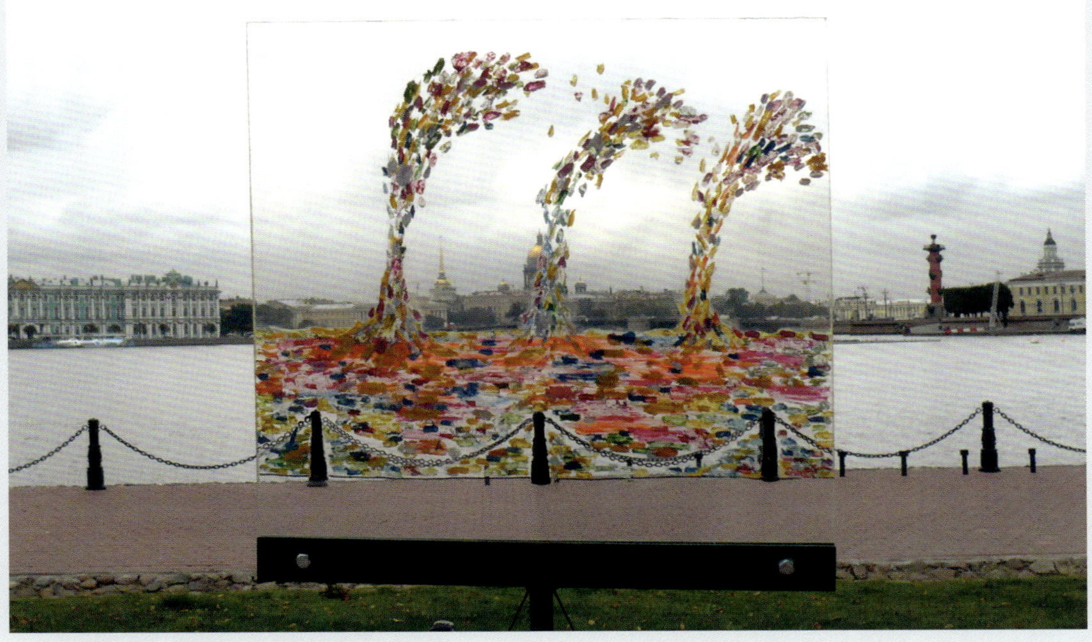

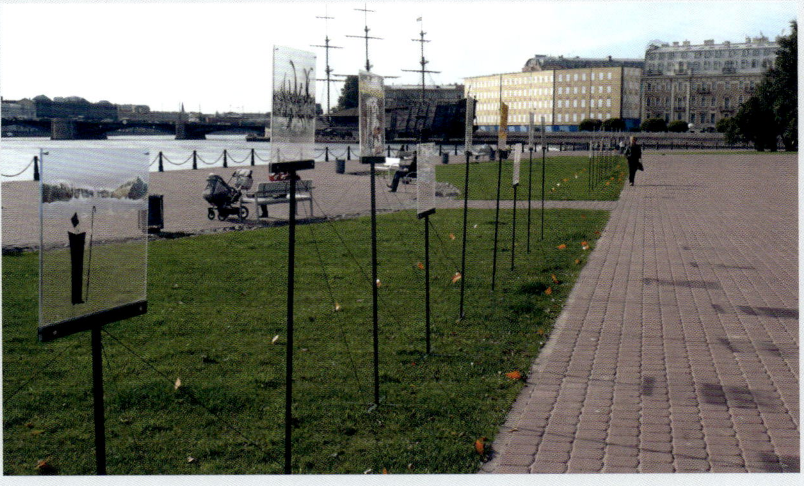

↗→
33+1 Art Community
The Stream
2008, part of the open-air installation, oil on plexiglass and metal

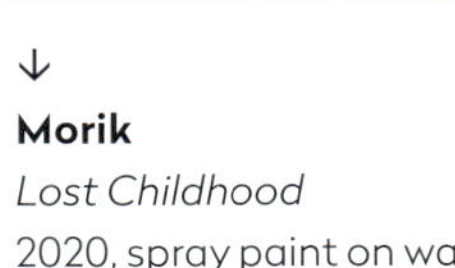

↓
Morik
Lost Childhood
2020, spray paint on wall

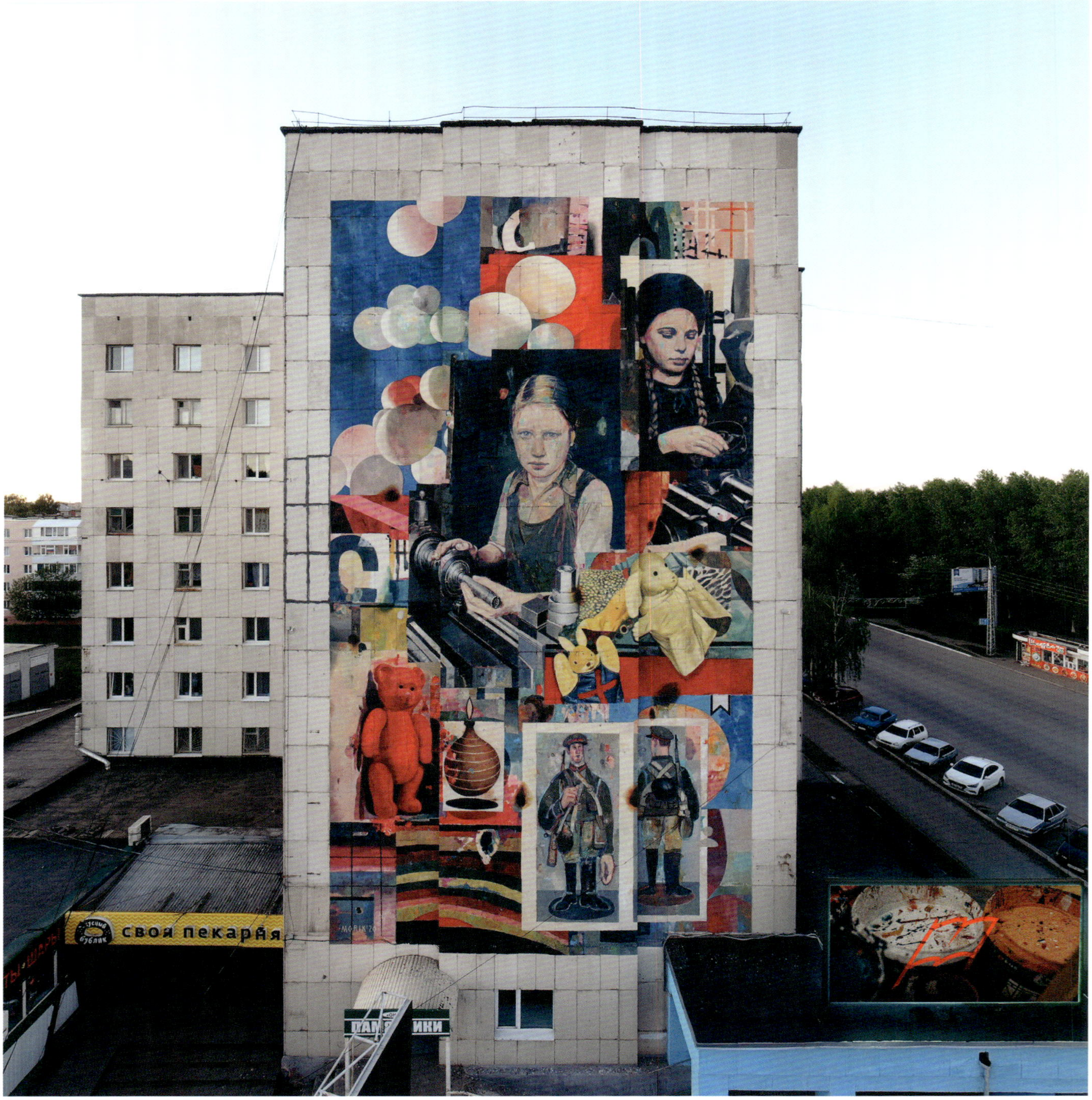

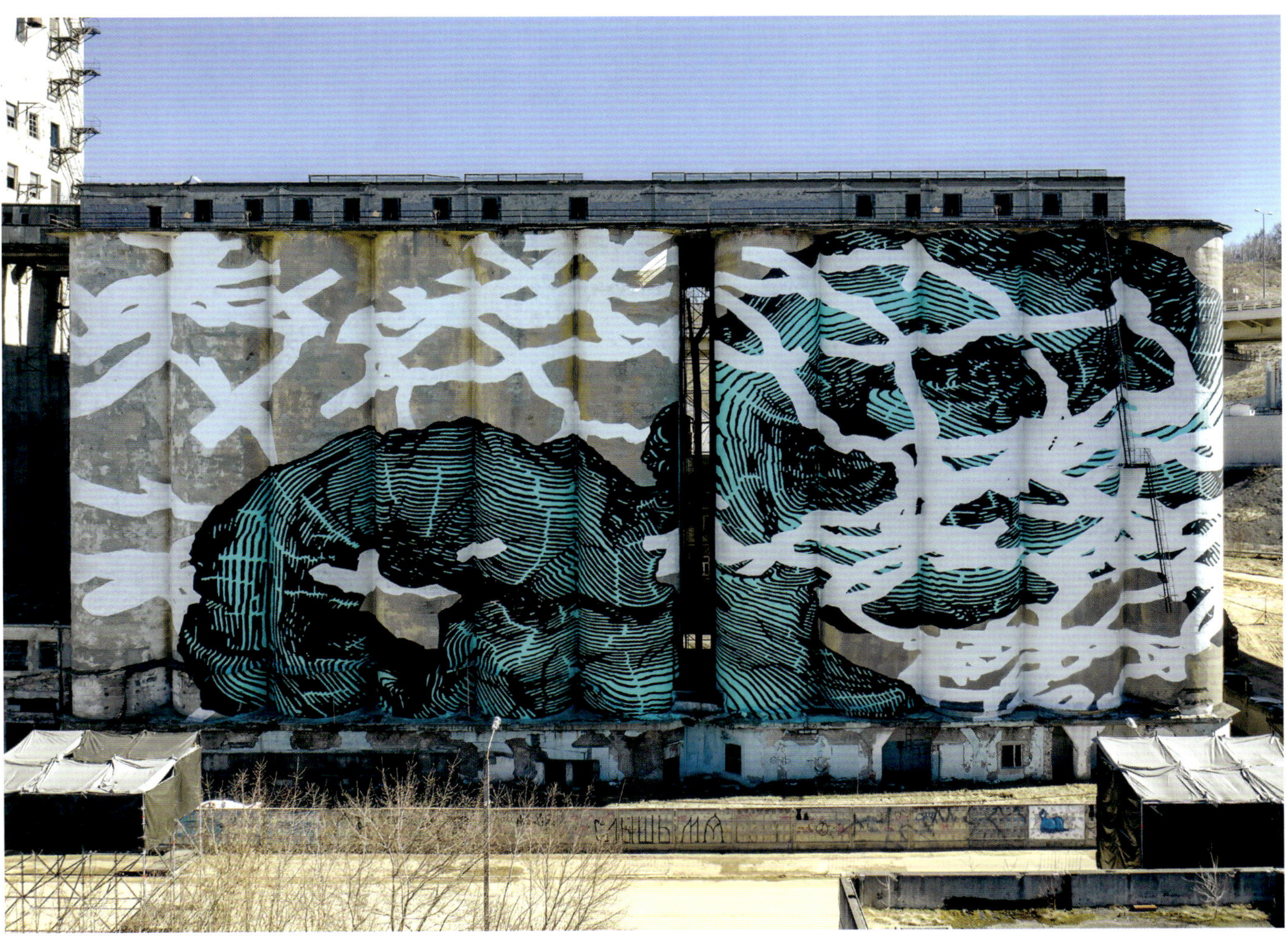

This is indicative, not only of the artistic situation in the Far East, but to some extent of Russian cultural attitudes in general. The Russian art world wishes to maintain a degree of cultural separateness.

Marat Danilyan ('Morik', b. 1986) and Andrey Berger ('Aber', b. 1985) from Novosibirsk in Siberia, became well known as the Morik & Aber duo in 2010 but went their own ways after a number of years together.

The mural by Morik illustrated was painted in Neftekamsk in the Republic of Bashkortostan as a commemorative project dedicated to the Second World War. Entitled *Lost Childhood*, it portrays girls having to abandon their toys and work in the war factories. They forsook their childhood and became adults to help their fathers win the war against the Nazis. It is noteworthy that this piece is a confident and unsolicited interpretation of the heroic past. Having abandoned the doctrinaire egalitarianism of the Soviet era, Russian public art retains a kind of nostalgia for large-scale gestures of this kind.

Andrey Berger is represented here by a painting on an abandoned flour mill created for the Intervals Street Art Festival, Nizhny Novgorod, in 2019. The mill stands on a high bank above the Oka River and the seemingly abstract image was, in fact, inspired by an old photograph of a fishing net taken in the middle of the last century. The work was saved as a video-installation after the mill was demolished in 2020.

In 2021, Berger painted the pillars of the bridge over the Moscow Canal near the city of Dmitrov where a section of the first Moscow – St. Petersburg bicycle route will pass under it along the Canal.[4]

↑
Berger, Andrey
Nets and Grids
2019, spray paint on wall

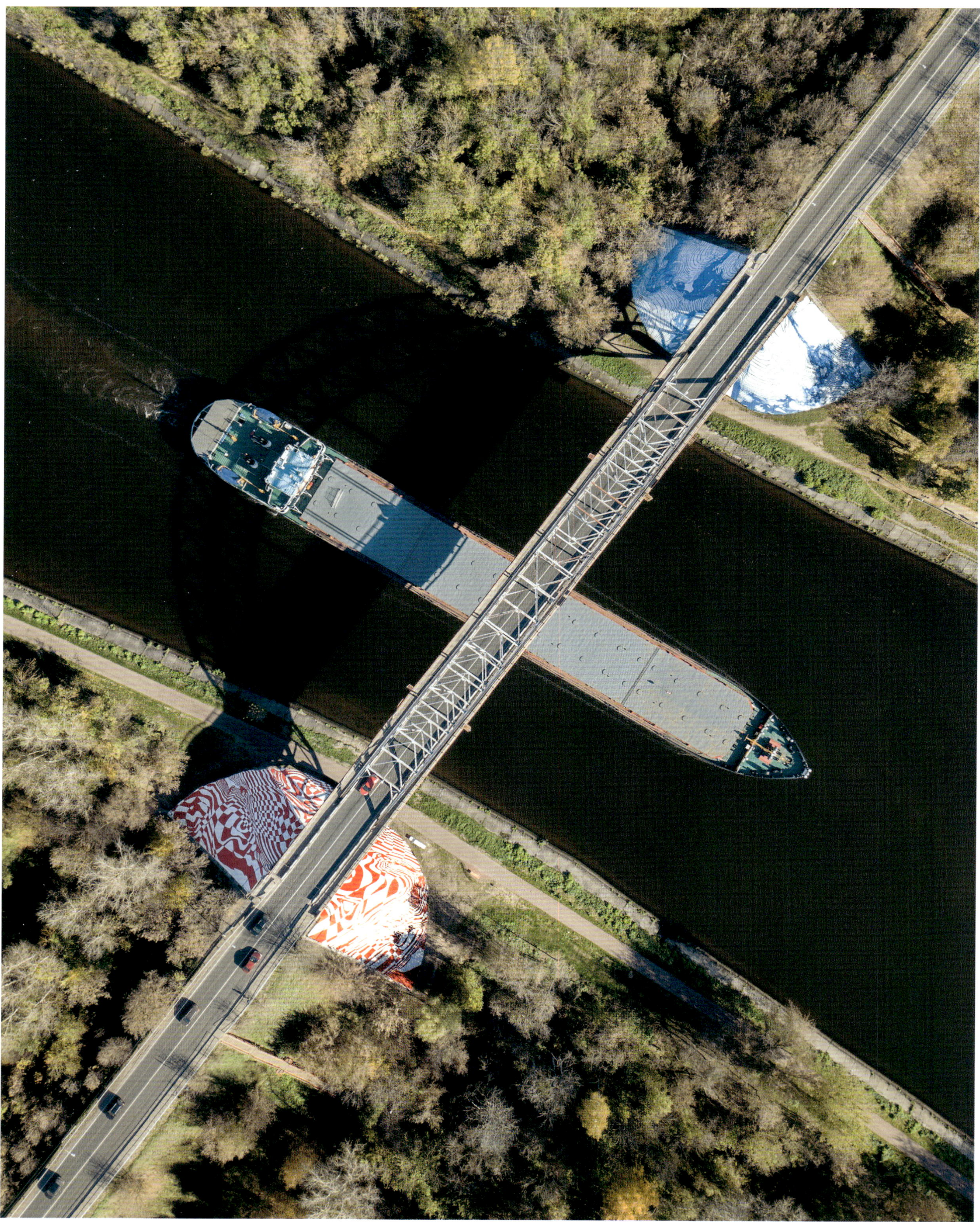

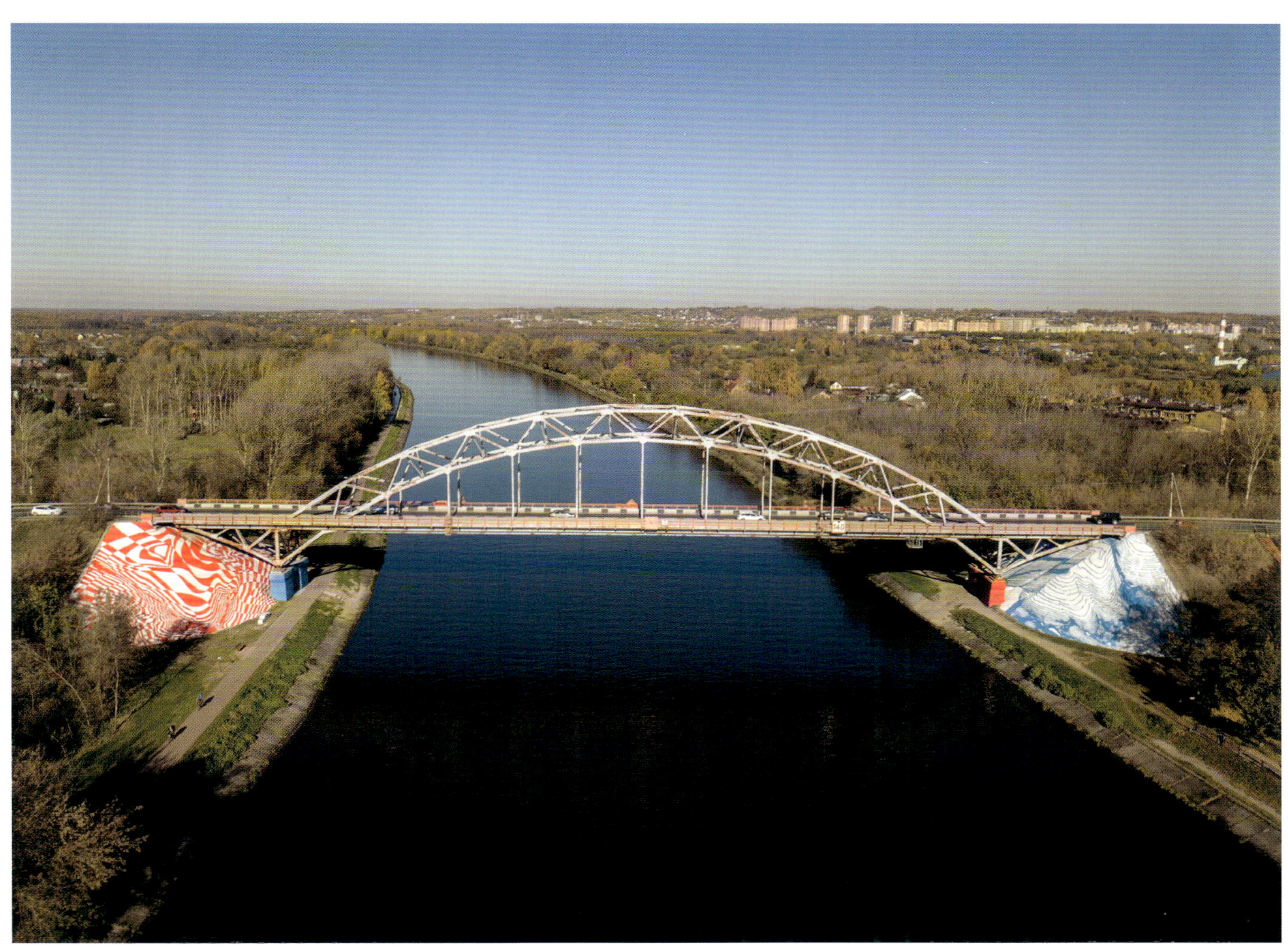

←
Berger, Andrey
Painted Pillars of the Rogachevsky bridge
2021, view of the bridge from above, the surface of the support, spray paint

↑
Berger, Andrey
Painted Pillars of the Rogachevsky Bridge
2021, overview of the bridge, the surface of the support, aerosol paint

According to the artist, the pillar on the Moscow side of the river was painted in dynamic white-red colours symbolizing its fast, intense rhythm while the pillar on the Saint-Petersburg side has smooth white-blue lines referring to the lyrical dimension of the city, its white nights and legendary canals.

In contrast to this, the still from *I Believe in One*, an on-going project by Anna Kabisova (b. 1984) and her husband Yevgeny Ivanov (b. 1983), transports you into a very different world, one intimately concerned with the cultural and religious past and present of the Caucasus. Kabisova graduated from the Rodchenko School of Photography and Multimedia in Moscow and returned with her husband and their daughter to Vladikavkaz, the capital of the Republic of North Ossetia-Alania, situated on the Terek river in the northern Caucasus. She is interested in the national tradition and ethnic identity of local people, how they realise themselves and how their cultural codes are revealed.[5] Kabisova and Ivanov presented their project at the Triennial of Russian Contemporary Art in Moscow in 2017.

Pavel Pletnev (b. 1981) comes from Omsk, once the military headquarters of the Siberian Cossacks during the time of the Russian Empire and which enjoyed huge industrial growth during and immediately after the Second World War. It is now a major centre for the petrochemical industry, and for the manufacture of synthetic rubber. It also produces agricultural machinery and both cotton and woollen textiles. The current population is a little more than one million people.

Pletnev's career began at the end of the 1990s as a graffiti artist, and his work is permanently on

→
Abishev, Marat
The Two of Them, front view
2019, spray paint, wall

↘
Abishev, Marat
The Two of Them, rear view
2019, spray paint, wall

Kabisova, Anna
Untitled, I Believe in One Project
2016, silver Bromine printing, contact print

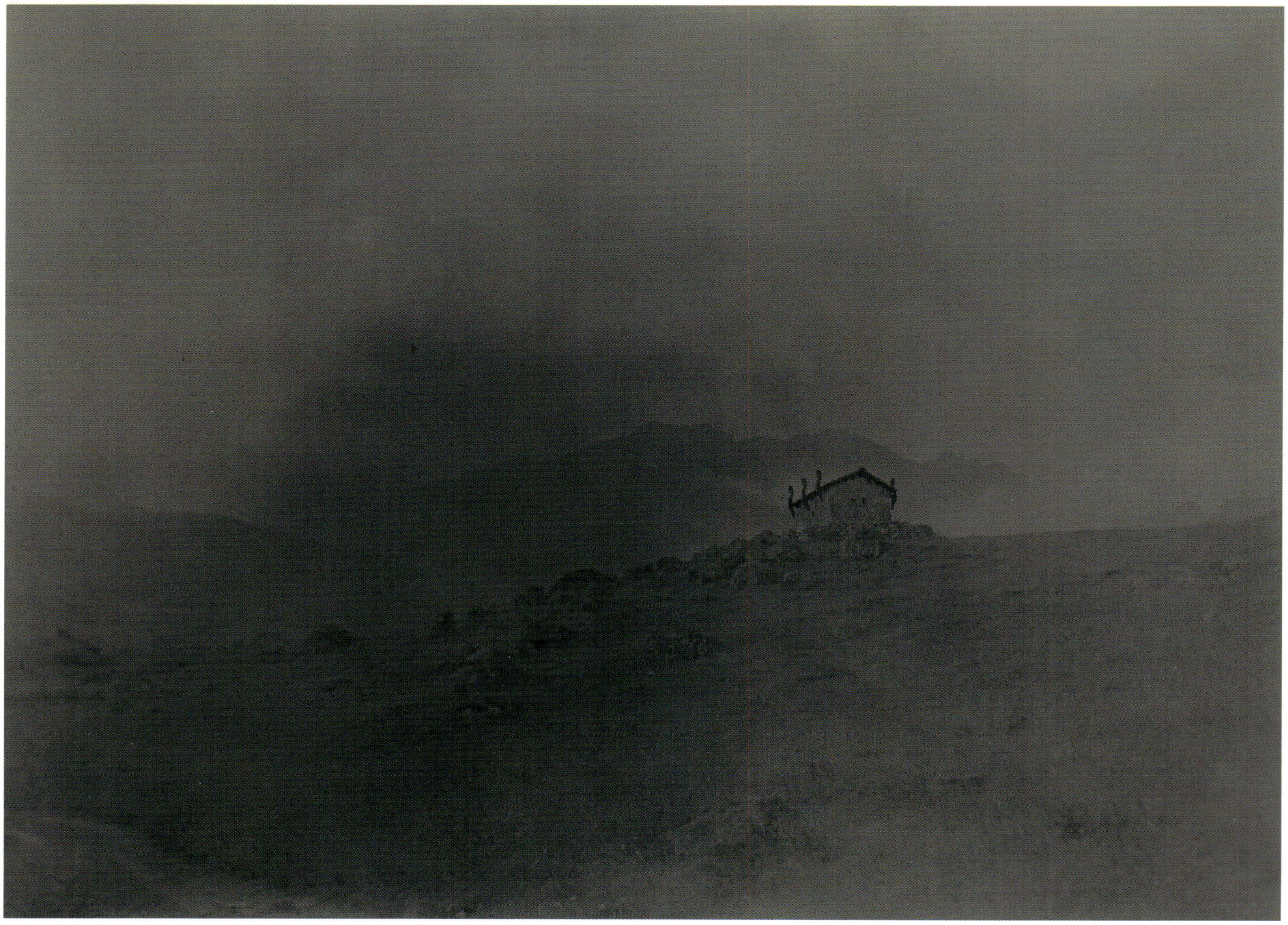

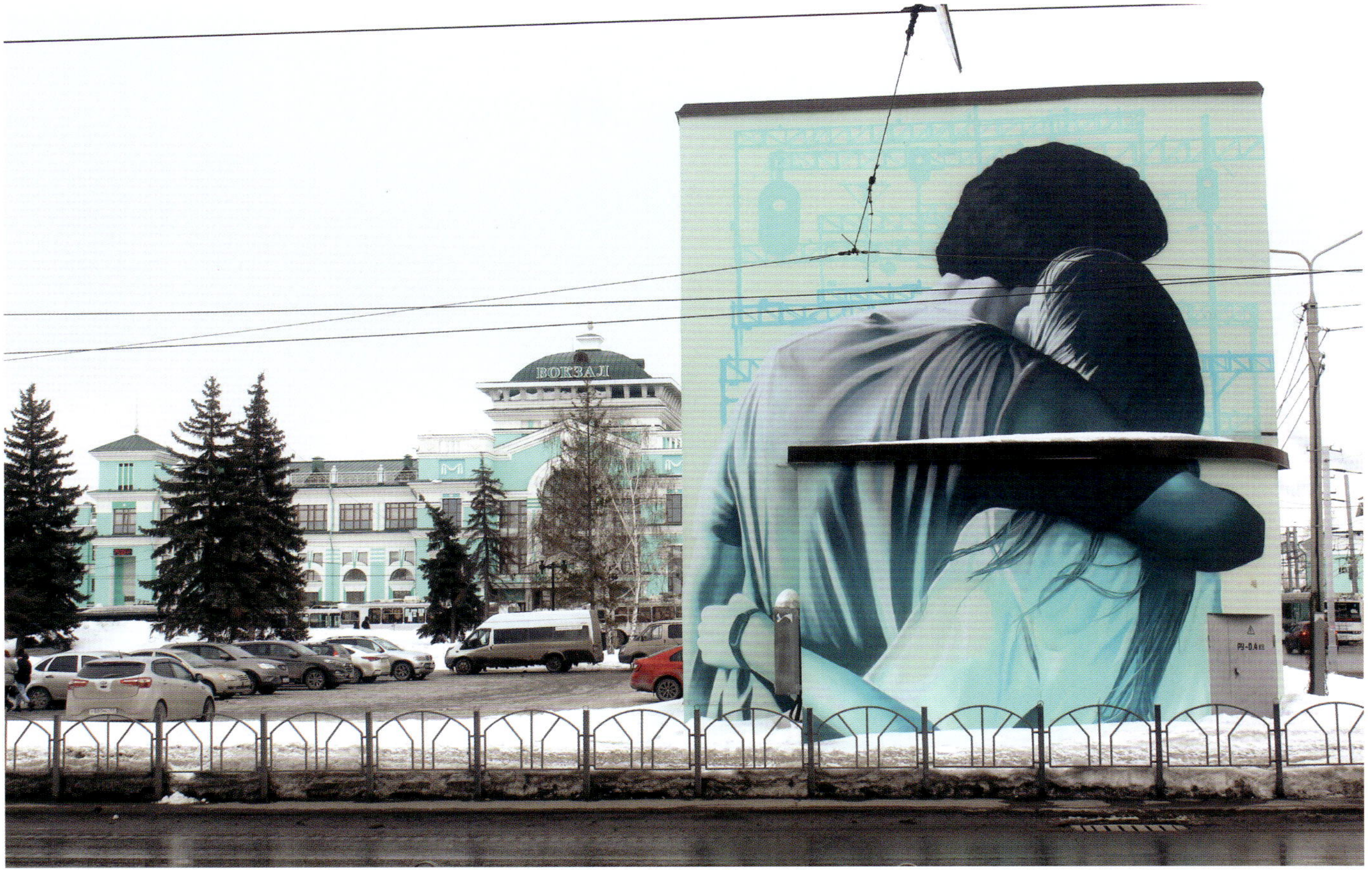

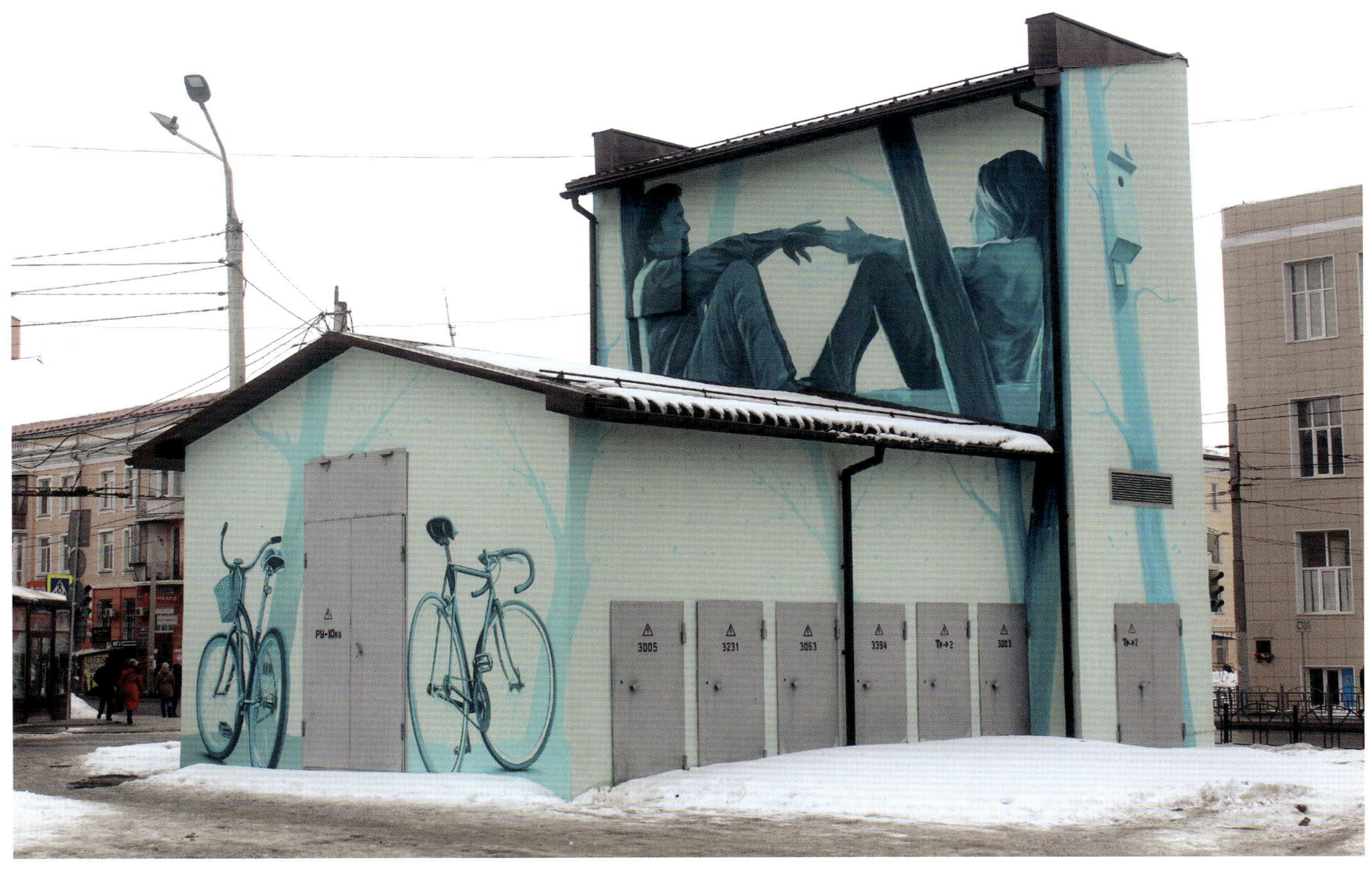
3005
3231
3063
3394

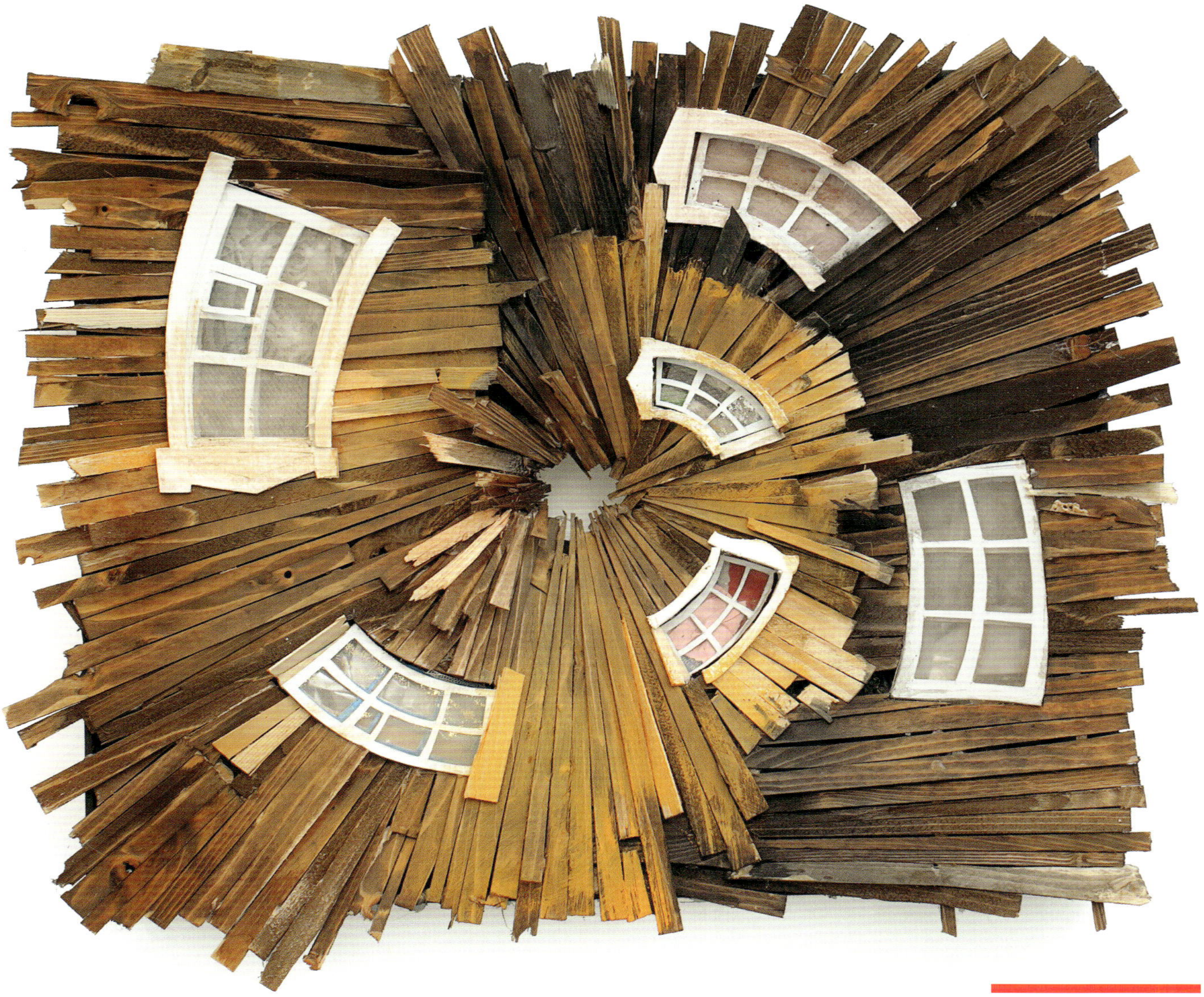

↑
Pletnev, Pavel
Funnel of Time
2021, mixed media on plywood

display at the Museum of Street Art in St Petersburg. He is currently both a mixed-media painter and a maker of three-dimensional works. His recent works *Funnel of Time* and *Acid House*, both from 2021, draw our attention to the chaotic rhythm of the cities and overwhelming urbanisation of our life, while at the same time representing a new and original take on the kind of quasi-realist Surrealism practised by Dali and Magritte.

Also, from Omsk is Marat Abishev (b. 1986), who is, like Pletnev, a maker of street art, and officially recognised as such. He was a participant, for example, in the Second Regional Festival of Omsk Street Art, which took place in 2019. He has noted on the internet that there is now often a clear distinction in Russia between street artworks blessed by regional authorities, and hit-and-run vandalism. 'Street art in many cities is used precisely for anti-vandalism purposes. One does not raise a hand to "put" something onto the worthwhile work of a colleague. We know all the graffiti artists, and they know us. If someone has marked a place, others do not come in – these are the unspoken rules.'[6] His large-scale romantic images occupy places reserved for major advertising images in Western societies, but perhaps survive for longer. Their very existence makes them a political statement, but they make no direct political statement in themselves.

Similarly, political statements are apparently absent from the impressive landscapes of the

Pletnev, Pavel
Acid House
2021, mixed media on plywood

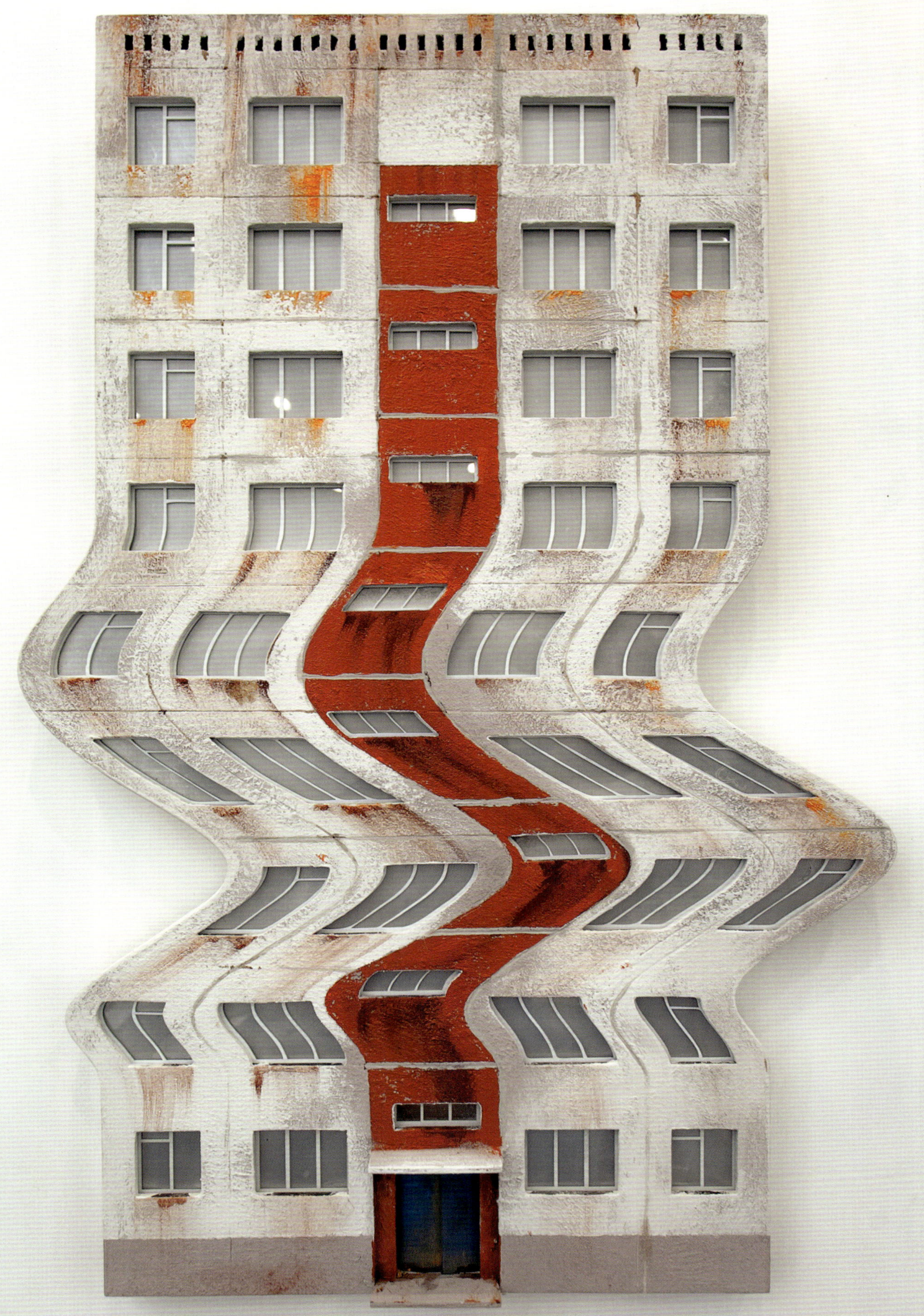

19

Kaliningrad photographer Anton Zabrodin (b. 1984). At a first glance the image illustrated, *Pine Trees on the Baltic Shore* (2020), expresses, purely and simply, a very Russian love of nature. That is, until you learn that it was part of a wider project about Bruno Taut, a renowned avant garde architect. Taut was born in the then-Prussian city of Königsberg (now Kaliningrad) and worked as an architect in Germany and Japan. This view of the Baltic Sea coast in Zacstrovie near Kaliningrad closely resembles the appearance of the coast in Akita prefecture in Japan, which Taut loved and used to visit when he lived in Japan in 1930. Both coasts, with their sandy beaches and pine trees, are still there but neither the old Königsberg nor the wooden Akita has survived. The former was completely destroyed during the Second World War, while the latter was wiped out by developers during Japan's 1960s property boom.[7] Zabrodin became a member of the Kaliningrad Union of Photo Artists after he took part in the *Irony as a Landscape* show at the Lumière Brothers Centre for Photography in Moscow in 2016.

Mayana Nasybullova (b. 1989) lives and works in Novosibirsk. One of her series embodies and

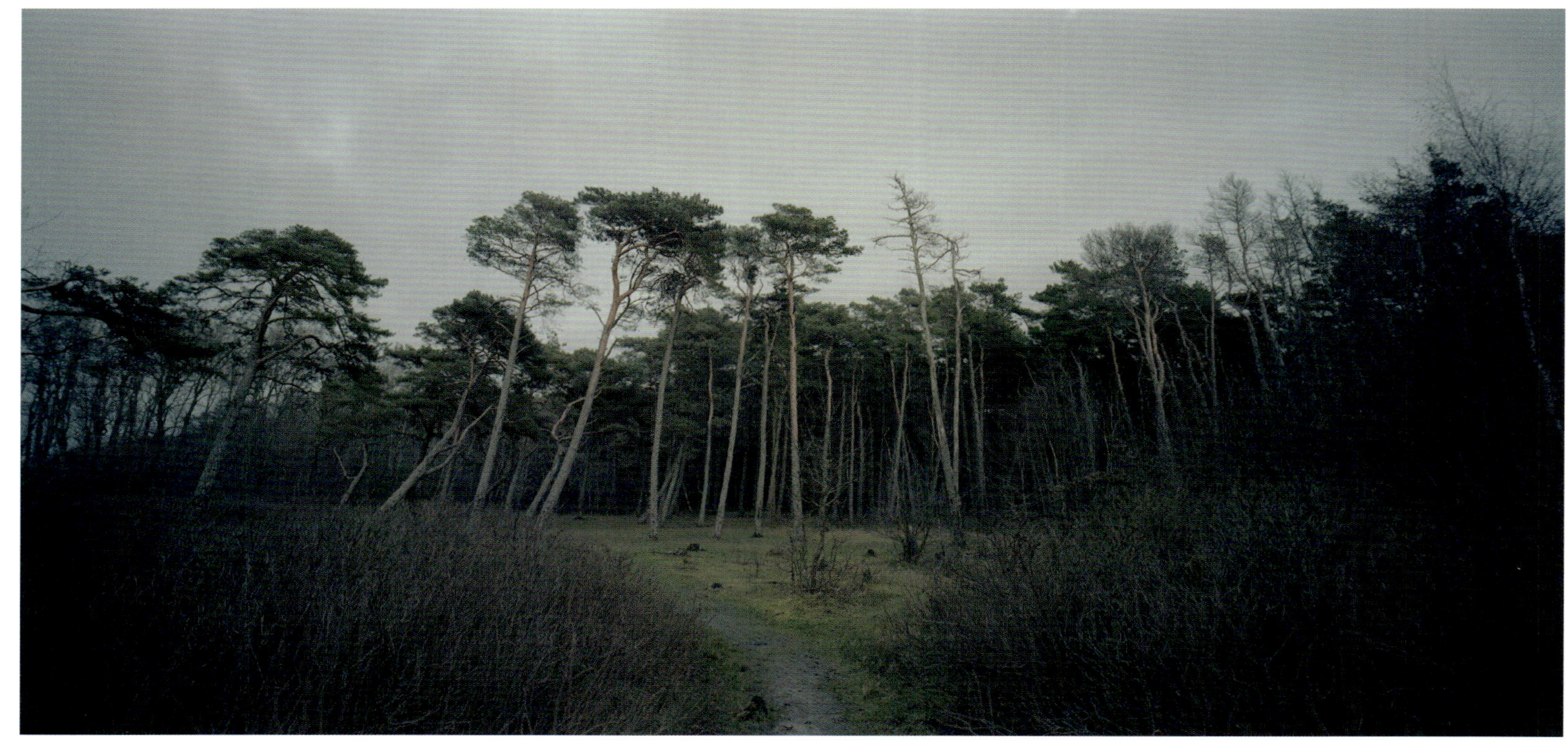

↑
Zabrodin, Anton
Untitled, Bruno Taut's Places Series
2020, colour photograph

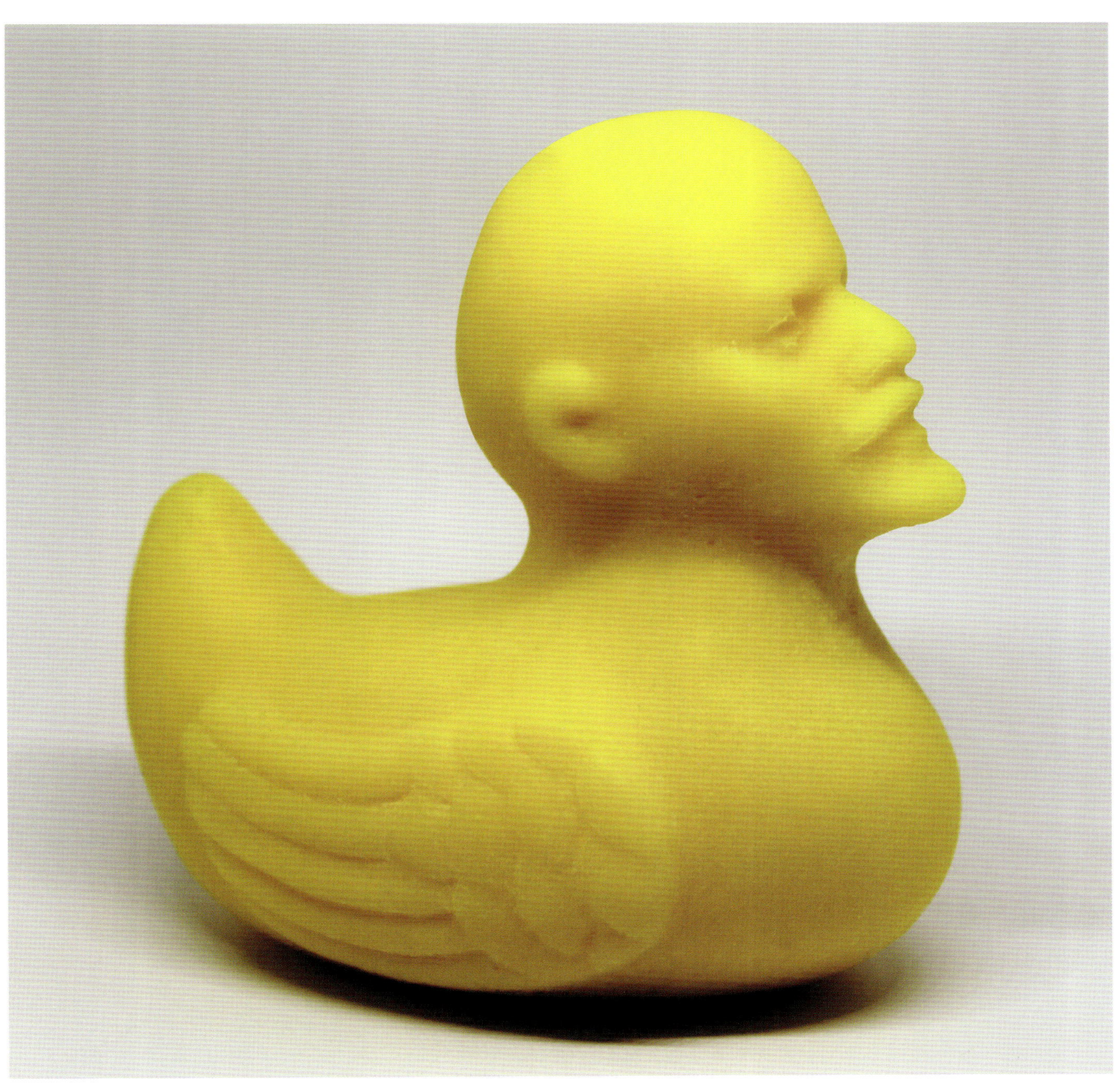

↑
Nasybullova, Mayana
Duckling Lenin, Lenin for the Soul Project
2016, acrylic, gypsum

satirises the Soviet cult of Lenin. In this example, Lenin is reincarnated as a rubber duck. In other items from the same series, *Lenin for the Soul*, (2015-2018) he appears as a roly-poly toy, a matryoshka doll and other well-known images. Another series, *Viva la Violence*, (2020) features torsos and body parts modelled realistically in gypsum and pierced with real knives.

In her online statement Mayana explains: "Viva la violence" is a sculptural manifesto, an aestheticization of violence — the dark companion of human history. This historical fact will not necessarily determine our future. With the growing popularity of video games and the increasing value of life, the level of violence is inevitably falling, despite our collective fears. One day, all the images of aggression and cruelty will be buried in works of art among the museum walls. Or maybe not".[8]

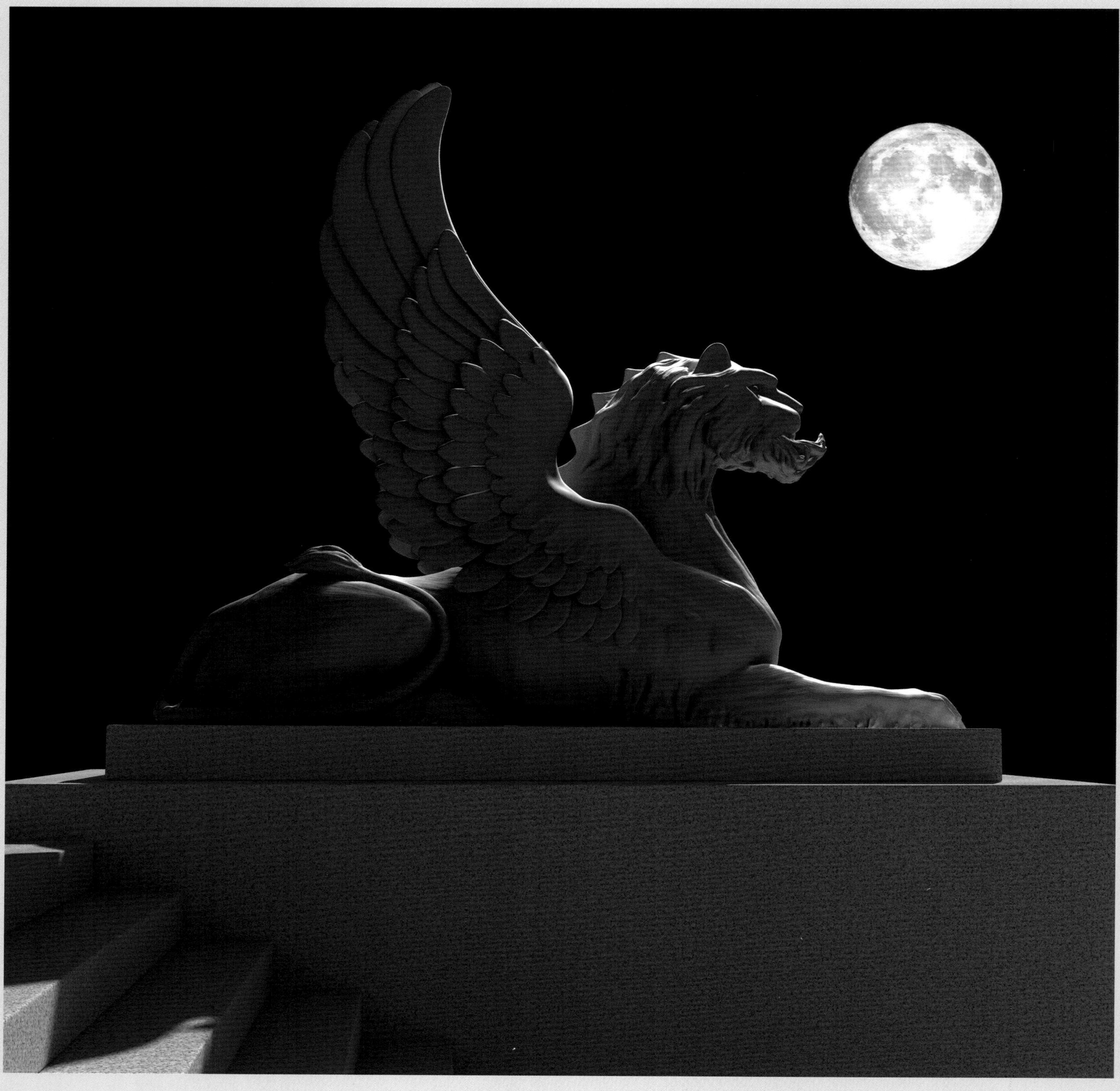

11 WOMEN'S ART

Olga Tobreluts (b. 1970) is one of the few Russian artists to have become well known in the West in recent decades. She was a relatively slow starter in the art world, she only began to be recognised in Russia in mid-1990s, under the influence of Timur Novikov (1958-2002). She is now a fully international artist and is exhibiting widely, both in Russia and elsewhere: in Hong Kong, Budapest, Berlin, Rome, Houston, Milan, Brussels and London. In Russia she was a pioneer in digital art, experimenting in abstract and figurative art, and also a member of the New Academism movement from 1994.[1]

Despite the fact that it is rooted in contemporary technology, her work is 'traditional' in the sense that it descends from a neo-classical tradition that has existed in Russia since the early nineteenth century. Examples shown here illustrate this link. Her other work is abstract and some of them are related to her experiments in digital art.

Another female artist from St Petersburg who waited even longer for world-wide recognition is Marina Alekseeva. Born in 1959, Alekseeva graduated from the Ceramics and Glass Department of the St Petersburg Stieglitz State Academy of Art and Design in 1984. Until 1994, the Academy carried the name of the sculptor Vera Mukhina (1889-1953), best known for her monumental sculptural group *Worker and Kolkhoz Woman*, one of the most famous monuments of Soviet art.

Alekseeva worked with different media and only began creating her 'Lifeboxes' – small boxes containing interiors of public places and private dwellings (*Two Rooms*, 2012) or recreating historic events (*Escape*, 2020, referring to Giacomo Casanova's famous escape from the Leads prison in Venice in 1756) against video-screen backgrounds – in the 2000s.[2] They brought her almost instant national and international success. Her work exists in many public and private collections including the State Russian Museum in St Petersburg, the Modern Art Museum and Multimedia Museum in Moscow, Fundacio Sorigue in Barcelona and the Sir Elton John Collection in the UK.

←
Tobreluts, Olga
Classic Walpurgis Night I
2010, vanish, digital printing on canvas

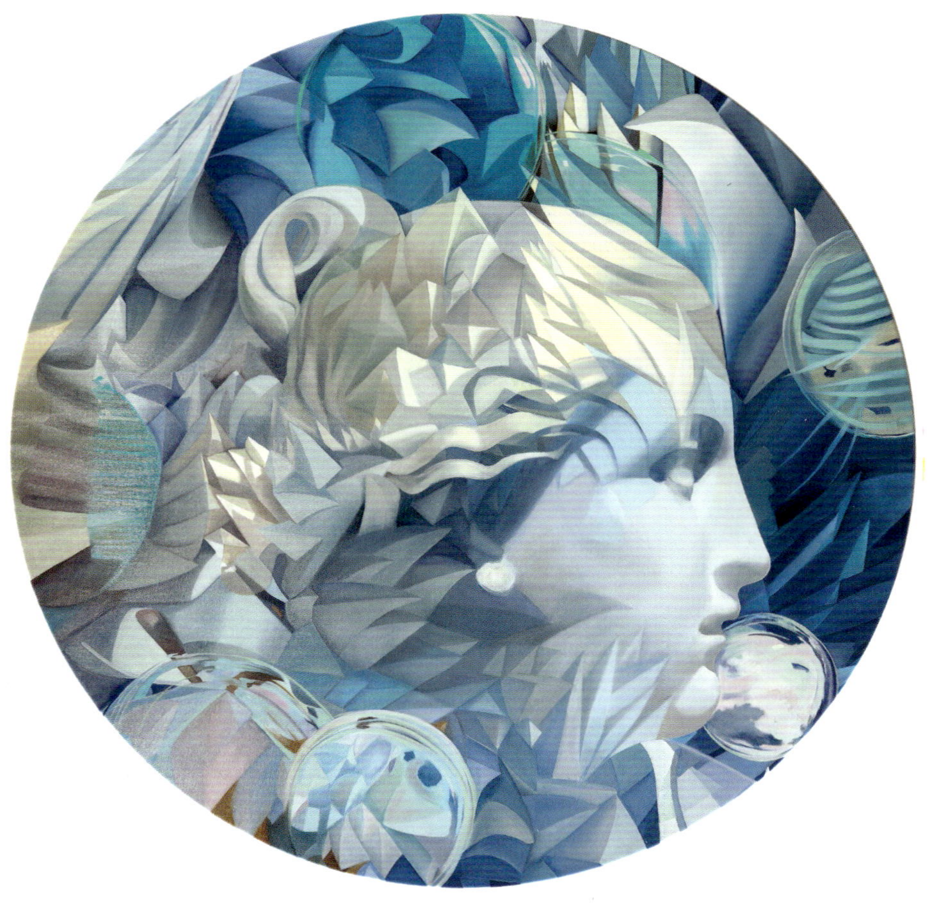

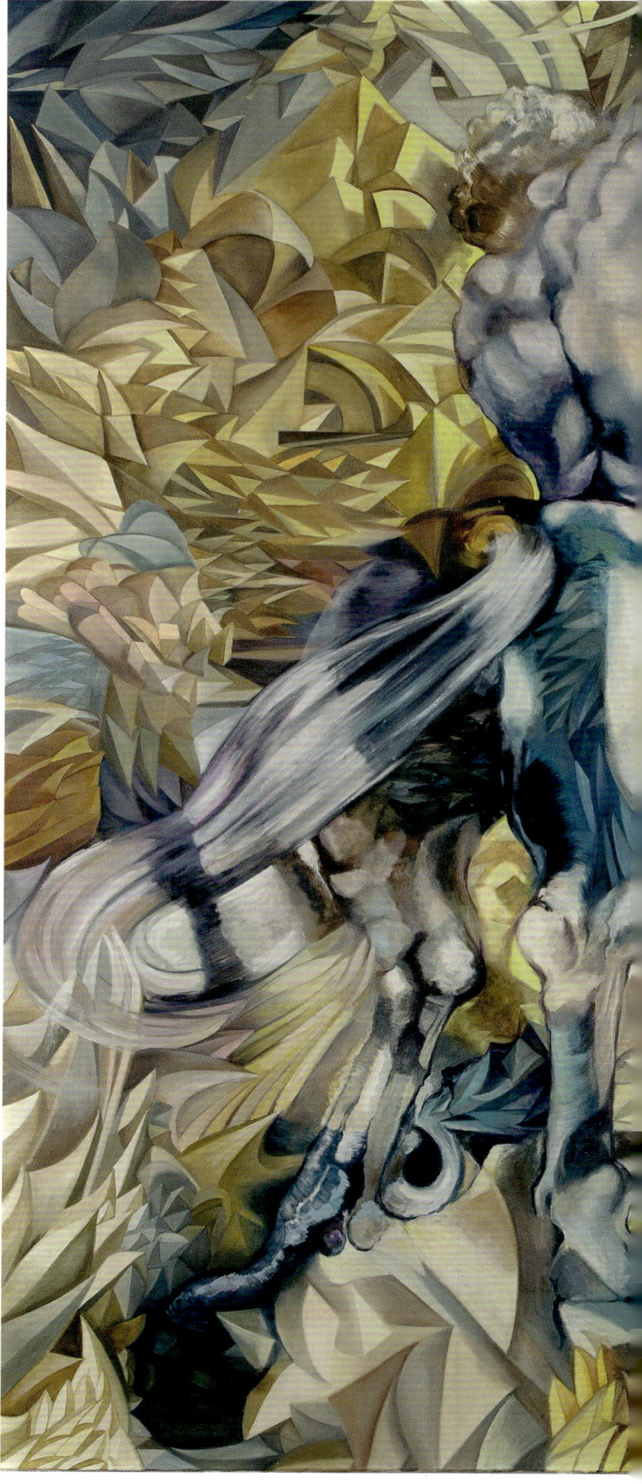

Tobreluts, Olga
Abduction
2021, oil on canvas

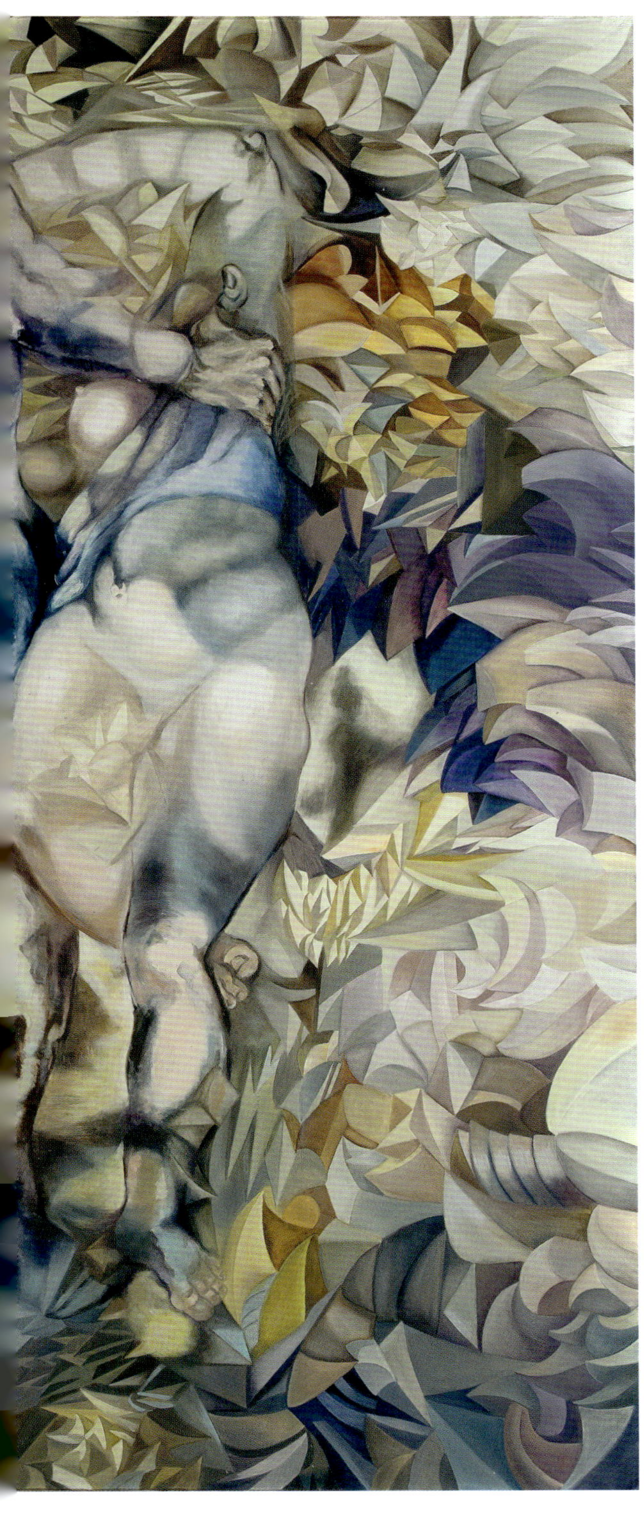

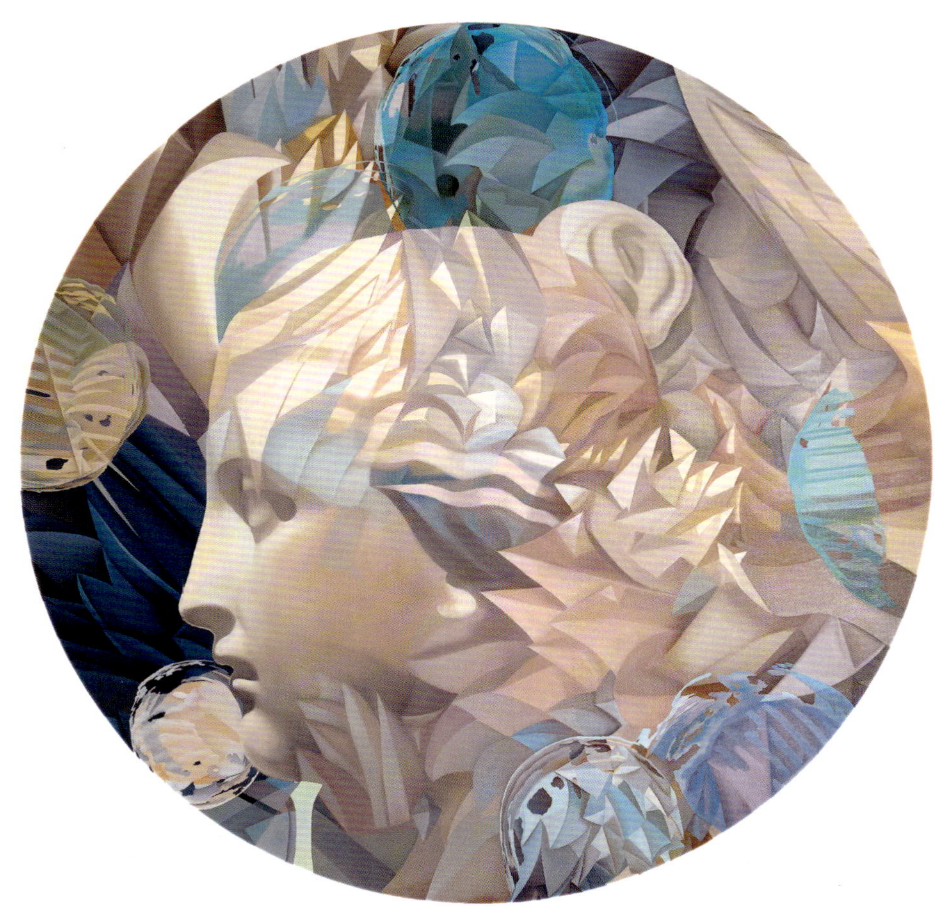

↓
Tobreluts, Olga
Transcoder
2019, oil on canvas

↘
Alekseeva, Marina
Escape
2020, mixed media, video

→
Alekseeva, Marina
Two Rooms
2012, mixed media. 1-channelled video, 2 interiors

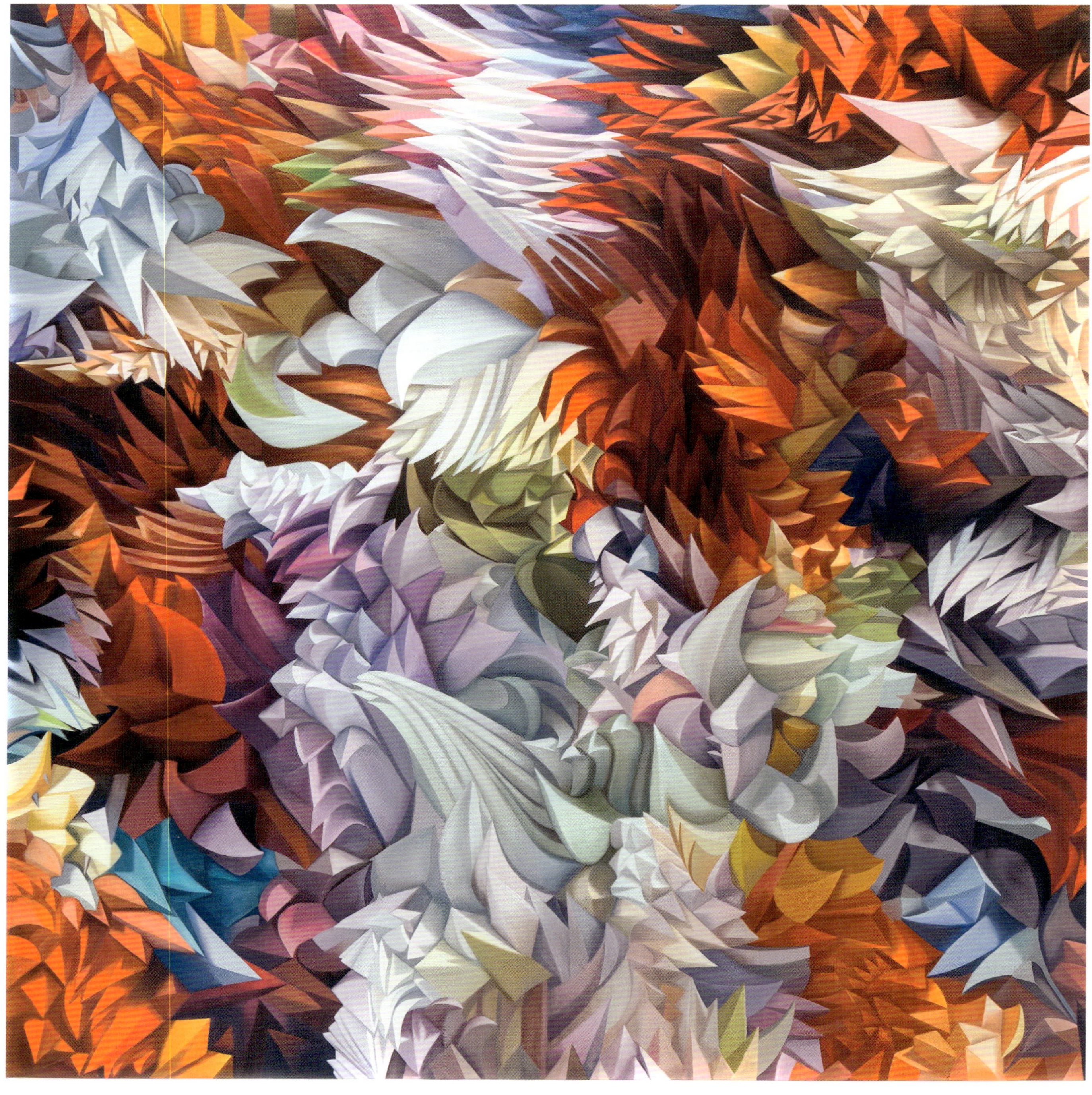

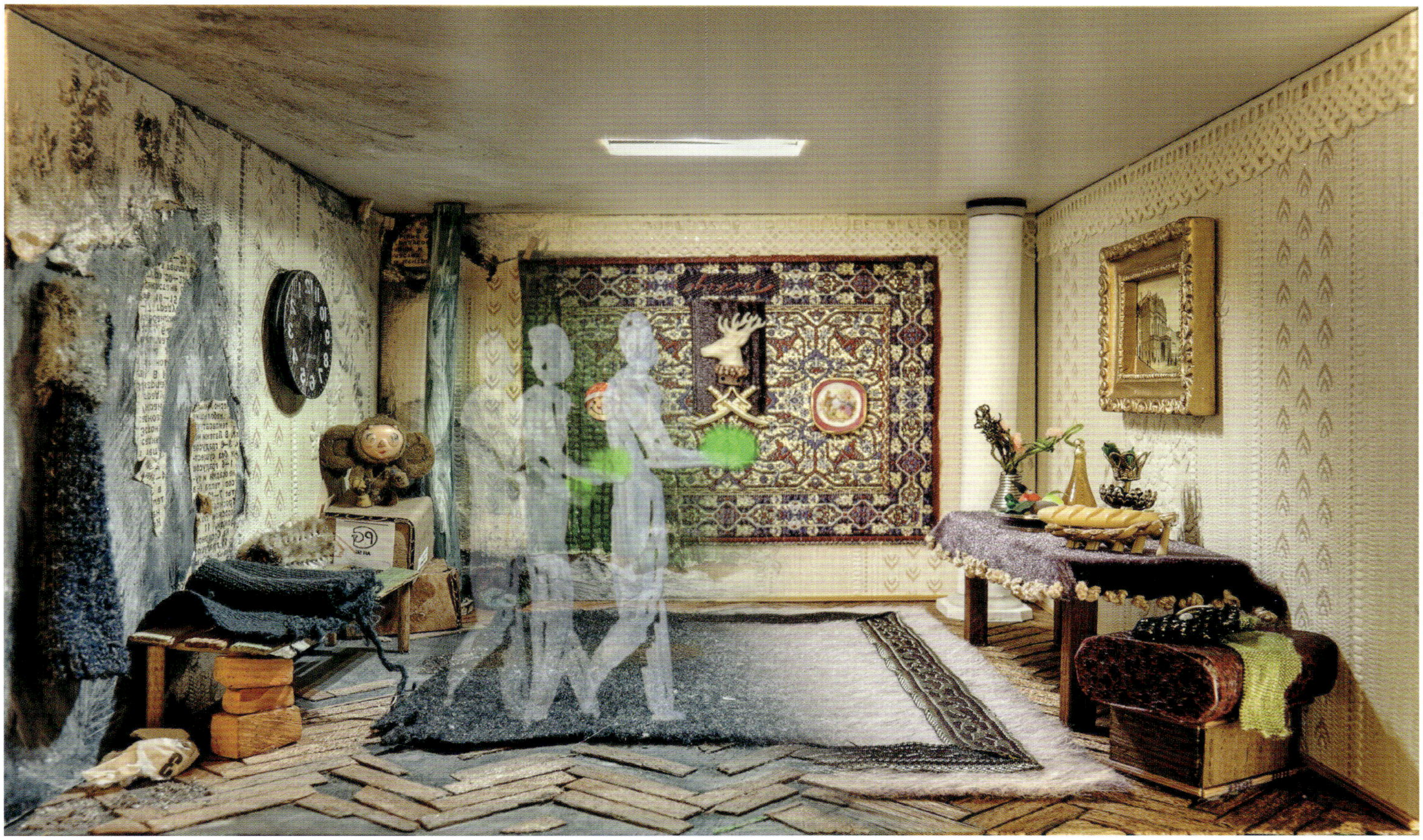

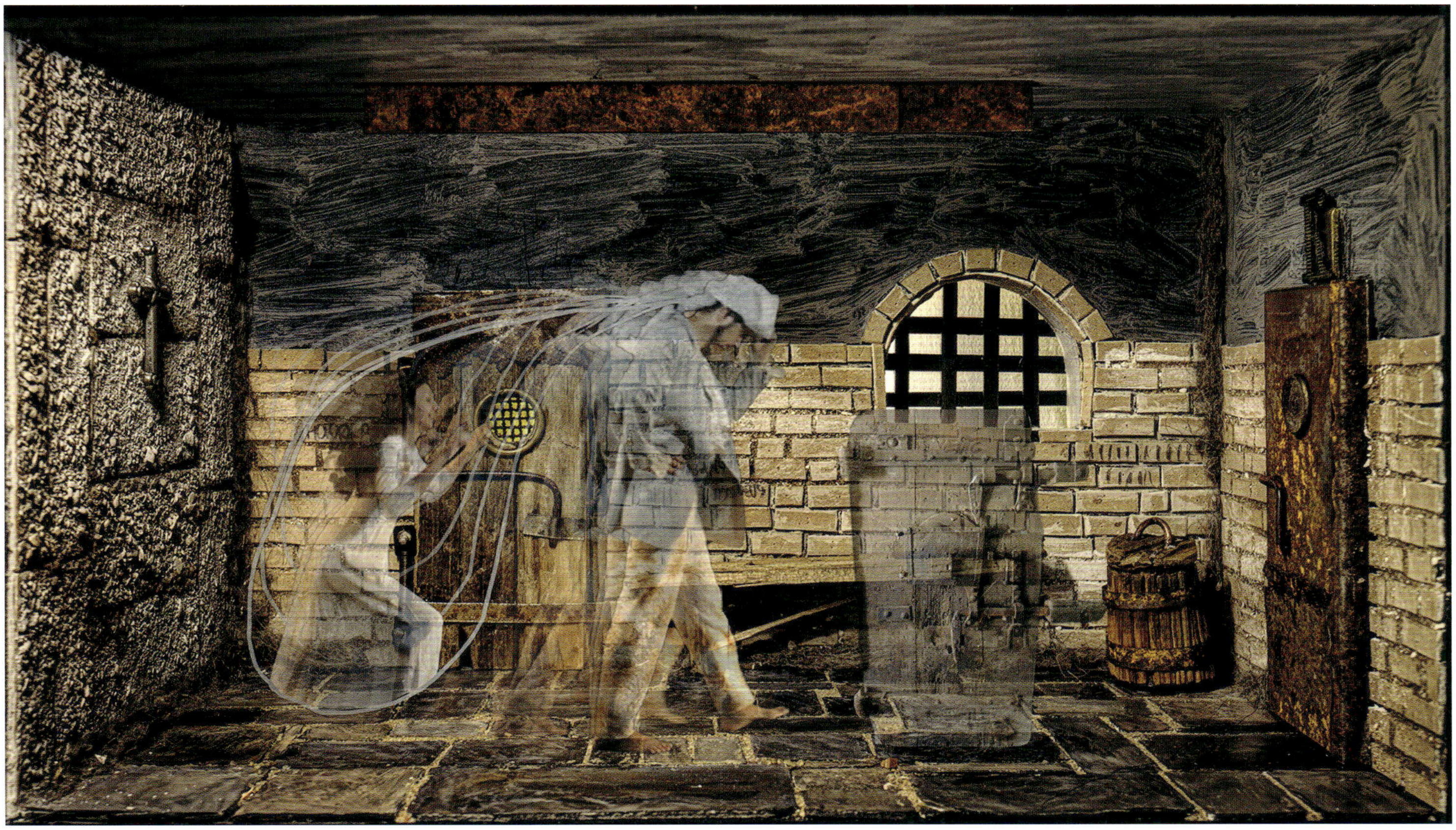

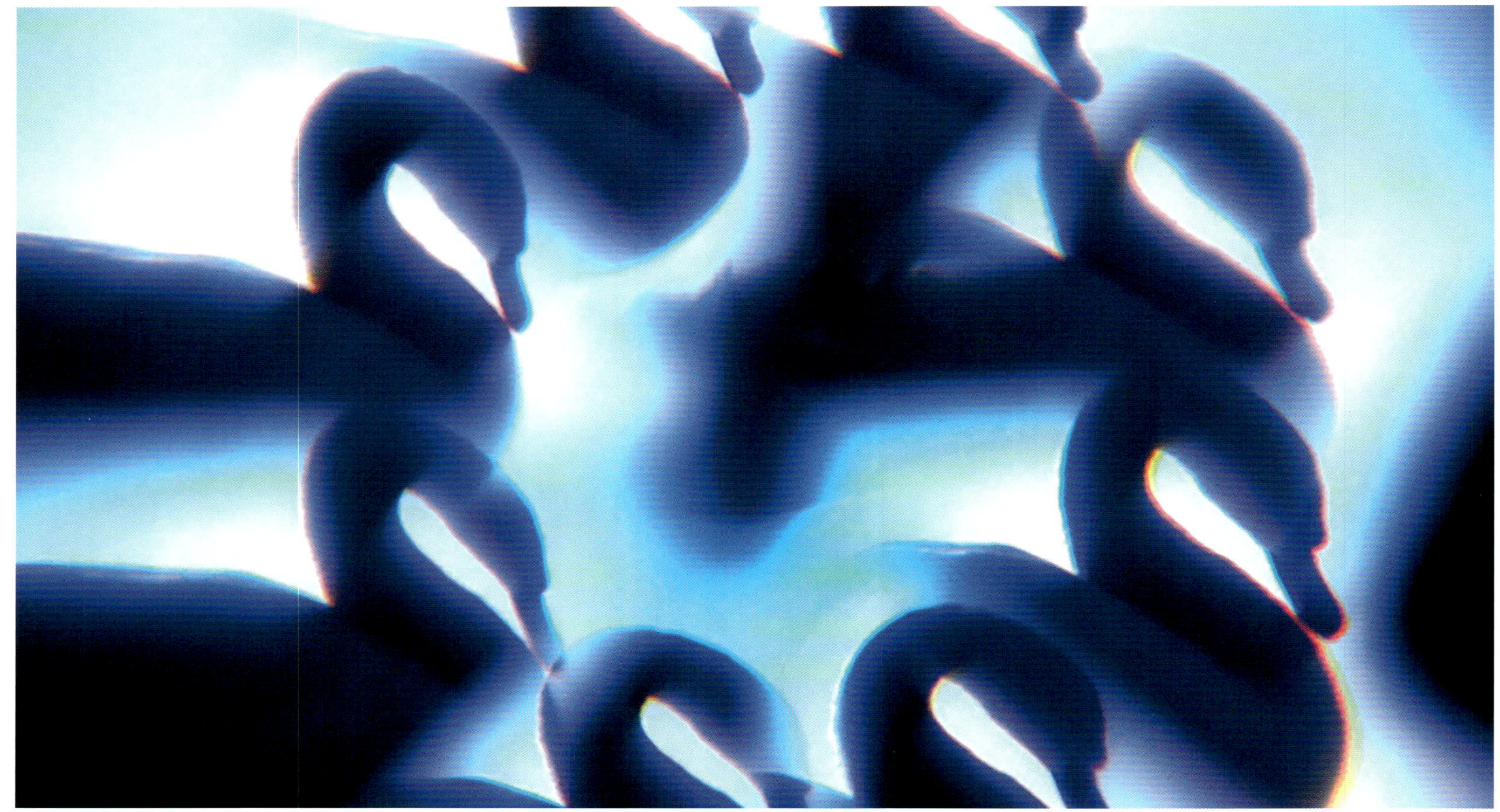

More directly involved in the world of textiles are two other female artists – Tatiana Akhmetgalieva (b. 1983) and Nadya Kosinskaya (b. 1981); both live in St Petersburg, but Akhmetgalieva also works in Moscow. She has produced art in a variety of different genres, often using thread as her primary material – unsurprisingly, as she studied at the Department of Artistic Textiles of the Stieglitz Academy's Faculty of Monumental and Decorative Art. She also works in the fields of graphics, installation and video and is represented here by a still from her *Love This Fiery Moments* video installation. Akhmetgalieva was a finalist for the Kandinsky Prize in 2010 and was awarded the Sergey Kuryokhin Contemporary Art Award twice in 2015 and 2016.

Nadya Kosinskaya graduated from the St Petersburg Roerich Art School in 2001 and the Faculty of Monumental and Decorative Painting of the St Petersburg Stieglitz State Academy of Art and Design in 2008. She is represented here by a piece called *Dress* (2019), made of nails fixed to plywood. She also paints, draws and uses thread to create both figurative and abstract works. The material is sometimes more loosely employed than in the item shown here.

↑
Akhmetgalieva, Tanya
Love These Fiery Moments
2016, video still

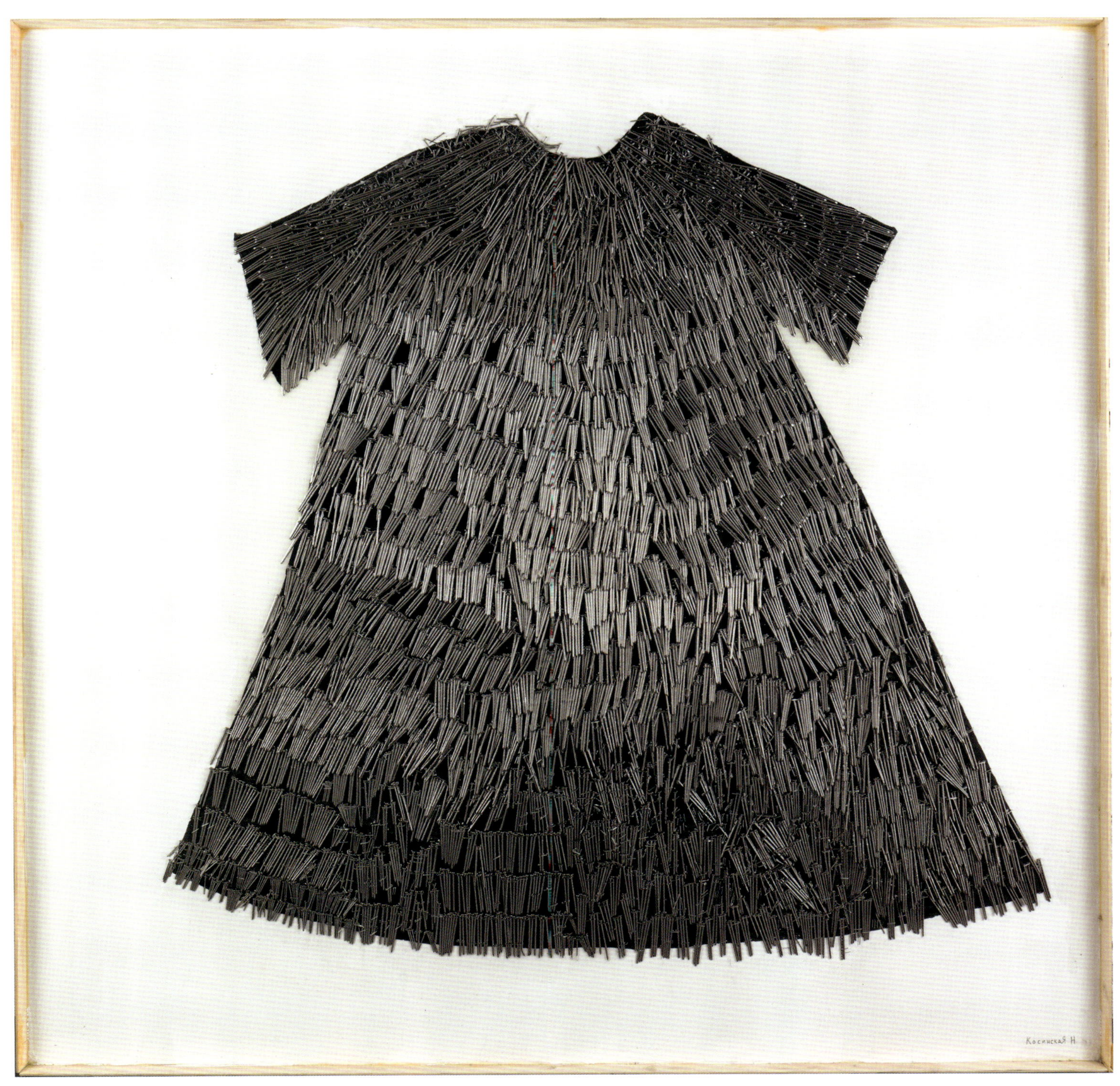

↑
Kosinskaya, Nadya
Dress
2019, acrylic, epoxy resin, staples, nails on plywood

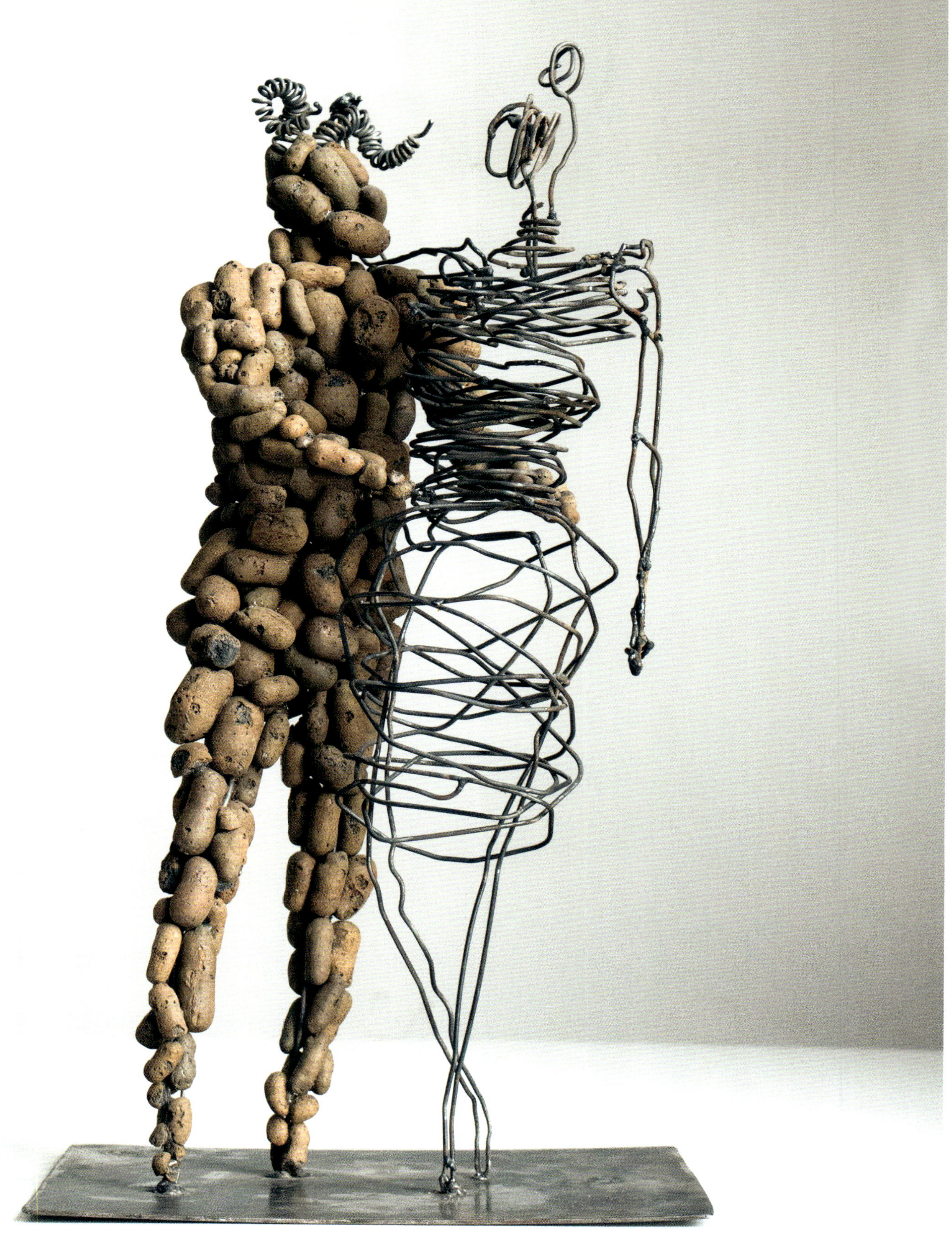

→
Dmitrieva, Marya
Rhizome
2014, acrylic, collage on canvas

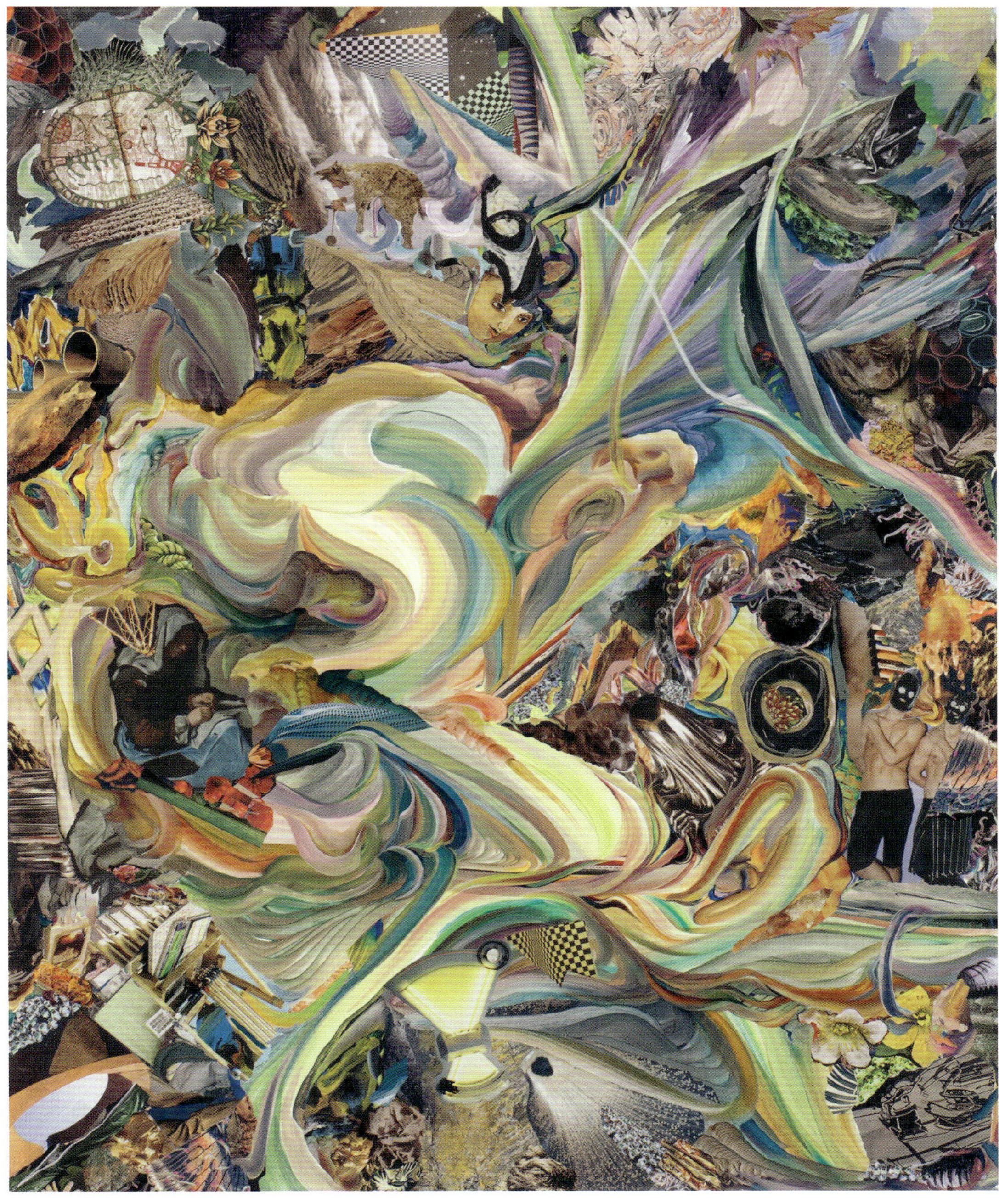

An inventive use of everyday materials can also be found in the sculptural work of Antonina Fathullina (b. 1982), who also lives and works in St Petersburg. Her work has been seen outside Russia, in the Canary Islands. The group of two figures illustrated here seems to have a certain kinship with the sculptures of Giacometti but is in no sense an imitation. One figure – a woman – is made of wire. The other figure – the man embracing her – is made of pebbles. Like other female artists in this section, Fathullina has a feeling for the creative possibilities offered by everyday materials.

Female painters in Russia employ a variety of styles. In her painting *Rhizome*, Marya Dmitrieva (b. 1983), who also works in St Petersburg, embraces a turbulent semi-abstract style. She is also a stage and cinema designer and a maker of installations. In her work as a painter she often uses collage. A website claims of her work that 'You can fall though the thin surface of the collage, like though a crust, into the crumbly quagmire of faceless time.'[3]

←
Fatkhullina, Antonina
Union of Air and Earth
2018, haydite, metal

Vika Begalska (b. 1975 in Dnipropetrovsk in Ukraine) lives in Moscow, where she has worked since 2000. She is a very active organiser in the Russian art world. In 2013 she founded the art platform Feminist Cuisine. In 2014 she founded an art group for sex workers. She was a nominee for the Kandinsky Prize in 2010. She has work displayed in the MAAC Foundation in Brussels, and in M HKA in Antwerp, as well as in the Moscow Museum of Contemporary Art and the Moscow National Centre for Contemporary Art. Her paintings, often in pale colours, embrace a wide variety of images. Often, as in *Girl with Raccoon* (2010), they are elegantly erotic, like the work of French eighteenth-century masters such as Fragonard.

They offer a marked contrast to the work of three other female artists included in this section, who similarly contrast with one another. Anya Zholud, born in Leningrad in 1981 but now living near Moscow, has work in a range of important Russian museums – the Hermitage Museum, the Museum of Nonconformist Art and the New Museum in St Petersburg, and also the Museum of Modern Art and the State Centre for Contemporary Art in Moscow. The wire sculpture shown here is not abstract, though it appears so at first sight. It is a simplified image of a candelabra. Zolud's painted images are also drastically simplified – for example, a flower in a vase, reduced to its very essence.

Taus Makhacheva (b. 1983) lives and works in Makhachkala, the capital of Dagestan and the fourth largest city in the Caucasus. Only a very small portion of its population is ethnically Russian: 5.4 per cent. The largest ethnic group – Avar – is just under 27 per cent. The remainder is comprised of a wide variety of the other ethnic groups that populate the Russian Federation. Makhacheva has a bachelor's degree in Modern Art from Goldsmith's College in London. She was a finalist for the Kandinsky Prize

→
Zholud, Anya
Sculpture, Anti-Chandelier Series
2018/19, paint, welding, metal

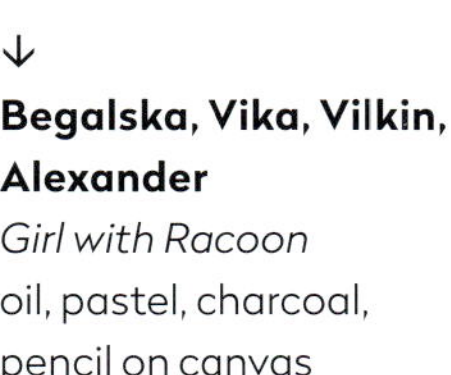

↓
Begalska, Vika, Vilkin, Alexander
Girl with Racoon
oil, pastel, charcoal, pencil on canvas

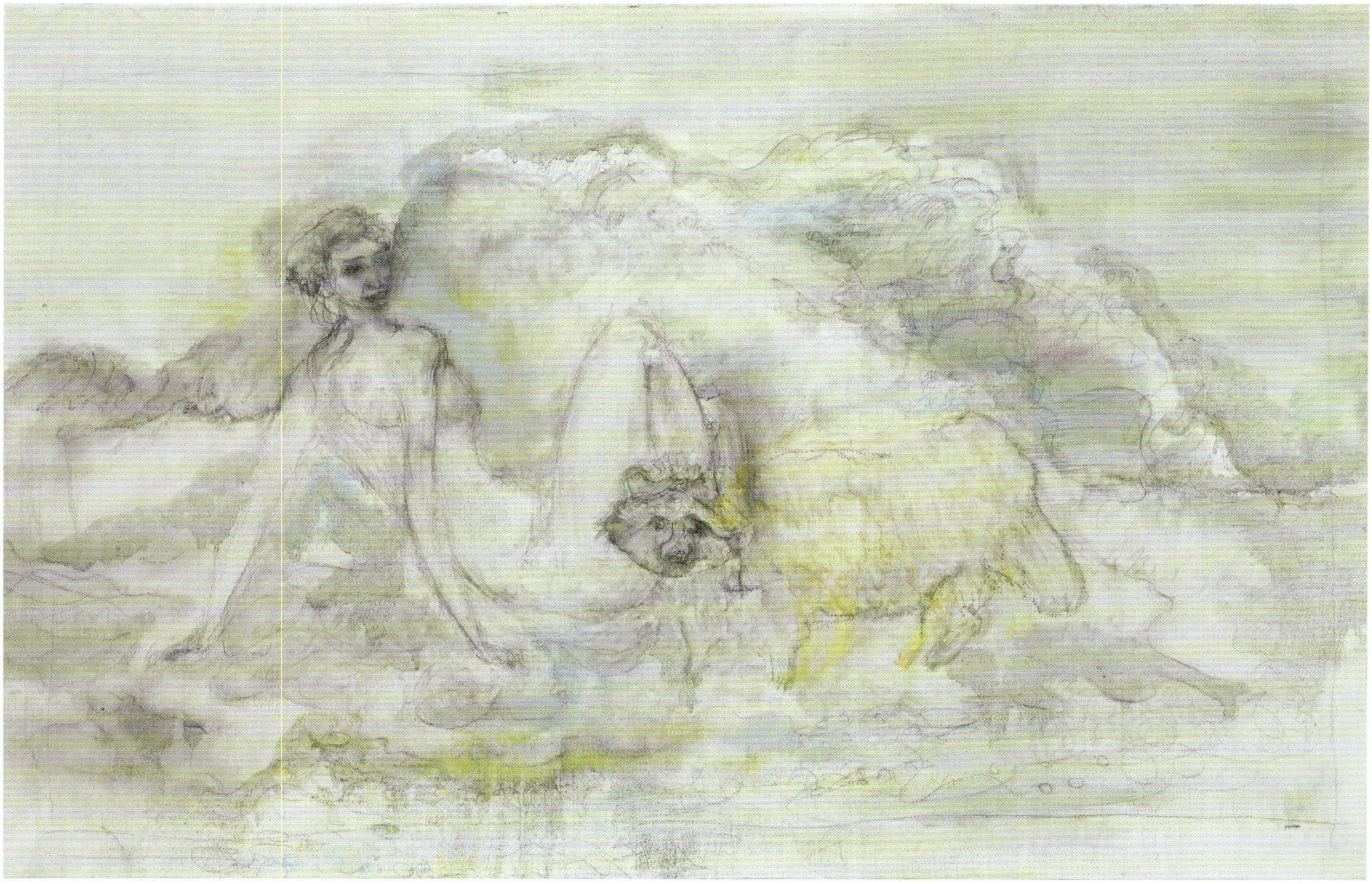

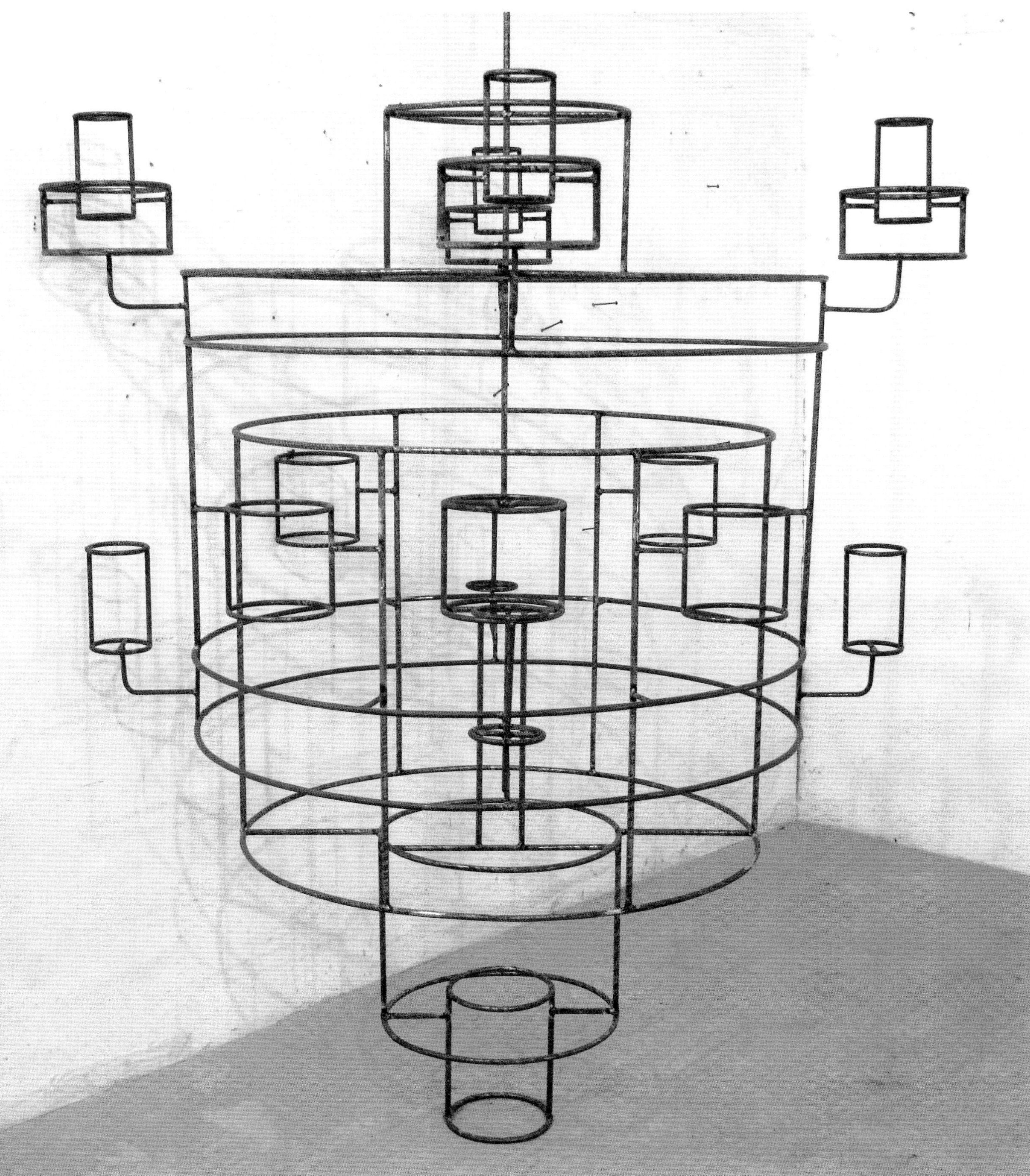

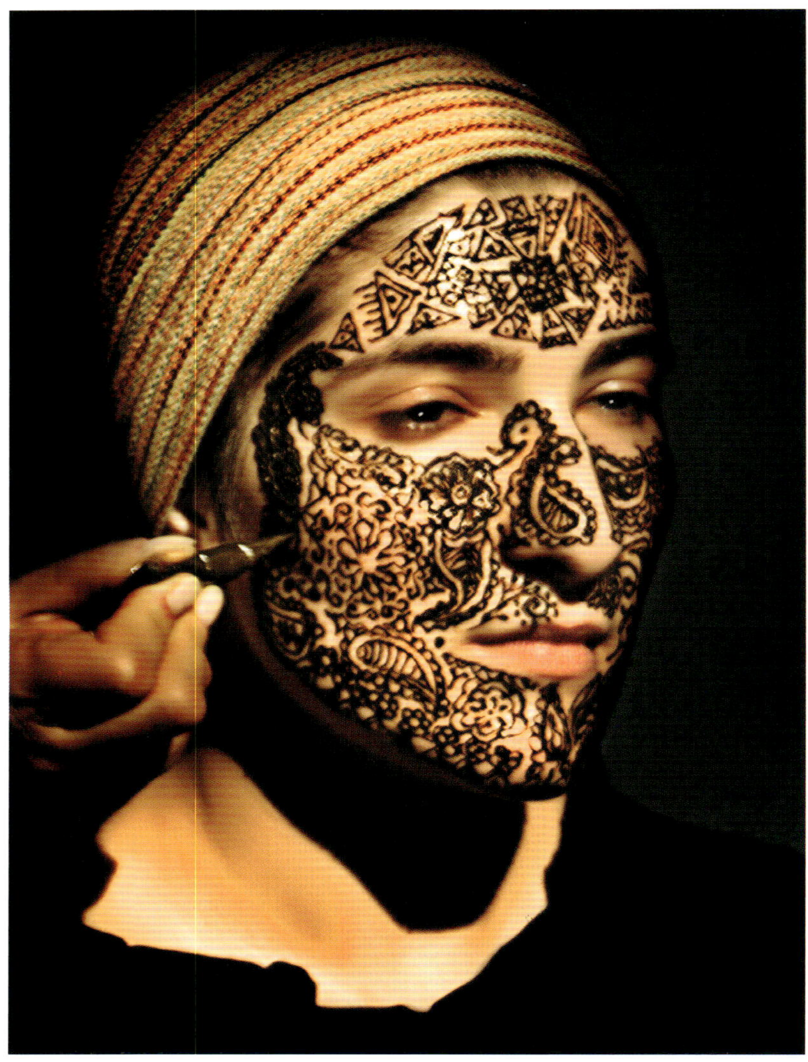

←
Makhacheva, Taus
Delinking
2011, photograph

↓
Makhacheva, Taus
Charivari
2019, mixed media installation, sound

→
Tereshko, Alena
It's an Apple
2019, photograph

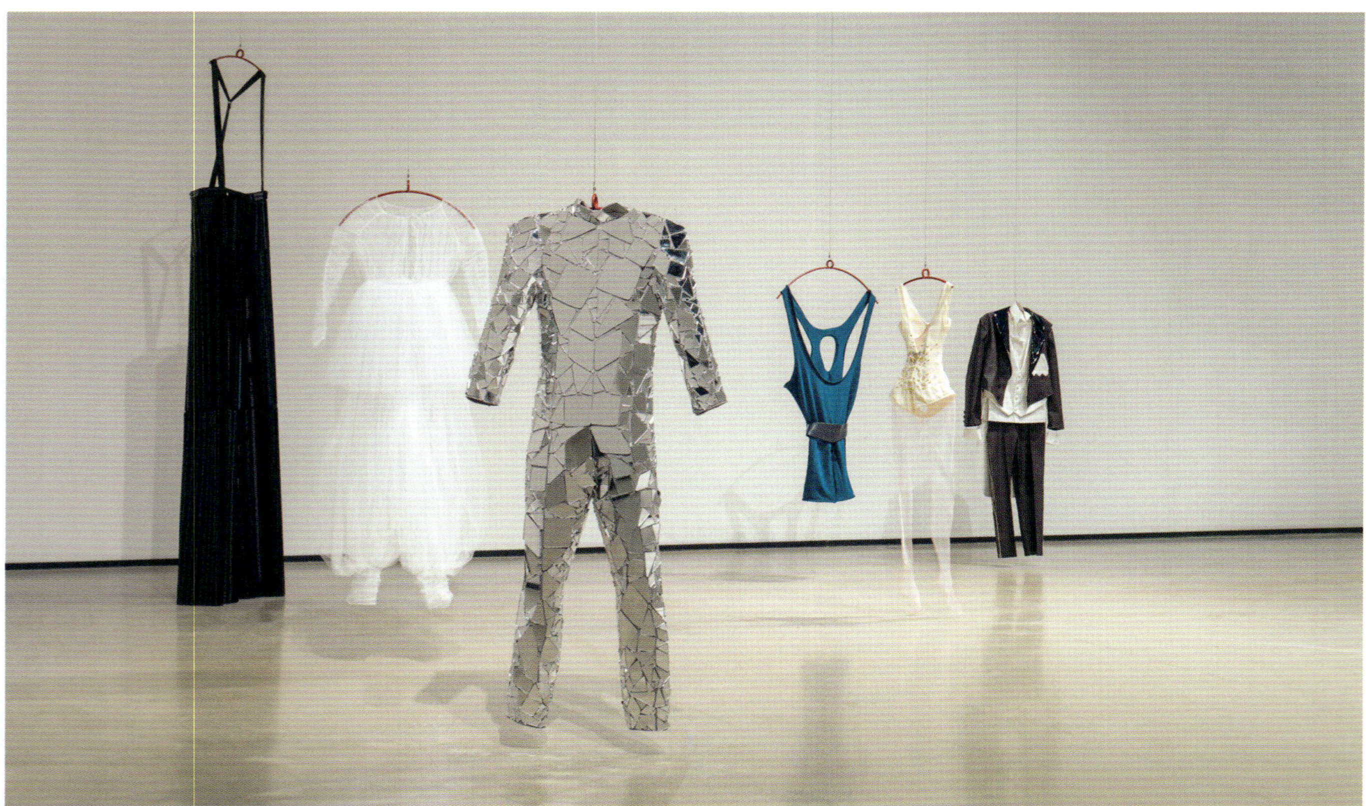

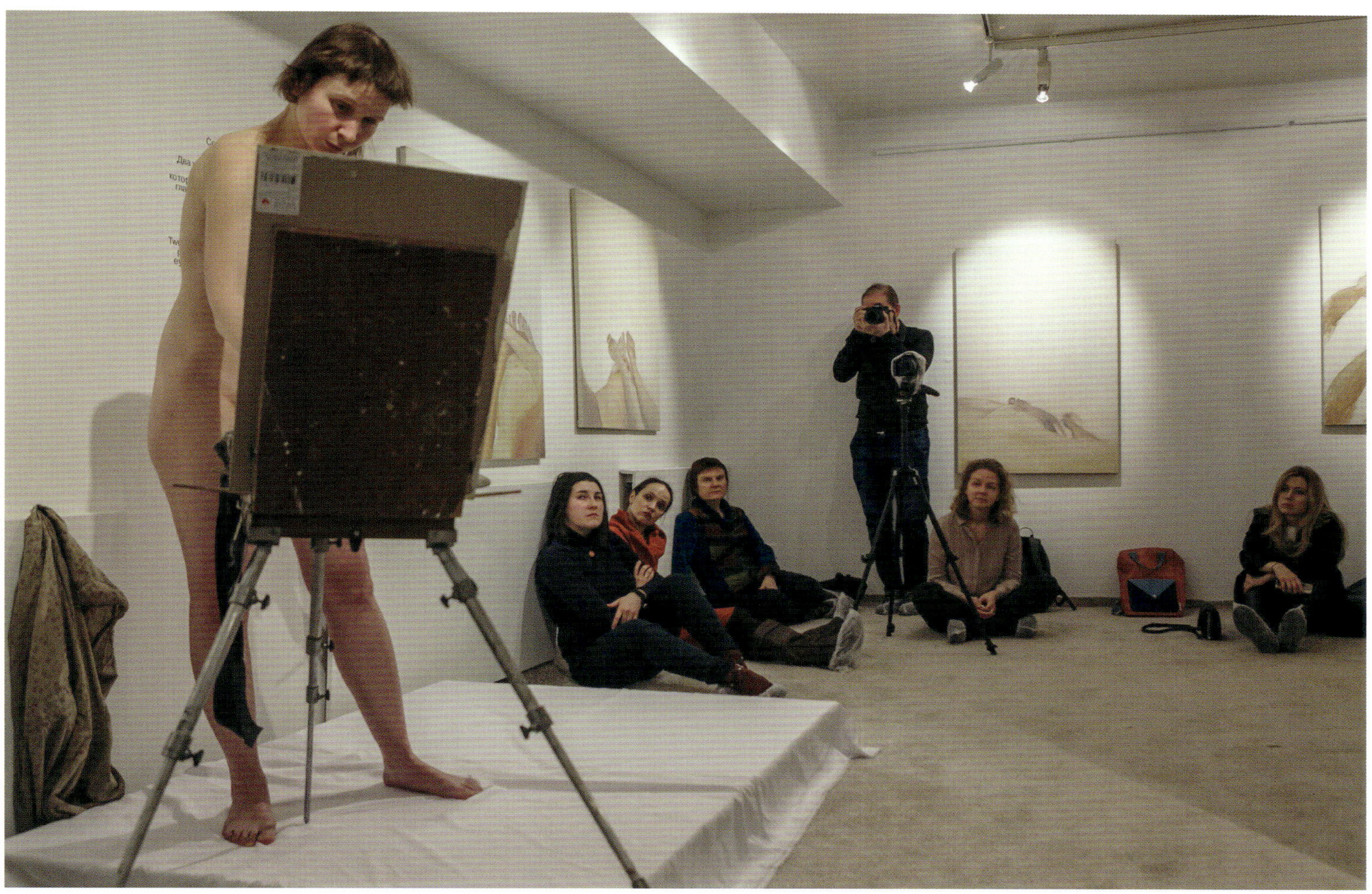

in 2011, exhibited in the Liverpool Biennial in 2012 as well as the Sharjah Biennial and in a special programme of the Fifty-Fifth Venice Biennale the following year. She has shown work in London, Milan, Düsseldorf and Tehran, as well as in France and Sweden.

Her *Delinking* performance is part of an extremely wide variety of work, often difficult to categorise. According to Taus, 'my face was painted with henna: Indian, African and Middle Eastern patterns. As soon as the whole face was covered with them, those places where the skin was still visible were also filled with henna: as a result the whole face was covered with a green mass. After the henna dried up, my face changed colour and became orange-brown; this new colour lasted about a week.'[4] Her activity illustrates the wide gamut of contemporary 'Russian' art like one of the artist's latest projects, *Charivari*, (2019) which, in her own words, has "post-Soviet context and references to circus in the actual 13 x 9 m installation and 7 unwearable costumes for the figures of circus ghosts"[5].

Finally in this section is an image from a video performance by Alena Tereshko (b. 1986), who lives and works in St Petersburg. She graduated from the St Petersburg Stieglitz Academy of Art and Design and the School of Young Artists Pro Arte. In 2017 she won the Media Prize offered by the Kuryokhin Foundation in St Petersburg. The image shows Tereshko naked during her *This is An Apple* performance at MoMA in 2019. Boldly erotic art, whose main instrument is the artist's own body, has been a constant element in Western avant-garde art almost from its beginnings. Here is evidence that the same impulse is alive and well, and currently flourishing in Russia.

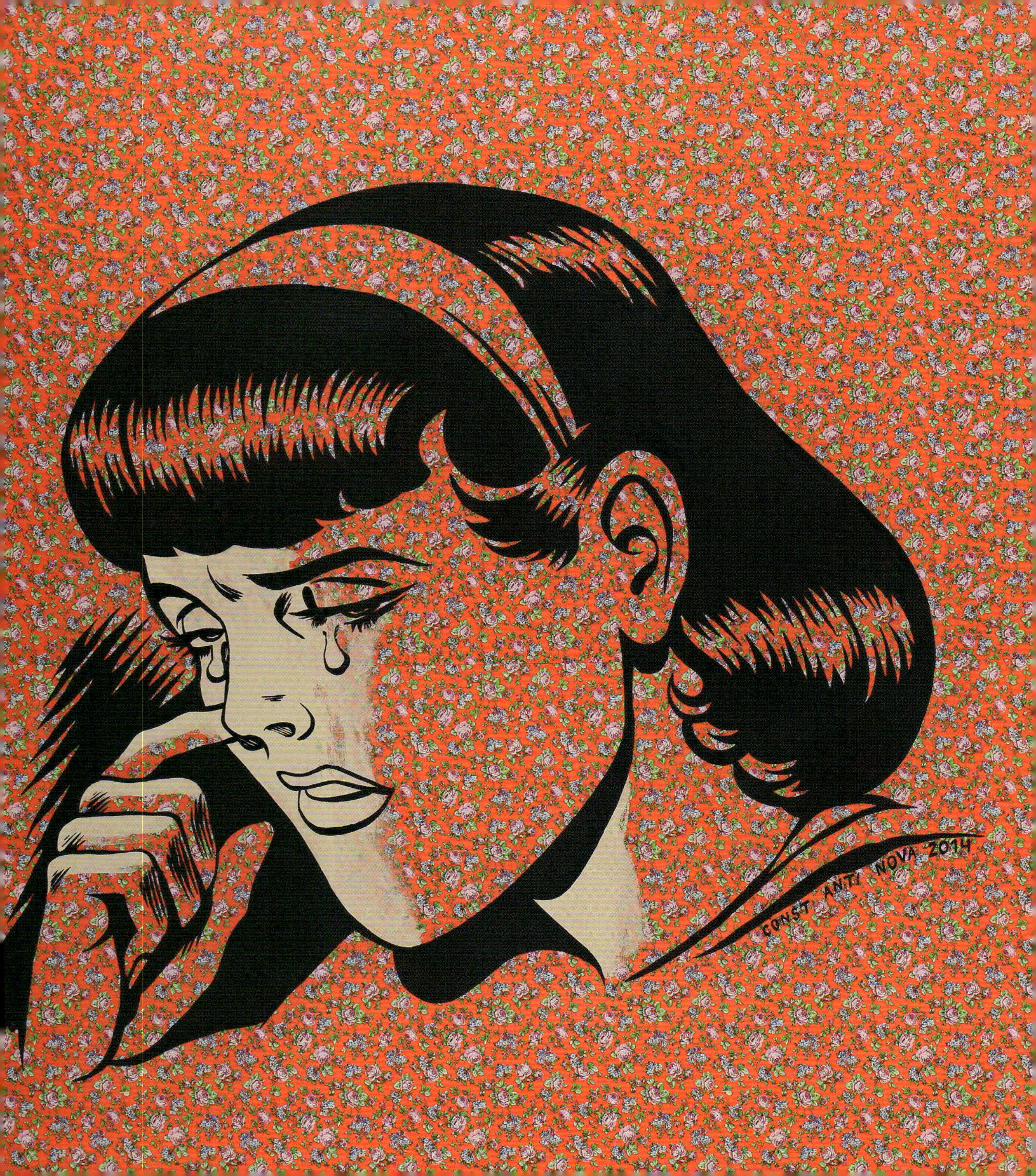
CONST ANTI NOVA 2014

12 CONCEPTUAL ART

For understandable reasons Pop Art never really took root in Russia. It manifested itself at the height of the Cold War and was quintessentially American. Even when Andy Warhol (1928-1987) seized on the image of Chairman Mao for one of his most famous series of paintings, he nevertheless presented his swubject to the viewer using exactly the same formula as that previously employed for his portraits of Marilyn Monroe – something rooted in the norms of American celebrity culture. The formula was derived from the way in which celebrities were presented to the American public through advertising, in particular by movie posters, and also through the images of them used in the American tabloid press. Direct observation of the subject played no part. It was the celebrity vibe that counted.

Russia did have, at that time, a kind of equivalent in the official portraits of the likes of Lenin and Stalin, but these images seem to have existed in isolation from the mainstream of Russian existing culture of the time. Warhol, on the contrary, was at the very centre of what was then taking place in American art and his work was seen as emblematic of the creative triumph of American capitalism. This was emphasised in touring exhibitions of his work in Europe.

In post-Communist Russia, a few tributes have now been paid to the influence of American Pop, channelling a vibe that is gradually fading from both American and Western European art. An example of this survival is Ludmila Konstantinova's (b. 1980) *Degenerreotype* series (2014). A press release issued in 2016 in connection with her solo show held at the privately owned but influential Erarta Museum in St Petersburg makes it clear that it would however be unwise to take the image illustrated here as an example of a slavishly uncritical imitation of an admired non-Russian model, by this time somewhat faded. The very title of the series also offers a clue: as a way of producing photographic images, daguerreotypes are long out of date.

The press release notes that Konstantinova works in a wide variety of styles and techniques,

←
Konstantinova, Ludmila
Untitled, Degenerotype Series
2014, acrylic on calico

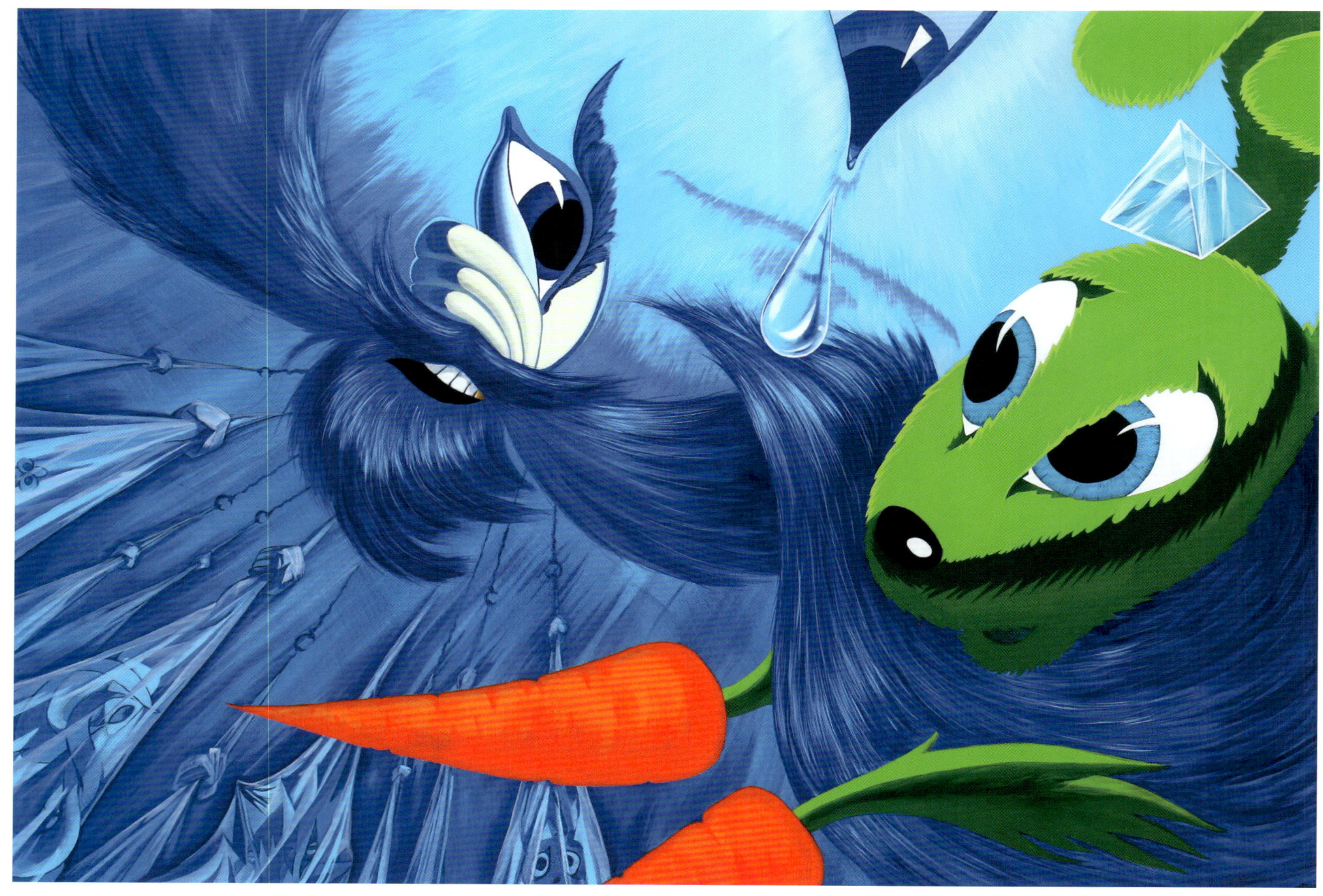

ranging from 'Suprematist abstractions to Pop Art simulations'. Her principle, it says, is the post-modernist one of 'conjoining the incompatible'.[1] The show was called, with obvious irony, *No Ambitions*. Konstantinova is more easily categorised as a Conceptualist rather than as an example of belated Russian Pop.

Other images featured in this section also show a sophisticated sense of design, of a kind that is now perhaps more familiar from top-level commercial work than from supposedly experimental art. An example is Rostan Tavasiev's series *A Drop of Creacin* (2017). Rostan explains that "Creacin has proven to be the strongest stimulant of creativity for both quantum neuromechanisms and biological beings. Civilization under the influence of creacin began to develop rapidly again".[2] Tavasiev (b. 1976), who lives and works in Moscow, has enjoyed considerable success in the post-Soviet art world. Short-listed for the Innovation Award in both 2006 and 2013, he has work exhibited in the State Tretyakov Gallery and in numerous other official collections.

↑
Tavasiev, Rostan
My Star, Episode 7
2017, acrylic on canvas

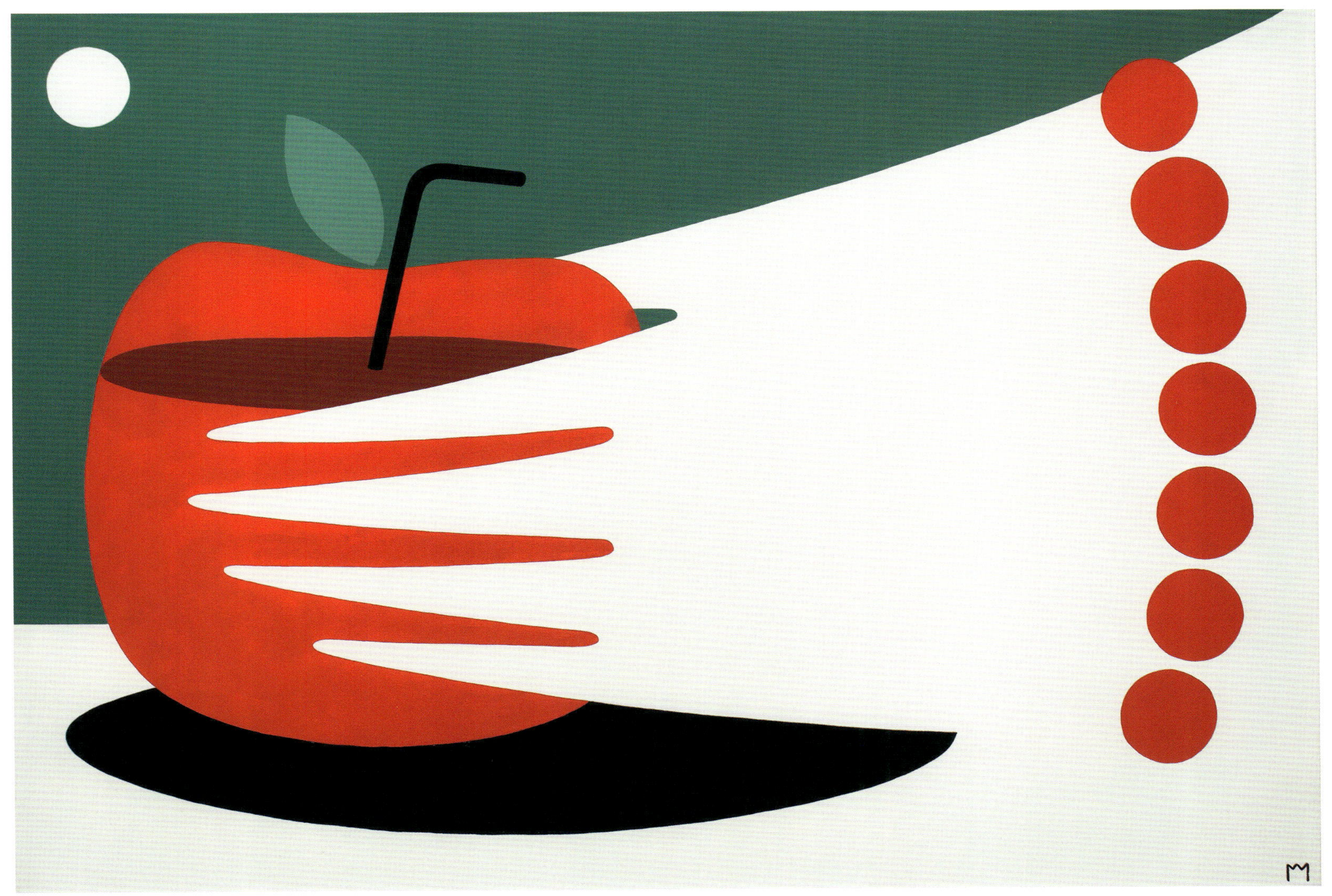

↑
Marker, Misha
Eva
2019, acrylic on canvas

Equally sophisticated is the work of Misha Marker, born a decade later in 1987, and therefore too young to be in any way influenced by the Soviet era. Marker's painting *Eve* represents an elegantly abstracted apple being seized by an even more radically abstracted hand. The composition is a perfectly poised example of contemporary graphic work, with forms reduced to their essence. Though he trained at an art school and has a degree as a 'teacher of fine arts', he now works anonymously as a 'street artist'.[3]

Much of the art in this section recalls familiar objects from the computer screen. For example, Maksim Svishchev's (b. 1982) rows of *Heads* (or *Masks)*,(2019), made of coloured clay, look like elaborated versions of emoticons. Among other things, this resemblance serves as a reminder that while Russia may now seem to exist in a separate cultural sphere, in technological terms it remains very much in step with what is taking place in the West.

Svishchev's practice covers a wide range – videos and sculptures, as well as what are described as

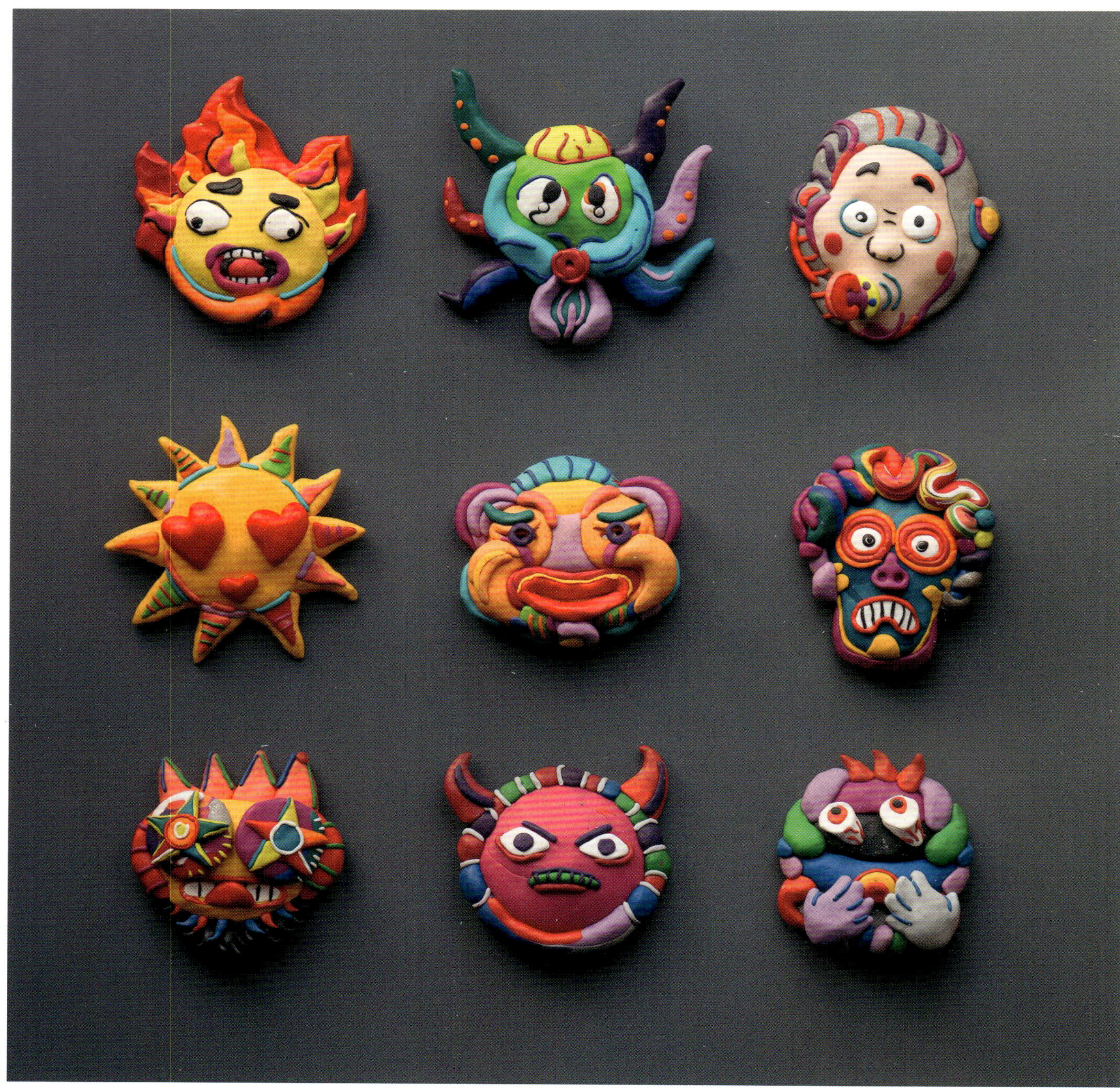

virtual or 'media objects', and his work has been widely shown internationally. In addition to shows in Moscow and St Petersburg he has exhibited in London, New York, Turin, Berlin, Seoul, São Paulo and Skopje. In addition, as he noted in a recent interview, he is now able to 'come up with a virtual form and present it anywhere on the planet'.[4]

If the technological situation in today's Russia is similar to what now also prevails in the West, what is perhaps less familiar is the pervasive sense of irony conveyed by many of these recent Russian conceptual artworks.

Semyon Motolyanets was born in 1982 in Belarus and graduated from the St Petersburg Stieglitz State Academy of Art and Design in 2009 where he now lives and works using a variety of media. The work shown here is a miniature monument entitled *Thirty-Five Years Left*, dated 2018. It is a pyramid

↑
Svishev, Maxim
Masks
2019, coloured polymer clay

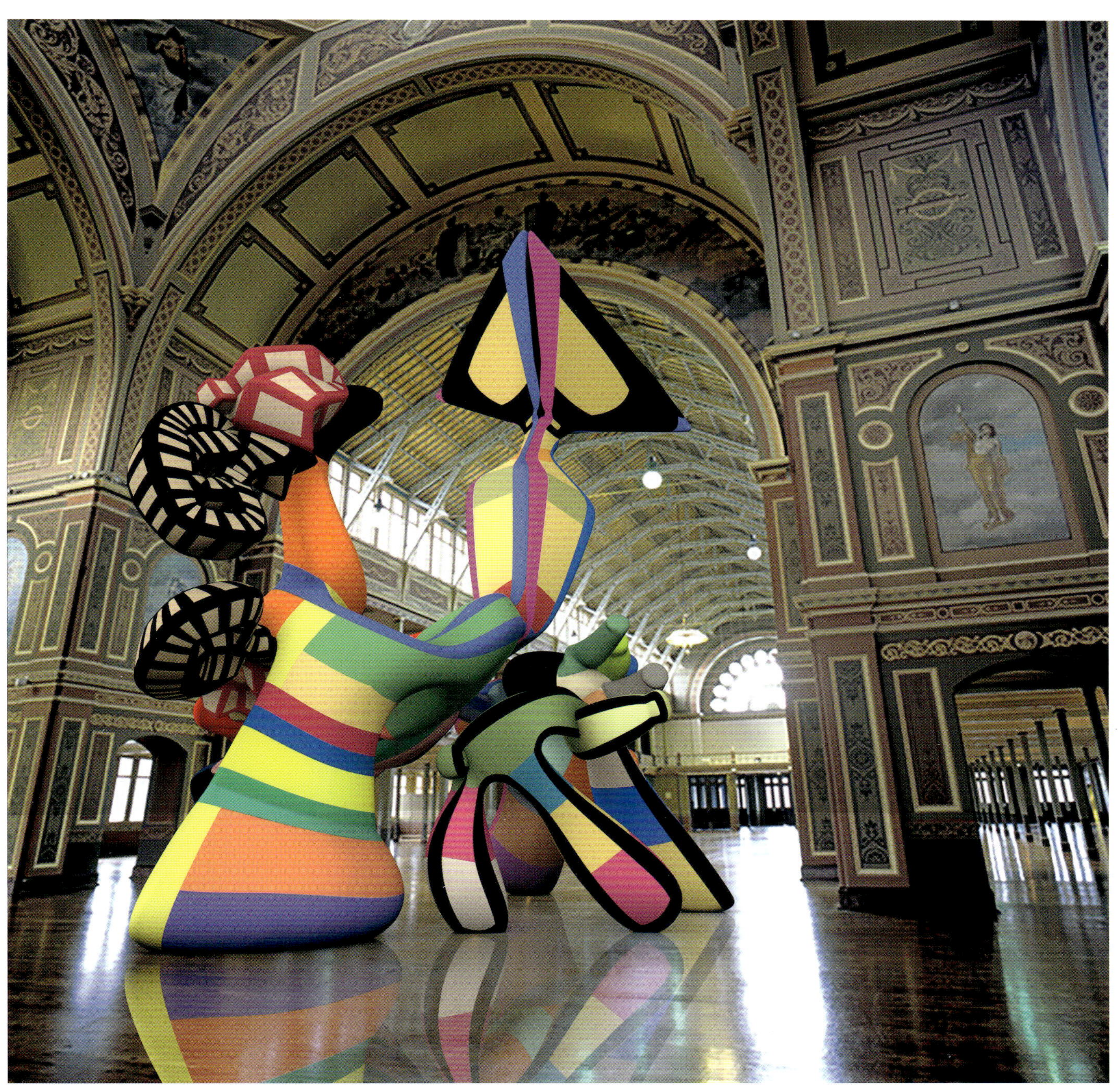

↑
Svishev, Maxim
TSVETASIS (virtual project)
2017, 3D graphics

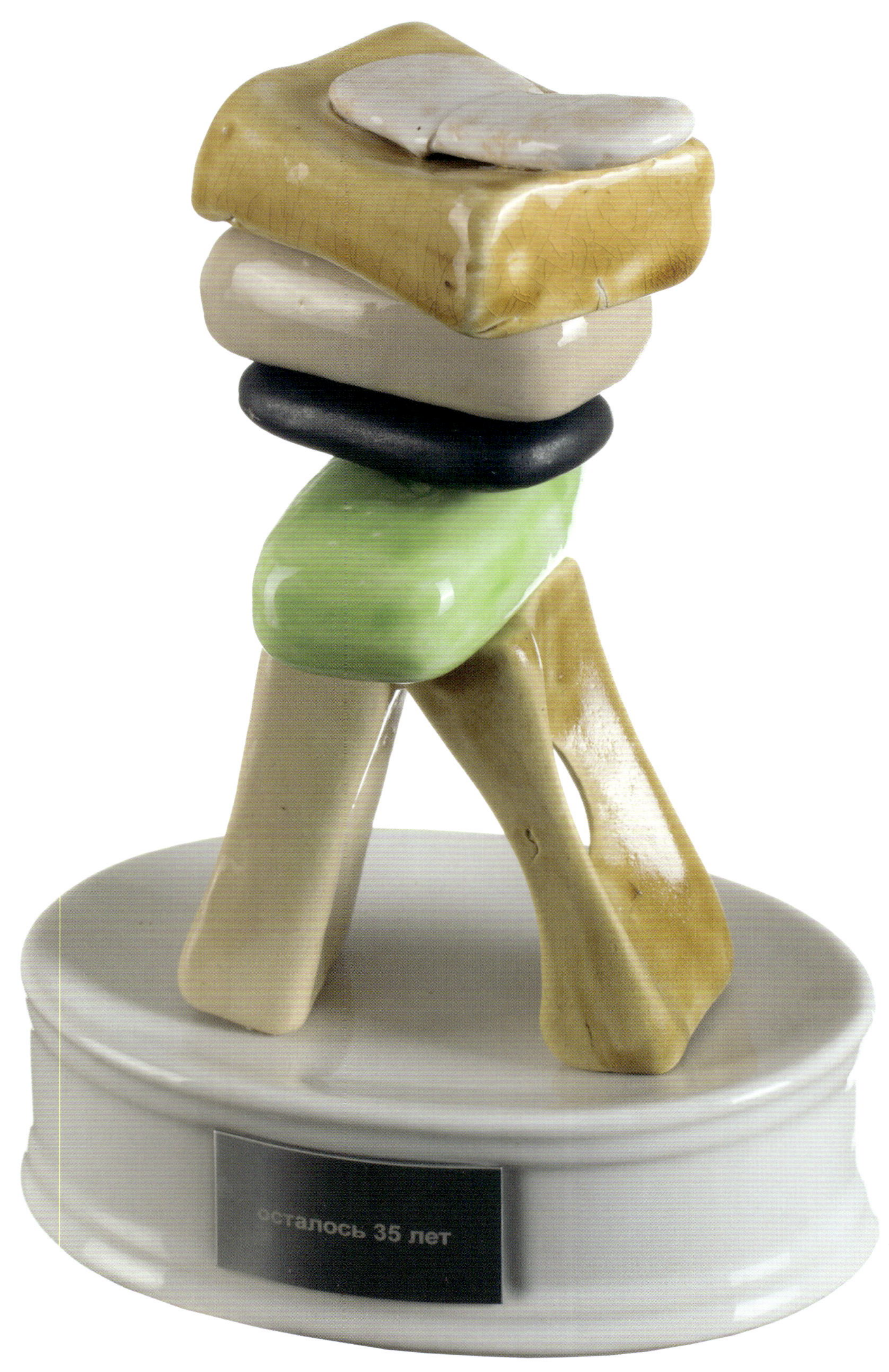
осталось 35 лет

←
Motolyanets, Semyon
Only Left 35 Years
2018, metal, ceramics, 21 x 16 x 16 см

→
Kuzkin, Andrey
Scary, 2007
black marker pen, porcelain cup

↓
Chtak, Valery
In My Case, In No Case
2016, acrylic on canvas

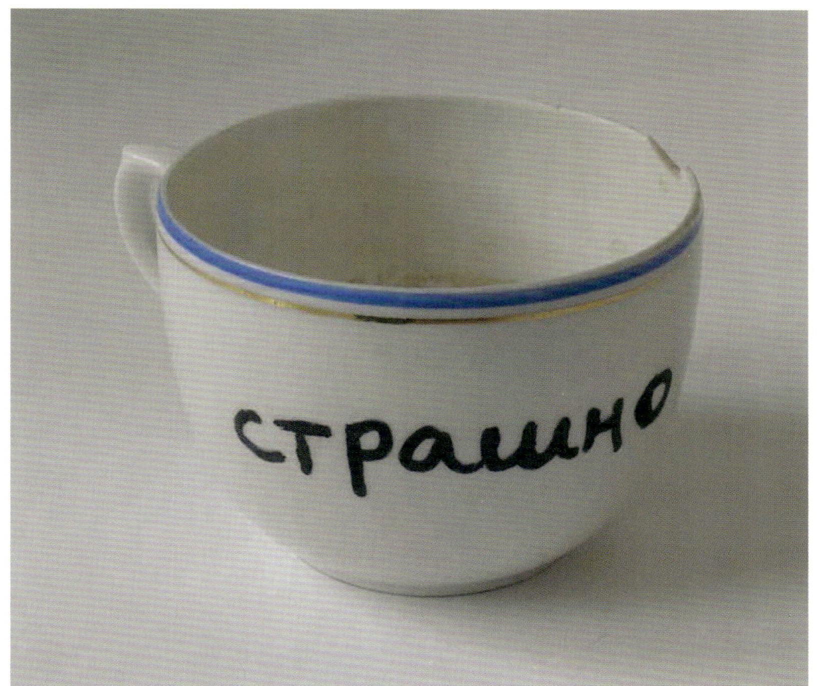

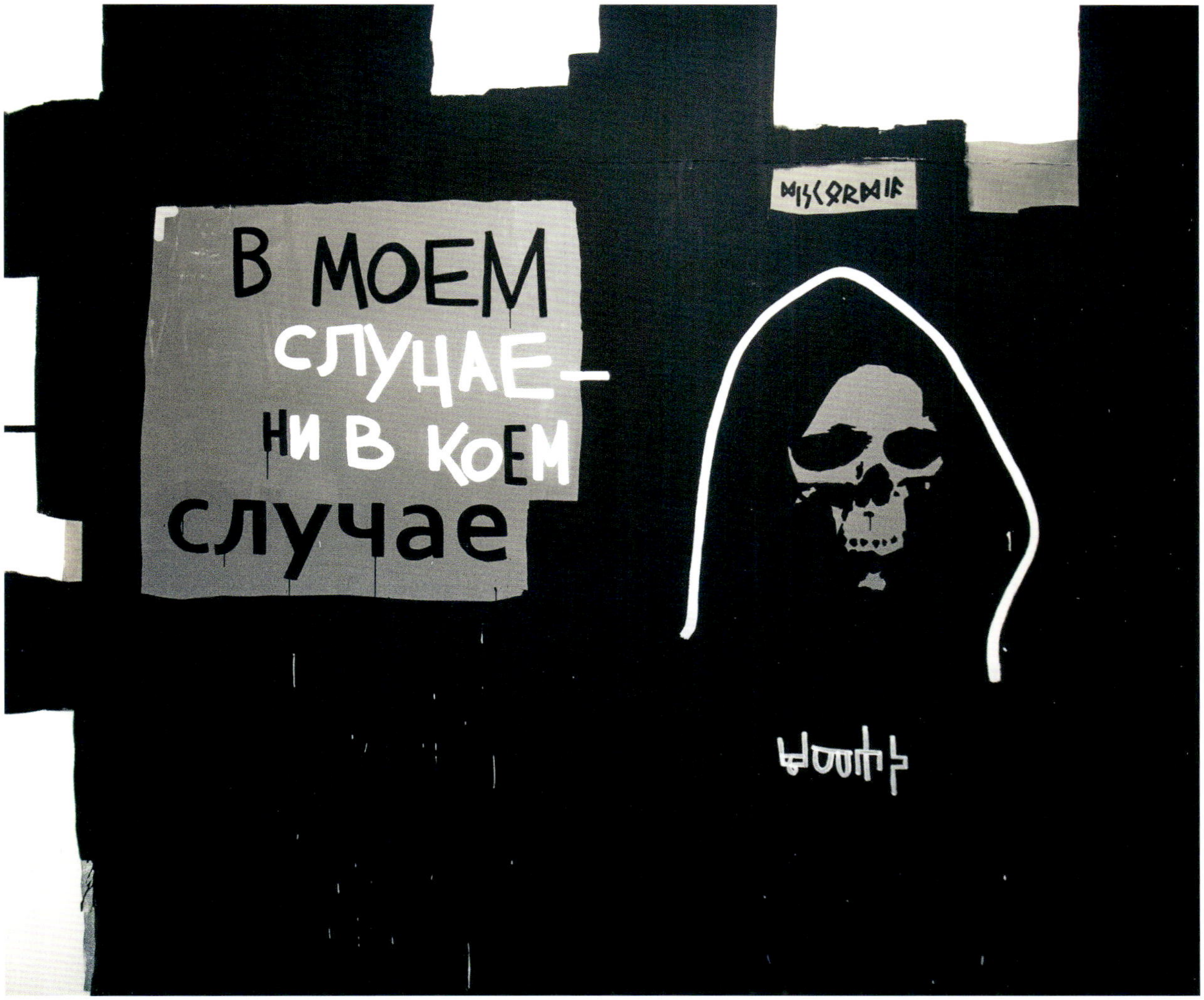

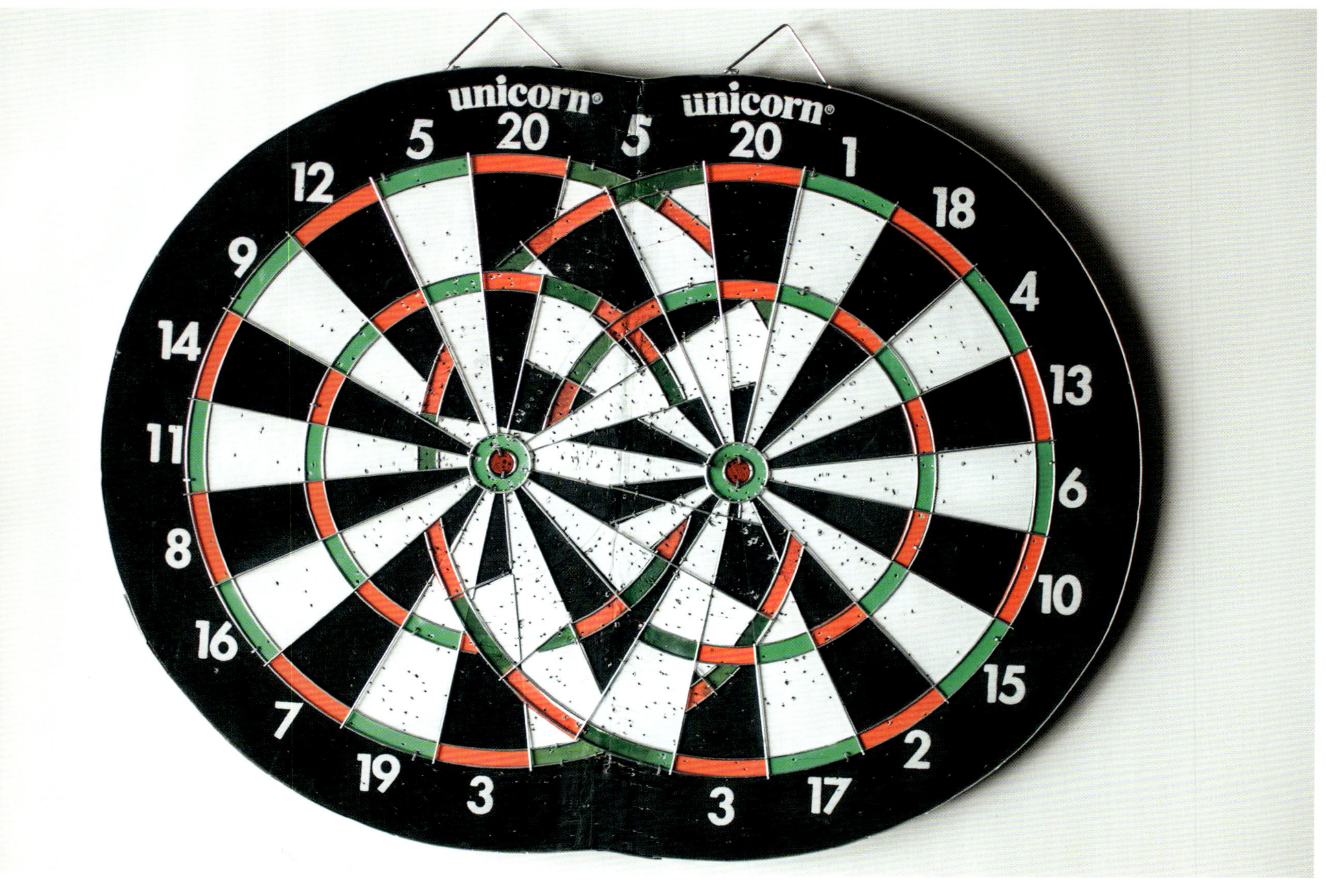

of soap pieces made of ceramic. There is the following comment on the internet website: "Soap is not used as a ready-made, but taken as an image, and its practical meaning is replaced by a metaphorical one. Shaky unstable pyramids made of glossy ceramic soap are an alternative to porcelain elephants standing on a chest of drawers in some bourgeois apartments. Small tablets on the base suddenly introduce the discourse of time: "Another 20 minutes", "Constancy lasts five hours", "Another 328 years" - and the works become an absurdist measure of either lost or remaining time".[5]

Andrey Kuzkin (b. 1979) is another young artist recently laureated in Russia. He won the Kandinsky Prize in 2016 and has also received a number of other major official awards. He has work exhibited in the collection of the State Tretyakov Gallery in Moscow. The object illustrated here consists simply of the word 'Scary' in Cyrillic characters, written with black marker pen on a chipped ceramic cup. It was produced in 2007.

An even more negative message is that offered in a black-and-white composition from 2016 by Valery Chtak (b. 1981). The image is a skull, peering out from under a hood. The Cyrillic inscription states: 'In My Case - No Way in one of his interviews the artist stated that he does not force people to

↑
Tregubov, Alexey
Hit It
2013, paint on metal and foam plastic

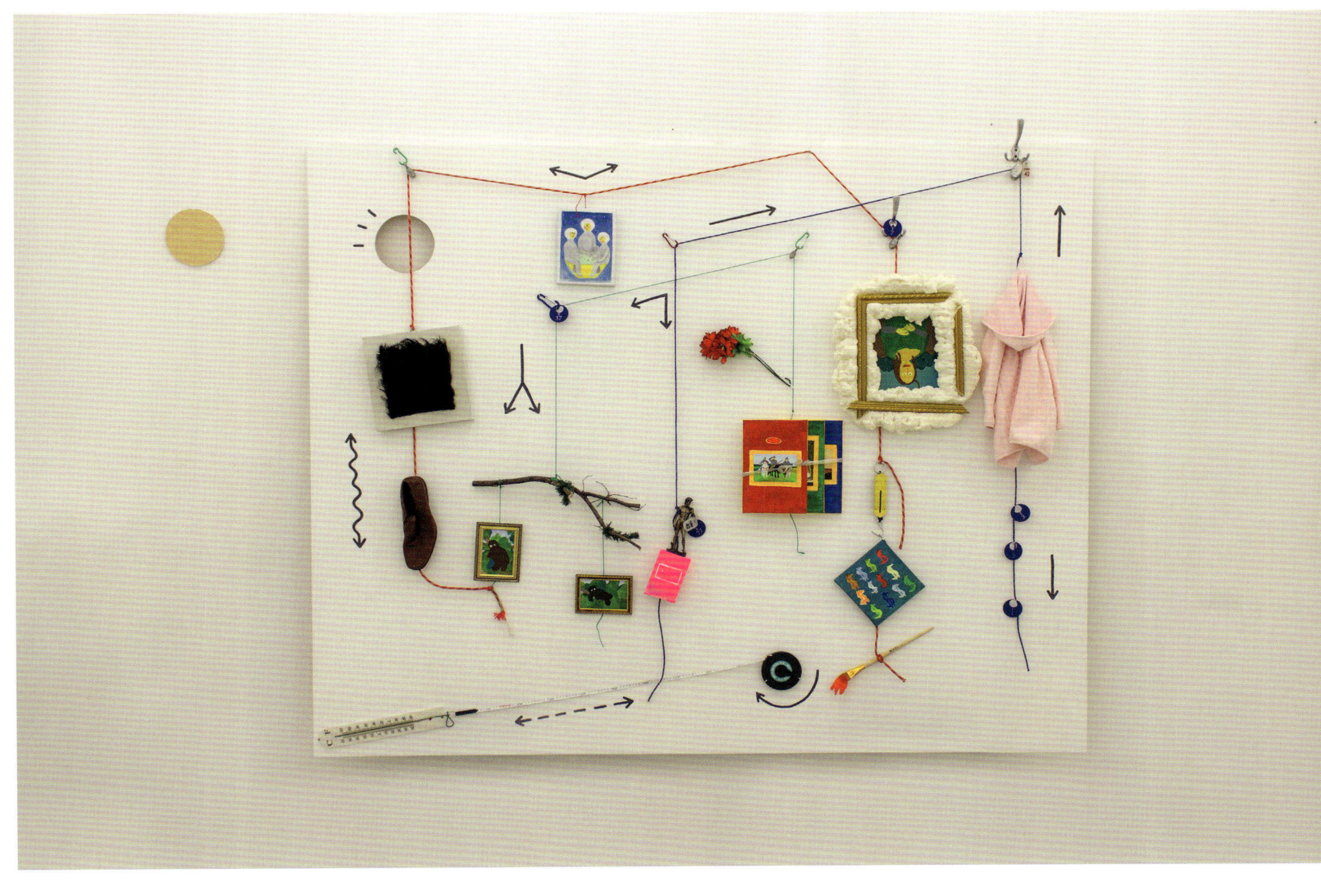

understand his art.[6] He too has work in the collection of the State Tretyakov Gallery and also exhibited in Paris and Athens

Even images by other Russian artists which at first glance seem less direct, sometimes suggest a sense of the challenges of the twenty-first century. Moscow artist Alexey Tregubov was born in 1979. He has been a nominee for the Kandinsky Prize (2012) and also for the Kuryokhin Prize. The piece called *Hit It* (2013) illustrated here is a double dartboard, which reads immediately as a metaphor for 'seeing double', as the boards confusingly overlap.

Finally, in this section is the duo EliKuka: Oleg Eliseev (b. 1985) and Evgeny Kukoverov (b. 1985), who work together in Moscow. They are generally regarded as the successors to the late-Soviet era Conceptualists Georgy Ostretsov (b. 1967) and Georgy Litichevsky (b. 1956). EliKuka's work is often interactive, and constructed to seem alive and familiar, while at the same time reassuringly undemanding. When Ostretsov formed the VGLAZ association of contemporary artists in 2010, EliKuka were part of it. A direct line of descent therefore exists between the Conceptualists who worked in the late-Communist/early Post-Communist epoch of Russian art and what is taking place now.

↑
Eli Kuka
World Order Simulators
2012, mixed media on canvas

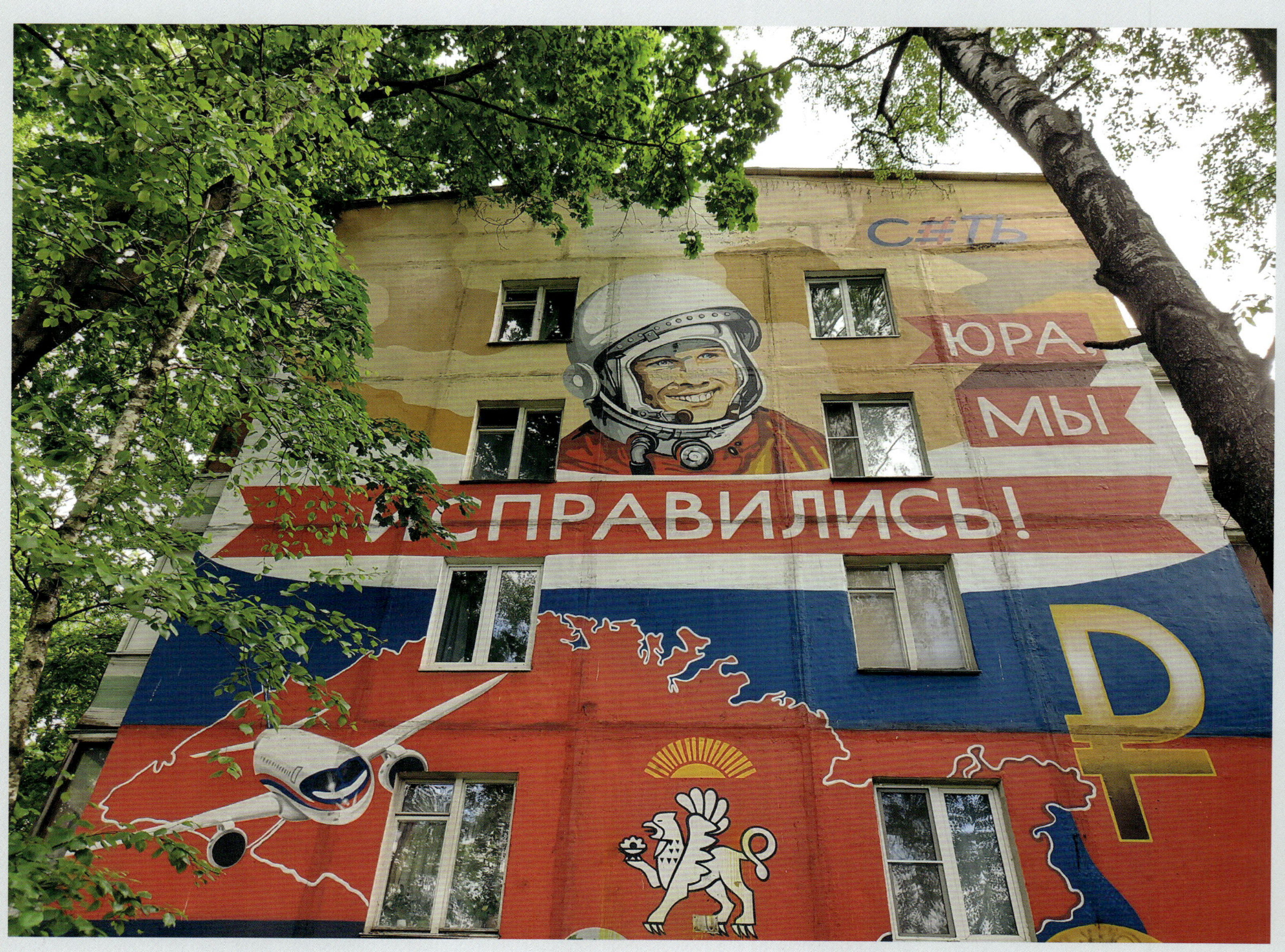
ЮРА,
МЫ
СПРАВИЛИСЬ!

13 STREET ART & GRAFFITI

A distinction needs to be made between Street Art and Graffiti, both now very much present in Russia. Street Art tends to be more permanent, and sometimes acquires an official or semi-official character. Graffiti are more hit-and-run and rely much more heavily on text. Sometimes they are composed entirely of text, albeit in a highly elaborate ornamental form.

Street images can partake of both qualities. This is true, for example, of works to be found in the 'Paint Moscow' graffiti area, which was established in the city in 2007, close to the Babushkinskaya Metro station. The images were created by both Russian and non-Russian artists, under the patronage of the MIAN group of companies, who used the event to celebrate their own twelfth anniversary.[1] Some of the paintings have since been altered – some would say vandalised – by fly-by-night anonymous graffitists.

The official mural illustrated here, also in Moscow, does not differ greatly from this series of predecessors. It is called *Yura, We Have Improved* and was painted by a group from Samara by the name of Nezo Street Art, formed in 2008, to celebrate the career of the Russian cosmonaut Yuri Gagarin. It responds to an image on the internet, which shows a monument to Gagarin, with the inscription 'Yuri, forgive us, we f—d it all up.' The composition made its appearance after the Crimean Peninsula became part of Russia in 2014.

Some Russian street art make use of text, while at the same time almost entirely excluding images, but still doesn't quite fit the descriptive term 'graffiti'. An extreme example is Slava PTRK's (b.1990) *Make Russia Grey Again* (2018) painted for a street art festival in Yekaterinburg – an otherwise featureless brick wall, with a few skyscrapers towering in the background. The four words of the title appear on the wall in block capitals in English. The instruction is clearly ironic and refers to a widely used slogan: 'Make Russia Great Again'. The monument is a satire on the dreariness of post-Soviet cultural life, as is made obvious by the title.

←
Nezo Street Art
Yura, We Have Improved!
2014, spray paint on wall

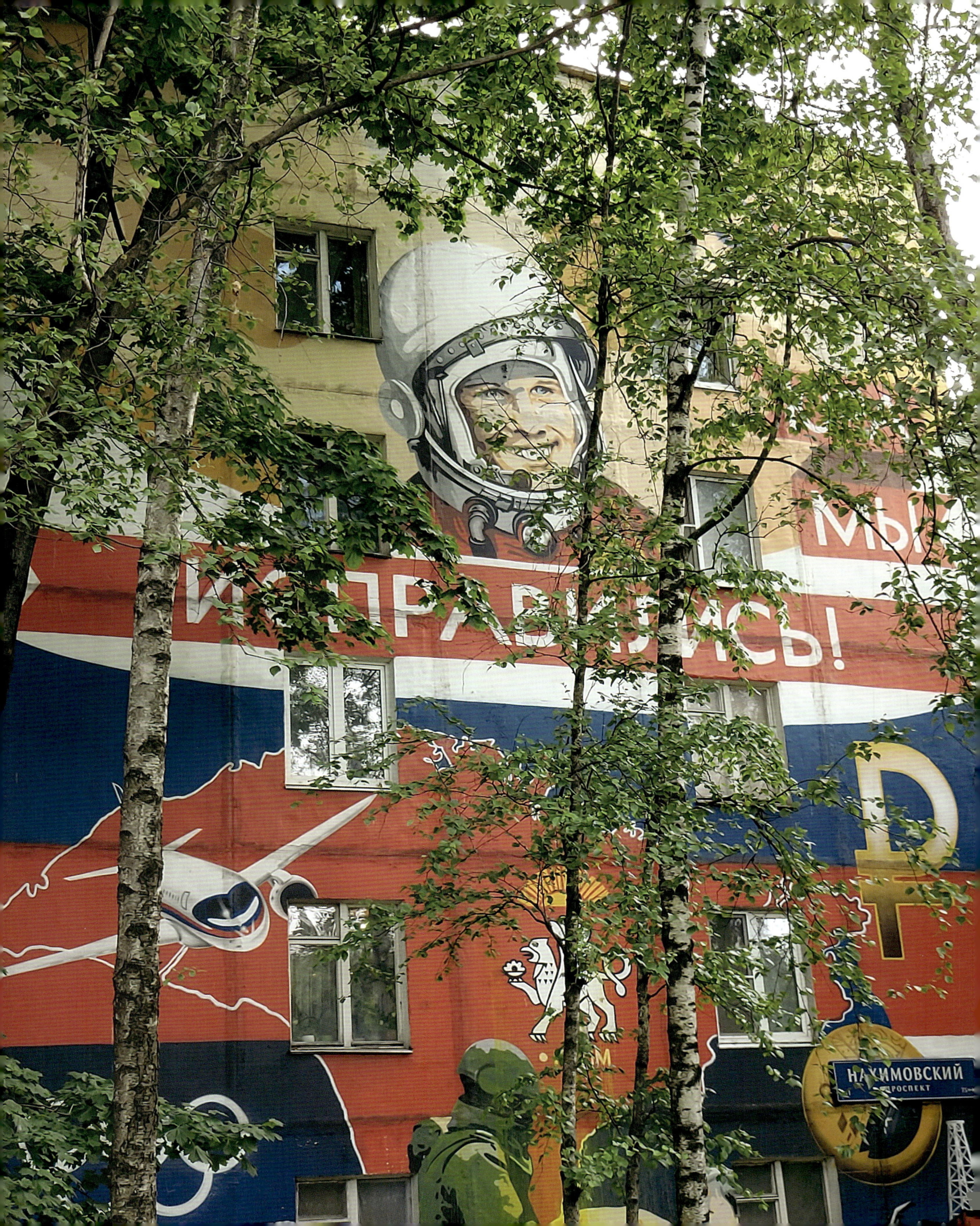
МЫ
НАХИМОВСКИЙ

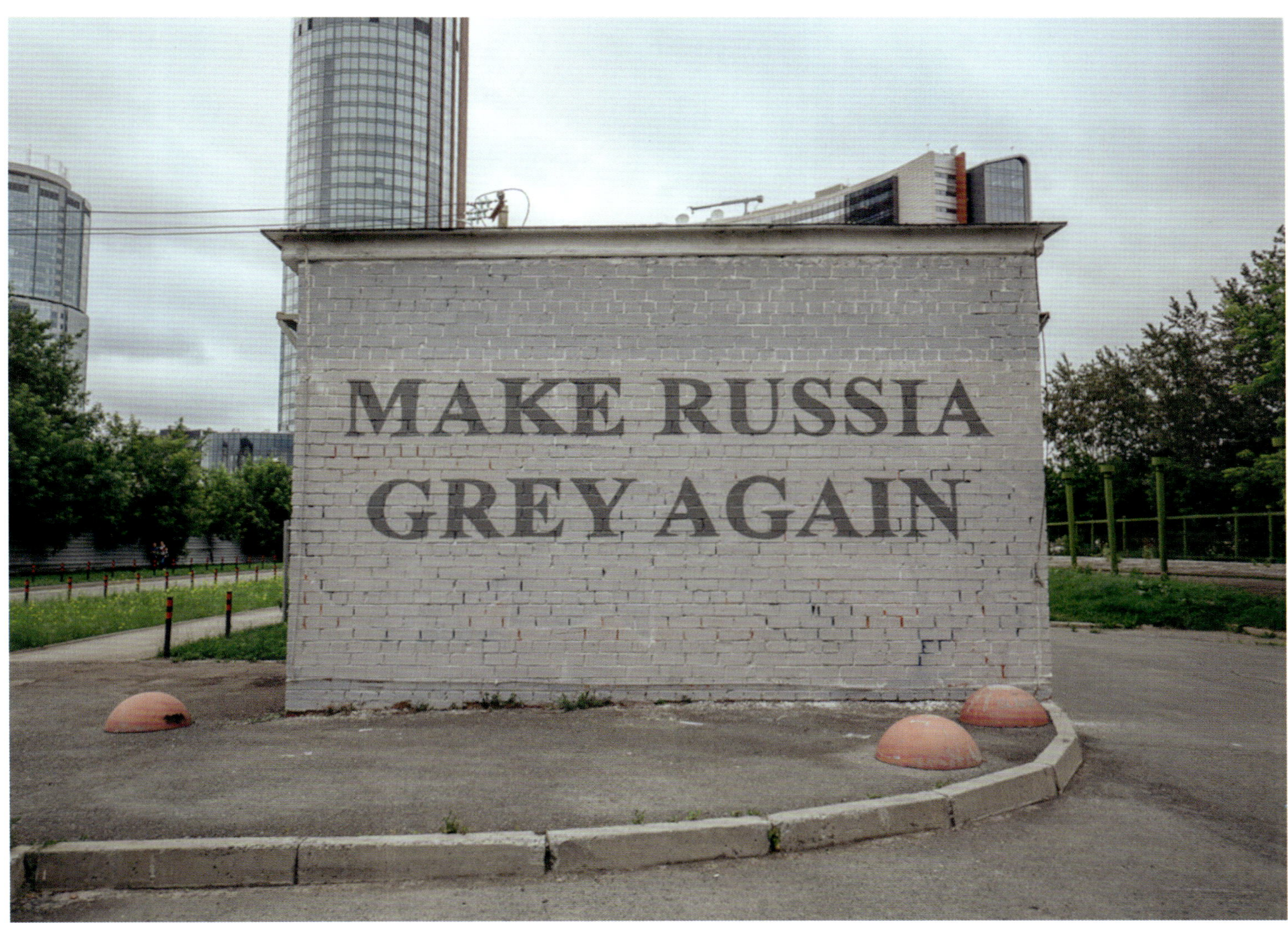

↑
PTRK, Slava
Make Russia Grey Again
2018, spray paint on wall

←
Nezo Street Art
Yura, We Have Improved!, overview
2014, spray paint on wall

One curious feature of some of these made-and-situated-in-Russia public artworks is this use both of the Latin alphabet and of words in English, not Russian. English, it seems, has become the *lingua franca* of today's contemporary art. English appears yet again in the thought bubble that features in Stas Bags' (b.1984) street art image of cow. 'Get milk,' it instructs the spectator, 'not art'. This is a painted image that might just as easily function indoors, rather than in its apparently outdoor location.

Also inscribed in English, and stubbornly un-graffiti-like, is Vladimir Abikh's image, *You Are Offline*. One work is located in Yekaterinburg, the second largest city in Siberia, and another in Kolomna, near Moscow. It mimics a computer screen, with cactuses and an approaching dinosaur, while the English text below informs the viewer that they are 'currently offline' and must 'interact with reality.'

A less moralising outdoor work is that by Pokras Lampas (b. 1991), the self-styled creator of the 'calligrafuturism' movement. He also produces outdoor works on a large scale. An example of the latter is an 11,000m^2 design made in 2018 for the RZhD Arena in Moscow. This is probably best seen in its entirety from the air, as it is shown here. It seems to possess no informative or moralising impulse. Its job is simply to be decorative. In March 2021 Lampas became one of the first Russian artists to sell his work as an NFT: a photograph of his drawing entitled *Transition* projected on the Chirkey Dam, the largest hydroelectric power station on the Sulak river in Dagestan in the northern Caucasus.[2]

Other Russian artists use more familiar graffiti-like forms. Kirill Kto (b. 1984) has, since the early 2000s, been a participant in major Russian street art groups, beginning with What For? (2002–2009)

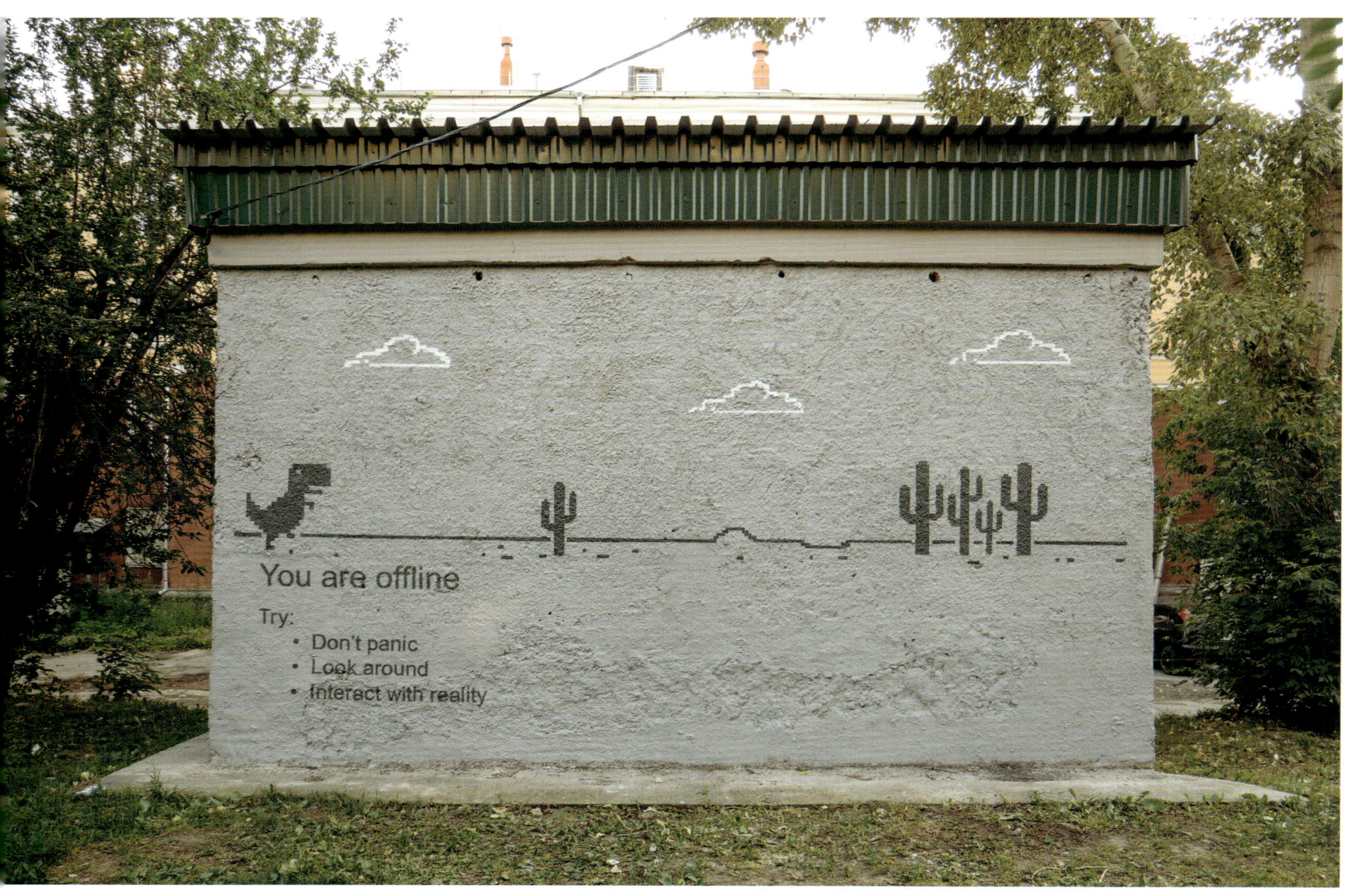

↑
Abikh, Vladimir
You Are Offline
2019, spray paint on wall

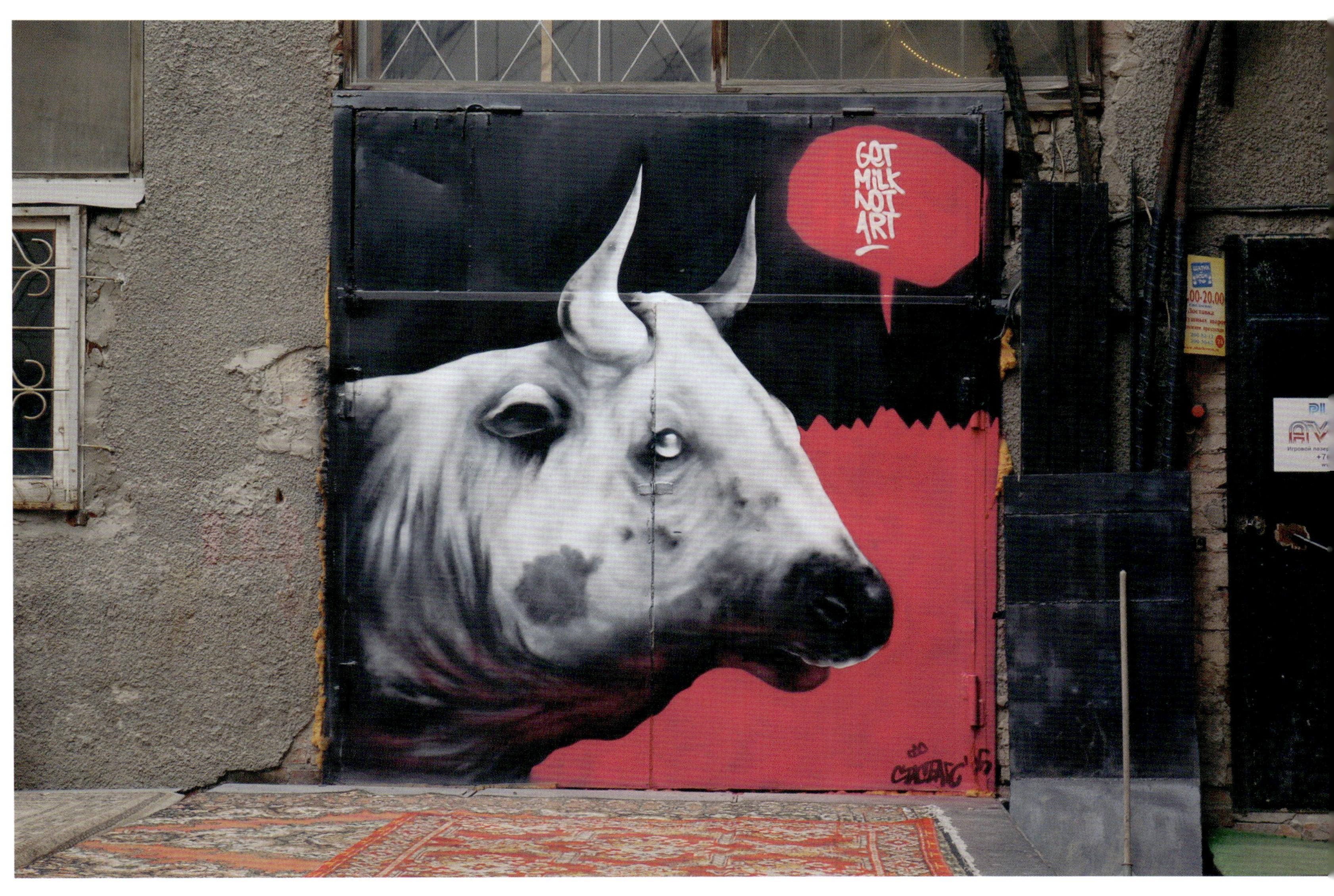

↑
Bags, Stas
Get Milk Not Art
2015, spray paint on wall

and No Future Forever (2005–2009): the titles suggest the prevalent mood in large sections of Russian society at that time. By 2012 Kto was listed in *ArtChronika* magazine as one of the fifty most influential people in Russian art – proof that graffiti art now has the power to cross once-seemingly impregnable cultural boundaries.[3]

The same is true, to some extent at least, of the graffiti art of Stas Dobry (b. 1985), although his outdoor compositions make little use of lettering, and are populated instead with a multitude of ghost-like figures.

One major point of difference does however seem to separate the images so far illustrated from the bulk of street art now being produced in Russia, which are basically not images as such, but elaborated text. This tendency is now rooted in graffiti art world-wide. As the name 'graffiti' suggests, this art form is as closely linked to the idea of writing as it is to the idea of picturing. Many Russian graffiti are inscriptions rather than actual images. They are unique to the language, and to the culture that produces them.

Graffiti art did not make a major impact during Soviet times. If graffiti appeared on walls, they were usually swiftly painted out, and those responsible, if caught, were subject to prison sentences

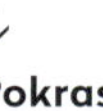

Pokras Lampas
We Have Our Own Way
2018, paint on tarmac

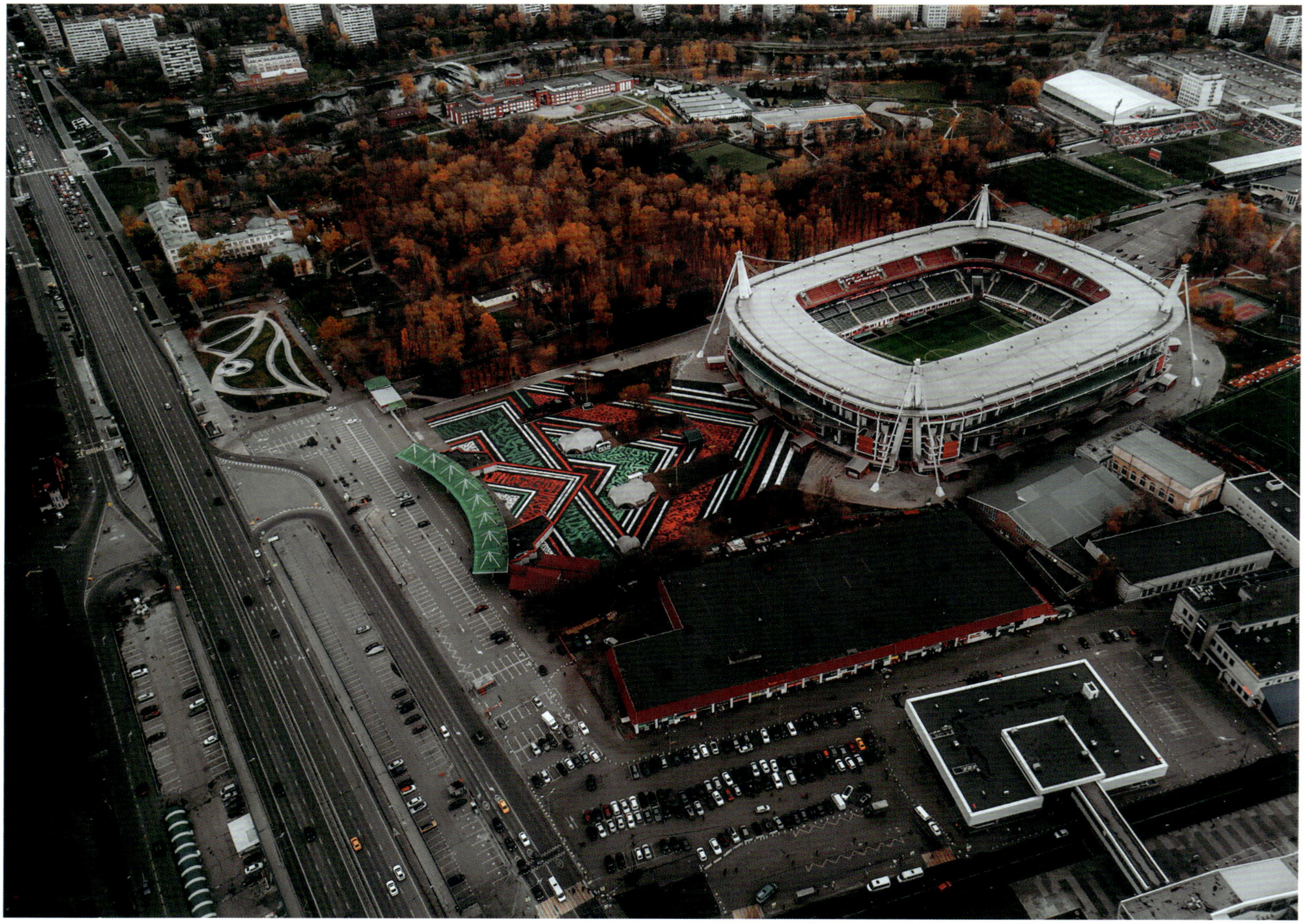

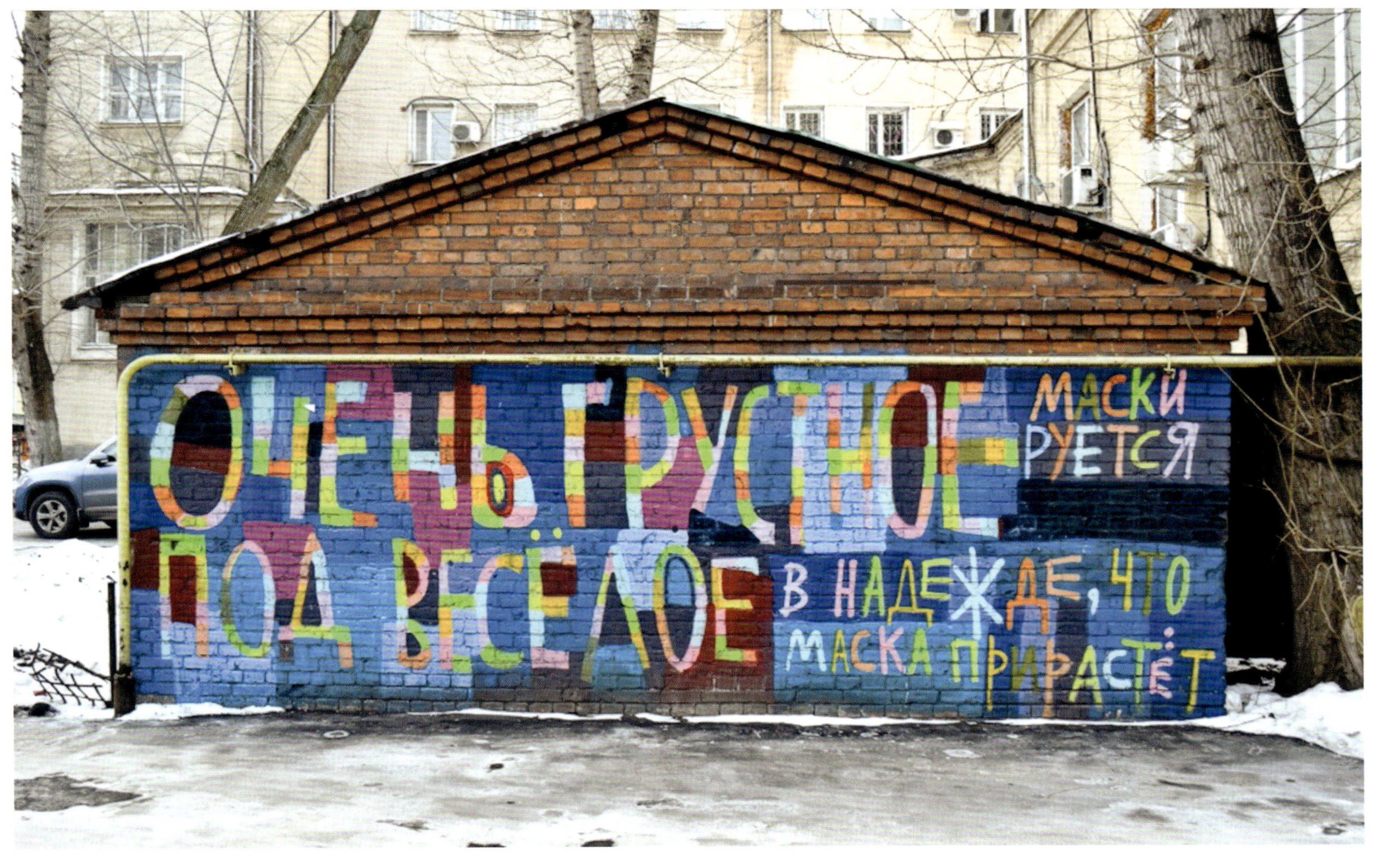

↑
Kto, Kirill
Sad Masks Itself as Jolly Hoping to Stay This Way
2012, spray paint on wall

for vandalism. Graffiti were regarded as the decadent products of Western individualism. Some knowledge of them percolated into Russia during the Gorbachev years, but nobody, even at a time when there was a brief Western revival of interest in Russian art, paid much attention to them. When graffiti appeared in Russian streets, they were classified by the Western world as part of a general climate of what was rather smugly described as 'dissidence'.

In the turmoil immediately following the collapse of the Soviet Union, the social and economic climate was not friendly to the appearance of new art forms, but these gradually started to appear toward the end of the 1990s, often initially under Western influences. One example was a blossoming of street graffiti. The movement initially arrived from neighbouring countries such as Latvia, and also perhaps from the Kaliningrad Russian enclave. By now, however, at least three generations of street graffiti artists have been working in Russia. Their work has been increasingly recognised officially, to the point where there is now a Museum of Street Art in St Petersburg, which was founded in 2009. No comparable institution seems to exist in the West.

One other artist of the current generation of Russian graffiti artists deserve mention here, not least because in his case he focuses on letter forms, rather than on immediately recognisable images. He, however, has become internationally known.

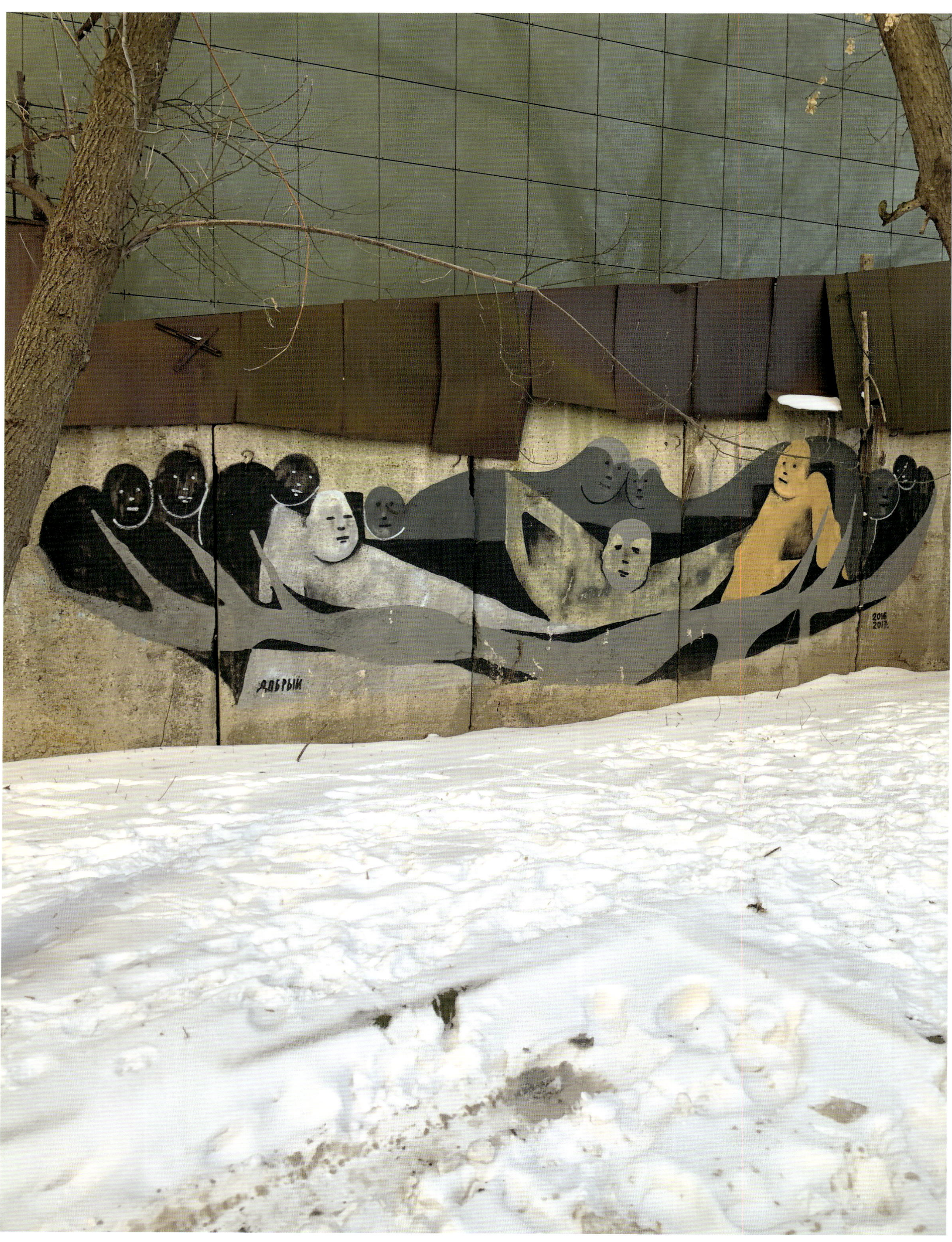
ДОБРЫЙ
2016
2017.

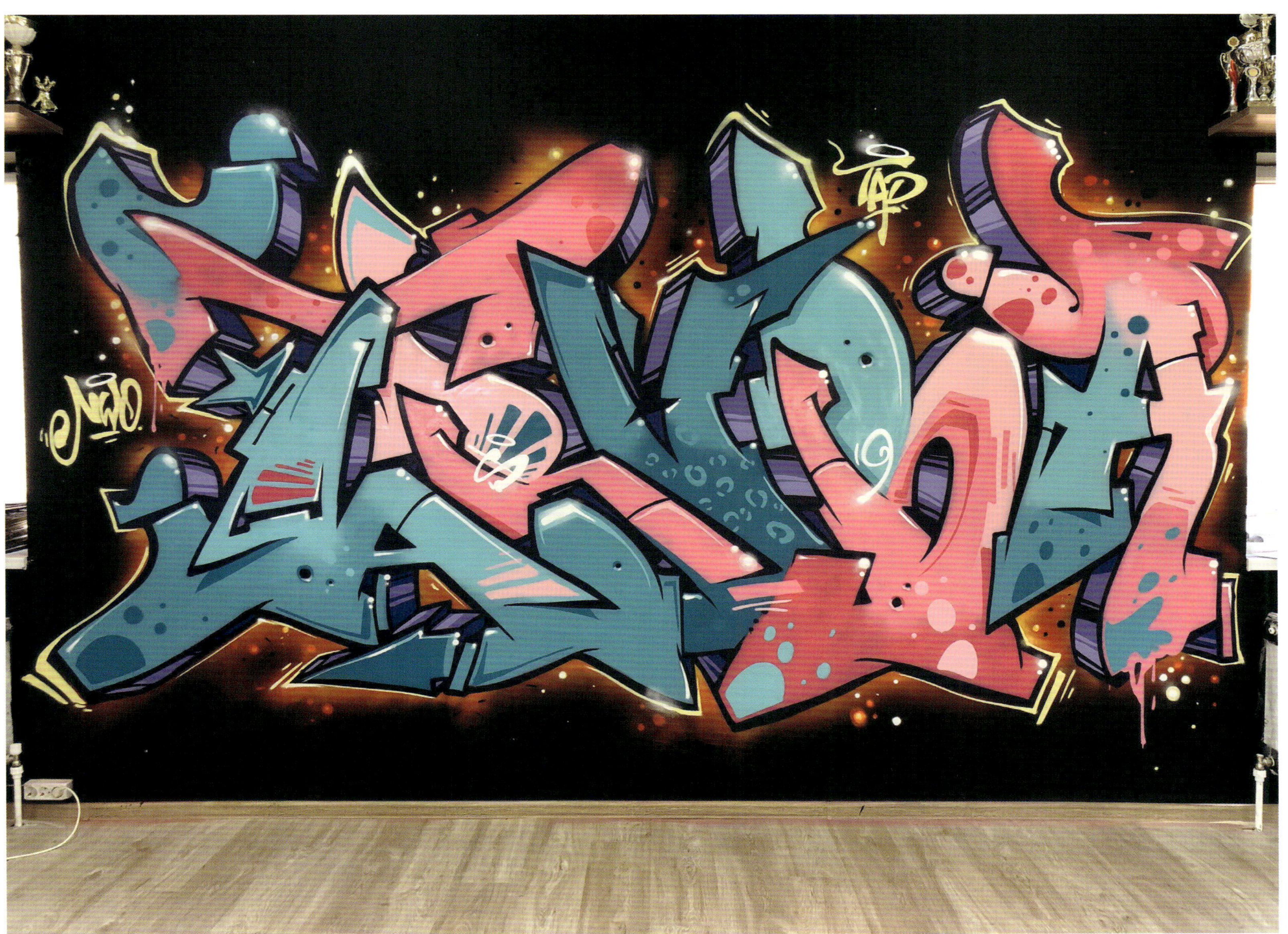

↑
Truba, Arseniy
Untitled
2021, spray paint on wall

Arseniy Truba (b. 1986) lives and works in Moscow but is also the Moscow representative of the TAD (Top 'n Dope) group in St Petersburg. He is an enthusiast for some distinctly non-Russian forms of popular music – i.e. funk and reggae – but is very much an active representative of contemporary Russian visual culture, participating not only in numerous street events within Russia but also in similar events abroad, taking inspiration from what he discovers there.[4] His animated letter forms have great visual force but do not immediately communicate specific meanings.

Most Russian street artists either run their own YouTube channels or own accounts on Twitter, Facebook and Instagram, sometimes having tens of thousands of followers. Their social media pages offer images of their work and show them producing it. In this sense, they are radical democratisers of art, full members of a now very recognisable international community of graffitists, found in most industrial and technological societies. Anyone with access to the internet can now appreciate their art.

←
Dobry, Stas
Untitled
2016–2017, spray paint on wall

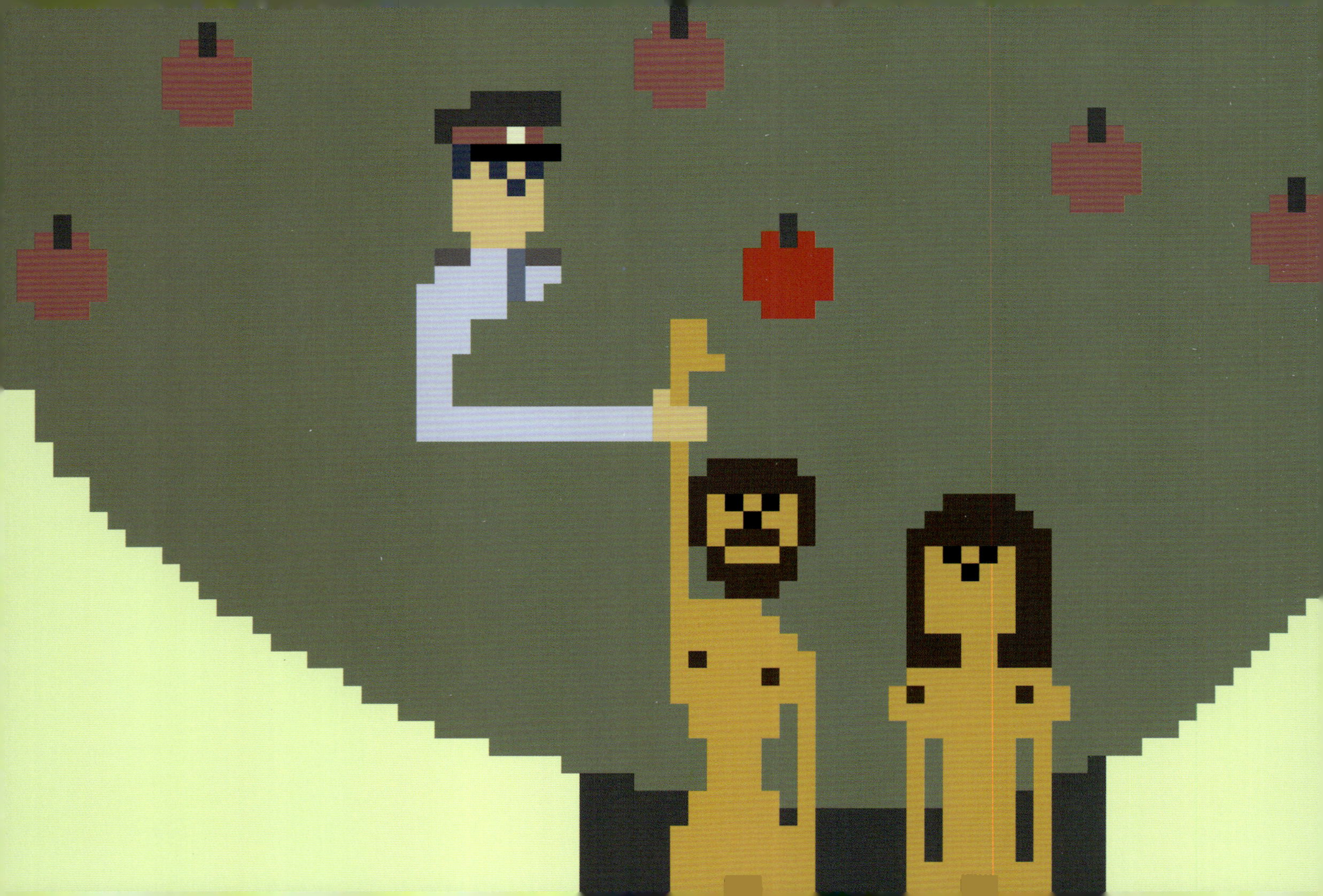

14 DIGITAL ART & THE NFT ART MARKET

The content of this chapter is by necessity a motley selection. Digitisation of images has become a technique used for all kinds of purposes. Although separate from the West in certain respects, Russian art continues to participate in the digital revolution and has by no means been left stranded technologically, also joining the rapidly expanding NFT market.

Sometimes the link to the digital world is directly obvious, as appears here for example in Ivan Tuzov's (b. 1984), *Et'*, – a pair of crudely pixelated naked figures being led out of Eden by an even more crudely pixelated police uniform clad Deity, under a sky patterned with pixelated forbidden fruit. The very crudity of these images implies that the world the figures inhabit is at the beginning (or the end?) of its existence.

Sometimes something is hidden under the surface of the introductory image. An example here is Albert Soldatov's video *Balthus* (2014), introduced by an image of a man and a woman playing cards: the image re-iterates, but does not directly copy, a composition by the French-Polish painter of that name, now in the collection of the Thyssen-Bornemisza Museo Nacional in Madrid. The video is made up of ten scenes derived from different Balthus (1908-2001) paintings, with an accompaniment of voice-over dialogues derived from social networks found on the internet. A text provided by the artist informs the viewer that 'The characters are frozen in an atmosphere of idleness and actualise the hovering as if in a trance [of] the consciousness of a modern man, a user of social networks and forums where information is presented in a fragmented form...' These 'superimposed narrated quotes from the internet express [the] infantile consciousness of a network user.'[1]

←
Tuzov, Ivan
Et
2013

One of the interesting things here is that this is definitely not populist artwork. It demands quite a high degree of sophistication from the viewer, both through its choice of images and through the use the artist then chooses to make of them. Soldatov (b. 1980) studied at the Rodchenko School in the department of new media and has been a winner of the Kandinsky Prize in the 'Young Artist, Project of the Year' category. He lives and works in Moscow.

Other artistic projects in this category are no less sophisticated. Kirill Savchenkov (b.1985) also lives and works in Moscow, where he studied and now teaches at the Rodchenko School. His *Anabasis* project of 2013, which consisted of a series of walks in the Bitsevsky Park and an exhibition in a former Cinema Hall in Yasenevo, an administrative district in Moscow. The park is one of the largest natural forest parks near Moscow. It is home to more than 500 species of plants, among them many fine trees - lindens oaks and firs - planted in the 19th century and is home to 33 species of mammals and 78 species of birds. As Savchenkov himself explains, 'many people find suburban landscapes sterile and anonymous, and I wanted to disprove that. I wanted to show that every housing block and every vacant lot contain certain histories and memories.'[2]

Although Egor Kraft's (b. 1986) work takes a different direction it is still closely linked to contemporary imaging technology. He also studied at the Rodchenko School, but also at the Vienna Academy of Fine Arts and Central Saint Martins in London. He now divides his time between Moscow and Berlin. He claims that his work 'spans across media, science, critical research, philosophy and art'.[3] The project illustrated here involves the digital reconstruction of damaged classical heads; in terms of where Russian art is now, this is a not atypical combination of the old and the extremely new. Many contemporary Russian artists are fascinated by the opportunities offered by the latest advances in technology.

Tim Parchikov's (b. 1983) *Burning News* offers a series of images of people standing in snowy landscapes, holding up burning newspapers. As they read, they are apparently unaware that the flaming paper is burning their hands. The artist recollects that the Bolsheviks, at the beginning of the twentieth century, published a newspaper called *Iskra* (Spark), because the aim of the publication was to ignite a revolution. Now, a century later, the flow of news is of such intensity that 'each new item torches and annihilates its predecessor.' The effect, says Parchikov, is 'one of anaesthesia'.[4] The mind sinks into a state resembling winter hibernation.

Kraft, Egor
Hellenistic Ruler
2018, marble, polyamide, machine learning algorithms

↘
Kraft, Egor
Colossal Head of Hercules
2018, marble, polyamide, machine learning algorithms

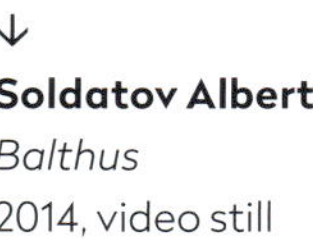

↓
Soldatov Albert
Balthus
2014, video still

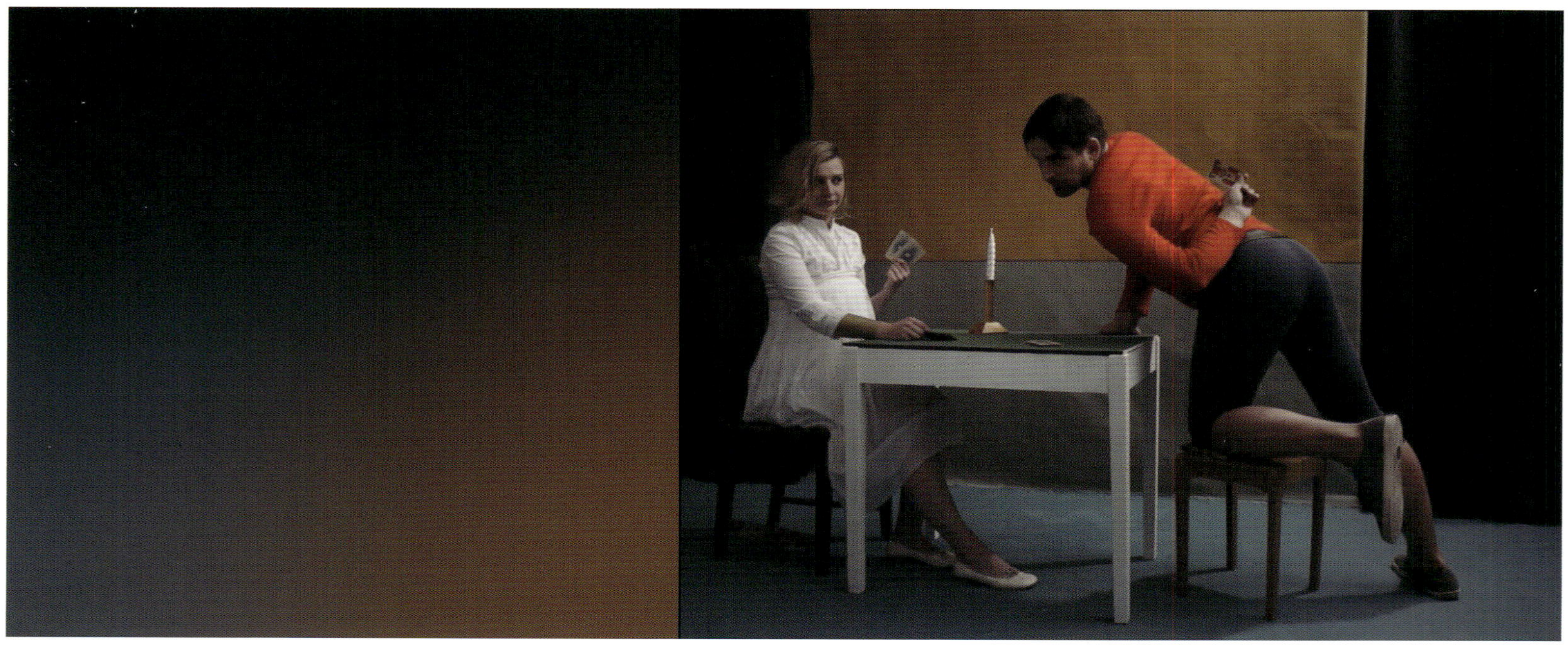

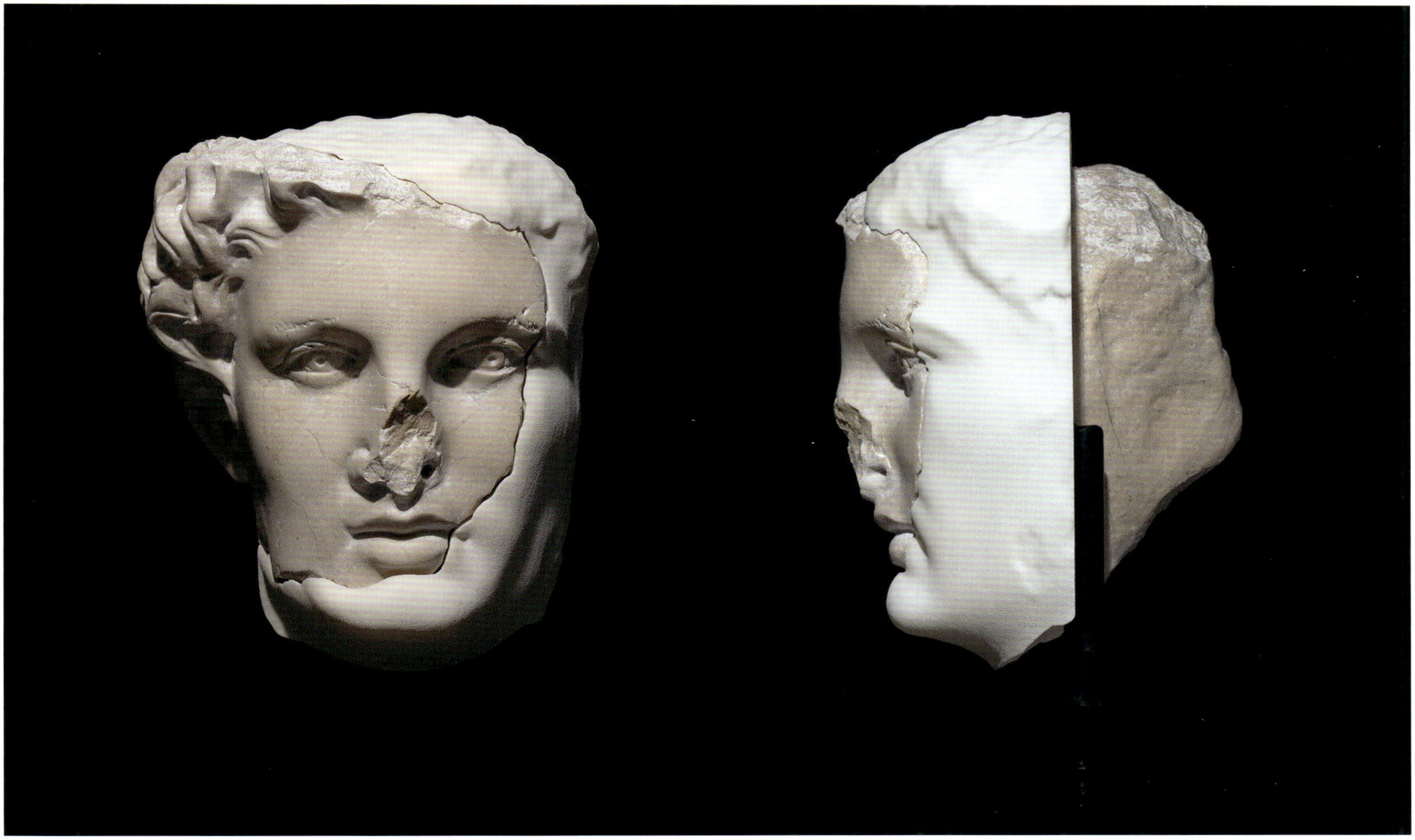

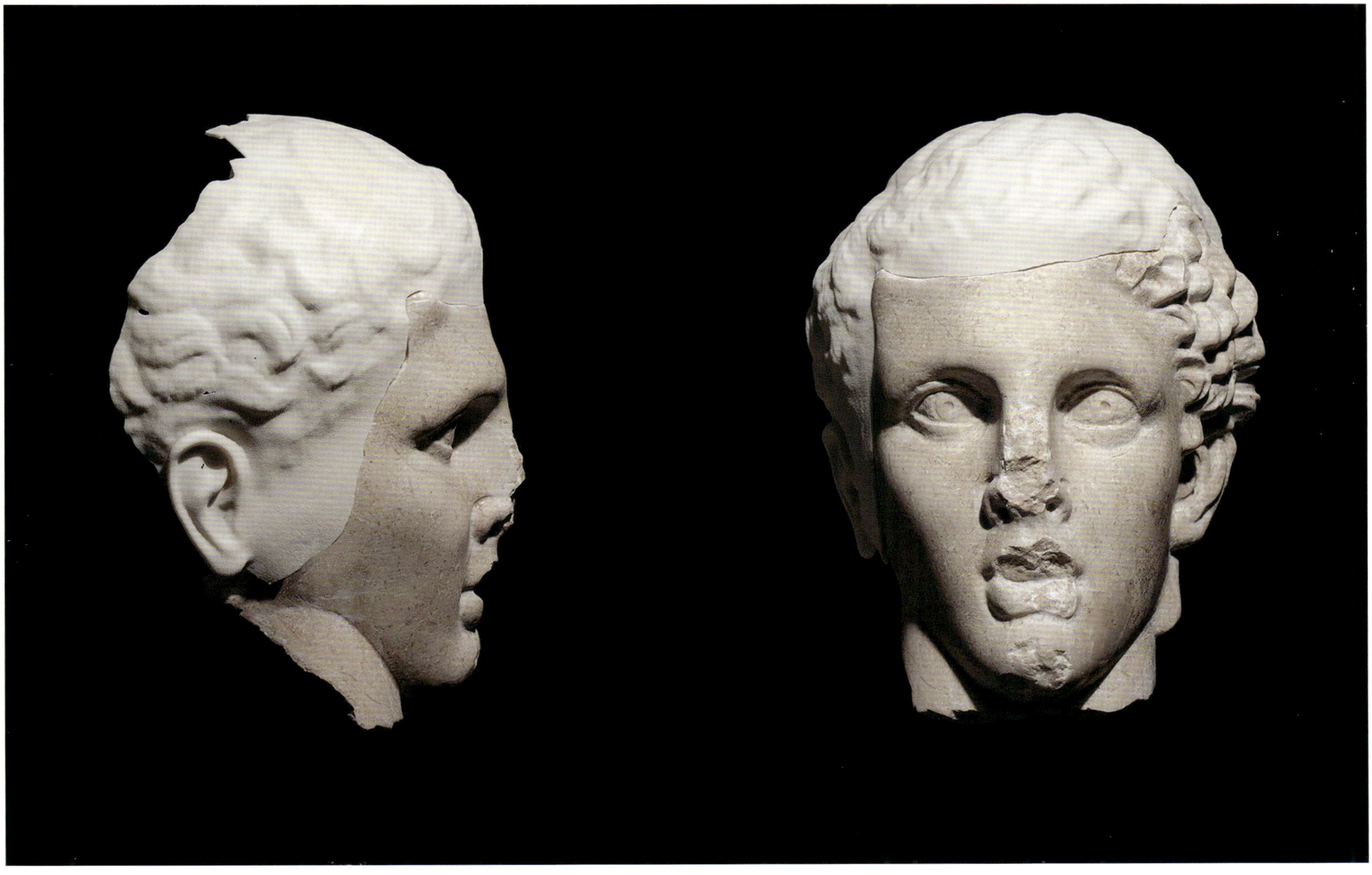

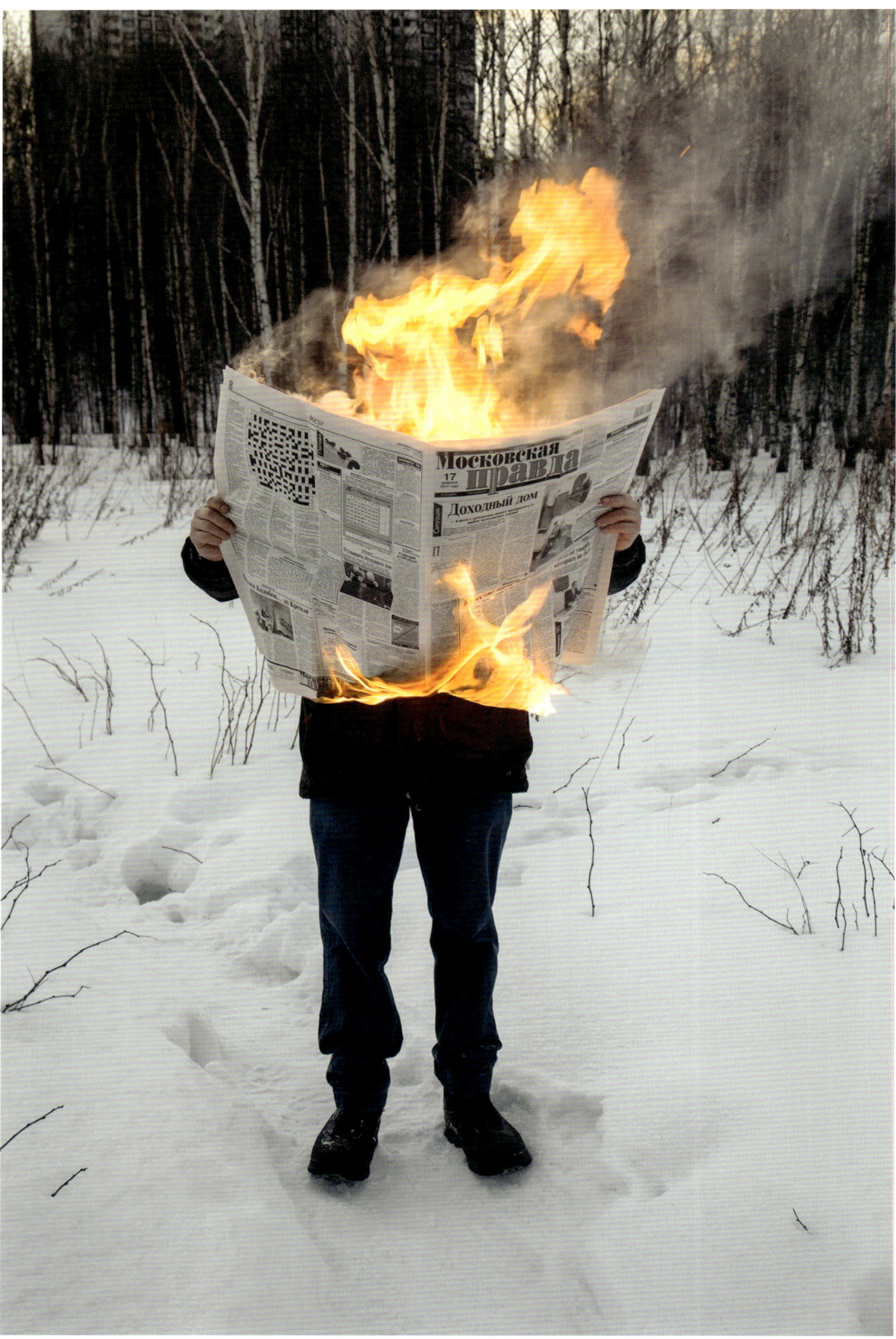

←
Parchikov, Tim
Burning News
2011, C-print

→
Dou, Oleg
Melting Worlds
2019, C-print face mounted with acrylic

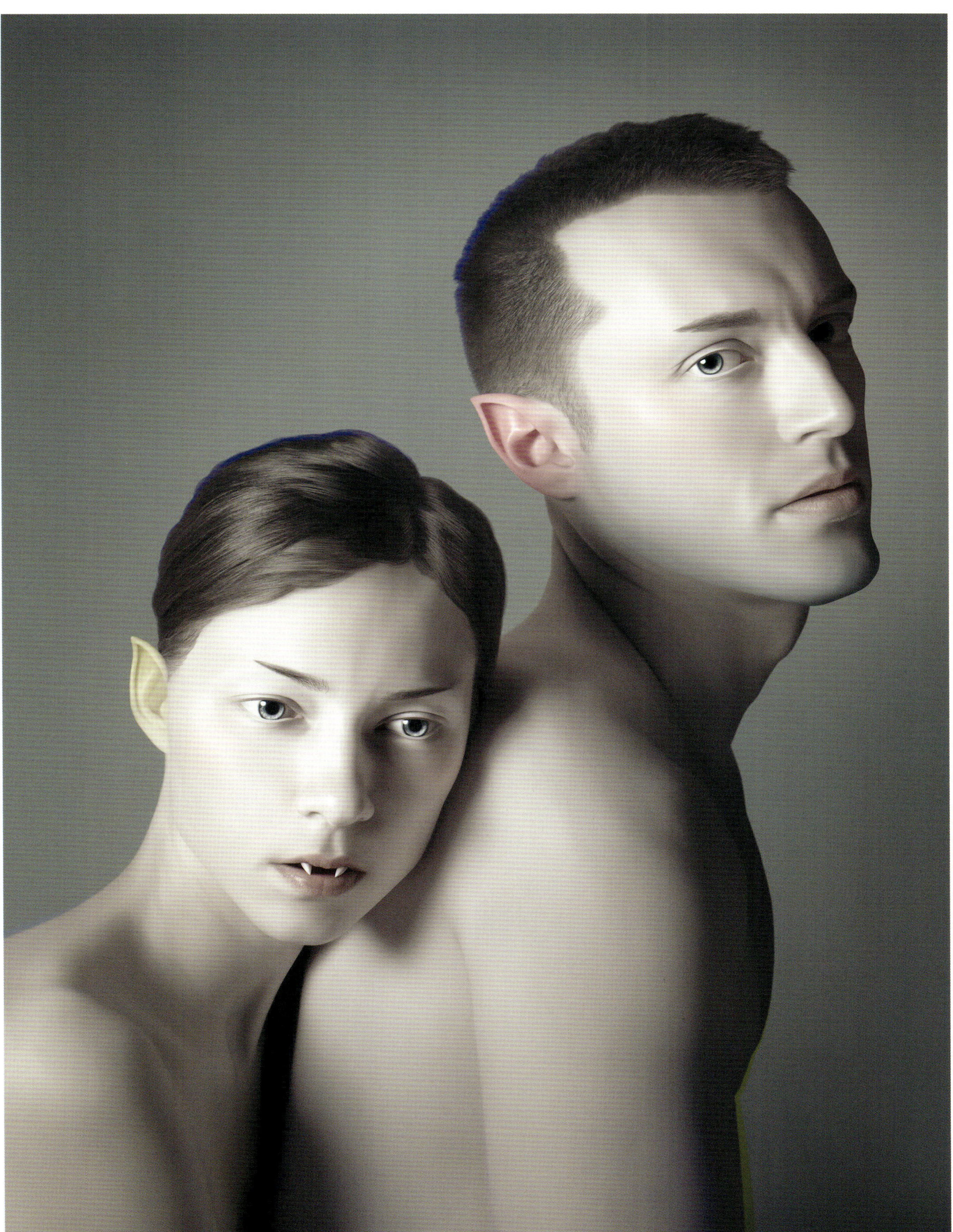

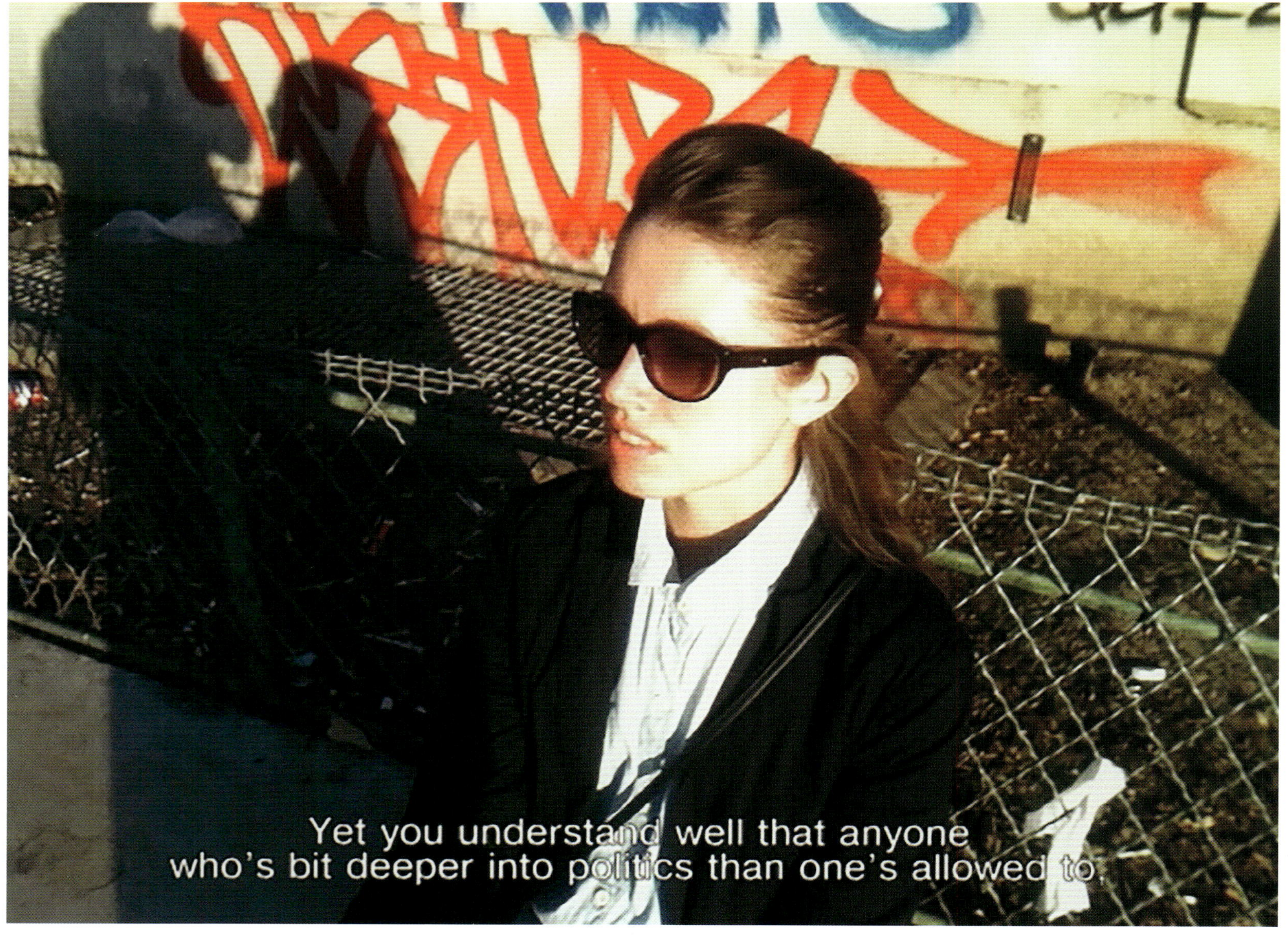

Oleg Dou (b. 1983) provides an even more minatory image: that of a handsome young couple, but it takes a second glance to see that one of them has the teeth of a vampire. Dou, born Duryagin, has, like many younger Russian artists currently at work, a considerable track record of foreign exhibitions – in Houston, Barcelona, Paris, Brussels and Seoul, as well as in the Netherlands and Poland. He has been a nominee for the Kandinsky Prize in Russia.

A winner of Kandinsky Prize 2013 is Evgeny Granilshchikov (b. 1985), again a graduate of the Rodchenko Institute. One of his best-known projects is a film called *Courbet's Funeral* (2014), described as 'a collage blending video poetry with documentation'.[5] It brings together both real-life footage and staged scenes. The real-life scenes include both images from the Prague Spring of 1968 and hastily filmed, upside-down images of riot police in Bolotnaya Square in Moscow. One notes the reference made by the title to a now distant revolutionary past, combined with the fluent use of contemporary visual techniques and possibilities.

↑
Granilshchikov, Evgeny
At Dawn Our Dreams Become Brighter,
2017, video still

The immediate ancestors of this kind of approach in contemporary Russian art are probably the

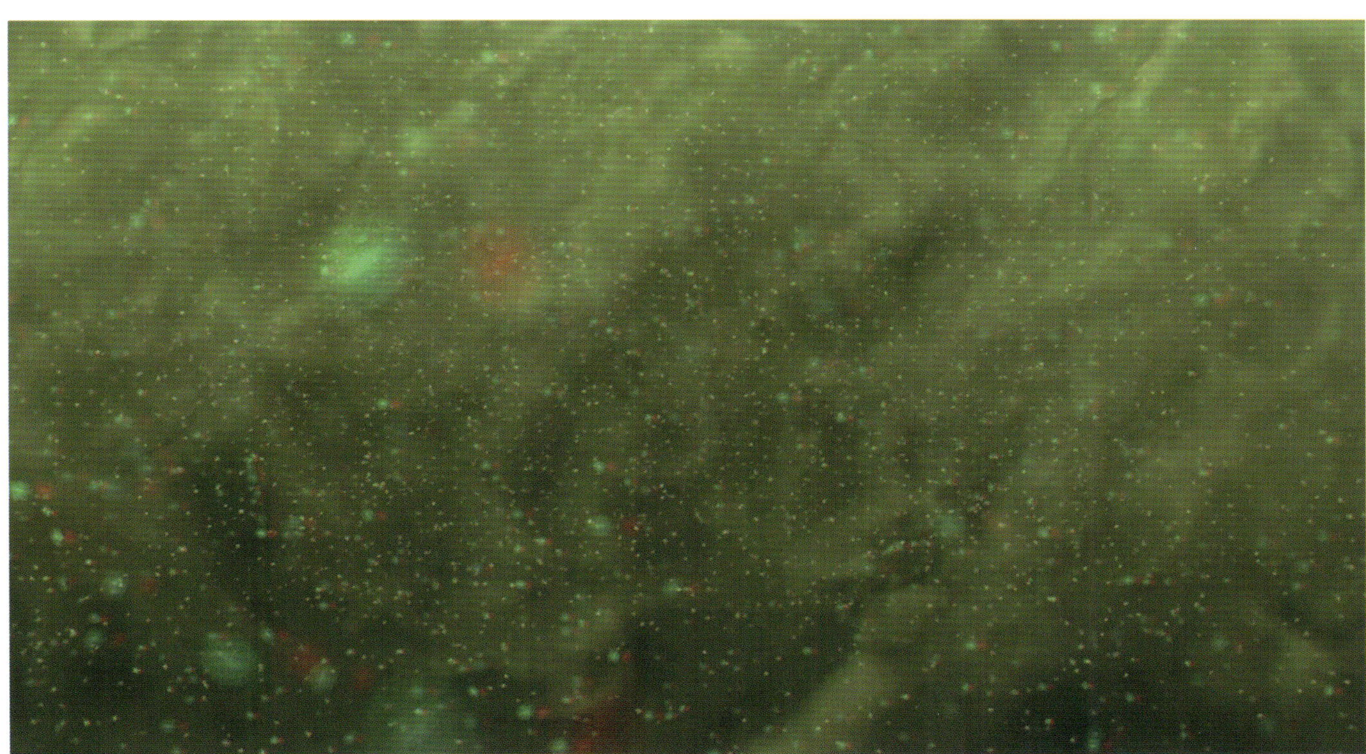

↑
Bluesoup
Murk
2013-2014, video still

Bluesoup Group, still active but formed as long ago as 1996. The group consists of three members: Daniel Lebedev (b. 1974), Alexey Dobrov (b. 1975) and Aleksandr Lobanov (also b. 1975). Valery Patkonen (b. 1972), one of the original founders, left the group in 2010. They live and work in Moscow. *Bluesoup* have exhibited at the XL Gallery in Moscow, which was founded in 1993 and is one of the oldest and influential in the Russian contemporary art. *Bluesoup* have also exhibited at the State Tretyakov Gallery and at many international venues like the Guggenheim Museum in Bilbao, Spain, the Hiroshima City Museum of Contemporary Art in Japan and the Gwangju Museum of Art in South Korea. Characteristic *Bluesoup* works feature images from nature, such as vast moving seascapes, abstracted to the point where the reference to the natural world almost vanishes. Unlike the work of Granilshchikov, who is ten years younger, the content of their art is not directly political.

The emergence and spread of NFT marketplaces opened new opportunities for Russian artists, both well-established and just starting out, to show and sell their art in digital form.

One of the first to join the NFT art market, apart from Pokras Lampas mentioned earlier, was the

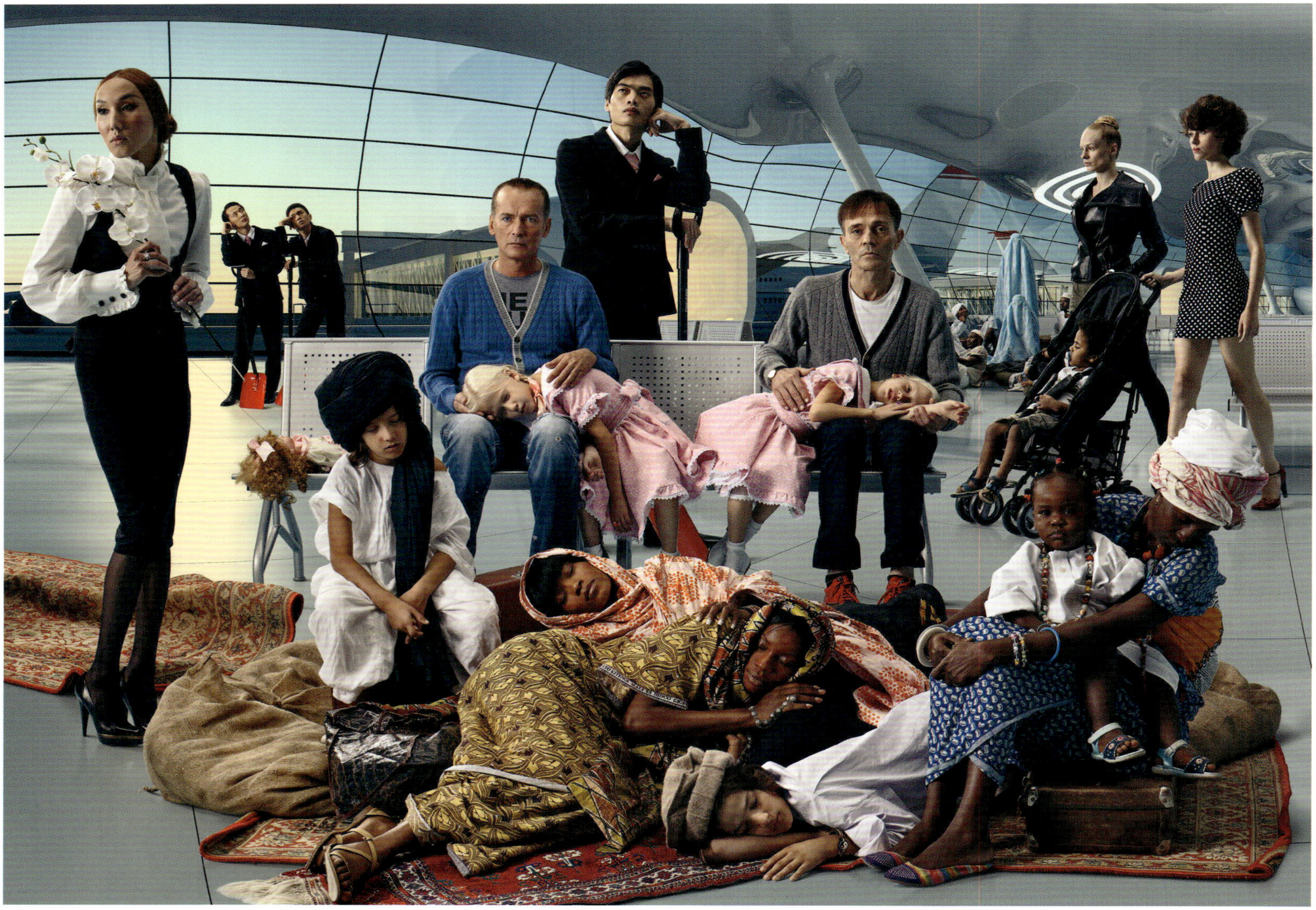

AES+F Group, perhaps, one of the most renowned Russian art collectives. It was formed by Tatiana Arzamasova (b. 1955), Lev Evzovich (b. 1958) and Evgeny Svyatsky (b. 1957) as AES in 1987. The group was joined by Vladimir Fridkes (b. 1956) in 1995 when it became known as AES+F.

According to their site, AES+F 'work at the intersection of traditional media, photography, video and digital technologies'.[6] The group's international recognition was upheld by *Last Riot*, the video-installation shown in the Russian Pavilion at the 52nd Biennale di Venezia in 2007. *The Twins* is one of AES+F's Allegoria Sacra projects, which won them the Sergey Kuryokhin Prize in 2011 and the main award of the Kandinsky Prize 2012. The group also won the NordArt Festival in 2014 and the Pino Pascali Prize in 2015 (18th Edition). They have held over 100 solo shows internationally and their works are shown in many international museums of contemporary art including Moderna Museet in Stockholm, the Art Gallery of South Australia in Adelaide, the Centre Pompidou in Paris as well as in Russian museums, including the State Tretyakov Gallery in Moscow and the State Russian Museum in St Petersburg.

In 2021 AES+F created *The Circle of Life* for the Nano Collection by Gentle Monster which perhaps represents the first occasion when an artwork destined for an advertising campaign was offered as an NFT[7].

AES+F
Allegoria Sacra, The Twins
2012, digital collage, c-print

AES+F
The Circle of Life
2021, video still

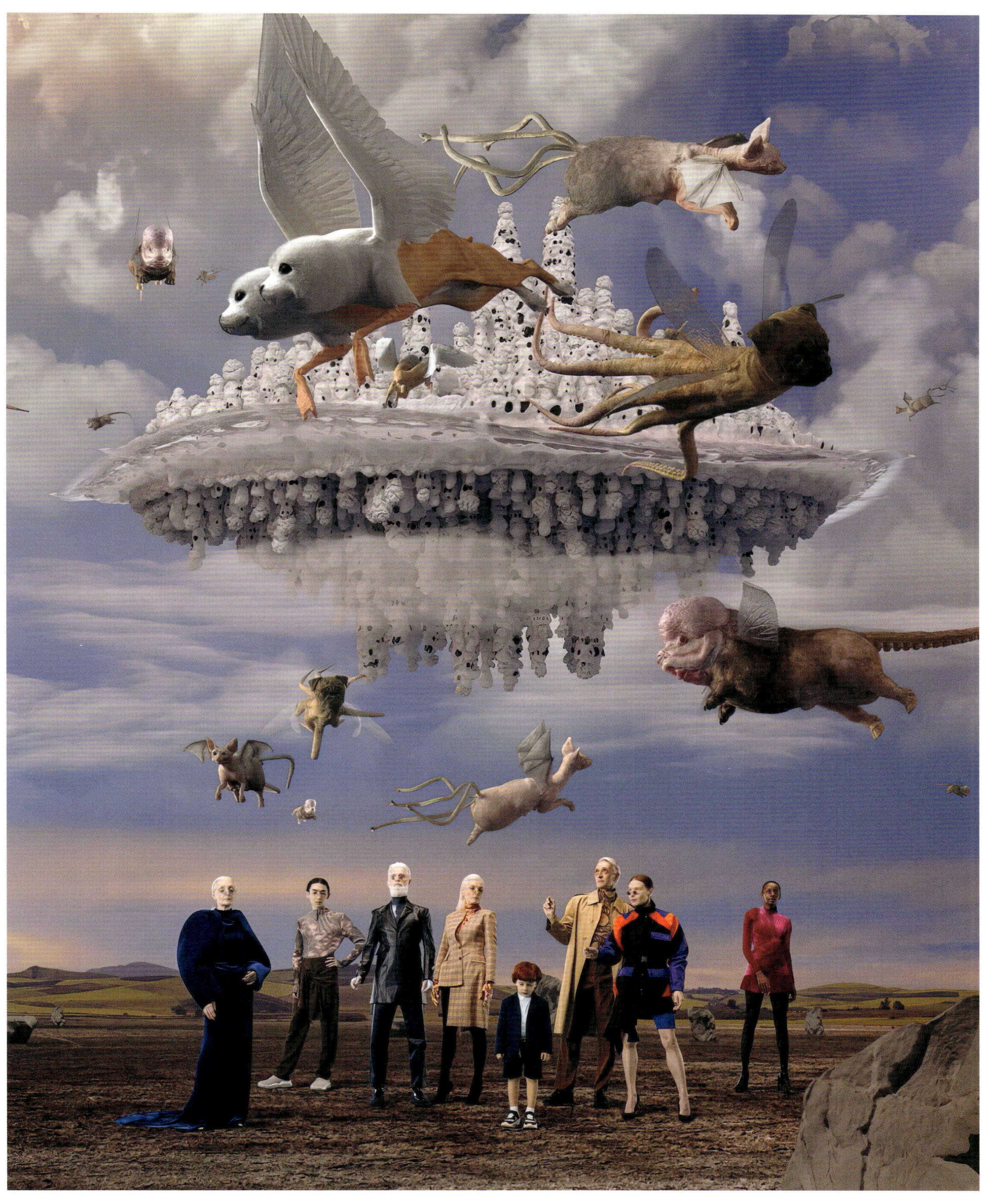

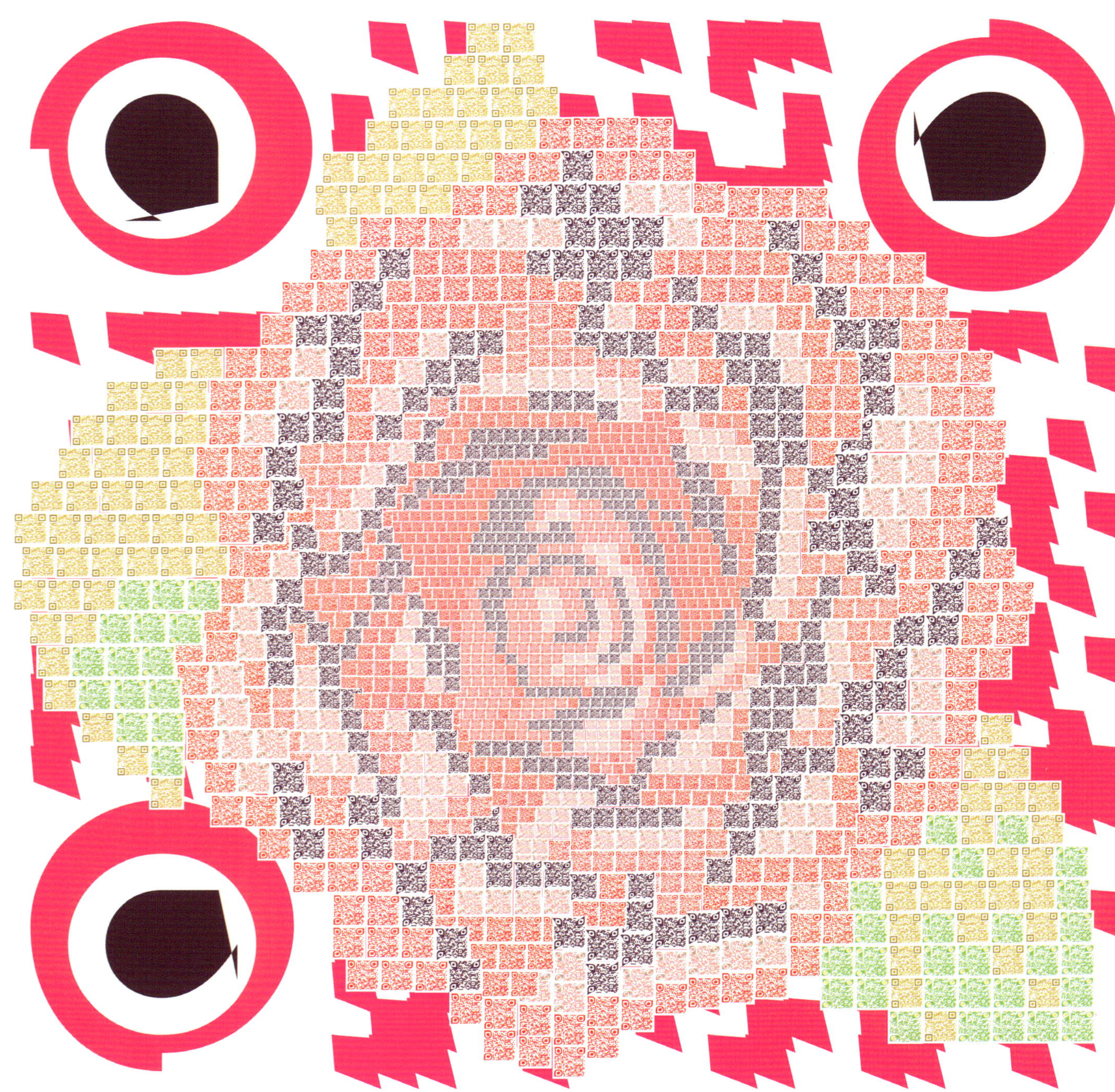

↑
Zabaluev, Sasha
Flower 11
2021, digital image with
QR-codes

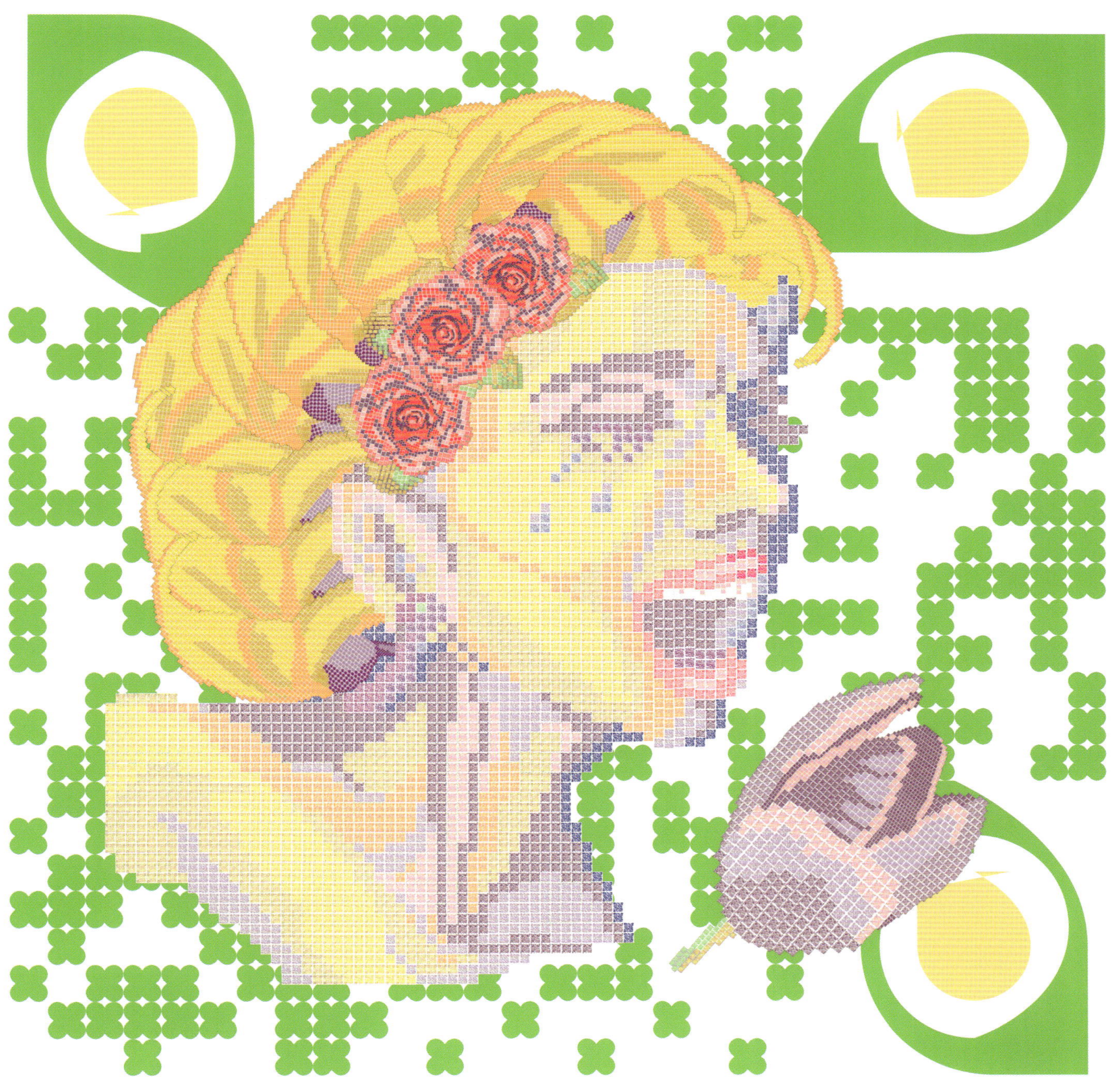

↑
Zabaluev, Sasha
Venus Flower 36.1
2021, digital image with QR-codes

The NFT art market has also opened its doors to 'virtual' newcomers like Sasha Zabalueva (b. 1986). She moved to Moscow from her native Rostov-on-Don in 2013 where she began to develop her expressive style with elements of feminine pop-art; however, dissatisfied with the result, she destroyed most of her *oeuvre*. Sasha moved on into digital art and responded to the emergence of NFTs and the spread of Covid-19 with her new project, *Color Digital* (*Color* means both a *colour* and a *flower* in Latin), making her art with the help of QR-codes.[8]

The ultimate effect of NFTs on the Russian and international art community is yet to be seen, but this new market undoubtedly expands the horizon for creativity and opens new avenues for art and owning artwork images, digital and non-digital alike.

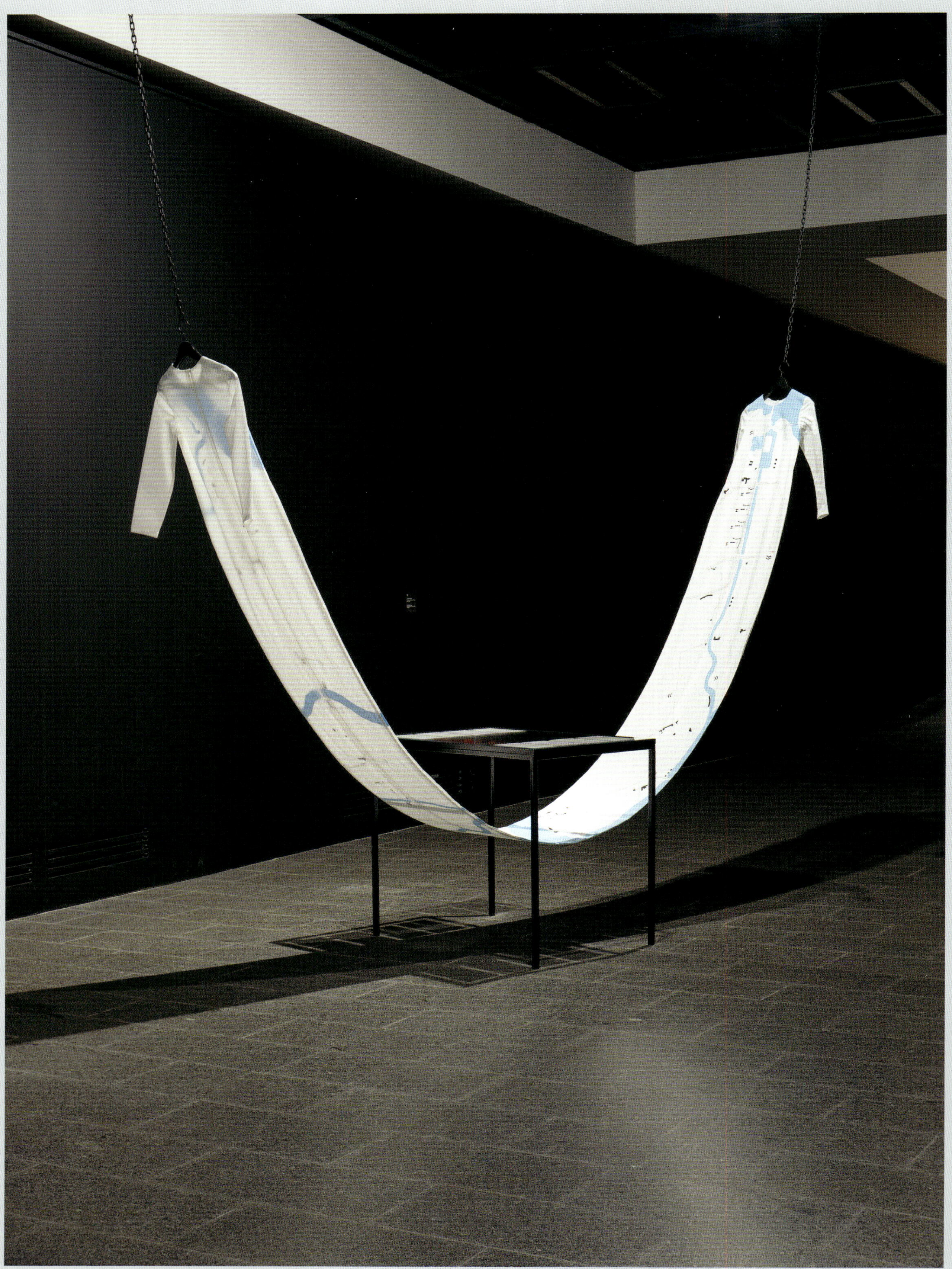

15
SCULPTURE & INSTALLATIONS

It has become an accepted aspect of contemporary art world today that 'sculptures' – that is to say three-dimensional artworks – can be created from any material, or any combination of materials: a fact already fully demonstrated in earlier chapters of this book. It is also accepted that three-dimensional objects, not necessarily art in their own right, can be combined in a given space, to produce something that qualifies as art in the mind of the viewer. These combination artworks are classified as 'installations'. Examples of art in both these categories have already featured in earlier chapters of this book, but it seems worthwhile to examine them again here, not least because they have been seen as particularly characteristic of Western avant-garde art – as opposed, for example, to the forms of artistic expression that seemed to be typical of the now-defunct Soviet Union.

An interesting example of installation art is Asya Marakulina's (b. 1988) installation *Seam Rule* shown at the Manezh Central Exhibition Hall in 2020. According to the artist, '*Seam Rule* was never intended as a project. Rather, it is a story about my secret behavioural practice in the city. Using the made-up rules of walking, as if weaving my body and time into the fabric of the streets, I tried to become a part of the city, in which I felt like a restless stranger. A peculiar game of "thread and a needle" and the rituals of "stitching" and "cutting" became my mainstay during my adaptation to St Petersburg. The texts are taken from my personal diary of those years.'[1] In Marakulina's case, a kind of leisurely peregrination round the space depicted becomes the artwork, not any of the separate items depicted.

←
Marakulina, Asya
Seam Rule, 2014-2015
2020, installation overview

One artist who pushes exhibition techniques further still is Ilya Fedotov-Fedorov (b. 1988). For example, in a show entitled *Preservation Instinct* (2018) he considered biological processes, and the ways in which these are presented in museum displays. With the help of these, 'he reveals the subjective nature of the acquisition of knowledge and its dependence on individual experience.'[2] To achieve this, he employed a wide variety of objects:

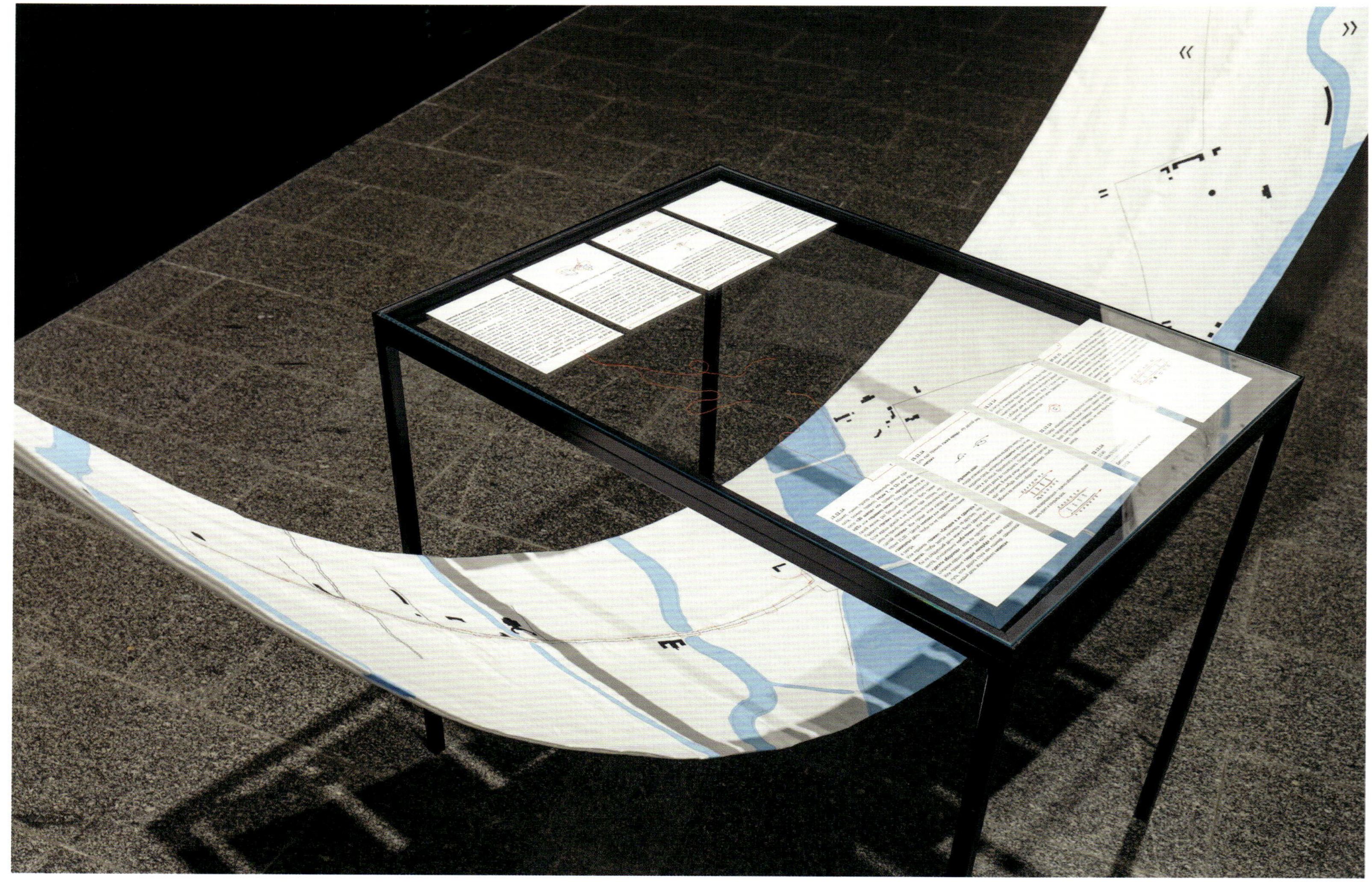

Models, samples, test tubes and laboratory flasks with unknown substances, as well as sketches, drawings, maps, and blueprints that seem, at first, to organise the 'collection' and put it in order. These objects are strange and mysterious, they seem to suggest the appearance of a 'post-human' world in which differences between organic nature and non-organic matter have been effaced and animals and plant species have mutated, adapted or changed so much that they have become unrecognisable.[3]

This provides a striking contrast to Alexander Povzner's (b. 1976) jokey sculpture *The Artist and the Canvas* (2019), in which a male figure punches his forearm through a canvas floating in front of him, as if determined to assert the superior merits of three-dimensionality.

Notwithstanding his avant-garde approach to art, Povzner has a strong academic background. He graduated from the Faculty of Sculpture of the Russian Academy of Painting, Sculpture and Architecture (now named after Ilya Glazunov) and the V. Surikov Moscow State Academy Art Institute, Faculty of Sculpture in 1997 and 1999 respectively. This was followed by a course at the Institute of Contemporary Art in Moscow in 2008–9.

↑
Marakulina, Asya
Seam Rule, 2014-2015
2020, central part of the installation

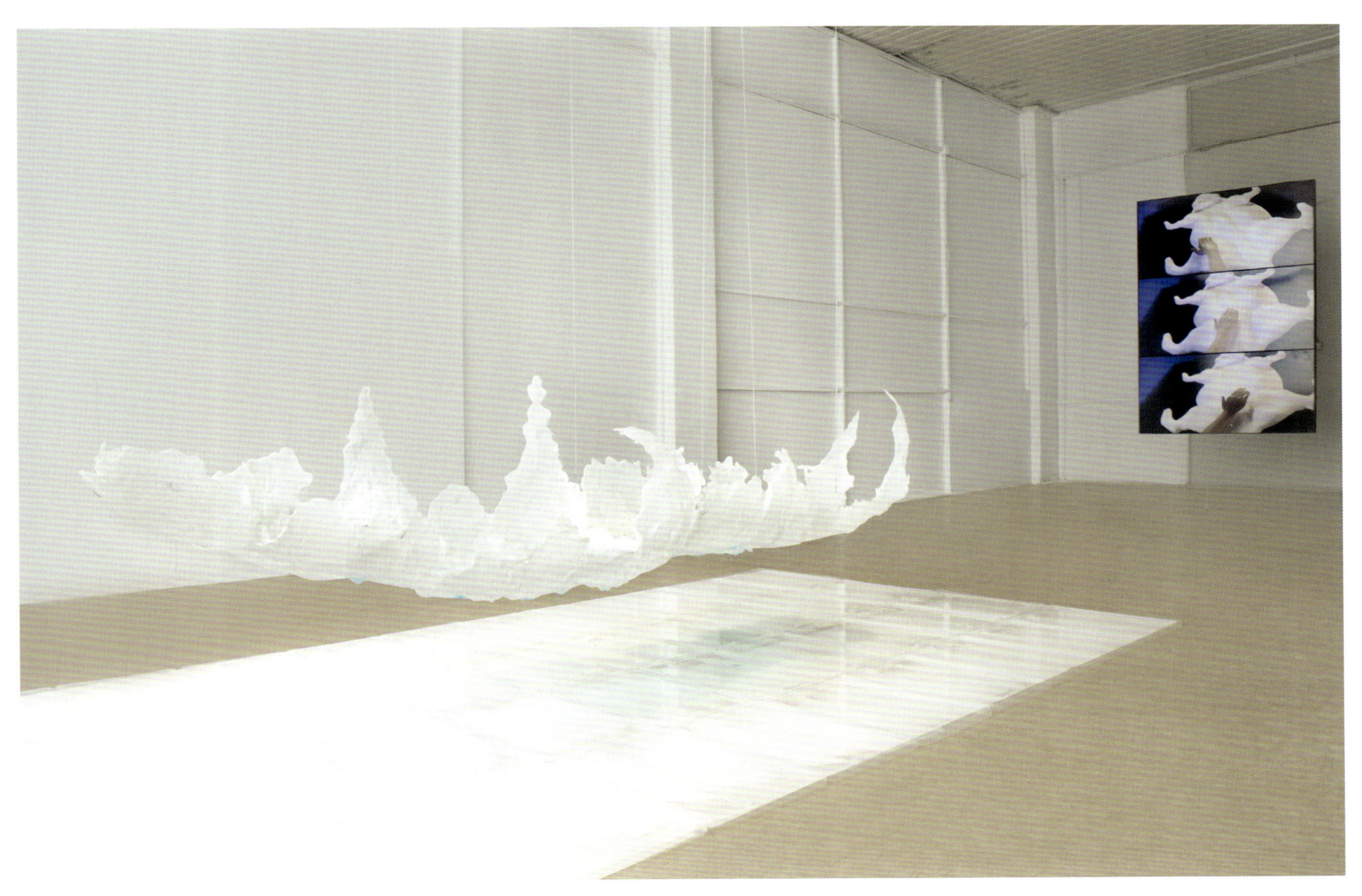

↑
Fedotov-Fedorov, Ilya
Exo-Ark
2019, mixed media
installation, video still

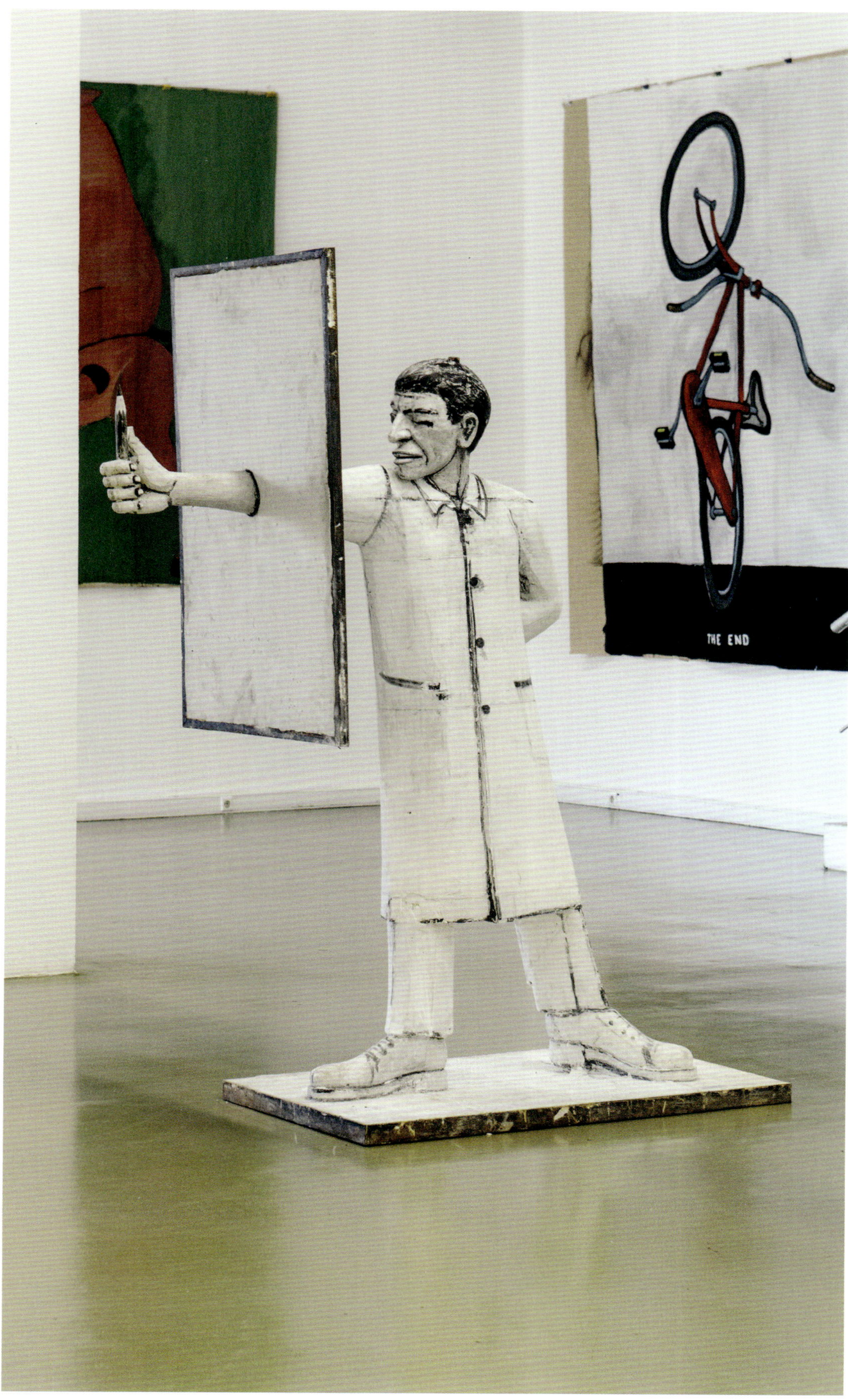

←
Povzner, Alexander
The Artist and the Canvas
2019, painted plaster

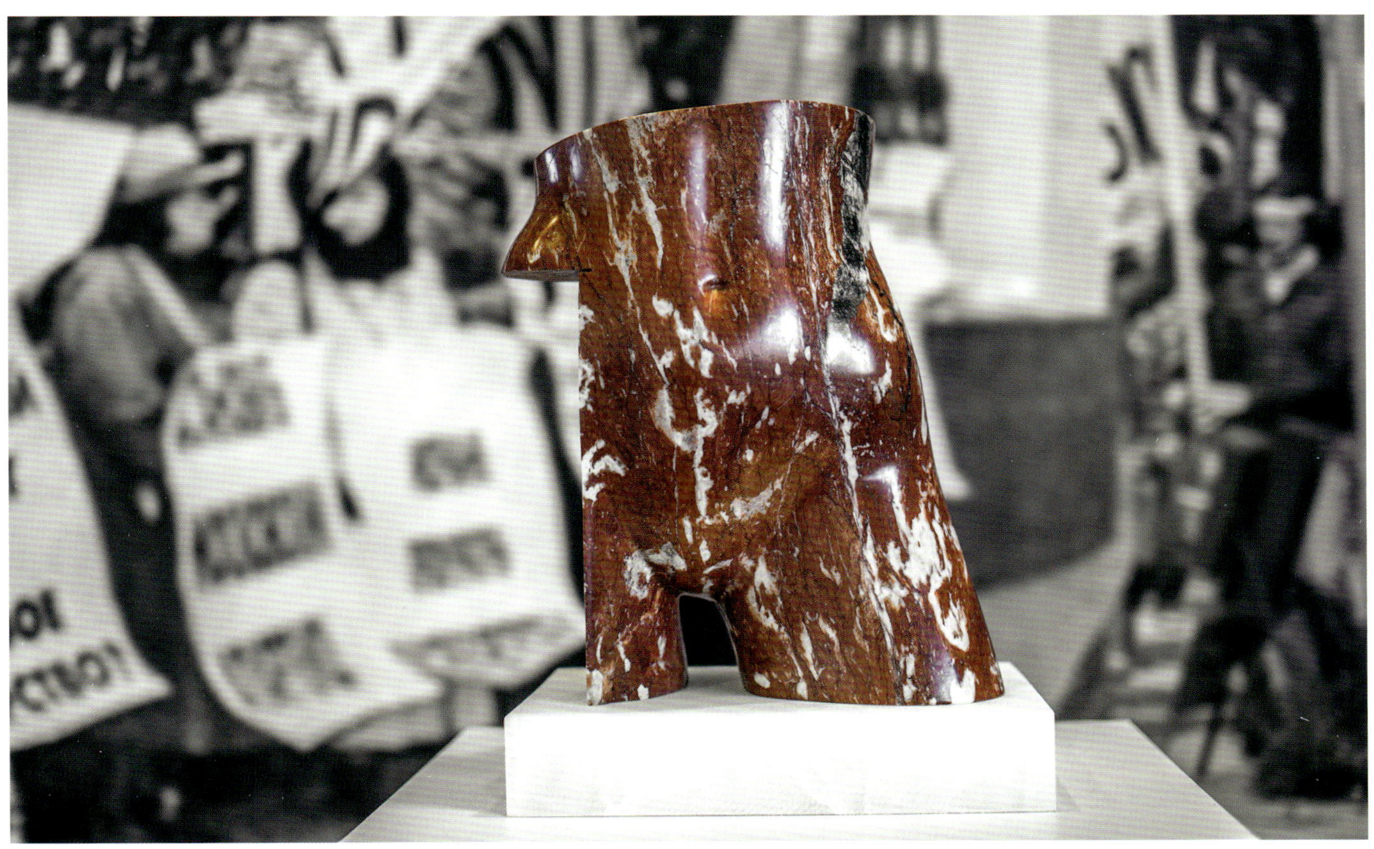

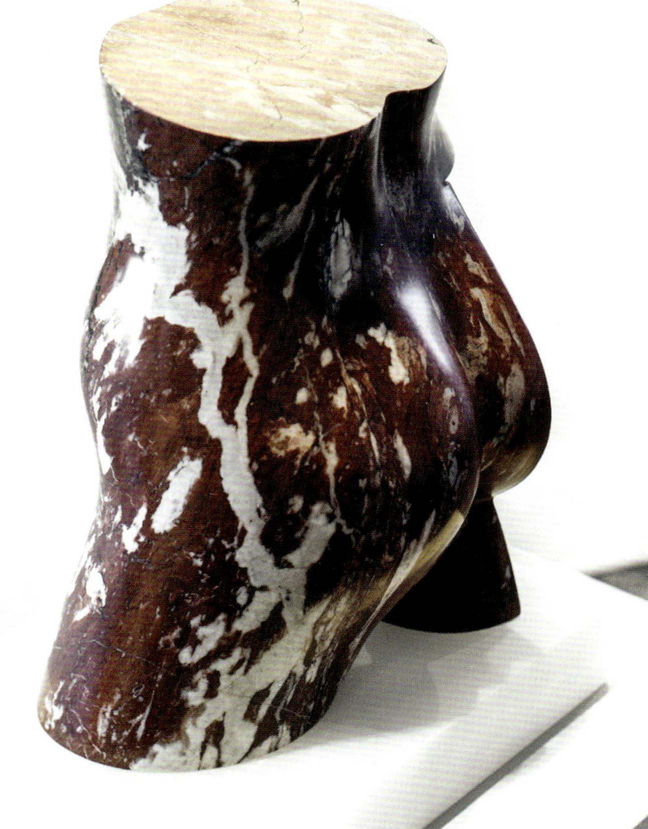

↑
Titova, Anna
Identikit
2017, marble, onyx, brass
(frontal view)

→
Titova, Anna
Identikit
2017, marble, onyx, brass
(side view)

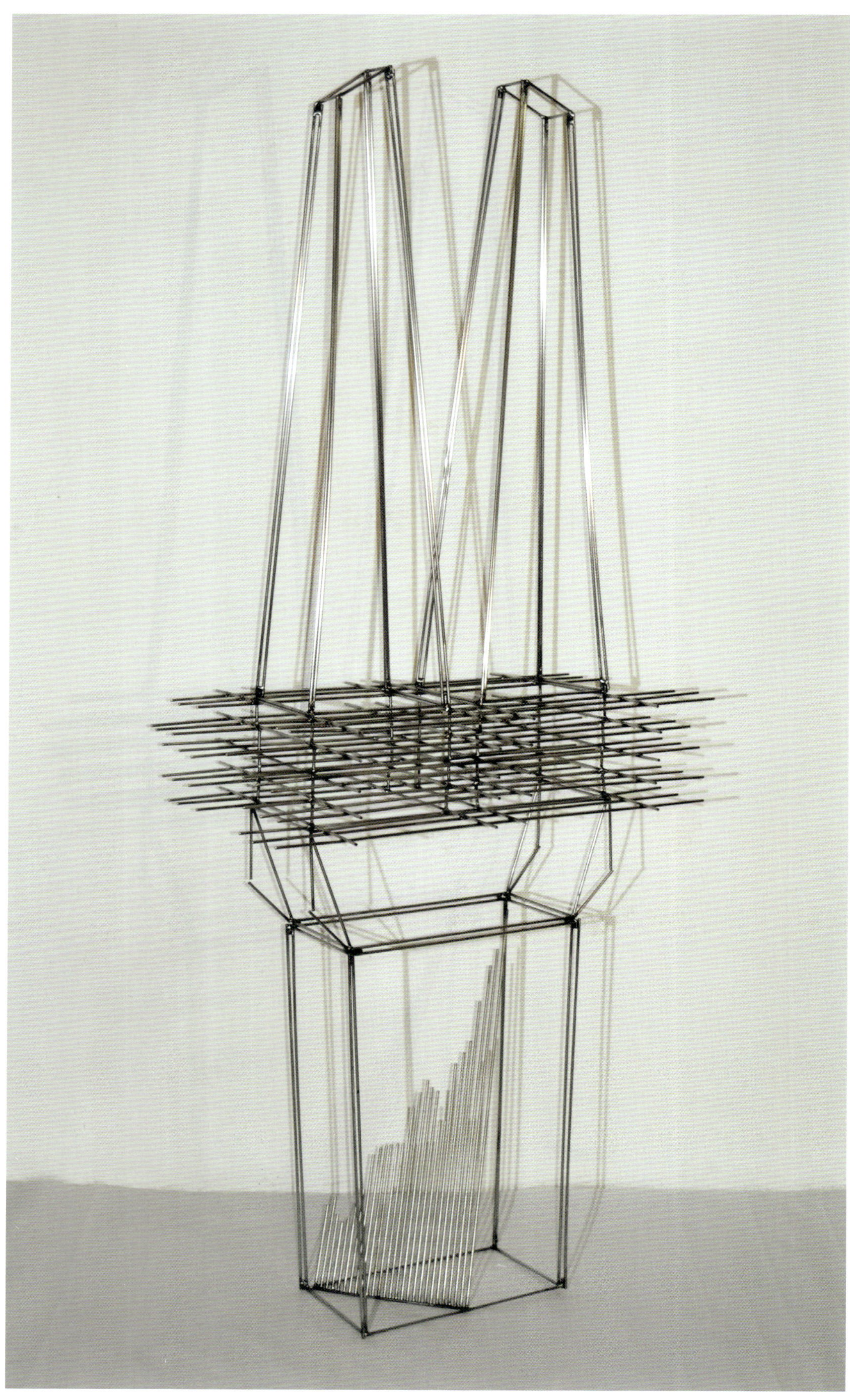

←
Bobkova, Liza
Love Tower
2016, stainless steel, welding (overview)

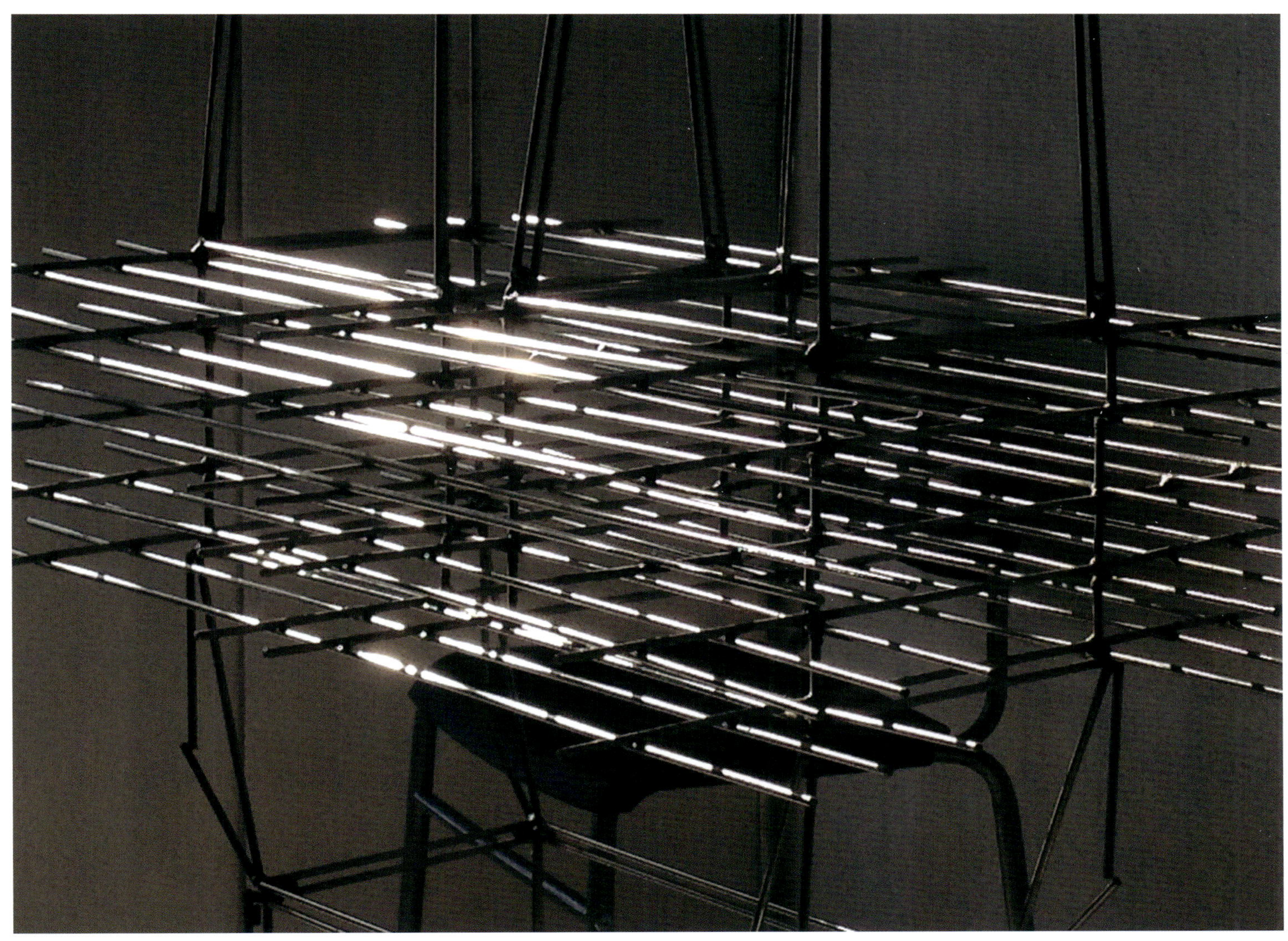

↑
Bobkova, Liza
Love Tower
2016, stainless steel, welding (central part)

This in turn can be compared with the sculpture of a torso by Anna Titova (b. 1984). By contrast, her biography is far from conventional. She was born in Ulan-Ude, the capital city of the Republic of Buryatia. However, her first exhibition took place not in Russia but in Glasgow where she studied at the Glasgow School of Art. Anna began her artistic career as a photographer and was nominated for the Kandinsky Prize in 2008 for her photographic work. She was awarded her MA at the Valand Academy in Gothenburg in Sweden and now concentrates on making art in three dimensions.

A number of Russian sculpture artists now focus on creating abstract rather than figurative art. Among them are Ilya Grishaev (b. 1984) – who lives and works in St Petersburg and is a member of the North-7 art group – and Lisa Bobkova (b. 1987).

Grishaev, like many Russian sculptors active today, produces art in a wide variety of genres. He describes his activity thus: 'I try to create plastic bodies. Assembled from forms aspiring to be signs… more obedient to poetic laws than to logic.'[14]

His abstract relief *Pas Tout* appears to be made up of looped strands of wire and provides a hint that its initial inspiration may have been a row of dancing figures, if one chooses to deduce this from the title and the work's appearance. The French word 'pas' after all has two quite separate meanings.

Like Grishaev, Lisa Bobkova (b.1987) lives and works in St Petersburg. Her *Love Tower* (2016) is made of rods of stainless steel and has an airy lightness that contradicts its title. No fairy-tale maidens are likely to be imprisoned here. It occupies space, but is essentially an abstract drawing in three dimensions. It looks back to the early years of Russian Modernism at the very beginning of the twentieth century.

Artur Dzharullaev (b. 1981) is yet another St Petersburg artist – a graduate from the Stieglitz State Academy, though he studied originally in Dagestan. *Oil Monsters* (2019) is one of a group of similar pieces he has made on this theme. They fall into a category, sometimes described as 'junk sculpture', which is also familiar from the work of artists of the same generation who live and work in the West but are more playful and high-spirited than their Western counterparts. Even more obviously than in Grishaev's work, they offer an oscillation between abstract and figurative impulses.

Other Russian sculptors of the current generation in this chapter embrace the figurative tradition, though in very different guises. These include Alexander Povzner (mentioned earlier in this chapter), Pyotr Diakov and Evgeny Antufiev.

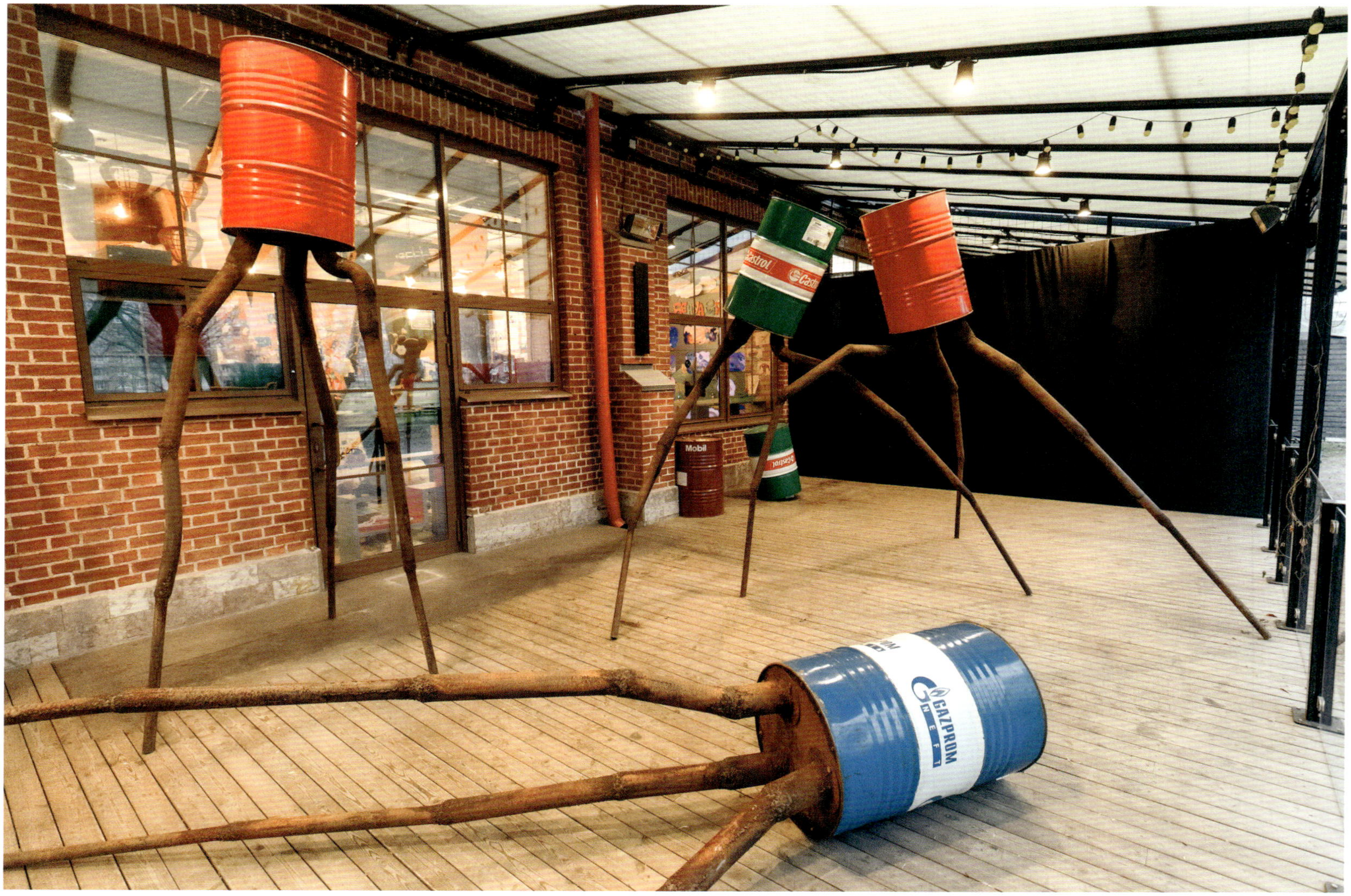

Dzharullaev, Artur
Oil Monsters
2019, 200 l barrels, steel plates, pipes, bolts

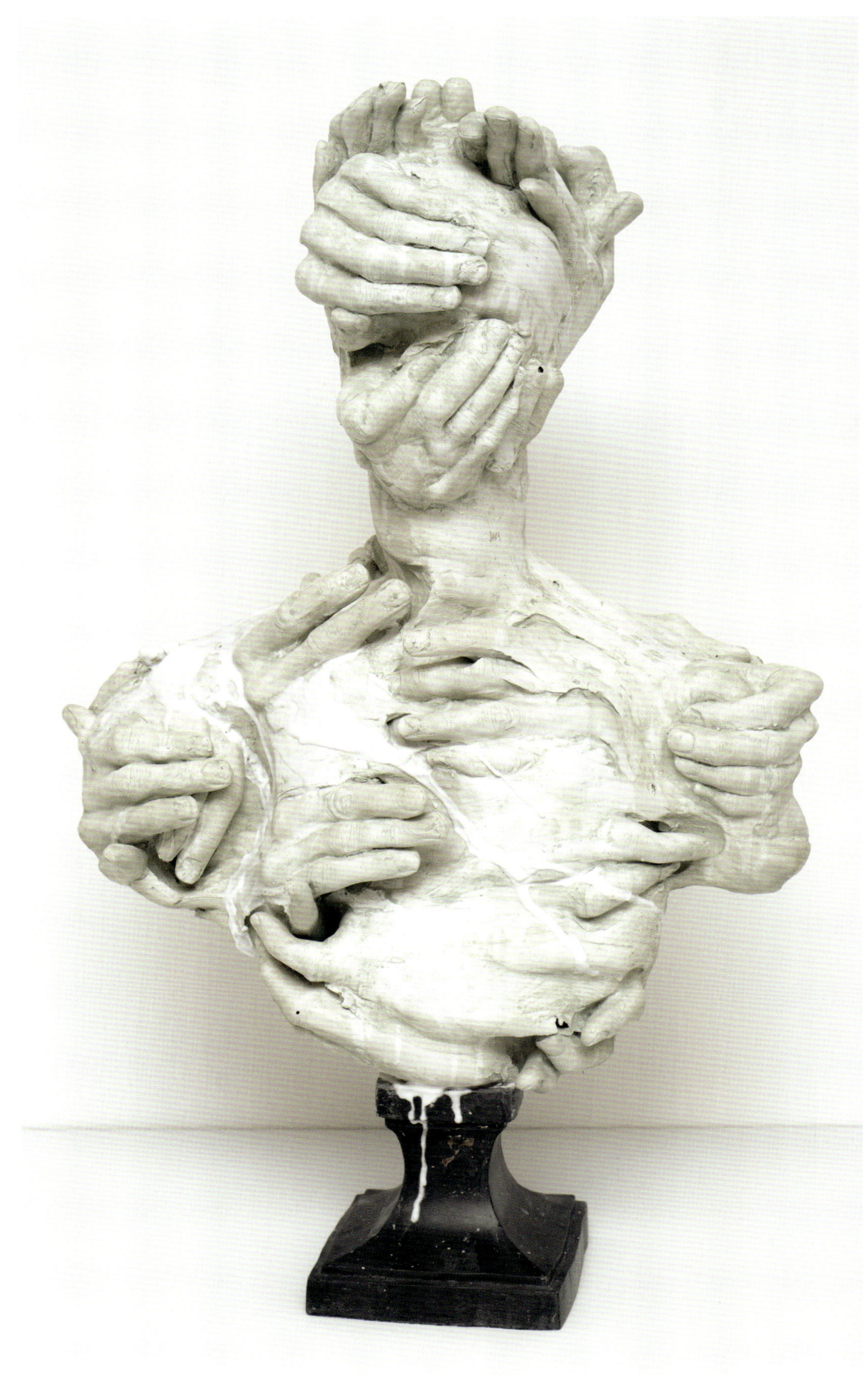

→
Diakov, Piotr
Bust
2018, acrylic composite, pigments

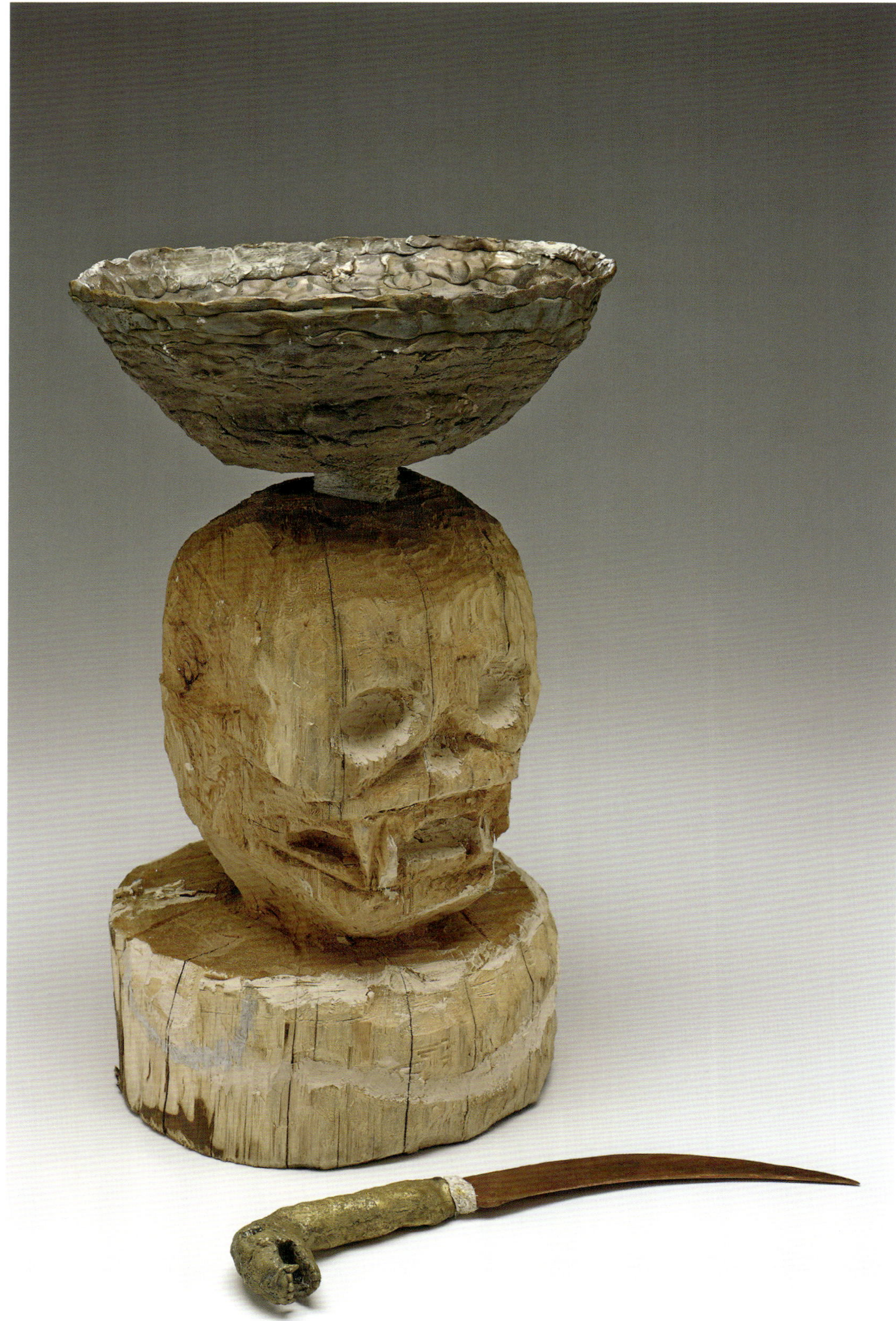

←
Antufiev, Evgeny
Untitled
2016, wood, bronze, textile, brass and copper, knife

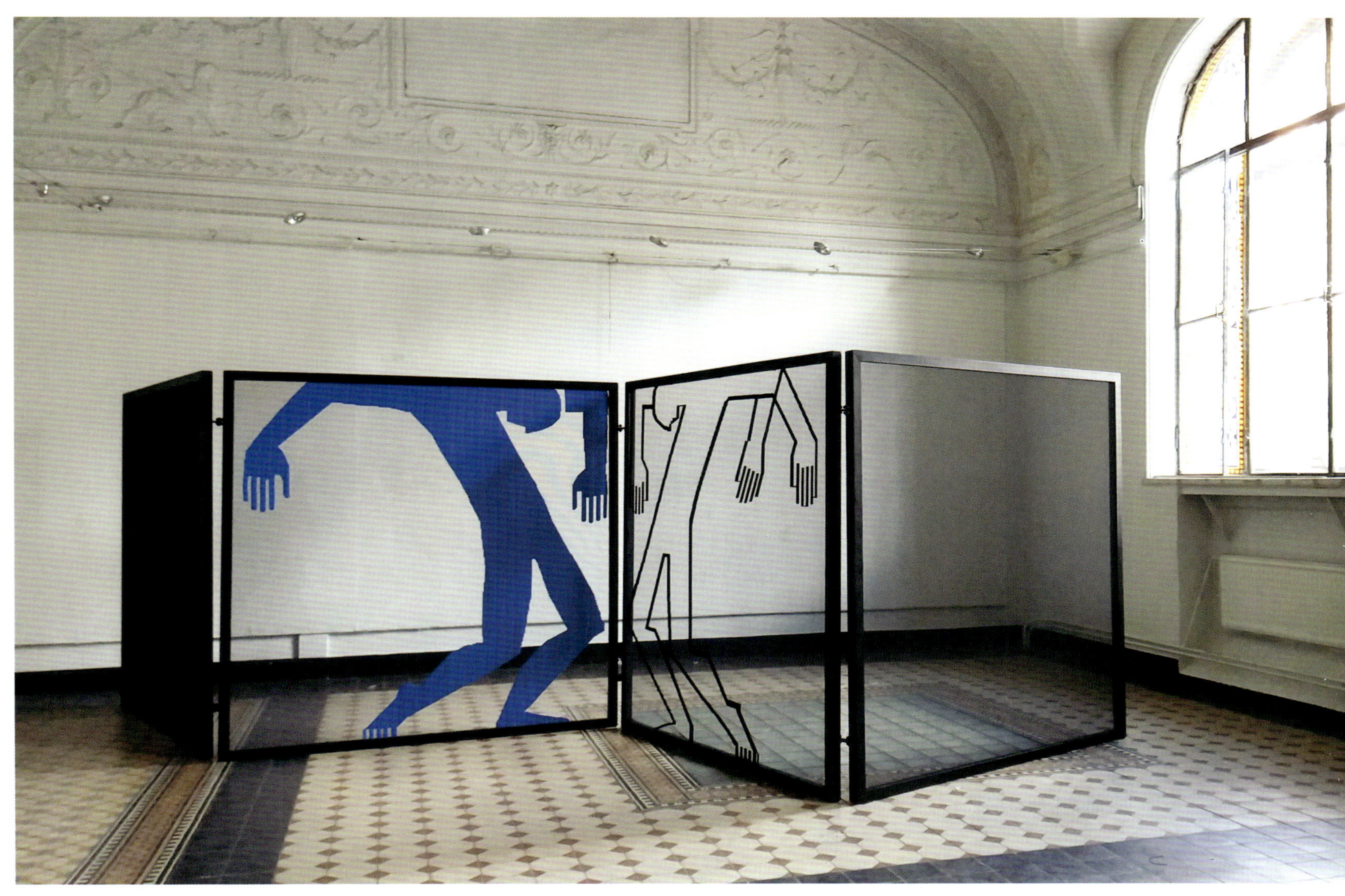

↑
Orlova, Polina
Avante-garde Body
2018, experimental weaving

Diakov (b.1983) creates busts which are a homage to the Baroque exemplars, but uses thoroughly contemporary materials, in this case, clay combined with acrylic resin. He has lived and worked in St Petersburg since 2005 and is a graduate of the Stieglitz State Academy of Art and Design and a member of the North-7 art group. Although his busts' relationship to European art of the past is obvious, they are nevertheless as contemporary in form as they are in their use of actual materials. One feels that they are evolving, or maybe just dissolving, as one gazes at them.

Evgeny Antufiev (b. 1986) lives in Moscow. His work consists of primitive-looking figures and objects that appear, at first glance, as if they belong in a collection of antiquities – trophies from some ancient but only recently unearthed ancient culture – one that modern scholarship has not yet quite managed to pin down, in terms of the actual time and place of their production. They share a sense of willed strangeness with Diakov's otherwise very different work – a deliberately constructed alienation that holds the spectator at arm's length. This is something not entirely uncommon in the history of contemporary art, from the Cubists and the Surrealists to the present.

Some artists, in addition, embrace aspects of the three-dimensional, without actually producing work that could be classified as either sculpture or installation – at least as these are usually

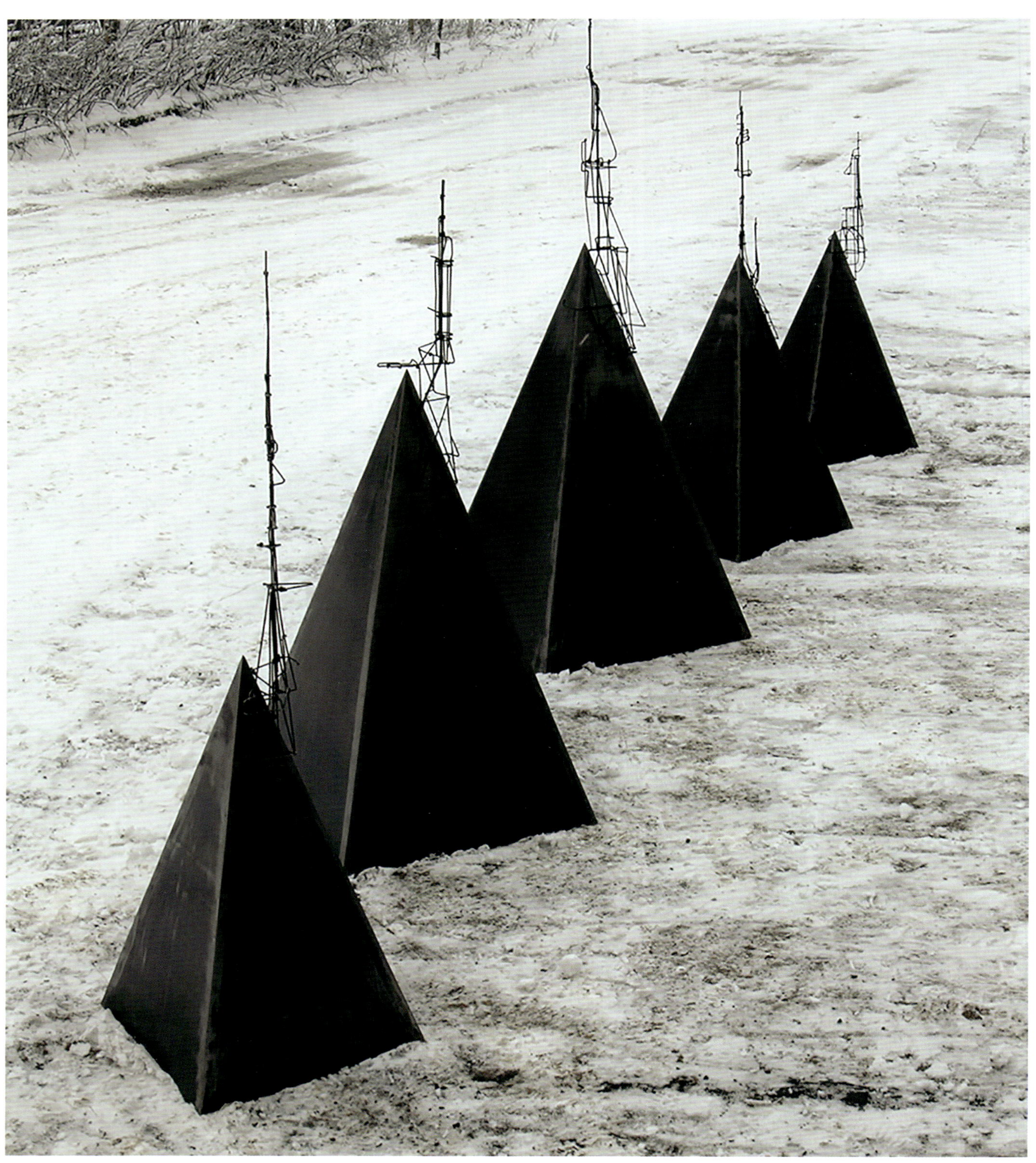

↑
Chumak, Anton
Crystallization, Salt project
2014 – 2016, installation, steel, welding

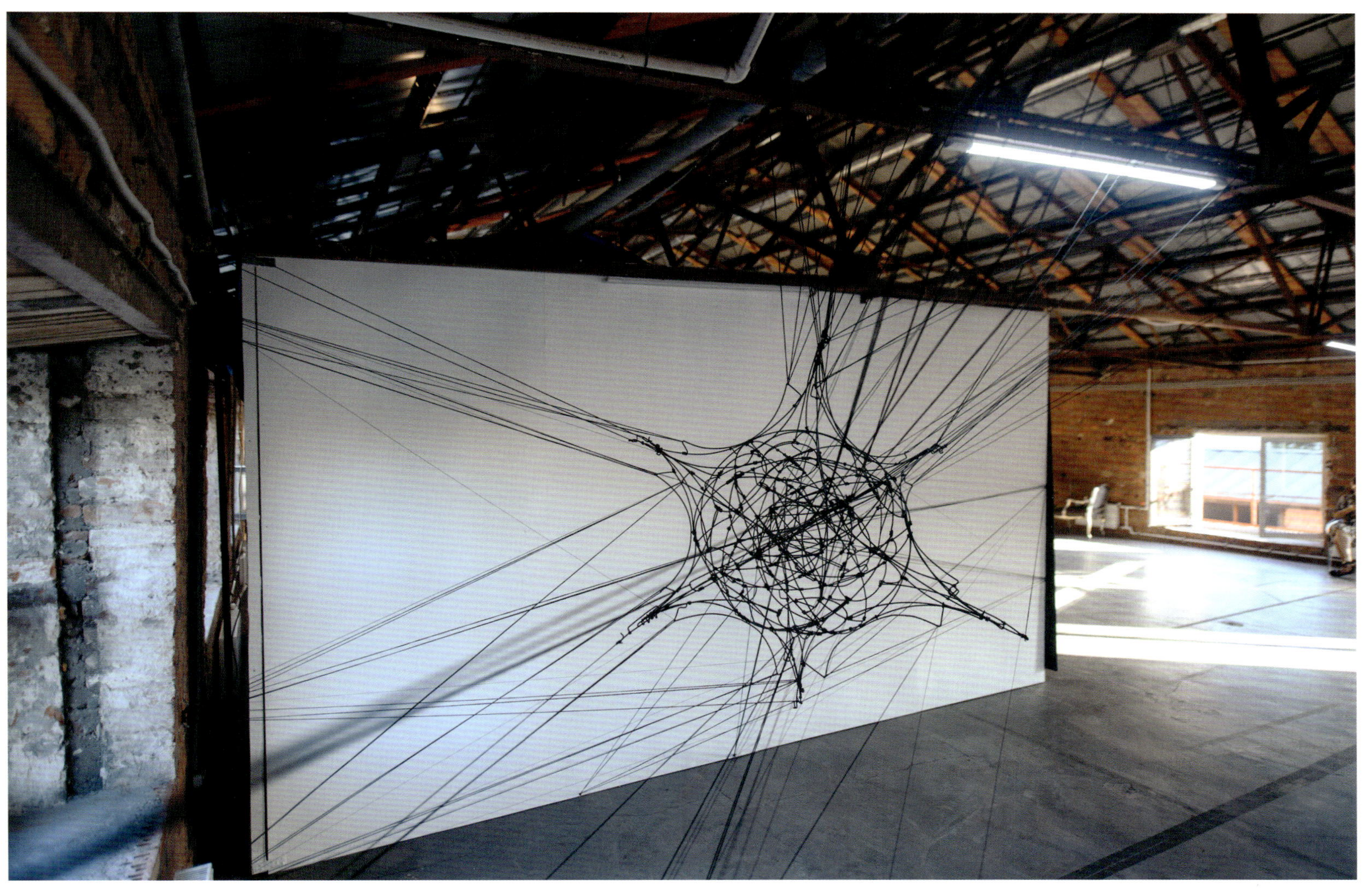

↑
Chumak, Anton
The Basis
2019, steel, welding, forging

understood. A case in point are the works of Polina Orlova and Anton Chumak, both living and working in St Petersburg. Like other Russian artists of their generation, they have embraced a wide variety of different artistic disciplines – graphics, textiles/canvas, installations and performances.

The example by Polina Orlova (b. 1989) shown here obviously owes its inspiration to Japanese screens, first fashionable in Europe in the second half of the nineteenth century. Like the sculptures of Evgeny Antufiev, Orlova's work has its roots in the past, and in a culture that seems exotic, both in Western European and Russian terms. The surprise here is the indication the work offers of cultural variety. Anton Chumak (b. 1980) was twice nominated for both the Kandinsky Prize and the Kuryokhin Prize. Installations from his project *Salt* and his later one, *the Basis,* explore the interdependence of humans and nature, ecology and culture.

The art now being created in Russia is as varied in the range of references it employs as anything currently being produced in the West.

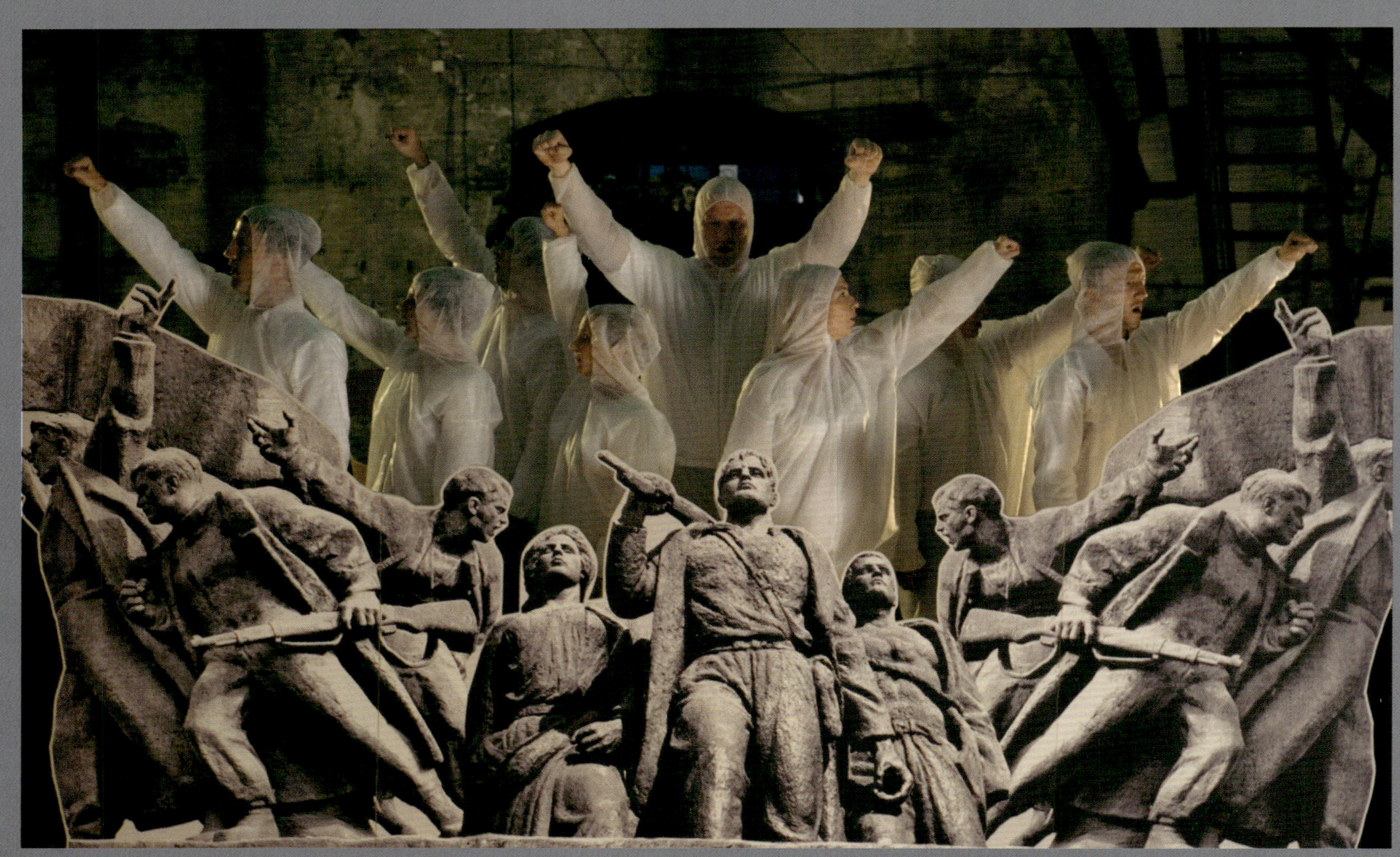

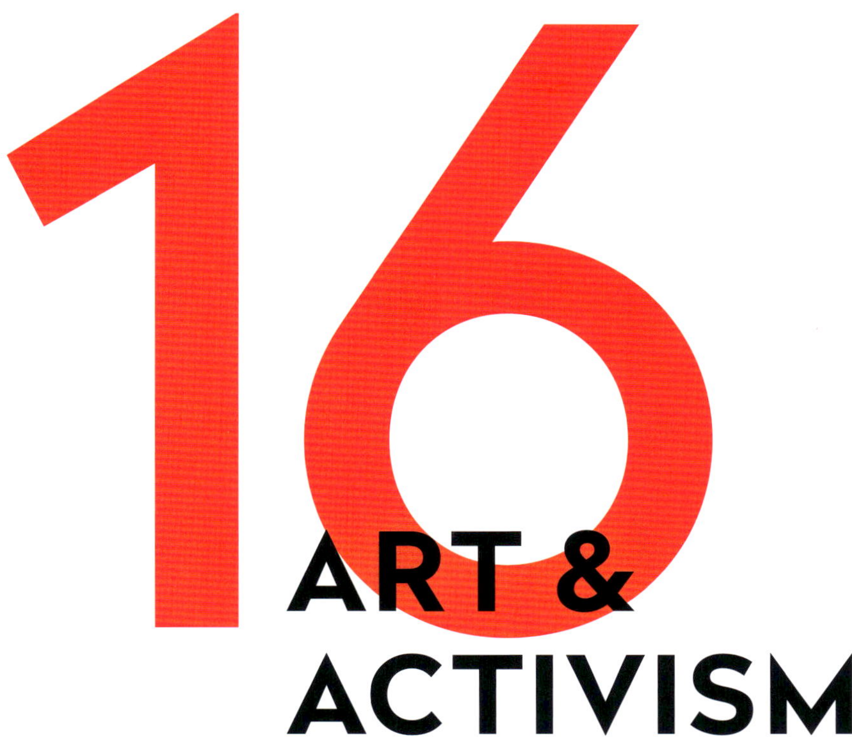

16 ART & ACTIVISM

There are now a number of politically and socially active art groups in Russia, and, in addition, some individual artists who have made reputations for themselves through activism which sometimes conflicts with official laws. The latter have on occasion established major reputations for themselves in the West, often – so it seems – convincing Western commentators that this is the only kind of genuinely new, post-Communist art activism and art that exists in the country: a small battalion of martyrs campaigning for free speech and freedom of expression.

The activist group best known in the West is probably Pussy Riot, an anonymous feminist punk rock and performance group founded in 2011 who embraced causes such as feminism and LGTB rights. However, the group's emphasis on political rather than artistic means to promote these and other causes, stirred controversy in the Russian art community, with condemnation by some, and others including them in university programmes.[1] The rest of society was left puzzled, offended or simply disinterested.

The group first achieved global publicity through an unauthorised performance staged by its four members within Moscow's Cathedral of Christ the Saviour in February 2012. It was halted by security officers and considered sacrilegious by the Orthodox clergy, churchgoers and a large proportion of the Russian population who are still very sensitive where the subject of faith and religion is concerned. Therefore, three of the group's members were arrested, convicted of 'hooliganism motivated by religious hatred' and sentenced to two years in jail. One of the three was later freed on probation, following an appeal.[2] One needs to consider what the reaction might have been had a British group staged a similar event in Westminster Abbey. The punishment might not have been as severe, but there would surely have been retribution of some sort. As of the summer 2021 most members of the group have left the country[3].

←
Chto Delat'
Partisan Songspiel, A Belgrade Story
2009, video still

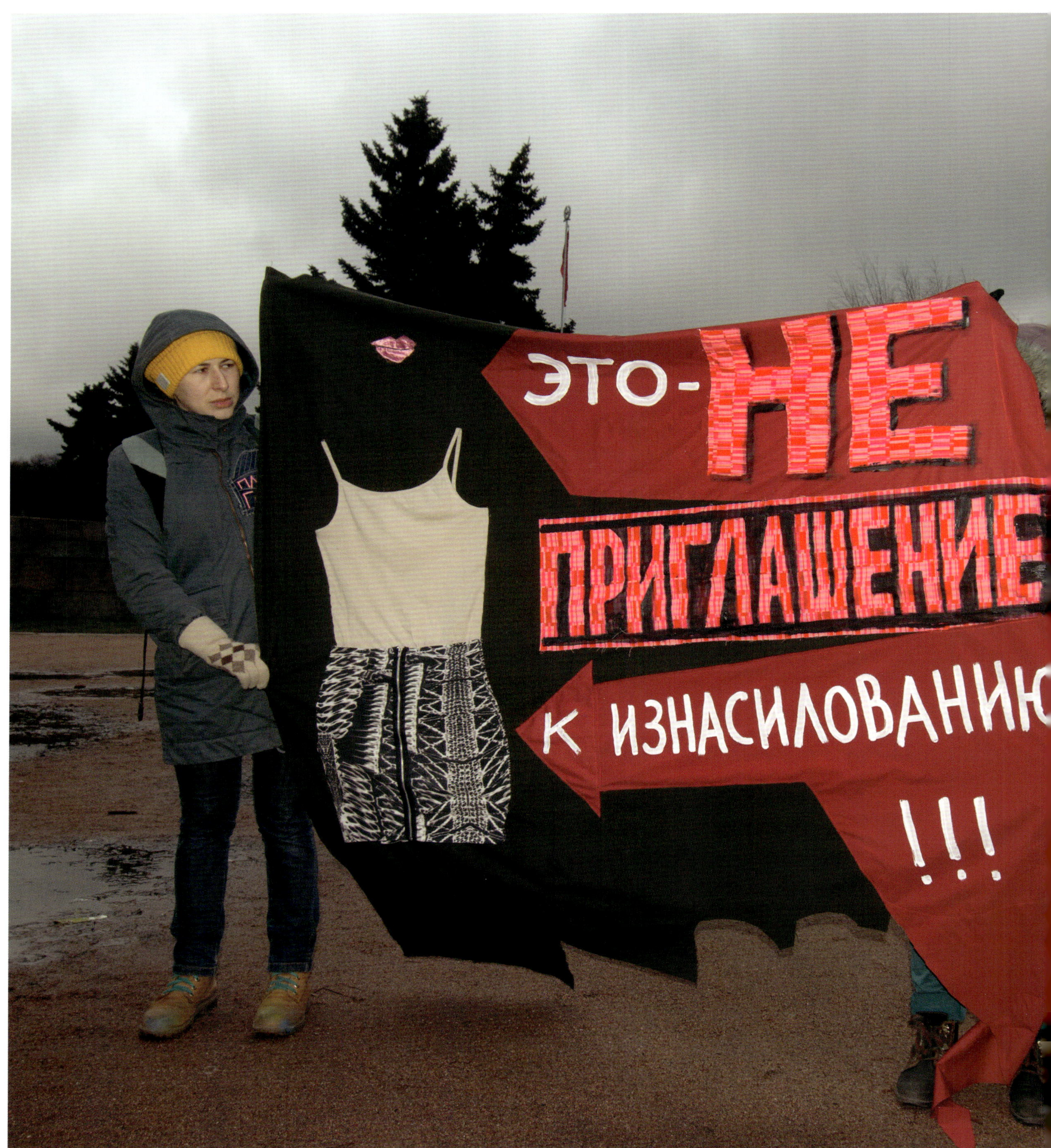
ЭТО-НЕ
ПРИГЛАШЕНИЕ
К ИЗНАСИЛОВАНИЮ
!!!

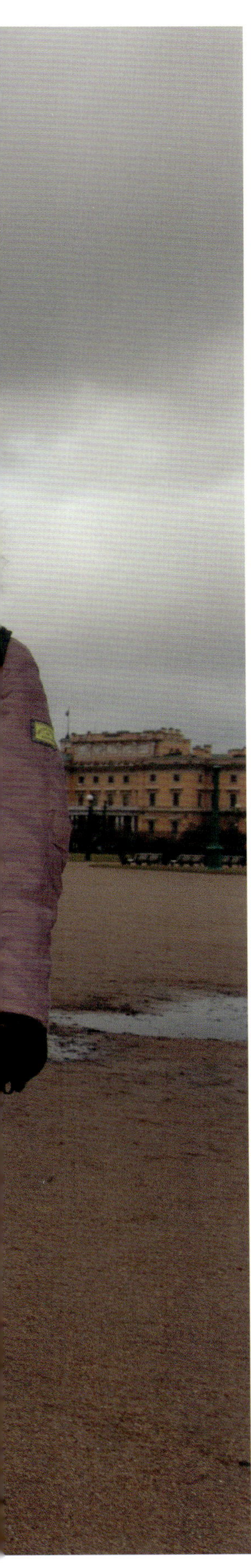

The above-mentioned collective was an offshoot of an arguably more important group, not confined to women, called Voina (War). According to the group's site, it was formed in 2005 by two activists, Vor (Thief) and Kozlenok (Kid) as 'a street collective of actionist artists who engage in political protest art'.[4] They have amassed a membership of more than 200 over the years and have engaged in a wide range of activities, including street art and pranks in public places. Voina has also been responsible for some deliberate public vandalism and hooliganism and therefore has been subject to a large number of prosecutions; they are determinedly non-official.

Despite this, the group was given an 'Innovation' prize in 2011 by the Russian Ministry of Culture. This is a major prize awarded in an all-Russian competition 'in the field of the contemporary arts'. The prize was awarded for the image of a giant phallus on the Liteiny drawbridge in St Petersburg, which the participants painted during the night of June 14, 2010. When the bridge was opened, the 65m drawing rose up erect in front of a building occupied by the St Petersburg FSB (Federal Security Service). Strange combinations of the official and the non-official are not unusual in contemporary Russian visual culture.

Provocations of this kind have in any case been commonplace throughout the history of avant-gardism – certainly from the time of the Dada Movement to the present. Members of activist art groups see themselves not as something specifically Russian but as part of a global anti-capitalist movement, whose pantheon of influences may well include not only Trotsky but Emmeline Pankhurst and Simone de Beauvoir

Another all-female art group that has been active both in Russia and Ukraine is the Shvemy (Sewing Co-op), founded in St Petersburg in 2015 as a graduation project by students from the School for Engaged Art.[5] Shvemy is simultaneously an art, a sewing cooperative and an activist project, built on the model of an alternative economic structure. The group examines conditions in the clothing industry. An official site notes that it 'makes actions and performances, questioning our clothes, ecology, work and rest time, using textile as a medium'.[6]

Shvemy was founded under the auspices of a much larger organisation called *Chto Delat'* – i.e. 'What is to be done?' – itself founded in 2003. The phrase comes from the title of an 1863 novel by Nikolai Chernyshevsky, which offered the possibility of a transformation of Russian society through the self-sacrificing use of scientific knowledge, and was one of the texts that inspired Bolshevism. Lenin used the phrase for the title of one of his own publications.

In current post-Soviet society, *Chto Delat'* sees itself as an agent for repurposing aspects of the Soviet intellectual past that are currently in danger of being misunderstood or simply forgotten. It publishes an English-Russian newspaper focusing on cultural politics in addition to running the School for Engaged Art in St Petersburg and backing a space called Rosa's House of Culture. It focuses on topics such as labour rights.[7]

←
Shvemy
This Is Not an Invitation to Rape
2015, photograph

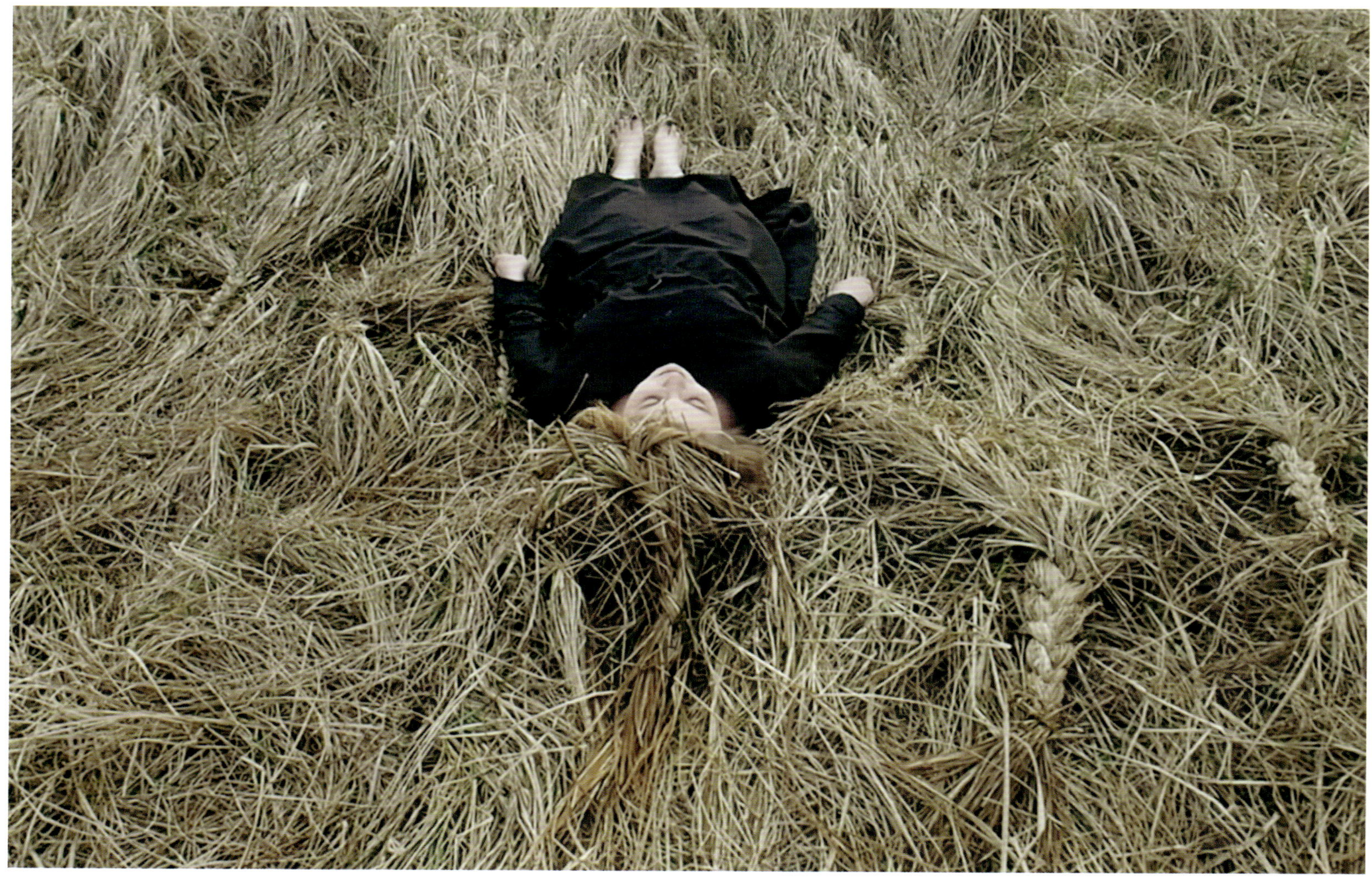

↑
Gentle Women
Art of Braid Weaving
2018, performance video still

The name 'Rosa' is a reference to Rosa Luxemburg (1871–1919), the famous Marxist, revolutionary socialist and anti-war activist, co-founder of the *Red Flag* newspaper, the central propaganda organ of the Spartacist uprising that briefly followed Germany's defeat in the First World War. She was summarily executed when the Spartacists were crushed by the government-sponsored *Freikorps*. To this extent at least, the Communist past remains unforgotten in today's Russia. Like the Orthodox faith, it is an integral component of Russia's, and of the world's history.

Another artists' group devoted to women's art, in a less deliberately controversial way, is the 'Gentle Women', founded in Kaliningrad in 2008 by Eugenia Lapteva (b. 1987) and Alexandra Artamonova (also b. 1987). They have exhibited frequently in St Petersburg and staged performances about female experiences and the female body. In many of their performances and videos they, along with other women who work with them, wear white wedding dresses, which often seem to get trashed. They are well aware that their work tends to arouse negative reactions in a male audience. Eugenia Lapteva has said in an interview:

Of course, through performances we experience our personal stories – love, breakups, betrayals, difficult relationships, despair. You visualise all this while you are in the frame. As soon as the video is edited, a different story begins, no longer your personal one – other women are experiencing it, and you look at your work with detachment.[8]

In addition, there are a certain number of individual artists, usually male, who call themselves 'art

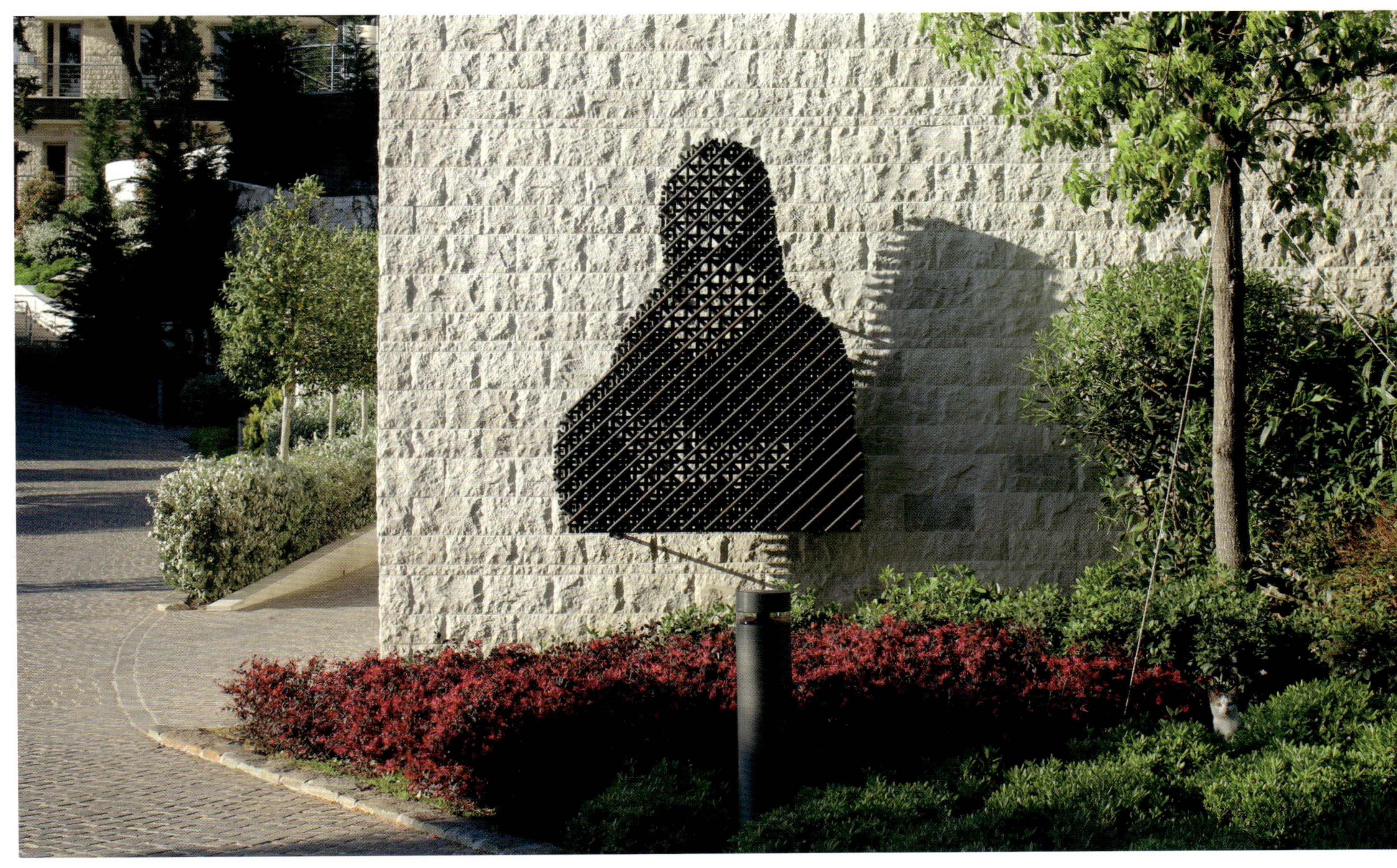

↑
Benkovich Konstantin
Mona Lisa
2018, steel pipes, welding

activists' and who have established reputations outside of Russia as people who, to a lesser or greater extent, have opposed current government policies at some point.

One of these artists is Konstantin Benkovich (b. 1981), who featured in a much-publicised show at the Saatchi Gallery in London: *Art Riot: Post-Soviet Actionism from 1990 to 2010*. Benkovich is best known for *Cry* (2018), the image of a head made of reinforced bars (rebar) and inspired by the famous Munch painting. It was briefly clamped to the balustrade on a Moscow bridge at the very spot where Boris Nemtsov, the former First Deputy Prime Minister of Russia and the leader of one of the main opposition parties, had been assassinated three years earlier. The alleged assassins, linked to the Chechen separatist movement, were subsequently arrested and convicted.

Benkovich graduated from the St Petersburg Stieglitz State Academy of Art and Design and specialises in making artworks from very ordinary, commonplace materials and components, mainly steel rebar using techniques such as welding to stick them together. Other more prominent works include *Mona Lisa* (2018), an outdoor sculpture at the art centre, Dukley Gardens, Budva, in Montenegro,[9] and *WTC (World Trade Center)* (2019), in memory of the September 11 2001 terrorist attacks in the USA, now in the collection of the State Russian Museum, St Petersburg.

Another activist artist is Artyom Loskutov (b. 1986). He was born in Novosibirsk where he was one of the organisers of Monstrations, the May Day apolitical art demonstrations which began in 2004. They have now spread to over thirty cities in Russia. They mock the realities of contemporary Russian life

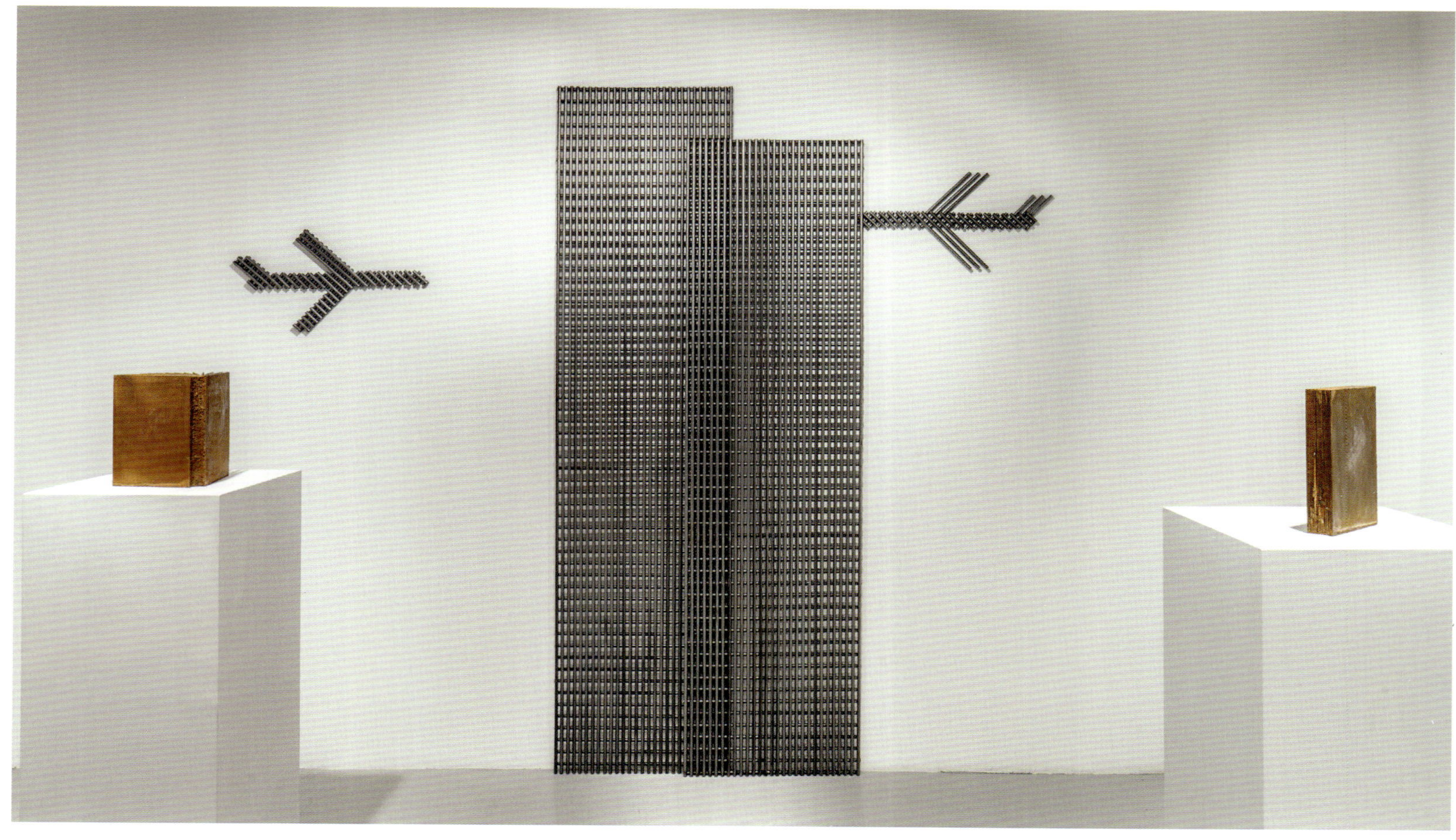

and although local authorities aren't keen on them, they nevertheless allow Monstrations to go ahead due to their non-violent and non-offensive character, recognising them as a kind of public art.

Loskutov became a winner of the Innovation 'Best Regional Project' Prize in 2010 for organising the Monstration in Novosibirsk. However, he was later informed by the local tax authorities that he could not register his art business there, or even practise art in the region, because of a previous drug-related criminal conviction[10]. Artyom then simply moved to Moscow where he has continued to make his art. In 2019 he announced the invention of a new style of painting which he called 'Dubinopis'. In this, paint is applied to the canvas with blows from a police baton. He has produced and sold more than thirty such works. In the summer of 2020, inspired by the protests in Belarus and the USA, Loskutov created two anti-totalitarian works, called respectively *Belarus* and *Black Lives Matter*.

Loskutov won the Innovation Prize once again in 2020, for his media project *Nothing will work without love*. It is worth noting that the Jury of the Innovation Prize 2020, stressing that 'Innovation is not only a competition of the best but also a common cause for all Russian professionals in the field of contemporary art',[11] decided to share the award among all the nominees to help them during the pandemic.

A third artist in this chapter, also featured in the Saatchi Art Riot exhibition, has established a somewhat more sombre reputation than the other two. He is Pyotr Pavlensky (b. 1984) who became famous (or infamous depending on your point of view) in Russia and abroad for staging deliberately provocative acts that upset the authorities. There is still a debate in the Russian art community about whether or not his actions should be considered as art.

Pavlensky has had a stormy career, with highs and lows. His work often involves nudity (his own),

↑
Benkovich, Konstantin
WTC (World Trade Center)
2019, installation, steel pipes, welding

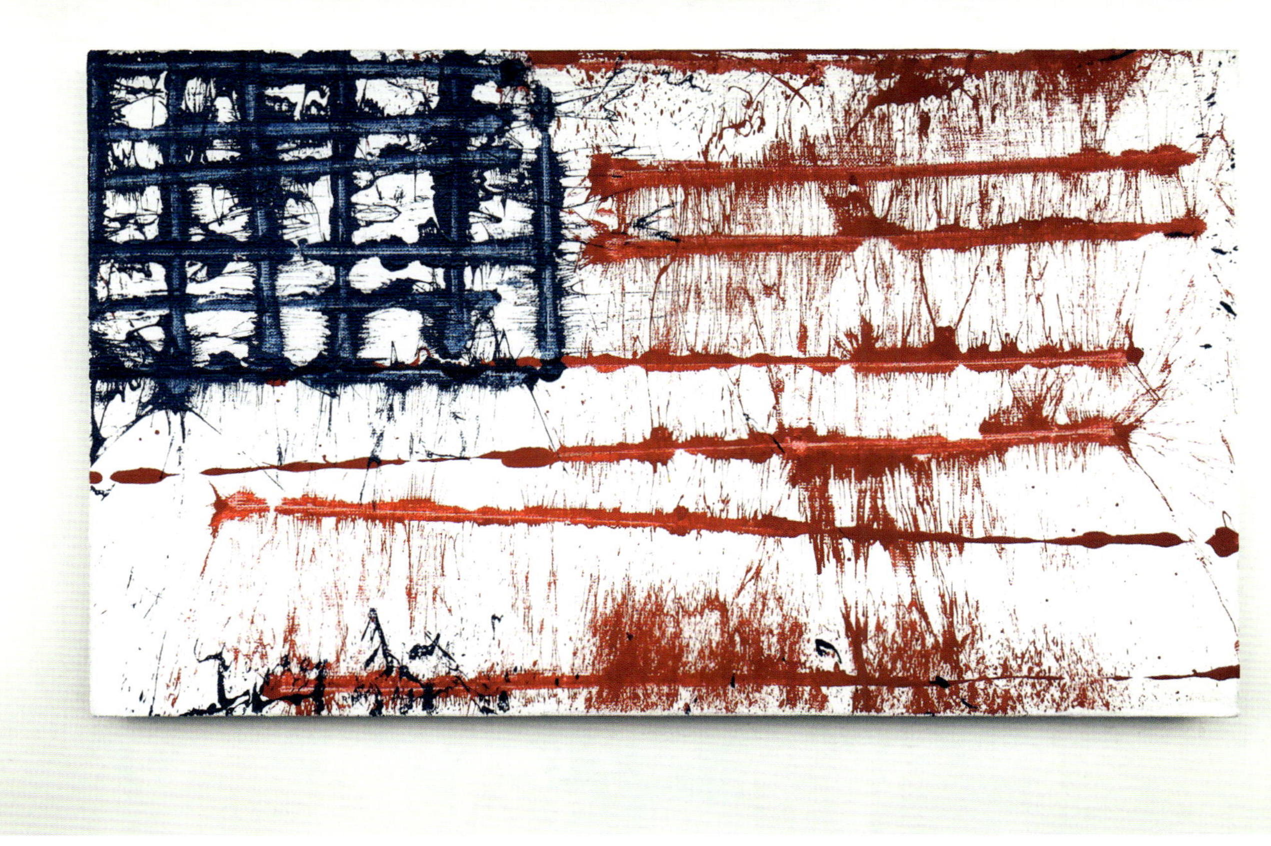

↑
Loskutov, Artem
America
2020, acrylic, vanish on canvas

and sometimes self-mutilation. In 2014 he cut off a part of his ear while sitting naked on the roof of the Serbsky Institute of Psychiatry in Moscow, thereby referencing its shady Soviet past. In 2015 he set alight the entrance door of the historic Lubyanka Building in Lubyanka Square, the central HQ of the FSB – the Russian intelligence services. The subsequent criminal proceedings barred Pavlensky from receiving the Innovation Prize in 2016. Several members of the jury left the competition and the remaining experts refused to vote on the visual artwork nomination[12].

After he was fined for the burnt door and ordered to pay damages of 980,000 roubles (or around £14,000 at the then prevailing rate), Pavlensky and his then partner, Oksana Shalygina fled to France, where they were granted asylum. Shortly afterwards they were both accused by a young actress of sexual assault. They claimed that the accusation was politically motivated. In October 2017, Pavlensky was sent to a psychiatric hospital for trying to set the Banque de France in Paris on fire. His partner posted photographs of this, with Pavlensky's captions denouncing bankers and calling for a 'great French Revolution'. He received a three-year prison sentence (with two years suspended) and was ordered in 2019 to pay €21,768 (around £20,000 at the prevailing rate) for material and moral damages.[13]

While still living in exile in France, Pavlensky ran into further trouble. In February 2020 a former government minister accused him of releasing a video on his website which showed him – the minister – masturbating. Pavlensky said that he had wanted to expose the minister's 'hypocrisy'. In the middle of the same month, he was arrested by the French police for stabbing two people at a New Year party six weeks previously. In October 2020 Shalygina, by this time separated from Pavlensky, accused him of 'sadistic rape' in her new book.[14]

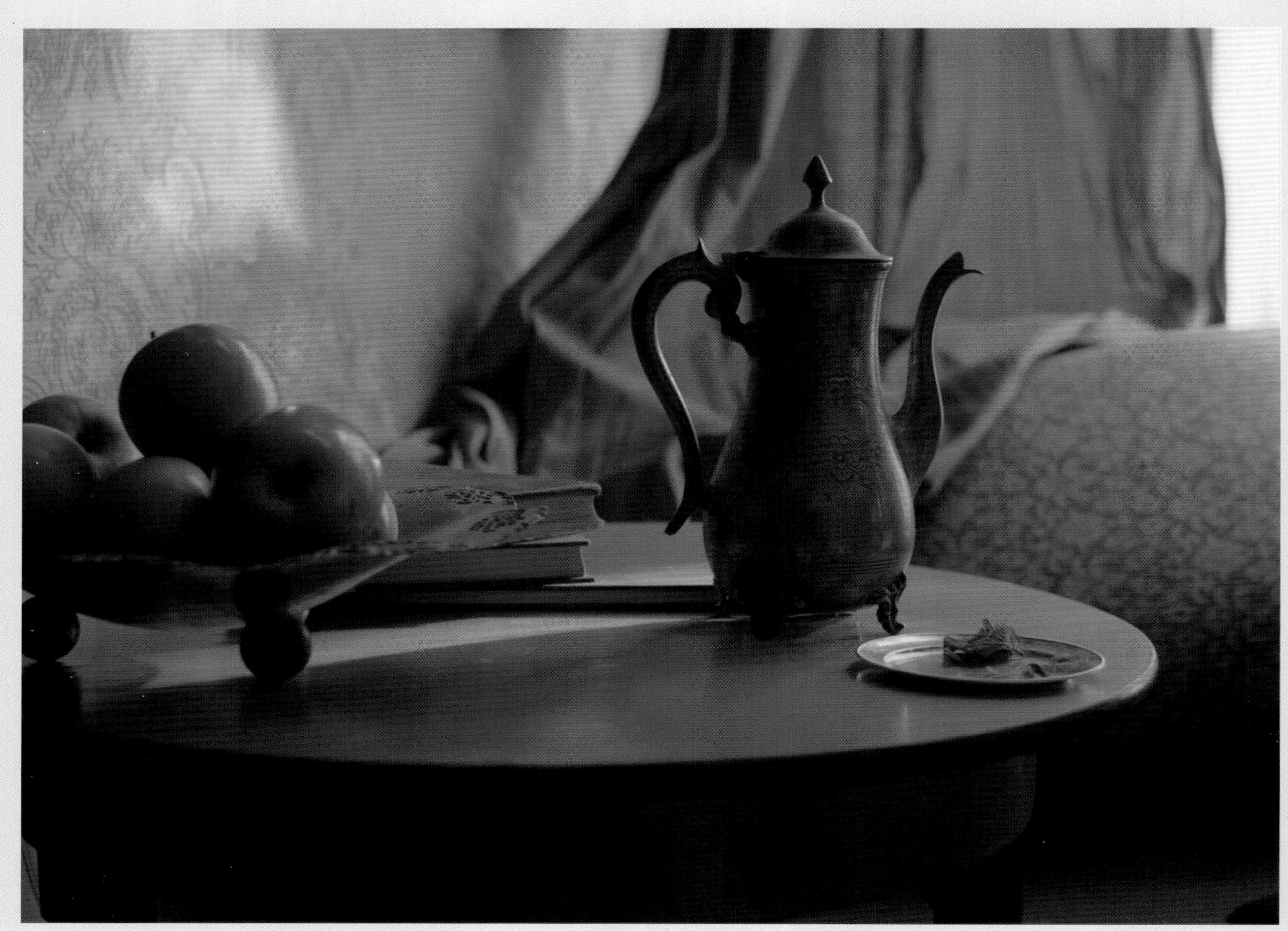

17 EXPATRIATE ART

One of the important freedoms that Russian people have been able to enjoy in the last thirty years is the ability to travel internationally. This has resulted in an exodus of students from Russia to study at numerous universities and colleges abroad. Artists were no exception to this and some of them stayed on to live and work in the countries of their choice after receiving their art degrees or completing their residencies. Interestingly, almost all of them continue to have strong links with Russia, exhibiting their work there and taking part in art competitions.

Polina Kanis was born in St Petersburg in 1985, studied at the Rodchenko Art School of Photography and Multimedia in Moscow and is now based in the Netherlands after completing art residencies and courses in Paris, Zurich and Amsterdam. Her recent video and sound project – *Toothless Resistance* – consists of two parts. Part 1 explores the *Friendship Tree*, a utopian project by Fyodor Zorin from the 1930s, which involves a political and ecological consensus still unattainable today. Part 2 reconstructs the room of Pyotr Kropotkin, a Russian philosopher who lived from 1886 to 1917, who believed that the key to evolution is cooperation and not competition. [1]

Another artist, Julia Zastava, was born in Moscow in 1982 but now lives in Vienna. She engages with eternal mysteries of love and hate, ugliness and beauty, using video and sound as well as working with watercolour and pencil on paper using fairy-tale and cartoon characters. She has held a number of successful solo shows in Paris, Vienna, Berlin and Moscow.

Genia Chef (b.1954), a Berlin-based artist, considers himself a founder of Post-Historicism, which involves interpreting past events in the form of a new mythology.[2] His art education began in Moscow and continued at the Vienna Fine Art Academy where he received the gold medal in the Fueger Gold Prize upon graduating in 1993. Chef held a personal show at the State Russian Museum in 2011. His work *Tsarevich Alexei*, shown here, is from the Family Album, dedicated to the memory of the last

←
Kanis, Polina
Toothless Resistance. The Room
2020, installation, video still

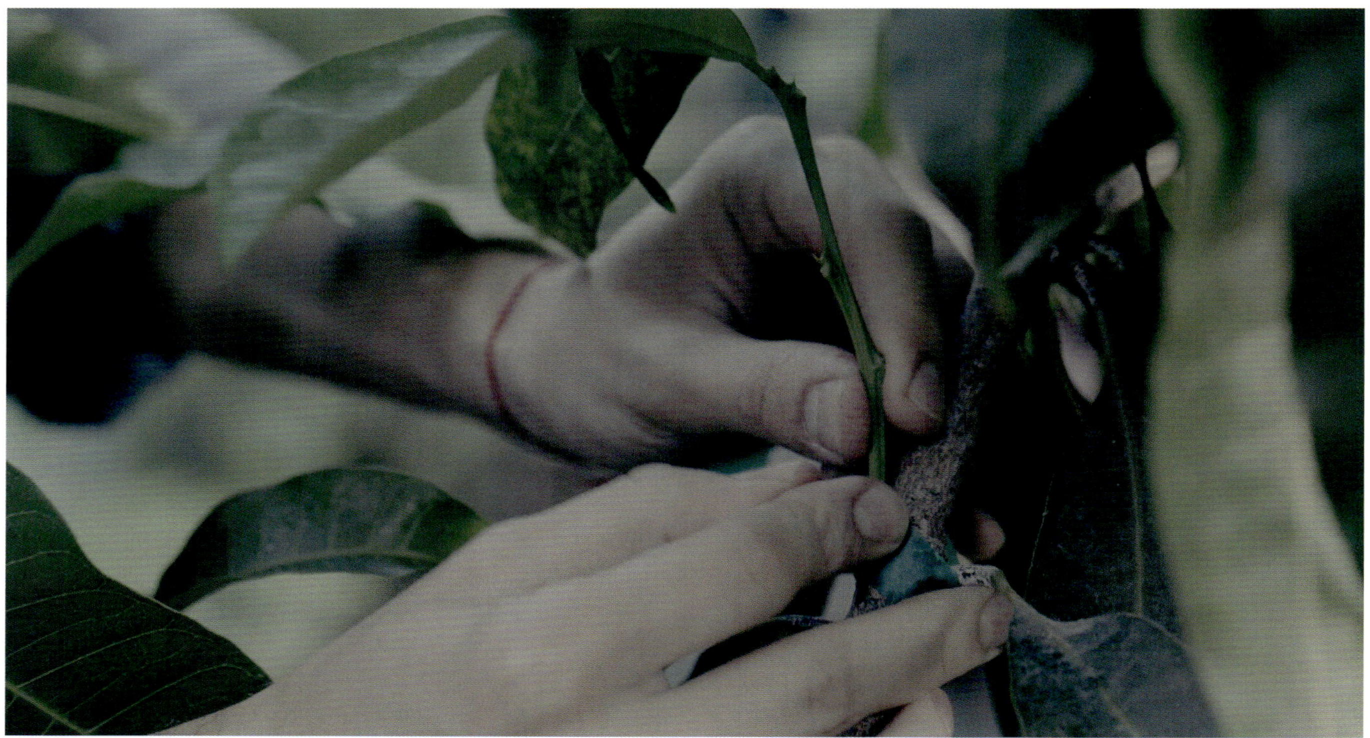

Russian Imperial family, which formed part of the *On the End of The World* show at the Novosibirsk State Art Museum in 2019–20.

His other work, also shown here, is from the NIBELUNGENLIED show inspired by the famous medieval German epic poem. The show began at the National Museum of Liechtenstein and will tour several European countries in 2021–2.

The art of Anya Myagkikh (b.1991), a Londoner originally born in Moscow and a graduate of the Chelsea College of Art and Design, heads in various directions. Some of her works are devoted to family iconography, others to her Mexican travels, but a large part consists of her 'unconscious' paintings: large and small fragments of aprons and tablecloths stretched over a hoop.

Colours and patterns in such works are formed by wiping brushes on an apron or using tablecloths for their intended purpose. Myagkikh's latest series of paintings, *Dudes (2020)*, continues her exploration of the boundaries of the abstract and figurative, using blobs of paint with the idea of taking her art further into the realm of NFTs.

↑
Kanis, Polina
Toothless Resistance. The Friendship Tree
2020, video still

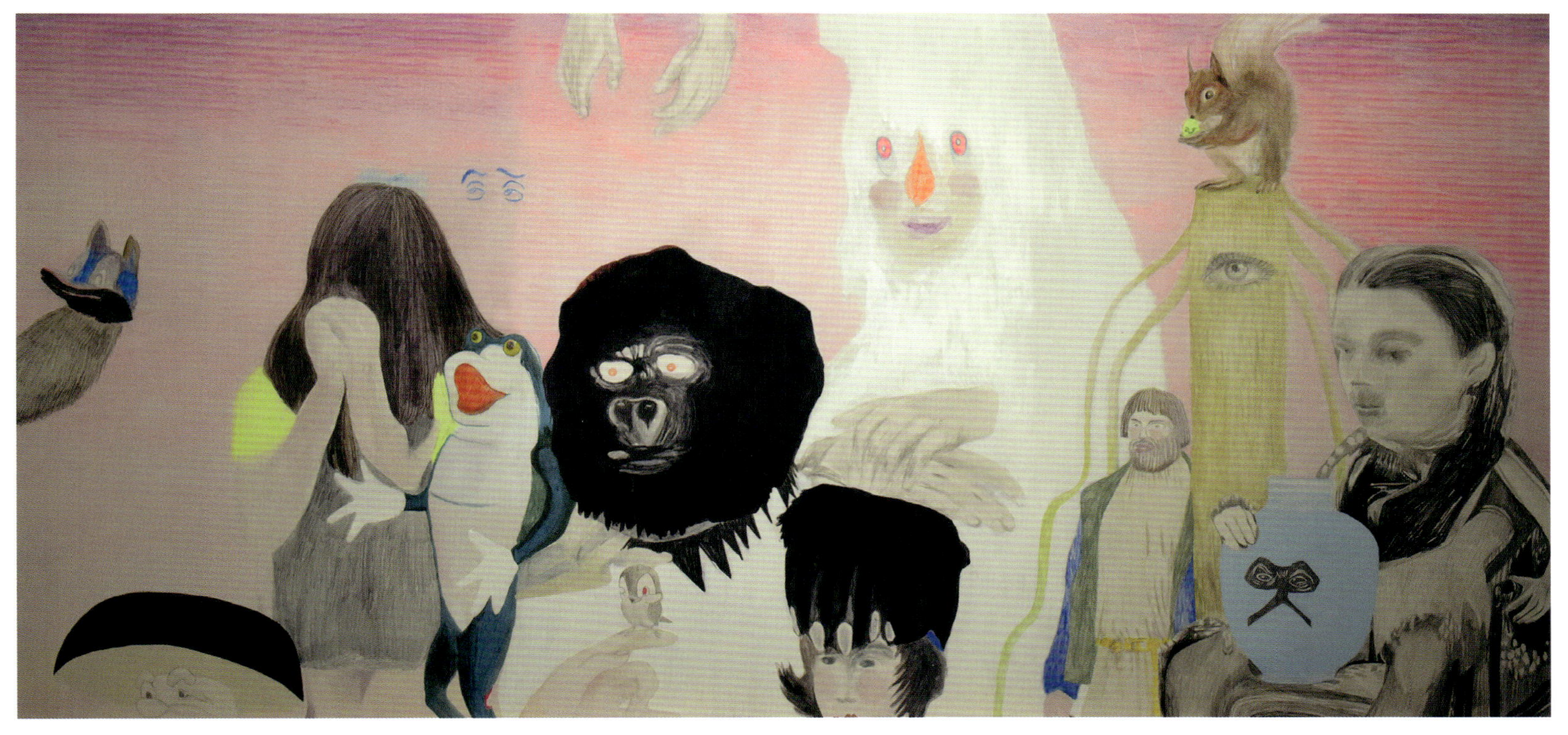

↑
Zastava, Julia
Untitled
2017, pencils, watercolour, acrylic on cardboard

Alexandra Lerman was born in St Petersburg in 1985 and studied at the Cooper Union School of Art and the Columbia University School of Art in New York where she now lives. In her work she uses video, photography, sculpture and performance. Her work was shown at the Whitney Museum of American Art, New York, in 2017 and Lerman was nominated for the prestigious Sergei Kuryokhin Prize in St Petersburg in 2019. She created a site-specific installation, entitled *Soldiers of the Sun, or the Right to the Future Time* at the Museum of Hygiene, St Petersburg, in 2019. Lerman used cyanotype, the image-making process employed by one of the first female photographers Anna Atkins to create her British Algae album in 1843, to make the images and also the song "The Return of the Giant Hogweed" of the British rock band Genesis as her video soundtrack.[3] The project, in the form of human-plant image interaction, deals with yet another human attempt to thoughtlessly change nature. After the Second World War, the virally invasive and photo-toxic giant hogweed plant was imported from the Caucasus to other parts of the Soviet Union in order to restore agriculture but it caused skin irritation and was even poisonous to people. Lerman also stresses that climate problems are indeed universal.

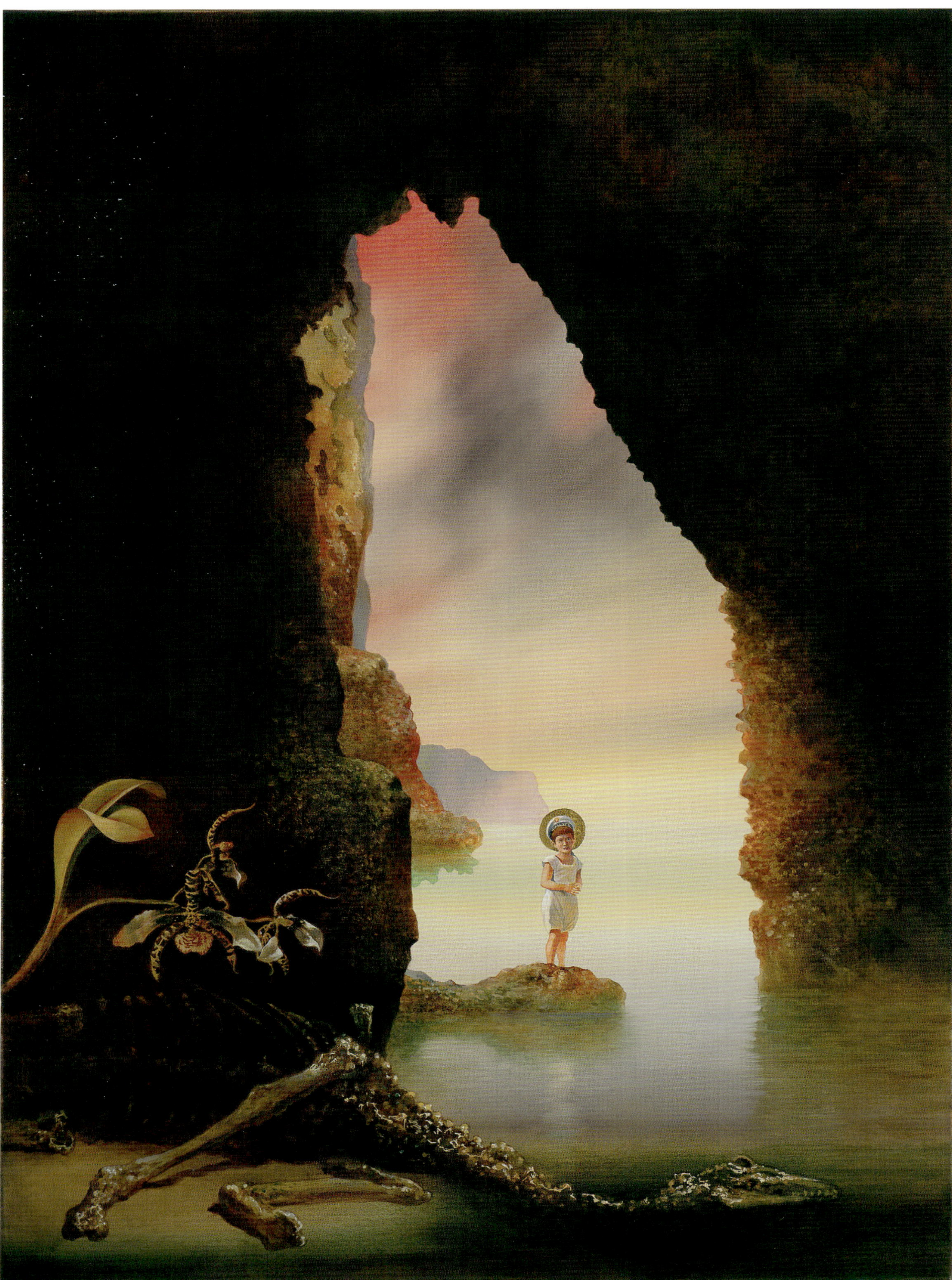

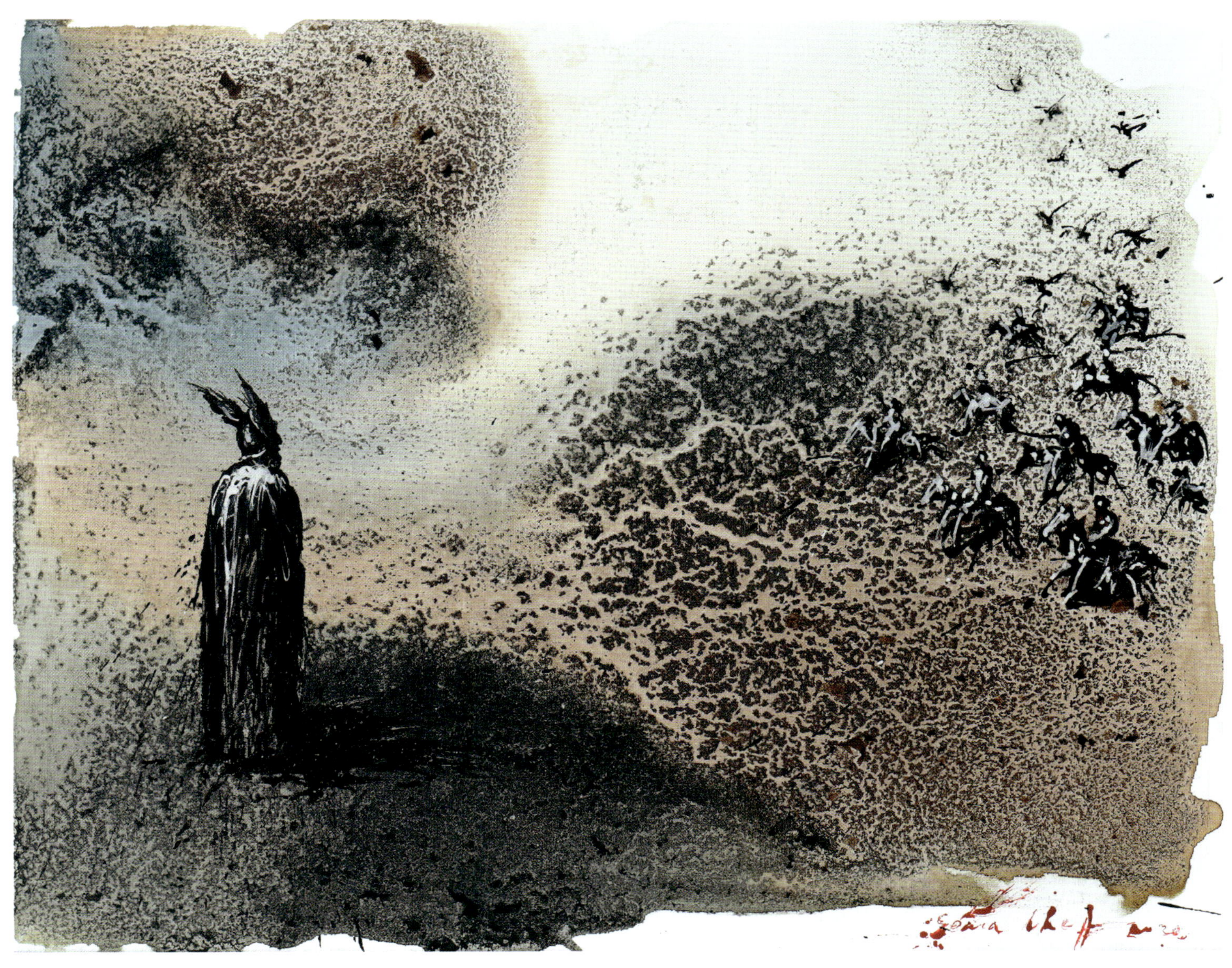

↑
Chef, Genia
Hagen Notices the Bavarian Warriors
2020, mixed media on canvas

←
Chef, Genia
Tsarevich Alexei
2013, oil and gold leaf on canvas

The last artist in this short chapter is also based in the USA. Nikolay Koshelev (b.1987) graduated from the Stroganov Moscow State Academy of Arts and Industry and studied at the New York Academy of Art. He lives and works in New York. His *Moon Pool. Archive* show appeared at the State Tretyakov Gallery in Moscow in 2021. It was inspired by Sergei Diaghilev's Russian Seasons in Paris in the 1910s and '20s, and tells the story of the work and life of an imaginary Russian artist hired by Diaghilev to design costumes and stage sets for one of his ballet productions.[4] This project allowed Koshelev to extend an invisible thread to the Russian Symbolist artists who were active more than a century ago and whom he has admired since his childhood.

We all now live in the world overwhelmed by an ever-changing flow of information. It is not easy to catch up and follow new trends and even more difficult to understand which of them will become fundamental and meaningful for our future. We hope and believe that the desire to move forward and the need to discover something new for themselves and for others will help Russian artists to reach even greater heights than before and to take a worthy place in the world culture of the 21st century.

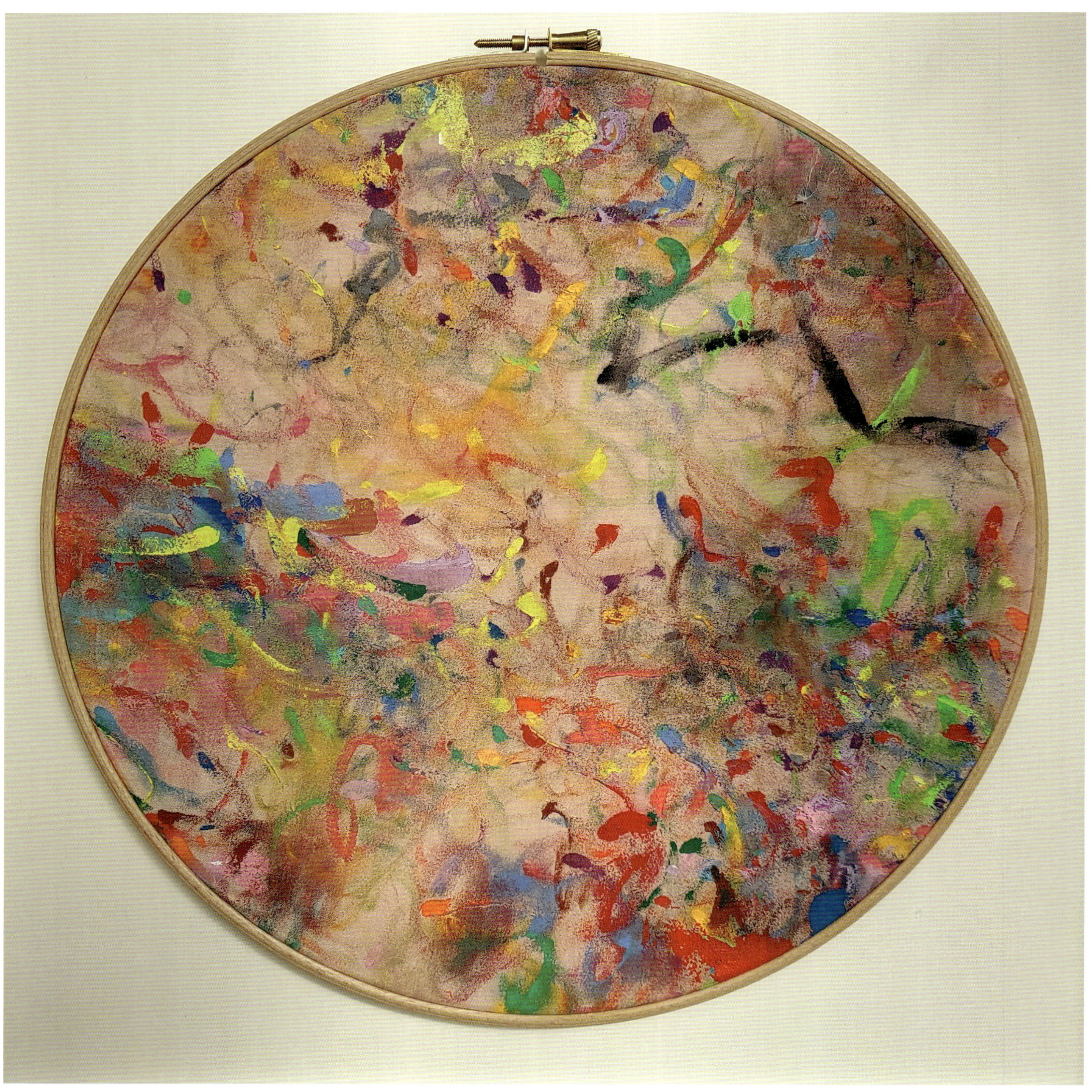

←
Myagkikh, Anya
Unconscious Painting
2015, acrylic on textile (apron)

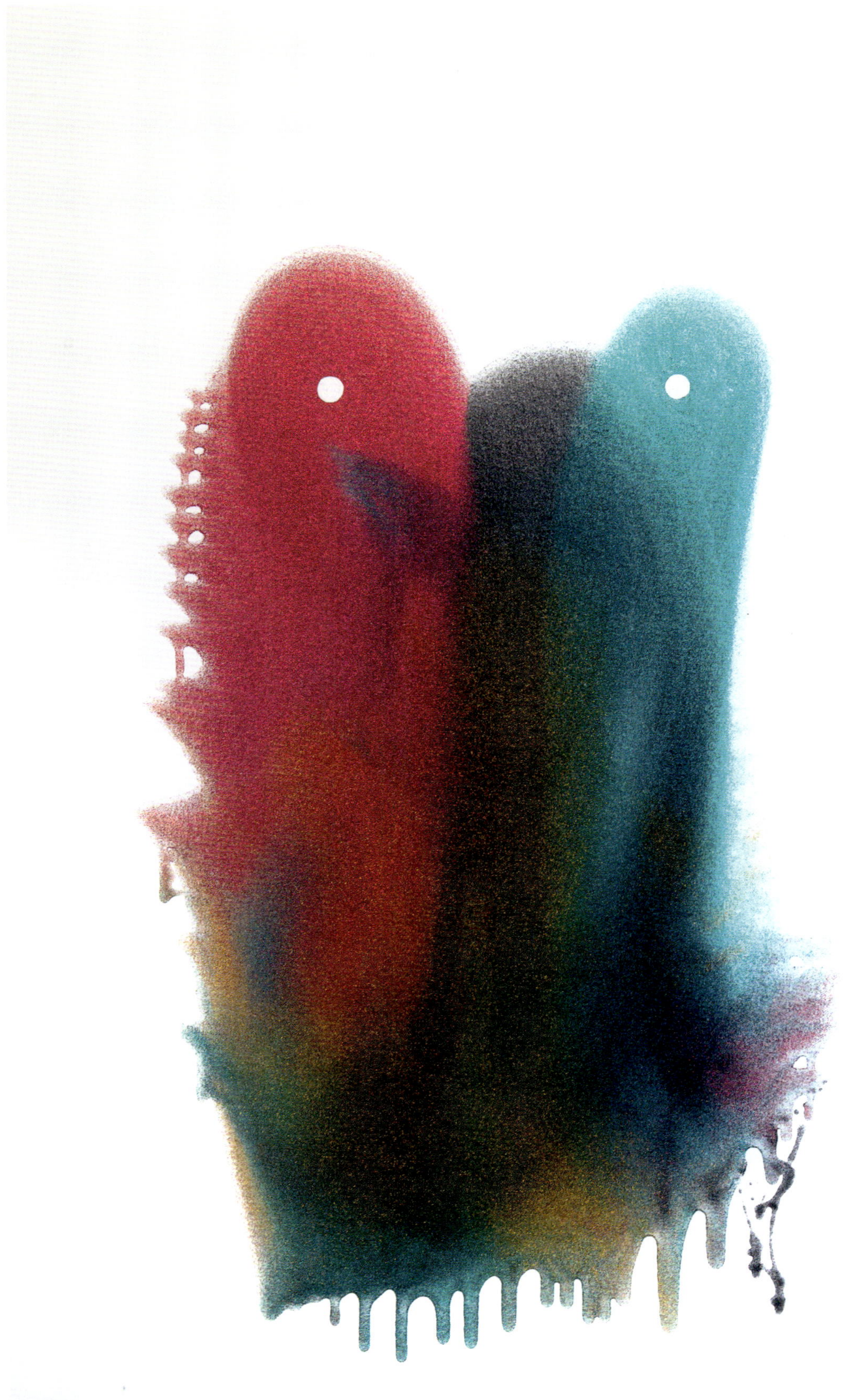

→
Myagkikh, Anya
Dude 19
2020, acrylic on canvas

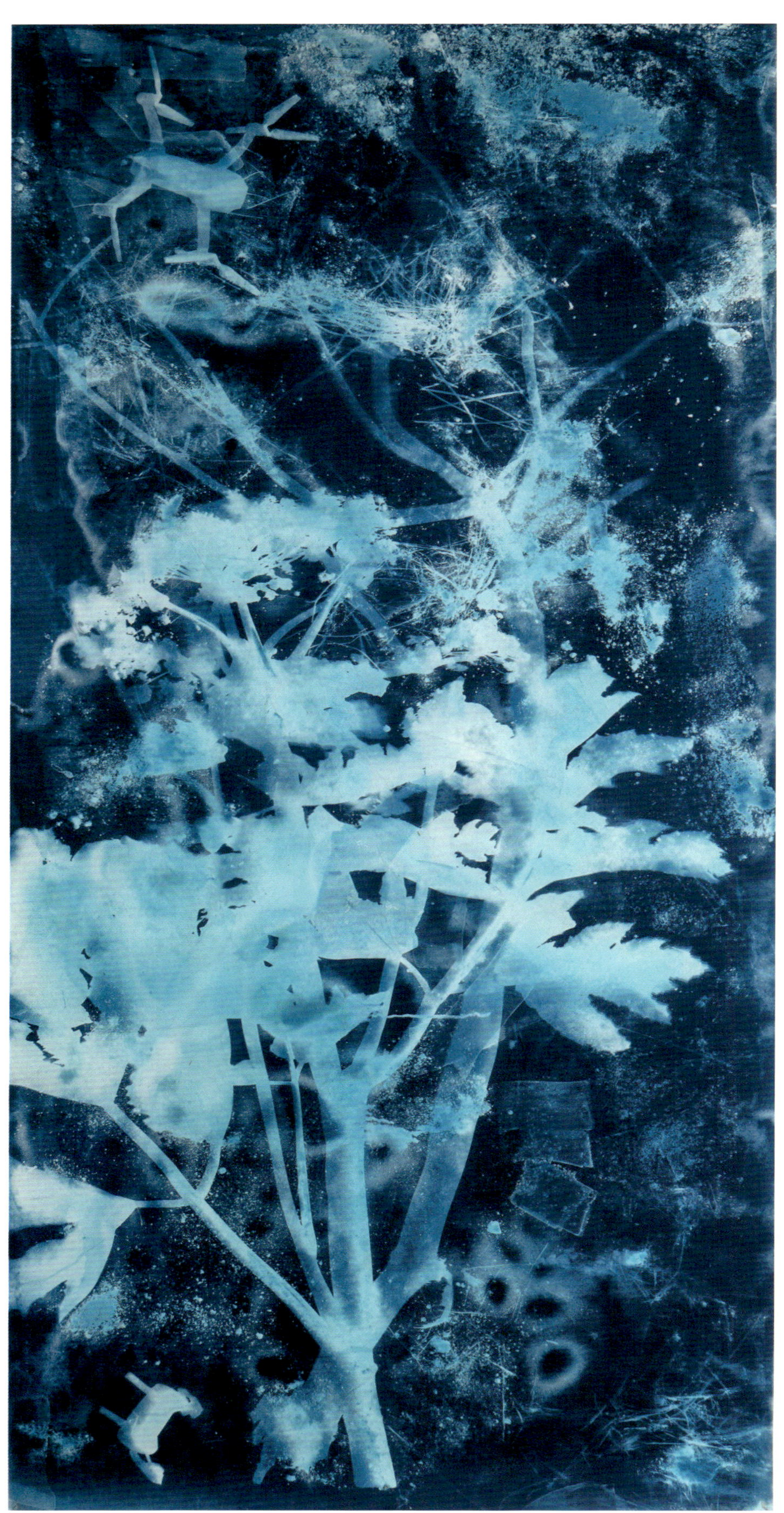

←
Lerman, Alexandra
Soldiers of the Sun #8
2018, cyanotype on watercolour paper

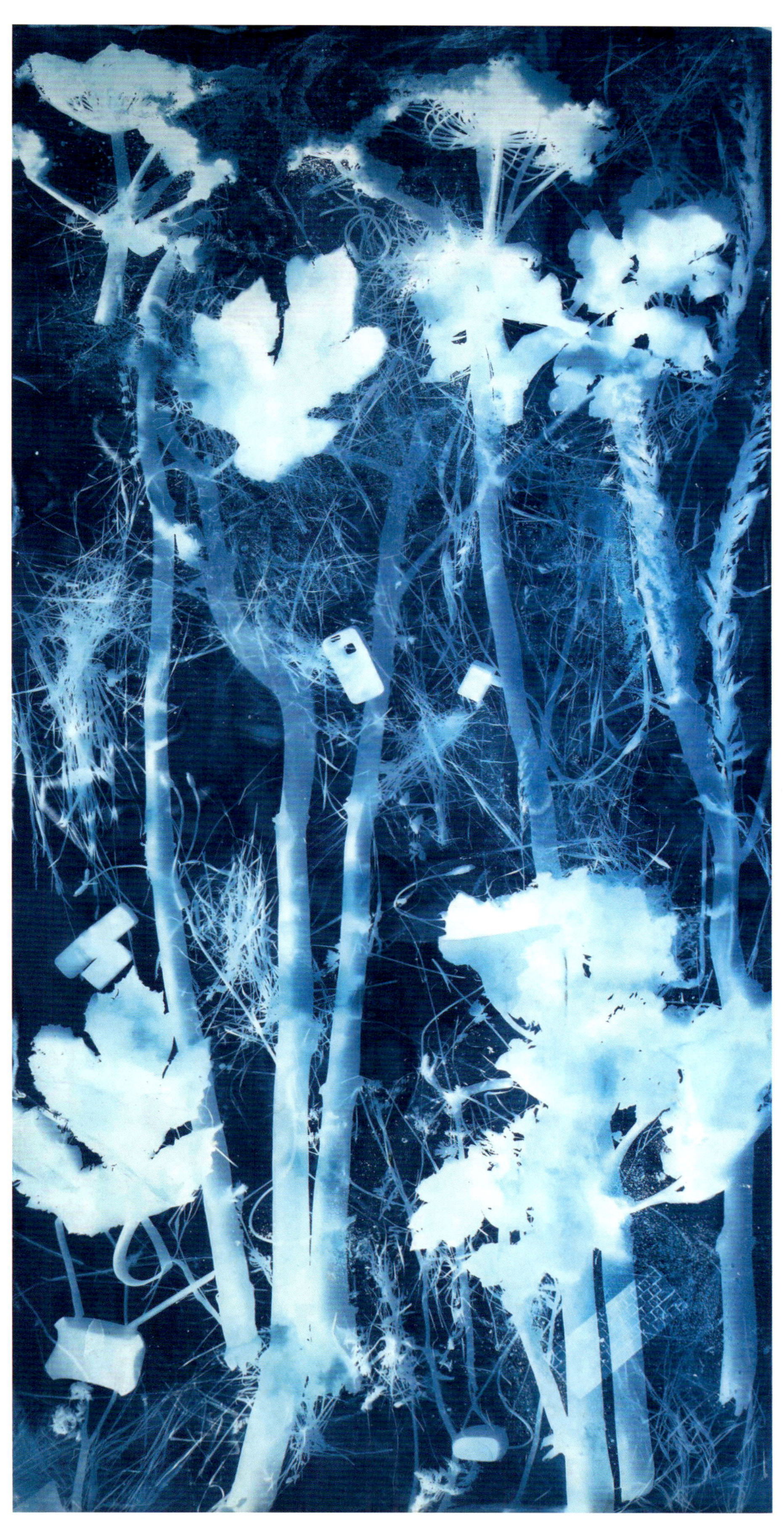

→
Lerman, Alexandra
Soldiers of the Sun #14
2018, cyanotype on
watercolour paper

ENDNOTES

Date of access: 14.01.2022

Foreword by Edward Lucie-Smith

1 https://www.arsenyzhilyaev.art/en
2 https://daily.jstor.org/how-alexander-pushkin-was-inspired-by-his-african-heritage/

Foreword by Sergei Reviakin

1 http://www.kandinsky-prize.ru/o-premii/?lang=en

Chapter 1 – From Past to Present

1 https://danilatkachenko.com/projects/motherland/
2 https://mokrov.ru/index/art/another-day-in-paradise.html

Chapter 2 - Nature and Landscape

1 https://en.wikipedia.org/wiki/Yuryev-Polsky_(town)
2 http://slonvboa.ru/oleg_borodin
3 https://izo-museum.ru/modern/vyistavki-i-sobyitiya/egor-plotnikov-minuta-do-probujdeniya
4 https://www.tretyakovgallerymagazine.com/articles/2-2019-63/pavel-nikonov-moving-towards-freedom-remembering-momentous-epoch
5 http://egorplotnikov.pro/en/page-about-me

Chapter 3 – Abstract and Surrealist Art

1 https://www.andrey-volkov.com/kopiya-intervyu
2 http://www.kandinsky-prize.ru/rinat-voligamsi/?lang=en
3 https://wsimag.com/art/55796-georgy-frangulyan
4 https://victoralimpiev.com/victor-alimpiev-there-there-and-there
5 https://mmoma.ru/files/booklet_novikov_eng.pdf
6 https://art.sredaobuchenia.ru/koshelev
7 http://www.crocodilepower.com
8 https://sample-art.com/en/artists/anna-andrzhievskaya

Chapter 4 – Icon Painters

1 http://test.trinity-church.ru/hram/vnutr.html
2 https://www.pravmir.ru/aleksandr-sokolov-ikonopis-udel-marginalov/
3 http://www.nsad.ru/articles/sergej-antonov-i-irina-zaron-v-ramkah-kanona-mozhno-zanimatsya-sovremennym-cerkovnym-iskusstvom
4 Ibid.
5 http://rsvetal.narod.ru/biogr.htm
6 https://orthodoxartsjournal.org/a-living-tradition-of-icon-painting/
7 Ibid.

Chapter 5 – Moscow

1 https://irinakorina.com/cv/
2 https://en.wikipedia.org/wiki/Anna_Parkina
3 https://www.widewalls.ch/artists/dima-rebus
4 https://dimarebus.com/fairy-tale/
5 http://mikaplutitsky.com/statement
6 http://mikaplutitsky.com/forest-deer-lesnoj-olen
7 https://artguide.com/posts/1779
8 http://romansakin.com/How-to-become-a-good-and-even-holy-person
9 http://www.district-berlin.com/en/school-without-centermoscow

Chapter 6 – St Petersburg

1 https://vladey.net/ru/artist/nestor-engelke
2 https://collections.vam.ac.uk/item/O722844/red-work-502-print-dontsov-philipp/
3 https://www.sobaka.ru/oldmagazine/glavnoe/12000
4 http://art-gorbunov.ru/en/portfolio-items/vertex/#main
5 https://imho-gallery.ru/ira-fyodor-bio/
6 https://ovcharenko.art/exhibitions/213-alexander-tsikarishvili-funny-soil-frutti-land/overview/

Chapter 7 – Central Russia

1 https://riavrn.ru/news/vladelets-galerei-kh-l-a-m-v-voronezhe-privykli-k-vyrazheniyu-sovremennoe-iskusstvo-/
2 http://vcsi.ru/vcsi/
3 http://www.kandinsky-prize.ru/nikolaj-alekseev/?lang=ru
4 Ibid.
5 https://mmoma.ru/exhibitions/gogolevsky10/ivan_gorshkov_fontan_vsego/
6 https://triennial-2017.garagemca.org/en/KirillGarshin
7 https://syg.ma/@kirill-garshin/orghanichieskaia-zhivopis-ili-sozdaniie-novoi-kartiny-iz-sokov-rastienii-i-ekologhichieski-pierierabatyvaiemykh-matierialov
8 https://www.alexeykorsi.com/
9 https://garagemca.org/ru/publishing/a-brief-history-of-street-art-in-nizhny-novgorod-by-alisa-savitskaya-artem-filatov

Chapter 8 – Along the Volga

1 https://realnoevremya.ru/articles/179550-avtor-graffiti-ronaldu-i-neymara-prochel-lekciyu-ob-iskusstve
2 Artist's press-release for the Energy Nation project, September 2021
3 https://vk.com/wall-57173485_1315
4 https://www.tretyakovgallery.ru/for-visitors/museums/filial-tretyakovskoy-galerei-v-samare
5 https://ru.wikipedia.org/wiki/%D0%97%D0%B0%D0%B9%D1%86%D0%B5%D0%B2,_%D0%90%D0%BB%D0%B5%D0%BA%D1%81%D0%B0%D0%BD%D0%B4%D1%80_%D0%9E%D0%BB%D0%B5%D0%B3%D0%BE%D0%B2%D0%B8%D1%87
6 http://syaylev.com/works/public-works/pillars-of-krasnoyarsk.html
7 http://www.mikhail-lezin.com/text_en.html
8 https://vivacity.ru/streetart/art-abstractov/
9 https://digitalina.ru/about/
10 https://samopoznanie.ru/trainers/aleksandr_aleksandrovich_gnutov-bajun/

Chapter 9 – Around the Urals

1 https://observatory.t-radya.com/and https://itsmycity.ru/2016-11-12/oni-yarche-nas-timofey-radya-sdelal-novuyu-rabotu
2 http://wheredogsrun.ru/en/2020/02/collector-2/
3 https://en.wikipedia.org/wiki/Gorodki
4 http://researcharts.ru/mari-research-telkov-ru
5 http://zeart.ru/en/info
6 http://www.artmnt.ru/collection.php?id=255
7 https://actiondice.ru
8 http://malyshchuk.com/ru/spirina#rec74604743

Chapter 10 – Across the Country

1 http://zipgroup.space/portfolio/dolphin/
2 https://www.pushkinmuseum.art/events/archive/2017/exhibitions/recycle/index.php?find=recycle%20group
3 https://primamedia.today/pavel-shu-gurov-chelovek-parohod/?from=37 was accessed on 21 April 2021 but not found as of 18 August 2021. The authors have a downloaded copy of the interview.
4 https://swe.minpromtorg.gov.ru/en/news/?tag=cy-cle+track+moscow+–+st.+petersburg
5 http://gradus.pro/anna-kabisova-mne-by-hote-los-zastat-cheloveka-v-moment-istiny/
6 https://www.omskinform.ru/news/137845
7 https://easteast.world/posts/1
8 https://vl adey.net/ru/artwork/6008

Chapter 11 – Women's Art

1 https://artguide.com/people/2675
2 https://www.theartnewspaper.ru/posts/8200/
3 http://kultproekt.ru/hudojniki/15024022016135615125/
4 http://os.colta.ru/art/projects/7748/details/22042/
5 Taus Mukhachev's letter to the authors dated 29 March 2021

Chapter 12 – Conceptual Art

1 https://www.erarta.com/en/calendar/exhibitions/de-tail/17df9945-e78e-11e5-8e29-8920284aa333/
2 https://www.annanova-gallery.ru/en/exhibitions/27/overview/
3 https://luna-info.ru/discourse/marker/
4 http://journal.masters-project.ru/maksim-svish-hyov-zvuchit-perelivaetsya-cvetami-meny-aet-formy-i-polnostyu-vyrazhaet-tvoi-emocii/
5 https://vladey.net/ru/lot/7495
6 https://primpress.ru/article/4493

Chapter 13 – Street Art and Graffiti

1 http://travelfotokor.ru/moscowstreet/izumrud/graffity/graffity.htm
2 https://forklog.com/hudozhnik-pokras-lampas-prodal-nft-s-proektsiej-svoego-risunka-za-16-eth/
3 https://kto.ru.gallery/
4 https://vivacity.ru/graffiti/truba/

Chapter 14 – Digital Art and NFT art market

1 http://www.kandinsky-prize.ru/al-bert-solda-tov/?lang=en
2 https://en.wikipedia.org/wiki/Kirill_Savchenkov
3 http://egorkraft.com
4 https://www.timparchikov.com/burning-news#1
5 https://www.whitechapelgallery.org/about/blog/evge-ny-granilshchikov-courbets-funeral/
6 https://aesf.art/page/short_biography/
7 https://superrare.co/artwork-v2/circle-of-life-24415
8 http://colordigital.art/

Chapter 15 – Sculpture and Installations

1 https://www.asyamarakulina.com/seam-rule
2 http://fragmentgallery.com/ru/preservation_instinct/
3 http://fedotovfedorov.com/works/1881
4 http://projectstart.ru/exhibitions/view/37/

Chapter 16 – Art and Activism

1 https://spb.hse.ru/ixtati/news/410001950.html
2 https://en.wikipedia.org/wiki/Pussy_Riot
3 https://observer.com/2021/08/three-members-of-pussy-riot-have-left-russia-to-avoid-constant-arrests/
4 https://en.free-voina.org/about
5 https://chtodelat.org/category/c_1/
6 https://moloko.plus/shvemy
7 https://chtodelat.org/
8 https://arterritory.com/ru/vizualnoe_iskusstvo/interv-ju/6186-skvoz_grjaz_led_i_plamen
9 https://www.dukleyhotels.com/en/leisure-wellbeing/dukley-art
10 https://www.interfax.ru/russia/327230
11 https://2020.artinnovation.ru/en/ceremony/
12 https://www.themoscowtimes.com/2016/02/18/pav-lenskys-threat-performance-barred-from-russian-art-award-a51860
13 https://en.wikipedia.org/wiki/Petr_Pavlensky
14 https://www.wonderzine.com/wonderzine/life/life-inter-view/253377-intervyu-oksana

Chapter 17 – Expatriate Art

1 https://www.polinakanis.com/
2 https://en.wikipedia.org/wiki/Genia_Chef
3 https://www.alexandralerman.com/soldiers-of-the-sun-or-the-right-to-future-tense-1
4 https://www.gq.ru/success/nikolaj-koshelev-interview

LIST OF WORKS

Measurements have height before width (followed by depth for three-dimensional works).

Image copyrights belong to individual artists or art groups unless stated otherwise.

Numbers in brackets refer to pages where works are illustrated.

Chapter 1
From Past to Present

Tkachenko, Danila, Motherland, Nr.1, 2016, archival pigment print on paper, various sizes (p.16)

Venkov, Dimitri, The Hymns of Moscovy, 2018, video still, DCP/2K/3K video, duration: 14'24 min (p.18)

Venkov, Dimitri, The Hymns of Moscovy, 2018, video still, DCP/2K/3K video, duration: 14'24 min (p.18)

Gronsky, Alexander, Untitled, Scheme Series, 2015, pigment print on paper, 13 x 18 cm (p.19)

Mokrov, Roman, Another Day in Paradise, 2017, installation, chaise longue, empty bottles, video, various sizes (p.20)

Otdelnov, Pavel, Stonehenge, 2013, oil on canvas, 200 x 250 cm, MOMMA collection (p.21)

Paperno, Alexandra, Colourization, Cinema of the Repeat Film Project, 2015, installation. 11 flags on the facade of the Circular Kinopanorama Pavilion at VDNKh, Moscow. Polyester silk, acrylic, 100 x 150 cm (each flag) (p.22)

Reshetnikov, Konstantin, Turnip 200, Import Substitution Series, 2020, steel, welding, turning and milling, paint, varnish, 16 x 5 x 5 cm, edition of 20 (p.23)

Poteryaev, Sergey, Untitled, Staraya Utka Series, 2013, digital print on paper, 45 x 30 cm (p.24)

Korotkova, Taisia, Transport of Radioactive Waste, 2014, wood, tempera, gesso ground, 50 x 60 cm (p.25)

Chapter 2
Nature and Landscape

Gimranov, Ilgiz, Life Like a Dream, 2018, acrylic on hardboard, 61.5 x 91.5 cm (p.26)

Gimranov, Ilgiz, Aren't Your Paws Frozen? 2017, acrylic on hardboard, 60 x 90 cm (p.28)

Shorin, Dmitry, Simeiz, 2020, oil on canvas, 137 x 192 cm (p.29)

Shorin, Dmitry, Pushkin, 2018, oil on canvas, 195 x 195 cm (p.30)

Pushnitsky, Vitaly, The Death of Orpheus Nr. 1, 2018, oil on canvas, 190 x 140 cm (p.31)

Kuraksa, Vasily, Solovetsky Island, 2018, oil on canvas, 80 x 95 cm (p.32)

Kuraksa, Vasily, Yuryev-Polsky, 2018, oil on canvas, 80 x 100 cm (p.33)

Borodin, Oleg, Untitled, Irony as a Landscape Series, 2016, digital print on paper, 30 x 30 cm (p.34)

Buravleva, Evgeniya, Rain, 2017, oil on canvas, 120 x 150 cm (p.35)

Miroshnikov, Stanislav, Dream, 2018, oil on canvas, 205 x 197 cm (p.36)

Plotnikov, Egor, Second Half of The Day, 2020, oil on canvas, 170 x 200 cm (p.37)

Chapter 3
Abstract and Surrealist Art

Volkov, Andrey, Family Secrets, 2007, oil on canvas, 170 x 200 cm (p.38)

Voligamsi, Rinat, Cross-landscape, 2013, oil on canvas, 120 x 160 cm (p.40)

Voligamsi, Rinat, Winter Day, 2015, oil on canvas, 120 x 120 cm (p.41)

Sitnikova, Natalia, Solar Wind-4, 2009, oil on canvas, 90 x 90 cm (p.42)

Alimpiev, Victor, Kathleen Ferrier, 2015, acrylic on canvas, 100 x 55 cm. Courtesy of Ovcharenko Gallery (p.43)

Novikov, Ivan, I Want to Be Afraid of the Forest, 2014, dry plants, tempera on canvas, 178 x 458 cm. Sergey Limonov collection, Saint Petersburg, Russia. Courtesy of pop/off/art Gallery. Photo: Vladislav Shatilo (p.44)

Kulkov, Vlad, Untitled, 2019, oil on canvas, 315 x 320 cm. Courtesy of Anna Nova Gallery. (p.45)

Koshelev, Egor, Snowball, 2017, oil on canvas, 80 x 60 cm. Courtesy of Ovcharenko Gallery (p.46)

Crocodile Power, My Mind Says No, 2018, plastic, resin, 99 x 44 x 33 cm (p.47)

Andrzhievskaya, Anna, City of Kitties, 2019, oil on canvas, 100 x 70 cm. Courtesy of Anna Nova Gallery (p.49)

Chapter 4
Icon Painters

Archimandrite Zinon (Theodor), View of the frescoes inside the Cathedral of St Nicholas the Miracle-Worker in Vienna, Austria, 2006 – 2008, various sizes © Protodeacon Victor Shilovsky, Secretary of the Diocese of Vienna and Austria of the Russian Orthodox Church (p.50)

Lavdansky, Alexander, Icon of Christ Pantocrator, egg tempera, gilding on gesso and wood, 1.5 x 1.3 m. The Agios Georgios Monastery, Mavrovouni, Larnaca District, Cyprus. © Kinovar (p.52)

Sokolov, Alexander, Icon of the Mother of God the Inexhaustible Chalice, 1993, silver riza, egg tempera and gold on gesso and wood. The Intercession Church of the Serpukhov Vysotsky Monastery. © Maria Vishnyak (p.53)

Sokolov, Alexander, Icon of the Holy Trinity, 2014, egg tempera, gold leaf, gesso and wood, 280 x 180 cm. Church of St. Alexander of Koman in Palermo, Italy. © Maria Vishnyak (p.55)

Soldatov, Alexander, Icon of the Mother of God, 2018, fresco, 185 x 75 cm, part of the iconostasis of the Church of the New Martyrs and Confessors of Russia in the city of Beslan, Republic of North Ossetia-Alania, Russia (p.56)

Soldatov, Alexander, Icon of Christ the Savior, 2018, fresco, 185 x 75 cm, part of the iconostasis of the Church of the New Martyrs and Confessors of Russia in the city of Beslan, Republic of North Ossetia-Alania, Russia (p.57)

Zaron, Irina, Icon of the Image of Edessa (or the Mandylion), 2015, egg tempera, gesso on wood, 65 x 59 cm. The Monastery of the Transfiguration of the Saviour, Valaam, Russia (p.58)

Zaron, Irina, Icon of St. Macarius of Egypt, 2015, egg tempera, gesso on wood, 80 x 60 cm. The Monastery of the Transfiguration of the Saviour, Valaam, Russia (p.59)

Antonov, Sergey, The Deposition from the Cross, 2010, dolomite, 71 x 58 cm. The Church of the Hieromartyr Antipas at the Kolymazhny Yard, Moscow, Russia (p.60)

Rzhanitsyna, Svetlana, Icon of Christ the Saviour on the Throne, 2021, egg tempera, gold, gesso on wood, 200 x 80 cm (p.61)

Rzhanitsyna, Svetlana, Icon of the Mother of God with the Child on the Throne, 2021, egg tempera, gold, gesso on wood, 200 x 80 cm (p.61)

Davydov, Andrej, Icon of Saint Paul with Saints, 2018, encaustic painting on wood, 40 x 32.5 cm (p.62)

Davydov, Andrej, Icon of the Nativity of Jesus, 2019, encaustic painting on wood, 54 x 45 cm (p.63)

Davydov, Philipp, Icon of Saint Patrick, 2017, egg tempera, gilding, gesso on wood, 50 x 34,5 cm (p.64)

Shalamova, Olga, Icon of Saint Hilda, 2016, egg tempera, gilding, gesso on wood, 50 x 28 cm (p.65)

Chapter 5
Moscow

Kroytor, Olga, Long Way, 2011, collage on cardboard, magazines, 85 x 109.5 cm (p.66)

Shuvaeva, Svetlana, Panic at the Pool, Crowd Character Series, 2015, acrylic markers on paper, 61 x 86 cm. Courtesy of Peter Lukacs (p.68)

Shuripa, Stanislav, Evening, Cityscapes Series, 2008, acrylic on canvas, 140 x 180 cm (p.69)

Korina, Irina, On Vacation, 2019, installation, various sizes. The City of Tomorrow exhibition at the State Tretyakov Gallery, Krymsky Val, Moscow, Russia. Photo: Anastasia Soboleva (p.70)

Machulina, Diana, Body of Labour, 2013, installation. Includes: The Fates, oil on canvas, 120 x 170 cm. Unharvested Strip of Wheat, UV digital prints on 50 transparent plastic plates, 60 x 100 cm each, wooden box 12 x 102 x 400 cm. Audio of the poem 'Unharvested Strip' by Nikolay Nekrasov read by Alexander Shavrin, duration: 1'10 min. A part of the film 'Even Cowgirls Get the Blues' (dir. Gus van Sent, 1993, USA), no sound, looped, duration: 00'04 min. A part of the film 'Call Me from Afar' (dir. German Lavrov, Stanislav Lubshin, 1977, USSR), no sound, subtitles, looped, duration: 00'28 min. Photo: Petr Zakharov (p.71)

Machulina, Diana, Unharvested Strip of Wheat, 2013, UV digital prints on 50 transparent plastic plates, 60 x 100 cm each, wooden box 12 x 102 x 400 cm (a part of Body of Labour installation). Photo: Petr Zakharov (p.72)

Machulina, Diana, The Fates, 2013, oil on canvas, 120 x 170 cm (a part of Body of Labour installation). Photo: Petr Zakharov (p.73)

Parkina, Anna, Untitled, 2011, collage on paper, 60 x 80 cm. Photo: Annik Wetter (p.74)

Rebus, Dima, The Woman, 2015, watercolour on paper, 50 x 70 cm. Courtesy of Artwin Gallery (p.75)

Plutitskaya, Mika, Library-II, Like the Merry-go-round in Childhood Series, 2019, oil on canvas, 120 x 160 cm (p.76)

Plutitskaya, Mika, Guest-IV, Like the Merry-go-round in Childhood Series, 2019, oil on canvas, 80 x 60 cm (p.77)

Ter-Oganyan, David, Face, 2014, C-print on canvas, 130 x 91 cm (p.78)

Ter-Oganyan, David, Beach, 2014, C-print on canvas, 130 x 186 cm (p.79)

Sakin, Roman, How to Become a Good and Even Holy Person, or Antennas and Semicircles, 2016-18, chamotte, paint and thread on wood, 160 x 110 x 20 см (p.80)

Yoffe, Alisa, Mama, 2021, acrylic on tiled wall, 310 x 310 cm. Photographed at the artist's studio at the Fabrika Centre of Creative Industries in Moscow, Russia. Photo: Evgeniya Filatova (p.81)

Chapter 6
Saint Petersburg

Kopeikin, Nikolay, Mr Cheburashka, 2012, acrylic on cardboard, 72 x 52 cm (p.82)

Kopeikin, Nikolay, The War of the Worlds, 2009, acrylic on canvas, 180 x 270 см (p.84)

Makarov, Kirill, Conversation, 2010, oil on canvas, 160 x 180 cm (p.85)

Plusch, Ivan, Glass Disease, 2015, wood, glass, leather, textile, height: 160 cm (p.86)

Plusch, Ivan, Flowers, 2019, oil and acrylic on canvas, 250 x 180 cm (p.87)

Engelke, Nestor, Wooden Danae, 2020, wood, 139 x 200 cm, from the series 'Hermitage Walks'. Courtesy of Ovcharenko Gallery (p.88)

Dashevsky, Alexander, Swimming Pool, 2012, oil on canvas, 110 x 180 cm (p.89)

Dontsov, Philipp, Red Work RM-31, 2002-2003, acrylic, resin, aluminium board, 59 x 59 cm. Courtesy of Anna Florkovskaja (p.90)

Gaponov, Ilya, Kuzbas Parallel, 2007, bitumen on canvas, 150 x 150 cm (p.91)

Gaponov, Ilya, Ammonia, 2021, bitumen and acrylic on canvas, 190 x 280 cm (p.92)

Tskhe, Leonid, Ruler, 2019, oil on canvas, 145 x 223 cm. Courtesy of Ovcharenko Gallery (p.93)

Gorbunov, Andrey, Transformation 3, Vertex Project, 2013-2014, acrylic, marker, vanish, paper on canvas, 180 x 180 cm (p.94)

Tsikarishvili, Alexander, Return of the Prodigal Son, 2019, mixed media (acrylic, oil, pastel, soil, textile) on canvas, 220 x 170 cm (p.95)

Drozd, Irina, Buzzy-Wuzzy Busy Fly, 2019, oil on canvas, 220 x 200 cm (p.96)

Drozd, Irina, Praying Squid, 2020, synthetic ceramics, height: 32 cm (p.97)

Chapter 7
Central Russia

Alekseev, Nikolay, Shell, 2014, steel, shell rock, wood, various sizes. The 'What if...' exhibition at the geological part of the Divnogorye open-air museum and nature reserve, Voronezh oblast, Russia (p.98)

Alekseev, Nikolay, Shell, 2014, steel, shell rock, wood, various sizes (overview). The 'What if...' at the geological part of the Divnogorye open-air museum and nature reserve, Voronezh oblast, Russia (p.100)

Gorshkov, Ivan, Untitled, Hyper- Jump and the Anteater Series, 2016, oil, spray, digital printing, stickers, felt on canvas diptych, 200 x 130 cm each part (p.101)

Zhilyaev, Arseny, Tsiolkovsky, Second Advents, 2016, installation, mixed media, various sizes. Courtesy of the Gazprombank Corporate Collection. Photo: New Holland and Alexey Bogolepov (p.102)

Garshin, Kirill, A Bear, Tanais Series, 2017, acrylic on canvas on board, 40 x 30 cm (p.103)

Toptunova, Elena (Lena Lisitsa), Three Townswomen, 2016, acrylic on board, 90 x 60 cm each. Nizhny Novgorod, Russia (p.104)

Nomerz, Nikita, The Detail, 2013, spray paint on wall, various sizes. Nizhny Novgorod, Russia (p.105)

Basay, Vasyo; Abikh, Vladimir and Zloyproduct, Easy Way to Stop Being a Street Artist, 2019, spray paint on wall, various sizes. Nizhny Novgorod, Russia (p.106)

Chernyshev, Vladimir, Boat, 2017, resin, tar, 30 x 220 x 80. Courtesy of Artwin Gallery. Photo: Ivan Erofeev (p.107)

Chapter 8
Along the Volga

Mavrin, Nikolay, After Storm in the Harbour, 2006, oil on canvas, 70 x 130 cm (p.108)

Kudinov, Dmitry (aka LIL-DEE), The Essence, 2021, spray paint on wall, various sizes. The Energy Nation Project, Zainsk, Republic of Tatarstan, Russia (p.110)

Kudinov, Dmitry and Sergey, Viva La France, 2018, spray paint on wall, various sizes. Kazan, Republic of Tatarstan, Russia (p.111)

Tsarev, Sergei, Annunciation, 2017, egg tempera, gesso on board, 140 x 100 cm (p.112)

Tsarev, Sergei, They All Ate and Were Satisfied, 2015, egg tempera and gesso on board, 80 x 80 cm (p.113)

Mavrin, Nikolay, Mundane and Spiritual, 2011, mixed media, found objects on board, 76 x 76 cm (p.114)

Syaylev, Andrey, Pillars of Krasnoyarsk, 2019, UV printing, two-component acrylic polyurethane varnish, ceramic tiles, tile adhesive, bricks, various sizes. Site-specific series. Krasnoyarsk, Russia (p.115)

Logutov, Vladimir, Untitled, Encounters Series, 2017, acrylic, airbrush, inkjet printing, mixed media on canvas, 144 x 96 cm (p.116)

Zaytsev, Alexander, Untitled (view of the roof of the Samara elevator from a window), 2016, acrylic on canvas, 80 x 80 cm (p.117)

Lezin, Mikhail, Untitled, 2014, acrylic on canvas, 104 x 61 cm (p.118)

Lezin, Mikhail, Untitled, 2016, acrylic on paper, 43 x 30.5 cm (p.119)

Art Abstractov, Avantgarde Series 98, 2020, spray paint on wall, 5 x 20 m. Tyumen, Russia (p.120)

Art Abstractov, Avantgarde Series 98, 2020, spray paint on wall, 5 x 20 m (overview). Tyumen, Russia (p.120)

Gnutov, Alexander, Ushkui (flat-bottomed boat), 2017, multicolour gel pens on paper, 21 x 29 cm (p.121)

Belousova, Alina, Neoincubator No. 13, 2019, printed circuit boards, radiators, 28 x 17 x 15 cm (p.122)

Belousova, Alina, Neoincubator No. 13, 2019, printed circuit boards, radiators, 28 x 17 x 15 cm (inside view) (p.123)

Chapter 9
Around the Urals

Radya, Tima, Brighter Than Us, 2016, installation, various sizes. The project at the Special Astrophysical Observatory of the Russian Academy of Science, Karachay-Cherkessia, Russia (p.124)

Seleznyov, Vladimir, Metropolis, Kazan, 2013, light-accumulating paint, bulbs, light switch, household waste, various sizes. Daylight view (p.126)

Seleznyov, Vladimir, Metropolis, Kazan, 2013, light-accumulating paint, bulbs, light switch, household waste, various sizes. (p.127)

Where Dogs Run, Collector, 2015, photograph of the media artist during the project. Wearable device: hand generator, gas analyser, satchel, speaker, microcontrollers, electronic components, pump, musical instruments, servo machines, LCD display, thermostat, tubes, solenoid valves, thermocouples, plywood, plastic, acrylic glass, foil, 80 x 60 x 60 cm. On the photo: Vladislav Bulatov. Location: Karabash, Cheliabinsk Oblast, Russia. The project was supported by the Austrian Cultural Forum and the Austrian Embassy in Moscow. Programming: Sergey Mashkov (p.128)

Slobtseva, Elena, Gorodki (Skittles), 2017, wooden and steel wire sculpture, 10 x 10 cm, height up to 150 cm, 3 x 2 m overall. The video screen at the back with a map of the city of Perm was made by Alexander Gulyaev and is not part of the work. Photo: Alexander Gulyaev (p.129)

Telkov, Fyodor, Carpenter with his Wife, Relatives and Friends, Sarsy village, Ural Mary: Traditional Garments Series, 2017, digital image (p.130)

Telkov, Fyodor, Priest, Mary Karshi village, Ural Mary: Traditional Garments Series, 2017, digital image (p.130)

Telkov, Fyodor, Women of Kurki village, Ural Mary: Traditional Garments Series, 2017, digital image (p.131)

Telkov, Fyodor, Local Historian, Big Tavra village, Ural Mary: Traditional Garments Series, 2017, digital image (p.131)

Zlye (The Evils), art group, Brainwash, 2013, spray paint, mounting foam, self-adhesive film, tin, 250 x 150 cm. Yekaterinburg, Russia (p.132)

Zlye (The Evils), art group, Brainwash, 2013, spray paint, mounting foam, self-adhesive film, tin, 250 x 150 cm (overview). Yekaterinburg, Russia (p.133)

Cherepanov, Anna and Vitaly, Cherepanov Set, 2021, mixed media, 65 x 40 x 12 cm (p.134)

Spirina, Svetlana, Six Hours of Melting Snow, 2016, performance video still (p.135)

Chapter 10
Across the Country

Zip Art Group, Layout of Utopias, 2017, installation, mixed media, various sizes. The Zip House of Culture Stop exhibition, MOMMA, Moscow, Russia. Photo: courtesy of MOMMA (p.136)

Recycle Group, Tower Raising II, 2014 – 2015, plastic mesh, 300 x 650 cm (p.138)

33+1 Art Community, The Stream, 2008, oil on plexiglass and metal, 1 x 1.5 x 30 m (part of the open-air installation). Saint Petersburg, Russia (p.139)

Morik, Lost Childhood, 2020, spray paint on wall, various sizes. Neftekamsk, Russia. Photo courtesy of Vitaly Kim, Dmitry Kudinov (p.140)

Berger, Andrey, Nets and Grids, 2019, spray paint on wall, 3,200 m². Nizhny Novgorod, Russia. Photo: Vanya Volkov (p.141)

Berger, Andrey, Painted Pillars of the Rogachevsky Bridge, 2021, aerosol paint on wall, various sizes (view of the bridge from above). Dmitrov, Moscow region, Russia. Photo: Alex Partola (p.142)

Berger, Andrey, Painted Pillars of the Rogachevsky Bridge, 2021, aerosol paint on wall, various sizes (overview of the bridge). Dmitrov, Moscow region, Russia. Photo: Alex Partola (p.143)

Kabisova, Anna, Untitled, I Believe in One Project, 2016, silver Bromine printing, contact print, 13 x 18 cm (p.144)

Abishev, Marat, The Two of Them, 2019, spray paint on wall, various sizes (front view). Omsk train station, Russia (p.145)

Abishev, Marat, The Two of Them, 2019, spray paint on wall, various sizes (rear view). Omsk train station, Russia (p.145)

Pletnev, Pavel, Acid House, 2021, mixed media on plywood, 89 x 61 x 4 cm. Courtesy of DIDI Gallery (p.146)

Pletnev, Pavel, Funnel of Time, 2021, mixed media on plywood, 48 x 63 x 7 cm. Courtesy of DIDI Gallery (p.147)

Zabrodin, Anton, Untitled, Bruno Taut's Places Series (part of Ikuru Kuwajima's project), 2020, colour photograph, various sizes. Kaliningrad Oblast, Russia (p.148)

Nasybullova, Mayana, Duckling Lenin, Lenin for the Soul Project, 2016, gypsum, acrylic, 10 x 11 x 6 cm (p.149)

Chapter 11
Women's Art

Tobreluts, Olga, Classic Walpurgis Night I, 2010, vanish, digital printing on canvas, 109 x 110 cm (p.149)

Tobreluts, Olga, Abduction, 2021, oil on canvas, left part of the triptych,175 cm, central part of the triptych, 270 x 360 cm, right part of the triptych, 175 cm (p.152-153)

Tobreluts, Olga, Transcoder, 2019, oil on canvas, 210 x 200 cm (p.154)

Alekseeva, Marina, Two Rooms, 2012, mixed media, single-channel video, two interiors, 42 × 46 × 40 cm (p.155)

Alekseeva, Marina, Escape, 2020, mixed media, video, 42 x 42 x 42 cm, edition of 3 (p.155)

Akhmetgalieva, Tanya, Love These Fiery Moments, 2016, video still, video duration: 4'10 min. Video: Tanya Akhmetgalieva. Sound: Victor Mazin (p.156)

Kosinskaya, Nadya, Dress, 2019, acrylic, epoxy resin, staples, nails on plywood, 150 x 150 cm. Courtesy of Igor Sukhanov, Saint Petersburg, Russia (p.157)

Fatkhullina, Antonina, Union of Air and Earth, 2018, haydite, metal, 35 x 20 x 17 cm (p.158)

Dmitrieva, Marya, Rhizome, 2014, acrylic, collage on canvas, 125 x 100 cm. From Mille plateaux, a nomadic experience show feat with Vlad Kulkov, Los Angeles, USA (p.159)

Begalska, Vika, Vilkin, Alexander, Girl with Racoon, oil, pastel, charcoal, pencil on canvas, 45 x 66,5 cm (p.160)

Zholud, Anya, Sculpture, Anti-Chandelier Series, 2018/19, paint, welding, metal, 180 x 160 cm (p.161)

Makhacheva, Taus, Delinking, 2011, photograph of the performance, performance duration: 1 week. Impronte Gallery, Milan, Italy (p.162)

Makhacheva, Taus, Charivari, 2019, mixed media, sound, various sizes (part of the installation). Architect: Maria Serova. Text: Alexander Snegirev. Costume design: Panika Derevya. Commissioned by the YARAT Contemporary Art Space. Courtesy of the Artist. Photo: Pat Verbruggen (p.162)

Tereshko, Alena, It's an Apple, 2019, photograph of the performance, performance duration: 1 hour, MOMMA, Moscow, Russia. Photo: Andrey Kachalyan (p.163)

Chapter 12
Conceptual Art

Konstantinova, Ludmila, Untitled, Degenerotype Series, 2014, acrylic on calico, 130 x 100 cm (p.164)

Tavasiev, Rostan, My Star, Episode 7, A Drop of Creacin Project, 2017, acrylic on canvas, 140 x 200 cm (p.166)

Marker, Misha, Eva, 2019, acrylic on canvas, 70 x 100 cm (p.167)

Svishev, Maxim, Masks, 2019, coloured polymer clay, 13 x 13 cm (p.168)

Svishev, Maxim, TSVETASIS, 2017, 3D graphics. The virtual project at the Royal Exhibition Building, Melbourne, Australia (p.169)

Motolyanets, Semyon, Only Left 35 Years, Soap Pyramids Series, 2018, metal, ceramics, 21 x 16 x 16 cм (p.170)

Kuzkin, Andrey, Scary, 2007, black marker pen, old porcelain cup, glass cover, 16 x 16 x 16 cm (p.171)

Chtak, Valery, In My Case, In No Case, 2016, acrylic on canvas, 128 x 162 cm (p.171)

Tregubov, Alexey, Hit It, 2013, paint on metal and foam plastic, 55 x 43 cm (p.172)

Eli Kuka, World Order Simulators, 2012, mixed media on canvas, various sizes (p.173)

Chapter 13
Street Art and Graffiti

Nezo Street Art, Yura, We Have Improved! 2014, spray paint on wall, various sizes (central part). The Gallery Around the Town project, Moscow, Russia (p.174)

Nezo Street Art, Yura, We Have Improved! 2014, spray paint on wall, various sizes (overview). The Gallery Around the Town project, Moscow, Russia (p.176)

PTRK, Slava, Make Russia Grey Again, 2018, spray paint on wall, various sizes. The Carte Blanche street art festival, Yekaterinburg, Russia (p.177)

Abikh, Vladimir, You Are Offline, 2019, spray paint on wall, various sizes. Yekaterinburg, Russia (p.178)

Bags, Stas, Get Milk Not Art, 2015, spray paint on wall, various sizes. Saint Petersburg, Russia (p.179)

Pokras Lampas, We Have Our Own Way, 2018, paint on tarmac, 11,000 m^2. RZD Arena, Moscow, Russia. In collaboration with FC Lokomotiv and Special One Agency. Photo: Ernest Em 19 TONES, BORSCH (p.180)

Kto, Kirill, Sad Masks Itself as Jolly Hoping to Stay This Way, 2012, spray paint on wall, various sizes. Moscow, Russia (p.181)

Dobry, Stas, Untitled, 2016-2017, spray paint on wall, various sizes. Moscow, Russia (p.182)

Truba, Arseniy, Untitled, 2021, spray paint on wall, various sizes. Moscow, Russia (p.183)

Chapter 14
Digital Art and NFT art market

Tuzov, Ivan, Et, 2013, digital image (p.184)

Soldatov Albert, Balthus, 2014, video still, video duration: 13' min (p.186)

Kraft, Egor, Hellenistic Ruler, Content Aware Studies Series, 2018, marble, polyamide, machine learning algorithms, custom software, original dataset, multi-channel video installation, 19 x 28 x 21 cm. Courtesy of the author and Anna Nova Gallery (p.187)

Kraft, Egor, Colossal Head of Hercules, Content Aware Studies Series, 2018, marble, polyamide, machine learning algorithms, custom software, original dataset, multi-channel video installation, 24 x 32 x 20 cm. Courtesy of the author and Anna Nova Gallery (p.187)

Parchikov, Tim, Burning News, 2011, C-print, 185 x 125 cm (p.188)

Dou, Oleg, Melting Worlds, 2019, C-print face mounted with acrylic, 160 x 120 cm. Edition of 8. (p.189)

Granilshchikov, Evgeny, At Dawn Our Dreams Become Brighter, 2017, video still, video filmed on mobile phone, duration: 7'30 min (p.190)

Bluesoup, Murk, 2013-214, video still, video duration: 00'45 min (p.191)

AES+F, Allegoria Sacra, The Twins, 2012, digital collage, C-print, 160 x 224 cm in Diasec®, 110 x 142 cm on Fine Art Baryta Paper. Copyright © AES+F (p.192)

AES+F, The Circle of Life, 2021, video still. Video, sound, duration: 1'37 min. Video artwork for the GENTLE MONSTER'S 2021 Nano Collection campaign. Copyright © AES+F (p.193)

Zabaluev, Sasha, Flower 11, 2021, digital image with QR-codes. From Color Digital series (p.194)

Zabaluev, Sasha, Venus Flower 36.1, 2021, digital image with QR-codes. From Color Digital series (p.195)

Chapter 15 Sculpture and Installations

Marakulina, Asya, Seam rule, 2014-2015, 2020, installation, walks, diary, cloth, various sizes (overview). Exhibited at the «Mimicry» section (curated by Sveta Usoltseva) of «Nemoskva» exhibition at the Manezh Central Exhibition Hall, Moscow, Russia. Courtesy of the Pushkin State Museum of Fine Arts (p.196)

Marakulina, Asya, Seam rule, 2014-2015, 2020, installation, walks, diary, cloth, various sizes (central part). Courtesy of the Pushkin State Museum of Fine Arts (p.198)

Fedotov-Fedorov, Ilya, Exo-Ark, 2019, installation, mixed media, various sizes. Video still, video duration: 8 min (p.199)

Povzner, Alexander, The Artist and the Canvas, 2019, painted plaster, 217 x 80 x 170 cm. Photo: Anastasia Soboleva / Spasibo Studio (p.200)

Titova, Anna, Identikit, 2017, marble, onyx, brass, 42 x 36 x 25 cm (frontal view). Courtesy of Artwin Gallery (p.201)

Titova, Anna, Identikit, 2017, marble, onyx, brass, 42 x 36 x 25 cm (side view). Courtesy of Artwin Gallery (p.201)

Bobkova, Liza, Love Tower, 2016, stainless steel, welding, 2 x 1 x 0.6 m (overview) (p.202)

Bobkova, Liza, Love Tower, 2016, stainless steel, welding, 2 x 1 x 0.6 m (central part) (p.203)

Dzharullaev, Artur, Oil Monsters, 2019, 200 l barrels, steel plates, pipes, bolts, 3-3,8 x 1,5-3 m. Photo: Mikhail Vilchuk (p.204)

Diakov, Piotr, Bust, 2018, acrylic composite, pigments, 73 x 42 x 26 cm (p.205)

Antufiev, Evgeny, Untitled, 2016, wood, bronze, textile, brass and copper, 56.5 x 33 x 32 cm, knife - 45.5 x 6 cm. Courtesy of Phillips (p.206)

Orlova, Polina, Avant-garde Body, 2018, experimental weaving. 200 x 800 cm (unfolded), 200 x 200 x 200 cm (when folded as a cube) (p.207)

Chumak, Anton, Crystallization, Salt Project, 2014 – 2016, installation, steel, welding, variable sizes (p.207)

Chumak, Anton, The Basis, 2019, steel, welding, forging, variable sizes (p.208)

Chapter 16 Art and Activism

Chto Delat', Partisan Songspiel, A Belgrade Story, 2009, video still. Video film, duration: 29'27 min. Produced by Biro Beograd – Biro for Culture and Communication, Belgrade, Serbia (p.210)

Shvemy, This Is Not an Invitation to Rape, 2015, photograph of the performance within the framework of the annual international campaign "16 Days for the Elimination of Violence Against Women", Saint Petersburg, Russia. Photo: Vadim Lurie (p.212)

Gentle Women, Art of Braid Weaving, 2018, performance video still, video duration: 5'18 min. The Curonian Spit, Kaliningrad Oblast, Russia (p.214)

Benkovich Konstantin, Mona Lisa, 2018, steel pipes, welding, 2 x 1,2 cm. Dukley Gardens, Budva, Montenegro (p.215)

Benkovich, Konstantin, WTC (World Trade Center), 2019, installation, steel pipes, welding, 2,5 x 1,2 m. Collection of the State Russian Museum, Saint Petersburg, Russia (p.216)

Loskutov, Artem, America, 2020, acrylic, vanish on canvas, 30 x 50 cm, painted with a police baton (p.217)

Chapter 17 Expatriate Art

Kanis, Polina, Toothless Resistance. The Room, 2020, installation, video still. Video, 3K, stereo sound, audio play, stereo sound. Full HD video duration: 24'09 mins (p.218)

Kanis, Polina, Toothless Resistance. The Friendship Tree, 2021, video still. Video, 2K, stereo sound. Full HD video duration: 24'09 mins (p.220)

Zastava, Julia, Untitled, 2017, pencils, watercolour, acrylic on cardboard, 100 x 210 cm (p.221)

Chef, Genia, Tsarevich Alexei, 2013, oil and gold leaf on canvas, 140 x 100 cm (p.222)

Chef, Genia, Hagen Notices the Bavarian Warriors from the cycle 'The Song of the Nibelungs', 2020, mixed media on canvas, 40 x 50 cm (p.223)

Myagkikh, Anya, Unconscious Painting, 2015, acrylic on textile (apron), 41 x 41 cm including the frame (p.224)

Myagkikh, Anya, Dude 19, 2020, acrylic on canvas, 100 x 70 cm (p.225)

Lerman, Alexandra, Soldiers of the Sun, No. 8, 2018, cyanotype on watercolour paper, 291 x 150 cm, Part of the Soldiers of the Sun or the Right to the Future Tense site-specific video and sound installation at the Contemporary Art in Traditional Museum Festival organized by ProArte Foundation. Museum of Hygiene, Saint Petersburg, Russia in 2019 (p.226)

Lerman, Alexandra, Soldiers of the Sun, No. 14, 2018, cyanotype on watercolour paper, 291 x 150 cm. Part of the Soldiers of the Sun or the Right to the Future Tense site-specific video and sound installation at the Contemporary Art in Traditional Museum Festival organized by ProArte Foundation. Museum of Hygiene, Saint Petersburg, Russia in 2019 (p.227)

INDEX OF ARTISTS & ART-GROUPS

Page numbers in *italics* refer to artworks.

INDEX

For artists and art groups, see index on pages 236-237

Published in 2022 by
Unicorn, an imprint of Unicorn Publishing Group
5 Newburgh Street
London
W1F 7RG
www.unicornpublishing.org

Project Manager:
Natalia Kambarova-Odoevskaya

English language
ISBN 978-1-9134-9172-7
Russian language
ISBN 978-19134-9198-7

Designed by Jonathan Christie
Printed by Fine Tone Ltd

10 9 8 7 6 5 4 3 2 1